In a B...

BED & BREAKFAST CAN BE FOUND IN:

a **Cod Jigging Home** where guests can participate in traditional cod fishing activities.

a **Fisherman's Cottage** on the east coast where you can watch whales and the world's highest tides.

a **Mountain Chalet** on the west coast with an everchanging panoramic view of the Pacific ocean and mountain ranges.

a **Special Needs Home** designed and fully equipped to meet the needs of the disabled traveller, with a ramp and a wheel-chair van for transportation. Hosts have information on accessible places to go.

a **Solar Home** which is solar powered.

a **Clown's Home** where the professional clown hostess has a collection of clown trivia and magical things to show.

an **Historic Farm Home**, on the former property of one of the Fathers of Confederation and the only farm to contain a village.

a **Downtown Metropolitan Residence** where they serve champagne in bed for breakfast and the *New York Times* along with it.

a **Christian Home** where the hosts, with extensive missionary experience in Africa, offer clergy and missionary specials.

a **Typical Canadian Farm** where guests are invited to help with chores and feed animals, and where the hosts serve huge homecooked meals from their own produce.

a **Modern East Coast Home** with a private beach and boat for charter.

an **Iceberg-viewing Home**, where guests can view icebergs from a twenty-seven-foot tour boat while eating lunch.

an **Historic Religious Home**, once a frequent stop by Brother André, founder of the famed Oratory in Montreal. Guests may request to stay in the room where he slept.

an **Opera Home**, where the baritone host teaches singing.

an **Angel's Home**, where guest rooms are called Michael, Raphael and Gabriel, and guests are watched over by all the angels of the house.

a **Peanut-free Home** with a peanut-free environment.

a **Horse-trainer's Home** where the hosts train Appaloosa horses using the "Whispering Method."

a **Skating Home** where you can put on your skates inside the back door and walk over to the longest outdoor skating rink in the world.

an **East Coast Fisherman's Home** — a base for deep sea fishing, clam digging and enjoying lobster suppers. Guests may join the hosts with hauling in lobster traps and preparing fishing nets.

an **Isolated Prarie Farm** where you can sit and relax in wide open spaces, tranqil surroundings, and listen to the wheat grow.

a **Church Home** in a converted church with the living room in the former church hall, high ceilings, stained glass windows and a unique atmosphere.

a **Northern Home** where you may be served smoked salmon, moose sausage or sourdough pastries for breakfast.

an **Island Home** accessible only by ferry. Spend a busy or quiet island day.

an **Indian Home** owned by a family specializing in Indian lore. Guests may sleep in a teepee or a trapper's tent.

a **Theatre Home** around the corner from the Shakespeare and Shaw Festival Theatres, where you can walk home after a late performance.

a **Ski Home** at the base of a ski hill or close to major slopes and groomed trails. Sip hot cider by the fireplace after a day on the slopes.

an **Authentic Norwegian Log Home** in nature's paradise, where alfresco dining on the beach and a singalong around the bonfire is a regular event.

a **Statutory Holiday Home** where guests are welcome to enjoy a Victorian Christmas or other holidays.

a **Native Home** on an Indian reserve, where one can experience Iroquois culture and a different historic theme in each guest room.

a **Caboose** of a converted railway car, where you can enjoy the view from the cupola and have breakfast in the hosts' home.

a **French-speaking Home** of a Quebec family. An ideal place to brush up on or learn the language.

a **Health Home** where there is a health centre for total mind and body rejuvenation.

a **Pianist's Home** where guests may enjoy an impromptu recital by the host.

a **Museum Home** where the host will be proud to show guests the on-site museum of early Canadian artifacts and tools.

a **Sea Home** where the fisherman-host can tell sea tales from his 30-year involvment in the local fishing industry.

a **Bridge-player's Home** where the host is involved in the local duplicate bridge club and loves to play a hand with guests.

a **Military Home** where the host will offer professional expertise in the region's military history.

an **Artist's Home** where the resident host artist will give lessons and where guests can watch her work at her easel.

a **Tea Room Home** where guests enjoy teas and clam chowder in a Victorian tea room located in the large pleasant sunporch.

a **Mummery Home** where every Wednesday in July and August a traditional Newfoundland skit, "Christmas and the Mummers", is put on by the hosts. Also included is a Christmas dinner.

an **Indian Island Haunts Home**, where hosts arrange boat trips to former Beothuk islands, with cookouts and overnight stays at a remote cabin.

THE CANADIAN BED & BREAKFAST
· GUIDE ·

FIFTEENTH EDITION
GERDA PANTEL

Penguin Books

PENGUIN BOOKS
Published by the Penguin Group
Penguin Books Canada Ltd, 10 Alcorn Avenue, Toronto, Ontario, Canada M4V 3B2
Penguin Books Ltd, 27 Wrights Lane, London W8 5TZ, England
Penguin Putnam Inc., 375 Hudson Street, New York, New York 10014, U.S.A.
Penguin Books Australia Ltd, Ringwood, Victoria, Australia
Penguin Books (NZ) Ltd, cnr Rosedale and Airborne Roads, Albany,
Auckland 1310, New Zealand

Penguin Books Ltd, Registered Offices: Harmondsworth, Middlesex, England

First published in Penguin Books, 2000

1 3 5 7 9 10 8 6 4 2

Copyright © Gerda Pantel, 2000

Acknowledgments
Manor House Bed & Breakfast, Indian Head, Saskatchewan

Manufactured in Canada

Typesetting E. H. Pantel

15th edition

Canadian Cataloguing in Publication Data

The National Library of Canada has catalogued this publication as follows:

Pantel, Gerda
The Canadian bed and breakfast guide

Began with 1983 ed.
Irregular.
Issues for 1983-1984 have title: Canadian bed & breakfast guide
Description based on 3rd ed. (1987).
ISSN 0836-5717
ISBN 0-14-029254-3 (15th ed.)

1. Bed and breakfast accommodations - Canada - Directories. I. Title.

TX910.C3P35   647'.9471   C88-039020-4

Visit Penguin Canada's web site at **www.penguin.ca**

To my parents,
the late Alfons Kemper and Hedy Kemper,
who brought their family to Canada,
but themselves never had an opportunity to discover
how beautiful this country really is.

Contents

Explanation of Signs and Symbols

▶   Guest Capacity (how many guests can be accommodated)

☎   Telephone

$ Rates (per night-Canadian Currency): S-single (1 person using 1 room); D-double (2 persons using 1 room with 1 double bed or 1 queen bed or 1 king bed or 2 twin beds);
F-family (constitutes parents with no more than 2 children in 1 room); Add. person (always refers to a 3rd person sleeping in the same room)

❄   Season (all homes operate year-round, unless otherwise stated)

🍽   Breakfast: (always included unless otherwise specified) Cont. (Beverage and toast); Full or Choice (varies with each host); Homebaked (something special i.e. homemade breads, muffins, pancakes, croissants, waffles etc.)

🍲   Meals (always on request and at additional charge and always with due notice)

🏠   Housing: Res.(residential); Hist.(historic); Sub.(suburban); others stated

▦   Rooms: S(with 1 single bed); D(with 1 double or queen or king bed or 2 twin beds); Ste(bedroom/s with sitting room & private bath); F(guest room for entire family with 2 or more beds). Lower level means basement or otherwise stated.

🛏   Beds: S(single); D(double); T(1 twin or 3/4 size); Q(queen); K(king); R(rollaway); P(pullout); others stated

🛁   Bath: sh.w.h.(guests share with host family); sh.w.g.(guests share with other guests); ensuite (entering from guest room); private (for one room only); other stated

★   In-house features: Air (central air-conditioning); F(fireplace); KF (kitchen facilities or access to kitchen); LF(laundry facilities, usually at additional charge) TV(guests are welcome to watch with family): others stated

✋   Restrictions: means NOT allowed (no pets, no children, no smoking); others stated. If "restricted" smoking is indicated, please ask hosts for detailed instructions.

〰   Languages: language <u>other than English</u> noted.

♥   Babysitting offered (at added charge and due notice)

🧍   On the property or in walking distance to...

🚗   Short drive or up to 1 hour drive to...

📢   Host specialties, comments and description of property and area.

✔   Membership (in a B&B organization or affiliation with local Chamber of Commerce or in a Farm Vacation Association)

What is Bed & Breakfast?

Bed & Breakfast is the next best thing to staying with relatives or friends!

Bed & Breakfast is a pleasant alternative to staying in a hotel rooom. In an age of expensive travelling, one can find comfortable and reasonable accommodation located in private homes across Canada. These homes offer a short-term stay for a paying guest in comfortable, cosy, friendly surroundings, close to travel routes and places of interest. And they offer a hearty breakfast!

Bed & Breakfast is geared to that certain type of traveller who is interested in getting to know people and places through personal contact. This all amounts to a unique change of pace and a more original way of travelling. It provides adventure and a relaxed atmosphere. Above all, it provides assistance and advice on a personal basis and an opportunity to make new and lasting friends.

In Canada, the Bed & Breakfast concept was pioneered by farmers and rural families offering their home atmosphere to city travellers for a rest and a change away from the rat race. Bed & Breakfast flourished in Montreal during Expo, and arose in Cape Breton Island around 1972. Over the years, the concept has grown immensely and become very popular. Today, there are Bed & Breakfast places in or near virtually every city and town from coast to coast. Bed & Breakfast is still growing rapidly in Canada. More and more people are taking advantage of this phenomenon, while others are being introduced to it by chance, and they love it.

Typical Bed & Breakfast hosts are people who are interested in sharing their genuine hospitality in a family atmosphere, and at the same time enriching their own lives through cultural exchange and friendship. Most B&Bs are hospitality oriented, not purely service oriented like a hotel. The hosts' main concern, above all, is to make guests feel welcome and comfortable and to help them have a wonderful holiday. Many hosts give a complimentary snack and coffee or tea upon arrival or in the evenings. Their homes are neat, clean and cosy, but not necessarily luxurious. Places to stay range widely, from a modest fisherman's cottage to a metropolitan apartment suite, from a historic rural mansion to a contemporary residence in suburbia, from a prairie ranch to a cosy mountain chalet.

New Bed & Breakfast homes are opening every year – you can even find B&B homes that have been bought or built especially for that purpose. And because some of these B&B's are run in the style of a hotel or inn, the hosts have completely separate quarters. These homes are usually decorated beautifully and furnished especially for guests. Breakfast may be served in a special guest breakfast room. These B&B's usually have more than 3 rooms for guests. These hosts are also very interested in their guests and certainly will give them as much attention as they can. However, in these larger B&B's, guests socialize mostly with each other, and less with the hosts.

Several attempts to establish a B&B Grading System have been made with criteria similar to that used in the hotel industry. This is a very difficult thing to do, as each B&B is so unique and cannot be "compared" with another. Some provinces have awarded "stars" to those B&B's who have chosen to join their grading system. Many B&B's however, cannot afford the extra cost involved. At this time, *The Canadian Bed & Breakfast Guide* does not indicate any "grade star" awards until a National criterion suitable for B&B accomodation is established and accepted from coast to coast.

Many B&B's are members of a local Bed & Breakfast organization or agency or may be affiliated with the local Chamber of Commerce or Provincial Department of Tourism. These organizations establish guidelines and standards for B&Bs, and also provide a referral system within the local area for guests who need a room.

About The Canadian Bed & Breakfast Guide

The *Canadian Bed & Breakfast Guide* has been compiled for quick and easy reference for use with official Standard Canadian Road Maps. These maps are available FREE from Tourist Departments in each province, or from the Canadian Government Office of Tourism in Ottawa.

Visitors to Canada will find that mileage shown on road-signs and on Canadian maps is in kilometres (1 km = 0.6 mile). Distances to each individual B&B home are shown in approximate kilometres in *The Canadian Bed & Breakfast Guide*.

Most B&B homes *operate year-round*, but some homes do not offer B&B during every month of the year. Seasonal availability is listed.

Guests are responsible for contacting individual hosts or agencies – the author does *not* arrange for reservations. Most hosts would appreciate advance notice. It is suggested that *guests contact the hosts ahead of time*, either by letter or phone. When enroute, travellers should stop early in the afternoon and decide how far they will travel that day, choose a B&B from the *Guide* and phone ahead. Hosts will appreciate the consideration and if they are booked for the night, they may refer the traveller to another B&B in the vicinity.

E-mail addresses & *Websites* are shown when they have been given to the author.

Arrival and departure times vary & should be arranged by the guests/hosts at first contact.

Many of the homes have been visited by the author on her personal travels from coast to coast. However, listings should not be taken as a recommendation. All the information in *The Canadian Bed & Breakfast Guide* was supplied by hosts in response to a questionnaire, and has been transcribed as accurately as possible. All the hosts have provided essential information about their home, but some have provided more description than others.

Rates are shown in Canadian currency. These rates are set by the individual hosts or local B&B organization, and are subject to change from year to year. The rates shown in this edition were supplied in the fall of 1996. There may be a small variance in the rate, as it is difficult for the hosts to anticipate changes in the next season.

When a reservation is made well in advance, a *deposit* for one night is usually expected. Host will generally refund the deposit if a cancellation is necessary and is made at least 48 hours in advance.

A *tax charge* may be added to the room rate according to local, provincial or federal regulations, but this varies with hosts and with areas. Some hosts are required to collect taxes, but this is shown in their listing only if the hosts have notified the author.

It is appreciated if parents bring sleeping bags as bedding for small children. When hosts have provided information about the *pets they keep in the house*, it has been indicated in this publication. If allergies are a concern, travellers should check beforehand when they make their reservation. Some *rooms may be in the basement* of the house. These are shown in the listing as "lower level, below ground or ground level". This should be clarified by asking about the layout of the house. *Accessibility* is indicated where applicable.

The *photos* included in *The Canadian Bed & Breakfast Guide* were supplied by the hosts and should only be regarded as a quick reference, since a black & white reproduction of an exterior photo cannot reveal a B&B's beautiful interior and ambience.

Maps shown for each province are not to scale. They are meant to be used for quick reference and show only relative locations that feature B&B's listed here.

If there is no listing in a place of your choice, write or drop in to the local Chamber of Commerce office or the local Tourist Bureau and inquire about any B&B's in that area.

The *Guide* is updated and revised regularly. Many entries could not be included in this edition due to limitations of space and late questionnaire returns.

The author would like to hear about travel experiences with *The Canadian Bed & Breakfast Guide*, as well as any suggestions that might make the *Guide* more useful.

How to use The Canadian Bed & Breakfast Guide

1) Refer to the Official Standard Canadian Road Map of the province you are visiting for the route you plan to take.

2) Determine where you would like to stay in a Bed & Breakfast or, decide how many kilometers or miles you want to travel on a specific day and then choose a B&B in the place or area.

3) Consult the indiviual maps shown at the beginning of each Province for locations listed in this edition of The *Guide*.

4) Look for your chosen location in *The Canadian Bed & Breakfast Guide*, referring to the PROVINCE ON THE BOTTOM of each page.. All locations are listed in alphabetical order within each province. This eliminates the need of an index. Nearby larger places are shown in brackets throughout the *Guide* for each listing.

   If your chosen B&B is booked and you need somewhere else to stay in that immediate or general geographic area, follow the "see also" reference to other choices listed in this edition of the *Guide*. "See also" is listed under most locations. For example: Hamilton (south-west of Toronto; see also Burlington, Dundas, Ancaster....)

5) If there is no reference to a town you are looking for, consult your Provincial map again and look for a nearest larger community. Once you've found it in the book, use the "see also" reference as a guide to a place nearby. It could be that a small change in your route will find you other accommodations and perhaps a look at an interesting part of the country you had not thought of visiting.

6) Refer to the handy key on the front flap for interpretation of signs and symbols in each individual listing, and use the key for a handy bookmark.

7) Where available, use the toll-free number for reserving B&B accommodation.

If you would like to be included in the next edition of *The Canadian Bed & Breakfast Guide*, please write for a Questionnaire to:

Gerda Pantel, 270 Juniper Ave., Burlington, ON L7L 2T3
Phone (905) 632-1996   Fax (905) 632-7686

Please submit cancellations, corrections or new entries
before Dec. 1, 2001

Find out more about Bed & Breakfast - send for the booklet:
"ALL ABOUT BED & BREKAFAST - Questions & Answers" 2nd ed.
by Gerda Pantel

This booklet will help you decide if B&B travelling or B&B hosting is for you. It is the result of collecting many inquiries each year, while preparing and updating the Canadian Bed & Breakfast Guide. Gerda answers questions about travelling the B&B route and about being a B&B host.
Please send cheque (or Int.money order) for Can.$7.00 to
Gerda Pantel, 270 Juniper Ave., Burlington, ON L7L 2T3
(not available from Penguin Books or in book stores)

British Columbia

Tourism British Columbia   tool-free 1-800-663-6000
1117 Wharf St., Victoria, BC   V8W 2Z2
Travel Information Center
562 Burard St., Vancouver, BC   V6C 2J6   (604) 683-2000

For ferry crossing schedules and information to Vancouver Island, Gulf
Islands and Queen Charlotte Islands contact:
B.C. Ferries Corporation
818 Broughton St., Victoria, BC   V8W 1E4   (250) 669-1211

Vancouver Island

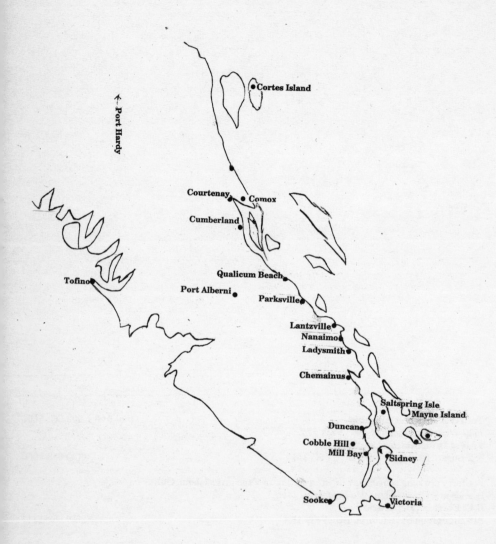

Cortes Island

← Port Hardy

Courtenay • Comox

Cumberland

Tofino

Qualicum Beach

Port Alberni

Parksville

Lantzville

Nanaimo

Ladysmith

Chemainus

Saltspring Isle

Mayne Island

Duncan

Cobble Hill

Mill Bay

Sidney

Sooke

Victoria

B.C Mainland

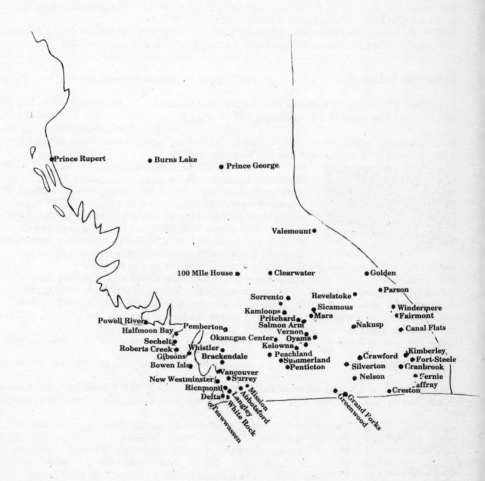

Prince Rupert ●   ● Burns Lake   ● Prince George

Valemount ●

100 MIle House ●   ● Clearwater   ● Golden

Sorrento ●   Revelstoke ●   ● Parson

Kamloops ●   Sicamous ●
Pritchard ●   ● Mara   Windermere ●
Powell River ●   Salmon Arm ●   ● Fairmont
Halfmoon Bay ●   Pemberton ●   Vernon ●   Nakusp ●   ● Canal Flats
Sechelt ●   Okanagan Center ●   Oyama ●
Roberts Creek ●   Whistler ●   Kelowna ●
Gibsons ●   Brackendale ●   Peachland ●   Crawford ●   ● Kimberley
Bowen Isle ●   Summerland ●   Silverton ●   ● Fort-Steele
Vancouver ●   Penticton ●   ● Cranbrook
New Westminster ●   ● Surrey   ● Nelson   ● Fernie
Richmond ●   Mission   Caffray
Delta ●   Abbotsford   ● Creston
Langley   Grand Forks
White Rock   Greenwood
Tsawwassen

Abbotsford

(east of Vancouver; see also Mission, White Rock, Langley)

Martens, Stan & Leona (Homestyle B&B)   ☎ (604) 853-9879, Fax (604) 853-9875
2156 Meadows St., Abbotsford, BC   V2T 3A6

From TCH1 take Exit 87 (Clearbrook Rd). Turn right on Marshall Rd, left on Meadows Street.

$45-50S $55-65D   ▶4
🍴 Full, homebaked   🏠 Res., ranch-style, view, deck   ■ 2D
(main floor)   🛏 2T(K),1Q   🛁 1Ensuite, 1sh.w.g.   ★TV/VCR
in common room, ceiling fans, private entrance, off-street parking,
guest quarters are separate   Ⓦ Designated smoking area, no pets,
not suitable for children   〰German
🏃 Mill Lake Park, Heritge House, fairgrounds, Seven Oaks/West
Oaks shopping malls, Recreation Centre, bus route No 5
🚗 Vancouver, Airport, Tradex Center, fish farms, riding stables, Fort Langley, Harrison Hot
Springs, Bridal Falls, Othello Tunnels, Game Farm
☞ Warm welcome in comfortable residential home with large deck and hot tub. Hosts will pick
up from Abbotsford Airport and/or Bus Depot. Special dietary consideration. ✔ B&B

Bowen Island

(north of Vancouver; see also Gibsons, Roberts Creek, Sechelt)

Paul, Bert & Lynn (A B&B Above The Sea At Twin Cedars)   ☎ (604) 947-9130, Fax 9150
Box Z-9, 1645 Whitesails Dr., Bowen Island, BC   V0N 1G0   1-888-811-3546
                                                    E-mail: twincedars@bc.sympatico.ca
From Vancouver, take Hwy1 north to Horseshoe Bay in West Vancouver. Continue on the ferry for
a 20min trip to Snug Cove, Bowen Island. Drive 8km to B&B.

$90S $105D $15Child $20Add.person $195F   ▶6
🍴 Full, homebaked   🏠 Rural, hillside, 2-storey, view from guest
rooms, oceanfront, patio, porch, deck, quiet, secluded   ■ 2D,1F
(upstairs)   🛏 1T,1D,1Q,cot   🛁 1Sh.w.g.   ★ F,TV in guest
sitting room, private entrance, hot-tub, off-street parking, guest
quarters are separate   Ⓦ Designated smoking area, no pets
🏃 Hiking (Cape Roger Curtis, Mt.Gardner, kayaking/swimming
(Tunstall Bay & beach), horseback riding (Evergreeen Acres)
🚗 BC Ferry to Snug Cove, scenic drives on Bowen Island, cab service on island
☞ Rustic hillside home located on the west side of the Island overlooking beguilling island of
Collingwood Channel with spectacular sunsets and close proximity to the beach. Relax in the
outside hot-tub on the forest's edge. Breakfast is served in the dining area surrounded on three
sides with windows overlooking the ocean and nature. Unique offering from the kitchen is a "Zone"
diet breakfast. There is a dog. Visa,MC ✔ B&B http://www.twincedars.com

Brackendale

(north of Vancouver; see also Whistler, Pemberton)

Vanderhoef, Sue & Marty (Glacier Valley Farm)   ☎ (604) 898-2810, Fax (604) 898-2844
Box 30, Brackendale, BC   V0N 1H0   Cell (604)892-7533, Email:gvfarm@mountain-inter.net

Located at Mile 16.5 Upper Squamish Valley Rd. Phone for directions.
$65-75S $80-95D $15 Add.person   🍽 Meals   ▶6-8
🍴 Full (farm-style)   🏠 Working farm, quiet, glacier-views from guest
rooms   ■ 3(upstairs)   🛏 2D,4T,1Q,cots   🛁 1Sh.w.g.   ★ F
🏃 Hiking trails, bird watching, fly fishing, river rafting, creek fishing
🚗 Squamish, shops, pubs, restaurants, buses, trains
☞ Large, rambling wooden farm house on working farm with sheep,
horses & farm animals, located in a very private and scenic valley,
surrounded by snow-capped mountains, waterfalls & green hillsides. Relax in
the cozy guest sitting nook. A perfect place to unwind. Visa,MC
http://www.bbcanada.com/547.html

Burns Lake

(west of Prince George)

Dicker, Mary & Noel (Loyola by the Lake B&B)   ☎ (250) 695-6396
Box 585, Burns Lake, BC   V0J 1E0   E-mail: mdicker@futurenet.bc.ca

Located on Colleymount Rd, Francois Lake. From Prince George, take Hwy 16 (Yellowhead) west
for 225km to Burns Lake. Take Hwy 35 south for 24km to Francois Lake. Proceed west past the
ferry terminal on Colleymount Rd for 4.5km. Look for B&B highway sign.

$50-55S $60-65D $10Add.person   (Family discounts)   ►6
🍴 Full, homebaked   🏠 Rural, 2-storey, view from guest rooms,
lakefront, quiet, covered veranda   ■ 2 (upstairs)   ⊨ 1Q,2T,2
large foamies   🚿Sh.w.h.(or private)   ★TV, off-street parking
⬤No pets, smoking outside   ⚬ French, some German
🧍 Wonderful lake (100 km long - fishing, boating, canoeing - pure
unpolluted water), walking, hiking, cycling, x-c skiing, Alpaca &
Llama ranch nearby, wildlife for photo enthusiasts
🚗 Omineca x-c ski trails, Eagle Creek Opal Beds, Nourse Creek Falls
🚌 Perfect retreat in comfortable home overlooking the lake, set amid rolling pastures, woodland
and the distant peaks of Tweedsmuir Park. Relax on the veranda or in the sunroom. Breakfast may
be served "al fresco"on the covered veranda. Families welcome. There is a cat outside.

Canal Flats

(north of Cranbrook; see also Fairmont Hot Springs, Windermere, Jaffray)

D'Silva, Adrian & Tracey (Findlay Creek Lodge)   ☎ & Fax (250) 349-5352
8807 Findlay Creek Rd., Box 9, Canal Flats, BC   V0B 1B0

Take Hwy 93/95 for 20km south of Fairmont Hot Springs. Turn on Findlay Creek Rd, follow signs.

$85-95S/D   🍽 Meals   ►6
🍴 Full, homebaked   🏠 Rural, 2-storey, acreage, view from guest
rooms, patio, deck, quiet, secluded   ■ 3D(upstairs)   ⊨ 3Q
🚿3Private   ★ F,satTV in guest lounge, ceiling fans, off-street
parking   ⬤Restricted smoking,no pets,not suitable for children
🧍 Hiking trails on property, viewpoints, picnic & B-B-Q spots,
inhouse gift shop
🚗 Championship golf course, public beach, natural hot springs,
trophy fishing lakes & rivers, kayaking, canoeing, Kimberley, Invermere
🚌 Warm welcome in peaceful and tranquil home, situated on 20 private acres with spectacular
lake and mountain views in the Columbia Valley. Breakfast is served in the guest dining room with
a river-rock fireplace and view of Columbia Lake. Relax in the hammock in the garden. Romance
and golf packages available. There is a dog in residence. Visa,MC

Chemainus *(on Vanc.Isle, south of Nanaimo; see also Saltsprings Isle, Ladysmith, Duncan)*

Blatchford, Larry (Castlebury Inn)   ☎ (250) 246-9228, Fax (250) 246-2909
9910 Croft St., Box 1432, Chemainus, BC   V0R 1K0   E-mail: birdsong@island.net

Phone for directions.
$325D   (plus tax)   ► 4
🍴 Full   🏠 Village, castles, view from guest rooms, porch, quiet,
secluded   ■ 2Ste(main & ground level)   ⊨ 2Q   🚿 2Ensuite
★Air,KF,LF,F,TV in suites, off-street parking, guest quarters are
separate   ⬤ No smoking, no pets, not suitable for children
🧍 Murals, art galleries, unique gift shops, Dinner Theatre, horse-drawn
tours, Native Art, tea houses, fine dining, beach, lake swimming, golfing,
kayaking, sailing charters
🚗 Bus, train, Airport, ferry
🚌 Whimsical and romantic medieval-style one room castles with giant marble soaking tubs, and
Juliet-Lookout to watch the sunrise/sunset on the sea. Breakfast Basket is delivered to suites.
Enjoy fruitful melancholy contemplation in very unique & memorable surroundings.
www.romanticbb.com

Chemainus (cont'd)

Blatchford, Virginia (Bird Song Cottage B&B)   ☎ (250) 246-9910, Fax 246-2909
Box 1432, 9909 Maple St, Chemainus, BC   V0R 1K0   E-mail: birdsong@island.net

Phone for directions.
$80S $105D $25Add.person   (plus tax)   ► 8
🍴 Full, homebaked   🏠 Village, hist., view from guest rooms, porch, quiet   ■ 3Ste(main & ground level)   ⊨ 1S,2T,1D,2Q
⊷3Ensuite   ★F, street parking   🖐 No smoking, no pets, children min. age 9
🚌 Bus, train, Airport, ferry
🏃 Murals, art galleries, unique shops, Dinner theatre, beach & lake swimming, horse-drawn tours, Tea Houses, fine dining, golfing, kayaking, sailing charters
🔫 Delightful lavender/white gingerbrad cottage, with bird theme guest rooms, and a potpourri of Victorian whimsey, surrounded by old-fashioned gardens and trickling fountains. Guest lounge with grand piano, celtic harp and a pump organ. Ideal place for special occasions, honeymoons & anniversaries. Relax in the garden sunporch with hand painted garden scenes. Enjoy a sumptuous morning fare. House specialty is "Bird Song Serendipity Tea" (a fun event - Victorian dress-up style - inquire for details). Breakfast is served on fine china in guest breakfast room. Special diets catered. There is a cat in residence.   www.island.net/~birdsong

---

Plater, Jane & Roy (Terrace Gardens Guest House)   ☎ (250) 246-2815
3114 Sunset Dr., RR1, Chemainus, BC   V0R 1K0

$50S $55-65D $10Child(under age 13)   (2nd night 25% discount)   ► 4

Phone for directions.
🍴 Full, homebaked   🏠 Village, 2-storey, view from guest rooms, deck, quiet   ■2(ground level)   ⊨1D,1Q   ⊷1Private
★F,TV/VCR in guest room, separate entrance, private hot tub(spa)   🖐One party only, children & pets welcome, designated smoking area   ～some Russian
🏃 Downtown Chemainus and 33 world famous murals
🚌 Nanaimo, ferries to Thetis/Gabriola/Saltspring Isls, Victoria
🔫 Spacious, beautiful home in "a hollow on a hill" overlooking Georgia Strait & mainland mountains. Breakfast is served in the dining room or adjacent upper deck. Relax in the hot tub and watch the moon rise over the water and the lights of Vancouvers' ski lifts in the background. Well travelled hosts enjoy music, theatre, books, golfing. ✔CC

Clearwater   *(north of Kamloops; see also 100 Mile House)*

Fischer, Joe (Trophy Mountain Buffalo Ranch B&B)   ☎ (250) 674-3095,
Box 1768, RR1, Clearwater, BC   V0E 1N0   E-mail: buffranch@hotmail.com, Fax (250) 674-3131

In Clearwater, turn at the Tourist Info Centre and proceed 20 km up Wells Gray Pk Rd.
$35-55S $50-60D $15-25Add.person   (plus taxes)   (packed lunches)   ► 13
🍴 Full, homebaked   🏠 Farm, log house, view, quiet, 70 acres
■ 8D (main & upper level)   ⊨ 3S,2D,3Q   ⊷ 2Private,
4ensuite   ★Air,F,LF, separate entrance   🖐Smoking outside, pets outside   ～ German
🏃 Horseback riding, hiking and x/c ski trails, mountain biking
🚌 Wells Gray Provincial Park, Trophy Mountain hiking area, Helmcken Falls, canoeing, river rafting, skiing, Clearwater
🔫 Hobby bison/horse farm with old log house built in 1926, completely restored for B&B. Hosts are outdoor adventure guides and well informed about the area and its many excellent outdoor activities. Visa,MC ✔CC

Cobble Hill
(south of Duncan; see also Mill Bay)

Simpson, Vicki & Gordon (Heron Hill B&B)   ☎ (250)743-3855,Fax (250)743-5821
3760 Granfield Place, RR2, Cobble Hill, BC   V0R 1L0   E-mail: heronhill@cvnet.net

From Hwy 1, north of Mill Bay, turn east on Hutchinson Rd towards Arbutus Ridge. Turn left onto Telegraph, then right onto Aros to Granfield.
$70S $70-80D $15Add.person   ► 6-8
🍴Full 🏠Rural, 2-storey, deck, view, quiet ■3D ⊨2T,1D,1Q,1R
⬛3Ensuite ★Fridge/microwave in guest sitting room, separate entrance to one room 🚭No smoking, no pets
🕯 Access to rocky beach, country roads
🚗 Arbutus Ridge Golf course, Shawnigan Lake, Cowichan Bay, Mill Bay Centre shopping, Duncan Native Heritage Ctr, Chemainus Murals, Nanaimo, Victoria
☞ Relax with a sea view of Gulf Islands and Mt. Baker. Hosts have been welcoming B&B guests for many years and assure a friendly approach and easy-going service. Enjoy the rural atmosphere with good access to shops and attractions. Home of the world famous "Cobble Cake". ✒B&B

Comox
(on Vancouver Isle east of Courtenay; see also Cumberland, Denman Isle)

Hendren, Dove & Michael (Foskett House B&B)   ☎ & Fax (250) 339-4272
484 Lazo Rd., Comox, BC   V9M 3V1   E-mail: foskett@island.net, 1-800-797-9252

Located 5.2 km from Comox. Follow boat launching signs on Lazo Rd. Turn left at green gate.
$65-75S $80-90D $20Add.person   (reservation recommended)   ► 5

🍴 Full, homebaked 🏠 Rural, ranch-style, hist., acreage, view from guest room, oceanfront at end of driveway, deck, veranda, quiet, secluded ■2D (main level) ⊨2Q,1P ⬛Ensuite
★TV,F, separate entrance 🚬Designated smoking area
🕯 Surrounding forest, boat launch, birdwatching, beachcombing
🚗 Skiing/hiking (Mt.Washington & Forbidden Plateau), fishing, ferry to Powell River
☞ 1920-built South African-style rancher with wrap around verandas, finished inside with cedar and a large beach stone fireplace in the great room, filled with collectibles and antiques, and a view of the Straits of Georgia. Located on 5 acres of forest in the Point Holmes area, retired hosts returned to the Comox Valley after years of city life in politics and Industry. Ideal spot for painters & photographers. There is a dog in residence. Heritage Tourism packages available. Visa,MC ✒B&B

Robb,Shirley & Alan(Alan&Shirley Robb's Levenvale B&B)   ☎(250)339-3307,Fax339-4036
2081 Murphy Ave, Comox BC   V9M 1V4   E-mail: alshirlrobb@bc.sympatico.ca

Enter Comox, turn right on Rodello just past Hospital. Look for 3rd street towards water.
$40S $55D $5-20Child/Add.person   ► 4

🍴 Full(Gourmet) 🏠 Res, split-level, view, deck, patio, very quiet ■2D (main & ground level) ⊨2T(K),1Q,1P
⬛2private ★F,LF, separate entrance, TV in suite sitting room, off-street parking 🚬Designated smoking area
🕯 Hospital, restaurants/pubs, marina/beach, shops, Filberg Park
🚗 Campbell River
☞ Well travelled hosts in central Comox home overlooking Comox Bay, furnished with interesting memorabilia/antiques. Enjoy the lovely garden & pond. Gourmet breakfast served with a flair on deck or in the formal dining room both with a glorious view of ocean, mountains & marina. Families & children welcome. ✒B&B

Cortes Island

(near Campbell River)

Hansen, Emilia & Gunnar (Blue Heron Bed & Breakfast)   ☎ (250) 935-6584
Potlatch Rd., Box 23, Manson's Landing., Cortes Island, BC   V0P 1K0

Take ferry from Campbell River (Vancouver Island) to Quadra Island. Drive to Heriot Bay and take
ferry to Cortes Island (45min). (20km from Whaletown Ferry Ldg near Smelt Bay Prov.Park).
$40-65S $45-70D $15Add.person   ▶ 4A,2Ch

🍳 Full, homebaked   🏠 Rural, res., ranch-style, acreage, view
from one guest room, oceanfront, patio, quiet   ▪ 1D,1F (main
level)   ⊨ 2T,1K,2R   🛁 1Sh.w.h., 1ensuite   ★ TV, separate
entrance, parking   🐾No pets, restricted smoking   〰 Danish
🚶 Beach and tide pools
📷 Spacious country home situated in garden setting on Potlatch
Rd. overlooking Sutil Channel toward Vancouver Island. Relax and
enjoy the special sunsets. There are pets.   ✐B&B

Courtenay

(on Van.Isle; south of Campbell R.; see also Comox, Cumberland)

Shipton, Mike & Maureen (Greystone Manor)   ☎ (250) 338-1422
4014 Haas Rd., RR6, Site 684, C2, Courtenay, BC   V9N 8H9

Located 3km south of Courtenay in Royston on Hwy19A. Turn on Hilton/Haas.

$60S $80D $20Add. person   ▶ 8A
🍳 Full, homebaked   🏠 Rural, older, view, waterfront, 1.5 acres, beautiful
flower gardens   ▪3D)upstairs)   ⊨1D,2T,1Q   🛁 2Ensuite, 1private   🐾No
smoking, no pets, child min age 12   ★Guest sitting room
🚶 Walking trails, rural setting, beach
🚐 Hiking, Denman/Hornby Islands, x/c & downhill skiing, ferry to Powell
River & Sunshine Coast
📷 Warm welcome in charming 1918-built waterfront home, with
breathtaking views across Comox Bay to the coastal mountains. Hosts came
from Bath (England) in 1990 and have brought with them their love of
gardening and created a beautiful English Flower Garden, a photographer
& Gardener's delight. Visa,MC ✐B&B http://www.bbcanada.com/1334.html

---

Cranbrook

(south-east BC; see also Kimberley, Ft.Steele, Fernie)

Dirom, Sandra & Robert (Singing Pines B&B)   ☎& Fax(604)426-5959,1-800-863-4969
5180 Kennedy Rd,SS3,S15,BoxA-9,Cranbrook,BC V1C 6H3   E-mail: singingpines@cyberlink.bc.ca

From Hwy 3/95 at Cranbrook, take Airport/Kimberley 95A North Exit & proceed 3.9km north.
Turn right at Kennedy, look for sign.
$80S $90-100D $20Add.person   ▶ 8
🍳 Full   🏠 Rural, ranch-style, acreage, view from guest rooms,
patio, large decks, quiet   ▪ 2D,1F (main level)   ⊨ 3Q,2T(extra
long)   🛁 3Ensuite   ★ F,TV/VCR & phone in guest rooms,
guest robes, private entrance, 2 guest lounges incl. hospitality
center, guest quarters are separate, outdoor hot tub, off-street
parking   🐾Designated smoking area, no pets, children min.age12
🚐 Wildlife & birdwatching, three Championship golf courses, downhill & x-c skiing, Fort Steele
Heritage Village, Museum of Rail Travel, Mining Railway, world class fishing, rafting, canoeing
📷 Warm and friendly welcome in comfortable home situated on 10acres of natural beauty with
views of the Rocky Mountains to the east and the Purcell Mountains to the west. Breakfast is
served on the covered deck. Enjoy nature's ever changing splendour. There is a large dog. CCards ✐
B&B www.bbcanda.com/singingpines

Cranbrook (cont'd)

Goss, Gladys (The Gables B&B)　　　　　　☎ (250) 426-7993, Fax (250) 426-7965
110-12th Ave South, Cranbrook, BC　V1C 2S1　　　E-mail: thegablesbb@bc.sympatico.ca

From Hwy 3/95 proceed to downtown area. Turn left at 1st St South, then right onto 12th Ave S.

$70-80S　$80-90D　$10Child/Add.person　　　　▶ 6A,3Ch
🍲 Full, homebaked　🏠 Hist., patio, porch,
quiet　■2(upstairs)　⊨2D,1Q　🛏3Ensuite　★ TV, stocked
bar-fridge in each room, off-street/street parking　♥
🚭Smoking outside, no pets, children min.age 5
🧍 Baker Hill Historic neighbourhood, Canadian Museum of Rail
Travel, shops, theatres, restaurants
🚗 Fort Steele Heritage Town, Wasa Lake, Trout Hatchery,
Cranbrook Heritage Tour, golfing, trail rides, boating, skiing
🖝 Uniquely renovated heritage-style home located in a quiet neighbourhood of "sunny" little
town (more sunshine than any other city in BC). Breakfast is served in the "one-of-a-kind" dining
room, in kitchen nook or on the sundeck. Relax in the front parlour with eclectic library. School-age
children welcome. Dog kennel available. Visa,MC ✓B&B

Murray, Gloria (Cranberry House Bed & Breakfast)　　☎ & Fax (250) 489-6216
321 Cranbrook St.N., Cranbrook, BC　V1C 3R4

Located right on the strip in Cranbrook. From Hwy 3/95, turn right at Van Horne St to Cranbrook
St to 3rd house on right. From Hwy 3/95 (Crowsnest Hwy) stay on Cranbrook St, continue

past Sandman Inn, go through lights and proceed to B&B on right.
$60S　$65-70D　(plus taxes)　　　　　▶ 8
🍲 Full, homebaked　🏠 Downtown, res., 2-storey, hist., patio,
porch　■4D (upstairs)　⊨ 4T,2Q　🛏 2Sh.w.g.　★Air,F,TV
in guest rooms, phone hook-ups, purified water, hot tub, off-street
parking　🚬 Smoking on patio, no pets, children min. age 12
🧍 Railway Museum, Cranbrook Heritage Walk, downtown core
🚗 Kimberley Ski Hills, Fairmont Hot Springs, Kootenay Trout
Hatchery, Fort Steele Heritage Town, Moyie Lake
🖝 Beautifully, refurbished, award winning Heritage home with antiques & quality decor.
Longtime hostess formerly operated a B&B in Moyie. Fax access available. Visa,MC,Amex ✓CC

Crawford Bay　　　　　　　　　　*(west of Cranbrook; see also Creston)*

Huiberts, Joan (Wedgewood Manor)　　　　　☎ & Fax (250) 227-9233
Box 135, Crawford Bay, BC　V0B 1E0

From Nelson go east on Hwy 3A cross Kootenay Lake by ferry (free) and drive 7km east to Crawford
Bay. From Creston go north on Hwy 3A along Kootenay Lake to Crawford Bay

$79S　$79-120D　$20Child　$20Add.person　　　▶ 12A,2Ch

🍲Full, homebaked　🏠Rural, hist., acreage, view, patio, quiet
■6D(main & upper level)　⊨1D,5Q　🛏6ensuite　★3F,
2private guest lounges, guest bicycles　🚭No pets, no smoking,
children min.age 4
🧍 Crawford Bay beach on Kootenay Lake (water still pure enough
to drink), canoe along pristine shoreline, golf at Kokanee Springs,
excellent walking/hiking from doorstep, Harrison Memorial
Church next door (handy for wedding party)
🚗 Kootenay Lake Ferry (longest free ride in NA), Ainsworth (sumptuous hot springs and cavern)
🖝 Historic, 1900-built Manor is situated on a 55-acres estate overlooking a small valley at the
foot of the Purcell Mountains and is furnished with pieces from the Victorian era with a library
lounge and front veranda. Honeymoon/anniversary/golf packages available. Visa,MC ✓B&B

Creston

(south-west of Cranbrook; see also Crawford Bay)

Allmeritter, Gertrud and Werner (Goat-River Lodge) ☎ (250)428-7134,Fax(250)428-4713
1108 Lamont Rd, RR1,S40,Box8, Creston,BC V0B 1G0   E-mail: allmi@kootenay.awinc.com

Located in Erickson, 0.5 km from Creston or 2km from Hwy 3W.
$45S $60-75D $10Add.person   E-mail: ✎ 6
🍴 Full (European)   🏠 Rural, res., bungalow, 7acres, view,
patio, heated swimming pool,riverfront   ■ 3D (main level)
🛏2D,2Q   🚪Private   ★TV in guest room, LF, sep.entrance,
private porch 🚭No smoking,no pets ~German
🏃 Wayside Gardens, museum, golf course
🚐 Kootenay Lake, Wildlife Center, golfing

☞ Home is located in the middle of 1000 fruit trees and cherry orchard with a beautiful view over the Goat River Valley. Enjoy the special honeymoon suite. There is a resident dog, cat & bird. ✎CC

Cumberland

(south of Courtenay, Denman Island, Comox)

Davis, Shelagh & D.Jackson (Wellington House B&B) ☎(250)336-8809,Fax(250)336-2321
2593 Derwent Ave, Box 689, Cumberland, BC V0R 1S0   E-mail: cma-chin@island.net

Take new Inland Island Hwy 19 to Cumberland, and follow signs to Dunsmuir Ave. Proceed
through the village, turn left towards Comox Lake and first right onto Derwent Ave.

$60S $75-80D $20Add.person   ► 8
🍴Full,homebaked 🏠Village, hillside, small acreage, patio, deck
porch, quiet, secluded   ■ 1D,2Ste(upstairs & garden level)
🛏1S,1D,2Q   🚪2Private,1sh.w.h.   ★TV/VCR in private guest
sitting rooms, KF in garden suite, ceiling fans, sep.entrance, guest
quarters are sep. 🚭Smoking on patio, children welcome
🏃 Original Mining Weigh Scale on property, village shops, Comox
Lake, restaurants, museum, hiking trails from property

🚐 Mt.Washington & Forbidden Plateau Ski Resorts, Filberg Lodge (Comox), golfing, ferries to
Powell River, Nanaimo and islands, sport fishing
☞ Country elegant suites in large modern home situated in a park-like setting in historic mining
village located in the foothills of the Beaufort Mountains. A perfect spot to relax and unwind.
Breakfast is served in large country kitchen. Hostess comes from England, and enjoys sharing the
peaceful surroundings with guests. There is a dog. Visa ✎B&B www.vquest.com/wellington/

Delta

(Vancouver); see also Tsawwassen, Richmond, White Rock)

Taylor, Jon & Margaret (The Ranch House) ☎ (604) 946-1553
7061 Ladner Trunk Rd., Delta, BC V4K 3N3

Located on Hwy 10 (Ladner Trunk Rd) in Delta, betw.Hwys 17/99.
$75S $85D $15Add.person   ► 6
🍴 Full, homebaked   🏠 Farm, ranch-style, acreage, view, porch
deck, quiet   ■ 3D,1F (main floor)   🛏1S,1D,2Q,crib, playpen
🚪2Sh.w.g.   ★ LF,F,TV in guest living room, private entrance,
off-street parking, guest quarters are separate   🚭 Designated
smoking area, no pets
🚐 Tsawwassen Ferries to Victoria & Nanaimo, US border,
downtown Vancouver, Grouse Mountain skiing, Vancouver Int. Airport
🏃 Reifel Bird Sanctuary, Burns Bog, hiking trails, bus to all areas of lower mainland
☞ Friendly country-style hospitality on small hobby farm with large backyard and located in the
Ladner area of rural Delta. There are 2 horses for viewing and petting. Relax in the hot tub on the
sundeck overlooking farmland and the captivating views of coastal mountains. For those guests
arriving and departing through Boundary Bay Airport, complimentary transportation is available.
There are 2 resident dogs. Visa ✎B&B http://www.bbcanada.com/2160.html

Duncan

(on Va.Isle north of Victoria; see also Cobble Hill, Saltspring Isle)

Gunnlaugson, Marjorie (Country Gardens B&B)   ☎ (250) 748-5865
1665 Grand Rd., Duncan, BC   V9L 5N7

From Swartz Bay Ferry, proceed on Hwy 17 to Hwy 1 and then north to Duncan. Turn right on Trunk Rd (first light after Silver Bridges) and follow Maple Bay signs to Grant Rd.

$45S $60D   ► 4A,1Ch
🍳Full, homebaked   🏠Rural, ranch-style, lake view, 2patios
■1S,2D   🚿Private   ★F,TV, wheel-chair access. ✋No
smoking, no pets, children min. age 13   ~~Dutch
🚐 Chemainus ("the little town that did") famous for its murals,
Native Heritage center (with magnificient world of North-west
Coast Indians) Whippletree Junction (crafts and antiques), ferries
🐾 Country charm in lovely cedar log home on private acreage.
Enjoy breakfast on the patios overlooking beautiful Quamichan Lake or tranquil garden with lily ponds. There is a pool with a waterfall & goldfish and there is a Briard in residence. ✓CC

Fairmont Hot Springs

(south of Golden; see also Windermere, Canal Flats)

McMillan, Bonnie & Ken (McMillan Chalet Bed & Breakfast)   ☎(250) 345-9553
Box 989, Fairmont Hot Springs,BC V0B1L0   1-800-856-9551 fax:(250) 345-2143
                                                 E-mail: kenmcm@rockies.net
Located at 5021 Fairmont Close. Take Hwy 93 to Fairmont Hot Springs. Turn east off Hwy at large Fairmont Resort sign, left on Hot Springs Rd, right on Falcon Rd, right on Fairmont Close.

$50-69S $60-79D $5-15Child $20Add.person   ► 6A,2Ch

🍳Homebaked (gourmet)   🏠Resort,Chalet-type, 3-storey, quiet,
mountain view,deck   ■3D(loft & lower level)   🛏2Q,1K,2T,cot
🚿1Sh.w.g.,2ensuite   ★F,TV in guest rooms   ✋Smoking outside
on deck, no pets
🏃 Five major golf courses, large natural hot spring pools,
recreational activities in Resort town
🚐 Scenic roads, fine dining, Windermere Lake, swimming,
boating, Invermere, Kimberley, Fort Steele Heritage town
🐾 Professional couple in comfortable chalet with large cathedral windows, situated in popular resort area. Relax on the deck and enjoy the beautiful mountain scenery. Convenient location near major route. Reservations please. Low season rates available. Visa,MC
www.bbexpo.com/bc/mcmchalet.htm

Fernie
(east of Cranbrook; see also Fort Steele, Kimberley, Jaffray)

Bowles, Barbara & Knud Larsen (Barbara Lynn's Country Inn B&B) ☎(250)423-6027,
691-7th Ave, Box 1077, Fernie, BC   V0B 1M0   1-888-288-2148,Fax(250)423-6024
E-mail: barbscountryinn@discoverfernie.com,

$40-65S $50-85D $60-130F $5-20Child (Extended stay/Senior/Cyclist rates)   ► 12-14

Located off Hwy 3 at 7th St.

🍴 Cont.(plus),homebaked 🏠Res, in town, view from guest
rooms, privacy deck, veranda ■ 5D,1F(upstairs) ⊨2T,4D,4Q,
bunk,futon sofa bed ⊿2Sh.w.g.,2ensuite ★KF,F, thermostats
in rooms, private entrance & parking, guest TV room with kitchen,
hot tub ⊕No smoking, no pets
🧍 Restaurants, pubs, stores, golfing, x-c ski/bike/walking trails,
tennis courts, Elk River abounds with fish

🚗Fernie Alpine Resort, Golf & Country Club, mountain climbing/hiking, Cranbrook Airport
🖝 Warm and friendly welcome in new home with country charm, and spectacular mountain
views, situated in the scenic Canadian Rocky Mountains. Hostess is a cycle tourist and loves to
share experiences with other cyclists. Ski packages available to ski ultimate snow in an area that is
fast becoming one of the great ski destinations in the world. (Average snowfall is 750cm and
liftlines are almost non-existent). Ski shuttle operated between town and the resort. Relax in the
hot tub after an active day and enjoy the congenial atmosphere. Host offers photography services to
anyone interested. Visa,MC ⌐B&B www.bbcanada.com/barbscountryinn

---

Fort Steele
(north-east of Cranbrook; see also Kimberley, Fernie)

Emery, John & Joanna (Emery's Mountain View B&B)   ☎ & Fax (250) 426-4756
Box 60, 183 Wardner-Fort Steele Rd., Fort Steele, BC   V0B 1N0

Located 2 km off Hwy 93/95. In Fort Steele, turn at Esso Stn. onto Wardner-Fort Steele Rd.
Proceed down hill over bridge and continue 1 km to house on right.

                $75-85S $85-100D $20Child/Add.person   ► 9
🍴 Full 🏠 Rural, 2-storey, acreage, view from guest rooms,
riverback, patio, porch, quiet, secluded ■ 3D incl.suite (upstairs)
+2cabins ⊨ 2T,2Q,1K,4cots ⊿ Private ★ Ceiling fans,
KF & separate entrance in cabin, off-street parking ⊕ Smoking
outside, no pets
🧍 Observe wild animals and birds in the marsh, stroll along the
Wild Horse River on north side of property

🚗 Golfing, skiing, Hot Springs, historic sites, mountain trails
🖝 Country home located on 14 scenic hectares along Wild Horse Creek and away from the
highways. Enjoy the breathtaking panoramic view of the majestic Canadian Rocky Mountains.
Hosts are well informed about the area and will provide directions to interesting historic sites.
Breakfast is served in main building dining room. There are 2 dogs in residence. Visa ⌐B&B
http://www.bbcanada.com/3207.html

Gibsons

(n/w of Vancouver; see also Bowen Isle, Roberts Creek, Sechelt)

Bailey, Sue & Gord (Marina House B&B) ☎ (604) 886-7888, 1-888-568-6688
546 Marine Dr., Box 1696, Gibsons, BC V0N 1V0   E-mail: marinahouse@sunshine.net

From Horseshoe Bay, take ferry (40min) to Langdale Ferry Terminal and proceed 4km south on the lower road. Located on the Sunshine Coast north of Vancouver.
$80S $90D $20Add.person   ▶ 6A
🍴 Full, homebaked 🏠 Res, hillside, 3-storey, hist., view from guest rooms, ocreanfront, porch, quiet ■3D(street level)
🛏2T(1K),2Q 🛁1Private,2ensuite ★TV in guest lounge, private entrance, off-street parking,boat ramp/mooring
ⓌSmoking on porches, no pets, not suitable for children
🚶 Beach walks, Gibsons Ldg & Molly's Reach (of "Beachcomber"
Fame), museum, shops, restaurants, mountain hiking, Sunshine Coast Transit Bus
🚗 Trails, beachwalks, golfing, fishing, sailing, secret coves, x-c skiing, Skookumchuck Rapids
☞ Heritage home (1931) restored to its original charm. A perfect destination for a weekend escape or stop-over on route around the inner-coast loop or home-base for kayak/canoe/cycle day-trips up the Sunshine Coast. Breakfast is served in the sunny breakfast room with exceptional ocean views. Breakfast picnic packages for early departure. Ferry pick-up avail.Visa,MC ✒B&B
http://wwww.wcbbia com/pages/marinahouse.html

Verzyl, Dianne and Bert (Ocean-View Cottage B&B) ☎ (604) 886-7943, Fax 886-4311
1927 Grandview Rd., RR5, Gibsons, BC V0N 1V5   1-800-231-9122

From Vancouver take ferry at Horseshoe Bay to Langdale (35 min). Proceed along scenic drive up the Sunshine Coast Hwy. Turn left at lower Rd, left on Pine Rd, right on Grandview Rd (#1927).
$75S $85D $120D(Cottage) $10Child $20Add.person   ▶ 4,2Ch
🍴 Homebaked(gourmet) 🏠Rural, acreage, view,quiet ■1D,plus

self-cont. cottage 🛏2T,1K,1Q 🛁2Private, soaker tub in cottage ★F,KF,TV in room ⓌNo pets,no smoking
💬French, Dutch
🚶 Beaches, walking and hiking trails, restaurants
🚗 Ferries to Vancouver, Powell River, Vancouver Island, golfing
☞ New home situated on the beautiful Sunshine Coast in quiet rural setting with a panoramic view of the sea/mountains. Relax
on the deck & watch Alaska cruise ships go by.Visa,MCB&B www.vancouver-bc.com/oceanview

---

Golden

(near Alberta border(Banff Nat.Park); see also Parson, Revelstoke)

Baier, Hubert & Sonja (Hillside Lodge) ☎ & Fax (250) 344-7281
1740 Seward Frontage Rd., Box 2603, Golden, BC V0A 1H0

$80-90S/D $10-15Child $20Add.person $98-115Chalets 🍽 Meals (plus tax)   ▶ 20
Located 13km west of Golden and 500m off TCH1.Follow signs.
🍴 Full, homebaked 🏠 Rural, Black Forest house & brand new chalets, acreage, patio, quiet, riverfront ■4D, 5Chalets 🛏10D
🛁4Private ★TV,F, private balconies or terrace, parking
💬German
🚶 Blaeberry River, hiking trails, bird/game watching, Wildlife Nature Reserve, fishing, whitewater rafting, kayaking, trail riding, golfing, Whitetooth ski-hill, x/c skiing, dog-sledding trips
🚗 Banff/Lake Louise Nat. Park, Rogers Pass, Glacier Nat.Park, Mummery Glacier, Kootenay & Yoho Nat.Parks, Radium Hot Springs, Columbia Icefields
☞ Quiet get-away home situated on 60 acres at Blaeberry River in the heart of the Rockies. Enjoy a brand new chalet or a room in the charming lodge. Relax on the porch, balconies or in the dining room with a spectacular view. Healthy meals are prepared by host chef in the evening & by the hostess for breakfast. There is a family dog; llamas, horses & goats are outside. CCards ✒CC

Golden (cont'd)

Kowalski, Ruth & André (H.G. Parson House)   ☎ (250) 344-5001, Fax (250) 344-2782
815-12th Street South, Box 1196, Golden, BC   V0A 1H0   E-mail: hgparsonhousebb@redshift.bc.ca

$72-77S $82-87D $10-20Child $15Add.person   (plus tax)   ► 6A,3Ch

Phone for directions.
🍴 Full, homebaked (buffet)   🏠 Res., 2-storey, hist., view, porch   ■ 3D(upstairs)   ⊨ 2T,2Q   ⌐ 1Private, 2ensuite ★F,TV,off-street parking   Ⓦ Designated smoking area, no pets   ⌁ French, Polish
🏃 Town walking trails, downtown area, summer/winter activities
🚗 Kootenay & Yoho Nat.Parks, Lake Louise, Radium Hot Springs, Rogers Pass, Emerald Lake

📢 Comfortable home built in 1893, completely furnished with antiques and collectibles and theme guest rooms; surrounded by beautiful Rocky Mountain scenery. Town is situated in the last of the natural wetlands. Relax on the front veranda or in the large private yard. Ideal place to stay a few days and visit the National Parks. Hosts know the area well and will plan personal activity packages for guests. Dog in residence. Visa,MC 🛏B&B   www.hgparsonhousebb.com

---

Perzinger, Erwin (Columbia Valley Lodge)   ☎(250)348-2508, Fax(250)348-2505
Box 2669, Golden, BC   V0A 1H0   E-mail: cvl@rockies.net, 1-800-311-5008

Located on Hwy 95 and 23 km south of Golden towards Radium Hot Springs.
$45-85S/D $10Add.person   🍴 Meals   (Senior's discounts)   (Off-season rates avail)   ► 35

🍴Homebaked 🏠Rural,acreage,view from guest rooms,patio,peaceful
■12units(main & upper floor) ⊨T,D,Q   ⌐Private ★Sep.entrance, licenced dining room, parking ⓌNo pets ⌁German
🏃 Columbia River, birdwatching, canoeing, photography, x-country skiing, horseback riding (on request)
🚗 Golden, Radium Hot Springs, Yoho, Banff & Glacier Nat.Parks
📢 European-style lodge with its unique touch and relaxed atmosphere, situated in a countryside setting surrounded by Rocky and Purcell Moutains and by the Columbia Valley Wetlands. Host is an Austrian Chef and serves European cuisine. Visa,MC 🛏CC www.bbcanada.com/2081.html

---

Grand Forks   *(south-east of Penticton; see also Greenwood)*

Fausten, Sharon & Richard (The Orchard Bed & Breakfast)   ☎ (250) 442-8583
5615 Spencer Rd., Grand Forks, BC   V0H 1H5

Located at 5615 Spencer Rd in Grand Forks. From jct of Hwys 3 & 41 (west of Grand Forks) go west to 2nd road on right (Spencer Rd). Turn right to first driveway on left.

$50S $60D $10Add.person   ► 4-6A
🍴 Full, homebaked   🏠 Rural, ranch-style, acreage, orchard view from guest rooms, deck, quiet   ■ 2D (main floor)   ⊨2T,1Q
⌐1Sh.w.g.   ★ LF,separate entrance, off-street parking
ⓌDesignated smoking area
🏃 Great hiking trail behind house, Fructova Heritage Centre
🚗 Jewel Lake (fishing), Christina Lake (public beach & park & golf course), Doukhobor Museum

📢 Experience warm country hospitality in attractive home nestled in a small working orchard with many varieties of fruit. Guests are welcome to pick fruit in season. Enjoy a beautiful view of the Sunshine Valley while having breakfast featuring fruits from the orchard. House specialty is fresh fruit crepes. 🛏 B&B

Greenwood

(south-east of Penticton; see also Grand Falls)

Dixon, Keith & Marilyn (Forshaw House B&B)   ☎ & Fax (250) 445-2208
197 Kimberley Ave.S, Box 288, Greenwood, BC   V0H 1J0

From east or west, take Hwy 3 into Greenwood. At museum, turn uphill to 1st house on left.
$40-55S $50-65D $10Add.person (Child free under age 6)   🍴 Meals   ▶9

🍲 Full, homebaked   🏠 Downtown, hist., 3-storey, quiet, porch,
deck ■3(main & upper level)incl.suite ↦1D,1Q,3S,2R
🛁1Ensuite, 2sh.w.g   ★F,TV,KF,one guest balcony, street
parking   🚭No smoking
🏃 Walks in old mining town with interesting Japanese history,
horseback riding, Greyhound bus stop, museum
🚗 Phoenix, old site of Coppermine, Grand Forks with Russian
history, hiking, canoeing, fishing, golfing, downhill/x-c skiing

📣 Friendly hosts in stately,1902-built Victorian-style home situated across from City Hall (&old
Supreme Court & Jail) of the smallest city in BC. Take a self-guided historic walking tour. ✐B&B

Halfmoon Bay

(north of Gibsons; see also Sechelt, Roberts Creek)

Burchill, Jack & Millie (Burchill's B&B by the Sea)   ☎ (604) 883-2400
RR2, Donley Site C17, Halfmoon Bay, BC V0N 1Y0

Located 50km north of the Langdale ferry slip.
$90S/D $25Child $35Add.person   ▶ 4A,2Ch
🍲Self-serve (provisions provided)   🏠 Rural, cottage, view from
guest rooms, patio, oceanfront, deck, swimming pool, quiet,
secluded   ■ 3 in self-contained cottage ↦1Q,1P, bunks
🛁1Private   ★ KF,F,private entrance, off-street parking
🚭No smoking, no pets
🏃 Tidal pools, walking trails

🚗 Langdale Ferry (to Vancouver), Saltery Bay Ferry, Powell River, scenic drive on Sunshine Trail
📣 Warm welcome in private and lovely cottage with a spectacular view. A great place for camera
buffs. Hosts are very knowledgeable about the area. Enjoy the saltwater swimming pool in season.
Breakfast foods are stocked for guests' convenience. There is a dog in residence. Visa
http://www.bbcanada.com/478.html

Jaffray

% (south-east of Cranbrook; see also Fernie, Ft.Steele, Kimberley)

Lyon, Doris & Doug (The Three Bears B&B)   ☎ (250) 429-3519
Box 209, Sand Creek Rd., Jaffray, BC   V0B 1T0   E-mail: threebears@cyberlink.bc.ca

From Hwy 3 south of Jaffray, turn onto Sand Creek Rd. Look for B&B sign at property entrance.
$50S $65D $15Child/Add.person   🍴 Meals   ▶ 8

🍲 Full, homebaked   🏠 Rural, split-level, acreage, view from
guest rooms, patio, porch deck, quiet, secluded   ■ 4 ↦S,Q
🛁2Sh.w.g.   ★ F,TV,LF,separate entrance, canoe/kayaks and
bikes for rent   🚭No smoking   〰German
🏃 Hiking, birding, tennis, golfing, fishing, kayaking, wildlife
viewing, cycling, bus to Cranbrook airport
🚗 Downhill skiing, canoeing, x-c and snocat skiing, hunting,
rafting, Jaffray, Cranbrook, US border

📣 Comfortable home on 5 acres of landscaped and forested land situated in the "South Country".
Relax on one of several decks or in the yard. Enjoy good conversation and cozy evenings around the
firepit or fireplace. Kennel provided for visiting pets. Picnic & packed lunches available. A perfect
4-Season destination. Visa ✐CC

Kamloops

(see also Pritchard, Salmon Arm)

MacQueen, Jack & Pat (MacQueen's Manor)
1049 Laurel Place, Kamloops, BC   V1S 1R1

☎ (250) 372-9383, 1-800-677-5338
Fax (250) 372-9384

Going east on Hwy1, take Exit 367 Pacific Hwy (going west take Exit 368), Proceed to Hugh Allen Dr, turn onto Gloaming and then onto Laurel Place.
$50S $65-75D $10Child $15Add.person   ► 4A,1Ch
✈ Apr1-Dec31   ⊘ Homebaked   🏠 Res., split-level, view, 2 private decks, quiet   ■3Ste(upst & ground level) ⊨2Q,1K,P
⊒1Private,2ensuite   ★ KF,LF,F,TV & coffee bar in guest room, off-street parking   🖐 Designated smoking area, no pets
🏃 Aberdeen Mall, restaurants, pub, golfing
🚗 Merritt, Salmon Arm, Vernon, Ashcroft Sun Peaks Ski Resort
☛ Warm welcome in new home filled with collectibles and friendly hospitality. Breakfast is served in antique furnished dining room overlooking the beautiful Kamloops Valley. There are 2 friendly dogs. Visa ⌇CC

Matter, Kitty (Matter House B&B)
225 McGill Rd., Kamloops, BC   V2C 1M2

☎ (250) 374-8011, 1-877-231-0022

Travelling on TCH Hwy1 from west, take Columbia St Exit.
From east or north, take Exit 370 to Columbia St. Proceed to 3rd traffic light, turn right on McGill Rd.
$40S $65D $15Add.person   ► 5-6
⊘Full,homebaked   🏠Res., split-level, view, patio, quiet   ■2D(ground & upper level) ⊒2Private ⊨2T,1Q,1S,1P ★Air,TV, guest living room,parking 🖐 No smoking, no pets ⌇German
🏃 Restaurants, shopping center
☛ Cozy home in quiet residential area with beautiful view of Kamloops river and the mountains. ⌇CC   http://www.bbcanada.com/1063.html

---

Zagar, Marion (Sunset Bed & Breakfast)
2667 Sunset Drive, Kamloops, BC   V2C 4K4

☎ (250) 372-2458

Located just off East Trans Canada Highway 1.
$25S $40D $10Child   ► 4A,2Ch
⊘ Cont., homebaked   🏠 Res., ranch-style, sun-deck   ■2S,1D (main & lower level)   ⊨ 2S,1D,1P,cot   ⊒ 1Private, 1sh.w.h.
★F,TV guest lounge, parking, bicycles available for guests
🖐No smoking, no pets, children min. age 10
🏃 Restaurants, shopping plaza, city bus passes in front of home, walking & cycling in pleasant residential area
🚗 Scenic drive in Shuswap Lake area, Merritt Castle Country, Wells Gray Provincial Park, golfing, fishing, excellent downhill & x-c skiing
☛ Quiet home surrounded by shade trees and situated in a very well established neighbourhood. Town is located in a semi-desert area, complete with sagebrush and tumbleweed and cacti.

Kelowna
(see also Okanagan Center, Oyama, Peachland)

Blake, Wayne & Marion (The Grapevine B&B)   ☎(250)860-5580,1-800-956-5580,
2621 Longhill Rd.,Kelowna,BC V1V 2G5   E-mail: grapevin@silk.net, Fax(250)860-5586

In Kelowna turn north off Hwy 97 on Dilworth Drive to Longhill Rd. Turn right onto Monford Rd for parking at entrance. $85-95D $20Add.person (plus taxes) 🍽 Meals ▶ 10 🍴Full, homebaked 🏠Rural, 2-storey, acreage,patio,porch,quiet ■3D,1F(upstairs) ⊨2Q,2K(T),1P ⊟2Private,2ensuite ★Air,LF, TV in guest rooms, sep.entrance, F (in guest living room) 🚭No pets, smoking outside, children minimum age 10 🚶 Hiking trail, cycling, walks

🚗 Wineries, golfing, skiing, hiking, hot air ballooning, restaurants, shopping centres, beaches 🦅 Cape Cod-style home situated on 1 acre in the wine region of the beautiful Okanagan Valley. Relax and enjoy the peaceful country setting and friendly hospitality. Delight in the many birds as they feed in the hillside garden. Hosts are gourmet cooks and serve unique, creatively presented breakfasts. Convenient location for business travellers. CCards ⌐CC

Breitkreuz, Bernie & Bettina (Bluebird Beach House B&B)   ☎ & Fax (250) 764-8992
3980 Bluebird Rd., Kelowna, BC V1W 1X6

Approaching Kelowna in the Okanagan Valley from Hwy 97, turn onto Gordon, cross Mission Creek, then right into Lexington and straight onto Bluebird (dead end).4hrs drive from Vancouver. $95S $95-140D $15Add.person ▶ 8-10 🌸Spring/Summer/Fall 🍴Full(Gourmet) 🏠Res., lakefront, 2-storey, view from guest rooms, quiet ■ 3Ste (upstairs) ⊨1D,2Q,2P ⊟3Ensuite ★ TV/fridge in guest rooms, private patios facing lake, separate entrance, off-street parking 🚭Smoking area, no pets, children min. age 10 🗨German 🚶 KF & barbeque in Beach Cabana (on property), private sandy beach & dock at back, 711-store, family restaurants, bus stop

🚗 Town Centre, shopping malls, Okanagan wineries, golfing, biking/hiking, horseback riding 🦅 Well travelled hosts in spacious custom-built home with tasteful, deluxe decor and located on beautiful Lake Okanagan. Ideal location for a restful luxury retreat and a paradise for swimmers, hikers and golfers. Enjoy gourmet breakfast at the beach Cabana. There is a resident old dog. Golf tee-time may be pre-arranged. Visa ⌐CC http://www.bbcanada.com/571.html

---

Durose, Paul & Lynda (Yellow Rose B&B)   ☎ & Fax (250) 764-5257
504 Curlew Dr., Kelowna, BC V1W 4K9   E-mail: yellowrose@direct.ca

Take Pandosy to Chute Lake, turn right on Lark, then right on Curlew. $70-85D ▶ 7 🍴 Full 🏠 Res., 2-storey, porch, quiet, deck, secluded ■3D (ground & upper level) ⊨ 1D,2Q,1P ⊟ 1Private, 1sh.w.g. ★Air,F,LF, ceiling fans, separate entrance, outdoor hot-tub, off-street parking 🚭 No smoking, no pets ♥ 🚶 Park, paved walking paths in well-lit safe neighbourhood 🚗 Downtown, restaurants, shops, golfing, excellent downhill skiing (Big White), wineries, airport, galleries

🦅 Lovely Victorian-style home in quiet exclusive residential area. Hostess is a caterer who loves to entertain and serves delightful meals. Relax in the gazebo or the hot-tub after a busy day at the local wineries. Breakfast is served on yellow rose china in special guest breakfast room. There is a cat in residence. Visa,MC ⌐B&B

Kelowna (cont'd)

Geismayr, Fred and Gaby (Crawford View)   ☎ (250) 764-1140/Fax (250) 764-2892
810 Crawford Rd., Kelowna, BC   V1W 4N3   E-mail: crawford_view@bc.sympatico.ca

In Kelowna, turn off Hwy 97 onto Gordon Dr S, then left onto Casorso. Keep right at stop and left
after bridge. Turn right onto De Hart, left onto Crawford Rd. Watch for 2nd driveway on left side.

$50-65S $65-75D $20Add.person   ► 6A,2Ch
🍽 Full   ♠ Rural, hillside, balcony, acreage, view, swimming
pool, patio, tennis court   ■ 3 (upstairs in separate building)
⊨2T,2Q   ▱3Ensuite   ★F,LF,TV & fridge in guest rooms,
sep.entrance, parking ⊛Smoking outside ⌁German,French
🕺 Golf course, orchards
🚗 Downtown Kelowna, Okanagan Lake, hiking trails, wineries,
Big White Ski area, Airport
🏹 Enjoy Austrian hospitality on 6 acre country estate within city limits and outstanding
panoramic view of lake, city and orchards. Breakfast is served in main building dining room
overlooking the pool. MC ✔B&B

Puderbach, Jo & Willi (Bird's Eye Bed & Breakfast)   ☎ (250) 764-2480
5142 Lark St., Kelowna, BC   V1W 4L3   Fax (250) 764-8497

From Hwy 97 in Kelowna, drive south onto Pondosy Lakeshore Dr.
Proceed to Chute Lake Rd and turn right onto Lark St.
$45-60S $60-70D   ► 4
🍽Full, homebaked   ♠Res., 2-storey, patio, deck   ■2D
(1Ste)(ground level) ⊨2Q,1R ▱2Private ★TV in guest room,
off-street parking   ⊛ No pets, smoking outside   ⌁German
🕺 Hiking, biking in nearby woods with view of Okanagan Lake
🚗 Beaches, wineries, downtown, shops, airport, restaurants/fine dining, Big White Ski Resort
🏹 Contemporary home with terraced rock garden and large patio in a quiet residential area. A
hearty breakfast is served in dining area or patio upon request. Visa

---

Senne, Reinhard & Ute (Casa del Sol B&B)   ☎ (250)470-2046, Fax (250)768-3392
3485 Fenton Rd., Westbank, BC   V4T 1V8   E-mail: casadelsol@telus.net, 1-800-261-4255

Follow Hwy 97 and turn into Glenrosard. Proceed for 3k to Fenton Rd on left.
$70S $80-110D $140F   ► 8A,2Ch

🍽 Full   ♠ Sub, 3-storey, acreage, view from guest rooms,
swimming pool, patio, porch, deck, quiet   ■ 2D,1Ste (main &
ground level) ⊨ 1D,3Q ▱ 3Ensuite   ★ Air,KF,F,TV &
ceiling fans in guest rooms, private parking, off-street parking,
jacuzzi-tub with lakeview, outside guest sitting area, bathrobes &
slippers for guests, guest quarters are separate ⊛Smoking
outside, no pets, children min. age 12   ⌁German
🕺 Hiking, mountain biking, horseback riding
🚗 Kelowna downtown, airport, lake swimming & watersports, Big White & Silver Star Resorts,
x-c skiing & snowshoeing, art galleries, Crystall Mtn, golfing, winetours & winetrain, dining
🏹 Completely renovated, award winning, contemporary California-Style home situated on
6.5acres overlooking the cities of Westbank & Kelowna with stunning lake & mountain views.
Breakfast is served in a spacious 10-window dining area overlooking Lake Okanagan or on the
sundeck (weather permitting). Relax by the fireplace or in the library or by the pool. Hosts will
provide reservations for horseback riding. Phone/Fax/E-mail services available. Discount for min
of 6nights (get 7th night free). Monthly rate upon request. There is a cat. Visa,MC ✔CC
httm://www.kanadanews.de/casadelsol.htm

Kimberley

(north of Cranbrook; see also Fort Steele, Fernie)

Wheatcroft, Gerry & Dorothy Robinson (Boundary Street House)
89 Boundary St., Kimberley, BC   V1A 2H4

☎ (250) 427-3510,
Fax (250) 427-3528

In Kimberley on Wallinger Ave, go 3 blocks north of Post Office to Boundary St. Turn left. Watch

for sign on right.
$60-65S $75-80D $15Add.person ► 6A
🏠Full,homebaked 🏠Downtown, older, 1.5 storey, patio, quiet
■3D(main & upper floor) ⊨1D,2Q ⊲1ensuite,1sh.wg. ★F,LF,
sitting area in rooms, parking ⦿Smoking outside, no pets
🧍 Downtown Kimberley, Pedestrian Mall, unique shops, galleries,
restaurants & coffee houses, nature trails, Cominco Gardens,
Prespyterian and United churches
🚙 Fort Steele Heritage Town, Canadian Museum of Rail Travel, St. Eugene's Mission & Church
🐾 Pretty (c1920) cottage-style home lovingly restored, furnished with comfortable period
antiques & family heirlooms & a wonderful view with rock gardens and Tamarack covered hillside.
Explore Kimberley and the area, soak in a claw-foot tub, read in the sitting room or day dream on
the patio. Enjoy a fresh wholesome breakfast. Visa ✓CC www.cyberlink.bc.ca/boundarystreet/

Ladysmith

(south of Nanaimo; see also Chemainus)

Hughes, Susan & Richard (Estuary Estate B&B)
302 Roland Rd, RR4, Ladysmith, BC   V0R 2E0

☎ (250) 245-0665, Cell 246-7781

Phone for directions.
$75S $95D $20Child/Add.person $125F ► 8
🏠 Full, homebaked 🏠 Res.,3-storey, view from guest rooms,
oceanside, porch, deck, quiet ■ 3(upstairs) ⊨ 3Q,R
⊲3Private ★ F, ceiling fans in guest rooms, off-street parking,
guest quarters are separate ⦿ Designated smoking area,
children min.age 10
🚙 Chemainus, murals, dinner theatre
🧍 Canoe/row boats on beach below the house, small mall, hiking trails, salmon spawning creek
🐾 Traditional new oceanside home, beautifully built and decorated, overlooking bird refuge,
sitting above an intertidal, stream-fed estuary with direct access to the beach and local trail head.
From the large picture windows watch bird life, bald eagles, herons etc. Breakfast is served in
special guest breakfast room. There is a dog in residence. ✓B&B

Langley

(Vancouver); see also Surrey, White Rock, Delta, Abbotsford, Tsawassen)

Dean, Heather & Darrell (Tramore House B&B)
26261-64B Ave., Langley, BC   V4W 3M7

☎ (604) 857-2618, Fax (604) 857-4918
E-mail: yodan@telus.net, 1-888-799-2618

From TCH1 east of Vancouver, take 264th St Exit North and travel 2km. Turn left onto 64B Ave
and to B&B on right. Located 13km north of the Canada/Lynden US border crossing.

$60S $70D ► 4A
🏠 Full 🏠 Rural, 2-storey, view from guest rooms, acreage,
deck, quiet ■ 2D(upstairs) ⊨ 2T,1D ⊲ 1Sh.w.g.
★F,LF,TV in guest rooms, game room, off-street parking
⦿Designated smoking area, no pets, no children
🚙 Regional parks, BC Game Farm, US border, antique stores,
Fort Langley, golfing, downtown Vancouver, Abbotsford airport,
Trinity Western University
🐾 Retired Military couple in lovely new English Tudor house, filled with fascinating memorabilia
of travels & foreign countries where hosts have lived. Situated on 5 acres, an ideal place for those
searching for a peaceful & serenic setting. Full English breakfast is served in the formal dining
room. There are 2 dogs & a Parrot. Visa,Amex ✓ B&B www.bbcanada.com/tramorehouse

Langley (cont'd)

Schwertner, Sylvia & Alan (Traveller's Joy B&B) ☎ (604) 533-2696, Fax (604) 533-3480
59 Wagonwheel Cr., Langley, BC   V2Z 2R1   1-888-550-6611

From Hwy 1 take Exit 66 south onto 232St. Follow the signs and turn left off Hwy 10 to stay on
232St. Turn left on 56Ave then first turn right onto Clovermeadow and Wagonwheel Cr.

$50S $80D $15Child $15Add.person   ► 4A,2Ch
🍳 Full, homebaked   🏠 Rural, res., 2-storey, acreage, quiet,
secluded   ■ 1D,1F(main & upper level)   ⊨ 2Q,1P
🛏1Private, 1ensuite   ★LF,F,TV in guest lounge, ceiling fans,
balconies, off-street parking, guest quarters are separate
♨Designated smoking area
🏃 Small Lake and park trail, golf course, shuttle service to
airport, downtown bus/skytrain

🚗 Int. Airport, downtown Vancouver, beaches, Provincial parks, historic sites, museums,
mountains, horse riding trails
🐎 Peaceful and comfortable home with large country garden situated in a quiet residential area
of small acreages. Friendly and informal hosts can provide information about day trips in the Fraser
Valley or Vancouver area. Parking space for RV. There is a cat. ✓B&B

Wong, Nola and Joseph (Nola's Garden B&B) ☎ (604) 533-3348
4675-209th St., Langley, BC   V3A 7E7

Take 232 St exit south off Hwy 1 to Langley. Turn left on Glover Rd, then left on No10 bypass,
cross Fraser Hwy (becomes 208St). Proceed to 47Ave. Turn left to house/3rd cul-de-sac right.

From Vancouver or USA border phone for directions.
$50-60S $60-70D $15Add.person   ► 6
🍳 Full, homebaked(after 8am)   🏠 Res., sub., multi-storey, view
from guest rooms, patio, quiet   ■1F,1D(upst)   ⊨2Q,1P(D)
🛏 1Private, 1ensuite   ★ F,LF,KF, TV in guest room,
sep.entrance, parking   ♨ Smoking outside only
🏃 Newlands Golf Club and restaurant, corner store, several
churches, bus stop

🚗 Downtown & historic Fort Langley, Cloverdale Rodeo, Vancouver, ferry to Vancouver Island,
airport, Game Farm, Abbotsford Air Show, Harrison Hot Springs, US border, Milner Downs
🐎 Australian hostess in casual friendly home with gardens of riotous colour, birds and fish pond.
Relax and enjoy the quiet area away from the sound of traffic. Information and maps supplied for
guests' continuing journey.

Lantzville
(north of Nanaimo; see also Parksville)

Martin, Sue & Dave (Home Again Bed & Breakfast) ☎ (250) 390-3863
6773 Philip Rd., Lantzville, BC   V0R 2H0

From Nanaimo travel north to Ware Rd. Turn left, proceed to top of hill to Philip Rd. Turn right

to house on left half-way down the hill.
$40S $55D $10Add.person $5Hot-tub   ► 4A,1Ch
🍳 Full   🏠 Rural, res., split-level, view, quiet   ■2D(upstairs)
⊨2T,1D,1P   🛁Sh.w.g.   ★F   ♨Designated smoking area
🏃 Winchelsea View Golf Course, beach (see seals, sea lions)
🚗 Ferries, airport, hiking, boating, theatres, restaurants
🐎 Comfortable and cozy home with view of the Winchelsea
Islands, Georgia Strait and mainland mountains in the background.
Good olde English breakfast is served in the dining room off the guest lounge. Relax by the fireplace
after a walk on the beach or in the secluded ivy-surrounded hot tub. There is a dog "Bill" and a cat
"Smudge" in residence. ✓B&B

Mara

(south of Sicamous; see also Vernon)

Bender, Fred & Anne (Lakeview Bed & Breakfast)   ☎ & Fax (250) 838-2283
92 Davy Rd., RR1, S2, C2, Mara, BC   V0E 2K0

From Sicamous, follow Hwy 97A south for 17 km. Look for B&B signs or phone for directions.

$55-65D $10Child $15Add.person   (weekly rates)   ▶ 6
🍳 Full, homebaked   🏠 Rural, bungalow, acreage, view from guest rooms, quiet, isolated   ■ 1D,1F (upstairs & lower level)   🛏 2S,1D,1Q   🚿 1Private, 1ensuite   ★TV, separate entrance   🚭No smoking, no pets   ∾ German   🚶 Hiking from back door   🚌 Beaches, golfing, fishing, boating, x/c skiing, hang-gliding, Salmon Arm, Vernon

🐾 Quiet mountain home with breathtaking view of Mara Lake and Shuswap River situated on wooded acreage. Relax and enjoy a wonderful breakfast served with warm hospitality in the solarium with view. ✓B&B

Mayne Island

(east of Ladysmith; see also Saltspring Island)

Engelhardt, Jurgen & Judith (Tinkerer's B&B)   ☎/Fax(250)539-2280
C31 Miners Bay, 417 Georgina Pt Rd, Mayne Island, BC   V0N 2J0   Email: tinkerers@gulfnet.pinc.com

Take BC Ferry from Tsawwassen on the mainland (near Vancouver) or from Swartz Bay on Vancouver Island (near Victoria).

$65-80S $75-90D $25Add.person   (plus tax)   ▶ 10
🎏 Apr15-Oct15   🍳 Full, homebaked   🏠 Village, rural, older, view from two guest rooms, multi-storey, oceanfront, quiet, wrap-around decks   ■2D,1F (main, upper & ground levels)   🛏3S,2D,1Q   🚿1Sh.w.g., 1ensuite   ★F,TV in guest room, 2 separate entrances, parking   🚭Smoking outside only, no pets   ∾German, Spanish   🚶 Miners Bay Village, government wharf, pub, restaurants

🚌 Georgina Point Lighthouse, Dinner Bay Park, Campbell & Bennet Bays, artists home studios
🐾 Home is one of the most colorful and whimsical buildings on the Island, surrounded by wonderful organic gardens of edible & medicinal herbs, flowers & fruit trees with magnificient views of Active Pass. Relax in one of the hammocks in the gardens, bicycle, hike, paddle, ramble through the idyllic landscape and marine scenery. Visit with Island artists in their home studios. Groups, families & international travellers welcome. Visa,MC ✓B&B
www.bbcanada.com/133.html

Mill Bay

(south of Duncan; see also Cobble Hill)

Beevor-Potts, Carole & Bob (Arbutus Cove B&B)   ☎ (250) 743-1435, Fax (250) 743-1410
2812 Wiltshire Rd., RR2, Mill Bay, BC   V0R 2P0   E-mail: arbutusc@cvnet.net, 1-877-743-1435

From Victoria take Hwy 1 north through Mill Bay to 2nd traffic light (past Mill Bay Centre). Turn east on Kilmalu Rd and proceed 2 km to Whiskey Pt.Rd. Turn left to Wiltshire Rd.

$60S $85D   ▶ 4A
🍳 Full, homebaked   🏠 Rural, ranch-style, acreage, view from guest rooms, oceanfront, patio, deck, quiet   ■ 2D (ground level)   🛏2Q   🚿2Ensuite   ★ F,TV in guest lounge, sep.entrance, canoe & bicycles for guests   🚭 No smoking, no pets, no children   🚶 Nature Park with walking trail, exploring beach frontage on Saanich Inlet, swimming

🚌 Three public golf courses, fishing charters/boat rentals, wineries, BC Forest Museum, Victoria
🐾 Spacious, new westcoast-style home situated on 2 wooded acres on the water with southerly view of beautiful Mill Bay. Relax in guest lounge, explore the area by bicycle, or use the canoe. Congenial hosts are knowledgeable of the local scene and can recommend good restaurants and activities. Breakfast is served in modern kitchen or on the spacious sundeck. Visa,MC ✓B&B

Mill Bay (cont'd)

Garbet, Dot & Jim (Maple Tree Lane B&B by the Sea)   ☎ (250) 743-3940
440 Goulet Rd., RR2, Mill Bay, BC V0R 2P0   1-877-854-2643, Fax (250) 743-3959

From Hwy 1, turn east onto Hutchinson Rd towards Arbutus Ridge, right onto Telegraph Rd, left onto LaFortune Rd, right onto Kilip Rd and left onto Goulet Rd. Look for signs on all corners.
$55-65S $85D $10-25Add.person (winter rates & 3days-plus discounts) 🍽 meals ▶ 5A,3Ch

    🍳 Full, homebaked 🏠 Rural, 3-storey chalet-type, acreage, view, oceanfront, swimming pool, hot-tub, patio, porch, deck, quiet ■1D,1F (main & lower level) ⊨2T,1Q,1P,crib 🛁2Private ★F,LF,TV in guest room, separate entrance (lower level), facilities for handicapped ⚜Designated smoking area 🚶 Arbutus Golf & Country Club, path leading to beach, canoeing 🚗 Mill Bay (shopping centre, marina, Chemainus (famous murals, dinner theatre, craft shops), Duncan (totem poles)

☛ Quiet oceanfront home. Enjoy the restful area and relax in the garden gazebo. Breakfast is cheerfully served in country kitchen, on deck, by the pool, on the patio or under the Old Apple Tree. Host will be delighted to have guests join him in a fishing venture. There are 2 cats. MC ✔B&B

Norton, Clifford & Mary (Norton's Green Bed & Breakfast)   ☎ (250) 743-8006
663 Frayne Rd., RR1, Mill Bay, BC V0R 2P0   E-mail: norton'sgreen@seaside.net

Take Island Hwy into Mill Bay, turn left on Frayne Rd. Driveway is on left before green mail boxes.
$50S $55-60D   ▶ 6
🍳 Full 🏠 Res, porch, quiet ■ 3D (main floor) ⊨1D,2Q 🛁 1Ensuite, 1sh.w.g. ★ F,LF,guest terry robes, off-street parking ⚜No smoking, no pets 🚶 Bay/beach/marina/waterfront park, restaurants, quaint shops 🚗 Victoria, Chemainus & Murals, Ladysmith, Duncan, Totems,
Native Heritage Centre, Brentwood College, Duncan, Victoria, Cowichan Valley wineries
☛ Warm welcome and friendly hospitality in new house in old-fashioned style with wrap-around balcony and pretty garden. Enjoy the relaxed atmosphere. Longtime hosts enjoy welcoming people from all over the world. ✔B&B

Mission   *(east of Vancouver; see also Abbotsford)*

Perdue, Fran & Martin (Fence Post Lane B&B)   ☎ (604) 820-7009, Fax (604) 820-4974
8575 Gaglardi St., Mission, BC V4S 1B2   E-mail: cherbert@netcom.ca, 1-877-833-7009

$50S $60-75D $10Child(under age 12) $15Add.person ▶ 4-5

From Lougheed Hwy No7 at 6.6km west of Mission, turn right on Chester, then left on Silverdale and right on Gaglardi St.
🍳 Full, homebaked (special diets accommodated) 🏠 Rural, ranch-style/back-split, acreage, view, patio, porch, deck, quiet, secluded ■ 2 (main & lower level) ⊨ 1Q,1D 🛁2Private ★F,separate large TV room, fans in guest rooms, quiet reading area ⚜ Smoking outside, no pets 🚶 Back-yard strolling (with bridge over creek), Community Hall
🚗 Restaurants, shops, golfing, Mission Raceway, Westminster Abbey, Harrison Hot Springs, hiking at Rolley Lake, Ruskin, Mission & Stave Falls Dams, Vancouver (commuter trains)
☛ Longtime B&B hosts in new, lovely decorated quiet country home, surrounded by beautifully landscaped acreage with creek and bridge in backyard. Guests can relax in the large entertainment room or enjoy the outside patios. Ideal place for anniversaries, special occasions or weekend get-aways. There is a resident cat. Visa,MC http://www.bbcanada.com/906.html

Nanaimo

(on Vancouver Island; see also Lantzville)

Dillon, Darlene & Russ (The Island View B&B)   ☎ & Fax (250) 758-5536
5391 Entwhistle Dr., Nanaimo, BC   V9V 1H2   E-mail: rdmts@islandnet.com

From Departure Bay Ferry Terminal follow Island Hwy 19A to Rutherford Rd. Turn right to Hammond Bay Rd, right to Entwhistle Dr. Turn left and down hill to B&B on left side. From Duke Point t Ferry Terminal take Hwy 19 to Mostar Rd., turn right and follow through lights at Hwy 19A. Road name changes to Rutherford Rd. Proceed as above.

$50S $60D $85Apt $20Add.person   ⓪Meals   ► 6A,2Ch
⬤ Full   🏠 Res., 2-storey, view from guest rooms, patio, quiet, deck ■1D,1F(ground level) ⊨2T,1Q,1P(Q),2cots ⊜2Private
★ F,KF,LF,TV in guest rooms, private entrance, guest quarters are separate, off-street parking   Ⓦ No smoking, no pets
🕺 Walks along rocky shoreline, park, pub, No2 bus in next block
🚗 Departure Bay Ferry Terminal, Parksville, Coombs Market Place, Cathedral Grove, Nanaimo, Chemainus

🔫 Warm & friendly hospitality in newly renovated home in a quiet area on 0.5 acre garden paradise. Relax on the deck, enjoy the beautiful sunsets & spectacular views. Breakfast is served in the main floor dining room at guests' convenience. Free pick-up & delivery in Nanaimo. ∕B&B

Grogan, Gloria & Gene (Beach Drive B&B)   ☎ (250) 753-9140
1011 Beach Dr., Nanaimo, BC   V9S 2Y4   E-mail: egrogan@pacificcoast.net

Phone for directions.
$35S $50D $25Add.person   n/c (Child under age 6)   ► 4
⬤ Homebaked   🏠 Res., split-level, oceanview   ■ 2D (ground level)   ⊨ 2T,1D   ⊜ Sh.w.g.   ★ TV,LF,separate entrance, parking   〰 Ukrainian, Irish
🕺 Beach access & beach combing, waterfront promanade to downtown, Castle & Protection Islands (short boat trips for island nature trails & Canada's only floating pub "Dingy Dock Pub")
🚗 Golf courses, Cathedral Grove with 1000 year-old trees, Indian shops with native works, Chemainus Murals, Parksville, Salmon Charter fishing, kayaking, Adventure Tours
🔫 Home overlooks Departure Bay Ferry Terminal on the Strait of Georgia. Enjoy the distant view of the Sunshine coast from the big bright sunroom where breakfast is served. Well travelled retired hosts enjoy golfing and are active with volunteer work and many hobbies. ∕CC

Matthews, Janette & Warren (Graycliff Cottage Waterfront B&B)   ☎&Fax(250)390-3203
7550 Lantzville Rd., Lantzville,BC   V0R 2H0   E-mail: graycliff@home.com, 1-888-801-1822

From Hwy1/Superior Rd, turn right on Lantzville Rd to B&B north of Woodgrove Mall/Nanaimo.

$75-90S $85-95D $15Child $20Add.person   ► 6
⬤Full   🏠 Village, raised bungalow, acreage, quiet, view from oceansuite, oceanfront ■3Ste (main floor & in separate building)   ⊨ 3Q,1P   ⊜ 3Ensuite   ★ TV in guest rooms, private entrance, outdoor hot-tub, off-street parking, guest quarters are separate   Ⓦ No smoking, no pets
🕺 Village of Lantzville, shops, restaurants
🚗 Parksville, Qualicum, Coombs Market, Cathedral Grove

🔫 Warm welcome in self-contained suites with coffee bar & small fridge and staircase to beach and panoramic view of Georgia Strait & coastal mountains. Watch beautiful sunsets , birds, wildlife & resident nesting Bald Eagles. Enjoy all the amenities of a good hotel in the personal setting of a B&B. Breakfast is served in guest breakfast room or in the guest room. There is a cat in residence (not allowed in guest quarters). MC ∕B&B www.shift.to/graycliff

Nanaimo (cont'd)

Molnar, Catherine (Carey House B&B)　　　　☎ (250) 753-3601
750 Arbutus Ave., Nanaimo, BC V9S 5E5　　　　E-mail: careyhouse@home.com

$35S $50D $55Ste ◙Meals (Reduced rates for 1week or longer)　　► 6A
Traveling north through town, turn left off Hwy at Townsite Ave, passing downtown to 3rd Ave on right. To ensure booking please phone or write.

◙Choice,homebaked ✪Res,quiet,older ▪1S,1D,1Ste ◲1Sh.w.g., 1private beds1S,1D,1Q ★Kitchenette & private entrance in suite
🚗 Downtown Nanaimo, ferry and bus terminal, golfing, dining
☛ Scottish hospitality. Centrally located quiet residential area with beautiful award-winning garden. Hosts are seasoned world travellers who have welcomed B&B guests for 15 years. Breakfast is served in antique-furnished dining room. There are resident pets.

Whyte, Nancy (Gateshead B&B)　　　　☎ (250) 754-3362
551 Nanaimo River Rd., Nanaimo, BC V9X 1E2

From Nanaimo follow signs to Bungy Zone. Located off TCH south of Nanaimo.
$40S $55D $10Child $10Add.person ◙ Meals　　► 7A,1Ch
◙ Full, homebaked, ✪ Rural, 2-storey, acreage, patio, porch, deck, quiet ▪ 2D,1Ste (main & ground level) ⊨ 1S,2T,2Q
◲ 1Private, 1ensuite, 1sh.w.h. ★ LF,TV in guest room, hot tub in solarium off one room, off-street parking ⊛ Smoking on deck, no pets ∾some French
🚶 Nanaimo River and swimming, shuttle available
🚗 Bungy Zone, Ladysmith, Chemainus and famous murals
☛ Olde English hospitality in park-like setting. Hostess is a former Chef. Relax in the patio hot-tub after a day of sightseeing or travelling. ↙B&B

Nelson　　　　　　*(west of Cranbrook; see also Silverton)*

Horsfall, Willa & Harold (Taghum Beach B&B)　　☎(250) 354-4906
3289 Granite Rd, RR2,S21,C19, Nelson, BC V1L 5P5

Located 7km south of Nelson. Phone for directions.
$50S $70D ◙ Meals　　► 6
◙ Full, homebaked ✪ Rural, 2-storey, older, acreage, view from guest rooms, riverfront, deck, quiet, secluded ▪ 3 (main & lower level) ⊨ 2S,2Q ◲ 1Sh.w.g. ★ LF,F,TV,private entrance, hot-tub, off-street parking, guest quarters are separate ⊛ Designated smoking area, no pets
🚶 Private sandy beach (dock/boat ramp), trails (hike/cycle)
🚗 Nelson, Kootenay School of the Arts, street-festivals & art walk, live theatre (summer productions & symphonies), public pool & gym, x-c & Whitewater ski area, golfing, Hot Springs, worlds longest free ferry ride, Kokanee Glacier
☛ Older, renovated farm house in semi secluded area with views of landscaped gardens to beach and situated adjacent to Regional Park. Enjoy the tremendous water view from the breakfast room and relax on the spacious decks with separate covered BBQ area or soak in the hot-tub under the clear skies of the Kootenays. Hosts are fond of the outdoors and knowledgeable of the area. There are 2 dogs & a cat in residence. Visa,MC.

Nelson (cont'd)

Maloff, Harry & Verna (Verna's Country Kitchen B&B)   ☎ (250) 229-4961
6497 Erindale Rd., Harrop, Nelson, BC   V1L 5P6

Located 22km north east of Nelson. Take 5min "Harrop" Ferry. Turn left on Erindale Rd.
$65S $97D $4Child $30Add.person   🍽 Meals   (plus tax)   ► 4A,4Ch

🍲 Full, homebaked   🏠 Rural, back-split, acreage, view from
guest rooms, lakefront, patio, porch, deck, quiet, secluded   ■2
(main and ground level)   ⊨ 1D,1K,1P,cot,crib   🛏 2Private
★KF,LF,F,TV in guest rooms, ceiling fans, hot tub, private
entrance, guest quarters are separate   👋 Designated smoking
area, no pets   ∾ Russian
🕴 Private sandy beach, fishing, wharf, x-c skiing, snowshoeing,
swimming, firepit/bonfires, hiking
🚗 Nelson (ride the old street car), Ainsworth Hot Springs, Kokanee Glacier, longest "free" ferry
🚙 Beautiful beachfront home on Kootenay Lake surrounded by breathtaking panoramic views of
snowcapped mountains and everlasting sun exposure. Breakfast is served in guest breakfast room.
Full menu available for additional meals, lunch to go or a romantic al-fresco dinner on the beach.
After a hectic day of travelling or sightseeing, relax in the hot tub or by the fireplace to ease tired
bones and watch the sunset on the lake, ending yet another wonderful day. ↙CC

Mather, Janeen & Mark Giffin (Emory House B&B)   ☎ & Fax (250) 352-7007
811 Vernon St., Nelson, BC   V1L 4G3   E-mail: emorybnb@kootenaynet.com

From Vancouver take Hwy 1 to Hope and Hwy 3 east to Castlegar, then Hwy 3A north to Nelson
and follow signs to City centre. Proceed to one street north of Baker St (main street in town).
$65-85S $70-90D $15Add.person   (plus taxes)   (off-season rates avail)   ► 11

🍲 Full   🏠 Downtown, 2-storey, hist., view from guest rooms
■ 2D,1Ste,1F (main & upper floor)   ⊨ 1S,1D,3Q   🛏 1Sh.w.g.,
2ensuite   ★ Air,TV,F, guest quarters are separate, off-street
parking   👋 No smoking, no pets, children min. age 10
🕴 Downtown Nelson, Aquatic & Fitness Centre, shopping mall,
Nelson Museum, restaurants, movie/live theatre, lakeside park
🚗 Granite Point Golf Course, Whitewater Ski Resort, hiking
trails, Kootenay Lake (fishing, beaches), Kokanee Glacier Nat.Pk
🚙 1926-built Heritage home furnished with restored antiques & local arts and nestled in the
centre of scenic town. Hosts have extensive experience in the hospitality industry (former Chef &
Restaurant Mgr). The convenient location makes exploring Nelson's heritage sights easy and
enjoyable. There are 2 resident cats. Golf & Ski Packages available. Visa,MC ↙CC
www.bbcanada.com/189.html

Stevens, Lynda & Jerry VanVeen (Inn the Garden B&B)   ☎ (250) 352-3226,
408 Victoria Street, Nelson, BC   V1L 4K5   Fax (250)-352-3284, 1-800-596-2337

Located 1 block south of Baker St. between Stanley & Ward Sts and across from Capitol Theatre.
$70S $150D $20-25Add.person   (plus taxes)   ► 20

🍲 Full, homebaked   🏠 Downtown, historic, view from guest
rooms, patio, porch, deck, terraced front gardens with steps
■5D,1Ste (2nd & 3rd levels)   ⊨2T,1D,5Q,1P,cot   🛏2Private,
1sh.w.g.,2ensuite   ★Separate entrance, off-street parking,
ceiling fans, guest lounge, bicycle/ski storage   👋No smoking, no
pets, children min. age 15(except in cottage)   ∾Dutch
🕴 Heritage buildings and walking tours, parks, restored trolley,
arts & craft stores, restaurants, live theatre, museum
🚗 Kokanee Glacier Park (hiking, skiing), Whitewater Ski Resort, Ainsworth Hot Springs, Caves
🚙 Friendly and relaxed atmosphere in beautifully restored Victorian home with comfortable
decor of plants, wicker & antique furniture. Located in picturesque Selkirk Mountain city with a
breathtaking view of lake and mountains. Enjoy the beautiful high terraced front garden with patio
and summer porch. Golf and Ski packages available. Also self-cont cottage available. Visa,MC.Amex

New Westminster *(Vancouver); see also Surrey, Richmond, Langley, White Rock, Delta)*

Field, Ethel (Royal City Bed & Breakfast)   ☎ (604) 521-5733
127 Queen's Ave., New Westminster, BC   V3L 1J4   E-mail: info@royalcitybedbreakfast.com

Located in Queen's Park area. Phone for directions.
$55-60S $70-75D $15Child   ► 4A,1Ch
🍳 Full, homebaked   🏠 Res., hist., river view, sundeck   ■ 2D
(upstairs)   ⊨ 2Q   🛁 2Private,   ★TV, parking, grand piano
for musical guests   ✋ Pets
🚶 Rapid Transit to downtown Vancouver, shopping mall,
Adventure Playground
🚗 International Airport, beaches, V.Island Ferry, Deer Lake
🐾 Grand old Heritage home, formerly the N.Nelson Mansion and built in 1913, with beamed ceilings, stained glass windows. Hosts enjoy sharing their comfortable home with guests. Delicious muffins are a house specialty. There is a resident dog and a cat. ↩CC
www.royalcitybedbreakfast.com

O'Shaughenssy,Anne & Ross Hood(Henley House B&B)   ☎(604)526-3919,Fax526-3913
1025-8th Ave, New Westminster, BC   V3M 2R5   E-mail: home@henleyhouse.com

Located on the north shore of the Fraser River and 16km east of the Centre of Vancouver and 24km

north of US border.
$60-75S $65-80D $10Child/Add.person $110F   ► 7
🍳 Full   🏠 Res, heritage home   ■3D(main & upper floor)
⊨ 1D,2Q,R   🛁 1Ensuite, 1sh.w.g.   ★ F,TV in 1 guest room
and in upstairs guest lounge, robes, slippers, hair-dryers,
air-conditioners, ceiling fans, street parking, guest quarters are
separate   ✋ No pets, smoking on balcony or garden deck, no
pets, children min. age 10
🚶 Restaurants, Massey Theatre (live Performances), park (tennis), bus stop from airport (hosts
will pick up guests from there), public transportation to downtown Vancouver
🚗 Fraser River Quay, Riverboat Casino, river cruises, museum, golfing, Simon Fraser University
🐾 1925 Heritage home in the craftsman-style, furnished with antiques & family trasures and
located in Greater Vancouver at historic New Westminster. There are 2 guest lounges with phones
and library of books and videos. Relax in the year-round hot-tub. Breakfast is served in the formal
dining room using handwoven linens, crystal, silver and bone china.There is a dog in residence.
Visa,MC   http://www.henleyhouse.com

Okanagan Centre

(north of Kelowna; see also Oyama, Vernon)

Blaskovits, Virginia (The Wild Flower B&B)   ☎ (250) 766-5217
932 Camp Rd., Okanagan Centre, BC   V4V 2H3   E-mail: blaskovits@cablean.net

From Hwy 97 at Winfield, take Centre North Rd on left (west) & follow winding road around to
Okanagan Lake. Turn right on Camp Rd. Located in Winfield just before Gray Monk Wineries.

$60S/D $20Add.person   ► 6A
🍲 Full, homebaked   🏠 Rural, res, 2-storey, lakeview from guest
rooms, patio, quiet   ■ 3D (ground & lower level)   ⊨ 1D,2Q
🛁 1sh.w.g.   star Air,TV in guest parlour, hot-tub on patio,
separate entrance   Ⓦ Smoking outside, no pets, not suitable for
young children
🏃 Pleasant walks down to the lake for a swim or up to the
well-known Gray Monk Cellars, birdwatching, mountain biking
🚐 Beaches/boat launch areas, Winfield/Kelowna/Vernon shopping, Silver Star & Big White
🐾 Spacious, elegant home, warmly decorated with antiques and with panoramic view of
Okanagan Lake, rich orchards lands and wild flower gardens. Located in a peaceful setting away
from main routes, yet close to various cities in the area. Relax in the hot-tub and enjoy the
panoramic view of the lake. Breakfast may be served on the large covered veranda or in the sunny
dining room. Enjoy a tranquil atmosphere & congenial hospitality. www.bbcanada.com/3515.html

---

100 Mile House

(north of Kamloops; see also Clearwater)

Scuffi, Roy and Louise (Nana's Bed & Breakfast)   ☎ (604) 791-5541, Fax (604) 791-5699
Comp.77 Tatton Rd. RR1, 100 Mile House, BC   V0K 2E0

From Hwy 97, take Tatton Rd, then Scuffi Rd. Located north of 100
Mile House. Phone for detailed information.
$35-40S $50-60D $5child   🍽 Meals   ► 4A,2Ch
🍲 Full   🏠 Rural, ranch-style, acreage, view, lakefront, patio,
quiet, isolated   ■ 2D,1Ste(main and lower level)   ⊨1D,2Q,1P,
2cots, crib   🛁 2Sh.w.g.   ★ F,TV,LF,KF, separate entrance,
parking, facilities for the handicapped, whirlpool tub, playpen,
highchair, toys, hot-tub outside   ♥   Ⓦ No smoking, no pets
🏃 Explore 6 acres of private land, horseback riding, hiking, x-country skiing, good bus route
🚐 Many lakes, fishing/golfing/hunting, excellent dining, 2 airports, 2 major Health Spas
🐾 Experience the super natural Cariboo. Relax and enjoy the beautiful view from the large
sundeck. Semi-retired couple in large family-orientated home, are very knowledgeable of the local
area. There are chickens, honey bees & a large heated greenhouse and garden. Children welcome.
Hosts will pick-up from train, bus or 108 Airport. ✔ CC

Oyama

(north of Kelowna; see also Vernon, Okanagan Center)

Parker, Yvonne & Elgin (Orchard Lane Bed & Breakfast)　　　☎ (250) 548-3809
13324 Middle Bench Rd., Oyama, BC V4V 2B4

Located 5.5km east of Hwy 97 (across the lake) at 13324 Middle Bench Rd. Phone for directions.
$45S $55-75D $10Child $15Add.person　　　▶ 6
🍴 Full, homebaked 🏠 Farm, 2-storey, view from guest rooms, deck, quiet, verandas, secluded ■ 3D (upstairs) ⊨ 1S,3Q, portable crib ⊲ 1Private, 1ensuite (sink in one room)
★Air,F,TV,LF, outdoor hot-tub, craft display room on site
🚬Designated smoking area, no pets
🚶 Orchard & tours, range land for hiking, biking, country walks
🚗 Lake access (swimming/boating), Silver Star (Vernon)/Big White (Kelowna) Ski Resorts & summer chairlift, golfing, fishing, winery tours, restaurants
🦅 New Victorian-style home, beautifully designed and decorated with large sprawling verandas & spiral staircase, with a panoramic view of the Central Okanagan Valley, nestled in a lush orchard surrounded by flower gardens, rockery and paths. Enjoy a tranquil retreat and breakfast served in the formal dining room or on veranda. Special diets on request. ✔B&B http://www.bctravel.com

---

Parksville

(on Van.Isle; north of Nanaimo; see also Qualicum B., Lantzville)

Chilton, Bob and Marg (Parksville Bed & Breakfast)　　　☎ (250) 248-6846
19 Jenkins Place, Parksville, BC V9P 1G4　　　E-mail: bobchil@nisa.net

From Island Hall go north to lights at Pym St. Turn left to Jenkins Place, and left again.
$50S $55-65D $15Add.person (off season rates avail) (Reservation please)　　　▶ 6

🍴 Choice, homebaked 🏠 Downtown, res., patio, quiet ■3D (upstairs) ⊨2T,1D,1Q,cot ⊲1Private,1sh.w.g. ★TV,LF,F, parking 🚬No pets, no smoking ♥
🚶 Wembley Mall, Community Park, tennis court, excellent fishing, beach, marina
🦅 Cozy home with country tranquility located in town. Hosts welcome guests over for a cup of tea. Enjoy the tasty breakfast. Families welcome. ✔B&B

Hetherington, Bob & Linda Teshima (Marina View B&B)　　　☎ (250) 248-9308
895 Glenhale Cr., Parksville, BC V9P 1Z7　　　Fax (250) 248-9408

Travel through Parksville on Hwy 19A past French Creek Market and turn right at light on Wright Rd and left on Glenhale Cr. Look for flag on top deck.
$70S $85-95D $20Add.person　　　▶ 6-7
🍴 Full, homebaked 🏠 Res., split-level, view, oceanfront, quiet, covered deck ■3(upst) ⊨2T,2Q,R ⊲2Ensuite,1private ★TV in guest lounge,parking 🚬No pets, no smoking, children min. age 10
🚶 French Creek Marina, excellent fishing, beachcombing, restaurant, store,
🚗 Englishman River & Qualicum River Falls, Cathedral Grove Prov. Park (large trees), beaches
🦅 Spectacular waterfront setting in the heart of vacationland with large deck overlooking the Strait of Georgia, islands and mountains beyond. Relax in the large solarium and watch the Alaska Cruise Ships sail by and catch a glimpse of seals and otters frolicking near the shore, as well as shorebirds & eagles. Savour a delicious breakfast of homemade preserves & fresh-baked goods served in gracious surroundings. Visa,MC ✔CC

Parson
(south of Golden; see also Windermere, Fairmont Hot Springs)

Dunphy, Brian and Suzette (Dunphy's Bed & Breakfast) ☎ (250) 348-2394
Box 22, Parson, BC   V0A 1L0

Located right on Hwy 95 and 3.2 km south of Parson. Watch for sign.
$40S $50D   🍽 Meals   ▶ 6A,2Ch
🍳 Full, homebaked   🐄 Farm   ■ 2S,3D (upstairs)   ⊨2T,3D
🛁1Sh.w.h.,1sh.w.g   ★TV,F,LF   ♿ Restr.smoking, no pets
🕴 Many types of farm animals to enjoy, large yard/creek on door step,
back country hiking
🚗 Heli/x-c skiing/snowmobiling, Radium/Fairmount Hotsprings,
Golden Dist.Museum, Invermere Ski Resort, Bugaboos Alpine rec area
🔫 Large farm house in excellent location from which to experience the majestic Canadian Rocky
Mountains during summer and winter time. Hosts are avid outdoor enthusiasts. ✒B&B

Peachland
(south of Kelowna; see also Summerland, Penticton)

Kennedy, Muriel & Dennis (Beatrice B&B)   ☎ 1-888-240-1491,Fax (250)767-2114
6083 Beatrice Rd., S1E,C29,RR1, Peachland, BC   V0H 1X0   E-mail: beatrice@silk.net

Take Hwy 97 to Peachland. Turn uphill at Princeton and proceed 1.1km. Turn right on Ellison &
immediate right on Beatrice.

$70S $80D $10Child $15Add.person   ▶ 6A,4Ch
🍳 Full, homebaked (Gourmet)   🏠 Res, hillside, view from guest
rooms, patio, porch, deck, quiet, secluded   ■ 3F,1Ste (main &
upper level)   ⊨ 5S,2Q,1K,R,P,cot   🛁1Private, 2ensuite
★Air,KF,LF,F,VCR,TV in guest rooms, ceiling fans, solar
telescope, private entrance, wheel-chair access, off-street parking,
guest quarters are separate   ♿ Smoking outdoor
🕴 Private garden decks, many fruit trees & grape vines & berries on property, village of Peachland
(with 8km of level beach), tennis courts, marinas, watercraft rentals, Kelowna Transit Bus
🚗 Summerland, Kelowna, Penticton, 30 wineries (sampling), numerous golf courses
🔫 Warm welcome in friendly modern home with a Great Room and situated in a "one of a kind"
location with a panoramic view of the whole of Okanagan Lake from Penticton to Kelowna. Relax
on one of the two restful view decks and enjoy the magnificient sunrise over Okanagan Mountain
Park or the spectacular sunset on Moon lit nights with twinkling stars. There is a dog in residence.
✒B&B   www.monday.com/beatrice

Pemberton
(north of Whistler, see also Brackendale)

Einarson, Christine & Fred (Alpen View B&B)   ☎ (604) 894-6787, Fax 894-2026
7406 Larch St., Box 636, Pemberton, BC   V0N 2L0   E-mail: ceinarson@bigfoot.com

$65S $75D $25Add.person $25Child (free under age 8)   ▶ 8
From Hwy 99 take Harrow Rd & turn left on Hemlock St to Larch St. Look for house on corner.
Located 25km from Whistler.

🍳 Full   🏠 Village, res., 2-storey, view from guest rooms, deck,
swimming pool, quiet   ■ 3(upstairs)   ⊨ 6T,1Q   🛁2Sh.w.g.
★Air,F,TV, off-street parking   ♿ Smoking outside, no pets, well
supervised children welcome
🕴 Playground park, One Mile Lake, swimming, walks around
lake, village of Pemberton, stores, high quality restaurants, bus to
Whistler and Vancouver, x-c skiing
🚗 Birkenhead Lake (boating), Whistler (skiing, snowboarding, golfing, Gondola ride), Lilooet
Lake (beach), hiking areas (Nairn Falls or Glacier hike), local scenic charter flights
🔫 Enjoy exceptional comfort and friendly hospitality and experience the peacefulness of
Pemberton's scenic farming valley, surrounded by snowcapped mountains. Located in a true
mountain paradise near the renowned Whistler Resort. Relax in the hot-tub after a day of outside
winter activities or in the pool after a busy hot summer day. There is 1 outside cat. MC ✒B&B

Pemberton (cont'd)

Hasan, Donna & Saad (The Log House B&B Inn)   ☎& Fax (604)894-6000, 1-800-894-6002
1357 Elmwood Dr., Box 699, Pemberton, BC V0N 2L0   E-mail: loghouseinfo@loghouseinn.com

Take Hwy 99 to Pemberton (32km past Whistler). Turn at Petro Canda and proceed cross railroad
tracks. Turn left at Nova Scotia Bank and right on Aster, continue to Dogwood. Turn right again

and up hill to log house on corner.
$85S $125D $160F $35Add.person   (plus tax)   ▶ 15
🍽 Full   🏠 Village, view from guest rooms, quiet, secluded
■7(main/upper & ground level)   ⊨ 2T,2D,4Q,1K   ⇔2Private,
5ensuite   ★ LF,F,TV & fans in guest rooms, guest lounge with
wood stove, guest robes, private entrance, off-street parking, guest
quarters are separate   🖐 Designated smoking area, no pets,
children min. age 5

🏃 Hiking, biking, golf courses, lakes, Whitewater rafting, skiing, Heli skiing, aerial sightseeing
🚐 Whistler/Blackcomb Resort
🔫 Exquisite, 5000 sq.ft.log home with wrap-around deck and hot-tub and beautiful views of
Mount Currie - a unique retreat in a splendid setting, among breathtaking scenery. The
Atrium-style interior reflects the natural beauty of logs and native artwork. The valley offers many
outdoor activities and it's nearness to Whistler allows guests to enjoy the resort whilst relaxing in
the tranquility of the Pemberton village. Fresh farm produce breakfast is served in guests breakfast
room. There is a small English Bulldog in residence. Pick-up possible upon request. CCards
↙B&B   www.loghouseinn.com

Penticton
          (s.of Kelowna; see also Summerland, Peachland)

Buchanan, Ruth (Paradise Cove)   ☎& Fax (250) 496-5896
Box 699, Penticton, BC V2A 6P1   E-mail: buchanan@vip.,net

Located at 3129 Hayman Rd., Naramata. From Westminster & Main Sts in Penticton, take the
Naramata Rd East. Follow for 13km to DeBeck Rd, left before the Fire Hall, right at Hayman Rd.

$60-655S $75-85D $115-125Ste $15Add.person   ▶ 6A
🍽Full   🏠Rural,res,two-storey,lake view,patio,quiet ■3D,1Ste
(main & lower level)   ⊨4Q   ⇔3Private,1sh.w.g.   ★TV/fridge &
beverage service in all rooms, F/KF/hot-tub in suite, wheel-chair
access   🖐No smoking, no pets,
🏃 Manitou Beach, Okanagan Lake, Riding Academy, 5 wineries
🚐 Kettle Valley Railway Tunnels, Country Squire Restaurant
🔫 Deluxe accommodation in modern home with panoramic view
of Lake Okanagan and situated in rural orchard surroundings. Very quiet. Widely travelled hostess
is a writer/editor. Ideal spot for honeymooners. Visa,MC ↙B&B
http://www.pcove.bctravel.com/okanagan/paradisecove

Penticton (cont'd)

Sturhahn, Otto & Ursula (House Victoria B&B)　　　　☎ & Fax (250) 492-3979
403 Woodruff Ave., Penticton, BC　V2A 2H7　　　　　　E-mail: sturhahn@vip.net

Entering Penticton from south or north via Hwy 97, continue on Eckhard Ave to City Centre. Turn

right on Latimer and proceed to B&B at corner of Woodruff.
$65-85S/D　　$25Add.person　　　　　　　　　　　　► 6
🍴 Full, homebaked　🏠Res., bungalow, deck, quiet　■3D (main
& lower level)　⊨2D,2S　🛏2Private, 1ensuite
★Air,TV/VCR, off-street parking, guest quarters are separate
🖐No smoking, no pets, children min.age 10　⚬German
🏃 Downtown, beach, convention/recreation facility, public
transportation, hikes and nature walks
🚐 Penticton Regional Airport, Skaha & Okanagan beaches, Apex Mountain Resort, golf courses,
boating, water skiing, Greyhound bus Depot, Keremeos (Grist Mill), historic train
🔫 Warm welcome in bright and cheery home. Breakfast is served in private dining room. Relax
in quiet surroundings, after a day at the Okanagan Wine Festival, the Penticton Peach Festival or a
busy day of sightseeing. Inquire about transportation to or from Airport or Bus. CCards ✓B&B

Port Alberni　　　　　　　　　　*(in the center of Van.Isle, west of Parksville)*

Visee, Dick and Jane (Lake Woods Bed & Breakfast)　　　☎ & Fax (250) 723-2310
9778 Stirling Arm Cr,S339,C5,RR3,Port Alberni,BC V9Y 7L7　　E-mail: lakewoodsbb@hotmail.com

From Hwy 4 west of Port Alberni, turn left on Faber Rd. Travel 4.8 km, turn right at stop sign.

$65-80S/D　　　　　　　　　　　　　　　　　　　► 6
🍴 Full, homebaked　🏠 Rural, multi-storey, view, lakefront,
patio, quiet　■ 3D (main and ground floor)　⊨2Q,1K
🛏1Sh.w.g., 1ensuite　★ F,TV, parking　🖐 Smoking outside
only, no pets　⚬ Dutch
🏃 Day trip on M.V. Lady Rose on Barclay Sound, forest & mill
tours, salmon fishing, walking trails
🚐 Pacific Rim National Park, Long Beach, Tofino, Ucluelet
🔫 Peaceful waterfront home overlooking the lake and expansive landscaped garden, situated on
the shores of beautiful Sproat Lake and easy distance for daytrips to the Westcoast and Pacific Rim
National Park. Enjoy a swim before turning in, or before breakfast. ✓CC
www.bbexpo.com/bc/lakewoods.htm

Port Hardy　　　　　　　　　　　*(on northern tip of Vancouver Island)*

Hamilton, Lorne and Betty (Hamilton B&B)　　　　　☎ (250) 949-6638
Box 1926, 9415 Mayor's Way, Port Hardy, BC　V0N 2P0

Travel up Hwy 19 to first 4-way stop. Turn left (Granville St - has hospital sign) and continue to
Mayor's Way. Turn left to first house on left.
$48S　$60-65D　　　　　　　　　　　　　　　► 6
🍴Cont,homebaked　🏠Res., split-level, view, quiet　■3(main &
lower levels)　⊨2T,1D,1Q　🛏2Sh.w.g.　★Separate entrance
🖐No smoking, no pets
🏃 Sea wall walk with lovely view of islands/mountains, downtown
park, museum, fishing dock
🚐 Storeys Beach, Telegraph Cove, Marble River, whale watching,
charter fishing, diving, hiking
🔫 Active host family enjoys fishing, hiking and meeting people. Friendly hospitality in area with
many attractions, lakes and rivers and year-around fishing. ✓CC

Powell River

(north-west of Vancouver)

Hollmann, Nancy and Alexander (Herondell B&B)   ☎(604)487-9528,Fax(604)487-1465
RR1, Black Point #29, Powell River, BC   V8A 4Z2   E-mail: herondel@prcn.org

Located halfway between Saltery Bay Ferry Terminal and Powell River City limits. From Vancouver, leave the bus at Lang Bay.
$40S $50D $15Add.person 🍴Meals   ▶ 8A,4Ch
🍽 Full (Lumberman's b'fast) 🏠Rural, older, 40 acres, front yard wildlife pond, isolated ■5D,1F(main & lower level) ★F,LF, separate entrance, parking ⊨4T,2D,1K,1R,1P ⊒1Private, 3sh.w.g., 1ensuite ⊛No smoking, children welcome ∾German
🎿 Nature trail through woods, saltwater beach, river swimming
🚗 Powell River, scuba diving, salmon fishing, Powell River Forest Canoe Route (5-day trip)
🔫 Very private wildlife refuge with visible waterfowl (occasionally bear, deer, cougar etc.) Early breakfasts only. Breakfast specialty is Eierkuchen and sour dough products (the "starter" has been in the family for over 50 years). Canoe/camping rentals/charters avail. CCards ✔CC

Randall, Roger and Shirley (Beacon B&B)   ☎ (604) 485-5563/Fax (604) 485-9450
3750 Marine Ave., Powell River, BC   V8A 2H8   E-mail: beacon@aisl.bc.com, 1-877-485-5563

Take Langdale Ferry from Horseshoe Bay (Vancouver) and drive along the Sechelt Peninsula to Earls Cove. Take Saltery Bay Ferry and drive 29.5 km north. Watch for Beacons.

$75-125S/D $20Add.person   ▶ 10A
🍽 Full, homebaked 🏠 Res., view, oceanfront, patio, quiet, hot tub ■1D,1F,1Ste (main & ground level) ⊨2T,4Q ⊒3Private ★F,LF,TV in guest room, wheel-chair access to suite, parking
⊛ Smoking outside only, children min age 12
🎿 Walk and explore nearby beaches and sea life
🚗 Canoe route portage 8 lakes (4-5 days), new golf course, biking, sunshine Coast Trail, Vancouver, ferry to Comox
🔫 Tranquil and congenial family surroundings in modern, waterfront setting. Enjoy the everchanging sights of Malaspina Strait, and the panoramic ocean views, including Vancouver Island's snowcapped mountains and the resident eagles, from the breakfast table. Fishing, dinner, sightseeing charters can be arranged. There is a friendly cat. Ideal place for groups or family reunions. Soothing hot-tub and on-site massage available. Visa,MC ✔B&B
http://www.vancouver-bc.com/beaconbb/

Prince George

(central BC; see also Burns Lake)

DeWit, Esther & Jerry (Tudor House B&B)   ☎ (250) 564-8433, Fax 564-5625
1720 Edmonton St., Prince George, BC   V2M 1X4   E-mail: dewit@princegeorge.com

From Hwy97 take Edmonton St towards downton.
$50S $60D $7.50Child $15Add.person   ▶ 6A
🍽 Full, homebaked 🏠 Downtown, 2-storey, view from guest rooms, patio, deck, quiet, secluded ■3(upst) ⊨1S,2Q,cot ⊒1Sh.w.g. ★ LF, off-street parking ⊛ No smoking, no pets ∾Dutch
🎿 Major shopping centre, restaurants, Tourism Office, hospital, Olympic Oval for walking, YMCA
🚗 Via & BC Rail Stations, Airport, Greyhound Bus Station
🔫 Pleasant, old-fashioned and warm hospitality in a beautiful, cozy character home. Dietary breakfast available on request. Free pick-up from railway and bus stations. There is a dog and a cat in residence. ✔B&B www.pgonline.com/bnb/tudorhouse.html

Prince George (cont'd)

Mead, Bob & Laura (Mead Manor Bed & Breakfast)   ☎ (250) 964-8436, Fax (250) 964-8449
4127 Baker Rd., Prince George, BC   V2N 5K2

Phone for directions.
$60S $70D   (Seniors Discounts avail)   ▶4A,2Ch
🍲 Full, homebaked   🏠 Res., split-level, deck   ◼ 2D (main &
ground level)   ⊨2Q   ⊲2Private   ★ F,TV,LF, off-street
parking   ⛹ Designated smoking area
🏃 College Heights Shopping Plaza
🚗 Downtown, Barkerville historic site, Fort St.James and museum,
lakes, trails (hiking, x-c skiing, snowmobiling), Tabor
Mountain Ski Resort, University of Northern BC, golfing
🐟 Warm, friendly hospitality in home tastefully decorated and situated in quiet location. ✔CC
http://www.bbcanada.com/356.html

Prince Rupert
(central BC on west coast)

Cox, Bryan and Mary Allen (Eagle Bluff Bed & Breakfast))   ☎ (250) 627-4955/7052
201 Cow Bay Rd., Prince Rupert, BC   V8J 1A2   E-mail: eaglebed@citytel.net, Fax (250) 627-7945

$45-55S $55-90D $5Child $15Add.person   (plus tax)(weekly & winter rates avail)   ▶10A,7CH

Located next to Cow Bay wharf across from P.R. Yacht Club.
🍲Cont.   🏠 1922-built downtown, older, waterfront,pier structure
◼4(main & upstairs)   ⊨4T,3D,5Q,crib,cot   ⊲3Private,1sh.w.g.
★ LF,TV/phone in guest room, exit to patio from each room
⛹Restricted smoking, no pets
🏃 Path along waterfront, downtown area, Northern Museum,
Mariner's Park, library, tennis courts, Performing Arts Centre,
Smile's Seafood Restaurant (a Prince Rupert landmark), fishing off
docks, Allied Pacific Processors (largest fish processing plant in
N.A.), Rushbrooke Floats (public boat launch and boat mooring at
entry to the Sea Walk hiking trail)
🐟 Renovated fishing home overlooking harbour, dock and yacht club, located on the shore in an
older area of town. Observe freighters, cruise ships and sail boats come and go, as well as
commercial fishing boats delivering and gearing up to depart. Knowledgeable hosts will gladly help
with itineraries and sometimes offer barbeque and fresh sea food meals. Families welcome.

Pritchard
(east of Kamloops; see also Salmon Arm, Sorrento)

Isaac, Lorne & Lynn (Alpine Meadows Bed & Breakfast)   ☎ (250) 577-3726,
RR1, McKim Rd., Pritchard, BC   V0E 2P0   Fax (250) 577-3654

Located east of Kamloops off TCH 1. Turn onto Hwy 97 (Vernon/Falkland), then left onto Duck
Range Rd and right onto McKim Rd. Watch for signs.
$35-45S $50-60D   ▶4
🍲Full,homebaked 🏠Farm,2-storey log home,view,patio,deck,
quiet ◼2D(walkout entry lower level) ⊲1Sh.w.g. ⊨1D,1Q
★2F,TV in guest lounge,private entrance, ample parking
⛹Designated smoking area, no children   ⚑ some German
🏃 Walking/hiking/cycling/x-c skiing/tobogganing on ungroomed
trails, large well sheltered dog kennel
🚗 Downhill skiing at Sun Peaks Resort, city of Kamloops, wildlife park & water slides, hunting
🐟 Unique log home with large rock fireplaces, nestled in 20acres of pines & meadows. Enjoy the
breathtaking view of the South Thompson River & Lake Kamloops and the beautiful sunsets.
Tranquility at its best. Breakfast is served in the dining room or on covered deck. House specialty is
wildflower honey from own honey bees. There is a very friendly dog and a cat in residence.

Qualicum Beach

(on Van.Isle, north of Nanaimo; see also Parksville, Lantzville)

England, Arlene & John (Blue Willow B&B)   ☎ (250) 752-9052 Fax (250) 752-9039
524 Quatna Rd., Qualicum Beach, BC V9K 1B4   E-mail: bwillow@island.net

From Nanaimo travel north on Hwy 19 and Qualicum Beach Exit. Follow Hwy 4A through the
village to waterfront. Turn right on Hwy 19A to Qualicum Rd. Turn right again at Quatna Rd. Or
via scenic route: take Parksville Exit from Hwy 19 and continue north to Qualicum Rd. Turn left,
then right at Quatna Rd.

$75S $85-100D   ► 6
🍳 Full, homebaked   🏠 Res., 2-storey, quiet   ■ 2D(main level)
plus garden suite (sep from house) ⊨1K(2T),1Q(house),
1Q,1D,2S(Ste)   ⇦Private   ★ TV in guest lounge, LF   🚭No
smoking   ⌇French, German
🏃 Beach, golf course, restaurants
🚗 Denman/Hornby Islands, Cathedral Grove Rainforest

☛ Elegant old Tudor home with leaded glass windows and beamed ceilings, amidst a show garden
of flowers, shrubs and tall West Coast conifers (featured on local Garden tours). Sumptuous
breakfast is served on hosts' collection of "Blue Willow" China. There is a long haired Dachshund.
http://www.bluewillow.bc.ca/

Sands, Dave & Audrie (Shoreline B&B)   ☎ & Fax(250) 757-9807
RR1, S152, C4, Bowser, BC V0R 1G0   E-mail: sands@nanaimo.ark.com

Located at 4969 Shoreline Dr in Deep Bay. From Hwy 19A, turn at Deep Bay. At tracks, turn right,
then make two left turns. Look for B&B at end of Shoreline Dr.

$65S $75D $30Add.person   ► 3A
🍳 Full, homebaked   🏠 Split-level, view from guest rooms, deck,
oceanfront, quiet   ■ 1D(ground level)   ⊨ 1S,1Q   ⇦Private
★ TV,private entrance, off-street parking   🚭 No smoking
🏃 Walks on beach (with large tide pools at low tide) or on quiet
paved roads, bird watching
🚗 Six golf courses, Horne Lake Caves, Coombs Country Market,
charter sailing, fishing, diving, Qualicum Beach

☛ Beautiful waterfront home with views of sea/islands/lighthouse and mountains on the
horizon, located in the heart of lighthouse country. Relax in the family room with library and TV or
in the established garden with guest seating and beach chairs. Knowledgeable hosts are enthusiastic
about the area. Breakfast is served on waterfront deck (weather permitting). There is a dog in
residence. Visa

Revelstoke

(west of Golden; see also Sicamous)

Akhurst, Susan & Bob Restall (Four Seasons Manor)   ☎ & Fax (250) 837-2616
Box 2628, Revelstoke, BC V0E 2S0   E-mail: fourseasonsmanor@cablelan.net, 1-877-837-2616

From Hwy 1 West, turn onto Victoria. Turn right on Mackenzie
(stop sign) & proceed 7 blocks. Located at 815 MacKenzie Ave.
$90-100S/D $15Add.person   ► 6-8
🍳 Full, homebaked   🏠 Res., view, 3-storey, veranda   ■3 (on
3rd floor)   ⊨3Q,2P   ⇦3Private   ★Bicycles for guests,
parking   🚭No smoking, no pets, not suitable for small children
🏃 Downtown, gift shops, restaurants, local walking tour, train
museum, riverfront walk, evening entertainment at Grizzly Plaza
🚗 Revelstoke Dam, Mt.Revelstoke Park, skiing snowmobiling, fishing, excellent hiking
☛ Warm welcome in 1905 Edwardian Paladian structure decorated in a romantic Victorian style.
Breakfast is served on deck of 2nd floor, weather permitting. Located in a quiet area away from
railway & highway traffic. Good place to plan for at least a two-day stay.
www.revelstokecc.bc.ca/vacation/4seasonsbb.html

Revelstoke (cont'd)

Astra, Joan and Olympe (Smokey Bear Campground & B&B) ☎/Fax(250)837-9573
Box 1125, Revelstoke,BC V0E 2S0   1-800-710-9573

Located 5 km west of Revelstoke on Hwy 1.
$35S $50-60D $10Child $15Add.person   ► 10A,5Ch
🍴 Full   🏠 Rural, 5 acre, patio   ■ 3D,1F (upstairs & ground level)   ⊨ 1D,5Q,1crib
🛁2Sh.w.g., 2ensuite   ★F,TV,LF, hot tub   👆 No smoking   ⁓ Russian
🏃 Flower Gardens, hiking, x-c skiing & snowmobiling
🚗 Mt.Revelstoke Nat.Park, Revelstoke Dam, Begbie Falls, Glacier National Park, Hot Springs
🐾 Inviting country home. Hosts are knowledgeable of the area. Ideal place for snowmobilers and groups. There is a dog & a cat. RV Park & hostel on property. Visa,MC ✓CC

Blackwell, Syd (Wintergreen Inn) ☎ & Fax (250) 837-3369, 1-800-216-2008
Box 1260, 312 Kootenay St., Revelstoke, BC V0E 2S0   E-mail: wintergreen@bctravel.com

$65-80S $75-90D $5Child (over age 6) $10Add.person   (plus taxes)   ► 24
Phone for directions.
🍴 Full   🏠 Res, 3-storey, view from guest rooms, patio, porch, deck quiet   ■8D,2F (main & upper level)   ⊨ 8T,7Q,1P
🛁Private, ensuite   ★Air,F,guest common area, ceiling fans, separate entrance, off-street parking, wheel-chair access, host quarters are separate   👆Smoking outside on deck
🏃 Historic Court House, downtown shops & restaurants, Railway Museum, riverside trails
🚗 Mt.Revelstoke & Glacier National Parks, Revelstoke Dam, historic "Last Spike of CPR" site
🐾 New B&B Inn, designed especially for guests' privacy and situated amid the splendor of majestic mountains at the gateway of 2 National Parks. World travelled host is a former educator. Free pick-up/delivery for buses. Visa, MC ✓CC

Ingram, Cliff and Donna (Alpine Lane Bed & Breakfast) ☎ (250) 837-6106
Box 1973, 487 Alpine Lane, Revelstoke, BC V0E 2S0

Located on TC Highway and 3km east of the lights. OR 1km west of eastern access to city. Watch for the orange trangles marking the road.
$40-55 $45-60 $10Child   ► 6
🍴Full,homebaked   🏠 Rural,split-level,acreage,decks,mountain view   ■1D,1Ste (upst)   ⊨1D,1Q,2S   🛁1Ensuite,1sh.w.g.(bidets)
★F,TV, sauna, parking
🏃 Hiking and x-c ski trails
🚗 Mt Revelstoke National Park Summit, Glacier Nat.Park, ski hill, Hydro Dam, golf course, snowmobile trails, Railway Museum
🐾 Relax and enjoy the friendly, casual atmosphere in the large spacious home situated at the base of Mt. Revelstoke. Surrounded by mountains, the house features a view from all rooms.✓CC

Revelstoke (cont'd)

Langinotto, Lisa (MacPherson Lodge)
Box 2615, 2135 Clough Rd, Revelstoke, BC   V0E 2S0

☎ (250) 837-7041, Fax (250) 837-7077
E-mail: bookrev@revelstoke.net

From TCH 1 take Hwy 23S for 7km. Turn on Clough Rd to home on left.
$60S $90D $5Child $15Add.person   ▶ 6A,4Ch
🍳 Full   🏠 Rural, log home, acreage, view from guest rooms, patio, porch, deck, quiet, secluded   ■2F,1Ste (upper & lower level)   ⊨2T,3K,3S,R,P, crib   🛁 3Private   ★ KF,F,TV in guest rooms, private entrance for suite, 1private guest balcony, off-street parking   👋 Smoking on covered porch   👄 French
🏃 Natural wilderness, trails (hiking, biking, x-c skiing)
🚗 Glacier National & Mt Revelstoke National Parks, Halcyon & Nakusp & Canyon Hot Springs
📣 Warm welcome in cozy hideaway nestled in the Columbia Valley and surrounded by picturesque beauty. Charming, knowledgeable hosts in beautiful, comfortable and relaxing location. Enjoy superb hospitality and good conversation. Small charge for kitchen privileges. Call for pick-up from Greyhound. There is a dog and a cat in residence. Visa,MC ✓B&B

Nelles, Rosalyne (Nelles Ranch B&B)
Hwy 23 S, Box 430, Revelstoke, BC   V0E 2S0

☎ & Fax (250) 837-3800, 1-888-567-4177

Located 2.2 km off TCH 1 at Revelstoke on Hwy 23 South.
$35-65S $45-75D $10Child $15Add.person   ▶ 22+
🍳 Full(hearty ranch-style)   🏠 Rural, large Horse-Ranch, acreage, view, patio, quiet   ■6 plus 1F (main & upper level)   ⊨5D,4Q,3T,1R   🛁 3sh.w.g., 4private   ★ F,TV in guest family room, sinks in some guest rooms, separate entrance, overnight horse accommodation available
🏃 Trail rides (horses), riding stables, x-c skiing, hiking
🚗 Revelstoke Dam, Mt Revelstoke Nat.Park (scenic drive) Williamsons Lake, Railway Museum
📣 Congenial hosts have been welcoming guests for 15 years in spacious ranchhouse on working horse ranch, set amid the majesty of the Selkirk Mountains. Enjoy the fresh mountain air and breathtaking scenery. There is a small pet poodle called "Handsome". Wilderness trail rides (hour rides) offered for experienced and inexperienced riders. Reservations recommended. ✓CC

Richmond   *(Vancouver); see also N.Westmin, Delta, White R, Surrey, Tsawwassen)*

Lewis, Joyce and Bob (Joyce's B&B)
10880 Granville Ave., Richmond, BC   V6Y 1R4

☎ (604) 278-8584

Located between No 4 and No 5 Roads.ph for directions.
$40-45S $45-55D   ▶ 5
🍳 Full, homebaked   🏠 Res., sub., split-level, acreage, patio, quiet   ■ 2D   ⊨2T,1D,1R   🛁1Ensuite, 1Sh.w.g.   ★TV in guest room, separate entrance, prarking   👋Restricted smoking, no pets, children min age 6
🏃 Aquatic center, jogging track, shopping malls, live theatre, restaurants, bus routes
🚗 Downtown Vancouver, International Airport, Ferries, easy access to Hwy 99
📣 Warm and friendly hospitality in comfortable home situated in quiet and convenient location. Hosts will pick up at airport. ✓B&B

Roberts Creek

(north-west of Vancouver; see also Gibsons, Sechelt, Halflmoon Bay)

Gaulin, Loragene and Philip (Country Cottage B&B) ☎ (604) 885-7448
1183 Roberts Creek Rd., Box 183, Roberts Creek, BC V0N 2W0

From Vancouver, take Hwy 1 and Horseshoe Bay-Langdale Ferry (40 min), and continue on Sunshine Coast Hwy 101 through Gibsons to Roberts Creek Rd (approx 35km).Turn left.

$85-125RoseCottage $99-145CedarLodge $50Add.person ► 8A
Full, homebaked (gourmet) Farm, older acreage, quiet
■ Cottage & lodge with cabin 4Q 3Private ★KF,wood stove, River Rock fireplace in lodge, wood-fired sauna, campfire circle No smoking, no pets, no children, one party only in lodge & cabin. French
Bicycling on beautiful beach avenue, golf course, French Gourmet restaurant, beach walks, shops galleries, bistro/cafe
Scenic coastline, hiking, swimming beaches, c/c skiing, fly-fishing, kyaking, mountain biking
Totally restored farmhouse, rustic cottage and lodge (a few steps away) surrounded by English Country style gardens and lawns. For all guests breakfast is brought to the door and cooked on antique wood stove (also tea and scones). Hostess is a spinner and weaver and raises sheep for fine spinning wool. Host is Vintage car truck & motorcyle restorer/collector and back country skier. There are 2 cats and an Irish Wolfhound in residence. Advance reservation necessary. B&B

Salmon Arm

(east of Kamloops: see also Pritchard, Sorrento)

Bodnar, Gisela (Silver Creek Guest House) ☎ (250) 832-8870
6820-30 Ave SW, Salmon Arm, BC V1E 4M1

At Flashing light west of Salmon Arm, turn off to Salmon River Rd. Follow road for 2.5 km, turn right on 30th Ave SW and drive for 1.5 km. Look forsign on left.

$25-30S $40-45D ► 6A
Choice Small ranch, patio ■ 3D(main level) 3D
1Sh.w.h.,1private ★TV,F,LF Restricted smoking, not suitble for children German
Bicycling, cross-country ski trails
drive Large Community center with swimming pool and hot tub, Shuswap Lake, beaches, boating, fishing, Salmon Arm, canoeing
Charming log house with beautiful view from deck of Mount Ida and Salmon River Valley. For a delicious breakfast, enjoy fresh farm eggs, homemade buns and jams and fruits in season. B&B

Evans, Robert (Sherwood Forest Bed & Breakfast) ☎ & Fax (250) 832-1863
2511-4th Ave.NE, Salmon Arm, BC V1E 2A7 E-mail: evansrg@shuswap.net

Arriving from west, turn right, from east turn left at 30th St.NE & TCH. Proceed to 5th Ave NE, turn right to 27th St, turn left to 4th Ave NE. Turn right to last house on right.

$70S $75D $10Child (under age 12) $15Add.person ► 4+
Full,homebaked Res., back-split 3-storey, quiet, view, deck
■1Ste(ground level) Private (with hot-tub) 1Q,2P
★F,TV/VCR in guest sitting room, small guest patio, off-street parking, sep.entrance, guest quarters are quarters No smoking,no pets
Video store, restaurants, swimming pool, curling rink, hiking trails, bus to downtown, College, bowling
Downtown Salmon Arm, Shuswap Lake (many beaches & picnic areas), winter sports & x-c skiing, great little fishing lakes, golf courses, Vernon, Kamloops
Comfortable, multi-level home in a quiet, private setting. There is a 25ft hibiscus tree in the solarium adjacent to the living room. Deluxe guest suite consists of 3rooms. Relax on the sunny little patio off the guest suite or join the hosts for interesting conversation in the large bright kitchen with a beautiful view of Shuswap Lake. "All-you-can-eat", wholesome breakfast chosen from Uncle Bob's selective menu is served in the dining room overlooking the lake. Host loves to show off his airplane under construction in the garage. CC http://www.bbcanada.com/980.html

Saltspring Island

(east of Duncan; see also Mayne Island)

Bischoff, Lynn & Ralph (Anchor Point B&B)
150 Beddis Rd., Saltspring Island, BC V8K 2J2
(250) 538-0110, Fax 538-0120
E-mail: info@anchorpointbb.com

Located 1km south of town of Ganges. Turn onto Beddis Rd & continue 100m towards Sail Club.

$125S/D $30Add.person (plus tax) 6A,2Ch
Full, homebaked Rural, hillside, acreage, view from guest rooms, patio, porch, deck, quiet, secluded 1D,2Ste (upstairs) 1D,2Q (incl.sleighbed) 1Private, 2ensuite ★ LF,F,TV, private entrance, off-street parking, robes & slippers, sitting areas in suites, guest quarters are separate No smoking,no pets,children min.age 12 German, French
Town of Ganges (a haven for artists, writers and craftspeople), galleries, town market, kayaking, sailing, bicycling, golfing
Butchart Gardens, Victoria, Chemainus
Traditional Cape-style residence with elegant decor, town & country atmosphere and a spectacular harbour view. A perfect place for a rejuvenating getaway. Relax in the outdoor spa, soaking in the views and starry skies or wander along the beach & wooded trails. Extensive classic movie collection inhouse (video/monitors delivered to guest rooms upon request). Breakfast is served in special guest breakfast room. There is a cat in residence. Complimentary transportation to and from ferry or float plane dock. Visa,MC B&B www.anchorpointbb.com

---

Bolton, Terry & Bev (Beddis House B&B)
131 Miles Ave., Salt Spring Island, BC V8K 2E1
(250) 537-1028, Fax (250) 537-9888
E-mail: beddis@saltspring.com

From Ganges, take Fulford-Ganges Rd south to Beddis Rd. Proceed 6 km to Miles Ave, turn left.
$135-165S $150-180D (plus tax) (weekly & seasonal rates available) 6A

closed Dec15-Jan31 Full, homebaked Rural, hist., view from guest rooms, acreage, oceanfront, porch, deck, quiet 3D (main & upper floor in new addition) 2T,1Q,1K 3Ensuite ★F/library in parlour, sep.entrance, oceanfront private decks/balcony, woodstove in each room, host quarters are separate No smoking, no pets, no children
Private clamshell beach in sheltered cove, prolific wildlife, many outdoor areas to relax, walks on quiet rural roads
Ganges Village, art galleries, craft studios, boating, Ruckle Provincial Park, Mount Maxwell
Restored Century Heritage farmhouse nestled peacefully beween the sea and an apple Orchard. Savour luxury oceanfront accommodation in a truly magical setting. Well travelled hosts enjoy sharing the diverse wonders of their island. Compl.afternoon tea/homebaking.Visa,MC CC www.saltspring.com/beddishouse

---

Leader, Harry and Ilse (Ocean Spray B&B by the Sea)
1241 Isabella Pt.Rd., Salt Spring Island, BC V8K 1T5
& Fax (250) 653-4273

Take ferry from Victoria (Swartz Bay) to Fulford Harbour on Saltspring Island. From Vancouver, take ferry from Tsawwassen to Long Harbour and drive through Ganges to Fulford Harbour.

$85D $10-15Child $20Add.person 4
Full (provided, but not served) Rural, acreage, oceanfront, 3-level, quiet Ste 2T,1P,cot Private ★Sep.entrance, KF, parking Restr.smoking German
Ecological Reserve, back country roads and forest trails
Roomy cedar home (built by architect of Frank Lloyd Wright School), is located on Satellite Channel with a panoramic view of the Gulf Islands and Mount Baker, situated on 5 acres of forested waterfront with the sea a stone's throw away from the bedroom deck, offering an ever changing scene of marine life. Visa/MC CC

Salt Spring Isle (cont'd)

Broad,Rick & Ruth-Anne(Anne's Oceanfront Hideaway) ☎(250)537-0851,1-888-474-2663
168 Simson Rd,Salt Spring Isle,BC V8K 1E2   E-mail: annes@saltspring.com,Fax(250)537-0861

Located on the north-west side of the Island off Sunset Drive.
$150-195D (off season) $185-230D (Summer)   ▶ 8A
🍴 Full (4-course Island b'fast)   🏠 Rural, res, 3-storey, acreage,
view from guest rooms, oceanfront, porch, guest balconies, quiet,
sandstone beach   ■ 4D(upstairs)   ⊨ 2T,3Q (incl canopy bed)
🛏 4Ensuite (incl.hydromassage tub & double tubs) ★F,TV,Air
(indiv.), balconies in 3 guest rooms, separate entrance, wheel-chair
access, elevator, outside hot tub, library, canoe &
bicycles for guests, host quarters are separate   Ⓦ No smoking, no pets, no children
🏃 Ocean, fishing, swimming, canoeing, kayaking, bird watching, cycling, craft/pottery studios
🚗 Golf course, tennis courts, movie theatre, swimming pool, shopping, restaurants, Art
Galleries, sailing charters, kayak rentals, hiking trails, pubs, Ganges, Vesuvius
📣 Luxurious, spacious (1996-built) home overlooking an everchanging panoramic seaview. Enjoy
the beauty and tranquility. Unwind among the Arbutus and Oak. Allergy aware and special diets
can be accommodated with advance notice. Enjoy morning coffee on the sun deck. Ideal place for
special occasion, get-away or honeymoon. CCards ✓CC

Tara, Helen (Water's Edge B&B)   ☎ (250) 537-5807, Fax (250) 537-2862
327 Price Rd., Salt Spring Island, BC , V8K 2E9

Take any one of 3 ferries to Saltspring Island and then Fulford-Ganges Rd to Beddis Rd. Turn
southeast for 2km to Price Rd and left 1km to waterfront. Located 4.2km south of Ganges Village.

$95-120S $120-150D $35-45Add.person   ▶ 7
🍴 Full, homebaked   🏠 Rural, waterfront on Ganges Harbour,
2-storey, seaview from guest rooms, patio, quiet   ■1D,1Ste
(ground level waterside)   ⊨1K.2Q,1S   🛏 1Ensuite, 1Private
★F,KF, rowboat, guest sitting room, separate entrance, parking
ⓌSmoking outside only
🏃 Shore walk at down tide, rowboating over magic chain of islands
in the harbour, kayaking, beachcombing, country walks
🚗 Village of Ganges, shopping, restaurants, 3 ferries, golfing, swimming, horseback riding
📣 Long-time island residents in contemporary home with country gardens, fish pond and covered
patio facing waterfront. Relax in the quiet comfort, watch the sun rise over the water, see the
abundant birds & sealife and marine traffic in the harbour. ✓B&B

Sechelt   *(n/w of Vancouver; see also Gibsons, Roberts Creek, Halfmooon Bay)*

Fedor, David & Brenda Wilkinson (Four Winds B&B)   ☎ (604)885-3144, Fax (604)885-3182
5482 Hill Rd., RR1, Blacks Site C33, Sechelt, BC V0N 3A0   E-mail: four_winds@sunshine.net

From Langdale (ferry from Vancouver), take Sunshine coast Hwy 101 through Sechelt and proceed
past Wakefield Inn to Hill Rd. Turn left.

$90-130S $105-145D $20Child   ▶ 4A,2-3Ch
🍴Full, homebaked   🏠Rural, view from guest rooms, deck, quiet,
oceanfront   ■ 2D (ground level)   ⊨ 2T,1Q   🛏2Private
★Guest robes, hot tub   Ⓦ No smoking, no pets
🏃 Rocky beach
🚗 Skookumchuck Rapids, kayak & canoe rentals, boat charters,
hiking trails, mountain biking, art galleries
📣 Architecturally designed home sitting on rocky oceanshore. Curl up in a window seat with the
sea just 20 feet away. Join the host family in the spectacular living room surrounded on three sides
by the ocean. Relax in the outdoor hot tub, fall asleep to the sound of waves lapping lazily on the
rocks below. Breakfast is served on the deck or in dining room. Hostess is a Registered Massage
Therapist and will take advance bookings for treatment and workshops. Ideal place for a weekend
retreat or a special occasion. There is a dog and a cat in host area. Visa,MC ✓CC
www.sunshine.net/fourwinds

Sechelt (cont'd)

Scholton, Bruce & Jean (Heron House on the Shores)   ☎ & Fax (604) 855-5429
C60, The Shores, RR2, Sechelt, BC   V0N 3A0

Located at 6490 N.Gale Ave. At Horseshoe Bay (Vancouver), catch ferry to Langdale and then take Hwy 101 to Sechelt. Follow Trail Ave to N.Gale Ave.

$85-135S/D   ► 6A

🍽 Full 🏠 Res., 3-storey, acreage, view from guest rooms, oceanfront, patio, porch, deck, quiet, secluded ■2D,1Ste (upstairs) ⊨1D,1Q ⊒1Ensuite, 1sh.w.g. ★ F,TV in guest rooms, soaker-tub in ensuite, sitting room with pooltable & shuffleboard, off-street parking Ⓦ No smoking no pets, not suitable for children

🏃 Private beach, swimming, golfing, park, old growth forest, public transportation
🚗 Downtown Sechelt, driving range, hiking, bike trails, kayaking, restaurants, pub
🛥 Large, elegant, beautifully decorated home with spectacular waterfront view, private swimming beach. Relax in the sitting room leading to decks and gardens. Enjoy the peace & quiet and a scrumptious English-Style breakfast. There are a dog and a cat in residence. Visa ✓B&B

Tucker, Corinna (Tucker's Inn B&B)   ☎ (604) 885-9077
RR2 Black Site C-11, Sechelt, BC   V0N 3A0   E-mail: tuckers_inn@sunshine.net

Located at 6966 Sunshine Coast Hwy 101. From Vancouver take Hwy 1 to Horseshoe Bay Ferry Terminal. Take Langdale/Sunshine Coast Ferry (40min ride). then Hwy 101 to Sechelt and 5km north of downtown.

$80-90S $90-120D $15-20Add.person   (plus tax)   ► 6A

🍽 Full 🏠 Rural, raised bungalow, acreage, view from guest rooms, ocean across street ■ 2Suites (ground level) ⊨ 2Q,1cot ⊒ 2Ensuite ★KF,F,TV/phone in suites, bathrobes, hair-dryers, private entrance, guest sitting room with fireplace, kitchenette and hot-tub, off-street 3 parking, guest quarters are separate Ⓦ Smoking outside ⁓ Spanish
🏃 Fishing, golfing, hiking, cycling, kayaking, boating, diving, bird sanctuary
🚗 Sechelt, shops, museums/galleries, Prov. Parks, wonderful restaurants
🛥 New Westcoast contemporary home built for B&B with luxury decor and located on 2.3acres with a natural creek, ponds and gardens and convenient beach access across the street. Breakfast is served in guest breakfast room or in guest suites. Ideal place for special occasions. Pick-up transportation available. Rates include breakfast & afternoon Tea. There is an outside dog. Pets welcome. Visa/MC ✓B&B   www.sunshine.net/www/2200/sn2277/

Sicamous   *(west of Revelstoke; see also Mara)*

Meyers, Ray & Phillis (Rainbow Valley B&B)   ☎ (250) 836-3268
Box 343, Sicamous, BC   V0E 2V0   E-mail: rainbowv@shuswap.net, Fax (250) 836-3008

Located at 1409 Rauma Rd and 2 blocks north of TCH.

$75-110S/D $20Child/Add.person   ► 10

🍽 Full, homebaked 🏠 2-storey ■ 1D,2F(upstairs ⊨5Q ⊒ 3Private ★ F,KF,LF,TV in guest rooms, separate entrance, ceiling fans, off-street & street parking Ⓦ Designated smoking area, no pets,
🏃 Beaches, shopping places, houseboating, gifts/crafts, restaurants, fruit stands, museum, golfing, Zoo, lake cruises
🚗 Scenic drive along Mara Lake to city of Vernon, large shopping malls, excellent downhill skiing
🛥 Newly-built house located with view of beautiful Canadian Rockies and Shuswap Lake and located in a quiet area. Breakfast is served in special guest breakfast room. Ideal place for weddings or family reunion-type gatherings and special occasions. Children welcome. Visa,MC

Sidney

Clegg, Averil & Maurice (Mandeville - Tudor Cottage by the Sea)   ☎ (250) 655-1587
1064 Landsend Rd., Sidney, BC   V8L 5L3   Fax (250) 655-3993

Located at north end of Saanich Peninsula, at intersection of Landsend Rd & West Saanich Rd. Phone for specific directions.
$75S $95D $20Child $35Add.person   ► 4A,4Ch
🍴 Full(West coast cuisine)   🏠 Rural, oceanfront forest acreage, 2-storey, hist., view from guest rooms, patio, porch, deck   ■2Stes (upstairs & ground level)   ⊨1S,2Q,1R,1P(D),crib   ⊲2Private
★TV,LF,F in one suite, kitchenette, private entrances, private patio, guest quarters are separate   👋Smoking outside, no pets
🚗 BC & Washington State Ferry Terminals, airports, Victoria, hiking trails (with excellent ocean views from higher points), Butchart Gardens, Vancouver Island attractions and virgin forests, Pacific Rim Nat.Park (with unspoiled beaches), good skiing
🎯 Retired Professional couple in picturesque classic English Tudor Cottage home with lawns & gardens leading to the beach. Enjoy the breathtaking views across the Satellite Channel to neighbouring Saltspring Island. Hosts are interested in the arts, music, travel, gardening and are active at the local Anglican Church. Breakfast is served in guest dining room. ✓B&B

Freeman, Mrs. Valerie (Seventh Haven B&B)   ☎ (250) 655-4197
9617-7th St., Sidney, BC   V8L 2V4

From Beacon Ave at 5th St, turn south to Orchard Ave, west to 7th St & south to B&B.
$45S $60D $10Child/Add.person   ► 4
🍴 Full   🏠 Res.,1-storey, garden view from guest rooms, patio, quiet   ■2D (main floor)   ⊨2T,1Q   ⊲1Ensuite, 1sh.w.h.
★ F,TV in one guest room, street parking   👋 No smoking, inquire about children and pets
🧍 Seaside town (shops, restaurants, marinas), beachfront & Anacortes Ferry, kayaking, sailing, short ferry trips, cycling, No70 bus to Victoria
🚗 Victoria, Butchart Gardens, Airport, Schwartz Bay Ferries
🎯 Charming cottage-style home with restful and cheerful atmosphere, located in Orchard Park. Hostess loves a good chat over a good breakfast, helping with daily plans and going the "second mile". ✓B&B

Shrimpton, Josie & Malcolm (Cartref Bed & Breakfast)   ☎& Fax (250) 656-1247
1345 Readings Dr., Sidney, BC   V8L 5K7   E-mail: cartref@islandnet.com

Phone for directions.
$60S $75-95D $10Child $15Add.person   ► 4A,2Ch
🍴Full, homebaked   🏠Rural, 2-storey, acreage, ocean view from terrace guest rooms, quiet   ■1D,1F(upstairs)   ⊨1T,1D,1Q,crib   ⊲Private   ★ LF,TV/VCR in guest sitting room   👋No pets, no smoking, only one party at a time
🧍 Nature trails, viewpoints
🚗 BC/US ferries, Sidney, Butchart Gardens, airport,Victoria
🎯 Warm and friendly welcome in new home (name is Celtic for "home") situated on a tranquil sunny hillside with view of Sidney Channel. Breakfast is served in the Conservatory or on the terrace by an ornamental waterfall. Recently retired hosts have travelled extensively and are knowledgeable about southern Vancouver Island. Coffee/tea & cookies always available. Extra space available for family & friends. Visa ✓B&B http://victoriabc.com/accom/cartref.html

Sidney (cont'd)

Siems, Susan (Borthwick Country Manor B&B)
9750 Ardmore Dr., Sidney, Victoria, BC   V8L 5H5

☎ & Fax (250) 656-9498
E-mail: msiems@coastnet.com

From Victoria travel 25 km north on Hwy 17A. Turn left on 2nd Ardmore Dr.

$130-169D $35Add.person   (Deposit required)   ► 10
🍴 Full, homebaked   🏠 Rural, 2-storey, acreage, view from guest rooms, quiet ■3D,1F(upstairs) ⊨2Q,1K,2T ⏤4Ensuite
★TV,outdoor hot-tub, guest bicycles, off-street parking 🚳No smoking, no pets, children min. age 12
🧍 Beach, golf course
🚗 Butchart Gardens, Butterfly Gardens, Airport, Vancouver ferries, Anacortes/Seattle-US ferries, sailing, boating, diving
🔻 English Tudor Country Manor house, tastefully decorated with some antiques, set in one acre of gorgeous landscaped gardens, and located in the beautiful Patricia Bay area of the Saanich Peninsula. Relax in the outdoor hot tub or stroll to the nearby beach. English hosts serve gourmet breakfast in the formal dining room or outside on the covered stone patio. Winter discounts available (Nov-Mar). CCards ✓CC ww.coastnet.com/~msiems/borthwick.html

---

Silverton   *(north of Castlegar)*

Iverson, Sue & George (Mistaya Country Inn & B&B)
Box 28, Silverton, BC   V0G 2B0

☎ & Fax (250) 358-7787

Located north of Castlegar Airport or Nelson on Hwy 6.
$45-55S $60-70D $15Add.person 🍽 Meals (plus tax)   ► 13
🍴 Full, homebaked   🏠 Rural, 2-storey ranch-style, acreage, view from guest rooms, porch ■ 4D,1F (upstairs)
⊨4S,1D,3Q,1P,1R, cot ⏤ 2Sh.w.g. ★ F,LF, guest lounge, outside firepit ★ Smoking on porch, no pets
🧍 90 acres of forest and pasture land, walking & x-c ski trails
🚗 Nakusp & Ainsworth Hot Springs, Sandon Ghost town, Idaho Peak lookout, Unique village of New Denver, Valhalla Prov.& Kokanee Glacier Parks
🔻 Spacious, comfortable country home overlooking a forest meadow and the Valhalla Wilderness Park. Experience a quiet vacation in the Slocan Valley, enjoy the wild flowers, magnificient scenery & wildlife or relax by the fireplace. Trail rides, riding lessons and overnight pack trips into the Selkirk Mountains. Wildlife viewing/canoe/kayak trips offered. Packed lunches & evening barbeques available. Visa,MC ✓B&B www.bctravel.net/mistaya

---

Sooke   *(south-west of Victoria)*

Lee, Daphne & Peter (Manzer Lodge)
3007 Manzer Rd., Sooke, BC   V0S 1N0

☎ & Fax (250)642-6632,1-877-642-6632
E-mail: manzerlodge@telus.net

From downtown Victoria, go over Johnson St Bridge to Tyee Rd. Turn right and follow all the way to Sooke. Look for 17-Mile-House Pub on right and then Manzer Rd 3rd road on left.

$95S/D   ► 4
🍴 Full English   🏠 Lodge-style, peaceful, 1-acre ■2D ⊨2Q
⏤2Ensuite ★ F in guest lounge, private balcony, hot tub on large deck 🚳 No smoking, no pets, no children
🚗 Galloping Goose Trail, Sooke Potholes, kayak & bike rentals
🔻 Comfortable home, tastefully and recently renovated and nestled high amongst the trees. Ideal place to explore the coastline with its bays, lakes and trails - or for a peaceful and tranquil rest.
www3.bc.sympatico.ca/manzerlodge

Sooke (cont'd)

Evans, Robyn (Gordon's Beach Farm Stay B&B)   ☎ & Fax (250) 642-5291
4530 Otter Point Rd., Sooke, BC   V0S 1N0   1-888-852-8881

From Hwy 1 take the Sooke-Colwood Exit following Hwy 14 to Sooke. Proceed through traffic lights
and continue on the West Coast Rd for 10km. Turn right up Otter Point Rd to 2nd house on left.
$70D $80-175Ste $15Child $15Add.person   🍽 Meals (lunch)   ► 6A,3Ch

🍳 Full   🏠 Farm, 3-storey, hillside, acreage, view from guest
rooms, patio, quiet, secluded   ■ 3(main & ground level)
⊨3Q,1R   ⌁ 2Private, 1ensuite   ★ TV/coffee makers in guest
rooms, private patios, beach hot tub and gazebo, separate entrance,
guest quarters are separate   ⍟ Smoking outside
🏃 Beach across road, whale watching, windsurfing, kyaking,
fishing, hiking, Storm Watch (winter)
🚐 Straight of Juan de Fuca (Gateway to Pacific Ocean), West
Coast Trails, marine parks, Botanical Beach, restaurants, Sooke & S.Potholes, Victoria
🔪 Custom-designed, contemporary home with an artistic blend of old and new and allergy-free
environment, situated on 10 acres in pasture with 180 degree view of the Juan De Fuca Straights
and Olympic Mountains. Guests may be surprised to see whales pass by during breakfast time.
Relax in the hot tub and watch the Sherringham Lighthouse as the sun sets. Breakfast is served in
the dining room, on the patio or in guest rooms. There is a resident cat and dog. Visa,MC ✓B&B
www.gordonsbeachbandb.com

Price, Helen & Gord (Water's Edge Cottage & B&B)   ☎ (250)642-5716,Fax(250)642-4864
5641 Sooke Rd., Sooke, BC   V0S 1N0   E-mail: watersedge@telus.net, 1-800-307-7556

$85D(Ste) $175D(cottage) $15Add.person(Child free under age6)(Weekly/monthly rates)► 8A,1Ch

Located on Hwy 14, 4km east of Sooke.
🍳 Cont., homebaked   🏠 Rural, 2-storey, older, 3acres, view
from guest rooms, harbourfront, deck, quiet, secluded   ■ 1Ste,
plus 2 private cottages   ⊨ 1S,1D,3Q   ⌁ 1Ensuite, 1private
★F,TV,KF,LF, ceiling fans, cozy wood stove, wheel-chair access in
cottages, private hot tub   ⍟ Designated smoking area
🏃 Galloping Goose Trail (hiking/biking), fishing & whale
watching (tour charters), beach, City Transport No 61
🚐 Sooke village, shops, unique dining places, Victoria, Port Renfrew, West Coast Trail/beaches
🔪 Quiet country home with newly renovated suite & charming, waterfront cottages. Relax on
the large deck or in the private hot tub, just feet from the water, and enjoy the magical views of
water & Olympic Mountains. A perfect spot for touring the incredible scenic Sooke area. Children
& pets welcome. Visa,MC ✓B&B http://victoriabc.com/accom/watersedge.html

---

Rolston, Marion (Ocean Wilderness Inn & Spa Retreat)   ☎(250)646-2116, Fax 646-2317
109 West Coast Rd., Sooke, BC V0S 1N0   E-mail: ocean@sookenet.com, 1-800-323-2116

$65-140S $85-175D   (Off-season discounts & winter specials available.   ► 12
From Victoria, take Hwy 14 along West Coast Road to Sooke
Village, go past the only traffic light and continue 13 km.
🍳 Full, homebaked (also served in guest room)   🏠 Rural, hist.,
acreage, view, patio, quiet, oceanfront, isolated   ■ 9(main and
upper level - all bed/sitting)   ⊨6Q,2K,2T(some canopy)
⌁9Private (3 soak-tubs for two)   ★Separate entrance, facilities
for the disabled, parking, outdoor reading areas, jetted hot tub in
garden Japanese gazebo   ⍟ No smoking
🏃 5 acres with ocean beach and marine life and forest trails, beachcombing, birdwatching, surfing
🚐 Victoria, Botanical Beach, Sooke River swimming, fine dining, wild west coast beaches
🔪 Old log house (authentic Norwegian cabin) with modern addition for luxurious guest
accommodation, furnished with antiques and with beautiful ocean and mountain views. "Where
eagles soar and old growth forest meets the sea". Massage, ocean nutrient treatment and seaweed
wrap for relaxation and revitalization. Salmon fishing and whale watching guides available.
www/sookenet.com/ocean

Sorrento

(north of Salmon Arm; see also Pritchard)

Langevin, Verna & Linda Eberle (Evergreen B&B) ☎ (250) 675-2568, Fax (250) 675-3188
Box 117, Vimy Rd., Sorrento, BC   V0E 2W0

Located in west end of village. Phone for directions.
$45S $55-75D   🍵 Afternoon Tea   ► 14
🍳 Full   🏠 Res., mountain view, acreage, beach access
■2D,1F(ground & upper levels)   ⊨ 4D,2Q,R   🚿2Private,
1Sh.w.g.   ★KF,TV lounge, separate entrance, 2 guest kitchens,
dry heat sauna, wheel-chair access   🚭Restricted smoking,
controlled pets
🕴 Small shopping center, restaurants, Shuswap Lake, boat trips,
tea garden with gazebo (for 15 people) in back yard, small bird aviary on site, Country Chapel
🚗 Golfing, Adams River Salmon Run, x-c skiing, Okanagan Fruit Valley, Blue Grass Festival
📯 Cottage-style home surrounded by evergreens in picturesque historic village. Congenial hosts
will serve breakfast in large guest breakfast room. Ideal place for small group, private retreats,
special occasions and weddings. ╰B&B

Summerland

(south of Kelowna; see also Penticton, Peachland)

Croft, Leslie (Solly House B&B) ☎ (250) 494-8032, Fax 494-8029
RR1,S6,C28, 6313 Solly Rd., Summerland, BC   V0H 1Z0   E-mail: krftcrft@cnx.net

From Hwy 97 exit east onto Solly Rd and proceed 3 blocks to house on right.

$65 $85 $15Add.person   ► 5
🍳 Full, homebaked   🏠 Res., older, heritage-style, view from
guest rooms, porch, deck, quiet, secluded, veranda   ■1S,2D (main
& upper level)   ⊨ 1T,1D,1Q   🚿 1Private, 2ensuite   ★F,TV,
ceiling fans in guest rooms, private entrance, guest quarters are
separate, off-street parking   🚭 No smoking, no pets, children
min. age 10
🕴 Beaches, restaurants, KVR walking/cycling trails, tennis courts
🚗 Downhill & x-c skiing, wineries, art galleries, shops, Kelowna
📯 Large, gracious Heritage-style home (ca 1910) with a gracious wrap-around veranda, a lovely
secluded yard and beautiful views of Okanagan Lake. Breakfast is served in guest breakfast room.
There is a dog in residence. ╰B&B www.bb.canada.com/sollyhouse.html

Surrey

(Vancouver); see also White R, Langley, Delta, N.Westmin, Tsawwassen)

Bury, Chuck and Glad (White Heather B&B) ☎ (604) 581-9797
12571-98th Ave., Surrey, BC   V3V 2K6

Follow Hwy 99 to 96th Ave. Travel west to 126th St and north to
98th Ave. Turn left.
$45-55S $55-65D $15Child(under age 12)   ► 4A,2-3Ch
🍳 Full, homebaked   🏠 Res., sub., view from guest rooms, patio,
quiet, sunroom   ■ 2D(main floor)   ⊨ 1Q,1D   🚿1Sh.w.g.,
2ensuite   ★F,parking   🚭 No smoking, no pets
🕴 Local bus routes connecting to all Vancouver bus lines and
sky-train, good restaurants
🚗Sky Lift, downhill skiing (Seymour/Grouse Mt/Cypress Bowl)
📯 Panoramic view of North Shore Mountains. Well-travelled hosts are knowledgeable about
local area, as well as Vancouver Island. Breakfast is served in garden-like sunroom with a beautiful
view. Located near Skytrain and easy, quick transportation to anywhere in Greater Vancouver.
Pick-up from cruise ships and airport. ╰B&B

Tofino
(on Vancouver Island's west coast)

Barton, Lynn (Clayoquot Retreat)   ☎ (250) 725-3305, Fax (250) 725-3300
Box 292, 120 Arnet Rd., Tofino, BC   V0R 2Z0   E-mail: lbarton@island.net

In Tofino, turn left on First St and right on Arnet Rd.
$70-80S $80-95D   ►6
🍴 Full, homebaked (buffet-style)   🏠 Village, 2-storey, acreage,
view from guest rooms, oceanfront   ■3(ground level)   ⊨2D,2Q
🛏3Private   ★ TV/fridge in guest rooms, hot tub, off-street
parking, private entrances, private patios   ⍟ Designated
smoking area, small pets considered
🕴 Tonquin Beach, town centre   🚐Pacific Rim National Park

🐾 Warm welcome in very quiet waterfront home with spectacular views of ocean and islands from every room. Hosts are long-time residents of this quaint small West Coast village. Enjoy a delicious buffet-style breakfast in your own room. Watch boats, eagles and occasional whales pass by, and relax in the oceanfront hot tub overlooking the surf. There is a cat and a dog. Two-day min in high season (July1-Oct15). Visa,MC ✍B&B

Burgess, Ralph & Wendy (Wilp Gybuu - Wolf House B&B)   ☎(250)725-2330
311 Leighton Way, Box 396, Tofino, BC V0R 2Z0   E-mail: wilpgybu@island.net,Fax1205

Take Hwy 4 across Vancouver Isle to Tofino. Phone for directions.
$75-85S $85-100D (off-season rates available)   ► 6A
🍴 Full, homebaked   🏠 Village, res., multi-storey, view, quiet
■3D(ground level)   ⊨2Q,2T   🛏3Ensuite   ★2F,TV,in guest
lounge, library, piano, F in guest rooms, private entrance,
parking   ⍟ No smoking, children min. age 12, no pets
🕴 Tonquin Park, ocean beach, whale watching, scenic cruises,
canoeing, kayaking, sport fishing, beachcombing, seaplane tours,
restaurants, gift shops, bus to/from east side of Island
🚐 Pacific Rim National Park & ocean beaches, golf course, airport
🐾 Contemporary, artistic West Coast cedar home overlooking Duffin Passage and the inside waters and islands of Clayoquot Sound. Host is a native Artist. Pick-up and delivery to bus/airport. There is a resident cat. Visa,MC ✍B&B

Dublanko, Joan (Chesterman's Beach B&B)   ☎ (250) 725-3726, Fax 725-3706
1345 Chesterman's Beach Rd., Box 72, Tofino, BC   V0R 2Z0   E-mail: surfsand@island.net

Located 3.5 km from the village of Tofino.ph or write for directions.
Accessible by direct Orient Express bus service from Port Alberni.
from $125-160S/D   (plus tax)   ► 12
🍴Cont.   🏠Village,beach-oceanfront,quiet   ■3Ste(main & upper floor &
sep.cottage)   ⊨T,D,Q,P   🛏3Private   ★F,KF, separate entrance, guest
fridge, facilities for the disabled
🕴 Pacific Rim National Park rugged coastline, beachcombing,
whale-watching, fine restaurants, marinas, art galleries, stores, native art
shops, boating, quiet paddle through the inlets, surfing, kayaking, sailing,
fishing, bird watching, Meares Island
🐾 Tranquil and private setting. Experience the open ocean, a beautiful beach and rolling surf right at the doorstep. Ideal romantic retreat - a favorite for honeymooners. Tours for wilderness viewing, fishing or scenic Hot Springs Cove arranged. Families welcome. There is a small dog. ✍
B&B   www.island.net/~surfsand

Tofino (cont'd)

Ironside, Ed & Mary Ellen (Water's Edge Bed & Breakfast)   ☎ (250) 725-1218
Box 635, Tofino, BC   V0R 2Z0

Follow Hwy4 west across Island to Tofino. Located at 331 Tonquin Park Rd.
$75-100S $85-105D $20Child $20Add.person   ▶6
🍴Full, homebaked   🏠Village, 2-storey, view from guest rooms, oceanfront,
deck, quiet   ■ 3D(main floor)   ⊨2T,2Q,R   🛁1Sh.w.g., 1ensuite &
jacuzzi   ★ Air, off-street parking   🖐 No smoking, no pets
🥾 Tonquin Park (boardwalk through rainforest to superb sandy beach)
Tofino centre with restaurants, galleries, Tour Companies (boat trips to Hot
Spring Cove, whale watching, Meares Island (big tree walk), scenic flights
🚗 Golf Course, Pacific Rim National Park (beaches, rainforest trails)
📷 Cliff-top home with spectacular sweeping views of several islands and
the open Pacific Ocean. There is access to the water by stairway to the rocks
and beautiful tidal pools. Well travelled hosts have lived in other countries, are knowledgeable
about the area and its attractions. Relax in the living room or on the deck and spot whales during
spring migration. Breakfast is served in the dining room, while watching many passing boats.
Pick-up from airport or bus. Visa,MC ✔B&B

Sloman, Val & James (The Tide's Inn on Duffin Cove)   ☎ (250) 725-3765
160 Arnet Rd., Box 325, Tofino, BC   V0R 2Z0   E-mail: tidesinn@island.net Fax: (250) 725-3325

On Vancouver Island, follow Hwy 4 west. Phone for direction.
$75-95S $85-110D $25Add.person   ▶7
🍴 Full, homebaked   🏠 Village, 2-storey, small acreage, view
from guest rooms, oceanfront, seaside deck ■1D,1Ste ⊨2T,3Q
🛁3Ensuite   ★Hot tub, jaccuzzi tub, F,TV/fridge, beverage bar,
pool table, cozy sitting areas in guest rooms, private entrances,
host quarters are separate   🖐 No smoking, no pets, children
min. age 12

🥾 Explore shoreline & tidal pools, stroll along sandy Tonquin Beach, harbour docks, village centre
(with shops, restaurants, galleries), whale watching tours, Hot Spring tours, kayaking, bus
🚗 Long Beach, Pacific Rim National Park, golfing, beaches,
📷 Commerical fishing family and lifelong Tofino residents in waterfront home with beautiful
view of Duffin Cove Passage, Meares Island, ocean and mountains. Large windows capture the
ever-changing shoreline, views and sounds of the sea. Ideal place for 2 couples in 2-bedroom suite.
Enjoy the beautiful views from the seaside decks or the relaxing hot tub. 2-night minimum in peak
season & long weekends. There is one cat (in host quarters only).

Wood, Janine (Solwood B&B)   ☎ (250) 725-2112, Fax (250) 725-2284
Box 468, Tofino, BC   V0R 2Z0

From Port Alberni travel west to Tofino. Located at 1298 Lyn Rd.
$55S $75-125D $10Child(free under age 5) $15Add.person   ▶8
🍴 Full, homebaked   🏠 Rural, res., 3-storey, view from guest rooms,
oceanfront, deck, quiet   ■ 1F,1Ste(main & upper floor)   ⊨2D,2Q,1P
🛁Private, 1sh.w.h.   ★ KF,private entrance, off-street parking, guest
quarters are separate   🖐 No smoking   〰 Spanish
🥾 Pathway to beautiful Chesterman's Beach from front of house
🚗 Pacific Rim Nat.Park, hiking, whale watching, Hot Springs, fishing, arts
festivals, village center, shops, restaurants
📷 Neo-Eastern longhouse with vaulted ceilings, large cedar beams, many
windows overlooking the surrounding gardens, and nestled in the forests of
Chesterman's Beach. Enjoy the relaxing atmosphere in the cathedral room, which receives the
sunrise through it's 9ft windows overlooking the forest. There are cats in residence. Visa ✔B&B

Tsawwassen

(Vancouver) see also Delta, Richmond, Surrey, White R., Ladner)

Troniak, Lyla-Jo & Bruce (Southlands House By the Sea)   ☎(604)943-1846,Fax 2481
1160 Boundary Bay Rd, Tsawwassen, BC   V4L 2P6   E-mail: btron@telus.net

Take Hwy99 to Hwy 17 (Exit 28) and proceed south to 56St in
Tsawwassen. Turn left to 12Ave, left again to B&B on left side.
$135-175D   (plus tax)   ▶ 14
🍽 Full, homebaked   🏠 Rural, 3-storey lighthouse tower and
2-storey carriage house, acreage, view from guest rooms, hot tub,
oceanfront, patio, porch, deck, secluded   ■ 5D,1Ste(2D) main &
upper level)   ⊨ 4Q,2K,1P   ⌑ 1Private, 4ensuite,
1sh.w.g(Ste)   ★ LF,F&TV in guest room, ceiling fans, hot tub,
guest room patios/decks, private entrance Ⓦ No smoking, ask about pets, children in suite only
🏃 Beachcombing in Boundary Bay Park, walking, biking, excellent bird watching (Pacific Flyway),
great restaurants, world known Reifel Bird Sanctuary and Burns Bog
🚐 Ferries to Vancouver Island & Gulf Islands, US border, International Airport, downtown Van.
🔫 Friendly hosts in beautiful sprawling West Coast country estate, located in the Sun Belt of
South Vancouver (35% less rain) with beautiful views overlooking ocean and mountains. West
Coast breakfast is served in the special guest breakfast room. Relax in the hot-tub or socialize in the
Great Room morning or evening. Visa,MC,Amex ✔B&B   www.southlandshouse.com

---

Valemount

(south-east of St.George)

Achterberg, Bill & Connie (Summit River B&B)   ☎ (250)566-9936,Fax:(250)566-9934
Box 517 Valemount BC   V0E 2Z0   E-mail: sumriver@vis.bc.ca

Located on the west side of Hwy 5 in Albreda and 22 km south of Valemount. Look for sign.
$50-60S $65-75D $12-15Add. person (plus tax) 🍽 Meals (group rates available)   ▶ 12-20A

🍽 Full, homebaked   🏠 Rural, riverfront, acreage, view, quiet,
isolated   ■3D,3F(main & upper level)   ⊨2S,8D,1R   ⌑5Private
★VCR,LF Ⓦ Restricted smoking ⌇Dutch
🏃 Fishing hole in glacier fed river, hiking, gold panning, x-c skiing
snowmobiling, horseback riding, frequent sightings of wild animals,
golfing, ATV trails
🚐 Village of Valemount, Mt Robson Prov.Park, Moose Marsh
canoeing, rafting float trips, heli skiing with expert ski guides
🔫 Old fashioned, cosy log house with country-style decor, surrounded by 40 acres of woods, fields
and stream, located in mountain valley, nestled at the base of Canoe Mountain, with a beautiful
view of the Albreda Glacier. Pick-up service from train/bus in Valemount available. Suitable for
large groups. There is a resident cat & a dog. Also 22 camp-sites available. Seniors discounts.
Visa,MC ✔CC   http://www.bctravel.com/north/summitriver.html

Brady, Mavis and Al (Brady's Bed & Breakfast)   ☎ (250) 566-9906
Box 519, Valemount, BC   V0E 2Z0   E-mail: brady@valemount.com

Coming north from Valemount or west from Jasper on Hwy 5, take
Blackman Rd. Turn on Buffalo Rd & continue to B&B.
$50S $60D   ▶ 4A,4Ch
🍽Full 🏠Rural, 160-acres, log house, view, inground swimming
pool, quiet, isolated   ★TV,F,parking ■2   ⊨2Q   ⌑Sh.w.g.
Ⓦ No smoking
🏃 Hiking/x-c ski (outside back door), variety of wildlife/birds
🔫 Comfortable, quiet mountain log home, built by the host family, situated on wooded acreage
with river (Salmon route) running through the property. Enjoy the sundeck for morning coffee and
the hearthstone fireplace at night. Relax in the gazebo or under a shade tree and take in the
magnificient panoramic scenery. ✔B&B

Vancouver

(see also Richmond, Surrey, Delta, Tsawwassen, White R.)
(see also North Vancouver & West Vancouver)

Barr, Jennifer & Larry (Kitsilano Point B&B)   ☎ & Fax (604) 738-9576
1936 McNicoll Ave., Vancouver, BC V6J 1A6

Located at north end of Cypress St & 1 block west of Burrard St.
$80-105S $90-115D $95-140Ste $20Add.person   ► 6
🍴 Full   🏠 Res., older, quiet   ■ 1D,1F,1Ste (upst)   ⊨2T,2D,3S,cot
⌂1Private, 1Sh.w.g., private basin & shower in each room   ★ TV,F
🖐No smoking, no pets, no children   ∿ some French
🏃 Kitsilano Beach with parks and pool, Vanier Park with museums,
Planetarium and Observatory, Short-cut to downtown, restaurants, stores,
English Bay, Granville Island & market (by foot ferry near house)
🚗 Stanley Park, Science Centre, Grouse Mountain, Airport, U of BC
🗣 Quiet, friendly hospitality in 1911-built house with secluded shaded
garden situated in very convenient location. Off-season rates available. ⌐B&B

Driver, Bernadette & Peter (Pacific Spirit Guest House)   ☎ & Fax(604)261-6837
4080 West 35th Ave, Vancouver, BC V6N 2P3   E-mail: pspirit@vancouver.quick.com

Located at the western end of 35th Ave.
$65S $75D $15Child/Add.person   ► 5A,1Ch
🍴 Gourmet   🏠 Res, 2-storey, older, patio, quiet   ■2(ground
level)   ⊨ 2T(1K),1D,R,crib   ⌂1Sh.w.g., sink in garden room
★ LF,F,TV, private entrance, street parking, guest quarters are
separate   🖐 Designated smoking area, pets inquire
🏃 Pacific Spirit Park (763hectares with lush rain forest, 50km
trails, walking, Mtn biking, horseback riding, picnic areas,, beach
access) tennis court, golf courses, fitness Centre, University of BC, good restaurants, shops, bus
No7 (Dunbar) to downtown
🚗 Stanley Park, museums, Gastown, Chinatown, Grouse Mtn, Capilano Suspension Bridge,
Granville Island, Victoria ferry
🗣 Quaint house in very convenient location. Hosts are long-time Vancouverites and happy to
share their knowledge of the city and the province with guests. Breakfast is served in
dining/breakfast room. Family friendly with children's video, games & toys. There is a cat in
residence. CCards ⌐B&B www.vancouver.quick.com/pspirit

Hainstock, Lyn (Penny Farthing Inn)   ☎ (604) 739-9002, Fax (604) 739-9004
2855 West 6th Ave., Vancouver, BC V6K 1X2   E-mail: farthing@uniserve.com

From airport drive towards downtown. Turn left on W12Ave, right on
MacDonald St and left on W6Ave. Look for house on north side.
Summer: $95S $170D $15child $20Add.person   (plus tax)   ► 8
🍴 Full   🏠 Res., hist., view from guest rooms, porch, quiet, secluded
■2D,2Stes (upst)   ⊨ 2T,1D,2Q,1K,2P   ⌂1Private, 3ensuite   ★F,
TV/coffee/bar/phones in guest rooms, fax/Email access, ceiling fans, street
parking, guest quarters are separate   🖐 Designated smoking area, no pets,
children min. age 12   ∿ some French
🏃 Beach, museums, UBC, bus stop
🚗 Downtown, Northshore, Grouse Mtn, Fort Langley, US border
🗣 Heritage house with antiques and stained glass, situated on a quiet
street in Kitsilano district. Enjoy the friendly and relaxed atmosphere. Hostess (originally from
England via Africa) was a potter/weaver/quilter and arranges art shows. Weather permitting,
breakfast is served in the garden surrounded with herbs and fragrant flowers. There are 3 friendly
cats. ⌐B&B www.pennyfarthinginn.com

Vancouver (cont'd)

Harris, Liz & Mike Graham (Walnut House B&B)   ☎ (604) 739-6941, Fax 739-6942
1350 Walnut St., Vancouver, BC   V6J 3R3   E-mail: info@walnuthousebb.com

From Burrard St., travel west 3 blocks on Cornwall. Turn right onto Walnut St to house on right.
$115-125S $125-135D   (plus tax)   (off-season & longer stay rates available)   ► 6

🍳 Full, homebaked   🏠 Downtown, 3-storey, hist., patio, porch, quiet   ■ 3D(upstairs)   ⊨ 2D,1K   🛏 3Ensuite   ★F,TV/VCR in guest rooms, ceiling fan, private entrance, off-street parking, guest quarters are separate   👋 Smoking outside, children min. age 12
🏃 Walking/jogging/biking paths, Granville Island, Kitsilano Beach, downtown area, 4thAve shops & restaurants, Vancouver & Maritime Museums, Pacific Space Centre, city bus No22

🐾 Restored 1912, romantic & friendly home located on a quiet street shaded by tall trees on Kitsilano Point and central to all Vancouver's attractions. Gourmet breakfast is served in guest breakfast room. There is a dog in residence. Visa,MC ✓B&B www.walnuthousebb.com

---

Holm Elke (B&B by Locarno Beach)   ☎ (604) 341-4975 (Cell)
4505 Langara Ave, Vancouver, BC   V6R 1C9

Phone for directions.
$75S $95D $25Add.person   (off season rates available)   ► 6
🍳 Full   🏠 Res., 2-storey, quiet   ■ 2F(upst   ⊨1T,1D,2Q, cot   🛏2Ensuite   ★TV, street parking   👋No smoking, no pets, children min. age 12   ∾German, French
🏃 Park opposite house, long sandy beach & beachside cafe, walking trails, boat rental, tennis, elegant dining, shopping street, direct bus line to UBC and City Center

🚗 UBC, City Centre, Airport, Stanley Park, northshore mountains
🐾 White Character home with newly renovated guest rooms, located opposite park on a quiet side street in an exclusive residential neighbourhood, just 200m from beach with panoramic views. Breakfast is served in guest breakfast room. ✓B&B

Iantosca, Rosina (Chambres d'hôtes Sunflower B&B)   ☎ (604) 522-4186, Fax 522-4176
1110 Hamilton St., New Westminster, BC   V3M 2M9   E-mail: yourhosts@sunflower-bnb.com,

Take Hwy 1 to Brunette St Exit (New Westminster). Proceed to 12th St, turn right, after crossing 6th Ave, turn right on Hamilton St.

$65S $75D   ► 9
🍳 Full, homebaked   🏠 Res., older, heritage-style, quiet, porch   ■ 4D (upstairs)   ⊨1D,3Q,cot   🛏 2Sh.w.g.   ★ F,TV in guest living room, reading room, slippers/robes, phone/fax, guest quarters are completely separate from host quarters, street parking   👋 No smoking, no pets   ∾ French, Italian
🏃 Shopping center, Riverboat Casino, Westminster Quay Market, restaurants, parks, library, museum, skytrain or buses to downtown Vancouver
🚗 Vancouver International Airport, downtown Vancouver, Greyhound Bus Stn, BC Ferries, golf courses, BC Place Stadium, Vancouver Trade & Convention Centre, Gastown, Stanley Park
🐾 French/Italian couple in Heritage house located close to the heart of Vancouver and the Internationl Airport. Enjoy a gourmet breakfast and wonderful hospitality in English, en francais and in Italiano. Ideal place for honeymoon, business trips or just holidays. There is a cat in residence. ✓CC http://www.sunflower-bnb.com

Vancouver (cont'd)

Johnson, Sandy and Ron (The Johnson House)   ☎ & Fax (604) 266-4175
2278 W34 Ave, Vancouver, BC V6M 1G6   E-mail: fun@johnsons-inn-vancouver.com

Located near 33rd & Arbutus Sts in the Kerrisdale/Shaughnessy area of Vancouver's West Side.
$75-145S $90-175D $25Add.person   ▶ 6A,2Ch

Full, hombaked ♣Res., hist. older, quiet, large porch, partial
view from guest rooms ■ 3 (upstairs) ⊨ 2Q,1K,1D(including
brass iron beds) 🚪1Private,2ensuite ★ TV,F,LF, parking,
fans 🖐No smoking,children min age 10 ↝French
♈ City transportation to downtown, restaurants, Kerrisdale &
Arbutus Shopping centres
🚗 U.B.C.,Granville I.,China & Gastowns,Van Duesen Gardens,
downtown, Stanley Park, Grouse Mountain
🔫 Restored 1920 Vancouver craftsman home, furnished with delightful antiques and collectibles,
including brass beds and carousel horses. Centrally located on a quiet street in one of Vancouver's
best neighbourhoods. Enjoy a bountiful breakfast and relax in the rock & rhododendron garden with
ancient sculptures. Recommended by Frommers & Fodors & "Best Places to Kiss". ↝B&B
www.johnsons-inn-vancouver.com

Kulash, Alida (Twin Hollies B&B) E-mail:twinhollies@bc.sympatico.ca, Cell (604) 916-1546
604 East 23rd Ave., Vancouver,BC V5V 1X8   ☎ (604) 876-1017, Fax 876-1029

From TCH1 take Grandview Hwy, turn left on Fraser St, right on 23rdAve.
$85S $95D $10Child $20Add.person   ▶ 8
🌀 Full ♣ Res.,hist., view, patio, porch, quiet ■ 2D,1F(upper level)
⊨1S,2Q,1K,1R 🚪2Private, 1sh.w.g. ★TV in guest rooms, ceiling fans,
off-street parking, guest quarters are separate 🖐Desig smoking area, child
min. age 14 ↝Russian, Croation, Dutch, German, Spanish, Afrikaans
♈ Queen Elizabeth Gardens, Antique Row, ethnic restaurants, Oakridge
Shopping Mall, Van Dusen Gardens, buses to downtown and skytrain
🚗 Whistler Resort, Harrison Hot Springs, Mount Baker, Hell's Gate
🔫 Charming Heritage home decorated with west coast art and artifacts
and surrounded by large trees. Enjoy the magnificient views of Vancouver
night lights and spectacular North Shore Mountains. Breakfast includes westcoast salmon among
other specialties. Hosts speak many languages and enjoy communicating with people from different
cultures. Visa,MC,Amex ↝B&B http://www.vancouver-bc.com/twinholliesbb/

Mitchell, Gus & Lani (Arbutus House B&B) ☎ (604) 738-6432, Fax 738-6433
4470 Maple Cr., Vancouver, BC V6J 4B3   E-mail: stay@arbutushouse.com

$85-155S $95-165D $25Add.person (plus tax) (off season rates available) ▶ 10
At Granville & 29th Ave turn west to Maple Cr. Turn right.

🎌 Mar-Oct 🌀 Full ♣ Res., 3-storey, older,
patio,quiet,deck ■2D,2F(main & upper level) ⊨ 2T,4Q
🚪2Private, 1sh.w.g. ★F,TV in guest lounge, TV/VCR,F in
some guest rooms, ceiling fans, off-street parking, some private
sundecks 🖐outside smoking, no pets, children min.age
12 ↝some French
♈ Van Dusen Gardens, Queen Elizabeth Park, Kitsilano Beach,
Granville Island, shops, restaurants, jogging, bicycling, public transit
🚗 Downtown, Lynn/Capilano Canyons, Grouse Mountain, North & West Vancouver, Steveston
🔫 Warm welcome in inviting 1920's character home, decorated with a charming blend of antique
& contemporary furnishings. Situated in jogging & bicycling friendly neighbourhood of exclusive
Shaughnessy. Enjoy the friendly elegant, yet casual atmosphere. Breakfast is served in the elegant
dining room or on the sundeck surrounded by fragrant gardens. Voted No.1 B&B (Survey by
readers) in Canadian Country Inns Magazine, 1999. There is a resident cat. ↝B&B
www.arbutushouse.com

Peloquin, Eugene and Janet (Peloquin's Pacific Pad)   ☎(604)874-4529,Fax 6229
426 West 22nd Ave., Vancouver, BC V5Y 2G5   E-mail: peloquin@vancouver-bc.com

$65-75S $85-95D $15Child $20Add.person (Reserve please)   ▶ 4A,2Ch

From Hwy1 use Grandview Exit and travel to Cambie St. Turn left, proceed to 22nd Ave. Turn left.
🍽 Full 🏠 Res., quiet ■ 1S,1D ⊨ 1D,2P, baby travel bed
🛁2Private ★ KF, TV in guest rooms, garden entrance, off-street parking 🚭No smoking, no pets 〰French, Ukrainian
🕺 Popular restaurants, shops, Q.E. Park, Bloedel Conservatory, hospitals, seabus/skytrain, bus to downtown. GM Place, theatres, BC Place Stadium
🚗 U.B.C., Horseshoe Bay Ferry Terminal, Oakridge Shopping center, downtown, Stanley Park
☛ Welcome to cozy comfortable home, situated in a quiet central residential area with easy access to Hwy 99, from USA, Airport and Ferry Terminals. Longtime hosts (14years) enjoy sharing helpful information about their picturesque city. hhttp://www.vancouver-bc.com/peloquin/

Sanderson, Corinne (Beautiful Bed & Breakfast)   ☎ (604) 327-1102, Fax (604) 327-2299
428 West 40th Ave., Vancouver, BC V5Y 2R4   E-mail: sandbbb@portal.ca

Located on the first block east of Cambie Street.
$95-125S $95-155D $135-235Ste $15-25Add.person   ▶ 10
🍽 Full 🏠 Res., sub., 3-storey, view from guest rooms, patio, porch, deck, quiet ■1S,3D,1Ste(upst) ⊨2T,2D,1Q,1P,1R
🛁2Sh.w.g., 1ensuite ★3F(pink-marble in suite), TV in some guest rooms, parking, balcony 🚭No smoking, no pets, children min.age 14 〰French
🕺 Major tennis court, 2 golf courses, Queen Elizabeth Park, large shopping center, VanDusen Gardens, hospitals, Vancouver's best restaurants, downtown bus, Victoria & Seattle buses
🚗 Grouse Mountain, Stanley Park, Reifel Bird Sanctuary, beaches, University, Airport, US border
☛ Gracious, new Colonial home with a view of north shore mountains & Vancouver Island, furnished with antiques,fresh flowers, and situated on a quiet street in central location. Enjoy the lovely garden incl. mini Japanese garden, pond & waterfall. Breakfast is served in formal dining room with silver, linens, antiques and great coffee. Luxurious suite has pink fireplace, balcony and North & South view. Hosts are well informed about the area & happy to help with plans. ✔B&B
http://www.beautifulbandb.bc.ca/

Selvage, Bob & Barb (Treehouse B&B)   ☎ (604) 266-2962, Fax (604) 266-2960
2490 West 49th Ave., Vancouver, BC V6M 2V3   E-mail: bb@treehousebb.com

$110-165Ste $20Child $30Add.person (Off-season rate available)   ▶ 8

Located on the west side near UBC and west of Granville St.
🍽 Full, homebaked (gourmet) 🏠Res.,3-storey,view from guest rooms, deck, quiet ■1D,2Stes(street & upperlevel) ⊨3Q,1P,1R
🛁1Private,2ensuite ★F,TV/VCR,fridges, guest robes/tea kettles/dryers/phones in guest rooms, 2jacuzzis, street parking 🚭Smoking outside, no pets, children min. age 10 or infants
🕺 Kerrisdale (shopping, restaurants), parks, golfing
🚗 UBC, downtown, ferries to Victoria
☛ Contemporary, multi-level home decorated with modern art and sculpture and located in one of the city's most prestigious neighborhoods. Relax in 2nd floor guest living room with marble fireplace or on the covered deck. Enjoy a calm, peaceful setting offering both privacy and hospitality. Breakfast is served in special guest breakfast room. CCards ✔B&B

Vancouver (cont'd)

Williams, D.& H. (Kenya Court Ocean Front Guest House) ☎ (604) 738-7085
2230 Cornwall Ave., Vancouver, BC   V6K 1B5

Located downtown on the Bay betw. Yew/Vine Sts, facing Kitsilano Beach. Phone for directions.

$95-165D ▶ 16A
🍴 Full   🏠 Downtown, apartment, view, patio, oceanfront, quiet ▦4
waterfront suites ⊨T,Q,K 🛁4Sh.w.g.   ★F,TV in guest room,
separate entrance, music room with grand piano   ✋No smoking, no
pets ⌇ Italian, French, German
🏃 Large heated outdoor salt-water swimming pool, English Bay, Kitsilano
Beach, tennis courts, Stanley Park, Planetarium, Maritime Museum
🚢 Vancouver Island and Gulf Island ferries (Horseshoe Bay &
Tsawwassen), Whistler
🚐 Spacious three-storey Heritage building with gracious antique
furnishings and spectacular ocean view from suites & from penthouse
solarium, where breakfast is served.

Town & Country Bed & Breakfast Reservation Service ☎ & Fax (604) 731-5942
Box 74542, 2803 West 4th Ave, Vancouver, BC   V6K 1K2

(Helen Burich, Manager) www.tcbb.bc.ca
Rates from $85-225D   (Deposit required)
Town & Country B&B in B.C. is a reservation service for Vancouver and Victoria (established in
1981). Homes have been inspected and vary from city townhomes to family homes in residential
areas to self-contained suites and even a few cottages, modest to luxurious, with both shared and
private baths. Rates vary according to location & facilities. Most homes are within 10-20 minimum
drive to city center. The Town & Country Reservation Service does not mail a list of B&B homes.

WestWay Accommodation Registry ☎ (604) 915-9786, Fax 915-9780
Box 48950, Bentall Centre III, Vancouver, BC   V7X 1A8 E-mail: westway@telus.net

(Zarina Jadavji)
Rates: from $35-110S   from $50-225D $10-25Add.person   (including breakfast)
WestWay Accommodations offers personalized reservation services representing 157 select homes
ranging from Victorian to modern; modest to luxurious; with elegant & s/c suites & cottages, some
with swimming pools, jacuzzi, sauna, views and waterfront. All homes are checked for comfort,
cleanliness and courtesy. Hosts are from different backgrounds and countries and speak French,
German, Spanish, Italian. Breakfasts range from full gourmet to continental. Most homes are
within 5-55 minutes drive or walk to downtown Vancouver, Stanley Park, Aquarium, theatres,
shopping malls, restaurants, art galleries, English Bay, fine beaches, parks, skiing, golfing, fishing
and other attractions.

North Vancouver
(see also Vancouver & West Vancouver)

Adems, Collin and Terrisa (Rockland House) ☎ (604) 987-5885
141 West Rockland, North Vancouver, BC   V7N 2V8

From TCH1 (on City's north side), take Lonsdale Rd north to West Rockland Rd. Turn left.

$55S $75-95D $30Add.person ▶4
🍴 Full   🏠 Res., 2-level ranch-style, ocean view, deck, quiet
▦2(ground level) ⊨2T,1Q 🛁1Sh.w.g. ★TV,KF, sep.entrance
✋No smoking, children very welcome
🏃 Play park outside back garden, public bus transit to Seabus and
Lonsdale Quay, hiking paradise
🚗 Downtown Vancouver, ski slopes, suspension bridge.
🚐 Retired hosts in home is situated on the quiet slope 1000 ft
up Grouse Mountain overlooking the city and the surrounding waters. Enjoy the magnificient view
from upper sundeck in the fresh mountain air. Family rates available. Longer stay rates. ✒B&B

North Vancouver (cont'd)

Chalmers, Sue (Sue's Victorian Guest House & Apartments) ☎(604)985-1523,1-800-776-1811
152 East 3rd, North Vancouver, BC V7L 1E6

From Hwy 99, go over Lion's Gate Bridge and take North Vancouver exit (Marine Drive becomes West 3rd) and look for house 1/2block east of Lonsdale. From Hwy 1, go over 2nd Narrows Bridge (Main becomes Cotton) then to East 3rd. Parking behind #152 & #158.
$60-75S $70-85D $25Add.person ►7
🌚Not incl. 🏠Hist.,highrise area,full width veranda at front ■2(upst)
⊨1Q,1S,2D ⚏Sh.w.g.,Victorian Soaker Baths,no showers ★TV,video, indiv. keys,guest fridge,phone in guest rooms ⓌNo smoking
🕴 Harbour (4blocks), Lonsdale Quay/restaurant on the water's edge, seabus terminal to downtown, Alaska cruiseship departure, restaurants, bus stops
🚗 Chinatown, Gastown, Stanley Park, Conference Center, IMAX Theatre
🔫 Lovely carpenter-gothic, modest sized, 1904-built home with original staircases, gingerbread on the front veranda, restored and upgraded for modern comfort. Bring
own slippers. Very convenient & central location. Long term/off-season rates available. Deposit required. Also available apartments in converted house next door.

Gruner, Sylvia & Gerhard (Pacific View B&B)   ☎ & Fax (604) 985-4942
139 West St.James Rd., North Vancouver, BC V7N 2P1

From Hwy 1 take Exit 18 (Lonsdale Ave) north, to St.James Rd W.
$65-80D ►4A+
🌚 Full 🏠 Res., 2-storey, view, backporch, patio, deck, quiet, panoramic view from some guest rooms ■2Ste (upper level)
⊨2Q ⚏ 2Ensuite ★ F,TV, spacious lounge with balcony, host quarters are separate, off-street & street parking ⓌNo smoking, no pets ﹏ Polish, German
🕴 Shopping, restaurant, parks, public indoor pool, local buses/sea bus connecting with Skytrain
🚗 Whistler Mountain Ski Resort, downtown Vancouver, Stanley Park, Horseshoe Bay
🔫 Home is situated in quiet residential neighbourhood. Breakfast is served in glass enclosed patio looking out on the garden. Families welcome. ↩B&B

Hartkopf, Gunter & Marianne (European B&B)   ☎(604)988-1792, Fax(604)988-1782
648 East Keith Rd., North Vancouver, BC V7L 1W5   E-mail: europeanbandb@home.com

Phone for directions.
$75-85S $95-115DD $20Add.person ►9
🌚 Full(European) 🏠 Res., multi-level, view from guest rooms, patio, quiet ■ 1S,4D (main floor) ⊨1S,2T,1K,2Q
⚏2Sh.w.g., 1private ★ F,TV in guest rooms, parking Ⓦ No smoking, no pets ﹏ German
🕴 Grouse Mountain, Capilano Suspension Bridge, Nature & Stanley Parks, beaches
🚗 Downtown Vancouver, Whistler Mountain, Harrison Hot Springs, Royal Hudson Train
🔫 Warm welcome in modern West Coast home centrally located. Breakfast is served on the terrace or in the dining room overlooking the garden. There is a Golden Retriever in residence.
↩B&B www.vancouver-bc.com/europeanbb/

North Vancouver (cont'd)

Malakieh,Josephine & Joe (A Lynn Canyon House B&B) ☎(604)986-4748,Fax986-4741
3333 Robinson Rd, North Vancouver, BC   V7J 3P7   E-mail: lynncanyonhouse@vancouverinn.com

Phone for directions.
$85-130S $90-135D   ►4
🍴 Full (Gourmet)   🏠 Res., 2-storey, view from guest rooms,
patio, deck, garden, gazebo, quiet, secluded, heated swimming pool,
pond   ■ 2D(upper level)   ⊨2Q   ⊲ 1Private, 1ensuite
★F,TV/VCR, hot-tub, extra large chess set in guest lounge, very
large parking lot, guest quarters are separate   Ⓦ Smoking
outside, no pets, children min age 12   〰 Italian, German
🏃 Various hiking/walking trails, waterfalls & spectacular scenery (adjacent to 617 acre Lynn
Canyon Park and Suspension Bridge), restaurants, cafes, shops, bus stop one block
🚐Downtown, Stanley Park, R.Hudson Train, Lonsdale Quay (sea bus), ferries to Victoria
🎯 Elegant, yet comfortable Cratfsman-designed Tudor home, brimming with tradition and
charm, coupled with a warm & friendly welcome and nestled in natural park surroundings.
Gourmet breakfast is a social event - enjoy a delicious multi-course fare. Join the hosts for
afternoon Tea in the clamatis-covered gazebo overlooking the beautiful secluded English garden.
Special diets can be accommodated. Visa,MC, ⌐CC http://www.vancouverinn.com

---

Massey, Ellison (Ellison House B&B)   ☎ (604) 990-6730, Fax 990-5876
542 East 1st St., North Vancouver, BC   V7L 1B9   E-mail: ellison@b-b.com, 1-800-561-3223

Follow Hwy 1 and signs to North Vancouver, take Lonsdale Exit and turn east on 1st St.

$40-60S $65-95D   ► 3A
🍴 Self-serve   🏠 Sub., raised bungalow, view from guest rooms,
patio, quiet   ■ 2 (main floor)   ⊨1D,1Q   ⊲ 1Sh.w.h.
★KF,LF,F,TV, street parking   🚭 No smoking
🏃 No 239 Capilano College bus to Lonsdale Quay
🚐Seabus to downtown Vancouver, Gastown, Chinatown, Stanley
Park, Grouse Mountain, Capilano Suspension Bridge, Lynn
Canyon hiking trails, Royal Hudson Steam Train
🎯 Comfortable home centrally located in a quiet residential neighbourhood. Long term rates are
available. Hostess operates Canada West Accommodations Reservation Service. There is a cat in
residence. CCards ⌐B&B www.b-b.com

Masterton, Delphine (Laburnum Cottage B&B Inn)   ☎ & Fax (604) 988-4877
1388 Terrace Ave., North Vancouver, BC   V7R 1B4

From Lions Gate Bridge take Exit for North Vancouver and travel east 1 block to Capilano Rd.
Turn left 1 km north to Paisley. Turn right, then to Philip. Turn right on Woods Dr, then left on

Terrace Ave and 100 yards to B&B.
$150-225D $30Add.person   (plus tax)   ► 16A
🍴 Full (gourmet)   🏠 Res., sub., acreage, patio, quiet secluded
■4D,2Ste (upst), small summerhouse cottage in garden for
honeymooners   ⊨2T,1D,4Q,1R,1P   ⊲5Private   ★very large
flood-lit parking lot   ⓌSmoking outside, no children
🏃 Capilano Fish Hatchery, Suspension Bridge, Grouse Mountain
Tramway, tennis courts, Par-3 Pitch & Putt, two bus routes
🚐 City of Vancouver & Lonsdale Quay (sea bus), fabulous restaurants
🎯 Charming home with Victorian air and antiques in romantic seclusion, is surrounded by virgin
forest (parkland) and beautiful award-winning English Garden. Gourmet breakfast is served in
guest breakfast room and in large country kitchen with AGA stove. Relax in the charming
Victorian drawing room. Home & gardens have been featured in several Magazines. Visa,MC ⌐CC

North Vancouver (cont'd)

Macek, Stefka (Mountain Bed & Breakfast) ☎ (604) 987-2725, Fax (604) 987-2171
258 East Balmoral Rd., North Vancouver, BC   V7N 1R5

From Hwy 1 take Lonsdale Ave Exit.ph for directions.
$45-50S $75-80D $15Child $20Add.person ◙iMeals   ►6A,4Ch
🍴 Full, homebaked 🏠 Res., split 2-storey, view, balcony, patio,
quiet ■ 2D(main floor) ⊨ 1D,2Q,2P ⊒ Private
★F,LF,TV in guest room, separate entrance, jaccuzi in suite,
parking 👋 No smoking, no pets ∾ German, Slovenian
🚗 Grouse Mountain, Capilano Suspension Bridge, Stanley Park,
downtown Vancouver

☛ Modern, newly renovated house with a friendly atmosphere and a beautiful view of the city of Vancouver. There is a cat in residence. Visa

---

Poole, Arthur and Doreen (Poole's Bed & Breakfast) ☎(604)987-4594,Fax 4283
421 West St. James Rd., North Vancouver, BC   V7N 2P6   E-mail: rapoole@lightspeed.bc.ca

From Vancouver (Route 1), turn north onto Westview, right on Windsor and then left on St. James.
$50S $65D   ► 4A,2Ch
🍴 Choice, homebaked 🏠 Res., sundeck, patio, quiet garden
■3D (garden level) ⊨1D,1Q,1T,cot,crib ⊒1Sh.w.g.(additional
upst) ★TV,LF,F 👋No smoking, no pets
🚗 Grouse Mountain Skyride, Capilano Suspension Bridge, Royal
Hudson Train, Lonsdale Quay, Sea Bus to City Center Stanley Park
& Aquarium, Gastown, Ferry to Vancouver Island

☛ Colonial-style home in quiet, lovely residential district. Convenient location to city center and attractions of Vancouver area. Retired hosts are happy to assist visitors with information about the city and area. Family/Children welcome. Winter Rates available. ✓B&B

Old English Bed & Breakfast Registry (since 1985) ☎ (604) 986-5069, Fax (604) 986-8810
1226, Silverwood Cr., North Vancouver, BC   V7P 1J3   E-mail: vicki-cbg@bandbinn.com

(Owner: Vicki Tyndall)
Rates: $85-175D   (including a hearty breakfast)
Old English B&B Resgistry has been providing a fast, reliable, informative service to its clients
since 1985. All homes have been inspected and each is selected with attention given to cleanliness,
ambiance & hospitality. The service would be delighted to assist with reservations. Visa,MC
http://www.bandbinn.com

Canada West Accommodations B&B Reservation Agency
Box 86607, North Vancouver,BC   V7L 4L2   ☎(604)990-6730,Fax(604)990-5876,
(Owner: Ellison Massey)   E-mail: ellison@b-b.com 1-800-561-3223
Rates: $50-85S $75-125D (including breakfast) (Deposit required)(Cancellation Notice 7 days)
A B&B reservation service covering British Columbia and Alberta, and including Greater
Vancouver, Victoria, Vancouver Island, The Okanagan, Whistler, Jasper, Banff, Calgary. The
B&B's offer one to three rooms & private bath. Weekly and monthly rates may be arranged in
North Vancouver. Credit card payment required to hold a reservation. www.b-b.com

West Vancouver

(see also Vancouver & North Vancouver)

Boden, John & Hawrelko,D (Creekside B&B)   ☎(604)926-2599/328-9400,Fax926-7545
1515 Palmerston Ave,West Vancouver,BC V7V 4S9   E-mail: donnajohnboden@bc.sympatico.ca

Take Exit 11 off Hwy 1 and proceed down 15th St to Palmerston. Turn right to house on right.

$114-169D   (2-day minimum stay)   ► 4A
🍽 Full, homebaked   🏠 Res., sub., acreage, patio, quiet
■2D(upstairs) ⊨1K,1Q 🛏1Private,1ensuite (with marble
jacuzzi and glass roof)   🚭No smoking, children min. age 10, no
pets ★F/refrigerator/coffeemaker in suite, LF, guest balcony,
complimentary guest robes & beverages, off-street parking
🚶 Shops, boutiques, parks, dining, beaches, skiing, hiking,
boating, natural wilderness, bus stop
🚗 Downtown, major shopping centres, summer and winter recreation, art galleries
📷 Contemporary Heritage home, architecturally designed, in one of Canada's most prestigious
communities. Totally private creek flowing through property among lofty native cedar trees. A very
natural setting tucked away in the centre of the city. Ideal for honeymooners. Dining &
Entertainment coupons available. Enjoy the wines and snacks in the guest rooms. Visa,MC

Gibbs, Gordon and Joan (Beachside B&B)   ☎ 1-800-563-3311, Fax (604) 926-8073
4208 Evergreen Ave., West Vancouver, BC V7V 1H1   E-mail: info@beach.bc.ca

Take Hwy 1 to West Vancouver, drive west along Marine Dr to Ferndale, turn left, then left on
Evergreen. From Horseshoe Bay, go East on Marine to Ferndale, turn right.
$150-250D $20Child(over age10) $30Add.person   (winter rates avail.)   ► 8
🍽Full, homebaked 🏠Res., sub., view from guest rooms,
oceanfront, patio, quiet, isolated ■3D,1F(main level) ⊨4Q
🛏4Ensuite 🚭No pets, no smoking ★TV,KF,2F, off-street
parking, separate entrance
🚶 Sandy beach at doorstep, Lighthouse Wilderness Park, excellent
gourmet restaurant, shopping mall
🚗 Gleneagles oceanside public golf course, Stanley Park, U.B.C.
downtown, Museum of Anthropology, Grouse Mtn, Sea-to-Sky Hwy
📷 Beautiful luxury waterfront home situated on a quiet cul-de-sac in an exclusive area of the
city, tastefully decorated in Spanish-style structure with stained glass windows and a panoramic
view of Vancouver's busy harbour. Enjoy the jaccuzzi on the beach, sit at the water's edge and
watch Alaska Cruise Ships pass by daily en-route to Vancouver Harbour. Hosts are world travellers
and certified tour guides. 50% Deposit required. Visa,MC ✓CC www.beach.bc.ca

---

Mulder, Bill & Jan (Gateway to Howe Sound B&B)   ☎ (604) 736-4163
Passage Island, 31-5858 Marine Dr., West Vancouver, BC V7W 2S2

Take Hwy 1 to Horseshoe Bay. turn south onto Marine Dr and proceed 2.5km to Fisherman's Cove.

$125D (water taxi included)   🍽 Meals   ► 2A
🥘Summer only 🍽 Full, homebaked 🏠 Rural, island home,
hillside, view from guest room, oceanfront, decks, quiet,secluded
■1D (ground level) ⊨1Q 🛏Ensuite ★F,private entrance,
sitting area with glass door, guest quarters are separate 🚭 No
smoking, no pets, no children, not suitable for individuals with
walking difficulties ⤳ Dutch
🚶 Quiet walks, tree-lined paths, Bus #250
🚗 Horseshoe Bay , scenic Marine Drive, downtown Vancouver
📷 Warm welcome in well-kept solar-battery powered home, uniquely situated on the rocks above
the ocean and surrounded by rocky and uneven terrain. Friendly hosts moved to Passage Island for
it's quietness, beautiful and peaceful setting.

Vernon

(north of Kelowna; see also Okanagan Center, Oyama)

Brookes, Keith & Colleen (Richmond House 1894)
4008 Pleasant Valley Rd., Vernon, BC   V1T 4M2

Fax (250) 542-3234
☎(250) 549-1767

From Hwy 97 in Vernon, turn right on 39St and left on Pleasant Valley Rd.

$65S $75D $15Add.person (longer stay rates available)   ▶ 6
Full, homebaked   Downtown, res., 2-storey, hist., view from guest rooms, covered veranda, deck, quiet   ■ 3(upstairs)   3Q   1Private, 2ensuite   ★ Air,F,TV/VCR in private guest lounge/library, outdoor hot tub, off-street parking, bicycles for guest (at nominal cost), guest quarters are separate   No smoking, no pets, children min. age 12   Spanish
Downtown shopping, antique stores, heritage walk, museums, art galleries, Winter Carnival, wine tours, Agrotourism, inhouse artist's studio and art gallery   Beaches, fishing, water sports, golfing, excellent downhill and x-c skiing at Silver Star Resort   Victorian Heritage home with antiques and elegant lounge situated on the East Hill of Vernon, surrounded by spectacular scenery. Relax in the outdoor hot tub. Gourmet breakfast is served with house-special blend coffee in the elegant dining room. Rooms are named "Tennyson" & "Emily Dickinson" and "Rossetti", and reflect the host's interest in literature. Hostess is an artist and her original paintings are displayed throughout the house. Dietary needs considered with prior notice. There are 3 cats and 2 dogs (kept separate from guest quarters). ✓B&B

Kennedy, Emmy (Falcon Nest Lodge)
5620 Neil Rd., Vernon, BC   V1B 3J5

☎ & Fax (250) 545-1759, 1-800-960-3331

From Hwy 97 in Vernon, take Silver Star Rd (48Ave) to East Vernon Rd. Turn right (BX School at corner) and continue to Dixon. Turn left, then right on Hartnell and proceed up on winding road following Lodge signs. Located on Neil Rd (large sign on roof of house visible on approach).

$40-45S $55-65D $125-165HoneymoonSte $85-95F(one room)   Meals   ▶ 16A,10Ch
Full, homebaked   Rural, ranch-style, view from guest rooms, acreage, heated swimming pool, patio, quiet   ■2S,3D,1Ste,1F (main/upper/ground level)   S,D,Q,K,bunks   3Sh.w.g., 1ensuite, jacuzzi   ★F,KF,TV in guest room, hot-tub, wheelchair access, sep.entrance   Smoking outside   German, Italian
Trails for hiking/mountain biking, x/c skiing from back door   Silver Star Ski Resort, downtown Vernon, Winter Carnival golfing, trail riding, hiking, Okanagan/Kalamalka Lakes beaches
Spacious country home, beautifully decorated, with many artifacts & paintings of local artists on display, situated on large property in the BX area of east Vernon with breathtaking view of lakes and Okanagan Valley. Relax in the jacuzzi after a busy day of travel or skiing and enjoy the Mini Resort atmosphere. New honeymoon suite with jaccuzi tub/fireplace and panoramic view. Breakfast is served in separate guest breakfast room. There is a large outdoor party tent by the pool, ideal place for weddings, re-unions, & special occasions. Also hostel facilities (dormitory-style) available, ideal for ski/hiking groups. Bed & Bale for horses/space for RV's. Small pets welcome. Minimum 2 nights. ✓B&B   http://www.monday.com/falconnest

Vernon (cont'd)

Cushing, Ruth-Maria and Peter Filas (The Maria Rose B&B)   ☎ (250) 549-4773
8083 Aspen Rd., Vernon, BC V1B 3M9   Fax (250) 549-4789

Located off Silver Star Rd and 9 km from the city. From Hwy 97 in town, take Silver Star Rd all the way up to Aspen Rd. Turn left, look for house on immediate right.
$40-60S $60-75D $20Add.person   (plus tax)   ▶ 10
🍳 Full, homebaked   🏠 Rural, 2-storey, separate guest house, acreage, view from guest rooms, patio, deck, quiet   ■ 4D (main & upstairs) (2 upst.rooms make a suite) ⊨2T,1D,1Q,1K,1R 🚫No smoking, small pets by arrangment ⌂2Ensuite, 1sh.w.g. ★F, separate entrances,TV/VCR in 3 guest rooms, LF for longer staying guests, sauna (winter only) ⌇German, Slavic understood
🏃 X-c skiing, hiking, country road walks, birdwatching
🚗Silver Star Mountain Resort, downtown Vernon, Okanagan beaches, wine tours
📢 Enjoy Royal treatment in mountain-side Coach House, situated among 7 acres of peaceful treed seclusion with a fabulous panoramic view. Located halfway between the city and Ski Resort. Guest rooms are named King, Queen, Prince and Princess, each with distinct character and elegantly furnished. There is a small charge for coffee/tea & warm-up kitchenette. Breakfast is served in main house guest breakfast room. Visa,MC ⌖B&B

Larson, Eskil & Sharon (Castle on the Mountain)   ☎ (250)542-4593,Fax(250)542-2206
8227 Silver Star Rd, Vernon,BC V1B 3M8   E-mail: castle.eskila@bc.sympatico.ca, 1-800-667-2229

Located 10 km east of Hwy 97 on 48th Ave (Silver Star Road). Phone for directions.
$65-155S $75-165D $10-20Child $30-45Add.person   ▶ 14A,2Ch
🍳 Full, homebaked   🏠 Rural, acreage, spectacular view, patio, quiet, isolated ■3(on 3 levels) +2 luxury suites (with jacuzzi & gas fireplaces), +self-cont.apartment ⊨T,Q,K ⌂5private ★Air,KF,LF, F,TV/VCR in guest lounge, sep.entrances, outside hot-tub (open year-round), slippers/robes,covered parking, playground 🚫No smoking, no pets
🚗 Silver Star Ski Resort (major x/c & Alpine ski area), Vernon
🏃 Mountainside hiking, camp/fire pit area for guests, art gallery and work studio on site, toboggan run, mountain biking,
📢 Long-time B&B hosts in spacious Tudor home with large deck situated on mountainside offering fabulous views over lakes & city. Enjoy the sunny south exposures in allergy-free environment. Ideal place for groups, honeymooners and special occasions. Hosts are artists and crafts people and have filled their home with art and handcrafted woodwork. The 2 suites, are called "Stargazer's Tower" & "Sailaway", ideal for that special occasion. CCards ⌖B&B

Schulte, Gisele & Frank (Wildwood B&B)   ☎ (250)545-2747, Fax (250) 545-0518
7454 Wildwood Rd, Vernon, BC V1B 3N8   E-mail: wildwood@junction.net, 1-800-545-1558

From Hwy 97 in Vernon, go up Silverstar Rd (48th Ave) for 6.5 km and turn left on Wildwood Rd.
$45-65S $65-95D $30Add.person   ▶ 8A,2Ch
🍳 Full, homebaked (Gourmet/vegetarian & special need diets)
🏠 Rural, acreage, Alpine-style, hillside, view from guest rooms, patio, quiet, isolated ■3(main & ground level) ⊨3Q,2P ⌂Private, ensuite ★Air,KF,F/TV/VCR in guest lounge, slippers & robes, separate entrance, parking 🚫 No smoking, no pets ⌇German, French
🏃 Bird Sanctuary, hiking trails, x-c skiing, biking
🚗 Downtown Vernon, Silver Star Ski Resort, Okanagan wineries, golf courses, beaches, canoeing
📢 Quiet Alpine country home with panoramic lake & mountain views. situated on wooded acreage next to bird sanctuary. Relax in the luxurious guest lounge with fire place & entertainment centre. Stroll through the garden and into the forest. Wake up to a gourmet or vegetarian breakfast. Special diets are accommodated. Golf & Ski packages and wine tours available. Hostess is a certified Practioner for Reflexology, Healing Touch & Footcare. Visa www.wwood.com

Vernon (cont'd)

Shantz, Karin & Steve (Melford Creek Country Inn & Spa) ☎ (250) 558-7910
7810 Melford Rd., Vernon, BC   V1B 3NS   E-mail: melford@melfordinn.com

On Silver Star Rd travel past Foothills Subdivision to Keddelston Rd (2km), turn left and travel 1km to Wilson Jackson Rd, turn right. Proceed to Melford Rd, turn left and watch for signs.

$69-119S $79-129D $25Add.person   ► 6-8A
🍲 Full, homebaked (gourmet)   🏠 Rural, acreage, indoor swimming pool, quiet   ■ 2D,2Ste (lower & upper levels) ⊨1K(sleigh bed), 2Q(brass/poster),1P   🛏1Ensuite, 2Private ★LF,3F(one in guest room), one guest balcony, guest robes, indoor spa facilities (heated pool, hot tub & sauna, massage service by appointment)   🚳No pets, no children   ⚬⚬ German 🏃 Hiking trails, biking, walking on rural roads or through treed areas that skirt the creek as it meanders through the fields
🚗 Silver Star Ski Resort, world class x-c ski trails, downtown, golfing, water sports, wineries
🛻 Distinctive, spacious French-style country chateau with cathedral ceilings and gothic windows and luxurious decor, nestled in a relaxed serene rural setting. Enjoy the pastoral view from huge glass wall in the living room and relax in the oversized kidney-shaped pool or by the massive floor to ceiling fireplaces. Hosts specialize in Honeymoon/Special Occasion packages. There are friendly resident pets. Visa,MC ✓ B&B www.melfordinn.com

---

Stewart, Joyce & Doug (Harbour Lights Bed & Breakfast)   ☎ (250) 549-5117
135 Joharon Rd., Vernon, BC   V1H 1C1   E-mail: harbourlights@telus.net, Fax (250) 549-5162

From downtown, take 30Ave west and continue on Bella Vista Rd all the way to Fleming Rd (winding road). Turn right and right again at Joharon.

$65S $75-85D $20Add.person   ►7A
❌ Not May   🍲 Full, homebaked   🏠 Sub., 2-storey, hillside, 2 acres, view, patio, very quiet, view from guest rooms   ■3D(main & ground level) ⊨3Q 🛏3Ensuite ★ Air, guest TV/VCR room, cozy guest sitting lounge with reading material, guest bar fridge   🚭 No smoking, no pets, not suitable for children 🏃 Beach, public boat launch, fishing, hiking
🚗 Downtown, shops, restaurants, shopping malls, Silver Star Ski Resort, wineries, golfing, Blue Heron waterside Rest/Pub, airport
🛻 Custom-built home with large picture windows overlooking beautiful Okanagan Lake and mountains from every room, situated on a quiet hillside in west end of town. Relax on the large shaded deck by grape vines overlooking lawn, flower garden, the lake and mountains. A great place from which to explore the Valley. Hosts enjoy travel, wine, cooking, sailing and good books. Join the hosts for a glass of BC wine or fresh lemonade and a welcome appetizer before making that all-important decision of where to dine. There is a dog and a cat in residence.Visa www.bbexpo.com/harbourlights

---

Tullet, Bill & Irene (The Tuck Inn Bed & Breakfast)   ☎ (250) 545-3252, Fax (250)549-3254
3101 Pleasant Valley Rd., Vernon, BC   V1T 4L2

In Vernon, take Hwy 97 to 30Ave. Turn east to point where 30Ave becomes Pleasant Valley Rd.

$40S $65-75D $15Child $20Add.person   🍽 Meals   (plus taxes)   ► 10A,2Ch

🍲 Full   🏠 Downtown, res., 2-storey, hist., view from 3 guest rooms   ■2D,2F(upstairs) ⊨2T,1D,3Q,2R,crib 🛏2Sh.w.g. ★Air,TV,LF,F, off-street and street parking   🚬Designated smoking area, no pets 🏃 Restaurants, movie theatre, live Playhouse, shops, museum, art galleries, churches, new Tea Room on premises
🚗 Silver Star Ski Resort, Kalamalka/Okanagan Lakes, beaches, water skiing, fishing, golfing
🛻 Award winning Heritage Home built in 1906 in very central location and furnished with antiques and collectibles from all over the world. Relax and enjoy the congenial hospitality and take a walk through town. Breakfast is served in the Tea Room. There is a cat. ✓CC

Arlidge, Rose Marie and Bruce (Charlotte's Guest House)   ☎ & Fax (250) 595-3528
338 Foul Bay Rd., Victoria, BC   V8S 4G7

From downtown Victoria follow Fairfield Rd east to Foul Bay Rd, turn right.
$90 per room $10Extra(one-night stay)   ► 4
🍴 Choice, homebaked   🏠 Res., sub., split-level, view, quiet   ■ 2D
⊨2T,1Q   ⊐2Private   ★ F,KF,LF, TV in guest room, separate entrance,
ample parking, phones, fully equipped snack room for guests   ♿ No pets
🚶 Gonzales Bay, sea & "view" walks, Oak Bay Village, marina
🚗 Butchart's Gardens, downtown Victoria, Beacon Hill Park, breakwater
🏴 Warm and attractive contemporary West Coast Garry Oak-shaded
house with spectacular views over the Straits to the snow-capped Olympics
in Washington State. Hosts operated a B&B in Ottawa for many years before
early retiring to their "beloved roots" on the West Coast. ✓CC

Baker, Jodi & Tim (A Palace on Dallas Oceanfront B&B)   ☎(250)361-9551,Fax385-1725
1482 Dallas Rd., Victoria, BC   V8S 1A2   E-mail: palacebb@brookenet.com

Travel south down Douglas to Dallas.Turn left & proceed 2.3km to B&B.
$90S/D $25Child/Add.person,(Child under age 6 free)   (+tax)   ► 10
🌞 Summer only   🍴 Full, homebaked   🏠 Res, 2-storey, hist., view from
guest rooms, oceanfront, porch   ■5F (main & upper level)   ⊐2Sh.w.g.
⊨3T,3D,1Q,1K,1R   ★ F,TV in guest rooms, off-street/street parking,
guest quarters are separate   ♿Smoking outside, no pets
🚶 Great beach across the street, windsurfing, sailing, kite-flying, diving,
hand-gliding, Beacon Hill Park, Craigdarroch Castle, Inner Harbour, Royal
BC Museum, Empress Hotel, buses Nos 2 and 10
🚗 Butchart Gardens, Goldstream Park, Ferry Terminals
🏴 Lovingly restored 1908-built oceanfront home with stunning ocean and mountain views and
12ft ceiling in guest rooms which are decorated with antiques. Located in a quiet neighborhood.
Dallas Rd is year after year voted best place to watch a sunrise, sunset, jog or walk the dog.
Breakfast specialties include smoked salmon eggs benny and lemon ricotta pancakes with blueberry
sauce. CCards ✓B&B   http://www.brookeline.com/palace

Boytim, Pauline (The Sea Rose B&B)   ☎ (250) 381-7932, Fax (250) 480-1298
1250 Dallas Rd., Victoria, BC   V8V 1C4   E-mail: searose@compuserve.com

$105-160S $115-170D $10-20Child $15-20Add.person   (plus tax)   ► 8+

From BC Ferries, follow Rte 17 to Mile 0. Turn left on Dallas Rd.
🍴 Full   🏠 Res., 3-storey, hist., partial view from guest rooms,
oceanfront   ■ 4Stes(main/upper/lower levels)
⊨2T,3Q,1K,3P,crib   ⊐ 4Private   ★ KF,LF,TV in guest
rooms, private entrance, off-street parking, wheel-chair access in
2suites, guest quarters are separate   ♿ No smoking, no pets
🚶 Clover Point, Beacon Hill Park, Cook Street Village, seafront
parkway with walking and benches, Bus No10
🚗 Downtown, Butchart Gardens, Craigdarroch Castle, Butterfly Gardens, Anne Hathaway
Thatched Cottage, Miniature World, Wax Museum, ferries to mainland and islands
🏴 Comfortable large home built in 1921, recently completely renovated and located on scenic
marine drive with un-interrupted sea and mountain views. Relax in the common area sunroom
overlooking the Strait of Juan de Fuca & Olympic Mountains. Breakfast is served in manager's
dining room. CCards

Victoria (cont'd)

Bender, Glenda (Bender's B&B)   ☎ (250) 472-8993, Fax (250) 472-8995
4254 Thornhill Cr., Victoria, BC   V8N 3G7

Phone for directions.
$50S $60D $25Add.person   (plus tax)   ► 10
🍽 Full   🏠 Res., bungalow, patio, quiet   ■ 4D,2F
⊨2T,3D,1Q,1R,crib,cot   ⊔4Sh.w.g., 2private   ★ TV in guest room, facilities for the handicapped   🖐 No smoking, no pets
🧍 Zellers shopping center
🚗 Uptown and Main Street, Butchart Gardens, ferries, airport
🔦 Warm & friendly hospitality. Breakfast served in solarium.

Denniston,Drew & Rosemary (The Denniston By The Sea)   ☎(250)385-5195,Fax5100
430 Grafton St., Victoria, BC   V9A 6S3   E-mail: denniston@pacificcoast.net, 1-888-796-2699

$75-125S/D $20Add.person   ► 10

Phone for directions.
🍽 Homebaked   🏠 Res., 3-storey, cliffside, oceanfront, older, view from guest rooms, patio, porch, deck, quiet   ■4 (upstairs)
⊨ 1S,2Q,2K,1R,1P   ⊔ 4Ensuite   ★ F,KF,LF,TV & coffee/tea maker in guest rooms, waterfront guest living room with fireplace, piano, extend.library, games, host quarters are sep.   🖐Smoking outside, no pets, conscientious parents required
🧍 Waterfront walkway, picnic tables, Saxe Point Municipal Park, Canadian Forces Base Esquimalt, complete Rec.Centre with heated swimming pool, shopping complex, numerous terrific restaurants
🚗 Inner Harbour, Empress Hotel, Parliament Bldgs, Royal BC Museum, day trips to West Coast trails & beaches, Butchart Gardens, golfing, Vancouver, Washington State's Olympic Peninsula
🔦 Cozy, comfortable, 1928-built waterfront Tudor-style home on a hill, once owned by famous concert pianist Madam Huntley Green, with a beautiful view across the ocean of Washington State's snowcapped Olympic Mountain Range. Enjoy the quiet & serene surroundings and watch the activities of bird/sea life along with the coming and going of ferries & ocean vessels.. Gift Certificates available. Wonderful Snowbird Program available during winter months. ✏B&B
http://www.bbcanada.com/1011.html

Dineen, Tana (Scholefield House B&B)   ☎ (250)385-2025, Fax(250)383-3036
731 Vancouver St.,Victoria, BC   V8V 3V4   E-mail: mail@scholefieldhouse.com, 1-800-661-1623

Located 4 blocks east of the Inner Harbour, 4 blocks south of Fort St, between Richardson and McClure.
$140-215S $150-225D   (plus tax)   ► 7
🍽 Full   🏠 Downtown, hist., 3-storey, patio   ■ 2D,1Ste (upstairs)   ⊨ 2Q,1K   ⊔ 3Ensuite   ★ F,TV in library, ceiling fans in guest rooms, separate entrance, street & off-street parking, guest quarters are separate   🖐 No smoking, no pets, children min. age 12
🧍 Inner Harbour, Empress Hotel, Royal BC Museum, Parliament, Old Town, Beacon Hill Park, whale watching, salmon fishing, ferries, shopping, restaurants, bus to downtown
🚗 Butchart Gardens, Goldstream Park, Sooke & West Coast trails, golfing, sailing, kayaking
🔦 Heritage house built in 1892, authentically restored and decorated with antiques and classic furnishings, situated on a quiet tree-lined street. Step back in time to the refined elegance of a by-gone era. A delectable 5-course champagne breakfast is served by the fireplace in the parlour and highlighted by herbs and edible flowers from the English Country Garden. Special off-season discounts up to 50%. There are 3 resident cats. Visa,MC ✏B&B

Victoria (cont'd)

Harris, Gail (Lilac House Country B&B)   ☎ (250)642-2809, Cell (250)885-6301
1848 Connie Rd., Victoria, BC   V9C 4C2   E-mail: lilac@pinc.com,

Take Hwy 14 west from Victoria towards Sooke and watch for "entering Sooke Disctrict" sign. Turn
left at Connie Rd to 4th house. Turn right and proceed across private bridge to house on top of hill.

$50-80S $70-95D $25Add.person   ► 6
🍴 Cont.(country breakfast on weekends)   🏠 Rural, acreage,
quiet, view   ■ 3(main & upper floor)   🛏 1Q,2D,2cots
🛏 1Private, 2sh.w.h.   ★ Woodstove, hot tub, off-street
parking   🚭 No smoking, no pets, children min. age 12
🕴 Trails through woods/hills on property, Galloping Goose Trail,
historic 17 Mile Pub, horseback riding & llama trekking
🚗 Matheson Lake, East Sooke Park, Sooke Museum, Potholes
& Harbour, French Beach, West Coast Trail

📷 Graceful, new custom, heritage-style home combining traditional architecture with modern
skylights and vaulted ceilings. Set on 5 acres with creek and surrounded by beautiful Sooke Hills.
Relax and enjoy the antiques, art and Pre-Raphaelite library, covered veranda, gardens and hot tub.
Honeymoon suite with large soaker tub. After 13 years of operating Lilac House B&B in the city,
hostess offers the same charm and hospitality amid the natural splendor of the countryside. There
is a cat "Teddy" in residence and there are 2 llamas "Sinbad" & Sterling Grey". Advance reservation
required. Visa,MC   http://vvv.com/~lilac

Hunt, Noreen & Garry (Medana Grove B&B)   ☎ (250) 389-0437,Fax (250) 389-0425,
162 Medana St., Victoria, BC   V8V 2H5   E-mail: medanagrove@home.com, 1-800-269-1188.

$110-135S/D $25Add.person   (off-season rates Sept-May)   (plus tax)   ► 4A
From Bellevue St travel south on Menzies to Simcoe. Turn left and then first right on Medana to
2nd house on right.

🍴 Full, homebaked   🏠 Downtown, res., 2-storey, older, porch,
quiet   ■ 2D(main & upper level)   🛏 1Q,1K,1R   🛏 2ensuite
★ F,TV in guest room, street parking, guest quarters are
separate   🚬 Designated smoking area, no pets
🕴 Inner Harbour, downtown, shopping, restaurants, Royal B.C.,
Museum, Parliament Buildings, Empress Hotel, Ferry Terminal,
oceanfront trails, whale watching tour operations, bus Rte 11
🚗 Butchart Gardens, golfing, Provincial parks, Vancouver & US ferry terminals, airport, beaches
📷 Lovingly restored 1908 character home, carefully decorated and furnished in keeping with the
period, including antiques and stained glass windows. Located in James Bay, a quiet neighbourhood
of mostly older homes. Hostess is the proud receiver of "Victoria Hospitality Award for Service
Exellence". Breakfast is served in the dining room.Visa,MC

Kennedy, Elva and Skip (Wooded Acres B&B)   ☎ (250) 478-8172/474-8959
4907 Rocky Point Rd., Victoria, BC   V9C 4G2   E-mail: ekennedy@pacificcoast.net

Located in the rural municipality of Metchosin between Victoria and Sooke.
$110S/D   (plus tax)   🍽 Meals   ► 4A
🍴 Full, homebaked (hearty country-style)   🏠 Rural, log home,
acreage, patio, quiet, veranda   ■ 2D   🛏 2Q   🛏 Private   ★ TV,
off-street parking, private hot tub   🚭 No smoking, no pets, not
suitable for small children
🕴 Wilderness hiking trail, beaches, birding, tennis court, fishing,
whale watching, variety of golf courses with beautiful facilities
🚗 Sooke Harbour House, elegant & pub-style dining, art shops
📷 Comfortable home is situated on over 3 acres of secluded "wooded park-like setting", which
guarantees tranqility and relaxation. Enjoy candlelight, a touch of wilderness & complete privacy in
hot-tub spa. Popular with honeymooners and for other special occasions. House specialties are
"privacy and good food". 🛏 B&B   www.lodgingvictoria.com/countryside

Victoria (cont'd)

Markham, Lyall & Sally (Markham House B&B)   ☎(250)642-7542,Fax(250)642-7538,
1853 Connie Rd.,Victoria, BC V9B 5B4   E-mail: mail@markhamhouse.com, 1-888-256-6888

Located halfway between Victoria and West Coast beaches. From ferries or Airport, take Hwy 17 to
Hwy 1, and to Hwy 14. Then all the way to Connie Rd (approx.45km). Turn left.

$95-195D   (reduced rate for one person) $25Add.person   ▶ 8
◑Full,homebaked(4-course) 🏠 Iris Farm, tudor-style, view, patio,
quiet ■4D(deluxe cottage) ⊨1K,2Q,2T ⬟4Private
★Woodstove, private hot-tub & Fireplace in cottage
Ⓦ Restricted smoking, no pets, children minimum age 12
🧍 10 acres of exquisite gardens, natural forest, woodland paths,
trout pond
🚗 Superb West Coast beaches, long hiking trails & bike paths

🐾 Quiet country living in spacious custom-built home situated on a knoll at the outskirts of the
City. Ideal place for honeymoon or special occasion. "Romance in the seclusion of honey-suckle
cottage at the edge of the woods. A Getaway to treasure". Enjoy afternoon tea in the lounge or
terrace overlooking garden/pond. CCards,JBC ↜B&B http://www.markhamhouse.com

---

McCarthy, Paul & Diana (Pitcairn House B&B)   ☎ & Fax (250) 384-7078
1119 Ormond St., Victoria, BC V8V 4J9   E-mail: ptcairn@victoriabc.com, 1-800-789-5566

From Fort & Government Streets, travel east on Fort St for 6 blocks to
Ormond St, turn left to house on right.
$65S $80-140D $20Add.person   ▶ 8A,2Ch
◑ Full, homebaked 🏠 Downtown, hist., patio, quiet ■2D,2Ste
(upstairs) ⊨ 2T,2Q,1K,cot ⬟ 1Sh.w.g., 1ensuite ★ Parking
Ⓦ Smoking on patio, no pets, children min. age 10 〰 French
🚗 Butchart Gardens, University of Victoria
🧍 Major downtown tourist attractions & harbour, bus (No11/14)

🐾 Victorian Heritage home (built in 1901) filled with period furniture, lace curtains, and stained
glass windows. Located centrally on Antique Row. Enjoy a hearty breakfast in the cozy dining room.
There are 2 small dogs in residence. Visa,MC

McGuire, Pat & Kathy (Eagle's Nest Bed & Breakfast)   ☎(250)658-2002,Fax(250)658-0135
4769 Cordova Bay Rd., Victoria, BC V8Y 2J7   E-mail: eagle@islandnet.com, 1-877-658-2002

$85-125D $15Add.person $15KF   (Reservation recommended)   ▶ 6
From Victoria Int.Airport or Swartz Bay Ferry Terminal, follow Patricia Bay Hwy (#17) to Royal
Oak Dr, then to Cordova Bay Rd. Look for long private driveway.
◑ Full 🏠 Res. ■ 3D,1Ste ⊨ 1D,2Q,1K ⬟Sh.w.g.,
1private in suite ★ KF/private deck, entrance & jacuzzi in
suite Ⓦ Smoking on outside deck, no pets, children welcome
🧍 Ocean/beachcombing, city bus route city, Mount Douglas Park
(500 acres of area to explore and hike)
🚗 Downtown, Commonwealth Pool & shopping centre, world
famous Butchart Gardens, public golfing, scenic drives,

🐾 Quiet, cozy, spacious, high-tech home with luxury modern accommodation. Hosts are
well-travelled and ready to offer tips on sightseeing, places to eat. Ideal place for honeymooners and
others wanting to get away for a special occasion. CCards www.victoria.com/accom/eagles.htm

Molloy, James & Linda & Jamie (Pension Molloy) ☎ (250) 414-0485, Fax 414-0486
1239 Pandora Ave., Victoria, BC   V8V 3R3 E-mail: innkeeper@home.com

Travel south on Blanchard to Johnson (one-way). Turn left to Fernwood, then left again
at Pandora (also one way).
$95-125S/D   (off-season Nov-Apr: 10-20% discount) ► 6
🍴Cont.,homebaked 🏠Downtown,res.,hist. ⊨2Q ⇋2Private
■2D(upstairs)+1suite ★Parking ✋Smoking in garden area,
inquire about children and pets
🏃 Downtown, Craigdarroch Castle, Victoria Art Gallery, Antique
Row, Cook St. Village, unique shopping
🚗 World famous Butchart Gardens, Anne Hathaway Cottage
🐾 Elegant Arts & Crafts Home built in 1910 with coal fireplace, rich oak panelling and stained
glass windows. Well informed hosts will gladly assist with travel plans. CCards

---

Monahan, Pat & Cathie (Benvenuto Bed & Breakfast) ☎(250)652-9254,Fx(250)652-4003
1024 Benvenuto Ave., Brentwood Bay, BC   V8M 1A1 E-mail: monahan@ampsc.com

$75S $85D $20Add.person   (long term rates available) ► 4-5A,2Ch
Located beside Butchart Gardens. Phone for directions.
🍴 Full, homebaked 🏠 Rural, res., 2-storey, porch, quiet
■2D(ground level) ⊨2S,1Q,2cots ⇋2ensuite ★F,LF,TV
in guest sitting room, VCR/movies provided, library ✋No pets,
smoking outside
🏃 Beautiful Waterfront Provincial Park with hiking/walking
trails, Butchart Gardens, Butterfly Gardens
🚗 Downtown Victoria, Sidney by the Sea, good restaurants
🐾 Newly renovated home for B&B with lovely decor and friendly atmosphere in a treed setting.
Guest area is on entry level, separate from household. Breakfast is served in the dining room.
Children welcome. Visa,MC ⌐CC

Richardson, Olga & Ken (Cedar Shade Bed & Breakfast) ☎ & Fax (250) 652-2994
6411 Anndon Place, Victoria, BC   V8Z 5R9 E-mail: cedarshade@home.com

From Swartz Bay BC Ferry take Hwy 17 (Patricia Bay Hwy) to Tanner Rd and turn right up hill to
Rodolph Rd. Turn right to Anndon Place and left to bottom of cul de sac. From Victoria take Hwy
17 past Sayward Rd and turn left on Tanner Rd - continue as above.
$50S $70-85D $20Add.person   (plus taxes) ► 6A,2Ch
🍴 Full(Gourmet) 🏠 Rural, res., split-level, view, patio,quiet
■3(ground level) ⊨2T,2Q,1P ⇋1Private,1sh.w.g. ★Air,F,
sep.entrance, facilites for the handicapped, off-street parking
✋No smoking 〰 Ukrainian
🏃 Bear Hill Reg.Park, Rodolph Park, Central Saanich Valley,
Pederson' Berry Farm, Trails, Beach.
🚗 Butchart Gardens, Elk Lake, Commonwealth Pool, Island
View Beach, Butterfly World, Cordova Bay Golf Course
🐾 Savour a taste of tranquility in comfortable home in quiet, private residential cul-de-sac
amidst big old cedars and douglas fir trees. Relax by the terraced rock gardens, cedar shaded fish
pond, water fall with fountain and herb garden and enjoy genuine Ukrainian hospitality. Breakfast
consists or organic & local food products. There are no chemical cleaning agents used in this house.
Hosts enjoy ballroom dancing, winemaking, flower & herb gardening. www.cedarshade.com

Victoria (cont'd)

Peggs, Joan (The Inn on St.Andrews)   ☎ (250) 384-8613, Fax (250) 384-6063
231 St Andrews St., Victoria, BC   V8V 2N1   E-mail: joan_peggs@bc.sympatico.ca, 1-800-668-5993

Phone for directions (map will be mailed if time permits).
$75S $85-110D $30Add.person   ►4
🍳Full,homebaked 🏠Downtown,res.,hist.,2-storey,city-view,quiet
🛏2Ste(upst) ⊨1T,2Q 🛁1sh.w.g.,1private, washbasin in one
room   ★F,TV 🚭No smoking
🏃 "Schoolhouse" (once Emily Carr's Studio), Inner Harbour,
ferry/ seaplane terminals, Parliament Buildings, RBC Museum,
the Empress Hotel, downtown shops, fine dining, ocean front
📣 Historic home, built in 1913 on the Carr-family property, is a designated heritage property in
James Bay. Enjoy modern comforts, wholesome food & old-fashioned hospitality. Visa,MC

Simms, Marion and Thomas (Marion's B & B)   ☎ (250) 592-3070
1730 Taylor St., Victoria, BC   V8R 3E9

Phone for directions.
$35-40S $50-60D $10Child $20Add.person (Deposit) ► 7A,3Ch
🍳 Full, homebaked 🏠 Res., bungalow, view, patio, quiet 🛏3
(main level) ⊨1S,1D,2Q 🛁1Sh.w.g.,1sh.w.h. 🚭No
smoking ★TV,F,LF,parking
🏃 Hillside Market Mall, Mount Tolmie, bus to downtown
🚗 Butchart Gardens, Empress Hotel, Oak Bay Village, China B.
📣 Cozy home located on quiet street overlooking spacious open
field and Mount Tolmie in the distance. Relax in a shower or jacuzzi bath. Beds are covered with
handmade quilts and cozy comforters. Transportation to and from bus depot can be arranged. Enjoy
the home away from home atmosphere. Two-days cancellation required.

Urban, Lois & Dana (The King's House Bed & Breakfast)   ☎ (250) 382-2460, Fax 388-9774
945 Dellwood Rd., Victoria, BC   V9A 6P2   E-mail: kingshouse@islandnet.com, 1-888-382-2424

From Airport/Sidney/Anacortes ferries, take Hwy17 and turn right on McKenzie Ave. Cross Gorge
Waterway, turn left on Craigflower and proceed 4 blocks to Dellwood on left.
$110-150S/D $20Add.person   (plus tax)   (off season rates available)   ►10

🍳 Full, homebaked 🏠 Res., 2-storey, balconies, patio, deck,
quiet 🛏 2D,1Ste(1or2 b-rooms)(upstairs) ⊨ 3Q,3P
🛁1Private,2ensuite (1double jacuzzi) ★ F,TV in one guest
room, ceiling fans, private entrance, off-street/street parking,
guest quarters are separate 🚭 Smoking outside & on balconies,
no pets, children min. age 10
🏃 Gorge Waterway, parks, historic sites, shops, golfing, pubs,
restaurants, No14 city centre bus
🚗 Downtown Victoria, Inner Harbour, Sooke, Butchart Gardens, Fisgard Lighthouse
📣 Friendly welcome in home full of warmth geared to the enjoyment of people. Well travelled
hosts enjoy making their guests feel comfortable. Each guest room is uniquely different. Enjoy the
social atmosphere of the sitting room where guests will find an amazing collection of limited edition
games. A hearty breakfast is served from a varied menu in the circular dining room. There is a cat
in residence (not in B&B area). Visa,MC, ✓B&B www.kingshouse.bc.ca

Victoria (cont'd)

Vernon, Linda & Martin (Gazebo B&B)
5460 Old West Saanich Rd., Victoria, BC   V8X 3X1

☎ 1-877-211-2288, Fax (250) 727-6605
E-mail: info@gazebo.victoria.com

Phone for directions.
$75-150S/D $25Child/Add.person   (plus tax)   ► 8
🍴 Full, homebaked   🏠 Rurl, 2-storey, acreage, view from guest rooms, patio, quiet, secluded   ■1D,1Ste,2F (main & upper level), plus two cottages   ⊨2T,3Q,2R   ⊐1Private,3ensuite
★LF,F,TV, 2private entrances, off-street parking, guest quarters are separate   ⊎Designated smoking area
🚗 Downtown Victoria and harbour, Butchart Gardens, R.BC.
BC Museum, scenic & coastal drives, golfing, whale-watching, Sooke, Butterfly Gardens, dining
📣 Warm welcome in manor house with themed guest rooms and cottages, surrounded by mature gardens and peaceful countryside. Multi-course breakfast is served in guest breakfast room. Hosts have many years experience in hospitality and derive much satisfaction from making their guests' visits memorable. Children and dogs welcome. Visa,MC ✓B&B   www.gazebo-victoria.com

---

Wait, Sally (Windlock on the Sea)
8560 West Saanich Rd., Sidney, BC   V8L 5W1

☎ (250) 652-2079, Fax (250) 652-2169
E-mail: swait@home.com

From Swartz Bay travel south on Hwy 17 to 2nd traffic light (McTavish Rd), turn right to end, left on West Saanich Rd, travel 2km. Located 27 km north of Victoria
$50S $85D $85Cottage   ► 6
🍴 Choice   🏠 Rural, acreage, view, oceanfront, large patio
■1D(main level), also separate selfcontained guest cottage   ⊨2Q,1P   ⊐2Private   ⊎No pets,no smoking
🚶 Beach combing on private beach, watch seals and otters playing, good birding and fishing in Saanich Inlet
🚗 Butchart Gardens, airport, Sidney & ferries to mainland
📣 Charming West Coast Cedar designed home located on beautiful Saanich Inlet with lovely views & fabulous sunsets. Featured accommodation is a lovely patioed cottage, set in picturesque and extensive xeriscaped (dry) garden. Hosts are in their 15th year of providing a unique B&B experience to many satisfied guests. Enjoy the relaxing atmosphere. A " Jack Russell" in residence (Marriage Commissioner next door!). ✓B&B   bbcanada.com/2124.html

---

Walsh, Gini and Peter (A B&B at Swallow Hill Farm)
4910 William Head Rd., Victoria, BC   V9C 3Y8

☎ & Fax (250) 474-4042
E-mail: info@swallowhillfarm.com

Take Hwy 1 to Colwood/Sooke Exit onto Hwy 1A, then Hwy 14, left on Metchosin Rd, then William Head Rd. Please phone first.
$80-85S $85-95D $25-30Add.person   (discounts avail.)   ► 4
🍴Full,homebaked   🏠Farm,view,quiet   ■2Ste   ⊨2T(K),1Q,2S,P
⊐2Private   ★Private decks, 1 Ste very private with separate entrance, sauna   ⊎No smoking, no pets
🚶 Nature Sanctuary (birds, deer, seal, otters), ocean beach, 46km hiking trail, historic (1870) church, museum & school, country store, restaurant & gift shop. Bus route
🚗 Victoria, Butchart Gardens, Sooke, Gulf Islands, Chemainus murals, Duncan, beaches, golfing
📣 Apple farm home with antiques and handcrafted furniture, in beautiful country setting near city. Enjoy the spectacular ocean & mountain sunrise view and a delicious farm breakfast. There are farm animals, a resident dog and wildlife. Friendly hosts love meeting people. CCards. ✓B&B
www.swallowhillfarm.com

Victoria (cont'd)

Werbik, Mila and D&V Booth (Humboldt House B&B) ☎(250)383-0152, Fax(250)383-6402
867 Humboldt St., Victoria BC V8V 2Z6   E-mail: rooms@humboldthouse.com

Located 2 blocks from downtown Victoria, BC's inner harbour.
$275-315S/D (plus tax)   (off-season rates available)   ▶ 10
🍴Full   🏠Downtown, 3-storey, Victorian, hist., view, quiet   ■5D(main &
upper level)   ⊨4Q,1K   🛁5Ensuite   ★F,private entrance, insuite
jacuzzi tubs, off-street & street parking   🐾No pets, not suitable for
childen, designated smoking area   ∾French, Czech, German, Cantonese
🚗 Butchart Gardens, ferries to mainland
🚶 Royal BC Museum, Empress Hotel, whale watching, downtown shops and
restaurants

📢 Luxury home, authentically renovated to reflect the Victorian era, especially suitable for
honeymoons, anniversaries or special retreats. Escape to the romantic luxury and to the most
unique hideaway of each room. House specialty is a gourmet/champagne breakfast tucked into a
basket and delivered through a two-way pantry into the privacy of each room. Visa/MC ⮕B&B
http://www.humboldthouse.com

Whistler   *(north of Vancouver; see also Brackendale, Pemberton)*

Gerig, Louise and Willy (Swiss Cottage)   ☎ (604) 932-6062/Fax (604) 932-9648
mailing: Box 1209, Whistler, BC   V0N 1B0   E-mail: louise@swisscanada.com, 1-800-718-7822

Location: 7321 Fitzsimmons Rd. In Whistler after 4th traffic light, turn right at White Gold Estate
and cross wooden bridge to Fitzsimmons Rd. Turn right and proceed to end and to house on right.
Winter: $98-145D   Summer $89-105D $25Add.person   ▶ 8

🍴Full, homebaked   🏠Res., village, quiet, riverside   ■2D,1F
(upstairs)   ⊨4T,1Q   🛁3Ensuite   ★TV,F,outdoor jacuzzi,
parking   🐾No smoking, no pets   ∾ German, French
🚶 Ski lifts, cross-country trail starts at doorstep, Whistler Village,
Lost Lake, golfing, tennis court by the house, biking, fishing,
hiking, canoeing
🚗 Garibaldi National Park, Cheakamus Lake, Brandywine Falls
📢 Swiss Chalet situated in excellent location. Enjoy all the
warmth and hospitality of a traditional Alpine B&B. Host's specialty is homemade breads. Hostess
is a ski-instructor. Visa,MC ⮕CC

Habkirk, Diana & Les (Brio Haus Bed & Breakfast)   ☎(604)932-3313,Fax(604)932-4945
3005 Brio Entrance, Whistler, BC   V0N 1B3   1-800-331-BRIO

In Whistler look for large Brio sign. Turn on Brio Entrance to 2nd property on right.
$70-85S(Summer) $85-100S(Winter) $80-120D(Summer/Winter $20Add.person (+ tax)   ▶ 8

🍴 Full, homebaked   🏠 Resort town, res., 3-storey, view from
guest rooms, porch,decks,quiet   ■2D,1F(upstairs)   🛁3Private
⊨2S,2T,1Q,1K   ★F,LF,TV in guest room, sep.entrance, guest
kitchen, off-street parking, jacuzzi moon tub/sauna, ski storage
🐾Smoking on decks, no pets
🚶 Across from Whistler Golf Course, on Valley (hiking) Trail,
0.5km to Whislter Village Centre, shops/restaurants/ski lifts
🚗 Brandywine and Narin Falls
📢 Charming European-style Alpine Home situated 0.5km south from Whistler Village town
center. Guests may prepare their own dinners in the guest kitchen, then relax around the fire in
the guest living room, or enjoy the moon tub and sauna. Hosts have been in the tourism business
for many years. Visa,MC,Diners ⮕B&B

Whistler (cont'd)

Huber, Erwin & Lisa (Chalet Luise)   ☎ (604)932-4187/Fax(604)-938-1531,1-800-665-1998
Box 352,7461 Ambassador Cr,Whistler,BC V0N 1B0   E-mail: info@chaletluise.com

Take Hwy 99 from Vancouver to Whistler. Approx 1km north of the village, turn right into White
Gold Estates on Nancy Green Dr. Right again on Ambassador Cr. Proceed 2 blocks to No. 7461.
$89-125S $95-210D $10Child $25Add.person   (plus tax)   ▶ 14

🍴 Full, homebaked(different specialties each day)   🏠 Res., view, patio,
balconies, quiet   ■8D(main & upper level, including superior suites)
⊨4T,4Q,4K   🛁 Private ensuite   ★LF,F's in rooms, whirlpool & sauna,
parking, ski/bicycle storage, separate entrance, guest lounge, beautiful
garden with patios   🚭No smoking, children min.age 8   〰German,
Italian, French

🚶 Whistler Village, ski lifts, shops, restaurants, x/c skiing & walking trails, biking, fishing
🚙 Alpine hiking, windsurfing, canoeing, sailing, golfing, horseback riding
🎿 Enjoy the authentic Swiss hospitality, ambiance and charm in a beautiful mountain setting.
Ski and summer packages available.Visa,MC ✔CC   www.chaletluise.com

---

Manville, Tim & Yvonne (Alta Vista Chalet B&B Inn)   ☎(604) 932-4900, Fax 932-4933
3229 Archibald Way, Whistler, BC   V0N 1B3   E-mail: avcb-b@direct.ca, 1-888-768-2970

Summer: $90S $130D $10Child   Winter: $100S $145D $15Child   (plus tax)   ▶ 16A,4Ch

From Vancouver, take Hwy 99 to Whistler. Turn left onto Hillcrest Rd (Alta
Vista Area), right onto Alpine Cres and left onto Archibald Way.
🍴Full, homebaked   🏠Village,European Chalet,view,patio,quiet   ■6D,2F
(main,upper & ground level)   ⊨6T,6Q,2R   🛁 6Private,2sh.w.g.   ★F,
guest lounge, games room with TV,VCR,guest fridge, jaccuzzi hot tub on
guest deck, secured ski storage,parking   🚭No smoking,no pets   〰French
🚶 Lake for swimming/canoeing/sailing/kayacking (rentals available), Valley
trail (canoe & bike rentals available), Whistler Village shops/restaurants
🚙 Horseback riding, ski lifts to Whistler and Blackcomb Mountain
🎿 Spacious European chalet furnished with pine and located on the Valley
Trail in a quiet forest setting overlooking beautiful Alta Lake. There is a dog
in residence. CCards ✔CC   www.altavistachalet.com

Myette-Spence, Ann (Golden Dreams B&B)   ☎ (604) 932-ANN'S(2667)/Fax (604) 932-7055
6412 Easy Street, Whistler, BC   V0N 1B6   1-800-668-7055

Take Hwy 99 north; once in Whistler, turn left at traffic light at Lorimer Rd and follow to Balsam
Way. Turn right and then next left on Easy St. Look for gold mailbox and sign on archway.
Winter:$95-125D   Summer:$85-95D $25Add.person $10Child   ▶ 6A

🍴Full,homebaked   🏠Resort village, mountainview, sundecks,
hot tub   ■3   ⊨2D,2Q,1cot   🛁1Sh.w.g.,1private   ★F,TV in
library lounge, kitchen   🚭No smoking, no pets
🚶 Valley trail & along golf course to village, x-c/downhill skiing,
restaurants,shops,hiking, bike trails at doorstep
🎿 Uniquely decorated rooms in Victorian, Oriental and Aztec
themes with sherry decanter, cozy down duvets. Nutritious
vegetarian breakfast served in country kitchen, including
home-made jams. Residence of Ex-National Ski Team coach. Children welcome. Visa/MC.

Nakayama, Bernadette & Ike (Sansou Whistler B&B) ☎ (604)932-3631, 1-888-611-4035
8084 Parkwood Dr., Whistler,BC V0N 1B8 E-mail: bandb@sansouwhistler.bc.ca, Fax 932-3681,

Phone for directions.
$89S $119D (Winter) $75S $95D(Summer) ► 6
Full, homebaked Sub, 3-storey, view from 2 guest rooms, deck ■ 3D(ground & upper level) 4T,1D 1Ensuite, 1sh.w.g. ★ F,TV, off-street parking No smoking, no pets German, Japanese
X-c skiing, snowmobiling/boarding, golfing, hiking, mountain biking, fishing, tennis, canoeing, kayaking, bus route to village
Village (gourmet dining, shopping, ski lifts)
Chalet-type mountain home with European hospitality and spacious living room, surrounded by breathtaking views located in popular resort town. A paradise for outdoor enthusiasts. Relax in the jacuzzi on the deck top. Enjoy a hearty breakfast. Visa,MC ✓B&B www.sansouwhistler.bc.ca

---

Plachy, Stan & Eva (Lorimer Ridge Pension) ☎ (604)938-9722,Fax(604)938-9155
6231 Piccolo Dr,Whistler,BC V0N 1B6 1-800-988-9002

Take Hwy 99 north to Whistler Village Centre. Proceed to Lorimer Rd. Turn left and then left again on Piccolo Dr. Look for house on left.
$99S $135D(Summer) $125S(Winter) $175D(Winter) (plus taxes) ► 16

Full, homebaked (buffet) Res., West-Coast style 2-storey, view from guest rooms, patio, deck, quiet ■ 8D(main & upper & ground level) 8T,4Q 8Private ★ TV,F(2 in guest rooms), separate entrance, off-street parking, hot tub, sauna, billiard room, ski lockers/ sports equipment storage, guest quarters are separate No smoking, no pets, children min. age 10 Czech
Whistler Village Ski Resort, biking trails, golfing, swimming, downhill & x-c skiing, hiking, dining, restaurants, horse-back riding, village bus route
Pemberton, Squamish, Shannon Falls
Cozy mountain lodge set in spectacular surroundings with a touch of West Coast architecture and fine Canadian hospitality. Enjoy the magnificient views of Blackcomb, Fissile & Rainbow Mts. Breakfast is served in guest breakfast room. There is a dog in residence. Visa,MC ✓B&B

Ruiterman, Paul & Helga (Renoir's Winter Garden B&B) ☎ (604) 938-0546,
3137 Tyrol Cr., Whistler, BC V0N 1B3 E-mail: renoir@dualmountain.com, Fax (604) 938 0547

$110-135D(Summer) $125-149D(Winter) $25Add.person (Single person rates avail.) ► 6A,2Ch

Take Hwy 99 past Whistler Creek traffic lights for 3km. Turn left at Blueberry Hill sign, left after 30 m and left after 250m.
Full, homebaked Village, 3-storey, view from guest rooms, deck, quiet ■ 2D,1F(main floor) 2T,1Q,1K.R 1sh.w.g., 1ensuite ★ LF,TV/VCR in guest rooms, spa hot tub, private entrance, off-street parking, guest quarters are separate No smoking, no pets, children min. age 5 German, Dutch
Golf Course (via trail), main village shops/restaurants
Black Comb & Whistler mountain ski lifts, hiking, biking, hangliding, canoeing, water-rafting,
New modern home with large rooms, tastefully decorated and situated at the foot of Whistler mountain overlooking Alta Lake. Enjoy the jacuzzi hot tub after a day on the slopes. Breakfast is served in the treetop dining room. Hosts will give a lift to skiers in the morning to the ski area. Extended stay & off-season rates available. Pick-up from bus loop/train station. Visa,MC ✓B&B

Stangel, Sue & Hal (Chalet Beau Séjour)　　　☎ (604) 938-4966, Fax (604) 938-6296
7414 Ambassador Cr., Box 427, Whistler, BC　VON 1B0　E-mail: sejour@direct.ca, 1-888-878-3310

Take Hwy 99 from Vancouver to Whistler. At 1km north of the village, turn right into White Gold
Estates on Nancy Green Dr. Turn right again on Ambassador Cr to 3rd house on left.
Summer:$85-99S/D　Winter:$105-120S/D　$10Child　$20Add.person　　　　　▶ 6A

🛏 Full　🏠 Res., village, 3-storey, view, deck, quiet　⊨3D
(upstairs)　⊨ 2T,2Q,1cot　🚗 3Private　★ F,TV, ski storage,
hot-tub, lounge, off-street parking ⓦDesignated smoking area
〰German, French, Spanish
🚶 Ski lifts, Whistler Village, lake, golf courses, ski trails, shops,
tennis, biking, restaurants, Whistler Valley bus service
🚣 Alpine hiking, sailing, horseback riding, canoeing, windsurfing
📣 Spacious new Alpine home with friendly Canadian hospitality
and relaxing atmosphere situated in central location. Complimentary transportation from bus or
train station and special off-season and ski packages available. Relax in the spacious guest lounge
with sundeck. Visa,MC ✔B&B　www.whistler-net/whistlerbnb/beausejour.html

---

Weh, Doris and Willi (Haus Stephanie)　　　　　　☎ & Fax (604) 932-5547
7473 Ambassador Crs., Bx 1460, Whistler, BC　VON 1B0

Winter: $100-125D $20Add.person　Summer: $80-95D　(Child free under age 5)　　　▶ 6

Coming north on Hwy 99, drive past village entrance, take second
road on the right (White Gold Estates). Stay on Nancy Green Dr
until it becomes Ambassador Cr.
🛏 Full　🏠Res., balcony, quiet　■3D,1F (main and upper
floor)　⊨ 2S,2Q　🚗 1Private, 2ensuite　★KF,separate
entrance, parking　♥　ⓦ No smoking　〰 German
🚶 Ski lifts, Resort village, cross-country trails
📣 Austrian-style house with European atmosphere and situated
in convenient location to the lifts and village activities.

White Rock　　　　　　*(Vancouver);see also N.Westminster,Langley,Delta,Tsawwassen)*

Gray, Pat (Dorrington Bed & Breakfast)　　　　☎ (604) 535-4408
13851-19A Ave, South Surrey, BC　V4A 9M2　　　　Fax (604) 535-4409

Phone for directions.
$85-105S　$100-120D　(minimum 2 nights)　　　▶ 4A
🛏 Full, homebaked　🏠 Res., 2-storey, small acreage, patio,
quiet　■ 2D (upstairs)　⊨ 1D,1Q　🚗 1Private, 1ensuite
★LF,separate entrance, outdoor hot tub, gazebo, tennis court &
ball machine & equipment, jaccuzzi tub in one guest room　ⓦNo
pets, no smoking, not suitable for children
🚶 Parks & heritage walking trails amid tall cedars/firs/maples
🚣 White Rock beach (with sun-hot sandy flats, promenade, sidewalk cafes), specialty shops
📣 Stately and comfortable home with themed guest rooms. Breakfast is served in the stunning
"Hunt Salon" with its river rock fireplace and 12 ft ceilings, or on the patio with cushioned rattan
chairs, overlooking the peaceful garden, tennis court and hot tub. Elegant picnic basket provided
and directions to gourmet markets. There is a miniature Dachshund in residence. Visa ✔CC
www.dorrington.com

White Rock (cont'd)

Hall, Iris and Bruce (Hall's Bed & Breakfast)   ☎ (604) 535-1225, FAx (604) 535-0088
14778 Thrift Ave., White Rock, BC   V4B 2J5   E-mail: halls@lifestyler.com

From Vancouver & airport go south on Hwy 99 to White Rock Exit (#10) onto King George Hwy
99A. Turn right at 148St & 32Ave. Continue on 148St (becomes Oxford in White Rock) to Thrift
Ave. Turn right.

$55-75S $65-90D   ► 6A
🍳 Full 🏠 Res., ocean view, patio, quiet ■2D,1Ste(main &
ground level) ⊨4Q ⌷3Private ★TV/VCR, large guest
lounge, kitchenette in suite, separate entrance, parking 🚳No
smoking, no pets, no children
🏃 Ocean and beach with promenade, shopping centers, arena,
curling rink, on bus route to Vancouver & surrounding areas
🚗 Downtown Van., Island ferries, Peace Arch Park, US-border
📣 Warm & friendly hospitality in a bright, comfortable and spacious home. Suite has 2 bedrooms
and occupies whole lower floor.↙CC http://www.lifestyler.com/halls

---

Windermere   *(s/of Golden; see also Fairmont Hot Springs, Parson)*

MacDonald, Scott & Astrid (Windermere Creek B&B)   ☎ & Fax (250) 342-0356
Box 409, Windermere, BC   V0B 2L0   1-800-946-3942

Location: 1658 Windermere Loop Rd. Phone for directions.
$80Ste $95Cabin   (plus tax)   ► 15
🍳 Full, homebaked 🏠 Rural, ranch-style, acreage, view, deck,
swimming pool, quiet ■ 1Ste(in main house), plus 5 log
cabins ⊨6Q,5P ⌷6private (with jacuzzi tubs in all cabins)
★Private entrance, host quarters are separate, parking
🚬Designated smoking area, not suitable for children, no pets
🏃 Miles of developed walking trails on property, many view points & picnic spots with benches,
non-sleeping (ca1880) pioneer log cabin open to guests, creekside hammocks, beaver ponds
🚗 Windermere (artist corner & public beach), Invermere, 2 Hot Springs (Fairmont & Radium)
📣 Log cabin, dating back to 1887, is very well laid out for B&B. Cabins were built in 1996 &
some are new for 2000. Situated on 107 forested acres backing on to crown land and the Kootenay
Park & golf course across the road. Breakfast is served in guest breakfast nook. Relax in the
sunroom or on the deck and enjoy the peaceful surroundings & beautiful views. Honeymoon, golf &
romance packages available. Visa,MC ↙B&B

When to stay in a B & B ?

You can stay in a B&B anytime of the year. Of course, it is most popular when on vacation. And there are many more B&B's available in the summertime.

You can stay in a B&B if you are a single traveller (on business or pleasure). Then, you are in the company of others, and socializing with strangers is so much easier.

You can stay in a B&B for a weekend. You might want to go to the country for a good rest, or you might want to go to the city for a shopping spree or a cultural event.

You can stay in a B&B when visiting friends and relatives (if they do not have enough room for you). There is probably a B&B around the corner.

You can stay in a B&B when attending a wedding in another town. Many churches have lists of B&B's located nearby.

You can stay in a B&B when visiting a sick relative or friend in another town. It makes for very comforting and convenient accommodation. Many hospitals keep lists of nearby B&B's for out-of-town relatives.

You can stay in a B&B even if you are not travelling by car. Many B&B homes are situated near excellent public transportation and many hosts will pick up and deliver from bus terminal, railway station or airport, sometimes at no charge.

You can stay in a B&B even if you are on a camping trip. Give yourself a treat and sleep in a comfortable bed once in a while, especially if the weather turns miserable and the gear is soaking wet.

You can stay in a B&B if you travel with your own trailer. Many B&B's have ample room and a hook-up for that purpose, and they usually welcome guests to join them in the house for breakfast.

You can stay in a B&B when you are hiking the trails. In Ontario there are many B&B's along the famous Bruce Trail and some of these hosts may even forward your car and gear for you to the next B&B on the trail.

You can stay in a B&B when taking part in acitivity groups, such as whitewater rafting, bicycling and wilderness tours etc. Ask for information when signing up for a trip.

You can stay in a B&B when relocating to another city. Is there a better way of getting the feeling of a new area than talking to the local people?

Northwest Territories
and
Yukon

Travel Arctic
Yellowknife, Northwest Territories   X1A 2L9
Tourism Yukon (CG)
Box 2703, Whitehorse, Yukon   Y1A 2C6

toll-free 1-800-661-0788

(867) 667-5340

Fort Smith NT   *(south of Yellowknife, near Alberta border)*

Calder, Linda & Bill Wade (Linda's B&B)   ☎ (867) 872-5787, Fax (867) 872-2166
13 Cassette Cr., Box 955, Fort Smith, NT   X0E 0P0   E-mail: bwade@auroranet.nt.ca

$65S $85D   🍽 Meals   ▶ 4
🍲 Full, homebaked   🏠 Res., round log home, porch, screend-in
deck, quiet ■2D(main floor) ⊨2T,1Q ⊲1Sh.w.g. ★F,TV,LF,
off-street parking, guest quarters are separate   ✋ No smoking,
pets welcome
🏃 Downtown, museum, many wooded areas, Slave River
🚗 Wood Buffalo Nat.Park with Pine Lake & Salt River & hiking
trails, float plane access to excellent fishing & canoeing
🎣 Enjoy warm northern hospitality in uniquely designed round log home with open concept
living area, skylights and stone fireplace, located in beautiful town at the gateway to Wood Buffalo
National Park. Log guest rooms are equipped with cedar panelled bathroom. Relax in the new wood
burning sauna situated just outside the house. Access to computer training classroom, multimedia
production & recording studio. There are dogs and a cat.

Yellowknife NT

MacIntosh, Tessa (Blue Raven Bed & Breakfast)   ☎ (867) 873-6328, Fax (867) 920-4013
37 Otto Dr., Yellowknife, NT   X1A 2T9

Take Franklin Ave (main street) toward "old town". Cross bridge to Latham Island and Otto Dr. Look for blue house on the hill.
$65S $80D $10Child $15Add.person   ▶6
🍴 Full   🏠 3-storey, view, lakefront, deck, quiet   ■2D,1F (main, lower & upper levels)   🛏2T,2Q,1P,cot   🛁1Sh.w.g., 1sh.w.h   ★F,LF,TV in guest rooms, off-street parking   ✋No smoking   ᴡᴡFrench
🚗 City Centre, museum, Legistlature, airport, beach

🏃 Charming historic restaurants, intriguing Northern souvenir outlets, bush/float plane bases, lake fishing tour

📯 Beautiful home perched atop Old Town's Latham Island on the shores of Great Slave Lake. Relax by the fireplace or on the spacious deck amidst pleasant home-stay atmosphere and enjoy the view of lake and the spectacular Northern Lights. Informative hosts (Lodge owner & photographer) are longtime Northerners. There are 3 children in the host family and a sweet Golden Retriever dog. Visa ✔CC

Dawson City YT

Nordic Steve & Tracy (5th Ave. Bed & Breakfast)   ☎ & Fax (867) 993-5941
700-5th Ave., Box 1241, Dawson City, YT   Y0B 1G0   E-mail: 5thave@dawson.net

$75-95S $95-115D $10Add.person   (plus tax)   E-mail: ✔ 16
🍴 Homebaked   🏠 Downtown, hist., view   ■3D,1F,1Ste (main & upper floor)   🛏2T,4D,2Q,2R   🛁3Ensuite, 1sh.w.g.   ★Sep entrance, KF in guest common room, parking   ✋No smoking
🏃 Robert Service Cabin, Jack London Exhibit, Visitor Reception, Palace Grand Theatre
📯 Newly decorated modern home with a historic finish in central location beside the museum, overlooking Victory Gardens. http://wwwyukonweb.com/tourism/5thavenue/index.html

Whitehorse YT

Pitzel, Carla & Garry Umbrich (Hawkins House)   ☎ (867) 668-7638, Fax (867) 668-7632
303 Hawkins St., Whitehorse, YT   Y1A 1X5   E-mail: cpitzel@internorth.com

Take Whitehorse City Centre Exit on Alaska Hwy. Follow 2nd or 4th Ave to Hawkins St.
$145S $175D(high season) $105S $123D(low season) $10Add.person   ▶8A

🍴 Full   🏠 Downtown, 2-storey, view   ■4(upstairs)   🛏4Q   🛁4Private   ★LF, jaccuzi, guest parlour, TV & balcony & fridge in guest rooms, parking   ✋ No smoking, no pets   ♥
ᴡᴡFrench, German
🏃 Restaurants, swimming pool, museums, shopping, riverboat, parks, waterfront, Gov't offices
🚗 Miles Canyon, ski/hike trails, dog sledding, fishing, canoeing
📯 Lavish, spacious and bright Victorian home with high ceilings located 2 blocks from the Yukon River. Experience one of the Yukon theme rooms. Young host family with 2 children. Hostess is a life-time Yukoner who weaves and studies languages. High season: May 1-August 31). CCards www.hawkinshouse.yk.ca

Alberta

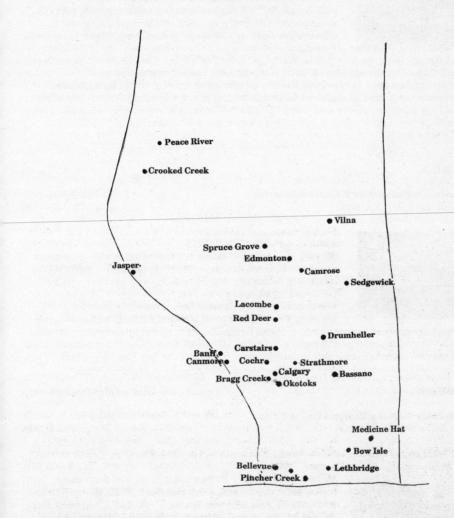

- Peace River
- Crooked Creek
- Vilna
- Spruce Grove
- Edmonton
- Camrose
- Jasper
- Sedgewick
- Lacombe
- Red Deer
- Drumheller
- Carstairs
- Banff
- Canmore
- Cochr
- Strathmore
- Bragg Creek
- Calgary
- Bassano
- Okotoks
- Medicine Hat
- Bow Isle
- Bellevue
- Lethbridge
- Pincher Creek

Alberta Tourism
10155-102nd St.
Edmonton, AB T5J 4L6

toll free 1-800-661-8888

Banff

(west of Calgary; see also Canmore)

House, Eleanor & R. Kunelius (Eleanor's House B&B)   ☎(403)760-2457 Fax(403)762-3852
125 Kootenay Ave., Box 1553, Banff, AB T0L 0C0   E-mail: info@bbeleanor.com

In Banff, travel through town over bridge, turn left and follow signs to Hot Springs. Turn left on

Kootenay Ave. Look for house with flag on right side.
$135S $145D   ▶4
❇ MidMay-MidOct   ⚏ Full, homebaked   🏠 Res., 2-storey,
view from guest rooms,quiet ■2D(upstairs) ⊨2T,1Q
⛌Ensuites ★F,TV in guest rooms on request, private entrance,
guest parlour (F/library/wet bar), off-street parking, guest
quarters are separate   🖐Restricted smoking, no pet, not suitable
for children

🚶 Banff Springs Hotel/spa/golf course, Banff Centre for Performing Arts, museums, Town Centre
🚐 Banff Upper Hot Springs Mineral Bath, Norquay/Lake Louise/Sunshine skiing
🐎 Newly renovated and enlarged mid-Century elegant home, situated within Banff Nat.Park
with mountain views from all windows and located in quiet prestigious neighbourhood. Breakfast is
served in large guest breakfast room. Former Nat.Park Warden & Hospitality/Travel worker, hosts
will provide personalized itineraries, to maximize important holiday time. Visa,MC ⌁CC
www.bbeleanor.com

Bassano

(east of Calgary)

Bulger, Joel & Kathy (Bar B Guest House)   ☎ (403) 641-4469
Box 126 Bassano, AB T0J 0B0   Fax (403) 641-4407

Located 12km west of Bassano and 6.5km east of the jct of Hwy 56.
$35-50 $45-60D $5-10Child   ▶6A,2Ch
⚏ Full, homebaked   🏠 Farm, 2-storey, older, view from guest
rooms, patio, quiet, isolated   ■ 2D,1F(upstairs) ⊨2D,1Q,2R
⛌1Sh.w.g.,1ensuite ★F,TV, parking with plug-ins 🖐No
pets, smoking on open patio
🚐 Crawling Valley, Bassano Dam, Calgary, Drumheller,
Dinosaur Prov. Park, Tyrrell Museum, Sisika Blackfoot Reserve

🐎 Personally designed, unique, spacious (1950) farmhouse set in a large, well-treed, quiet yard
surrounded by prairie scenery and featuring decorative stonework & paintings by local artists. Host
is a historian specializing in ranching frontier history. There is a farm dog. Visa,MC ⌁B&B

Bellevue

(west of Lethbridge; see also Pincher Creek)

Rinaldi, Jerry & Becky (Burmis Bed & Bales)   ☎ & Fax (403) 628-2150, 1-800-345-2841
Box 430, Bellevue, AB T0K 0C0   E-mail: burmisbb@agt.net

Located 10km east of Bellevue off Hwy 3 and 4.5km south on Hwy 507. Phone for directions.
$60S $75D $65F $20Add.person 🍴Meals   ▶9A,2Ch

⚏ Full, homebaked   🏠 Farm, split-level, view from guest
rooms, patio, porch, deck, quiet, secluded ■ 2D,1F (upstairs)
⊨2D,2Q,1S   ⛌ 1Private, 1sh.w.g.   ★ F,LF,TV in guest room,
outdoor hot-tub, private entrance   🖐 No smoking, no pets
🚶 Crowsnest River (excellent for world class fly fishing), hiking
and sight seeing trails, abundance of wild life
🚐 Waterton National Park, US-border, Head-Smashed-In Buffalo
Jump, Frank Slide historic site

🐎 Peaceful and quiet home on Horse Ranch in the foothills of the Rocky Mountains. Relax on the
large wrap-around deck, enjoy the trickling sound of the Crowsnest River and the smell of
homebaking and cooking. Breakfast is served in separate guest breakfast room. ⌁B&B
http://www.telusplanet.net/public/burmisbb/

Bow Island

(west of Medicine Hat)

Brosz, Elroy & Pat (Mom & Dad's Bed & Breakfast)   ☎ (403) 545-2381
439-3Ave East, Bow Island, AB   T0K 0G0

Located on eastern edge of Bow Island. Look for signs inside town limits along Hwy 3.
$30S $40D $65F   📧 Meals (packed lunches)   (Longer stay rates available)   ► 8A,3Ch
⬛ Full, homebaked (Western style)   🏠 Village, res., 2-storey
◼ 4D,1F (main & upper level)   ⊨ 1S,2T,3D,cot   ⚬ 1Private,
2shw.g.,1ensuite   ★ F,LF,TV, table tennis, bocci, croquet,
parking   ♥   ∾ some German & French
🏃 Public swimming pool, tennis courts, ball diamonds, golf course,
fishing (trout), Bean Plant, restaurants, churches
🚐 Spitz Sunflower Plant, Forty-Mile Reservoir (Canada's largest
pump Station), boating, fishing, Alberta Birds of Prey Centre,
Ostrich Farm, Etzicom Windpower Museum, Writing-on-Stone Provincial Park
📢 Well travelled and gracious hosts in spacious and comfortable modern home in the town of
Bow Island. Relax and rest or take part in various studies or any of the many activities. ⌐ CC

Bragg Creek

(west of Calgary)

Bilben, Rolly & Judy (Countryside Inn & B&B)   ☎ (403) 949-2805, Fax (403) 949-3371
Box 669, Bragg Creek, AB   T0L 0K0

Take first left turn south of Bavarian Inn to first house on left.
$65-100S $75-115D   ► 6A
⬛ Full   🏠 Village, ranch-style bungalow, acreage, patio, deck,
quiet, secluded   ◼ 3D (main floor)   ⊨ 3Q   ⚬ 3Private
★F,LF,TV in guest rooms, off-street parking, guest quarters are
separate   Ⓦ No smoking, no pets, no children
🏃 Meadows of wildflowers, hiking/biking trails, arts/craft shops,
galleries, fine restaurants, Kananaskis Day Park, Elbow River
🚐 Banff, Canmore, Kananaskis Country, Calgary, Rocky Mountains
📢 Spacious home nestled on a quiet lane among tall evergreens. Gourmet breakfast includes
Grand Marnier Waffles or Eggs Benedict. Relax in the reading room around the warm stone
fireplace after a day of enjoying scenic Kananaskis Country. Hosts have been in the hospitality
industry for over 17 years. There is a bird in residence. ⌐B&B

Calgary

(see also Cochrane, Okotoks, Bragg Creek)

Bates, Brian & Charlotte (Paradise Acres B&B)   ☎ (403) 248-4748
Box 20, S2, RR6, Calgary, AB   T2M 4L5   Fax (403) 235-3916

Take TCH Hwy 1 east from the city to Paradise Rd (6.5km). Turn south 1km to No 243105.
$65S $75D $15Add.person (one only)   ► 6A
⬛ Full, homebaked   🏠 Rural, 2-storey, acreage, view from guest
rooms, deck, quiet, secluded   ◼5D(main & upper level)   ⊨5Q
⚬2Private,3ensuite   ★ TV,F,ceiling fans, off-street parking
Ⓦ No smoking, no pets
🚐 Golf course, Lake Chestermere, Calgary Airport, downtown
Calgary, Stampede Grounds, major shopping centre, Kananaskis
Country, Olympic Park
📢 Warm welcome and friendly hospitality in spacious new luxurious home surrounded by quiet
countryside with city access. Relax by one of the marble fireplaces and enjoy the city & mountain
views. Breakfast is served in special breakfast room. CCards ⌐B&B

Calgary (cont'd)

Brink-Scrimgeour, Helen G. (Brink Bed & Breakfast)   ☎ (403) 255-4523
79 Sinclair Cr SW, Calgary, AB   T2W 0M1

Located in Southwest Calgary, Springwood off Elbow Dr. Phone for detailed directions.
$55-80S/D $5Extra(for 1 night stay)   🔟 Meals   ►4

🛏Full,homebaked   🏠Res,split-level,patio,quiet   ■1D,1Ste
(main/upst.,incl. popular honeymoon suite) ⊨1D,1Q
🛁1Sh.w.g.,1ensuite   ★F,LF,TV in guest room, barbeque
🕇 Direct bus route to Southland Station of LRT (Light Rail
Transit), walk & bike paths, Jewish Synagogue "House of David"
🚐 South-Centre, Heritage Park, Fish Creek
🎏 Comfortable, country-style home with a relaxed atmosphere,
situated in quiet residential area. Congenial hostess is a retired
Nurse and a Teddy Bear Enthusiast. Breakfast served in dining room overlooking the large deck
and attractive landscaped back yard. Afternoon Tea and picnic baskets available. ✐B&B

Carsted, George & Helen (A Home Away From Home)   ☎ & Fax (403) 257-0425
135 Mount Reliant Pl.SE, Calgary, AB   T2Z 2G2   E-mail: carstedg@cadvision.com

Located at south end of Deerfoot Trail (Hwy2) at 22X Hwy & McKenzie Lake Blvd.

$25S $50D $5Child $75F   🔟 Meals   ► 2A,1Ch
🍴 Cont.   🏠 Res., sub., 2-storey, view, porch, deck, quiet
■1S,1D (upstairs)   ⊨ 1S,1D   🛁 1Sh.w.g.   ★ F,LF,TV,
elect.Air Filters, off-street parking   🖐 No smoking, no pets
🗣German, Polish
🕇 Bow River (good fishing), Fishcreek Park (walking & cycling
trails), golfing,
🚐 Downtown, Stampede Grounds (July), Banff National Park
🎏 Large home located on the banks of the Bow River with terraced back yard and flower garden.
Relax on the front porch and enjoy the lovely evening air. There is a triple car driveway. Retired
hosts are a former Teacher & and Nurse and are interested in health issues, geography & politics.
Enjoy evening tea in congenial company.

Donnelly, John & Mary (Aurora House B&B)   ☎ (403) 932-4162, Fax (403) 932-4068
Box2, S5, RR2, Calgary, AB   T2P 2G5   E-mail: marengo@telusplanet.net

Travel west of Calgary city limits on TCH1 for 30km to Sibbald Creek Trail (No68). Turn south for
500m and take first right turn (west) onto private gravel road. Continue on main road west for

5km. Driveway on left opposite horse arena.
$60S $85D $20Child/Add.person $160F   (plus tax)   ► 4
🍴 Full, homebaked   🏠 Farm, bungalow, hillside, view, patio,
deck, quiet, secluded   ■2(ground level)   ⊨1D,1Q   🛁1Sh.w.g.
★LF,F,TV, piano/pool table for guests   🖐No smoking, no pets
🕇 Nature trails, Alborak Stable (hunter/jumper/dressage facility),
lake, canoeing, birdwatching
🚐 Calgary Airport, downtown, Spruce Meadows, village of Bragg
Creek, Canmore, Banff, Kananaskis Country Recreation area, golfing, x-c skiing & ski resorts
🎏 Warm welcome in home situated in the wooded foothills far away from bright lights allowing
the night sky to show its splendor. Relax on the deck or patio or by the fireplace. Breakfast is
served in the dining room or continental style, if guests prefer. Horse stay-overs are permitted with
special arrangements. Hosts are a retired Teacher and a Petroleum Engineering Consultant. They
run a cow/calf operation on the farm. Visa

Calgary (cont'd)

Hancock, Sharon (Sharon's B&B for R&R)   ☎ & Fax (403) 251-2288
244 Cantrell Dr. SW, Calgary,AB   T2W 2K6

$45S $60D $10Child $15Add.person $85F   🍴 Meals   (weekly rates available)   ►8
Phone for directions.
🍳 Full, homebaked, self-serve   🏠 Res., raised bungalow, view,
decks, quiet   ■ 2 (main & lower level)   ⊨ 1S,2Q,1P,crib
🚿2Private   ★ KF,LF,F,TV/books/games/videos, car plug-ins,
off-street & street parking   👋Smoking outside, no pets
🧍 Shopping, theatres, restaurants, library, kids playgym, walking,
cycling, picniking in Fish Creek Pk, Transit No29 and LRT stop
🚗 Downtown, museum, churches, dining, golfing, fishing,
University of Calgary, Calgary Tower, Saddledome, Stampede Park, Kananaskis Country
🔫 Warm and friendly Christian home situated across from beautiful Fish Creek Park. R&R
stands for "Rest & Relaxation". Enjoy sitting out on the front deck with a lovely view. Hostess
enjoys swing dancing, reading & gardening. Office space with fax and computer access, small
exercise room and bicycle available for guests. Airport pick-up & drop-off for a small fee. There is a
cat "Mr.Baily" in residence. Celiac hostess will prepare glutin-free meals, if requested. "May God
bless and keep you safe throughout your travels". Children welcome. Visa ✓B&B

Knight, Kathryn & Ken (A Good Knight B&B)   ☎ (403) 270-7628, Fax (403)283-4242
1728-7th Ave. NW, Calgary, AB   T2N 0Z4   E-mail: goodnite@telusplanet.net, 1-800-261-4954

From TCH1 (16Ave NW), turn south on 19th St NW, left on 8Ave NW
(bottom of hill), then right on 18St and left on 7Ave.
$60-85S $70-150D   ► 6
🍳 Full, homebaked(gourmet)   🏠 Res., 2-storey, porch, quiet   ■ 3D
(upstair)   ⊨3Q   🚿 2Ensuite,1private (1jacuzzi)   ★ F,LF, TV/coffee
maker in guest rooms, parking   👋 No smoking, no pets
🧍 L.R.T. station (Light Rail Transit to university, stadium, downtown and
stampede grounds), shopping, restaurants, parks
🚗 Stampede, Heritage Park, Spruce Meadows, Rocky Mountains
🔫 Newly-built, Victorian-style "In-Fill" home in quiet established
neighbourhood with custom pine and willow furnishings. Young hosts are
lifelong Calgarians and have a unique Teapot collection. Hostess is a Home-Ec teacher and serves
scrumptious and innovative breakfasts. There are two little girls in the family. Accommodation
includes a romantic suite with cathedral ceiling and private balcony. Visa,MC ✓B&B
www.agoodknight.com

Larson, Valinda & Helmut Schoderbock (Inglewood B&B)   ☎ & Fax(403) 262-6570
1006-8thAve SE, Calgary, AB   T2G 0M4

From TCH (16th Ave) go south on Centre St to Calgary Tower (9th Ave). Turn left (east) and
proceed to 9th St, turn left again and continue 1 block to 8th Ave SE.

$70-100S $80-125D   ► 8A
🍳Full, homebaked   🏠Downtown, res, 2-storey, view from guest
rooms, river at back, deck, quiet   ■ 3D,1Ste(upst)   ⊨4Q
🚿4Ensuite   ★ TV, room keys, guest bike storage, off-street
parking   👋No smoking, no pets   ⚑ German
🧍 Calgary Stampede, Olympic Saddledome, Zoo, Calgary Tower &
City Centre, Glenbow Museum, world class fly fishing on Bow
River, bicycle/walking trails, light rail transit system (LRT)
🚗 Planetarium, Airport, Heritage Park, Olympic Park, City Look-Out
🔫 Young couple in large Victorian-style home built in 1992, situated next to the Bow River in
very central location. Ideal place for scenic walks. Bring your own bike. ✓CC

Calgary (cont'd)

Lloyd, Jonathon (Calgary Westways Guest House)   ☎ (403) 229-1758, Fax (403) 228-6265
216-25Ave SW, Calgary, AB   T2S 0L1   E-mail: calgary@westways.ab.ca

$45-90S $70-120D $15Child $20Add.person ⬛Meals (plus tax) (Deposit required)   ▶ 7
From downtown take McLeod Trail South access to 25Ave and continue past Elbow River to B&B
 on right side.
🍴Full(hearty) 🏠 Downtown, 3-storey, hist., porch, deck, quiet ⬛4
(upstairs) ⊨2Q,2K ⬛4ensuite ★F,LF,KF, TV/VCR,Air in guest
rooms, hot-tub on deck, street/off-street parking ⓌDesig.smoking area,
children min. age 6, inquire about pets
🚶 Stampede Grounds, downtown, Lindsey Park Sports Arena, 4th Street
restaurants, Mission Bridge Micro Brewery, LRT & busses
🚐 Kananaskis Nat.& Fish Creek Prov.Pks, Calgary Zoo, Calaway Pk,
Olympic Pk, Int.Airport
📣 1914-built Heritage home with original features/leaded glass windows,
situated in the heart of downtown. Host has been in the hospitality business
for over 20 years. Visa,MC,Amex ✐B&B www.westways.ab.ca

McLeod, Karen (Sweet Dreams & Scones Bed & Breakfast)   ☎ & Fax (403) 289-7004
2443 Uxbridge Drive NW, Calgary, AB   T2N 3Z8   E-mail: sdreams@cadvision.com

 $70-90S $80-120D $135-180Ste   ▶ 8
From Hwy 1 (16th Ave NW), turn north onto Uxbridge Drive.
🍴 Homebaked (gourmet) 🏠 Res., 2-storey ⬛3D,1Ste
(upstairs) ⊨2T,1D,2Q,1K(four-poster) ⬛1Private,
3ensuite ★ F,TV,LF, off-street parking Ⓦ No smoking, no
pets, children min. age 10
🚶 University of Calgary, Olympic Skating Oval, Foothills
Hospital, restaurants, city bus #9 (2 blocks)
🚐 Downtown, LRT(Light Rail Transit), Calgary Zoo, Olympic Pk, three shopping centers
📣 Spacious home with wonderful decor (combination of antiques, quilts, collectibles and rustic
willow) and warm hospitality. Relax in the huge private yard with lovely garden. Hats & accessories
available for sale as keepsakes. Hosts are avid antique collectors, skiers and very knowledgeable
about the City. House specialty is breakfast scones. Visa ✐B&B www.cadvision.com/sdreams

---

Palmquist, Dennis & Beth (Rosedale House B&B)   ☎ & Fax (403) 284-9568
1633-7A St NW, Calgary, AB   T2M 3K2   E-mail: rosedale@cadvision.com

Travelling on Trans Canada Hwy (16th Ave N) proceed 8 blocks west of Center St. Turn south on
7A St to 2nd house on right side
$75S $90D $15Add.person   ▶ 8A,2Ch
🍴Full, homebaked 🏠Downtown, res., 2-storey, patio ⬛3Stes
(below ground level with high ceilings) ⊨4Q,1R,crib ⬛3Ensuite
★TV in guest room, F/LF in guest lounge, double jacuzzi, small
fridge in each room, parking ⓌSmoking outside 〰French
🚶 Downtown area, restaurants, shopping, bus & LRT stops, Bow
River bank, Jubilee Auditorium
🚐 University of Calgary, Airport, Calgary Zoo, Heritage Park, Spruce Meadows
📣 Spacious estate home with extenive oak woodwork and country decor situated in the city's
most established and popular neighbourhood of Rosedale, close to downtown and major roadways.
Professional host family has travelled worldwide extensively and is happy to share favorite spots in
and around the City. There is a small dog in host quarters. ✐B&B
http://www.cadvision.com/rosedale/index.htm

Calgary (cont'd)

Pantel, Evelyn (Evelyn's Bed & Breakfast)   ☎ (403) 286-5979
107 Silverbrook Rd NW, Calgary, AB   T3B 3H9

$30-35S $50-60D $10Child $15Add.person 🍽Meals (Off season rates avail)   ▶ 2A,2Ch

Phone for directions. Will mail map and meet guests if necessary.
🍹 Full (unique) 🏠 Res., bungalow, patio, quiet ■3D(main & lower floor) ⊨2D,1Q 🛏1ensuite, 1private, 1sh.w.h.
★KF,LF,TV in guest room, pool table, bar, parking ✋No pets
〰some French
🏃 Bow River with adjoining park & mountain view, bicycle/walking path, bus service
🚗 LRT to downtown, University of Calgary, Olympic Park
🔫 Country-style home, close to spectacular Rocky mountains, situated on a quiet pretty residential street on the western side of the city fringe with quick access to Banff Hwy. 〰B&B

Romanzin, Valerie & Gerry (B&B In Meadow Splender)   ☎ & Fax (403) 288-6902
251080 Range Rd 32, Calgary, AB   T3Z 1E7   E-mail: inmeadow@cadvision.com

Phone for directions.
$60S $75D   🍽 Meals   (Reservations recommended)   ▶ 4
🍹 Full, homebaked 🏠 Rural, raised bungalow, acreage, view from guest rooms, quiet ■ 1D,1Ste (ground level) ⊨ 2Q
🛏1Private,1ensuite ★TV in great room, F/fridge & microwave, guest library, separate entrance, guest quarters are separate ✋No smoking 〰some French
🏃 Bow River, fishing, horseback riding, golfing & driving range, country walks, small aircraft flights, local artisan crafts, landscaped garden
🚗 Calgary, Zoo, Olympic Venues, Western Heritage Centre, Bragg Creek & Cochrane village shops, whitewater rafting, Kananaskis Country, Canmore, Banff, skiing, hiking
🔫 Bright & comfortable home, tastefully decorated with fine furniture, Western art and country ambiance. Crafts & wares of local artisans are displayed throughout the house. Enjoy the tranquil landscape of rural life and spectacular panoramic view of the Canadian Rocky Mountains. Breakfast is served in guest dining area. There is a cat in residence. Visa,MC 〰B&B

Russell, Elva B. (Russell's Bed & Breakfast)   ☎ (403) 249-8675
2806 Linden Dr SW, Calgary, Alta   T3E 6C2

Located just north of Glenmore Reservoir/Glenmore Park & 6 blocks south of Crowchild Trail/Glenmore intersection southwest.
$45S $80D   ▶ 7
🍹 Choice 🏠Res., 2-storey, quiet ■3(upstairs) ⊨3T,1D
🛏1sh.w.g. ★F,TV, parking ✋No pets, restricted smoking,
🏃 Glenmore Reservoir & Park, bus stops, restaurants, shopping
🚗 Downtown, Performing Arts Center, Glenbow Museum, Heritage & Prehistoric Parks, Calgary Zoo, Kananaskis Country
🔫 Comfortable & spacious executive home, tastefully decorated, situated in quiet residential area. Informed hosts can help with travel plans, tours, directions in this beautiful busy city and interesting, picturesque areas nearby. Enjoy gracious Western hospitality. 〰CC

Calgary (cont'd)

Seetal, Josephine & Raghu (Shangarry B&B)   ☎ (403) 271-5704, Fax 278-9364
432 Wilderness Dr. SE, Calgary, AB   T2J 1Z2   E-mail: shangarry@canada.com

Phone for directions.
$70S $85-95D $20Add.person   ►6
Not Dec20-Jan3   Full, homebaked   Sub, bungalow, patio   3D (main & lower level)   2T,1D,1Q   Sh.w.g. ★ LF, table tennis, Grand Piano, off-street parking   No smoking, no pets, inquire about children
Large shopping centre, library, Leisure Centre with wave pool, restaurants, bus route to Light Rail Transit
Downtown, Stampede, Spruce Meadows, Calgary Zoo, Fish Creek Park (walking/biking)
Warm and friendly hosts in bright, spacious and elegant home, backing onto private golf course and situated in a unique Canadian City. Relax on the patio overlooking the golf course or feel free to tinkle the ivories on the grand piano in the living room. Hostess is originally from Dublin and enjoys sharing life and cooking with guests. A traditional breakfast (including Irish Fry) is served in guest breakfast room. House specialty is Newfoundland pancakes. There is a small dog in residence. Visa ✓B&B   www-5.cybersurf.net/~jseetal

---

Sharpe, Marde (Bankview House B&B)   ☎ & Fax (403) 245-5385
1809-21 Ave SW, Calgary, AB   T2T 0N5   E-mail: bankviewhouse@home.com

Phone for directions.
$75S $85D $10Child $95F $15Add.person   ►4A,2Ch
Full, homebaked   Downtown, 2-storey, hist., view from guest rooms, swimming pool, koi pond, patio, porch, deck, quiet, secluded   1D,Ste,1F (upst)   2Q,1P   2Private, 1ensuite   ★ Air, F, TV & bar-fridge in guest rooms, private entrance, internet & fax service, off-street parking   No smoking, no pets, children min. age 6
17th Ave (art galleries, boutiques, antique shops), many great restaurants, Stampede Grounds
Kananaskis Country, Banff, Cochrane
Centrally located home, built in 1913 with elegant Edwardian charm and tin ceilings. Relax in the secret garden or in the heated inground pool, listening to the water falling into the koi pond. Breakfast is served in sepearate guest breakfast room. Featured in several magazine articles. Suitable for business clientele. There is a dog in residence.   www.bbcanada.com/2885.html

---

West Margaret (Riverpark Bed & Breakfast)   ☎ (403)257-0757
86 Mountain Park Dr SE, Calgary, AB   T2Z 1S1   Fax(403)257-5830, Cell(403)807-2599

Phone for directions.
$50S $65-70D $15Add.person   ►4-5
Full, homebaked   Res., 2-storey, view from guest rooms, patio, deck, quiet   1D(upstairs), 1Ste(lower level)
2Q,R,futon   2Private   ★F,TV in guest room, phone for guests's use, private sitting room, off-street parking   No smoking, no pets, no children
Walking, cycling, lovely nature trails along the river with great abundance of Canada Geese, bus stop (#93) to Light Rail Transit
Downtown, Spruce Meadows Equestrian Center, Stampede Grounds, Canada Olympic Park
Spacious modern home with grounds bordering on park. Congenial hosts know the area well. Located 10 min from the Spruce Meadows Equestrian Center. Enjoy scrumptious breakfasts.

Calgary (cont'd)

Whittaker, Carol & Earle (Big Springs Estate B&B) ☎ (403) 948-5264, Fax (403) 948-5851
RR1, Airdrie, AB T4B 2A3   E-mail: bigsprings@bigsprings-bb.com, 1-888-948-5851

$90-125S/D $25Add.person (plus taxes)   ►6
From Airdrie travel 12km west on Hwy 567, south 2.8km and west 7km. From Cochrane travel
8km north on Hwy 22 and east 14.4km on Hwy 567. (30km from Calgary Airport and fast on
country roads).
🍳 Full (Gourmet)   🏠 Rural, bungalow, hillside, acreage, deck,
patio, quiet, secluded   ■ 5D (ground level
walk-out) ⊨1D,1K,3Q,1S   ⊇3Ensuite,2private   ★ F,LF,TV
in guest lounge, thermomasseur tub & pedestral sink in exquisite
Bridal Suite, sep.entrance, hot-tub under the stars, sauna, piano,
guest quarters are separate   ⓦ Smoking outside, no pets
🏃 Private nature path (leisure walks on 35 pastoral acres in
hillside valley), explore rock outcroppings and wild flowers, ideal photographing
🚗 Calgary, Airport, Banff, Kananaskis Country, Banff-Canmore Corridor, Airport
🐾 5500 sqft secluded home situated on 35acres in a private peaceful setting, overlooking a valley.
Relax in the English Garden sitting room with furniture groupings arranged so the garden
atmosphere continues to the surrounding green of the outdoors. Silver service gourmet breakfast is
served in the dining room. Hosts are certified and experienced cooks. Ideal place for first & last
night stay for mountain vacations and insure quick & easy access to airport.
Romantic/corporate/weekend packages available. Visa,MC ✓B&B www.bigsprings-bb.com

---

Wood, Dori (Lions Park Bed & Breakfast)   ☎ (403) 282-2728, Fax (403) 289-3485
1331-15 St NW, Calgary, AB T2N 2B7   E-mail: doriwood@home.com, 1-800-475-7262

Phone for directions. Located 2 blocks south of TCH, between downtown & UofC.
$70-85S $75-125D $10Add.person   ►7
🍳 Full, homebaked   🏠 Downtown, res., 2-storey, view
■1D,1F(upstairs), plus 1Ste ⊨3S,1D,2K   ⊇1Private,
2ensuite ★F,LF,TV in guest living room, sep entrance, air filter,
parking ⓦNo pets, no smoking
🏃 Jubilee Auditorium, S.A.I.T., University of Calgary , North Hill
Shopping Centre, Riley & Conf.Parks, Bus & Light Rail Train
Systems, Kensington, Eau Claire Market, downtown, Planetarium
🚗 Canada Olympic Park, Bragg Creek, Canmore, Kananaskis, Calgary Zoo, airport, Calaway &
Heritage Parks, Spruce Meadows, Banff, Dinasaur Provincial Park
🐾 Long-time hostess in spacious executive home in central location. Enjoy a nutritious
breakfast, served in private dining room or in the garden. Ideal place for business or vacation
travellers. Relax in the comfortable atmosphere. Visa,MC ✓B&B www.lionsparkbb.com

---

Zorn, Barb & Gary (Hilltop Ranch B&B)   ☎ 1-800-801-0451
Box 54, Priddis, AB T0L 1W0   E-mail: hilltopr@cybersurf.net

Located at 24202-178 Ave SW, Calgary and 25km south-west of the city of Calgary on Hwy 22X.

$60-75S $75-95D $30Child/Add.person   ►8
🍳 Full, homebaked   🏠 Rural, bungalow, hillside, acreage, view,
patio, deck, quiet, secluded   ■ 2D,1F(ground level)
⊨2S,1D,2Q   ⊇ 2Ensuite,1private   ★ F,TV,KF,LF, guest
lounge, guest quarters are separate   ⓦ Designated smoking area,
children min. age 4
🏃 Hiking, golfing, wildlife & bird watching
🚗 Banff, Kananaskis Recreation area & Park, Spruce Meadows, Calgary downtown, Stampede
🐾 Warm welcome and Western hospitality on beautiful hobby ranch surrounded by 57acres and
park-like ranch setting, with view of the Rocky Mountains. Enjoy a hearty ranch breakfast in the
morning and romantic walks under stars and moon in the evening. Carriage & sleigh rides
available. There is a Boxer dog and a cat in residence. Overnight horse stabling available in eight
new box stalls. CCards ✓B&B www.discoveralberta.com/hilltop/

Camrose

(south-east of Edmonton; see also Sedgewick)

Taylor, Elaine & David (College Lane B&B)
4602-49 St., Camrose, AB T4V 1M5

☎ (780) 672-2882
E-mail: drtent@telusplanet.net

$55-65S $65-75D $10Add.person ◖◗Meals (plus tax) ► 6

From Hwy13(48Ave),south on 50St,east on 47Ave,south on 49St.
🍽 Full 🏠 Downtown, hist., porch, quiet ■ 2D,1Ste(upst)
⊨2D,1Q 🛏 1Private, 2,ensuite ★ TV,LF,separate entrance,
off-street parking 🐾No smoking, no pets
🚶 paved hiking trails (15km), x-c ski trails, Augustana University
College, shopping, Camrose Historical Museum
🚙 Edmonton, museums (Ukrainian Heritage, Reynolds, Donalda
Antique Lamps), Steam Train rides, world's smallest airport

🐽 Fully renovated heritage (1912) home furnished with antiques and situated on large treed lot
bordering the College Campus. Well travelled hosts enjoy exchanging travel stories with guests
from around the world. Experience a small city in the unique parkland of central Alberta and learn
about the area pioneers. Breakfast is served in special guest breakfast room. Visa

---

Canmore

(west of Calgary; see also Banff)

Ciaramidaro, Carmelo & Anneke (Stella-Alpina B&B)
1009-9th Ave, Canmore, AB T1W 1Z5

☎ & Fax (403) 678-2119
E-mail: martino@agt.net

Phone for directions.
$70S $79D $25Add.person ► 4A,2Ch
🍽Full 🏠Downtown, split-level, view from guest rooms,quiet
■1Ste,1F (lower level) ⊨ 2S,2Q 🛏 2Private with jacuzzi tubs
★F,LF,TV in rooms, off-street park., guest area is sep. x-c ski
waxing facility 〜Italian/Dutch/German/French/Spanish
🚶 Bow River with great walking trails, excellent fishing & hiking
& mountain biking, public tennis court, downtown Canmore, excellent restaurants, art galleries
🚙 Banff, Banff National Park, Lake Louise, several major ski resorts, Nordic Ski Centre
🐽 Quiet home with rustic interior, spruce woodwork throughout, located on a cul-de-sac across
from a wooded reserve. Hosts have a wealth of international hospitality experience, including on
cruise ships world-wide, and are very knowledgeable about the area's flora and fauna. Special
gourmet breakfast includes smoked salmon, wild mushroom/and or herb omelette with herbs from
own garden. There is a dog in residence. Children welcome. Visa, MC ⌐B&B

Clark, Roberta (Bach & Bed - A Musical Offering)
626-2nd St., Canmore, AB T1W 2K6

☎ (403) 678-2665
E-mail: -robcel@telusplanet.net

From Exits off the Trans Canada Highway, follow signs to the
Town Centre (Main Street). Turn left on 7th Ave, left on 2nd St.
$85D ►2
🍽 Full, homebaked 🏠 Downtown, 2-storey, quiet, views
■1D (main floor) ⊨1Q 🛏 1Private ★ Separate entrance,
garage parking 🐾 No smoking, no pets, children welcome
🚶 Main street stores, restaurants, Bow River Valley walking
🚙 Nordic Centre, golf courses, x-c & downhill skiing

🐽 Bavarian-style home nestled among Spruce & Alberta Wild Rose. Hostess teaches music and
loves guiding her guests to the activities they are interested in. Plenty of delicacies served for
breakfast. Resident cats are comfortable with guests & wild rabbits relax on the lawn. ⌐B&B

Canmore (cont'd)

Cole, Alan & Sharon (McNeill Heritage Inn)   ☎ & Fax (403) 678-4884
500 Three Sisters Dr., Canmore, AB   T1W 2P3

$100S/D(winter) $135S/D(summer) $10Add.person   (plus tax)   ► 13
From TCH travel through Canmore on 8th (Main) St.Turn left on 8th Ave, crossing the Bow River
on Rundle Dr., then right on Three Sisters Dr.

🍴 Full, homebaked   🏠 Village, 2-storey, hist., acreage, view,
riverfront, porch, quiet, secluded ■5D ⊨2T(K),4Q 🚗5Private
★F,TV room, separate entrance, off-street parking, guest quarters
are separate 🖐No smoking, no pets, not suitable for children
🕴 X-c skiing/hiking from back door, fishing, golfing, restaurants
🚗 Banff, Kananaskis Country, Lake Louise, Calgary
📣 Warm and friendly hospitality in historic home situated on the
Bow River. Relax on the veranda or by the cozy fireplace. Hosts are outdoor recreation oriented and
can advise on good places for activities. Breakfast is served in the old fashioned dining
room.Visa,MC ✓B&B

Driard, Marie-Joelle (ReNaissance B&B)   ☎ & Fax 403-678-1675
252 Lady MacDonald Dr, Canmore, AB   T1W 1H8   E-mail: renaisbb@telusplanet.net

Phone for directions.
$85S/D $10child $130Ste(for2) $20Add.person   ► 6
🍴 Full, homebaked   🏠 Res., 2-storey, view from guest rooms,
patio, deck, quiet ■1D,1Ste (upper & ground level walkout)
⊨2Q,P 🛏 1Private, 1sh.w.h. ★ LF,F,TV & private entrance
in suite, off-street/street parking 🖐 No smoking, no pets,
inquire about children 〰 French
🕴 Cougar Creek & Canyon, hiking trails, mountain biking, Alpine Club of Canada
🚗Downtown, shops, restaurants, museums, golfing, back country outings, Nordic Center, hiking,
x-c/downhill skiing, Banff, National & Provincial parks, Banff Centre for the Arts, Banff Springs
Hotel, Kananaskis Country, Lake Louise, Spray Lakes, City of Calgary
📣 Charming and bright new home situated on Mount Lady MacDonald & Grotto Mountain
Foothills in quiet location with a beautiful view of the Rockies. Hostess is an artist and outdoor
enthusiast with experience in the toursim industry. Enjoy a hearty breakfast before a day of
travelling or outdoor activities. Visa ✓B&B www.bbcanada.com/1096.html

---

Ess, Bob & Gabi (Amble Inn)   ☎ & Fax (403) 678-6497
438-2nd St., Canmore, AB   T1W 2K4

From Hwy 1 follow signs to business district (8th St). Turn south, toward Three Sisters Mountain
onto 2nd St. Proceed to B&B on corner of 4th Ave. (Parking on 4th Ave side).

$80S $98D $20Child/Add.person   ► 4
❋ Summer only 🍴 Full (Gourmet) 🏠 Downtown, 2-storey,
view from guest rooms, deck, quiet ■ 2D (main floor) ⊨2K
🛏 2Private ★ F,TV, guest room airconditioners, private
entrance, wheel-chair access, jacuzzi, guest quarters are
separate 🖐No smoking, no pets 〰 German
🕴 Town Center, restaurants, unique shops, galleries, creek &
river walks
📣 Warm welcome in large home with balconies and magnificient views located in the heart of the
Eastern Slopes of the Canadian Rockies. After a day spent visiting the attractions or using the
recreational opportunities, relax in comfortable surroundings. Special diets can be accommodated.
Breakfast is served in guest breakfast room. There is a small dog in residence ✓B&B

Canmore (cont'd)

Foff, Vera & Mark (Grandview Chalet)
112 McNeill Dr., Canmore, AB T1W 2R8

☎ (403)678-9911 Fax:(403)678-9923
E-mail: foff@telusplanet.net

From downtown Canmore follow signs to "Spray Lakes" and "Nordic Center". At the turn continue straight and take first left onto Carey Dr & left again on McNeill Dr. Look for 3 flags on balcony.

$70-100S/D $10Child/Add.person   ►4
🔴 Full   🏠 Res., 2-storey, view from guest rooms, quiet
■2D   ⊨2Q   🛏2Ensuite   ★ F,TV in guest rooms, private entrance, off-street parking, guest quarters are separate, tea room with fireplace   ⊘ No smoking, no pets   ∞French,German
🏃 Bow River Embankment, downtown, restaurants, shops, Nordic Centre (built for 1988 Olympic Games in Calgary)
🚐 Banff, Spray Lakes, Kananaskis, Lake Louise, Sunshine

🐾 "Empty nester" with European background in new executive chalet in quiet neighborhood with magnificient views of the Rocky Mountains. Hosts love to ski, hike, bike, play tennis and bridge. Table tennis champions (discout for anyone who can beat them). Distinctive sign of the house is the three flags hanging off the main balcony. Breakfast served in special guest breakfast room. There is a German Shepherd "Cayla" in residence. Visa ✔B&B www.grandviewchalet.com

---

Gailus, Andrea & Fred (Cougar Canyon Bed & Breakfast)
3 Canyon Rd., Canmore, AB T1W 1G3

☎ & Fax (403) 678-6636
E-mail: gailusaf@telusplanet.net, 1-800-289-9731

Location: 3 Canyon Rd. From TCH1 exit at Hwy 1A Canmore. Follow Hwy 1A toward Exshaw, turn left at Elk Run Blvd. Proceed to Canyon Rd and turn right. Look for house on left.

$75-95S/D   ►4
🔴Full(Gourmet)   🏠Res., 2-storey, view, patio, quiet, back creek
■2(upper level)   ⊨ 2T,1Q   🛏 2Ensuite   ★F,TV/VCR, library in guest loft ⊘No smoking, no pets   ∞German
🏃 Cougar Canyon hiking trail at back door
🚐 Town centre, shopping, casual/fine dining, galleries, Bow River trout fishing, Mordic Center downhill/x-c skiing, mountain biking, Banff Nat.Park, Sulphur Hot Springs, Kananaskis

🐾 Modern home especially designed for B&B, with beautiful mountain views, situated on the sunny side of town. Tea & coffee are provided in the cozy guest loft. Share the fireplace at breakfast around the dining room table. Well travelled family enjoys skiing & hiking. Calgary airport pick-up available. There are resident pets. Visa,MC ✔B&B www.canadianrockies.net/cougarcanyon

---

Herspiegel (Off Our Rockies B&B)
175 McNeill, Canmore, AB T1W 2R9

☎ & Fax (403) 609-3009
E-mail: rockies@telusplanet.net

Phone for directions.
$90-110D $20Child/Add.person   (winter rate available)   ►5A
🔴 Full   🏠 Res, 2-storey, view, patio, deck, quiet   ■2D(ground level)
⊨2Q   🛏 2Ensuite   ★ TV, coffee room, guest deck   ⊘ No smoking, no pets, no children   ∞ German
🏃 National Trail, Bow River and embankment, Nordic Center, Canmore (quaint shopping/restaurants), x-c skiing, golfing
🚐 Banff & Banff National Park, Lake Louise, Kananaskis, 5 world class downhill ski resorts, Calgary
🐾 Fabulous new home located at the base of Nakoda Egaday Mountain - surrounded by some of the most picturesque scenery in the world. Take a walk from the backdoor and into wilderness. Hosts love to pamper their guests. Breakfast is served in guest breakfast room. There is a dog in residence. ✔B&B www.offourrockies.com

Canmore (cont'd)

Hyink, Matt & Christine (An Eagle's View B&B)   ☎ & Fax (403) 678-3264, 1-877-609-3887
6 Eagle Landing, Canmore, AB   T1W 2Y1   E-mail: eaglelan@telusplanet.net

Take Town Centre Exit. Turn left at lights (Benchland Trail), then right again on Eagle Landing.
$100S $110D $20Child/Add.person   (Off-season discounts)   ▶ 4A,2Ch

🍽 Full, homebaked   🏠 Res., 2-storey, view, patio, deck, quiet
■2D (main & street level)   ⊨2Q,cot,crib   ⬛2Ensuite
★LF,F, private entrance, guest sitting room, guest quarters are
separate   ⊕ No smoking, no pets   〰 Dutch
🚶 Cougar Creek area (hiking/walking), downtown with quaint
shops & restaurants, Silvertip Golf Course (extreme golfing)
🚐 Banff, Banff Nat.Park, Lake Louise, Kananaskis Wilderness
Area, Nordic Centre, excellent downhill ski and hiking areas
📣 Quiet and luxurious home with friendly atmosphere and surrounded by spectacular mountain
splendor located in new neighborhood. Relax in the comfortable guest sitting room after a busy day.
Special diets considered with notification. Breakfast is served in guest breakfast room. CCards
✔B&B   www.aneaglesview.com

Kamenka, Pat & Ann (Hidden Falls B&B)   ☎ (403) 678-3604, Fax (403) 678-6594
Box 8073, Canmore, AB   T1W 2T8   E-mail: info@hiddenfalls.com, 1-888-678-3600

Located at 107 Three Sisters Dr. From Hwy 1 proceed to downtown (Main St). Turn left at 8th Ave

and follow Nordic Centre signs. Look for house on right (sign).
$110S/D   (Special rates for 3nights min.)   ▶ 8
🍽 Full   🏠 Res., 3-storey, view from guest rooms, waterfall at
back, deck, quiet, secluded   ■4D(upstairs)   ⊨2T,3Q
⬛4Ensuite ★F,TV in guest lounge, separate entrance, two guest
rooms with balconies, outdoor firepit, off-street parking   ⊕No
smoking, no pets, children min. age 12
🚐 Banff, Kananaskis Country, Lake Louise, Calgary
🚶 Olympic Nordic Centre, Beaver dam, hiking/cycling and x-c ski trails, fishing, waterfall
📣 New, bright, large home in unique setting with park-like privacy. Enjoy the stunning views
and soothing sound of the falls at night. Hosts are longtime area residents and gladly help with
sightseeing & activity plans. Rooms are named after area mountains. Relax on the large property by
the little brook or by the old barn - a painter's delight. Breakfast is served in special guest breakfast
room. Spectacular scenery & frequent wildlife visits make this an ideal place for photography
buffs.   www.hiddenfalls.com

Mazzucchi, Albert and Connie (Bird's Nest)   ☎ (403) 678-2294
1005-15th Street, Canmore, Alberta   T1W 1V3

Canmore is located 22 km east of Banff. Phone for directions.
$65D $15Add.person   ▶ 3
🍽Choice, homebaked   🏠Res., bi-level, view, patio, quiet
■1(lower level)   ⊨1S,1Q   ⬛Private   ★TV,parking   ⊕No
pets, no smoking, child min age 8   〰Italian, German
🚶 Nordic Centre, museum, hiking trails, excellent dining facilities
🚐 Banff, Lake Louise, 5 major ski resorts, 200km x-c ski trails
📣 Friendly atmosphere in home located in new area abundant
with recreational facilities and excellent services and circled by the rugged Rockies. Enjoy a hearty
breakfast and watch the many different species of birds hosts love to feed.

Canmore (cont'd)

Middleton, John & Joan (By the Brook B&B)   ☎ (403) 678-4566, Fax (403) 678-4199
4 Birchwood Place, Canmore, AB T1W 1P9   E-mail: b+b@expertcanmore.net

Phone for directions.
$85S $115D $20Add.person (Off-season rates available)   ▶ 5A
◑ Full, homebaked 🏠 Res., 3-storey, view from guest rooms,
quiet, 2 decks ■ 2F(main floor) ⊨ 1S,2Q ⌑2Ensuite
★LF,F,TV/ceiling fans in guest rooms, off-street parking 🖐 No
smoking, no pets, not suitable for children
🧍 Downtown, restaurants, galleries, shops, walkway system along
mountain stream, golfing, x-c skiing, hiking, fishing

🚗 Five Ski Hills, Banff, Kananaskis Country, dog-sled rides, snowmobiling, white water rafting
🎿 Large modern home with Bay window sitting areas in guest rooms and tranquil environment.
Relax in the hot tub or sauna or by the fireplace. Experienced travellers (hiking, biking, skiing,
fishing in the area) hosts are happy to help with guests plans and itineraries. Breakfast is served in
special guest breakfast room. Gift Certificates available. Visa,MC ↙B&B

Okamoto, Hisashi(Jack) & Hiroko(Jill) (Spring Creek B&B) ☎(403)678-6726,Fax 5877
1002-3rd Ave., Canmore, Alta T1W 2J8   E-mail: hokamoto@expertcanmore.net

Located on corner of 1st St and 3rd Ave.
$75-95D (minimum booking 2 nights)   ▶ 6
◑ Choice 🏠Res., view, patio, quiet, isolated ■2D(upstairs)
⊨2Q,2P,2T ⌑ 2Ensuite, 1private ★LF,TV in guest sitting
room, guest quarters are solely on 2nd floor. parking 🖐No pets,
no smoking 〰 Japanese
🧍 Bow River, dining, golfing, hiking, skiing, shops, watch wildlife
graze nearby, white water rafting, helicopter tours

🚗 Calgary, Banff, Chair-lift to Sulphour Spring, Lake Louise, Kananaskis Country, skiing, hiking,
🎿 Bright, spacious home built especially for B&B on Spring Creek nestled under picturesque
Three Sisters Mountain in the Bow Valley. Enjoy the fresh air and pure water and the beautiful
mountain views from guest room windows. Host is a retired airline pilot and photographer and
hostess is a flower arrangement & Japanese brush-writing teacher and good at Koto harp playing.
Large format pictures are displayed throughout the house. Full breakfast is served in the main
dining room on the first floor. Visa,MC ↙B&B http://www.expertcanmore.net/springcreek

---

Segstro, Jac (Jac'N'Sarah's B&B)   ☎ & Fax (403) 678-2770, 1-800-600-3816
10 Riverview Place, Canmore, AB T1W 2B9

Please call for directions.
$50S $75-85D $20Add.person $5-10Child   ▶ 8
◑ Choice, homebaked 🏠Res.,views,quiet cul-de-sac,large decks
■2D,1Ste ⊨3Q,2T ⌑1Sh.w.g. plus tub,1sh.w.h. ★F,LF,KF,
large skylight in #2 guest room for starlit views from beds, separate
entrance 🖐No smoking 〰Dutch,some French & German
🧍 Quiet and scenic walks at the doorstep, restaurants, galleries, gift
shops, dike holding back the Bow River (at back door step)

🚗 Nordic Centre, Hot Springs, hiking, mountaineering, skiing, Banff Nat.Park, Kananaskis
🎿 "Rooms with a difference - Hospitality with a flair". House is situated on a quiet cul-de-sac
which backs onto the Bow River with a beautiful view of the Rocky Mountains and Foothills. Ideal
place to use as a base from which to experience the Kananaskis, Bow Valley, Banff & Lake Louise
areas of the Rocky Mountains. Host is a marriage commissioner and performs civil marriages.
Early reservation recommended. Two-day min. stay during high season. There is a dog in residence.

Canmore (cont'd)

Tarnowski, Roseanne & Grant (The Quilters Inn) ☎ & Fax (403) 678-6785
702-2nd St., Canmore, AB T1W 2K7 E-mail: quilters@telusplanet.net

From Main Street (8th St) in Canmore, turn left at 7th Ave. Proceed to 2nd St, turn left and continue to house on left (at stop sign). Located at corner of 6thAve & 2ndSt. Look for quilt flags.

$55S $75D ► 4A
Full, homebaked Downtown, 3-storey, view from guest rooms, quiet ■ 2D (lower level) 2T,1K 1Sh.w.g. ★ TV in guest sitting room, guest robes, separate entrance, off-street parking, guest quarters are separate No smoking , no pets, not suitable for children
Downtown shops, restaurants, Bow River, extensive walking trail system, helicopter tours, fabric shop
Nordic Center, Banff Nat.Park, Bragg Creek, Kananaskis Country, Calgary, Sunshine & Lake Louise world class ski resorts
Warm welcome and friendly hospitality in contemporary-style home decorated with family treasures, antiques and quilts. Hostess is a quilter and Home Economist. Studio space and classes are available. Enjoy the beautiful mountain setting, providing peace, serenity and inspiration. Ideal place for two couples. ✓B&B

Carstairs

(north of Calgary; see also Cochrane)

Carroll, Lynn & Terry (Gray Fox Ranch & Bed & Breakfast) ☎ (403) 337-3192
RR2, Carstairs, AB T0M 0N0 E-mail: barfx@cadvision.com

From Hwy 2 north of Calgary proceed on Hwy 2A, west on Rte 580.
$60S $70-85D ► 8A
Full Farm, ranch-style, 2-storey, porch, quiet ■ 3D (upstairs) 2T,2Q 1Sh.w.g,1ensuite (clawfoot soaking tubs) ★ F,LF, separate entrance, library, reading room, old fashioned cookstove No pets, desig.smoking area, no children
Sign Language
Nature walks on ranch
4 Golf courses, fishing, horseback riding, white water rafting, rodeos
Victorian-style farmhouse with special ambiance of Elegance & Romance on a working cattle ranch. Decorated in English Country and situated in rolling farmland dotted with trees & wildlife close to the mountains & Banff. A wonderful place to relax and rejuvenate while creating that very special memory. Silver service gourmet breakfast served at guests' convenience.

Cochrane

(north-west of Calgary; see also Carstairs)

Degraw, Neil & Marilyn (Mountview Cottage B&B) ☎ (403) 932-4586, Cell (403) 660-5268
Box 8,S4,RR1, Cochrane, AB T0L 0W0 E-mail: degraw@nucleus.com

Proceed north through Cochrane on Hwy 22. Turn left at first road and drive 4.4km, turn left at stop sign. Continue 1km, turn left at Mountview Estates. Look for B&B sign in front of No27.

$55S $75D $20Add.person ► 6
Full, homebaked Rural, hillside, view, acreage, deck, quiet
■3D(main & ground level) 3Q,cot 2Sh.w.g. ★TV,F, outdoor hot-tub, pool-table Desig.smoking area, no pets
Cochrane, rodeos, Calaway Amusement Park, Calgary, Fortress Ski Resort, Kananaskis Country, craft & specialty shops, Spruce Meadows horse jumping, golfing
Warm welcome and friendly hospitality in comfortable home, situated in a park-like setting with a beautiful view of valley and mountains (180 degree on the horizon). Stroll the large grounds, rest on a bench and take in the country atmosphere and "the most magnificient view in the West". There is a corral for horses. ✓B&B
http://www.bbexpo.com/ab/mountview.htm

Cochrane (cont'd)

Howell, Ray & Fran (Timber Trail)   ☎ & Fax (403) 932-4995
Box 1313, Cochrane, AB T0L 0W0

From Calgary, take Hwy 1A west to Cochrane. Continue west on Hwy 1A for 7 km. Turn on Grand Valley Rd and follow for 21 km. Turn at red barn mailbox and proceed 1km.

$45S $75D   ▶4
🍴 Full, homebaked 🏠 Farm, Cape Cod, 2-storey, acreage, isolated ■2D(upstairs) ⊨1D,1Q 🛏1Sh.w.g. ★F,TV,LF, front porch swing, parking
🧍 Farm animals & ostrich on grounds, birdwatching, walks & x/c skiing on forested trails
🚗 Cochrane, craft & art shops, 3 golf courses, Banff, Calgary & Cochrane shopping, restaurants, Stampede, Kananaskis Country

🐎 Warm welcome on horse,cattle & ostrich ranch with Cape-Cod country farm house nestled in a spruce and pine forest. Breakfast is served on the front porch or back deck, weather permitting. Relax on the front porch swing. Rooms are named "Cowboy's Roost" (old west-style) and "Cowgirl's Dream" (flowers & country antiques). ✏B&B

Peterson, Elsa & Mike Madsen (Dickens Inn B&B) ☎ (403) 932-3945,Fax 932-9775
RR1, Cochrane, AB T0L 0W0   E-mail: dickens@nucleus.com

From Hwy 1, take Cochrane Turnoff (Hwy 22) and drive north to Hwy 1A. Go west 2 km to Horse Creek Rd. Turn north 7km.

$75-85S $85-95D   ▶6
🍴 Full, homebaked 🏠 Rural, 2-storey, acreage, view from guest rooms, porch, quiet, isolated ■ 3D (upstairs) ⊨ 3Q (four-posters) 🛏 3Ensuite ★ F,TV Ⓦ Designated smoking area, no pets, no children
🚗 Town of Cochrane, Kananaskis Country, Canmore, Calgary, Banff Nat. Park (hiking, skiing)

🐎 Large, beautifully decorated Victorian-style home, designed and built as a B&B, with a panoramic view of surrounding mountains. Relax on the wrap-around porch. Well travelled and informed hosts enjoy crafts and woodworking. Ideal country getaway. Visa,MC ✏B&B
www.bbexpo.com/ab/dickens.htm

Crooked Creek   *(east of Grand Prairie; see also Peace River)*

Isaac, Flo (Flo's Country Cottage B&B & Home Bakery) ☎ & Fax (780) 957-2508
RR1, S3, Box1, Crooked Creek, AB T0H 0Y0 E-mail: flosbnb@hotmail.com

$50S $65D $10Child $15Add.person (plus tax) 🍽 Meals ▶6
Located between Grand Prairie & Valleyview, south of Hwy43 on the paved Ridge Valley Rd (on route to Alaska).

🍴 Full, homebaked 🏠 Village, Cape Cod 2-storey, view from guest rooms, porch, quiet ■ 1Ste (upstairs) ⊨ 1D,1Q,1P
🛏1Private (for suite) ★F, ceiling fans, off-street parking, guest quarters are the whole upstairs Ⓦ Designated smoking area, no pets 〰 some Spanish & Dutch, American sign language
🧍 Bison Ranch, Country Stiches Quilt Shop, coffee shop, fire pit in backyard, bakery on site
🚗 Swan Lake (full of trout), Sturgean Lake (boating, fishing), hiking, golfing, picnicking

🐎 Warm welcome in "Country Cottage" with warm interior, enhanced by the aroma of fresh baking and surrounded by flower beds and shrubs and vines climbing the veranda posts. Located in the hamlet of Ridge Valley. The little bakery is at the side of the house. Hostess bakes breads, & cinamon rolls for sale from the home, and on weekends for the Grand Prairie farmers' market. Enjoy an evening snack at the kitchen table or in the guest sitting room upstairs. One party only at a time. There is a dog and a cat in residence. Visa ✏B&B www.vvw-teg.net/flosbnb

Drumheller
(north-east of Calgary)

Hamilton, Norah & M.Robertson (The Inn at Heartwood Manor) ☎(403)823-6495
320 N.Railway East, Drumheller, AB T0J 0Y4 1-888-823-6495, Fax (403)823-4935
E-mail: heartinn@telusplanet.net
Coming from Calgary go straight through to the 4-way stop, turn left, and proceed two blocks down

on the right side. $79S $89-179D
$10Add.person (+tax) ▣Extra
▣ Full 🏠 Downtown, hist. ■ 4S,15D,1Ste,11F main & upper
levels ⊨ 1S,10D,12Q,3K,3cots ⚷Private ★ Air,Fs,TV in
guest rooms, ceiling fans, jet tubs, 4private entrances, wheel-chair
access, off-street/street parking ⓦDesignated smoking area
〰 some French
🏃 Fossil Museum, Aquaplex, Reptile World

🚗 Royal Tyrrell Museum, Roseland Dinner Theatre, East Coulee School Museum, half-day and
full-day Digs
🐾 Originally built before 1921 and refashioned, large Country Inn with fashionable rooms and
eclectic mix of new and old, suitable for romantic holidays, as well as business stays. Full Manor Spa
Packages offered. Breakfast is served in special guest breakfast room. Champagne breakfast is
available. Families welcome. Visa/MC http://www.discoveralberta.com/heartwoodmanor

---

Nimmo, Bryce & Rosalie (Taste the Past B&B) ☎(403)823-5889,Fax(403)823-4516
281-2nd St.W.Box 865. Drumheller, AB T0J 0Y0 E-mail: taste@telusplanet.net,

Phone for directions.
$60S $75D $10Add.person ►6
▣Gourmet 🏠Downtown, 3-storey, hist., veranda ■3D
⊨2T,2Q,cot ⚷ 3Private ★ Guest room, off-street parking in
rear ⓦ Smoking outside
🏃 Red Deer River, waterpark, tennis court, bicycle/walking paths,
restaurants, shops

🚗 Royal Tyrrell Museum, scenic canyons, Hoo Doos, Badlands, golf course, trail rides
🐾 Spacious turn-of-the-Century brick home, one of the areas original grand mansions, renovated
and restored with antique decor and romantic atmosphere. Specialty breakfast is served in sunny
breakfast room. Energetic hosts are knowledgeable on local tourism. Visa,MC

Edmonton
(see also Spruce Grove)

Amyotte, Emile & Jeannine Roy (L'Amy du Roy B&B) ☎ (780) 465-3225, Fax(780)462-9651
8514-86 Ave, Edmonton, AB T6C 1J5 E-mail: amyduroy@telusplanet.net

Located in s/e Edmonton, beside Bonnie Doon Shopping Centre.
$50S $60D $10child ►6A,2Ch
▣ Full, homebaked 🏠 Res., bungalow, deck, quiet ■2D,1F
(lower level) ⊨1D,1Q,1R,crib ⚷ 1sh.w.g., 1private
★LF,TV in guest sitting room, coffee/snack station for guests,
off-street parking ⓦSmoking on deck, no pets 〰 French
🏃 Shopping Centre, Old Strathcona, St.Jean Faculty (UofA),
Edmonton Transit

🚗 Downtown, Coliseum, Muttart Conservatory, West Edmonton Mall, Convention Centre
🐾 Retired couple in new, spacious and sunny home situated in quiet cul-de-sac in the heart of the
Francophone area. French Canadian-style breakfast served in the spacious kitchen or on deck,
weather permitting. Guest accommodation is in bright full lower level. Children of all ages
welcome. MC ✔B&B http://www.bbexpo.com

Bayne, Bill & Anna (Victorian Rose B&B)   ☎ (780)903-0242, Fax (780)459-1306
43 Glenhaven Cr., St.Albert, AB   T8N 1A4   E-mail: vrose@icrossroads.com

Located north of Edmonton and 2km west of Hwy2 via downtown St.Albert.

$50S $65D $10Child   ► 2A,1Ch
🍳 Full, homebaked 🏠 Rural, bungalow, deck ■ 1(main floor) ⊨ 1Q,1cot 🛏 1Ensuite ★ F,TV & coffee bar in guest room, hot-tub, off-street parking 🚭 No smoking
🧍 Outdoor Farmer's Market (Western Canada's largest), historic downtown, Father Lacombe Chapel, Heritage Museum
🚐 Downtown Edmonton, West Edmonton Mall, University of A.
🎯 Warm welcome and friendly hospitality with Victorian-style atmosphere. Join the hosts in the sitting room by the cozy fireplace, or relax in the hot-tub and enjoy the outdoors after a tiring day of travelling and sightseeing. Gourmet breakfast is served in the dining room with candlelight and fire in the fireplace. Gift Certificates available. Visa ✓B&B

Brooks, Ernie & Ethel (Brooks Place B&B)   ☎ (780)438-6048 Fax437-7889,1-800 599-7770
3230-104A St., Edmonton, AB   T6J 2Z6   E-mail: brookspl@connect.ab.ca

Take Calgary Trail to 34Ave and proceed west to 106St. Turn south to 32A Ave and east to 104A St, then north.
$55S $65-75D $15Add.person   ► 6A,1-2Ch
🍳 Full, homebaked 🏠 Res., sub., 2-storey, deck,quiet ■1Ste ⊨2Q,1D 🛏1Private,1Ensuite ★LF,TV,VCR coffee bar, ceiling fans, off-street & street parking, entire 2nd floor for guests
🚭No smoking,no pets
🧍 Shopping Mall, restaurants, bowling, City bus
🚐 W.Edmonton Mall, Airport, Old Strathcona/Fringe Festival, University, Sky Reach Centre
🎯 "Empty-nester" hosts in modern southside home located on a quiet street with easy access to all attractions in the city. Hosts have welcomed people from around the world for over 30 years and draw on this experience to offer warm and sincere hospitality to their guests. Special dietary needs will be considered with advance notice. Gourmet-style breakfast is served in the dining room. Chilren under age 6 free. Family rates available. Visa ✓B&B www.bbexpo.com/ab/brooks.html

---

Carr,Ruth & Paul(Carr's Streetside Garden B&B)   ☎&Fax(780)474-7046
11318-63rd St, Edmonton, AB   T5W 4E8   1-877642RUTH(7884)
                                              E-mail: streetsidebb@compusmart.ab.ca

Phone for directions.
$50-70S/D $10Add.person   ► 4A
🍳 Full, homebaked 🏠 Res, 2-storey, hist., view of garden from guest rooms, veranda, patio ■ 3D (upstairs) ⊨1Q,2T,1D 🛏1Sh.w.g.,1private ★TV,LF, guest robes/slippers, 6-soaker tub, off-street parking 🚭No smoking, no pets
🚐 Art galleries, Muttart Conservatory, Elk Island Nat.Park (buffalo), Citadel Theatre (live), Winspear Concert Hall
🧍 Highland Historic Walking Tours (guided), paved trail network (walking & biking & x-c skiing), golfing in panoramic river valley, restaurants, unique shops
🎯 Friendly home with a unique blend of antiques and contemporary decor, a gracious retreat in a quiet neighbourhood close to Agricom & Hwy16. Gourmet-style breakfast and evening teatime are served. Guests are welcome to stroll, sit or paint in the garden. Kitty Carr is the resident cat. Visa,MC ✓B&B

Champigny, Kathy & Paul (Kountry Komfort B&B)
4601-42 St., Beaumont, AB   T4X 1H1

☎ & Fax (780) 929-2342
E-mail: kountrykomfort@home.com

Phone for directions.
$45S $55D $10Child $10Add.person   ► 4A,1Ch
▣Full   ♠Res.,small town,1.5-storey,view,deck,quiet,swimming
pool, secluded   ■1D,1F (upstairs)   ⊨1S,1D,1Q   ⊒1Sh.w.g.
★F,TV,LF, off-street parking   ⍟Smoking outside   ⌇French
⚕ Town of Beaumont, hist.church, golfing, restaurants, shops,
parks, walking trail
🚗 City of Edmonton, Int.Airport, West Edmonton Mall, U of
Alberta, Old Strathcona, Miquelon Prov. Park (swimming, boating, fishing), Ukrainian Village,
🐾 Comfortable new home backing onto a wooded area in quiet community with French Cdn
Village Theme evident in its architecture. Phone, fax, computer available for the business traveller.
Hosts are very helpful with information about area tourist attractions. Silver service breakfast
served in the dining room. Parking available for guests flying out of International Airport.
Visa ⌐B&B- www.bbcanada.com/kountrykomfort

Cooper, Linda & Alan (Chateau Memory Lane (West Edm.B&B)
8719-179th St., Edmonton, AB   T5T 0X4

☎ (780) 489-4161
Fax (780) 444-2476, 1-877-489-4161
E-mail: memorylanebb@hotmail.com

$40-45S $45-65D $10Add.person   (off-season rates/Oct-Apr)   ▣ Meals   ► 10
From West Edmonton Mall drive to 178St and west on 89Ave. Proceed south on 180St. Follow loop
around to B&B (West Edmonton B&B).

▣ Full, homebaked   ♠ Res., raised bungalow, view from guest
rooms, porch, quiet, deck   ■2S,2D,1F(main level)   ⊨2S,2D,1Q,R
⊒1Shw.g., 1sh.w.h. 1ensuite   ★ F,TV,LF,KF, games & toys for
children, off-street parking, guest quarters are separate
⍟Designated smoking area
⚕ West Edmonton Mall, excellent restaurants, Dinner Theatre,
pubs, bus terminal & airport shuttle service
🚗 Space Science Centre, Fort Edmonton Park, Old Strathcona, Stadium, Coliseum, U of A
🐾 Large home with spacious grounds and relaxing deck, located in quiet neighborhood. Congenial
hosts are happy to please and help. "Give us just one night... we will give you a memory". Breakfast
is served in special guest breakfast room. Pick-up & return from airport/bus/train available
(nominal charge). There is a small dog and a cat in residence. ⌐B&B

Hanlon-Karrel, Carol & Bryan Karrel (Karrel's Sleepover B&B)
15615-81st St., Edmonton, AB   T5Z 2T6

☎ & Fax (780) 456-5928
E-mail: karrels@compcocity.com,1-877-456-5928

Located north of 82nd St off Yellowhead Hwy.
$50-60S $60-70D $80-90F   ► 4A,3Ch
▣Full, homebaked   ♠Res, split-level, quiet, deck   ■1S,2D(upst)
⊨1S,1D,1Q   ⊒1Sh.w.g.,1ensuite   ★F,TV,ceiling fans, off-street
parking, guest quarters are separate   ⍟Desig.smoking area
⚕ Small lake & park area, bus route & LRT (Light Rail Transit)
🚗 Skyreach Center, golfing, City Centre, shopping mall,
restaurants, W.Edmonton Mall
🐾 Hearty welcome in deluxe, well appointed home in quiet residential of north end of the City.
Hosts are a retired Military couple and enjoy welcoming guests from worldwide. Enjoy the
comfortable ambiance. Relax on the deck in the pretty, secluded back yard. There is a cat.
Vis,MC ⌐B&B www.bbcanada.com/659.html

Longley, Doug & Joan (Barratt House B&B)　　☎ (780) 437-2568, fax (780) 430-1669
4204-115 St., Edmonton AB　T6J 1P4　　　　　　　E-mail: longley@telusplanet.net

Located 3 blocks south of Whitemud Freeway. From west travel to 119St, from north/south/east to
11St. Proceed to 40thAve, then to 115St, north to 42Ave.
$55-60S　$65-75D　$10Add.person　　　　　　　　　　　► 4
🍴 Full, homebaked (Gourmet)　🏠 Res., 2-storey, deck, quiet
■ 2D(upstairs)　⊨ 1D,1Q,cot　⊒ 1Private, 1ensuite
★TV,LF, off-street & street parking　🖐 Smoking on deck
🚶 Park/ravine walks, bus No50 to Southgate Transit Centre
🚗 Downtown, Airport, West Edmonton Mall, Kinsman Aquatic
Centre, over 30km paved river valley trails, University of Alberta
🔫 Attractive spacious home in quiet residential south-west area of the city. Relax in the inviting
family room or outdoors on the flower filled deck overlooking a beautiful landscaped yard. Hosts are
friendly and caring Christian couple and enjoy a warm and relaxed atmosphere. Gourmet-style
breakfast is served in the dining room. Special dietary needs will be accommodated with prior
arrangement. There is a cat in residence. Visa ✒B&B

Peske, Lothar & Yolande (Woodbend B&B)　　　☎ (780) 470-0043
9-26320 Twp Rd 514, Spruce Grove, AB　T7Y 1C8　　E-mail: woodbend@hotmail.com

Located 10km s/w of West Edmonton Mall. Call for directions.
$40S　$60D　　　　　　　　　　　　　　　　　　► 8
🍴 Full　🏠 Rural, raised bungalow, acreage, deck, quiet,
secluded　■ 2D,1F (main & lower level)　⊨2T,1Q,1K,1P,
cot,crib　⊒1Private, 2ensuite　★F,TV/VCR,guest sitting/dining
room, separate entrance, off-street parking guest quarters adjoin
main house　🖐 Smoking outside　〰German
🚶 Devonian Botanical Gardens, Clifford E.Lee Nature Sanctuary
🚗 Golf courses, West Edmonton Mall, downtown Edmonton, Spruce Grove, Stony Plain, Devon
🔫 Large Alpine-style country home with quiet and peaceful atmosphere, situated in the wood in
secluded setting. Breakfast is served in the guest breakfast room. There are outdoor dogs. Visa,MC
✒B&B　http://www.bbcanada.com/629.html

Rogers, Monica (Sentimental Journey B&B)　　☎ (780) 963-3215, Fax (780) 963-9785
24, 53103 Range Rd. 14, Stony Plain, AB　T7Z 1X2　　E-mail: monicar@telusplanet.net

Location: 6 Diamond Dr., Hubbles Lake. Situated 8.5 km west of Stony Plain on Hwys 16A. Turn
north on Range Rd 14 to Diamond Rd. Turn right, then 1st left and proceed to 6 Diamond Dr
$45S　$55D　　　　　　　　　　　　　　　　　► 4A
🍴 Full　🏠 Rural, cedar structure, view, lakefront, patio, quiet,
sun deck, spa, solarium　■2D　⊨2D(main floor)　⊒Sh.w.g.
★TV,F,LF, parking　🖐 No smoking, children min.age 12
🚶 Lakeside walking trails, swimming, cross-country skiing
🚗 West Edmonton Mall, charming town of Stony Plain, Andrew
Wolf Wine Cellars, Multicultural Heritage Centre, Victorian Tea
House, golfing
🔫 Unique accommodation in comfortable cedar cluster home with 5 roofs, built into the hillside
and situated on tranquil Hubbles Lake. Hostess is artist and a Loon enthusiast and has been
welcoming guests in her home for many years. Relax in the spa and solarium. Canoes available to
observe loons. Picnic table at lake side. ✒B&B

Jasper
(west of Edmonton near BC border)

Carter, Bob & Glenda (Wyndswept Bed & Breakfast)   ☎(780)866-3950, Fax(780)866-3951
Box 2683, Hinton, AB   T7V 1Y2   E-mail: wyndswep@agt.net

$75(and up) $35Add.person   (min.2 nights, book early for June to Sept)   ▶ 6A
Located at 12 Folding Mountain Village, Jasper East. On Hwy 16E, 4km past Park East Gate, follow directional signs.
Full, homebaked   Village, 2-storey, hillside, acreage, view from guest rooms, quiet, decks   2Ste (main & garden level)   1Q,2K,1T   2Private   ★ F,LF, satTV,VCR in guest rooms   Smoking outside, no pets
Flower gardens, firepit, gazebo, viewing decks, bird watching
Town of Jasper & Nat.Park, Hinton, Columbia Icefields, Miette Hot Springs, Marmot Basin
Large custom-built home, specially designed for B&B, the view, and to fit into the hill. Located in the village on the side of Folding Moutain with a spectacular panoramic view - a painter's & photographer's paradise. Hosts are avid naturalists, long time residents of the area, and willing to share off-beaten tracks. Enjoy a heart/healthy/hearty breakfast in the the big country kitchen, while watching the clouds dance over the mountain ranges. Visa,MC ✓B&B   www.wyndswept.com

---

Jober, Shawna & Gerry (Jober's Cottage)   ☎ (780) 852-3893
Box 894, 705 Geikie St., Jasper, AB   T0E 1E0

Phone for directions.
$45S $60D $10Child/Add.person   ▶ 6
Compl.coffee/tea   Downtown, res., bungalow, patio, quiet, secluded   1D,1F (lower level)   2T,1D   1Sh.w.g.   ★ TV in guest rooms, off-street/street parking, guest quarters are separate   No smoking, no pets
Hiking trails to Pyramid Bench and to Old Fort Point & Valley of the five lakes (begin at back door), downtown shops, restaurants
Columbia Ice Fields, Miette Hot Springs, Maligne Lake, Mt.Robson Provincial Park (BC), excellent skiing areas
Warm welcome in modest home with renovated rooms located in picturesque mountain resort town. Host is a retired Rail Conductor and loves to hike with guests. Hosts are long-time Jasper residents and know the area well. There is a dog in residence. ✓B&B

Kan, Mrs. Marilyn Leslie   ☎ (780) 852-3009
Box 1940, 222A Cabin Creek Dr., Jasper, AB   T0E 1E0

Located at 1222A Cabin Creek Drive. Phone for directions.
$45-60S/D $20Add.person   ▶ 4
NONE (Complimentary coffeee/tea, self-serve   Res., quiet   2D   2T,1D   Sh.w.g.   ★Private entrance, handicap access may be arranged   No pets, no smoking
Town centre, mountain lakes, hiking trails begin across street.
All the attractions in Jasper National Park (Columbia Icefields, Miette Hot Springs, Maligne Lake), Mt Robson Prov Park (BC)
Quiet comfortable residence, located at edge of town. Main floor guest rooms have a southern exposure, with a view of the garden and the mountains along the Icefield Parkway. Host's interests include local history, environmental issues and travel. ✓CC

Robinson, Mrs. Jean

☎ (780) 852-4527

Box 640, Jasper, AB T0E 1E0

From Hwy 16 East or West travel into town. Look for 808Connaught Dr at west end of main street.

$50S/D (off season rates available - Oct1-April30) ► 6

☒Not included 🏠Downtown, village, bungalow, quiet, view from guest rooms ■1D,1F(main floor) ⊨3T,1D,cot ⊲1Sh.w.g.

★F,lounge for guests, street parking ⚠No smoking, no pets

🚶 Town Centre, walks in forest across the street, ski bus for Marmot Basin pick-up, x/c skiing on groomed trails

🚗 Mount Edith Cavell with the hanging Angel Glacier, Maligne Lake, Columbia Icefields, world-class downhill skiing

🐎 Hosts, born and raised in Jasper, have welcomed B&B guests for a long time, are avid birders and have hiked all the trails and fished in most of the lakes. They will gladly share their local knowledge with visitors. Enjoy the breathtaking beauty and magnificient views in this active year round resort town. There is a resident dog. ✍CC

Yates, Denise & Gordon (Mountain Splendour B&B English Style)

☎ (780) 866-2116

Box 6544, Hinton, AB T7V 1X8   E-mail: mtnsplen@telusplanet.net Fax:(780)866-2117

Located in Jasper East at #17 Folding Mountain Village on the Yellowhead Hwy 16 and 4 km east of Jasper Park.

$85-135D $25Add.person ► 7A

☒ Full 🏠 Rural, village, 3-storey, acreage, view from guest rooms, patio, wrap-around deck, private upper balconies, quiet ■ 2D ⊨ 2Q,3R ⊲2Ensuite ★ F,LF, satTV in private guest lounge, outdoor spa ⚠ No smoking, no pets, no children

🚗 Town of Jasper, Miette Hot Springs, Athabasca Falls, excellent x-c & downhill skiing (Athabasca Lookout, Nordic Centre, Marmot Basin), Columbia Icefields

🐎 Lovely new home with beautiful panoramic mountain view in a peaceful setting where nature abounds. Relax and enjoy the warm English-style hospitality. Visa,MC

Zaffino, Lorraine & Luigi (Angels on Aspen B&B)

☎ (780) 852-3749, Fax 852-3266

2B Aspen Cr., Box 373, Jasper, AB T0E 1E0   E-mail: lulo@telusplanet.net

Phone for directions.

$65-85S/D $10-15Add.person (Reserv.recommended) ► 7

☒Cont.(May-Oct only) 🏠 Res.,, 2-storey, patio, quiet ■3 (lower level) ⊨2T,2Q ⊲1Ensuite,1sh.w.g. ★TV in guest rooms, private entrance, street parking, guest quarters are sep.

⚠ Smoking outside, no pets, children min. age 12 〰 Italian

🚶 Downtown with interesting shops and restaurants, hiking, cycling, golfing, birdwatching, x-c skiing

🚗 Athabasca Falls, Miette Hot Springs, Mt.Edith Cavell, Mt Robson, Columbia Icefields, Marmot

🐎 Warm welcome in relaxing and comfortable abode situated in a quiet residential area of beautiful and popular resort town. The town is situated in the heart of Jasper National Park and surrounded by some of the most breathtaking wonders of the world. Guest rooms are called "Michael's", "Raphael's" and "Gabriel's". After a long day of travel or sightseeing, guests can relax peacefully, knowing "they will be watched over by all the Angles on Aspen". There is a dog in residence. CCards ✍B&B www.telusplanet.net/public/lulo

Lacombe

Sawyer, Corinne & Dave (On the Lake B&B)
RR1, S2, Box32, Lacombe, AB T0C 1S0

☎ (403) 748-3237
E-mail: cjsawyer@telusplanet.net

From Hwy2 take Hwy12 west to Lacombe. Phone for directions.
$85S $95D   ▶4A
🍴 Full, homebaked   🏠 Village, raised bungalow, hillside, 2acres,
view from guest rooms, patio, deck, quiet, secluded   ■2D (street
level) ⊨2Q 🛏2Ensuite ★ F,TV/VCR/library in guest
lounge (with billiards, beverage stand), guest quarters are
separate ✋ No smoking, no pets, not suitable for children
🧍 Adjoining Aspen Beach Prov.Park (with biking & walking
trails), sandy beaches, swimming, birdwatching, marsh walk, private beach path
🚗 Edmonton, Red Deer, Rocky Mountain House, Prairie Steam Excursions, 30 golf courses
🗨 Warm & friendly welcome in lakeside home with water fountains in & out and in which the
host's antique(vintage) gas pump collection provides ambient lighting throughout the house.
Bicycles provided for guests. Breakfast is served in the dining room with a panoramic view of Gull
Lake and park. House specialty is Puff Pancakes with wild Saskatoons from the property. B&B has
received the 1999 award for Excellence by the Red Deer Convention & Visitors Bureau. ✓B&B
www.bbcanada.com/2843.html

Lethbridge

Chell, Ruth (Chellsea House B&B)
9 Dalhousie Rd.W., Lethbrtidge, AB T1K 3X2

☎ (403) 381-1325, Fax 381-0228
E-mail: chellsea@telusplanet.net

Travel south on University Dr., turn right onto McGill Blvd.
Continue for 3 blocks to Dalhousie Rd. Turn right.
$50S $80D   ▶4
🍴 Full, homebaked   🏠 Res., bungalow, patio, quiet   ■2D
(main floor) ⊨2T,2Q 🛏1Ensuite, 1sh.w.g. ★Air,F,TV,
parking ✋No smoking, no pets, no perfumes, ask re children
🧍 Two man-made fishing lakes and parks, U.of Lethbridge,
recreation/shopping centers, walking/hiking, city bus stop
🚗 Head-Smashed-in Buffalo Jump, Writing-on-Stone Archaeological Park, Dinosaur
museum/birds of Prey Sanctuary, Japanese Gardens, Remington Carriage House, Mormon Temple
🗨 Modern home with antiques and original oil paintings, situated in pleasant heart-of-Alberta
town. Enjoy the timeless elegance and comfort. Breakfast is served in antique furnished country
kitchen, or on the covered patio or courtyard (weather permitting). ✓B&B

Haynes, Helen (Forsyth House B&B)
715-3rd St.South, Lethbridge, AB T1J 1Z4

☎ (403) 320-5344
E-mail: hhaynes@telusplanet.net

From Calgary on Hwy 3 continue on Scenic Drive past 6th Ave South to 4th St South. Turn left to
7A Ave South, left to 3rd St South and left again to B&B.

$40-45S $60D   (long term rates available)   ▶4A
🍴 Cont., homebaked 🏠 Downtown, 2-storey, hist., view from
guest rooms, deck, quiet ■ 2D(upstairs) ⊨2D,1R
🛏1Sh.w.g ★ F,TV in guest rooms, separate entrance, off-street
& street parking, guest quarters are separate ✋ No smoking, no
pets, not suitable for children
🧍 Downtown, Gault Museum, Southern Alberta Art Gallery,
University of Lethbridge, Community College, YMCA, Coolie walks
🚗 Fort McLeod, Buffalo-Jump-Head-Smashed-In, Wakerton National Park
🗨 Tastefully restored 1906-built quiet home furnished with antiques througout, situated at the
edge of the Coolies looking over to the University. Formerly from Toronto, retired teacher has
many varied interests, including golfing, bridge playing. Breakfast is served in special guest
breakfast room. Computer access available. http://www.bbcanada.com/1452.html

Medicine Hat

(south-east corner of province near SK border, see also Bow Island)

Groves, Joy & Gary (Groves B&B)
Box 998, Medicine Hat, AB T1A 7H1

☎ & Fax (403) 529-6065
E-mail: groves.bb@memlane.com

From Medicine Hat, take Hwy1 to Hwy3 (to Lethbridge). Proceed 3km to Holsom Rd, turn right and continue 6.7km to RR70. Turn right, travel 3.3km to Twp Rd130. right again & 1.6km to B&B.
$35S $50D $10Child $15Add.person $70F   🍴 Meals   ▶6A,4Ch

🍲 Full, homebaked   🏠 Rural, bungalow, view from guest rooms, acreage, swimming pool, deck, quiet, horseshoe pit   ■3F (main & lower level)   ⊨1D,2Q, cot, crib, mattress for children   🛁2Ensuite, 1sh.w.h.   ★LF,F,TV & ceiling fans in guest rooms, private entrance, guest fridge, pool-table, games, trampoline, off-street parking   🚭 Smoking outside
🕺 Swimming, biking, picnicking, fire pit, hiking in nearby hills
🚗 Cypress Hills Provincial Park, Writing on Stone, Red Rock coulee, excellent skiing
🚙 Quiet country home, with beautifully landscaped acreage and magnificent panoramic view of the South Saskatchewan River. Evenings, relax around the firepit or take a dip in the deck-side pool. There is a dog in residence. Large dogs & horses can be housed in outside kennel & corral or indoor in a travel carrier. Extended stay/return visit discounts. ✍B&B bbcanada.com/grovesbb

---

McShannock, Patty & Kelley (McOhanak B&B)
364-8th St.SE, Medicine Hat, AB T1A 1L7

☎ (403) 527-6603
E-mail: ronock@shockware.com

Phone for directions.
$50S $60D $15Child   ▶6A,1Ch
🍲 Full (country-style)   🏠 2-storey, hist., veranda, heated indoor swimming pool, quiet   ■3D(upstairs)   ⊨3Q,cot   🛁 1Sh.w.g. (with antique clawfoot tub)   ★F,TV,1guest room air-conditioner, off-street/street parking   🚭 Desig.smoking area, no pets
🕺 Historic downtown, walking paths, golf courses, parks, city bus
🚗 Cypress Hills Provincial Park, Echodale Park (with man-made Lake in the Prairie), airport
🚙 Restored 1912 Victorian home, warmly furnished with antiques & collectibles – a step back into another era. McOhanak is the Gaelic spelling of hosts' last name, which was first recorded in Kilmashenochan, Scotland in 1456. Breakfast is served in special guest breakfast room. Relax on the wrap-around veranda and let the worries slip away. Visa http://www.bbcanada.com/2798.html

---

Okotoks

(south of Calgary; see also Bragg Creek)

Turner, Lynn & Ian (Lineham House B&B
33 Elma St., Okotoks, AB T0L 1T3

☎ (403) 938-6182

Take Hwy 2 south from Calgary to Hwy 2A into Okotoks, turn left at bottom of the hill on Elma St.
$60S $75D $15child/Add.person $150F $10Dog   🍴Meals   ▶6A,2Ch

🍲 Full   🏠 Downtown, hist., 3-storey, view from guest rooms, patio, porch, deck, quiet   ■3D(upstairs)   ⊨2T,2D   🛁1Sh.w.g., 1sh.w.h (incl.antique clawfoot tub)   ★F,TV,guest common room, off-street/street parking, guest quarters are separate   🚭 Designated smoking area, children min. age 5
🕺 Walks along the river/parks/pathways, shops, restaurants, Cultural Centre, Greyhound bus from Calgary
🚗 Big Rock (largest glacial erratic in NA), Calgary, Stampede
🚙 1906-built elegant home (reg.historic site), lovingly restored to the charm and elegance of an era gone by and tastefully decorated with a blend of antiques, unique pieces, art & crafts. Located in the foothills of the Rocky Mountains. Enjoy friendly Western hospitality. Ideal place for intimate gathering, business retreat or workshops. Knowledgeable hosts will be happy to help with itinerary. Country breakfast is served in separate breakfast room. Picnic lunches or special dinners can be arranged. There is a friendly dog in residence. Visa ✍B&B

Peace River

(northern Alberta)

Kelly, Irene (Kozy Quarters B&B)   ☎ (403) 624-2807
11015-99th St, Box 7493, Peace River, AB   T8S 1T1

Phone for directions
$50S $60D   (Bridal room on request)   ► 8A
🍽 Full, homebaked, self-serve   🏠 Res, hist., 2.5-storey, view,
frontriver, porch, quiet   ■ 4(upstairs)   ◄ 2T,2D,1Q
🛁1Sh.w.h.   ★ F,TV, off-street parking   ✋ No smoking
🚶 Downtown area, stores, restaurants
🚗 Museum, River Boat Tours, golfing, skiing, local arts & crafts,
trout farm, nature trails

📢 Large home, tastefully renovated to enhance its historic character, located in a tranquil garden setting and the sole survivor of buildings constructed by the RCMP since 1916. Ideal place for business or pleasure stays. Breakfast is served in guest breakfast room. Visa ✔B&B

Pincher Creek

(west of Lethbridge; see also Bellevue)

Lewis, Ken and Dorothy (Beau-K-Ranch)   ☎ Fax (403) 627-2234
Box 1720, Pincher Creek, AB   T0K 1W0   E-mail: dmklewis@telusplanet.net

From traffic light in Pincher Creek, go 9km south on Hwy 6 to small cemetery on right. Turn

left and proceed .2 km to 1st house on right.
$35S $45-55D $5Child $10Add.person   🍽 Meals   ► 6A,4Ch
🍞Homebaked   🏠Farm, view, quiet   ■2D(main floor/ground
level)   ◄1D,2Q,(1P in ground level family room)   🛁3Private
★F,LF,wheel-chair access,trampoline,hot tub   ♥ ✋No smoking
🚶 Horseback riding, hiking,
🚗 Head-Smashed-In Buffalo Jump, Waterton Lakes Int. Peace
Park, Oldman River Dam, Frank Slide Interp.Center, Ft McLeod

📢 Quiet country home on a working ranch in tranquil and very scenic surroundings, located in the Foothills.✔B&B

Red Deer

(midway Calgary/Edmonton; see also Lacombe)

Ellerby, John & Donna (Country Home B&B)   ☎ & Fax (403) 347-0356
RR1, Site 7, Red Deer, AB   T4W 5E1

On Hwy 2 travel 3 km north of Red Deer. Turn west on Hwy 11A and drive 12 km to Range Rd 11.

Turn north (right) to first house on left.
$35S $55D $5Child   ► 6
🍽 Full   🏠 Farm, ranch-style, acreage, quiet   ■ 3(main and
lower level)   ◄2D,2T, host quarters are separate   🛁2shw.g.
★LF,KF,TV in guest sitting room, private lower entrance,
parking   ✋No smoking,
🚶 Walk on country roads
🚗 Red Deer, lake/beachfront/swimming/sailing, golfing

📢 Warm and friendly hospitality in pretty rural setting and quiet, peaceful location. House specialty is fresh ground wheat pancakes, breads and jams. Breakfast is served in family dining room. Ideal location for business or pleasure visitors.

Red Deer (cont'd)

Uiterwyk, Susan (Dutchess Manor Spa & Guesthouse) ☎ (403) 346-7776
4813-54 Street, Red Deer, AB   T4N 2G5

Coming from south, proceed to city centre. Turn right on 55St, right on 48Ave and right on 54St. From north take 67St turn-off to city entre. Turn left on 55St and proceed as above.
$50S $70D   (plus tax)   ▣ Meals   ► 6A

🍲 Full or Cont (caters to vegetarian diets)   ⌂ Downtown, hist., 2-storey, patio, porch, quiet ■1S,2D(upstairs) ⊨2T,1D,1K ⌕Sh.w.g. ★ TV,LF, separate entrance, private deck, off-street parking 🖐No pets, no children, designated smoking area ⌇Dutch, French, German

🏃 City parks & Recreation areas, downtown, shopping, hospital restaurants, theatres, museums, courthouse, bus stop across street 🚗 Golf courses, x/c ski trails, theatre

🐾 Cozy 1905-built home with lots of original woodwork, decorated in European style and located in old area of city. Guest rooms have Dutch names. Hostess operates a full service aesthetic salon and giftstore on main floor. Spa packages (evening, day or weekend) and steamroom/water massage tub on premises available. "Come to Dutchess Manor for a Dutch Re-treat". ↙B&B

Sedgewick   *(south-east of Edmonton; see also Camrose)*

Tanton, Ron & Helen (Wheatland Meadows Berry Inn) ☎ (780) 384-3539
Box 450, Sedgewick, AB   T0B 4C0   E-mail: wmcf@telusplanet.net, Fax (780)384-2764

Phone for directions.
$45S $55D $7.50Child(over age10)   ▣Meals   ► 8
🍲 Full, homebaked, self-serve, buffet ⌂Farm, hillside, view from guest rooms, deck, quiet, secluded ■ 3F(ground level) ⊨2D,3Q,1K,2cots 🚗 3Private ★ KF,LF,F,TV in guest rooms private entrance, wheel-chair access, guest quarters are separate 🖐 Designated smoking area, no pets

🏃 Private Orchard with sweetness gardens (berries), selection of birdhouses next door, excellent hunting for White Tail, Mule Deer and Moose

🚗 Sedgewick (Hardisty Lakes), Camrose (shopping), Forestbury (oil field and coal mine), golfing

🐾 Warm welcome in peaceful and tranquil surroundings located on main flyway for ducks, geese and big game in North America. Breakfast is served in guest breakfast room. A "Berry Special Place". U-pick berries available.. Ideal place for honeymoon or family reunions. Camping facilities on property. CCards www.comcept.ab.ca/cantravel/berryinn.hmtl

---

Trekofski, Mona & Joe (Ms Mona's Bed & Breakfast) ☎ (403) 384-3936, Fax (403) 384-3730
Box 504, Sedgewick, AB   T0B 4C0

Phone for directions.
$45S $55D   ▣ Meals   (plus tax)   ► 6
🍲 Full, homebaked   ⌂ Res., 2-storey, hist., porch, deck, quiet ■ 3D (upstairs) ⊨ 2D,1Q 🚗 3Private ★ Air,LF,F,TV in guest rooms, separate entrance, off-street parking, winter plug-ins, large dining room/gathering area with hot tub

🏃 Town of Sedgewick, archives, town park, Rec Centre, curling, bowling, hockey, golfing, x-c skiing
🐾 Comfortable home (1912) on the highest point in town with Victorian-style decorated rooms. Relax in the hot tub or by the fireplace & enjoy down-home country atmosphere.Visa,MC ↙B&B

Spruce Grove

(north of Edmonton)

Henitiuk, Mike & Audrey (Stonesthrow B&B)
46 Fairway Dr., Spruce Grove, AB   T7X 3K3

☎ (780) 962-0829, Fax (780) 962-9465
E-mail: 75211,45@compuserve.com

Travel west from Edmonton on Yellowhead Hwy 16 to Century Rd (turn-off at Spruce Grove). Proceed south on Century Rd to Grove Dr, west to Links Rd, and north on Fairway Dr.
$45S $60D $5Child $15Add.person   🍽 Meals   ► 4A,2Ch
🌞Summer only 🍞Homebaked 🏠Res., 2-storey, view from guest rooms, patio, deck, quiet ■ 1S,2D(upstairs) ⊨ 1D,1Q,2R ⇱1sh.w.g.
★F,KF,LF,TV 🖐 Designated smoking area, no pets ⤳ French
🏃 Golf course at back, walking trails, shops, public swimming, restaurants
🚗 West Edmonton Mall (world's largest shopping Mall), downtown Edmonton, Stony Plain Multicultural Centre, Devon Botanical Gardens
🗣 Quiet city place with a view of the Glory Hills north of Spruce Grove and golf course at back. Watch the golfers on the links from the back yard or try a round or two. Well travelled hosts enjoy exchanging travel experiences. Transportation to and from airport, train or bus terminal and City of Edmonton available. Visa/MC(to hold room) ↙CC

Strathmore

(east of Calgary)

Sproule, Winston and Vera (Sproule Heritage Place B&B)
Box 43, S14, RR1, Strathmore, AB   T1P 1J6

☎ (403) 934-3219

Located east of Strathmore on Hwy1. Travelling west go 7.8km west from jct 561. From Calgary (going east) travel 14.5km east of Strathmore. Watch for B&B highway sign.
$65-95S/D   ► 6A
🍳 Full, homebaked 🏠Rural, hist., veranda ■3D(upst)
⊨1D,2Q ⇱1Sh.w.g.,1private ★TV, separate entrance
🖐No pets, smoking on open veranda, not suitable for children
⤳Russian, Ukrainian
🚗 Rocky Mountains, Tyrrell Museum, Drumheller, Calgary (40Km)
🗣 Charming 1920 Heritage home surrounded by prairie scenery (an Alberta Registered Historic Resource farmsite). House was chosen by Hallmark (USA) for 1987 Christmas & 1991 Alberta Gov't Telephone for filming. Restored by the hosts to its original beauty and furnished with antiques, and replicas handmade by the hosts.

Vilna

(north-east of Edmonton)

Lavoie, Yvette & Robert (Country Garden B&B)
Box 545, Vilna, AB   T0A 3L0

☎ (780) 636-2029

Phone for directions.
$35S $45D $15Add.person   ► 6
🍳 Full, homebaked 🏠 Rural, bungalow, acreage, deck, sun room, quiet ■ 1S,2D(main floor) ⊨1S,2Q ⇱3Private ★ KF,LF,TV 🖐 Designated smoking area ⤳ French
🚗 Smokey Lake (World Pumpkin Weigh-off in Oct), great hunting and fishing areas
🗣 Warm welcome in spacious log-style home. Relax in the sun room off the kitchen or on the deck. Hostess is well known for her cooking/baking and can usually be found in the kitchen.

B & B Travel Tips

B&B travelling can be most enjoyable, when it is planned ahead and when there is ample time to socialize.

When travelling B&B, you get more than just a bed to sleep in, because you are making a personal contact in a strange place.

Plan your trip at home in the comfort of your living room, researching the maps of the provinces you want to visit, and then write or phone the B&B hosts, to see if the room is available for you. When you have B&B confirmations, you will relax and enjoy your trip much more.

If you are on the road and decide to stay in a B&B, do phone ahead from a nearby phone (best: take a break at lunchtime and choose the B&B for the coming night). The hosts will appreciate your consideration and if their rooms are booked, they can also direct you to another B&B host. (This is not convenient, if you appear at the door in the evening without prior notice.)

Contacting the B&B hosts ahead of time is a big advantage. You will not only have a room waiting for you that night, but you have already "broken the ice." The hosts will be welcoming you at the door and you are not a stranger any more.

Do remember that you are entering a private house as a guest – (even though you are paying something) – the hosts are still doing you a favour by inviting you into their homes and you must observe whatever house rules exist. If you keep this in mind, your stay will be very enjoyable.

Do not expect the same service you usally get in a hotel. The service in a B&B is completely different. It is even better, because of all the little things the hosts will do for you and the information they will give you (many extras that cannot be bought in a hotel!). In fact, they will be happy and so proud to tell you all about the local attractions/events/history of their hometown.

Breakfast is almost always memorable! Most hosts will ask in the evening what you would like for breakfast and at what time (you can sleep in if you wish!). Go ahead and tell them if you would like porridge or something special. You will be pleasantly surprised.

On the day of departure, you should leave after breakfast and with all your belongings! It is not fair for the hosts to have to store your luggage, while you are making some side-trips before leaving town. Remember, they have to get the room ready for the next guests.

If you stay more than one night, you can go and come at your pleasure. But do let the hosts know when you will be back, especially if you plan to be late. They might even give you a key, and then you can let yourself in quietly.

As a B&B guest you have all the privacy you want in your own room. Hosts take the cue from you - if you do not want to socialize, they will understand.

All hosts are very obliging to special needs, but as a guest you must always remember that these extras are usually given by the hosts out of friendliness and a desire to please.

Most guests find it more convenient to pay in the morning at breakfast, when there is usually more time. Some hosts will ask for this to be settled upon arrival. It is wise to ask the hosts what they would prefer.

Do tell the hosts all about yourself and where you come from and what you do day in and out. They will be eager listeners. After all that's why they are inviting people into their homes – so the world comes to them!

Saskatchewan

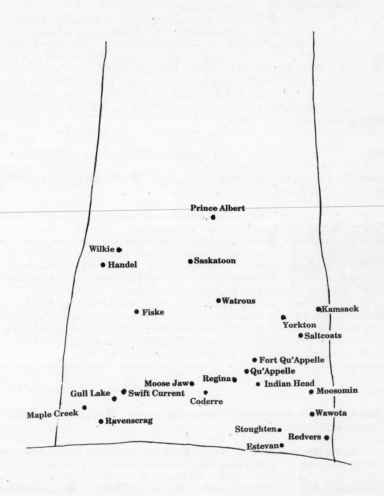

Prince Albert

Wilkie ●
● Handel
● Saskatoon

● Watrous
● Fiske
● Kamsack
Yorkton ●
● Saltcoats

● Fort Qu'Appelle
● Qu'Appelle
Moose Jaw ● Regina ●
Gull Lake ● ● Swift Current ● Indian Head ● Moosomin
Coderre
Maple Creek ● ● Wawota
● Ravenscrag
Stoughten ●
Estevan ● Redvers ●

Tourism Saskatchewan
1919 Saskatchewan Dr.
Regina, SK   S4P 3V7

toll-free 1-800-667-7191

Coderre

(south-west of Moose Jaw)

Lepine, Carol & Leonard (Carol's Guest House)   ☎ (306) 394-2016
Box 101, Coderre, SK   S0H 0X0

Located 100km south-west of Moose Jaw on Hwy 363, or 50km north of Gravelbourg on Hwy 58.
$30S/D $40F   ⦿Meals   ►6
💧 Full, homebaked   🏠 Village, raised bungalow, quiet   ▣2D
(main floor)   ⊨2D,1P   ⚎2Private   ★KF,LF,TV in guest
room, private entrance, wheel-chair access, street parking, guest
quarters are separate
🦮 Outdoor dog kennel on site, small pasture for boarding of larger
animals, Community Center (ideal for large gatherings)
🚗 Chaplin Marsh (a bird watcher's paradise) Ducks Unlimited
Project, Old Wives Lake, Gravelbourg Cathedral, Shamrock Regional Park (heated pool, golfing,
skiing, snow-shoeing), Wood River (fishing, canoeing, hiking, hunting)
🐖 Completely separate house designated for guests only (next to host family home) located in a
peaceful little farming community and close to scenic Wood River. Experience a taste of country
life. Breakfast is served in separate guest breakfast room. Hosts will be happy to help set up any
tours or events guests would like. ✔ B&B

Estevan

(s/e of Regina, near US border; see also Redvers, Stoughton)

Hemus, Kaye (Turn-of-the-Century B&B)   ☎ (306) 634-6405, Fax (306) 634-7456
1309-3rd St., Estevan, SK   S4A 0S1

Located 10km from US border on Hwy 475. Phone for directions.
$45-50S $50-55D   (plus tax)   ►6
💧 Full, homebaked   🏠 Downtown, hist., deck, quiet   ▣ 3D
(main level)   ⊨2D,2T   ⚎1sh.w.g., 1ensuite   ★ Air,TV,
off-street and street parking   ⓦ Smoking outside only
🦮 Heritage Town Walking Tour, Estevan Nat. Exhibition Centre,
Aquatic & Leisure Centre, golfing
🚗 Rafferty/Alameda Dams, Shand Power Stn & Greenhouse
Estevan & area self-guided driving, mine & energy tours (free), summer theatre (July/Aug)
🐖 Heritage home with plenty of oak, brass, stained glass windows, antique furnishings and
Victorian lace. Elegance & hospitality in the Energy City. Enjoy a peaceful, quiet and refreshing
rest in beautiful surroundings. Family or group rates available. Visa ✔B&B

Fiske

(south-west of Saskatoon; see also Handel)

Siemens, Bob & Charlene (Longview Farm & B&B)   ☎ (306) 377-4786, Fax 377-2071
Box 53, Fiske, SK   S0L 1C0

From Hwy 1 at Swift Current, take Hwy 4 north to Rosetown, then Hwy 7 west to Fiske. Proceed
1.5 km south and 1.5 km east.
$40S $50D   ⦿ Meals   (plus tax)   ►4
✴Summer only   💧 Full, homebaked   🏠 Farm, 2-storey,
quiet   ▣ 2D(main & upper level in guest house)   ⊨2Q,1S
⚎1Sh.w.g.   ★LF,KF, parking   ⓦ No smoking   〰 German
🦮 Nature walks through pastures, rustic cottage on property
🚗 Petroglyphs at Herschel
🐖 Warm welcome on working farm in western Saskatchewan
farm country. There are cattle, sheep and chickens. "Come, share our love of the land". Bring a
chicken ormanent to add to hosts' "roost" (collection) and get discount on first night. ✔B&B

Fort Qu'Appelle

(east of Regina; see also Qu'Appelle, Indian Head)

Whiting, Jill & Jerry (Company House B&B)   ☎ (306) 332-6333
Box 1159, 172 Company Ave., Fort Qu'Appelle, SK   S0G 1S0   E-mail: chbbt@sk.sympatico.ca

Located 1 block from The Hudson Bay Store, next to Town Office.
$50S $60D   (Family rates available)   (plus tax)   ▶ 6
🍲 Full, homebaked   🏠 Res., hist., older, sweeping veranda,
quiet   ■ 3D(upstairs)   ⊨ 2D,1K   🛁2Sh.w.g. clawfoot tub &
jacuzzi   ★Air,F,parking, TV in private guest lounge
🖐Smoking outside only, no pets   ♥   ∿some French
🏃 Beaches, fishing, canoeing, birdwatching, tennis, shopping
🚗Mission Ridge golf club/skii hill,Echo Prov.Park,Ft Museum
🚚 Charming home, built in the early 1900, with 10 ft ceilings, chandeliers, bevelled glass
windows and ceramic cherry wood fireplaces. Enjoy friendly Prairie hospitality in a relaxed rural
setting of popular Saskatchewan resort town. Hosts have lived in many regions of Canada and are
delighted to welcome guests. ✔B&B www.bbcanada.com/392.html

Gull Lake

(west of Swift Current; see also Maple Creek)

Magee, Beatrice (Magee's Farm & B&B)   ☎ & Fax (306) 672-3970
Box 428, Gull Lake, SK   S0N 1A0   E-mail: b.magee@glen.com

Take Trans Canada Hwy west from Gull Lake for 13.3km. Turn left at "Carmichael" sign, then 6km
south to "Magee" sign. Turn left and go for 2.5km to 1st farm on left.
$25-30S $35-50D $10-15Child(under age 12)   🍽 Meals   ▶ 6

🍲 Choice, homebaked   🏠 Farm, ■ Modern cabin   ⊨S,D
🛁 Sh.w.g.   ★ F,KF   🖐 Pets welcome
🏃 Working grain and livestock farm grounds
🚗 Town of Gull Lake, Indian historic site, lookout, trout fishing
🚚 Mixed working farm. Hosts were involved in 4H and are very
interested in photography. Hunters welcome. There is a resident
dog and cat. Reservations only accepted. ✔B&B

Handle

(west of Saskatoon; see also Wilkie)

Schoeler, Howard and Shirley   ☎ (306) 658-4347
Handle, Saskatchewan S0K 1Y0

From Saskatoon, take Hwys 14 and 51 past Biggar and continue on paved road.
$30S $40D   🍲$3 Each   🍽 Meals   ▶ 4A,3Ch
🍲 Choice, homebaked   🏠 Farm, view   ■ 1S,2D   ⊨D,S
🛁2Sh.w.h.   ★ TV,F
🚗 Towns of Biggar, Unity and Wilkie
🚚 Fully equipped working grain farm in wheat-farming centre
and situated in a quiet setting, excellent location for a night of
relaxation after a day's travelling. Enjoy the wide-open spaces.
Hosts delight in giving visitors a short tour of the area.

Indian Head   *(east of Regina; see also Qu'Appelle, Fort Qu'Appelle)*

Sanders, Murray & Christy (Manor House Bed & Breakfast)   ☎ (306) 695-3853
Box 159, 501 Woodward Ave, Indian Head, SK   S0G 2K0   E-mail: m.sanders@sk.sympatico.ca

Phone for directions.
$40S $50D   🍽 Meals   ▶ 11
🍴Cont., homebaked 🏠Res., 2-storey, hist., deck, porch, quiet
■1S,5D(upst)   ⊨1S,5D   ⚲2Sh.w.g.   ★F, TV,LF   🖐No smoking, no pets
🚗 Qu'Appelle Valley, PFRA Tree Nursery, PFRA Experimental Farm, Regina
☛ Comfortable home, built in 1904 as a Duplex was once a focal point of the town renowned for its perennial gardens and fish pond and situated in one of the oldest towns in Saskatchewan. Now a single dwelling and upgraded to modern comfort retaining as much of the original character & charm as possible. Relax and enjoy the congenial hospitality. Visa www.meliorgraphics.com/manorb&b

---

Kamsack   *(north of Yorkton)*

Brock, Don & Marleen (Border Mountain Country B&B)   ☎& Fax (306)542-3072
Box 1233, Kamsack, SK   S0A 1S0   E-mail: donaldbrock@hotmail.com

From Kamsack travel 7km east and 3km south on Hwy 5, 5km east on Side Rd.
$35S $45D $5-10Child(free under age 6) $10Add.person   🍽 Meals   ▶ 4A,4Ch

🍴 Full, homebaked 🏠 Farm, bungalow, view, porch, deck, quiet,secluded ■2F(lower level) ⊨2T,1Q,3R,crib ⚲1sh.w.g.
★LF 🖐 Smoking outside
🏃 Scenic valley area for hiking, cycling, horseback riding (guest owned horses), bird/wild animal viewing, hunting (Elk, moose, deer, black bear), farm animals including Arabian horses
🚗 Kamsack, Duck Mountain Prov.Park and Ski Area, National Doukobour Heritage Village, restaurants, Trans Canada Trail
☛ Cozy, country-style bungalow with a pleasant mixture of old and new. Property adjoins thousands of acres of accessible wildlife lands and gorgeous Duck Mountain Prov.Park (Aspen forest gives way to Pine). "Empty-Nester" hosts are familiar with the surrounding area and enjoy outdoors. Bed/Bale for guest horses. There is a small resident dog. Full service camping available.
MC ⁀B&B www.bbcanada.com/1144.html

Maple Creek   *(west of Swift Current near AB border; see also Gull Lake, Ravenscrag)*

Sorensen, Karen (Cypress Hills Bed & Breakfast)   ☎ (306) 662-3377
Box 1090, Maple Creek, SK   S0N 1N0

Located 37 km south of Maple Creek on Hwy 21, then 2.5 km west and 2.5 km north. Look for signs
$40S $50D $5Add.person   🍽 Meals   ▶ 4
🍴 Cont. 🏠 Rural, 2-storey, 160 acres, deck, patio, quiet
■1Ste(main floor), host quarters are upstairs ⊨ 1D,1P,cot
⚲Ensuite ★ KF,TV in suite, guest lounge, separate entrance, parking 〰 Danish
🏃 Hills and forests for walking, large vegetable garden, wild berries in season, outdoor fire pit
🚗 Maple Creek ("Old Cow Town"), Cypress Hills Prov.Park
☛ Situated on secluded large 160 acres of unspoiled nature with abundant wildlife. Hosts have retired from Tourism business and travelled extensively. There is a "Kitty" in residence. ⁀B&B

Maple Creek (cont'd)

Goronzy, Ben & Carol (Memories B&B)   ☎ (306) 662-2756
Box 996, Maple Creek, SK S0N 1N0

Located at 219 Hood Street. From TCH1 turn south on Rte21 (8km) to Maple Creek. Turn left on Hood St to last house on right.
$45S $55-65D $10Add.person $60F (Child free under age 12) $10Cot (plus tax) ▶ 8
    🍲 Full, homebaked 🏠 Village, res., 2.5-storey, hist., patio, quiet ■ 2D,2F(upstairs) + cottage ⊨2T,3D,2Q,cot
🛁Sh.w.g. ★ TV, fan in one guest room, street parking
Ⓦ Designated smoking area, no pets
🚶 Downtown, shopping, eateries, coffee shops, Old Timers Museum, Jasper Cultural Center, golf course
🚗 Maple Creek Airport, Swift Current, Medicine Hat (Alberta), Cypress Hills Interprovincial Park, Fort Walsh Nat.Park
📷 Historic brick house with theme guest rooms and located on a double treed lot. A gallery of family art drapes the walls, including original survey maps, dating back to the late 1800, rescued from the attic caves. Tea & goodies served evenings in the dining room. Breakfast is served in guest breakfast room. Also cottage available for families. Pick-up from Greyhound Depot (phone ahead). There are 2 cats and a dog outside. Reservations advised for June/July/Aug. ↙B&B

Moose Jaw   *(west of Regina)*

Oberding, Sharon & Tony (Prairie Rose B&B)   ☎ (306) 692-6101
196, 325-4th Ave SW, Moose Jaw, SK S6H 5V2

Located at the corner of 9th Ave NW & Hwy 363. From TCH turn south on 9th Ave NW and drive through city. Turn west on Hwy 363 to B&B on south side.
$35S $45D $10Child(under age 10)(free under age 5) $8Bed/Bale (plus tax) 🍽 Meals ▶8
🍲 Full, homebaked 🏠 Farm, 2-storey (2 houses joined), older, deck, swimming pool, quiet, secluded ■ 4 (upstairs) ⊨ 3S,1D,1Q,crib 🛁 1Sh.w.g. ★ TV in guest lounge, ceiling fans, private entrance, hot-tub, guest quarters are on upper level Ⓦ No smoking
🚶 Sukanen Ship, 15 Wing Miltary Base (Nato Flight Training Center), Airshow featuring Snowbirds (July), downtown Moose Jaw, Temple Gardens Mineral Spa, Tunnels of Little Chicago
🚗 Regina, Regina Airport, Buffalo Pound Prov.Park, White Track ski area
📷 Unique construction of two houses joined together and situated in ideal location close to the city, but far enough to avoid any noise. Great breakfasts are served in the guest breakfast room. Hosts are very hospitable and love interacting with guests. Discounts for groups and extended stays available. Bring something with a Rose on it and receive 5% off first night rate. Wheel-chair cces room available on request. ↙B&B

Reilly, Patricia & Gerald (Redland Cottage B&B)   ☎ (306) 694-5563
1122 Redland Ave., Moose Jaw, SK S6H 3P3

Phone for directions.
$45S $60D $5Child $75F 🍽 Meals   ▶ 4
🍲 Full 🏠 Res., bungalow, hist., porch, quiet, veranda ■2
(main floor & attic suite) ⊨3D 🛁2sh.w.g. ★KF,LF,F,TV, ceiling fans, off-street & street parking, guest quarters are separate Ⓦ Designated smoking area
🚶 Downtown, historic Mineral Water Health Spa, beautiful Cres.Park, Moose Jaw Tunnels, murals
🚗 Kinsmen Aquatic Centre, CFB Moose Jaw, Snowbirds Flying Team
📷 Restored home to reflect its Prairie beginnings with Prairie antiques in one guest room and Victorian decor in the other. Relax on the open veranda and enjoy breakfast (weather permitting). There is a poodle in residence. Home was featured on 1999 historic homes tour. Visit the homestead cabin in the back-yard. ↙CC

Moosomin

Rousay, Peter & Joy (Windover Guest House)   ☎ (306)435-4336, Fax (306)435-3821
Box 1204, 902 Windover Ave., Moosomin, SK S0G 3N0   E-mail: p.rousay@sk.sympatico.ca

In Moosomin, turn south off TCH1 on Hwy 8 (Main St). Proceed to 4th intersection, turn right one block to B&B on corner of Windover Ave & Gordon St. (front door faces Gordon St).

$40S $50D $10Add.person   ► 4A
🍽 Full, homebaked(7-9am) or Cont.(self-serve) 🏠 Downtown,
2-storey,hist.,porch,deck ■2D(upstairs) ⊨2D ⌐1Sh.w.g.
★TV/air-conditioners & ceiling fans in guest rooms, in-house
fax/copier & internet access, off-street parking 🚫No smoking,
inquire about children and pets
🏃 Quilt shop, gift & antique shop, art studio, swimming pool,
tennis courts, restaurants

🚗 Qu'Appelle Valley, Moose Mountain, golf course, Bear Claw Casino, tea house, museum, rodeos
📷 Queen Anne Victorian (ca 1890), yellow brick home with many original features, stained glass windows and eclectic blend of antiques as well as family heirlooms and personal favorites. Situated on Canada's "Main Street" Trans Canada Hwy 1. Hosts are passionate about the preservation of historic buildings. They invite their guests to share their delight in the friendly ghosts of this Century home. Enjoy a delicious breakfast including traditional Red River Cereal, served in formal dining room. There is a dog in residence. Watkins Products available. ✔ B&B
http://www.bbcanada.com/1644.html

Prince Albert

Tuek, Teresa & Brian (Serenity Spa House)   ☎ (306) 763-7727, Fax (306) 764-1044
250-20St., Prince Albert, SK S6V 4G4

Phone for directions.
$49S $89D   (plus tax) 🍽 Meals   ► 9A,1Ch
🍽 Full 🏠 Res, 4-storey, hist., patio, deck, swimming pool, quiet
secluded ■ 1S,3D,1F (main & upper floor) ⊨ 1S,3D,1Q,cot
⌐*4sh.w.g., 1sh.w.h. ★ KF,LF,F,TV in lounge & one guest
room, airconditioners, ceiling fans, off-street/street parking, guest
quarters are separate 🚫 No smoking
🏃 Diefenbaker House, Keyhole Castle, Lakeland Art Gallery, golf
course, Kinsmen Water Park, two large malls, bus stop
📷 1912 historic home, previously owned by the 2nd Explorer to the North Pole. Total relaxation health experience offered, including sea mineral pool, electronic toning beds, infra-red pain relieving unit and more. Owned by master herbalist providing massage, reflexology & pampering services. Breakfast is served in the guest breakfast room. There is a dog in residence. Guests may enjoy a complimentary sitdown tea at the Lakeland Art Gallery. Visa,MC ✔B&B

Qu'Appelle

(east of Regina; see also Fort Qu'Appelle, Indian Head)
☎ (306) 699-2328

Mader, Ken and Jo (Bluenose Country Vacation Farm & B&B)   ☎ & Fax (306) 699-7192
Box 173, Qu'Appelle, SK   S0G 4A0

Located 4.8 km north of the Trans Canada Highway on Hwy 35. Watch for signs.
$52S $70D $3Pets   (Family rates on request)   🍽 Meals   (plus tax)   ▶ 12

🍴 Full, homebaked   🏠 Working grain farm, 3-storey, indoor heated swimming pool, quiet   ■ 3 (upper floor), 2Stes   🛏3D,2Q cots   🚻5private   ★Air,TV, separate entrance, wheel-chair access   ⚲Restricted smoking
🧍 Mini golf & children's playground on property, Bluenose Agriculture Interpretive Centre, farm animal zoo, nature trail
🚗 Qu'Appelle fishing lakes and resorts, boating, Regina, Dominion Experimental Farms, horseback riding
🚩 Majestic fieldstone (turn-of-the-Century) English style home, built in 1904, with walls up to 3ft deep, with a striking silhouette - a landmark on the prairie landscape. There is a Country Tea Room on premises and a historic Church Hall for day bus tours, weddings, retreats. Relax and enjoy the fresh country air and beautiful sky-wide sunsets - an agriculture experience with country elegance. Saskatchewan hospitality award winners. Vacation packages available. Visa,MC ✓B&B

Ravenscrag

(south-west of Swift Current near US border; see also Maple Creek)

Saville, Jim (Spring Valley Guest Ranch)   ☎ (306) 295-4124
Box 10, Ravenscrag, SK   S0N 0T0

Call ahead for directions.
$40S $60D $15Child   🍽 Meals   ▶ 8
🍴 Full   🏠 Farm, older, quiet, isolated   ■ 4D (upstairs)   🛏4D   🚻 1Sh.w.g.   ★ KF,LF   ⚲Restricted smoking
🧍 Pleasant wooded valley (exceptional in spring-time) and abundant wildlife, horseback-riding arranged, leather shop, family museum, Hutterite colony, camping facilities
🚗 Cypress Hills Prov. Park (golfing, swimming, boating, craft
shops), historic Fort Walsh, Wallace Stegner House, White Mud Pits, Fossil Research Center
🚩 Early-Century (1913-built) character home in ideal location for naturalists, photographers and those who can appreciate the beauty of total darkness, silence and solitude. Also available large log home with banquet facilities for weddings, family re-unions, retreats and workshops. ✓B&B

Redvers

(s/e of Regina near MB border: see also Moosomin, Estavan, Stoughton)

Sylvestre, Lorna & André (Sylvestre's Bed & Breakfast)   ☎ (306) 452-3854
Box 429, Redvers, SK   S0C 2H0   Fax (306) 452-6195

Located 14 km west of Redvers on Hwy 13. Phone for directions.
$40S $50D $10Child   🍽Meals   (plus Tax)   ▶ 10
🍴 Choice, homebaked   🏠 Farm, 2-storey, quiet, large yard   ■1D,2F(upstairs)   🛏 T,D   🚻 Sh.w.h.   ★ TV,LF, parking   〰 French
🧍 Quiet walks with clean prairie air in native grasses & wild flowers, abundant birds and some wild animals of interest to photographers and naturalists
🚗 Kenosee and White Bear Lakes (swimming, boating, golf courses, waterslides, entertainment)
🚩 Enjoy the peace and tranquility of a rural Saskatchewan farm and relax in the old farm home and large yard. Hosts enjoy meeting people from all over the world and offer true & friendly Saskatchewan hospitality. Farm tours available. Visa ✓B&B

Regina

Mogg, Cheryl, E. (Crescent House B&B)
180 Angus Cr., Regina, SK S4T 6N4
☎ (306) 352-5995
E-mail: cheryl.mogg@dlcwest.com

From Albert St., turn west on 15th Ave to Angus St. Turn south to College
Ave, where Angus St becomes Angus Cres.
$50-55S $55-60D $10Add.person   (plus tax)   ► 5
🍳 Full, homebaked   🏠 Res., 2-storey, hist., porch, deck, quiet   ■2
(upstairs)   ⊨ 1D,1Q,cot   ⌁ 1sh.w.g.   ★ Air,LF,F,TV in one guest
room, private entrance, off-street parking   🖐 Designated smoking area,
compatible pets welcome
🚶 Wascana Park, Royal Sask.Museum, Albert Street Bridge, Legistlative
Assembly, Devonian Pathway, Cathedral Shopping District, Collections Art
Gallery, downtown business district
🚗 Exhibition Park, Taylor Field, RCMP Museum, Sask.Science Centre
☛ 1927-built character home with sunny south addition and many antiques, located in the
prestigious Cresents area. Relax on one of the three decks or in the tree-shaded backyard. Modem &
fax access for business travellers. Low fat and special diet available. Pick-up and delivery from
airport can be arranged. Winter plug-ins for automobiles. Guests are welcomed by 3 very friendly
non-shedding, retired champion Soft-coated Wheaten Terriers. ✏CC

Powell, Gail (Morning Glory Manor)
Box 1364, Regina, SK S4P 3B8
☎ (306) 525-2945, Fax (306) 352-6515

Phone for directions.
$45-65S/D   (Reduced rates for longer stay)   ► 4
🍳 Cont.(extended)   🏠 Downtown, 2-storey, older, view from
guest rooms   ■ 2D(upstairs)   ⊨ 4T   ⌁ 1Sh.w.g.   ★ Air,F,
off-street parking   🖐 Smoking on patio, no pets, children under
1 or over age 10 welcome
🚶 Downtown, Wascana Lake Park, performing arts centre,
museum, art galleries, University of Saskatchewan, Science
Centre, Imax-Theatre
🚗 Qu'Appelle Valley, lakes, nature preserve, sportsplex
☛ Charming character home built in 1923 featuring plenty of oak, beveled glass and beautiful
views. Relax by the fireplace or in the delightful sunroom and enjoy the tranquil surroundings.

Saltcoats
(south of Yorkton)

Farquharson, Joan & Walter (Blue Heron House)
142 Crescent Lake Rd., Saltcoats, SK S0A 3R0
☎(306)744-2214, Fax(306)744-2612
E-mail: farq.blueheron@sk.sympatico.ca

Located on Yellowhead Hwy and 26 km from Yorkton. Phone for directions.
$50S/D   (plus tax)   (Family rates available)   ► 16

🍳 Cont(plus)   🏠 Village, 2-storey, view from guest rooms, deck,
lakefront, patio, quiet   ■2(ground level)   ⊨ Q,T   ⌁ Sh.w.g.
★Air,F,LF,TV in guest lounge, extensive library, limited
wheelchair access, parking   🖐No smoking, no pets
🚶 Spacious garden, playground, public park, excellent birding
opportunities, local museum and library, good cafes
🚗 Shopping Mall, antique/craft shops, Western Dev.Museum,
three Provincial Parks, golf course
☛ Warm and friendly hospitality in home overlooking Anderson Lake. Enjoy good conversation
and relaxed, peaceful surroundings. Spiritual guidance, opportunities for counselling and Thematic
Retreats available. Hosts are knowledgeable about local and ethnic history of the province. By
pre-arrangment Natural History guided tour with well-known Naturalist Guides may be booked.
Also available: 2bedroom bungalow "Katies Cottage" and "The Guest House (for 8). Visa,MC

Saskatoon

Clay, Barb and Lynne Fontaine (Brighton House)   ☎ (306) 664-3278, Fax 664-6822
1308-5th Ave N, Saskatoon, SK   S7K 2S2   E-mail: brighton.house@endoramail.com

Upon entering the City, take Circle Drive to Idylwyld Drive. Turn east on 33rd Street to 5th Ave North and look for house 2 blocks down Ave.

$40S $50D $60Ste $10Add.person   ► 8A,2Ch
🍴Homebaked 🛏Res., older, patio, quiet ■2D,2Ste (1st floor & attic)
🛏3Q,1D,2R,2cribs 🚪2Private,2sh.w.g. ★TV,KF,LF, elegant antique gas fireplace ✋Smoking outside
🏃 River, University, YWCA, theatre, galleries, downtown, city bus route
🚗 Historic Batoche, Western Development Museum, Forestry Farm/Zoo
🎺 Gracious character home (affectionately known as the "Gingerbread House"), with the warmth of country and furnished with antiques, beautifully renovated to preserve it's original appearance & atmosphere of a by-gone era. A "beary" warm welcome for all ages. Complimentary use of bicycles. Relax in the outdoor hot tub after a long busy day. Ideal spot for honeymoon/anniversaries.Visa,MC ✓B&B

Dyck, Jed & Helen (Chic-A-D Acres B&B)   ☎ (306) 931-7119
GS 316, Box 21, RR3, Saskatoon, SK   S7K 3J6   E-mail: chicadacres@sk.sympatico.ca

From Saskatoon, travel west on Hwy 7, south on Hwy 60 for 10km, west on Vanscoy Rd (No762)

for 3km, and south on gravel road for 2.4km. Watch for sign.
$40-55S/D   ► 4
🍴 Full, homebaked 🛏 Rural, 2-storey, acreage, view from guest rooms, porch, deck, quiet, secluded ■ 2D (upstairs) 🛏 2D
🚪 1Sh.w.g. ★ F,Air,TV in spacious lounge area, guest quarters are separate ✋ No smoking, no pets
🏃 Walks through natural woodland and virgin prairie and open meadows (perchance observe white-tail deer)
🚗 Pike Lake Prov. Park, Moon Lake Golf & Country Club, downtown Saskatoon, Sask.Berry Barn
🎺 Newly constructed country home nestled among acres of natural trees with pastoral views of sheep and horses and natural flora of the area. Ideal for a quiet country retreat. Nutritious breakfast is served in the large country kitchen. Hosts are educators who enjoy meeting people and they love the many aspects of country living. There is a dog in residence.

Noonan, Mari (Calder House Inn)   ☎ & Fax (306) 665-7263
848 Saskatchewan Cr.E, Saskatoon, SK   S7N 0L4

Located 3.5 blocks from both Broadway Bridge or University Bridge via 25th St off Idylwylder Hwy11 or College Dr (Hwy5).
$50S $75D $10Child $120F   (plus tax) 🍽 Meals   ► 8
🍴 Full 🛏 Downtown, hist., 3-storey, view from guest rooms, riverfront, quiet ■3D,1F (main & upper level) 🛏1S,3D, cot, crib 🚪 4Private ★ F,TV, off-street/street parking
✋Designated smoking area, no pets, children min. age 12
🗣French, Russian
🏃 Downtown shops, restaurants, University, hospital, skiing & biking trails, Lydia's Celtic Pub, Amigos Nite-Club, Broadway Theatre, coffee shops, Mendel Art & Gordon Snelgrove Galleries, Innovation Place, Synchrotron Site
🎺 Historic home reflecting its history, fully renovated situated by the river in the front yard. Enjoy the intimate hotel atmosphere. There is a dog in residence. www.link.ca/calderhouse

Stoughton

(south-west of Regina; see also Redvers, Estevan)

Mitchall, Don & Marjorie (Marje's Garden B&B/Campgrounds)   ☎& Fax(306)457-2845,
Box 425, Stoughton, SK S0G 4T0

From Stoughton travel 4.8km northwest on Hwy33, 3.2km north & 0.8km east. Watch for signs.

$45D   ► 6A,2Ch
⬛Full   🏠 Farm, older, view from guest rooms, patio, quiet,
secluded   ■ 3(upstairs) plus cottage house   ⊨ 2D,1Q
🛁1Sh.w.g., plus outdoor facilities for campers & cottage
★F,TV in guest rooms, ceiling fans   ⓦ Designated smoking area
🕇 Farm grounds with orchard and gardens
🚙 Public swimming pool, 9 hole grass green golfing, museum in
Stoughton, Rte66 Snowmobile Trail

🐃 Beautifully restored 1928-built home with rustic decor, surrounded by flowers and vegetable
gardens and orchard. A 3 generation historic home. Ideal place for hunters (best upland game &
goose & white tail hunting). Cottage is in former garage and next to outhouse with hot shower &
sink and is shared with the campground. There are plug-ins for campers. ✒B&B

Swift Current

(west of Regina; see also Gull Lake)

Green, Dixie & Dave (Swift Current Heritage B&B)   ☎(306)773-6305,Fax(306)773-0135
Green Hectares Farm, Box1301, Swift Current, SK S9H 3X4

From Hwy 1 exit at Swift Current Tourist booth (22nd Ave NE) and travel north on Hwy 4 to

Walker Rd at right and proceed 1km to farm. Watch for sign.
$36S $60D   (plus tax)   (Child rate available)   ► 6
✳ April1-Nov1   ⬛ Full, homebaked   🏠 Farm, at edge of city,
2-storey, hist., view from guest rooms, creek at front, deck, quiet
■3D (main floor)   ⊨ 2T,2Q   🛁 1Sh.w.g., 1sh.w.h.   ★ TV,F,
off-street parking   ⓦSmoking outside
🕇 Swift Current Petroglyphs 500 m from door (historic rock

carvings & paintings). Swift Current Creek flows through farm property (canoeing, fishing)
🚙 Swift Current & Wheatland Malls, museum, Frontier Days Fair, Doc's town, art gallery
🐃 Working cattle ranch and irrigation farm with comfortable farmhouse located near all
activities. Appaloosa horses in training with "horse whispering" methods, kept close to house. Large
host family (including visiting grandchildren in summer) are interested in Archaeology and trail
riding. Enjoy and relax in congenial surroundings. Bed & Bale & camping on request. ✒B&B

Watrous

(south-east of Saskatoon)

Munro, Alex and Esther (West Wind - The Graf House)   ☎ (306 946-3821
Manitou Beach, Watrous, SK S0K 4T0

Located 5 km north of Watrous. Follow signs to Manitou Beach, turn left at golf course.
$55S $60D $95Ste   🍽 Meals   (plus tax)   ► 8
⬛ Full, homebaked   🏠 Village, hist., multi-storey, view, quiet,
decks   ■ 4D (ground level)   ⊨ 4Q   🛁 4Private,2sh.w.g.
★TV in breakfast room, games room & pool table, parking
🕇 9-hole grass green golf course across the road, mineral water
spa, small mall, tennis courts, unique horse-hair floor dance hall,
picnic grounds, paddle boats, cross-country skiing
🚙 Town of Watrous, shopping, bowling, restaurants
🐃 Historic house (1917-built in a neighbouring town, recently
moved to its present location and extensively restored and enlarged) is nestled into a hill, just below
the golf course. Enjoy breakfast in the breakfast room with an incredible view, relax on the guest
deck. Host operates the local Specialty Meat Shop and hostess restores houses and furniture. ✒CC

Wilkie

(north-west of Saskatoon; see also Handel)

Sander, Joe & Marcy (Plains Bison B&B)
Box 403, Wilkie, SK S0K 4W0

☎ & Fax (306) 843-3146
E-mail: acs@sk.sympatico.ca

Located 4km west of Wilkie on Hwy14.
$55S $65D $10Child $75F   ▣ Meals   ► 6A,4Ch
⊕ Full, homebaked   🏠 Farm, bungalow, view, quiet, deck
■2D,1Ste(main & lower level)   ⊨ 3D,R,crib   ⊑ 1Ensuite,
1sh.w.g   ★ KF,LF,F,TV in sitting room, bicycles to rent
⊕Designated smoking area, no pets   ⚬ German
🏃 Walking & cycling trails, snowmobiling, x-c skiing
🚗 Wilkie, swimming pool, fishing at Scott Dam, excellent hunting (wild game/waterfowl) in fall
Warm and friendly welcome on Bison Ranch surrounded by beautiful Prairie landscape located in Central Saskatchewan. Hosts will conduct tours of the ranch. Guests may take part in the feeding & care of the buffalo, and learn their characteristics and gentle ways. Breakfast is served in the gazebo or deck, weather permitting. Ideal place for wedding and reunion guests. ✓B&B

Yorkton

(north-east of Regina, near MBborder; see also Saltcoats, Kamsack)

Musey, Ann & Zenon (Lazy Maples B&B)
111 Darlington St.West, Yorkton, SK S3N 0E9

☎ (306) 783-7078

$36.75S $47.25D $10Add.person   ▣ Meals   (spec. discounts & family rates available)   ► 7
Located in northwest part of Yorkton, close to Yellowhead Hwy 16.
⊕ Full, homebaked   🏠 Res., raised bungalow, patio, quiet
■2D(in 1suite) (lower level)   ⊨ 2D,1P,1R   ⊑ 1sh.w.g.
★TV,VCR,KF,LF, bicycles, exercise cycle, off-street parking, plug in   ⊕Smoking outside, pets outside   ⊕ Ukrainian
🏃 St.Mary's Church, corner store, Sonja's Flower Garden, mini golf, ecologic walking park, city bus
Semi-retired couple in totally renovated home with large perennial flower garden & cozy backyard. Hosts are familiar with city and area tourist attractions/events and have conducted many church and area tours. Hostess is involved in the local Cultural Center. Breakfast (incl. perogies) is served in the dining room. Ukrainian souvenirs are available. Visa ✓CC

Manitoba

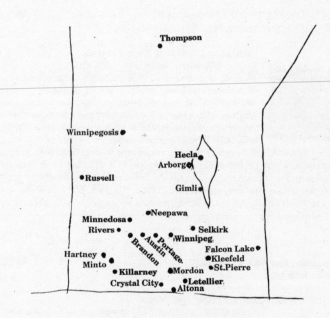

Thompson

Winnipegosis

Hecla
Arborg
Gimli

Russell

Neepawa
Minnedosa
Rivers
Selkirk
Portage
Austin Winnipeg
Brandon Falcon Lake
Hartney Kleefeld
Minto St.Pierre
Killarney Mordon
Crystal City Letellier
Altona

Travel Manitoba (Tourism Dep't)
155 Carlton St.   7th floor
Winnipeg, MB   R3C 3H8

toll-free 1-800-665-0040

Altona
(south of Winnipeg near US border; see also Letellier, Morden)

Siemens, Ed & Ruth (Schwartz Heritage House B&B)　　　☎ (204) 324-1233
Box 1671, No245, 10thAve NW, Altona, MB　R0G 0B0

From Winnipeg, travel 108km south on Hwy 75. Proceed west on
Hwy 14 for 18km, then south on Hwy 30 for 10km.
$45S　$55D　$15Child/Add.person　🍽 Meals　　　► 8A,4Ch
🍵 Cont., homebaked　🏠 Res., hist., 3-storey, deck, quiet
■4D,2F (upstairs)　🛏 2D,2Q　🛁 1Sh.w.g.　★ Air,TV, street
parking　👋 No smoking, no pets, children min. age 5
🚗 Downtown Winnipeg, beach and campgrounds, golf course
🏃 Outdoor Community swimming pool, park, Nature Sanctuary

🐾 Theme rooms enhanced with antiques add interest to recently modernized Heritage house
(built in 1902). Breakfast is served in the spacious dining room. Enjoy spectacular Manitoba
sunsets from the 2nd-storey guest room and a warm friendly atmosphere. Dog and bird in residence.
Visa ✏B&B

Arborg
(north of Winnipeg; see also Hecla Isle, Gimli)

Phelps, Charisse & Carly (A Touch of Home B&B)　　　☎ (204) 376-2260
Box 495, 11 Hay Portage Place, Arborg, MB　R0C 0A0

Located on junction of Hwys 7 and 68.
$40S　$50-55D　(plus tax)　🍽 Meals　　　► 7
🍵 Full, homebaked　🏠 Rural, res., bi-split level, deck, quiet
■ 3(upper and lower levels)　🛏 1S,1D,1Q,1P　🛁 Private
★Air,TV/VCR in guest room, ceiling fans, private lounge,
playpen, high-chair, off-street parking, guest quarters are
separate　👋Designated smoking area, no pets, children welcome
🚗 Lake Winnipeg and beaches

🐾 Warm welcome by mother & daughter team in cozy home with private back yard and large
deck off the dining room, where breakfast is served. Located in a quiet bay in the village along the
Icelandic River. Relax and enjoy rural hospitality at its finest and a complimentary tray afternoon
or evening with special lemon blueberry muffins fresh from the oven. Ideal place for special
occasions, hunters or vacationers. Alternate arrangements are possible with advance notice. ✏B&B

Austin
(west of Portage La Prairie)

Jones, Cecil & Judith (The Oak Tree B&B)　　　☎ (204) 637-2029
Box 35, Austin, MB　R0H 0C0

$45S　$55D　$75F　$10Child/Add.person　🍽 Meals　　　► 5A,2Ch
Located 5km south of TCH at east entrance to Austin.

🍵 Full, homebaked　🏠 Farm, bungalow, patio, deck, quiet,
secluded　■ 2(main & lower level)　🛏 2D,1S,crib,bunkbeds
(children in sleep bags)　🛁1Sh.w.g.(in lower level)　★F,TV,LF,
some wheel-chair access　👋No pets
🏃 Farm grounds, x-c skiing, snowshoeing
🚗 Golf courses, Manitoba Agricultural Museum (Pioneer village,
large display of agricultural machinery), Annual Threshermen's
Reunion & Rodeo (July), Spruce Woods Park, Carberry Desert

🐾 Modern home full of family heirlooms and collectibles; surrounded by six golf courses. Enjoy
the shaded yard and landscaped gardens, where wildlife, birds & nature abound. Ideal place for a
short or longer golfing holiday. Tee time can be booked, if required. End the day with a weiner roast
at the outdoor fire pit. Breakfast is served in family dining room and bag lunches are available.
Semi-retired hosts are active in the community and involved with local historic book publishing.
Children welcome. ✏B&B

Brandon

(west of Portage La Prairie)

Soloway, Ivan & Paulette (Casa Maley)
1605 Victoria Ave, Brandon, MB   R7A 1C1

☎ (204) 728-0812 Fax (204) 728-6287
1-877-729-2900

Located two blocks east of junction of Hyws 10/1A.
$40S $50D $60F 🍽 Meals   ▶ 4A,4Ch
🍴 Choice, homebaked   🏠 Downtown, res., older, patio, quiet
■3 (upstairs)   ⊨1S,1T,1D,1Q,cot ⚱2Sh.w.g.
★Air,2TV,3F,LF, garage parking plus parking for 4 cars, sinks in
2 guest rooms ⚜No smoking
🕺 Brandon U., Daly House Museum, Architectural walking tours,
antiques, Keystone Recreation Center, restaurants, shops
🚗 Canada Winter Games Sportsplex, golfing, Spirit Sands Desert
🐾 Designated Heritage, 1912-built European-style, 3-storey Tudor house with red brick exterior,
fairy-tale Gingerbread-house appearance and spacious interior decor and beautiful quarter-cut oak
and wainscotting in foyer, dining room and grand staircase. Hosts enjoy welcoming people from all
over the world. Transportation and pick-ups by appointment can be arranged. Visa,MC 🛏B&B

Szmon, Terry & Pam (The White House Bed & Breakfast)   ☎ & Fax (204) 726-4280
1705 Middleton Ave., Brandon, MB   R7A 1A8   E-mail: whitehse@mb.aibn.com

From TCH turn off at McDonalds Restaurant onto North Service Rd (Middleton Ave). Turn west to

Chalet Motel and look for white house on west side of Motel.
$40S $50D $10Child/Add.person   🍽 Meals   (plus tax) ▶ 8
🍴 Full, homebaked   🏠 Sub., 2-storey, hist., 2-acres, porch,
quiet, veranda   ■3D,1F(upstairs)   ⊨1K,1Q,3D ⚱3Sh.w.h.,
1ensuite   ★Air,LF,F, TV in guest rooms, off-street parking
⚜Smoking on back deck, no pets
🕺 Golf course, large treed property
🚗 Riding Mountain National Park, International Peace Gardens,
Lake Minnedosa, Classic Rock Festival, Spirit Sands Provincial Park (sand hills)
🐾 Congenial hosts enjoy meetin gpeople and sharing with them the beauty of their home filled
with many fine antiques and collectibles, as well as the surrounding property which resembles
country-like living in the city. Ideal place for special occasions. Enjoy the famous home-cooked
breakfasts served in special guest breakfast room and the relaxing atmosphere. Special breakfasts
requests may be accommodated. There is a dog in residence. 🛏 B&B bedandbreakfastmanitoba

---

Crystal City   *(s of Portage-La-Prairie near US border; see also Killarney, Morden)*

Hildebrand, Judy (Poplar Lane B&B)   ☎ (204) 873-2194
Box 443, Crystal City, MB   R0K 0N0

Travel 7km south of Crystal City on Hwy 34, then 3km west to end of road.
$40S $50D $10Child   ▶ 8
🍴 Full   🏠 Farm, 2-storey, hist., view from guest rooms, quiet
secluded   ■ 3D (upstairs)   ⊨ 1D,2Q,1P ⚱ 1Sh.w.g.,
1ensuite   ★ TV,LF ⚜ No smoking, no pets 〰 German
🕺 Hiking along creek & ravine on property, x-c skiing, canoeing
🚗 Holiday Mountain Ski Resort, golf courses, Rock Lake
(boating, fishing, swimming)
🐾 Warm hospitality in recently renovated 1905 farm house,
enhanced with hardwood and character furnishings and situated on operating sheep farm. Feel free
to visit the sheep, llama and horses. Explore the valley of the meandering Cypress Creek.
Experience a relaxing country stay with abundance of home cooking and baking.

Falcon Lake

(west of Kenora (ON), near Ontario border)

Vlasman, Mike & Yuki (Falcon Trails Resort)   ☎ & Fax (204) 349-8273
General Delivery, Falcon Lake, MB   R0E 0N0   E-mail: relax@falcontrails.mb.ca

From Trans Canada Hwy, take Falcon Lake Exit past stop sign and proceed on road into the lakeforks. Take the right fork (southshore Rd) and continue to the very end.

$45-55S/D $65-75F   (plus tax)   ► 6
🍵 Cont. 🏠Rural, lakefront, lodge, view from guest rooms, porch, acreage, deck, quiet, secluded ■3Ste(upstairs) ⊨6T(K)
🛁1Sh.w.g.   ★ KF,F,private entrance, library, guests quarters are in private wing 🚭No smoking, no pets, children min. age 6 〰Japanese
🏃 Hiking, biking, canoeing, swimming, x-c/downhill skiing, snowshoeing, skating
🚗West Hawk Lake, Alfred Hole Goose Santuary, South Whiteshell Trail/part of Trans Canada T.
🐾 Rustic luxury in stylish Lodge situated on the granite of the Canadian Shield at the secluded end of Falcon Lake in the beautiful Whiteshell Provincial Park and surrounded by spectacular natural scenery. Relax in the great room by the massive granite fireplace after a day of outdoor adventures & travelling or in the private outdoor hot tub. There are also luxurious post & beam chalet-style guest cabins (self-contained). Ideal and unique setting for workshops, conferences, meetings & family reunions. Breakfast is served in guest breakfast room. Attractive group rates available. CCards, ✔B&B http://falcontrails.mb.ca

---

Gimli

(on Lake Winnipeg; see also Arborg, Hecla Isle)

Orestes, Darcy & Philip (Ash Grove B&B)   ☎ (204) 642-5345
Box 93, Camp Morton, MB   R0C 0M0

Located 80km north of Winnipeg, just off provincial Hwy222 on Rd324 in Camp Morton.
$45S $55D $5Child $110F   ► 7

📅May-Sept(long weekends), open only Thurs-Sunday & Monday on long weekends) 🍵 Cont, self-serve 🏠 Village, 2-storey, hist., gazebo, quiet, secluded ■4
(upstairs) ⊨1S,2D,1bunkbed 🛁Sh.w.g. ★ TV, library
🚭Designated smoking area, pets negotiable 〰some French
🏃 Lake Winnipeg and beach, Camp Morton Prov.Prk (hiking & biking trails, playground & Recreation Area), bus stop at corner 🚗 Several golf courses, Resort town of Gimli
🐾 Charming & comfortable old house, formerly a Roman Catholic Nunnery, located on 2acres of park-like lawns & gardens and backing onto Prov.Park. Relax in the gazebo, listen to the abundance of songbirds in the wooded grove. Breakfast is served in guest breakfast room. There are 2dogs and 2cats outside, who get along well with others. Children welcome. Visa ✔B&B

Hartney
(south-west of Brandon; see also Killarney, Minto)

Whetter, Margaret (River Park Farm Guest Home)   ☎ (204) 858-2407, Fax (204) 858-2390
Box 310, Hartney, MB   R0M 0X0

Located on Hwy 21 and 1 km west of the town.
$40S $50D $10Child   🍽 Meals   ► 10
🍴Full,homebaked   🏠Farm,hist.,3-storey,view,quiet,riverfront
■4D plus attic suite (all upstairs)   ⬛2Sh.w.g.   ⊨8S,1D,1P,1R
★Air,F,TV in guest room   🖐No smoking
🎴 Souris River, small dock with canoe, nature trails along river
bank, golfing, horseshoe pit, restored farm buildings (barn and
shop)part of a mixed farming operation
🚐 Lauder Sand Hills Wildlife Management area, Souris Agate pits, swinging bridge, Peace Garden
📣 Restored turn-of-Century house and farm buildings (built 1910-1913), furnished with period
antiques. Enjoy a vacation center and learn about country living at its best; a place of Canadian
culture and beauty in a very scenic setting. Abundance of wildlife can be seen on the property and
along the river. A great place for retreats and seminars. Hosts are involved with English as a
second Language Homestay program. Guided canoe trips available. ✓B&B

Hecla Island
(north of Winnipeg in Lake Winnipeg, see also Arborg, Gimli)

Holtz, Sharon and Dave (Solmundson Gesta Hus)   ☎ & Fax (204) 279-2088
Box 76, Hecla Island, MB   R0C 2R0   E-mail: holtz@mb.sympatico.ca

Located within Hecla Island Provincial Park in the heart of Lake Winnipeg, accessible via Hwy 8.
$55S $60-75D   🍽 Meals   ► 8A,4Ch
🍴 Full, homebaked   🏠 Village, hist., acreage, view, lakefront,
quiet, veranda   ■4(main & upper floor)   ⊨2D,2Q,2cots
⬛2Sh.w.g.,1ensuite   ★TV,KF,parking   🖐Smoking
🎴 Woodland lakeshore for walking, church & museums in historic
Icelandic fishing village. hiking, cycling, angling
🚐 18-hole golf course, beaches, interpretive programs, trails
📣 Luxurious European-style hospitality in newly renovated &
completely modern comfortable home located in an original Icelandic settlement. Each room has a
view of the lake. Relax on the veranda and enjoy the beautiful view of Lake Winnipeg and the
tranquil and peaceful atmosphere. Host is a commercial fisherman and dinner specialty is Manitoba
Pickeral (Walleye). There are cats, dogs, ducks. Visit the in-house gift shop. Off-season rates
avail.Visa,MC ✓B&B www.heclatourism.mb.ca

Killarney
(south of Brandon; see also Crystal City, Minto)

Krueger, Linda & Henry (Country Comfort B&B)   ☎ (204) 523-8742 Fax (204) 523-8511
Box 808, Killarney, MB   R0K 1G0

Located 4km south of Hwy 3 between Killarney & Boissevain.
$40S $55-60D $10child   (Reservations appreciated)
🍽Meals   ► 6+
🍴 Choice   🏠 Modern ranch-style   ■ 2F (lower level with
entrance)   ⊨ 2T,2D,1Q,1R,2P   ⬛ 1Sh.w.g.   ★ KF,TV in
guest sitting area, private entrance   ♥   🖐 No smoking, no pets
🎴 Quiet country walks, bird & animal watching, x-c skiing,
ski-dooing, biking
🚐 International Peace Garden, US border, Boissevain Outdoor Art Gallery (murals), Killarney
Lake, Bottineau Winter Park (downhill skiing), Brandon, Turtle Mt Prov. Park, excellent hunting
📣 Warm welcome and friendly Manitoba hospitality in newly renovated farm house with cozy
comfort in a country setting. Relax after a day of sightseeing or travelling and partake in many
recreational and entertainment facilities provided. ✓B&B

Kleefeld

(south-east of Winnipeg; see also St.Pierre Jolys)

Davidson, Cliff & Donalene (The Stationhouse B&B)   ☎ (204) 377-4790
Box 88, Kleefeld, MB   R0A 0V0   E-mail: stationhouse@bigfoot.com

$40S $50D $10Child (free under age 6)   🍴Meals   ▶ 4A,4Ch

Located 1km west of Kleefeld on College Ave. Phone for directions. 🍳 Full, homebaked 🏠 Rural, 2-storey, hist., acreage, deck, quiet, patio, secluded ■2D,1F (upstairs) ⊨ 2T,1D,1Q,P 🛁1Sh.w.g.   ★ F,TV,ceiling fans, off-street parking, guest quarters are separate ✋ Smoking outside, no pets 🏃 Village of Kleefeld (Honey Capital of Manitoba), beautiful park (with pagodas for cooking, tennis, play structures & ice-skating), x-c ski & snowmobile trails, grocery store
🚗 City of Winnipeg, Royal Winnipeg Ballet & Orchestra, golfing, swimmming, museums
📣 Canadian Pacific Railway Station built in 1927 with the former large waiting room serving as the living room, surrounded by 5 acres of poplar & oak trees and wild berry bushes. Hosts are railway enthusiasts and have collected many railway artifacts, literature & historic items. There is an extensive model railroad currently under construction. Breakfast is served in guest breakfast room. There is a dog in restricted area. Vis ✔B&B http://www.mts.net/~davidso/

Letellier

(south of Winnipeg near US border; see also Altona)

Derksen, Dennis and Sheila (Fraser House)   ☎ (204) 737-2284/737-2361,
33 Main St., Letellier, MB   R0G 1C0   Fax (204) 737-2081

Located 16 km N of US border on Hwy 75. Phone for directions. $40S $50-60D $7.50Child   (Children welcome)   ▶ 4A,2Ch 🍳 Homebaked 🏠 Rural, older, quiet, front porch ■ 1D,1F (upstairs) ⊨ 2D,1P 🛁 1Sh.w.g.(no shower) ★ TV,LF, parking ✋No smoking, no pets, children welcome 〰 French 🏃 Park, tennis court.
🚗 Golfing, fishing, swimming, shopping
📣 1916-built home, furnished with wonderful antiques enhancing its Victorian decor and situated in the heart of Manitoba's bustling agricultural area in a French community. Enjoy a quiet walk, cycle, or play a game of tennis. Visa,MC

Minnedosa

(north of Brandon; see also Rivers, Neepawa)

Graham, Pat & Darrell (The Castle)   ☎ (204) 867-2830, Fax (204) 867-5051
149-2nd Ave S.W., Box 1705, Minnedosa SW, MB   R0J 1E0   E-mail: castlebb@escape.ca

From Hwy1 at Brandon, take Hwy10 north to Minnedosa. At Town Center, go west on 2nd Ave SW.
$45S $55-77D $99(Honeymoon Ste) $10Child   (plus 10% in July/Aug)   ▶ 10A,3Ch

🍳Homebaked 🏠Village,hist.,3-storey,quiet,riverlot ■2D,1F,1Ste (upstairs),host quarters on top floor 🛁1Sh.w.g, 3ensuite ⊨S,D,Q,P,T,3cots ★F,parking ✋Restricted smoking, no pets 🏃 Town center, restaurants, Lake Minnedosa with beach and park, golfing, tennis, Pioneer Museum, bird walk,boating, skiing 🚗 Brandon, Neepawa (Margaret Laurence Museum), Clear Lake, Riding Mountain Nat.Park
📣 Victorian home (ca1901) known locally as "the Castle", a redesigned and restored Heritage landmark of Queen Anne architecture. Located on the Little Saskatchewan River on a quiet street in a lovely setting. Suitable for retreats, business travel, reunions, honeymoon, anniversary. Wedding night and anniversary packages available. MC ✔B&B

Minnedosa (cont'd)

Proven, Susan (Fairmount B&B)　　　　　　　　☎ & Fax (204) 874-2165
Box 633, Minnedosa, MB R0J 1E0

From jct of Hwys 10/16 north of Minnedosa, proceed 6.6km north on Hwy 10 (towards Riding
Mt.Nat.Park). Turn left on Fairmount Rd and continue 6km to farm.

$40S　$50D　$10Child/Add.person　🍽 Meals　　▶ 7
🍲 Full　🏠 Farm, 3-storey, hist., view from guest rooms,
lakefront, porch ■2D,1F(upstairs) ⊨1S,2T,2D ⊒3Private
★TV,LF　🖐 No smoking, no pets　⌁Spanish
🕴 Woodland and waterbirds, walking trail around Prairie
waterways, beaver house, x-c skiing, ox-cart historic trail
🚗 Brandon, Riding Mtn.Nat.Park, Margaret Lawrence Museum
(Neepawa), Rock Concert (Minnedosa), Agassiz Ski Resort

📢 Restored 1914-built farmhouse with stained glass windows and furnishings in the style of
early Canadiana situated on third generation working farm, on the edge of a pond and a sheltered
natural spruce grove. Relax while sheep graze on the pastures by the water. Spend summer
evenings around the bonfire or in the cozy attic rec-room in the winter. Hostess loves to cook for
guests, using natural farm products ("just like Granny"). Breakfast is served in special guest
breakfast room. ⌐B&B

Minto　　　　　　　　　　　*(south of Brandon; see also Hartney, Killarney)*

Fraser, Ernest & Donna (Fraser Family Farms & B&B)　　☎& Fax (204) 776-2176
Box 93, Minto, MB R0K 1M0　　　　　　　　　　　E-mail: ffamfarm@escape.ca

Located 8km east of Minto off Hwy23. Watch for riverside municipality sign, turn south.
$40S　$55D　$10Child　$30Add.person　🍽 Meals　　　▶ 2A,4Ch
🍲 Full　🏠 Farm, bungalow, quiet　■ 1F (ground level)　⊨ 1S,1P, crib　⊒ Ensuite
★KF,LF, facilities for the handicapped, separate entrance, electric hook-up　🖐 No smoking
🕴 Horseback and hay riding, small petting animals
🚗 International Peace Gardens, Turtle Mountains Provincial Park, Boissevain (murals, famous
Turtle Derby, quaint shops, restaurants), Whitewater Lake, Brandon, US border (ND)
📢 Warm country welcome on working farm with beef cows and horses. Stay a few days and learn
about country living or just enjoy the peace & quiet. Hosts' daughter gives riding lessons for guests.
Coffee & meals provided for bus tours. There is a resident dog. ⌐ MFVA

Morden　　　　　　*(south-west of Winnipeg, near US border, s/a Altona, Crystall City)*

Cordrey, Gary & Ginny (Rose Briar B&B)　　　　　☎& Fax (204) 822-4446
886 Gilmour St., Morden, MB R6M 1R9

From Wpg. follow Hwy3 south to Morden. Turn north on Mountain at RCMP, left at crosswalk.

$45S　$55-60D　　　　　　　　　　　　　　▶ 4
🍲 Full, homebaked　🏠 Downtown, rural, res., bi-level, view
from guest rooms, patio, quiet, sunroom　■ 2D (lower level)
⊨ 2T,1Q　⊒ 1Sh.w.g.　★ F,TV in guest sitting area, fans in
guest rooms, private entrance, off-street parking, guest quarters
are separate　🖐 Smoking outside, no pets, children min. age13
🕴 Golfing, lake and beach, fishing, fossil digs, x-c skiing, hiking,
biking, art and craft shops, museums, auctions, festivals
🚗 Outdoor drama walk through maze, min.golf, skiing
📢 Warm welcome in southern Manitoba home with modern conveniences and old fashioned
hospitality. Savour delicous home-cooked breakfast. Relax by the wood burning fireplace in the cozy
sitting area or in the sunroom, after a busy day of sightseeing or travelling. Hosts are long-time
residents of the area and look forward to assisting their guests. Ask about fabulous holiday
packages. Visa ⌐B&B

Neepawa

(north of Brandon; see also Minnedosa)

MacPhee, Joe & Glenda (The Garden Path B&B)   ☎ (204) 476-3184
Box 928, 536 Second Ave., Neepawa, MB R0J 1H0

Located on the Trans Canada Yellowhead Hwy 16 at the corner of 2nd Ave in town.

$59-69S/D $10Add.person   ▶ 7A,1ch
🍴 Full, homebaked, buffet   🏠 Res., rural town, hist., 2.5-storey, porch   ■3D (upstairs)   ⊨ 2T,2Q,cot   🛁1Sh.w.g.,1Ensuite
★F,off-street parking   🚭 No smoking, no pets
🧍 Margaret Laurence Home, Riverbend Park, World Lily Capital Festival (July), Trans Canada Trail route
🚗The Lily Nook, Neepawa Golf & Country Club, Mt Agassiz Ski Centre, Riverside Cemetary, Riding Mt.Nat.Park (Aug)

📣 Spacious yellow brick home (ca 1903) completely renovated, containing much of the charm and character of its early heritage, and situated in rural town, the proud receiver of "Manitoba's Most Beautiful Town" & "Communities in Bloom" Awards. Breakfast is served in the formal dining room or on the casual sun porch. Leisure time may be spent in the spacious living room with its fireplace, piano, books, games and garden view. The grounds are well suited for strolling. "Baseball, feline & garden languages spoken here". There are 3 resident cats. Visa,MC ✔B&B

Portage-La-Prairie

(west of Winnipeg; see also Austin)

Rud, Marnie & Barry (Rud's on the Lake Bed & Breakfast)   ☎ & Fax (204) 857-9231
Box 974 Main Station, 10 Pine Cr., Portage-La-Prairie, MB R1N 3C4   1-877-857-4917
    E-mail: brud@portage.net

In Portage turn south off Sask Ave (at any light) towards lake, turn right at lake and proceed past Yellowquill School/College to Pine Cr. OR: From Hwy 1 east or west turn north from Portage

by-pass onto Yellowquill Trail, turn right onto Pine Cr at stop sign.
$55-60S/D $15Add.person   (plus tax)   ▶ 6A,1Ch
🍴 Full   🏠Res, acreage, bungalow, view, lakefront, swimming pool, patio, deck, quiet   ■ 3(lower level)   ⊨ 1S,1D,1Q, cot,crib   🛁 1sh.w.g.   ★ Air,F,TV/VCR in guest room, coffee/tea in guest lounge, off-street parking   🚭 No smoking
🧍 Fishing in Assiniboine River, waterfowl & wildlife seen on property, canoes/paddle/row boat available

🚗 Winnipeg, golfcourses, Delta Beach & Marsh, Austin Machinery & Fort La Reine Museum
📣 Comfortable home in park-like setting on the shore of Crescent Lake. Relax by the heated pool. Enjoy the perennial flowers & beauty of the property over a homecooked Western breakfast.

Rivers

(north of Brandon; see also Minnedosa)

Kroeger, Lynn & Jake (Cozy River Inn B&B)   ☎ & Fax (204) 328-4457
Box 838, Rivers, MB R0K 1X0

Take Hwy 1 west from Brandon to Hwy 270. Proceed north to Hwy 25 and west to Rivers. Look for B&B 1km east of town.
$60S/D $10Add.person   ▶ 4A,4Ch
🍴 Cont., homebaked (self-serve)   🏠 Rural, bungalow, view from guest rooms, riverback, quiet, deck   ■ 2Stes (in separate cottage)   ⊨ 2Q,1P   🛁 2Private   ★ TV in guest room, separate entrance, fridge/coffee maker/ toaster oven in each suite   🚭 Designated smoking area, no pets
🧍 Town of Rivers, gravel pit & dam
🚗 Watersports, fishing, hunting, wildlife, bird watching, x-c skiing, snowmobiling, curling, tennnis, golfing, Lake Wahtopanah Provincial Park with sandy beach, Brandon, Souris, Minnedosa
📣 Guest house with theme rooms is separate from main dwelling and situated on Little Saskatchewan River surrounded by trees and park-like yard. Hosts enjoy music & crafts. Enjoy the cozy and peaceful atmosphere and friendly surroundings. Breakfast is served in suites. Visa ✔B&B

Russell

(south-west of Dauphin, near SK border)

Tweet, Ward & Linda (Boulton Manor B&B)　　　☎ & Fax (204) 773-3267
Box 1468, 322 Memorial Ave. South, Russell, MB　R0J 1W0

Phone for directions.
$50-60S　$60-70D　$100Ste(for 2)　$15-20Add.person　▶ 11
🄳Full, homebaked　🏠Res., 2-storey, hist., deck/balcony　■4D (incl
2Ste)(main & upper level)　🛏 2D,2Q,2R,1P　🚿2sh.w.g.
★F,LF,off-street parking　🖐Smoking on deck,no pets
🏃 Restaurants, shops, public pool, Beth Naylor costume Museum
🚗 Golf course, historic sites, fishing, Asessippi Park & ski hill, Riding
Mtn Nat. Park, air strip, Ukrainian & Native Culture

📢 Century home with spacious grounds & backyard wood. Browse through the collection of
antiques, books, letters and photos and imagine the trials of early Manitoba life. Breakfast is served
in the dining area or on the front deck. Hosts are knowledgeable about history of the area and about
nearby cultural and recreational sites. Reduced rates for 2 or more nights. ✎CC

Saint Pierre-Jolys

(south of Winnipeg; see also Kleefeld)

Lavergne, Raymond & Nicole (Gîte de Forest)　　☎ (204) 433-7870/7758, Fax 433-7181
512 Au Cote, Saint Pierre-Jolys, MB　R0A 1V0　　　E-mail: rlavergne@pli.mb.ca

Phone for directions.
$50S/D　$15Child　　　　　　　　　　　　　　▶ 5A,2Ch
🄳Full,flexible　🏠Rural, bungalow, deck, solarium　■1S,1D,1F
(main & lower level)　🛏 1S,1D,1Q,P　🚿1Private, 1sh.w.g.
★Air,KF,LF,F,TV,off-street parking　🖐 No smoking, no pets
〰 English (household language is French)
🚗 Provincial Park in Saint-Malo, beach, golfing, bison farm
🏃 Art Gallery (Riviere-Aux-Rats), museum, historic Goulet
house, fine restaurants (French cuisine), walking trails (soon to be part of Trans Canada Trail)
📢 Renovated home located in the centre of dominantly French speaking town. Relax in the
4-season solarium which houses fireplace and library. Enjoy the fire pit and swing in the back yard.
Breakfast can be enjoyed in the solarium. Hosts are of Acadian & French descent (1976) and are
proud of their roots and happy to share their heritage and knowledge of the area. Local tours for
groups of 30 or more can be organized. Visa ✎B&B

Selkirk

(north of Winnipeg)

Mannhart, Alex & Margrit (Fox-Estate B&B)　　　☎ (204) 482-9200
Box 9, Group354, RR3, River Rd 1168, Selkirk, MB　R1A 2A8　　Fax (204) 482-6260

From Winnipeg, take Main St North (becomes Hwy9) through Lockport and past East Lower Fort
Garry. Turn right on River Rd and continue 3km. From Selkirk
take Eveline St South to the town limits, where it is River Rd.
$45S　$55D　　　　　　　　　　　　　　　　▶ 8
🄳 Full　🏠 Rural, hist., 2acres, view from guest rooms, patio,
riverfront, porch, deck, quiet　■4D(upstairs)　🛏2S,3D
🚿2Sh.w.g.　★F,TV, private entrance, private parking lot
🖐Designated smoking area, no pets, not suitable for children
〰Swiss German
🏃 Historic stone church, small park, river walkway, fishing, bus line to Winnipeg
🚗 Airport for float-planes, fishing, hunting, golfing, Marine Museum, Oak Hammok Marsh,
Prairie Dog Railway, Lower Fort Garry Museum, Winnipeg Airport, downtown Winnipeg
📢 Beautiful, historic Estate nestled on the banks of the Red River. Each floor has its own
private lounge and glassed-in veranda. Hosts are artists and crafts people and have filled their home
with interesting art and handcrafted work. There is a small dog in residence. Visa

Selkirk (cont'd)

Sarginson, Laurel & Robert (Evergreen Gate B&B)   ☎ (204) 482-6248
1138 River Rd., Box 68, G349,RR3, Selkirk, MB R1A 2A8   E-mail: rsargins@sirnet.mb.ca

Take Hwy 9 (Main St) north from Winnipeg, turn right on River Rd directly north of Lower Fort
Garry. From Selkirk follow Eveline St. Look for No 1138.

$50S $60D $10Add.person   ► 4
🍴 Cont.(large choice)   🏠. Semi-rural, riverfront, acreage, quiet,
private, screened porch, deck ■2D(or Ste) ⊨2Q ◁1Sh.w.g.
★TV lounge, kitchenette, bicycles available   🖐No smoking, no
pets, families welcome   ∾ French
🏃 Walking, cycling, fishing, Lower Fort Garry
🚗 Golfing, Oak Hammock Marsh, Selkirk Marine Museum, Lake
Winnipeg beaches, Bird's Hill Park, downtown Winnipeg

☛ Warm welcome and friendly hospitality in unique contemporary home situated in peaceful
park-like surroundings high above the historic Red River. Ideal place for birdwatching (white
pelicans), for business travellers, weekend get-aways or visiting Manitoba's Interlake. Visa ↩B&B

Thompson   *(northern Manitoba)*

Doorenbos, Anna and Robert (Anna's Bed & Breakfast)   ☎ (204) 677-5075
204 Wolf Street, Thompson, MB R8N 1J7   E-mail: info@annasbnb.mb.ca

Take Hwy 6 north from the Perimeter Rd in Winnipeg (760 km to Thompson).

$40S $50D   📷 Meals   ► 2A
🍴 Full   🏠 Bungalow, quiet, deck, gazebo ■1Ste(self-cont -
main level) ⊨2T ◁Private ★Parking,sep entrance, phone
& TV in den 🖐No smoking,no children,no pets ∾Dutch
🏃 Northern Zoo, indoor swimming pool with waterslide, shopping
centers, Heritage Museum, on local bus route
🚗 Paint Lake Provincial & Pisew Falls Heritage Parks, Sasagui
/Odei River Rapids, Ospwagan/Troy Lakes stocked trout fishing

☛ Thompson is the depot centre for travellers to Churchill, other Northern Communities and
fly-in fishing lodges. Enjoy true Northern Hospitality in spacious home with large guest suite.
There is a greenhouse connected to the cozy and informal living room. Hosts originally came from
Egypt and Indonesia and they enjoy cooking oriental foods. Airport, train and bus pick-up available
for a nominal charge. ↩CC

Winnipeg   *(see also Selkirk)*

Auriat, Anna (Aubrey B&B)   ☎ & Fax (204) 775-1433
292 Aubrey St., Winnipeg, MB R3G 2J2

Located just south of Portage Ave (main street in City)
$35S $50D $10Child   📷 Meals   (plus tax)   ► 4A,1Ch
🍴 Choice   🏠 Downtown, 3-storey, quiet ■2D(upstairs) ⊨4S
◁1Sh.w.g. ★TV,KF,LF, ceiling fans, guest bikes available, off-street &
street parking   🖐 No smoking, no pets, children min. age 12
∾Ukrainian
🏃 Assiniboine River, shopping, bus stop for all routes
🚗 Beaches, horse races, Stadium, historic places, gambling casino
☛ Comfortable home situated on a quiet street with mature elms/ashes.
Relax alone or join the family for a chit chat. Special rate for longer stays.

Clark, Andy & Mirelle (Maison Grosvenor B&B) ☎ (204) 475-9630
824 Grosvenor Ave., Winnipeg, MB R3M 0N2

Take Hwy 95 (Corydon Ave) and turn north on Lilac St, right on Grosvenor.
$50S $60D $15Child 🍽 Meals ▶ 6A
🍷 Full 🏠 Res., 2.5-storey, older, patio, quiet
■3D(upstairs) ⊨3Q,cot ⟋2Sh.w.g., 1sh.w.h. ★ F,TV in guest sitting
room, airconditioners, off-street parking, guest quarters are separate
🖐Designated smoking area, no pets, children min.age10 ⋙ French
🚶 Corydon Ave & Osborne Village (galleries, boutiques, cafes, bistros,
patios), restaurants (Greek, Italian, Continental, Korean, Chinese), city
transportation in front of house
🚗 Assiniboine Park & Zoo, malls, Airport, Centennial Concert Hall, The Forks Market
📢 Beautiful 1914 Queen Anne Revival character home with oak-beamed ceilings, built-in oak
buffet and original stained glass windows, located in the city center's district of exciting, charming
& distinctive cultural and Continental character (Fort Rouge & River Heights). Guest rooms are
called "Green Room", Santa Fe Room", and Whimsical Room." Breakfast is served in guest breakfast
room. Special diets will be accommodated. There is a resident cat (isolated when guests are
present). ✍B&B

Clark, John and Louise (West Gate Manor) ☎ (204) 772-9788 Fax (204) 772-9782
71 West Gate, Winnipeg, MB R3C 2C9 E-mail: jclark@escape.ca

Located in City Centre. Phone for directions.

$45S $60-65D $10Add.person ▶ 8
🍷Full,homebaked 🏠Downtown, hist., sunroom, quiet
■4D(upst) ⊨2Q,3D,1T,cots ⟋2Sh.w.g. ★ F,1guest sitting
room, off-street parking 🖐 No smoking, children min. age 11
🚶 Antique shops, restaurants, shopping, bus depot, Winnipeg Art
Gallery, University of Winnipeg
🚗 Polo Park Mall, Winnipeg Arena/Stadium, Convention center,
CNR Station, The Folks Market
📢 Situated in historic, picturesque Armstrong Point area of the city, where Winnipeg's elite
built during the turn of the Century. Home is decorated in Victorian splendour with each room
reflecting its own period and theme. Ideal central location from which to explore the city.

Ellie, Peter & Eugenia (Ellie's Bed & Breakfast) ☎ (204) 772-5832, Fax (204) 783-1462
77 Middle Gate, Winnipeg, MB R3C 2C5 1-877-653-1462

From Portage Ave or Broadway Ave West proceed to Furby. Turn south to Middle Gate.

$45S $55-65D 🍽 Meals ▶ 6
📅 Apr-Dec 🍷 Full, homebaked 🏠 Res., split-level, quiet
■ 3D (upstairs) ⊨2T,2D, crib ⟋2Sh.w.g. ★ F,TV,LF,
off-street parking 🖐 No smoking, no pets ⋙ Ukrainian
🚗 Museum, Art Gallery, The Forks, Assiniboine Park,
downtown, shopping centres, Misaracordia Hospital, Convention
Centre, Winnipeg Arena & Stadium, University of Manitoba
📢 Bright and cheerful large modern home located in historic
Armstrongs Point area in the heart of the city surrounded with trees and peaceful atmosphere.
Hosts are well travelled and love to cook and they are known for their superb omelet. Pick-up from
bus, airport or train at additional charge. ✍B&B

Ingalls, Ann & Ray (Ann's Prairie Charm Bed & Breakfast)   ☎ (204) 253-3636
190 Greenview Rd., Winnipeg, MB R2N 4C6

$40S $50D $10Child (age 5-12) (free under age 5)   ▶4

From South Winnipeg Bypass (Rte 100) go 5.5 km south on Rte 200, then east on Greenview Rd.

🍴 Cont., homebaked   🏠 Rural, sub., split-level, acreage, porch, quiet, secluded   ■ 2D (upstairs)   ⊨2T,1D   ⬜1Sh.w.g.   ★F,TV,LF   ✋ Smoking outside
🧍 Surrounding prairie farmland
🚗 University of Manitoba, downtown Winnipeg, restaurants, shopping, Steinbach Mennonite Museum

🐾 Charming, modern home furnished comfortably with antiques and family heirlooms surrounded by park-like setting on the prairie. Located in the southeast corner of Winnipeg with easy access from major routes. Enjoy quiet country living in the city. Tourists, business and professional guests welcome. There is a dog in residence. Weekly rates available.

Jones, Arlene and Bob (Bannerman East B&B)   ☎(204)589-6449,Fax(204)528-5937
99 Bannerman Ave., Winnipeg, MB R2W 0T1

Located close to Portage/Main Sts junction in North Winnipeg.

$38S $48D $10Child (under age 12)   ▶3
🍴Full   🏠Res.,patio,quiet   ■1S,1D(upstairs)   ⊨1S,1D   ⬜1Sh.w.g., 1sh.w.h.   ★TV,KF,LF,parking   ✋No smoking,no pets
🧍 Excellent ethnic and continental restaurants, public transportation, historic St. John Park Anglican Church(1820), historic "Forks" site, Museum of Man & Nature, Concert Hall, Ukrainian Cultural center, shopping, theatres, Folklorama sites & Rainbow Stage (July/Aug)

🚗 Lower Fort Garry, Steinbach Mennonite Museum, MB Stampede (Morris), Emerson (USA border), Mint Factory, Lake Winnipeg, International Airporrt, Railway Station, Bus Depot
🐾 Well-traveled hosts (B&B in Europe and Eastern Canada) in comfortable home and pleasant surroundings. Enjoy warm hospitality in convenient location. ✓B&B

Lobreau, Francis and Anya   ☎ (204) 256-9789
137 Woodlawn Ave., Winnipeg, MB R2M 2P5   E-mail: flobreau@home.com

Located in South Winnipeg, off St. Mary's Rd (Rt 52), with easy access to Trans Canada Hwy or South Bypass (Hwy 100).

$40S $50-55D   ▶4-6
🍴 Choice   🏠Sub.,4-level split-level,acreage,quiet   ■3D(upst)   ⊨1Q,2D   ⬜1Private, 1Sh.w.g.   ★TV,KF,LF,F, parking   ✋No pets, no smoking   ∽French,Polish
🧍 Major Shopping Centre, University of Manitoba, City transit, St. Vital Park, Riel House
🚗 Quick access to downtown attractions, St. Boniface

🐾 Comfortable home with antique furnishings, located on a half acre of landscaped grounds in a quiet neighbourhood near the Red River. Warm up by the fireplace on cool evenings. Relax in the hammock or play a tune on the grand piano. Pick-up service available at added charge. ✓B&B

Winnipeg (cont'd)

Neufeld, Elsa & Werner (Elsa's Place B&B)   ☎& fAX (204) 284-3176
796 Pasadena Ave., Winnipeg, MB   R3T 2T3   E-mail: elsavern@escape.ca

From Pembina Hwy travel on Dalhouse to Silverton, left on Laval to house on corner of Pasadena.

$40S $50 $10Child   ► 6
🍴 Full   🏠 Res., bungalow   ■2S,2D (main & lower level)
🚪2D,2K   🛏 1Sh.w.g.   ★KF,LF, off-street/street parking
✋No smoking, no pets   ∿ German
🚗 St.Vital Shopping Mall
🎯 Warm & friendly welcome in comfortable city home. Hosts are retired farmers and enjoy travelling, reading, quilting and antiques and learning how to use the computer. ✒B&B

Preweda, Delann and Larry (Cozy Cove Bed & Breakfast)   ☎ (204) 256-4430
13 Nichol Ave., Winnipeg, MB   R2M 1V6

Located 2 blocks west of Trans Canada Hwy at St. Mary's Rd.
$40S $50D $10Child   ► 4A,2Ch
🍴Full & Cont. 🏠Res., bungalow, sunroom, quiet ■1S,2D(lower level) 🚪1S,2D 🛏Private ★Air,TV,LF,VCR, bikes available for guests, private sitting room, parking ✋No smoking, pets welcome
🧍 Excellent transit service
🚗 The Mint, The Forks, downtown, Osborne Village, hospital

🎯 Enjoy warm hospitality in quiet, spacious, attractive home with sunroom overlooking a beautiful yard. Well-traveled hostess enjoys exchanging experiences. Host is an avid fisherman/hunter. Breakfast includes fresh muffins and homemade breads & jams. One-day fishing excursions available. There is a dog & cat in residence. ✒B&B

Taylor, Joe & Bev Suek (Twin Pillars Bed & Breakfast)   ☎ (204) 284-7590,
235 Oakwood Ave., Winnipeg, MB   R3L 1E5   E-mail: tls@escape.ca Fax (204) 452-4925

Take Rte 16 & Osborne St south to Oakwood Ave (east off Osborne)
$38-40S $48-50D $55Ste $10Add.pers   (Child under age 8 free)   ► 8A,2Ch
🍴Cont.(generous) 🏠Res., 3-storey, hist., porch, deck,quiet ■3D,1Ste (2nd/3rd floor) 🚪2T,2D 🛏1Sh.w.g.,1sh.w.h. ★LF,KF,TV & balconies in some guest rooms, separate entrance, off-street parking ♥ ✋Designated smoking rooms ∿ some French
🧍 Old movie theatre, park across street, restaurants, public transportation (bus #16), Municipal Hospital
🚗 Osborne Village shopping, downtown, Canoe & Golf Club, The Forks Market, Winnipeg Zoo, Museum of Man & Nature
🎯 Turn-of-the-Century Heritage house with antique furniture and twin pillars on front, situated in a quiet residential area. Enjoy a friendly, homey atmosphere and conversation with congenial hosts. Only unscented, non-allergenic soap is used in the household. Children welcome. There is a resident dog in host area only. Catering to groups available. ✒CC
www.escape.ca/~tls/twin.htm

Winnipeg (cont'd)

Thevenot, James, Judy (Six Pines Ranch) ☎ (204) 633-3326
Box 27B, RR2, Winnipeg, MB   R3C 2E6 E-mail: sixpines@gatewest.net

Located south of Stonewall. On Sturgeon Rd (Rd 8E) travel 4.2km north to Perimeter Hwy,
between Hwys 6/7. Look for 69058 Sturgeon Rd (Hwy 8E)
$69D $25Child(age 3-7 in same room)   (plus tax)   🍽 Meals   ► 8

🍲 Full   🏠 Farm, 3-storey, hist., acreage, view from guest
rooms, quiet, secluded   ■3D(2ndfloor)   ⊨ 2T,2D,futon, crib
🛁1Sh.w.g.   ★KF,LF,TV in sitting room, fans in guest rooms,
guest quarters are separate, play area, horse shoe pits
🚭Smoking in smoking parlour, no pets
🏃 Parklike setting farmyard, horse trails, golf course, farm tours,
Halloween tours, camping facilities out back (larger groups)
🚗 Lower Fort Garry (National Historic Fort), Oak Hammock
Marsh Interpretive Centre, Fort Whyte Nature Centre, Winnipeg, International Airport
📷 Victorian homestead, built in 1811 with beautiful douglas fir banister leading all the way to
the 3rd floor. There is an old fieldstone granite/limestone Blacksmith Shop on the property.
Breakfast is served in the turn-of-the-Century formal dining room. Relax on the beautifully
landscaped grounds and enjoy the peace and serenity of country living not far from the city. Nightly
bon-fires under the stars (weather permitting). Enjoy a tour of the farm &/or help with the daily
chores. Pick-up at airport, bus depot or train station. The ranch has been the location for movies
and TV episodes. There are dogs and cats.✓B&B www.sixpines.mb.ca

---

Bed & Breakfast of Manitoba (Reservation Service) ☎(204)661-0300, 1-877-304-0300
434 Roberta Ave., Winnipeg, Man   R2K 0K6 E-mail: info@bedandbreakfast.mb.ca
(Paula Carlson)
Rates:$45-90S/D   (including full breakfast). Advance reservation highly recommended.
Organized in 1980, Bed & Breakfast of Manitoba represents a variety of quality inspected homes in
Winnipeg and throughout rural Manitoba. Friendly and knowledgeable hosts will make guest feel
welcome and will do their best to ensure that they leave with fond memories of this fine province.
Call or write for a full colour brochure with descriptions of each home and current rates.

Winnipegosis   *(north of Dauphin)*

Lytwyn, Jim & Sherry (Twin Spruce Lodge) ☎ (204)656-4765, Fax 656-4785
Box 203, Winnipegosis, MB   R0L 2G0 E-mail: slytwyn@mb.sympatico.ca

Located 58km north of Dauphin on Hwy20. Turn east at junction of PTH364 and continue for 6km.

$65S $75D $10Child/Add.person $90F (plus tax)   ► 9
🍲 Self-serve   🏠 Farm, ranch-style, view from guest rooms,
quiet, secluded, screened deck   ■ 3(main floor) and guest
house   ⊨5S,2Q,2P   🛁 Private   ★ KF,F,TV in guest rooms,
ceiling fans, private entrance, wheel-chair access in guest house,
off-street parking, hot-tub on screened deck, guest quarters are
separate   🚭 Designated smoking, no pets indoors (outdoor
kennel for dogs)
🏃 Walking trail, excellent wildlife area, hiking, birding, snowmobiling, fishing, watersports
🚗 Golf Course, museum, stores, restaurants, Canada's first pink firetruck
📷 Large private guesthouse with deluxe comfort & hospitality. Suited for country vacation
packages and a great place for fishing and hunting enthusiasts (all inclusive fully guided packages
available with meals included). Cuddle up by the fireplace and enjoy the reading material or the
satellite TV and VCR. Relax in the hot-tub and leave the stress behind after exploring Manitoba's
parkland. ✓B&B

Ontario

Ontario Travel
77 Bloor St. West, 9th Floor,
Toronto, ON   M7A 2R9

(English) 965-4008
(French) 965-3448
toll-free (English) 1-800-668-2746
(French) 1-800-668-3736

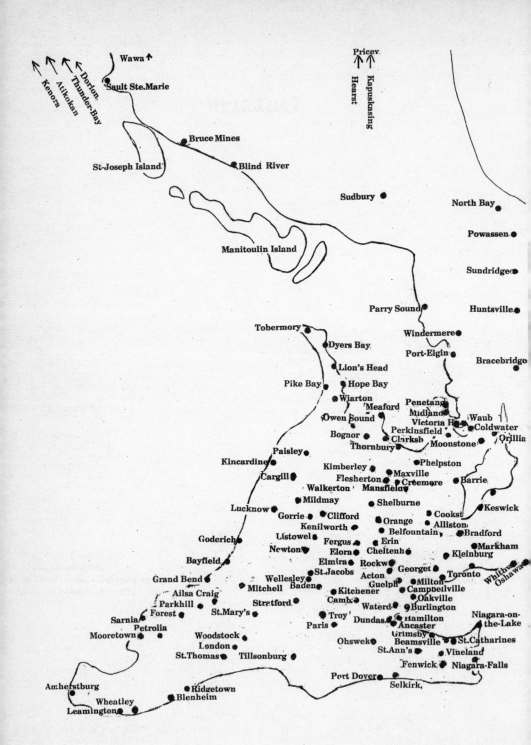

Wawa ↑

Sault Ste.Marie

← Kenora
← Atikokan
← Thunder-Bay
← Dorion

Pricev. ↑
↑ Kapuskasing
Hearst

Bruce Mines

St-Joseph Island

Blind River

Sudbury

North Bay

Powassen

Sundridge

Manitoulin Island

Parry Sound

Huntsville

Windermere

Port-Elgin

Bracebridge

Tobermory

Dyers Bay

Lion's Head

Pike Bay   Hope Bay

Wiarton

Meaford   Penetang
Midland
Owen Sound   Victoria H   Waub
Perkinsfield   Coldwater
Bognor   Clarksb   Orillia
Thornbury   Moonstone

Paisley

Kincardine   Kimberley   Phelpston

Cargill   Flesherton   Maxville
Walkerton   Creemore   Barrie
Mansfield

Mildmay   Shelburne
Keswick

Lucknow   Gorrie   Clifford   Orange   Cookst
Kenilworth   Alliston
Listowel   Belfountain   Bradford

Goderich   Fergus   Erin
Elora   Cheltenh   Markham
Newton   Rockw   Georget   Kleinburg
Bayfield   Elmira   Toronto
St.Jacobs   Acton   Whitb
Grand Bend   Wellesley   Guelph   Oshawa
Ailsa Craig   Mitchell   Baden   Kitchener   Campbellville
Parkhill   Stratford   Camb   Oakville
Forest   St.Mary's   Waterd   Burlington
Sarnia   Troy   Dundas   Hamilton   Niagara-on-
Petrolia   Paris   Ancaster   the-Lake
Mooretown   Grimsby
Woodstock   Ohswek   Beamsville   St.Catharines
London   St.Ann's   Vineland
St.Thomas   Tillsonburg   Fenwick   Niagara-Falls

Port Dover

Amherstburg   Ridgetown   Selkirk,
Wheatley   Blenheim
Leamington

Ontario

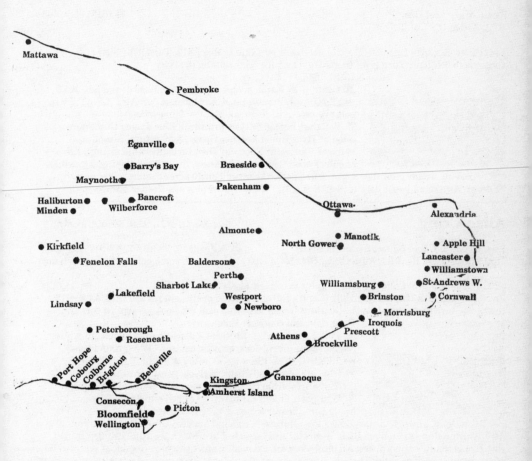

Mattawa

Pembroke

Eganville

Barry's Bay

Maynooth

Braeside

Pakenham

Haliburton
Minden

Bancroft
Wilberforce

Ottawa

Alexandria

Kirkfield

Almonte

North Gower

Manotik

Apple Hill

Lancaster

Williamstown

St-Andrews W.

Fenelon Falls

Balderson

Perth

Williamsburg

Sharbot Lake

Lakefield

Westport

Newboro

Brinston

Cornwall

Morrisburg

Lindsay

Iroquois

Peterborough

Roseneath

Athens

Prescott

Brockville

Port Hope
Cobourg
Colborne
Brighton

Belleville

Kingston

Gananoque

Amherst Island

Consecon
Bloomfield
Wellington

Picton

Federation of Ontario B&B Accommodations
Box 437, 253 College St., Toronto, ON   M5T 1R5

☎ (416) 515-1293
E-mail: info@fobba.com

Rates vary in the different parts of the Province. Breakfast is always included in the price quoted. FOBBA is not a Reservation Service. FOBBA is the Feration of Ontario Bed & Breakfast Accommodation, working since 1986 to set professional standards for Ontario B&Bs. There are more than 500 members across the province. Each B&B meets FOBBA standards for cleanliness, comfort and safety, and each host is knowledgeable about the events, attractions and special points of interest in their area. There is a warm welcome and only happy surprises at FOBBA B&Bs. Call of write for free guide booklet. Many members are listed individually in this Guide.   www.fobba.com

---

Acton
(west of Toronto; see also Rockwood, Georgetown)

Toth, Marg and Les
RR1, Acton, ON L7J 2L7

☎ (519) 853-1065

From Hwy 401, take Exit 320 (Hwy25) north and go 14km to Reg Rd12. Turn left (west) and continue to 6th Line. Turn right (north) and look for 6th house on left side.

$35S $45D $10Child   ► 4
🍽 Cont.   🏠 Rural, acreage, ranch-style,huge deck,quiet ■2D
🛏2T,1Q   🛁1Private,1sh.w.h.,whirlpool   ★Air,F,LF,KF,TV in guest rooms   ⓦ No smoking   ∾ Hungarian
🏃 Walking, biking, (bicyles provided), Blue Spring Golf Course
🚙 Old Hyde House Leather Goods, Agricultural Museum, Mohawk/Woodbine Raceway, Glen Eden (downhill skiing), Kelso and Rockwood Conservation Areas, Bruce Trail (hiking, x-c skiing)

🔖 Spacious, sunny bungalow situated in a park-like setting on 10 acres of quiet wilderness. There are two small house dogs (downstairs only). Well behaved pets can sleep in garage.

Ailsa Craig
(north-west of London; see also Parkhill)

Lee, Bruce & Carol (Quiet Streams B&B)
26215 Coldstream Rd.,RR1, Ailsa Craig, ON   N0M 1A0

☎ & Fax (519) 232-9592/3,1-877-416-5565
E-mail: quietstrms@golden.net

$60S $80-95D $8Child $115F   (plus tax)   🍽 Meals   ► 4A,5Ch
From Hwy401 take Hwy402 at Exit81 (Centre Rd) and proceed north towards Parkhill. At Exit19 (Petty St), turn east toward Nairn. Continue 5.5km to Coldstream Rd. Look for sign on corner.

Turn right and continue 1km.
🍽 Full, homebaked   🏠 Rural, hillside, acreage, view from guest rooms, patio, porch, deck, quiet, secluded   ■ 3 (ground level)
🛏 2S(K),1Q,P   🛁1Sh.w.g.,1sh.w.h.   ★Air,LF,F,private entr., wheel-chair access, off-street parking, guest quarters are sep., fax/E-mail/Internet for business guests   ⓦ Smoking outside
🏃 Sign-posted nature trails on property, pine trails & woods, Apple Lane, beaver crossing, croquet corner

🚙 Ailsa Craig, Murrays X-mas House (fine European cuisine) London, Grand Bend, Sarnia
🔖 Warm welcome in unique B&B, decorated and furnished to create a beautiful country retreat, with scenic country atmosphere. An ideal place for a romantic quiet getaway. Breakfast is served in dining room or deck or patio. There is a dog and a cat in residence. (dog is allowed in kitchen only). Inquire about hair care, foot care and nursing assistance. Visa ⌐B&B www.quietstreams.on.ca

Alexandria
(n/e of Cornwall;see also Maxville,Apple H.,Willamstown,Lancaster)

MacDonald, Ed & Audrey (Maple Lane Guest Home B&B) ☎(613)525-3205,(905)666-0517,
No.21320,RR2,Glen Robertson Rd,Alexandria, ON K0C 1A0   E-mail: maple-lane@sympatico.ca

From Hwy 401 take Exit 814 and go north to Alexandria. At 1st traffic light turn right at Lochiel St

(Glen Robertson Rd) and proceed 6.5 km east to Gate Post 21320.
$45S $55D 🍽Meals   ►6
📅May-Nov. (other by special arrangement) 🍳Full,homebaked
🏠Hist., view from guest rooms, porch, secluded, veranda ■3D
(main & upper level) 🛏2T,2D 🚿2Sh.w.g. ★Air (partial),
TV avail.for guests 🚭Smoking outside, no pets ⚘French
🏃 Quiet country roads for hiking & biking, private nature trails
🚗 Maxville Highland Games, Nor'wester & Dunvegen Museums

📣 Century home with hand hewn beams, pine floors, loft and "Old Country" atmosphere,
nestled among mature maples on 100 acres in a truly peaceful setting. Relax on the sun porch or in
the evening around a crackling campfire (hostess frequently involves her well-known Marionettes
to participate in the fun). Hostess teaches French (ideal place for French Immersion guests). Golf
packages available. There is a friendly resident dog "Maggie-Muggins" (not allowed in guest area)
✓B&B http://www.bbcanada.com/1068.html

Alliston
(north of Toronto; see also Cookstown, Bradford, Mansfield)

Davies, Valerie and Wally (Fintona Farm)   ☎ & Fax (705) 435-5685
RR1, Alliston, ON L9R 1V1

Located 6.6 km west of Alliston on Hwy 89 and 5.3 km east of Airport Rd on Hwy 89. Turn south
onto dirt road on Con 3 of Adjala. Look for 1st house on s/e corner of 3rd Con & 30 SR (1km)
$45S/D   ►4

🍳Full 🏠197-acres farm, hist., view, patio, quiet ■2D(upst)
🛏2D 🚿Sh.w.g. ★Air,LF
🚗 Hiking, fishing, cycling, downhill or x-c ski Loretto/Mansfield
📣 Fully restored 1874-built farm house surrounded by mixed
farm land. There is a north-south 2000ft grass runway
(N44.07/W79.57) with 2 tie-downs available, for those who would
like to fly in. Ideal location for Bruce Trail hiking. Several good
restaurants close by.

Kooistra, Clara & Sid (Gramma's House B&B)   ☎ (705) 434-4632
146 Victoria St.East, Alliston, ON L9R 1K6   Fax (705) 434-4771

From Hewy400, take Exit75 & Hwy89 west through Cookstown (becomes Victoria St. in Alliston).
$50S $65D $10Child $25Add.person $100F 🍽Meals   ►6A,2Ch

🍳 Full, homebaked, self-serve 🏠 Village, 2-storey, hist., porch,
deck ■2D,1F (upstairs) 🛏1D,2Qcot 🚿1sh.w.g.,
sh.w.h. ★ LF,TV, private entrance, off-street parking, guest
quarters are separate 🚭 Smoking outside, no pets, children
min.age 4 ⚘ Friesian/Dutch
🏃 Movie theatres, cafes, stores, Nottawasaga Golf Course, Camp
Bordon, Honda Plant (tours), fishing, Potato Festival, Simcoe
Pioneer Museum

🚗 Cookstown Outlet Mall, antique shops, Barrie Ski Hills, Lake Simcoe, Pearson Int.Airport
📣 Semi-retired couple with farming background in a classic Victorian home with a bright and
cheerful atmosphere, located in a growing and friendly town. Relax on the covered porches or on the
large back deck overlooking the naturally treed yard. Hosts have raised a large family (now have 19
grandchildren) and enjoy meeting people from various backgrounds. ✓B&B

Almonte

(south-west of Ottawa; see also Pakenham)

Matheson, Patricia (The Squirrels) ☎ (613) 256-2995
Box 729, 190 Parkview Dr., Almonte, Ont. K0A 1A0

From Ottawa going west, follow Queensway to Almonte cut-off and then Hwy 44 for 14 km to house situated diagonally opposite Almonte Community center.

$35S $50D 🍽 Meals ▶ 5
🍳 Full, homebaked 🏠 Village, ranch style,view,acreage,quiet
■1S,2D(main level) ⊨1S,4T 🛏1Sh.w.g. ★ TV, large
guest lounge, parking ⚌No smoking ⤳some French
🏃 Community center/park, public swimming pool, shops &
restaurants x-country skiing, Mississippi Valley Textile Museum
🚗 Downhill skiing, golfing, Tait MacKenzie Museum, Naismith
Basket Ball Museum

📣 Unique very spacious home with cathedral ceilings surrounded by almost an acre of landscaped gardens, providing plenty of privacy for guests. Hostess is a world traveller and has many interesting memorabilia around the house. Farm-style breakfast is served in sunroom. ⤳CC

Vetter, Pat & Frank (Menzies House 1853 Bed & Breakfast) ☎ (613) 256-2055
80 Queen St., Almonte, ON K0A 1A0 (613) 256-8714

From Ottawa take Hwys 49/44. After entering Almonte, turn left at first stoplight onto Queen St. From Toronto, take Hwys 7 & 15. Take first exit to Almonte driving along Perth St., Bridge St.

and then over bridge to Queen Street.
$65 $80D (picnic lunches at additional cost) ▶ 4
🍳 Full, homebaked 🏠 In town, 2-storey, hist., view from guest
rooms, 250 ft. riverfront, swimming pool, patio, gazebo, quiet
■3D (upstairs) ⊨2T,1Q,1K 🛏1Ensuite, 1sh.w.g.
★F,KF,TV/VCR (available in library), air-conditioning in guest
rooms ⚌No pets, no smoking
🏃 Specialty stores, antique shops, art galleries, Textile Museum
🚗 Ottawa, canoeing, golfing, scenic drives in Lanark County
📣 Designated (1853) Heritage home situated on the Mississippi River in the center of historic town. Enjoy English-style afternoon tea, stroll along the riverfront garden, read/relax by the pool. http://www.bbcanada.com/541.html

---

Amherstburg

(south of Windsor; see also Wheatley, Leamington)

Honor, Robert and Debra (The Honor's) ☎ (519) 736-7737
4441, C4, RR2, Amherstburg, ON N9V 2Y8 E-mail: dhonor@mnsi.net

From Amherstburg, go out Simcoe St/Pike Rd to 4th Con., turn
right. Look for 13th house on east side. (send for detailed map)
$45-55S $55-65D $55Ste $5Child ▶ 4A,2Ch
🎏 July/Aug.(other by arrangement ▣Choice 🏠Farm, view,
older, patio, quiet ■2D(upstairs) ⊨2D,cot 🛏1Private,
1ensuite ★Air,TV ⚌No smoking, no pets ⤳French
🚗 Historic Amherstburg, Fort Malden Nat. Hist. Park,
birdwatching, Black History Museum, Point Pelee, Windsor
📣 Tree shaded cottage-style home in quiet and peaceful country setting, overlooking farm and woods, but close to Metropolitan activities. There are 3 cats & a dog in the house. ⤳B&B

Amherst Island

Thompson, Bob & Corrinne (Anniversary House B&B)
RR1, Stella, ON K0H 2S0 ☎ (613) 389-8190, Fax (613) 389-1858

From Hwy 401, take Exit 593 to Hwy 133 south to Millhaven. Turn right on Hwy 33 to Ferry dock.

Ferry leaves every hour on half hour. Drive 3km west to B&B.
$60-70S/D $15Child ► 6A,2Ch
🍲 Full, homebaked 🏠 Rural, 2-storey, acreage, view, lakefront,
patio, deck, quiet ■ 3D(upstairs) ⊨ 2T,2Q,P,cot,crib
🛁1sh.w.g., 1ensuite ★ Air,TV 🖐 No smoking, no pets,
inquire about children
🏃 Swimming at lakeside, bird watching, quiet roads for walking
and cycling (guest owned bikes), x-c skiing, Island sand beach
🚗 Historic Kingston, 1000 Islands, Fort Henry, Marine Museum of the Great Lakes
🔫 Large, modern designer waterfront home situated on an island in Lake Ontario. Enjoy the
peaceful island country atmosphere and a different sunset every evening. Relax on the dock, explore
the island and its beautiful scenery, or read a favorite book in the den or in the great room.
Breakfast is served in the dining room. There is a dog outside. ✓B&B

Ancaster

Wentworth, Dan and Dorothy (Duck Tail Inn Bed & Breakfast) ☎ (905) 648-3596
1573 Butter Rd. West, Ancaster, ON L9G 3L1

From Hamilton or Toronto on Hwy 403, take Copetwon Exit and continue south on Hwy 52,
crossing Hwy 2/53 onto Trinity Rd. Proceed through 2 concessions, then turn right (west) onto
Butter Rd. Go one concession and look for Duck mailbox and a cannon on front lawn.

$50S $65D ► 4A
🍲 Choice 🏠 44-acre farm, view, ranch-style, patio, quiet,
isolated, pond with ducks ■ 2D(main level) ⊨ 2T,1Q
🛁1Ensuite, 1sh.w.h., jacuzzi for guests ★ Air,TF, separate
entrance 🖐Restricted smoking, children min. age 4
🏃 Private museum on property (Early Canadian Artifacts & Tools
- free tours), quiet country roads
🚗 War Plane Heritage Museum, Caledonia Boat Farm, Mohawk
Chapel, Mount Hope Airport, Brantford, Hamilton, Niagara Falls
🔫 Modern country home overlooking rolling fields and pond, situated near picturesque Niagara
Escarpment. Enjoy the very restful country atmosphere. Hostess hatches ducks. There is tasteful
duck decor all through the house. Relax in the large sunroom, furnished with wicker, overlooking
the garden and pond. A cat lives in residence. ✓B&B

Woods, Shirley & Larry (Tranquility Base B&B) ☎ (905) 648-1506, Fax (905) 627-2818
110 Abbey Close, Ancaster, ON L9G 1K7

From Hwy 403 west of Hamilton, take Wilson St East Exit, then first turn left at fire hall on

Meadowbrook Rd, and right on Abbey Close.
$55S $65D $20Child 🍽 Meals ► 4A,1Ch
🍲Full, homebaked 🏠Res., 2-storey, deck, quiet ■3(upstairs)
⊨1K,2T,1D 🛁 1Sh.w.g. ★ Air,F,TV, off-street parking
🖐No smoking, no pets
🏃 Centre of old village of Ancaster, shops, restaurants
🚗 Downtown Hamilton, Copps Coliseum, Hamilton Place,
Dundurn Castle, Canadian Heritage War Plane Museum, Mt.Hope
Airport, Ancaster Old Mill, Niagara Falls, Kitchener/Waterloo Mennonite area, Toronto
🔫 Warm welcome and friendly hospitality in comfortable, large modern brick home located on a
quiet cul-de-sac. Well travelled hosts have been collecting Victorian cranberry, crystal, dolls, art and
other antiques for more than 25 years and these are displayed through the house. A justifiable fine
local reputation as a talented cook is reflected in memorable breakfasts, served in guest breakfast
room. The coffee pot is usually on. Visa ✓B&B

Apple Hill
(north of Cornwall; see also Lancaster, Williamstown, Alexandria, Maxville)

McIntosh, Stewart and Christena (Tanglewood Farm)　　　☎ (613) 527-2884
RR2, Apple Hill, ON　K0C 1B0

From Hwy 401 take Exit 789 & Hwy 138 north to Hwy 43. Travel
east 5 km to Pidgeon Hill Rd, then south 2 km to McIntosh Rd and
left to first farm (5 km west of Apple Hill).
$30S　$50D　$12Child(under age 12　🍽 Meals　▶ 4A,2Ch
🍳 Full　🏠 Farm home　■ 3D (upstairs)　⊨ 2D,2T
🛁1Sh.w.g.　★TV,F　🚭No smoking, no pets
🚶 Hiking, walking, cross-country skiing, maple bush
🚗 Glengarry Highland Games, Cornwall, Seaway Valley

🐾 Feel the warmth and welcome of country hospitality and relax in rural tranquility. Enjoy
delicious homecooking and fresh vegetables from the garden.

Athens
(west of Brockville; see also Newboro, Westport)

Thompson, Chris & Marie (The Apple Grove)　　　☎ (613) 924-1463, Fax (613) 924-1417
10 Elgin St.S., Box 478, Athens, ON　K0E 1B0

From Hwy 401, take Exit 696 (Brockville) onto Hwy 29 and go north app. 24 km. At fork in road,
follow signs for Hwy 42 & Athens. At main intersection, turn left on Elgin St S to 5th house.

$55S　$60-75D　$10Add.person　🍽 Meals　▶ 5A,2Ch
🍳 Full, homebaked　🏠 Village, hist., 2-storey, quiet, sundeck,
Victorian veranda　■2D,1F(main & upper level)　⊨1S,2D,2Q
🛁1Ensuite,1sh.w.g.　★Air,TV,guest parlour,sep.entr.,parking,
wheel-chair access in one room　🚭No smoking　💬French
🚶 Walking tour of the Murals of Athens, restaurants, cycling
🚗 Charleston Lake & Prov.Park (year-around outdoor activities),
swimming, hiking, x-c skiing, Brockville, Thousand Islands

🐾 Gracious, circa 1886-built Victorian home with shaded front porches, white pillars, large back
sundeck and large quiet rooms. Situated on a shaded street of historic village; in the heart of United
Empire Loyalist country. Hosts have a motorboat at the lake for touring. There is a cat. 🖋CC

Atikokan
(west of Thunder Bay)

Elder, Mary (The Cedar Rail B&B)　　　☎ (807) 597-8707
23 Birch Rd., Box 252, Atikokan, ON　P0T 1C0

Take Hwy 11 west from Thunder Bay or east from Fort Frances to Hwy 11B and proceed north for
3km into Atikokan.
$52-60S　$62-70D　$25Child　▶ 2A,1Ch
🍳 Cont., homebaked, buffet　🏠 Res., 2-storey, view over back
garden, patio, quiet, secluded　■ 1(main floor)　⊨ 1D, air-bed
for child　🛁 1Private　★ Air,TV, private guest sitting room,
off-street parking　🚭 Smoking outside, no pets
🚶 Golf course, curling rink, arena, swimming pool, library,
museum, mining attraction displays, town centre, x-c ski trails
🚗 Quetico Provincial Park with Information Pavillion, abandoned Steep Rock iron mine site
🐾 Friendly and experienced hosts in well-maintained and landscaped home, with bird feeders in
back yard and located in a quiet residential setting. Local birding information available. Hosts are
knowledgeable about local history, natural history and tourism activities. Breakfast is served in
sunroom or dining room. 🖋B&B　http://www.bbcanada.com/2942.html

Baden

(east of Stratford; see also Wellesley)

Banbury, Sarah & Family (Banbury Farm B&B)　　　　☎ (519) 634-5451
1942 Wilby Rd., RR2, Baden, ON　N0B 1G0　　　　　　　　1-888-892-0666

Take Hwy 401 to Hwy 8 west towards Kitchener and continue on Hwy 7/8 west towards Stratford to Waterloo Reg Rd 12. Turn right (north) and travel through Petersburg and St. Agatha. Take 1st

crossroad (Wilby Rd) west to 1st farm on right.
$40S $60D $20Add.person 🍴Meals　　　　　　► 7
🍷 Cont., homebaked　🏠 Farm, older, pleasant view,
veranda ■1D,1F(upst) ⊨1S,2T,1D,1P 🛁 2sh.w.h. ★TV,F,LF
🖐No pets, smoking downstairs, child min. age 6　〰 French
🏃 Walking, cycling, cross-country skiing
🚗 Kitchener/Waterloo, Stratford, Golf courses, two Universities, farmer's markets, St.Jacobs Mennonite Country

🎯 Attractive 86-acres farm with horses and emus. Enjoy the comfort, space & hospitality. Relax on the screened veranda overlooking paddocks with split rail fencing, fields & trees. Riding instruction available. There are 2 dogs in residence. 🖊B&B

Hill, Jane & Graham (Dappled Pegasus Bed & Breakfast)　☎ (519) 634-8379, Fax 634-8725
RR2, Baden, ON　N0B 1G0　　　　　　　　　　　E-mail: lerwick@golden.net

Located just west of St.Agatha. Take Hwy 7&8 west from Kitchener to RegRd12. Turn north thru Petersburg to St.Agatha. Turn west on RegRd9 and look for B&B sign at first farm lane on left.

$60S　$75D　　　　　　　　　　► 7
🎏 April-Dec 🍷 Full, homebaked　🏠 Farm, 2-storey, hist.,
150 acres, view from guest rooms, heated swimming pool, porch,
quiet, newly added Conservatory, isolated　■ 3 (upstairs)
⊨1S,1Q,2D 🛁 1Sh.w.g. 🖐 No smoking, no pets
🏃 Nature Trails, restaurant, shops, churches, pub, golfing
🚗 Waterloo/Kitchener, Stratford Festival Theatres, Baden
(Castle Kilbride), Elora, St.Jacobs, farmers' markets

🎯 1840's built stone farmhouse, lovingly restored, decorated with antiques situated amidst 150 acres of gently rolling rich farmland and forest. Unwind in a casual country atmosphere, sleep with the gentle sounds of wind sighing through the leaves & the soft nickering of horses; awaken to a dip in the sparkling pool followed by a hearty breakfast served in sunny windowed breakfast room resplendent with plants. There are 2 dogs & 3 cats & 3 horses. Enjoy a quiet get-away.

Balderson

(south-west of Ottawa; see also Perth)

Miller, Ann (Woodrow Guest Ranch & B&B)　　☎ 1-800-582-2311, Fax (613)267-1766
RR1, Balderson, Ontario　K0G 1A0　　　　　　　　　E-mail: rchapman@ripnet.com

Located at 3062 Concession 8A, Drummond on the outskirts of Perth. Take Hwy 511 off Hwy 7 to the village of Balderson, turn right on Concession 8A Drummond to house No 3062

$60-75D　$15child (under age 12 in parent's room)　► 6
🍷Full, homebaked　🏠96-acre working farm ■3D(upstairs)
⊨K,T 🛁Central, ensuite ★satTV & video library,F in guest
lounge, guest dining room 🖐No pets 💙
🏃 Village of Balderson, Prov. Parks (beaches, fishing, boating,
fishing), x/c ski & snowmobile trails, nature trail to explore
🚗 Glenair Kitten, Heritage Silversmiths,Brown Shoes &
Balderson Cheese Factory outlets, Ottawa, Kingston

🎯 Hilltop Century Victorian farmhouse (1884), set in pleasant country garden shaded by maples, overlooking horse paddocks. 1-4 day Horselovers "All Inclusive Breakaway Packages" offered. In winter enjoy x-c skiing or relaxing by the fire. Visa,JCB 🖊CC www.travelinx.com/woodrowfarm

Bancroft

(N. of Peterborough; see also Haliburton, Wilberforce, Maynooth)

Brundage, Diane & Elizabeth Inglis (Teddy Bear B&B)   ☎ (613) 332-4678, Fax 2307
26541 Hwy62,Gen.Del.,L'Amable, ON K0L 2L0   tedbear@bancom.net, 1-877-332-BEAR

Situated on Tait Lake at Green's Corner (Hwy62 & Bay Lake/Detlor Rds) and 9km couth of
Bancroft. Look for signs on highway.

$45-55S $60-75D $20-30Child/Add.person $100-135F   🍽 Meals   ► 8A+,4Ch+

🍴 Full   🏠Rural,2-storey,older,acreage,quiet,lake view from 2
guest rooms, lakeback, porch ■4F(upstairs & lower level)
🛏3Q,2T,5R,2playpens 🚿2Sh.w.g.,1sh.w.h. ★Air,F,TV,LF,
fans,heaters, onsite parking Ⓦ Designated smoking area, pets
outside only

🏃 Private beach (Tait Lake), snowmobile trails, fishing
🚗 Rock Hound Gemboree, Teddy Bear Picnic Parade (Aug),
antiques, scenic tours with cavalcade of fall colours, The Gut,
forestry tours, Algonquin Prov.Park (canoeing, hiking, x-c skiing, snowmobiling), Bancroft
🎯 Warm & friendly hospitality in B&B situated on a quiet lake. Relax by the lake & take in the
view from the deck or unwind by the fireplace. Breakfast is served in guest breakfast room or on
deck with view of Tait Lake (weather permitting). Retreat Packages for couples or small groups and
Corporate Brainstorming Packages available including either a massage or an outdoor activity.
Gift Certificates. CCards ⬅CC www.mwdesign.net/tedbear.html

Leenders, Kathleen & Albert (Leender's Lakeside B&B)   ☎ & Fax (613) 339-1055
RR3, Bancroft, ON K0L 1C0   E-mail: leebb@mail.bancom.net, 1-888-255-8222

From Bancroft travel south 18km on Hwy 28. Located 2km north of Silent Lake Prov.Park.

$50S $60D $10Child $20Add.person   🍽 Meals   ► 6

🍴 Full, homebaked   🏠 Rural, res., 2-storey ranch-style,
1.5acres, view from guest rooms, lakefront, patio, back deck,
quiet ■4D(upper & lower level)   🛏 2T,2D,1Q   🚿2Sh.w.g.
★ F,KF,LF,TV, guest quarters are separate Ⓦ No smoking
🗣 Dutch
🏃 Fishing on Paudash Lake, marina, boat launch, hiking,
restaurants, Greyhound bus stop
🚗 Bancroft, Playhouse Theatre, "Gemboree", rock hunting
🎯 Comfortable home located on Anderson Lake with beautiful decor and tanquil surroundings
abounding in natural beauty. An ideal place for artists, photographer, bird watchers and nature
lovers. Browse through the assortment of "Kathleen's Kreations" in the on-site studio. Scumptuous
breakfast is served in large dining room with a view of the lake. Special package rates on request.
Snowmobilers, hunters, skiers welcome. Visa ⬅CC www.bbcanada.com/1972.html

---

Barrie

(north of Toronto: see also Phelpston)

Richmond, Pam & Bob (Richmond Manor)   ☎ (705) 726-7103
16 Blake St., Barrie, ON L4M 1J6   E-mail: richmond.manor@sympatico.ca

From Hwy 400, take Exit 96 (Dunlop St) & travel 3km east to Blake St. Look for first house on left.

$55-65S $70-80D $15Child $135F $20Add.person   ► 5

🍴 Full, homebaked   🏠 Res., 3-storey, hist., acreage, view from
guest rooms, porch, quiet ■ 2D(upstairs)   🛏 1D,1Q,1R
🚿1Sh.w.g., 1sh.w.h.   ★ F,TV in private sitting room, ceiling
fans, off-street parking Ⓦ Smoking on porch, no pets
🏃 Walking & bicycle trails along Kempenfelt Bay (Lake Simcoe),
sandy beaches, marina, parks, downtown shopping & dining
🚗 Canada Wonderland, Rama Casino, skiing, Toronto
🎯 Ivy-covered Georgian-style home (ca 1911) with traditional elegance situated on forested
property and waterfront. Home is included in local Christmas House Tour. There is an in-house
folk artist. Breakfast is served in formal dining room. Enjoy many folk art treasures. ⬅B&B

Blackstock, Hugh & Jane (Heavitree House B&B) ☎ (705) 721-0483
RR1, Shanty Bay, ON L0L 2L0 E-mail: heavitreehouse@sympatico.ca

On Hwy 400, travel north from Barrie and continue on Hwy 11 north towards Orillia. Five km past junction, take Oro-Medonte Line 3 south to 2nd house on right.
$40S $55D ► 6
Homebaked · Rural, 2-storey, hist., acreage, view, porch, quiet · 3D(upstairs), guest quarters are separate · 2T,2D · 2Sh.w.g. ★ TV,F & woodstove, separate entrance, parking · No smoking, no pets, children welcome
Walk or bike on country roads, large perennial garden, croquet
St.Marie among the Hurons & Martyr's Shrine, Wye & Tiny Marsh Wildlife Centres, historic Naval & Military Establ., Leacock & Norman Bethune homes, boat cruises, theatre, fine dining
1860's farm house with open vistas surrounded by rolling countryside. Relax in the parlour with fireplace, piano, games & books or on the screened-in porch. Well travelled hosts (including Nepal & Africa) enjoy hiking, gardening & birding. Breakfast is served in separate guest breakfast room. Visa ✓CC www.bbcanada.com/1485.html

---

Kirby, Charita & Harry (Cozy Corner Bed & Breakfast) ☎ (705)739-0157
2 Morton Cr., Barrie, ON L4N 2T3 E-mail: cozy@bconnex.net

Take Hwy 400 north to Exit98 (Bayfield North). Turn left at Livingstone (Walmart Plaza) to 2nd stoplight. First right again to 2nd street on left. Look for home with picket fence.

$95Ste ► 6A
Full · Res., 2-storey, patio, porch, quiet · 2Ste (upstairs) · 2Q · 1Sh.w.g, ensuite ★ Air,F,LF,TV in guest rooms, jacuzzi in suite, guest quarters are separate, off-street parking · Smoking on patio or porch, no pets, no children
Spanish, German
Downhill and x-c skiing on doorstep
Georgian Bay & Wasaga beaches (world's longest fresh-water beach), Saint-Marie-among-the-Hurons, Canada's Wonderland, Toronto, x-c & downhill ski runs
Charming brick home with old world ambiance reflecting hosts' European backgrounds. Situated on a quiet residential street in the center of 4 major malls, restaurant & entertanment. Hosts are a former Teacher/Governess and a German/British-trained Chef. Gourmet breakfast is house specialty. Visa ✓B&B

O'Kane, Carol & Mike (O'Kane's Bed & Breakfast) ☎ (705) 835-3554
General Delivery, Hillsdale, Barrie, ON L0L 1V0

From Toronto, take Hwy 400 north to 400 Extension (to Sudbury/Parry Sound) and continue to Exit 121. Drive north on Hwy 93 for 3 km to Hillsdale and look for B&B on right at Albert St.

$45S $55D $5Child Meals ► 7
Full, homebaked · Village, 2-storey, hist., wrap-around porch, patio · 3D(upstairs & ground level) · 2T,1Q,1K · 1Sh.w.g., 1sh.w.h. ★F,TV, off-street parking · Designated smoking area · Portuguese, Spanish
Antique and gift shops, pottery, honey factory
Midland, Penetanguishene Summer Theatre, Barrie, Horseshoe Valley & Mt.St.Louis downhill skiing, Hardwood Hills
125-year old cottage-style home renovated with modern comforts and a large country kitchen, surrounded by picturesque farm and orchard lands and located midway between Barrie and Midland. Hosts have lived many years in Central & South America and are interested in people and their journey in life. ✓B&B

Barrie (cont'd)

Robinson, Ross & Val (Oak Ridge B&B) ☎ & Fax (705) 725-8214
29 Doran Rd, Box 11, Midhurst, ON L0L 1X0

$55S $65D $15Child $25Add.person $100F ▶9

Phone for directions.
🕩 Full 🏠 2-storey, older, acreage, view from guest rooms, swimming pool, patio, porch deck, quiet, secluded ■3F(upstairs & lower level) ⊨2D,1Q,1P,1R ⬦1Private, 1sh.w.g.
★Air,LF,F,TV, ceiling fans, private entrance, off-street parking, guest quarters are separate ✋ Designated smoking area, no pets, children min. age 10 ∽ German
🏃 Hunter Russell & Ganaraska Trails
🚗 Beaches of Barrie & Wasaga Beach, Midland, Penetang, Rama Casino, boat cruises on various lakes, skiing at Horseshoe & Snow Valley & Collingwood, restaurants
☛ Warm welcome in gracious home in a quiet 2acres park-like setting with manicured gardens. Relax on the private decks by the pool overlooking the treed ravine. Breakfast is served in Post & Beam eating area. Hosts enjoy helping guests. Visa ⌐B&B www.bbcanada.com/2209.html

Barry's Bay *(sout-hwest of Pembroke; see also Eganville)*

Deakin, Mary Helen & Don (Barry's Bay B&B) ☎ (613) 756-1023
Box 217, 77 Sandhill Dr., Barry's Bay, ON K0J 1B0

Located in town just off Hwy 60.
$40S $50D ▶4
🕩 Full, homebaked 🏠 2-storey ■ 2D(upstairs) ⊨1D,1Q
⬦1Sh.w.g. ★Private guest entrance ✋No pets,no smoking
🚗 Historic sites, art galleries, boating, kayaking, canoeing, river raft trips, fishing, tennis, artists' studio tours, craft shops, Madonna House, Pioneer Museum, heritage log structures, flaming leaf tours, downhill & nordic skiing, mountain biking, golfing, excellent shopping
☛ Comfortable home, tastefully decorated with Nottingham lace, cozy wool duvets & fine china and furnished with antiques. Enjoy the friendly atmosphere and a hearty breakfast, walk around the spacious grounds or relax by the fireplace in the bright living room. Experience magnificient year-round scenery & Madawaska Valley hospitality. ⌐B&B http://www.bbcanada.com/191.html

Bayfield *(south of Goderich on Lake Huron)*

Cassidy, Joan & Peter Karstens, (Brentwood on the Beach) ☎ (519) 236-7137,
RR2, Zurich, St. Joseph Shores 1, ON N0M 2T0 Fax (519) 236-7269

St.Joseph Shore Phase I is located off Hwy 21 between Bayfield & Grand Bend. Look for sign.
$135-225D $25Add.person ▶20
🕩Choice, homebaked 🏠Village, ranch-style, indoor swimming pool, lakefront ■10(incl.2honeymoon suites) ⊨2T,4Q,4K
★Air,7F(incl in 3guest rooms),TV,KF, whirlpool,sauna,
⬦10Ensuite ✋No pets, no smoking ∽German, French
🏃 Sandy beach at back, golf course, tennis, x-c skiing
🚗 Pinery Prov. Park, marinas, shops, Stratford/Blyth theatres, Huron County Playhouse
☛ Relax and escape the stresses of everyday life in a B&B with luxury Country Inn atmosphere. Enjoy spectacular sunsets, walks, swimming in a spa-like environment. Breakfast served in large sunroom overlooking Lake Huron. Ideal place for honeymooners & special occasions and winter retreats. Rest and rejuvenate on the 60ft balcony and screened-in porch. Gift Certificates available. Also available: (0.4km) 4 off-site (1b-room) condo-style cottages & 2b-room cottage on separate site. Visa,MC ⌐B&B www.brentwoodbnb.com

Bayfield (cont'd)

Pakenham, Carol & Ted (Magnolia Manor Bed & Breakfast)   ☎ & Fax (519)233-3181,
RR1, Varna, ON   N0M 2R0   E-mail: magmanor@tcc.on.ca, 1-800-216-5968

Located on County Rd3 and 8km from either Hwys 4 or 21 and
approximately 8km from Bayfield.
$50S $75-90D $15Add.person   (winter rates avail.)   ► 8
🍳 Full, homebaked   ⌂ Rural, plantation, 2-storey, hist., 3acres,
swimming pool, pond, patio, porch, quiet   ■ 4D(upstairs)
⊨1S,1D,3Q   ⟶3Private, 1sh.w.h.   ★ F, guest parlour with
TV, ceiling fans, plant-filled sun room, ample parking   ✋ No
smoking, no pets, no children

🕴 Walking trail on property, village of Varna
🚐 Bayfield, Bannockburn Cons.Area, fine dining, Blyth Festival/Grand Bend Playhouse
🐾 Impressive Estate in a Southern Plantation setting, a haven of peace and tranquility far
removed from the hustle & bustle of city living. Languish in the shade of the weeping willows, have
a swim in the pool, or relax in front of the field-stone fireplace or plant-filled bright and breezy sun
room. There are a cat and 2 dogs in residence. A wonderful place for a rest. Winter-, mid-week
special and business rates available. Visa,MC ✓B&B www.tcc.on.ca/~magmanor

---

Soper, Clair (Clair on the Square B&B)   ☎ (519) 565-2135
Box 158, 12 The Square, Bayfield, ON   N0M 1G0

Phone for directions.
$95S $110D $30Add.person   ► 6
🍳 Full, homebaked   ⌂ Village, 2-storey, hist., acreage, deck,
pond, quiet   ■ 3 (upstairs)   ⊨ 1T,3Q   ⟶1Private,2ensuite
★2F, guest room airconditioners, ceiling fans, off-street parking
✋ Smoking in the garden, no pets   ∾French, Latin
🕴 Bayfield with shops & restaurants, beach, Bayfield River
🚐 Stratford and Blyth Theatres, London, Mennonite Country, Lake Huron beaches, hiking
🐾 Classic Victorian yellow brick home (ca 1850) lovingly restored and situated on the west side of
Clan Gregor Square. Relax in the beautifully landscaped garden with pond or in the comfort of the
music-filled living room. Breakfast is served in the dining room or on the deck. Celebrations for
8-20 can be arranged. Consider spending Thanksgiving, Christmas or New Years. Alternative diets
may be accommodated on request. ✓B&B www.com2interactive.com/clair

---

Beamsville   *(west of St-Catharines; see also Grimsby, Vineland, St.Anns)*

Lianga, Vic & Nancy (Grapeview Guesthouse)   ☎ (905) 563-5077
4163 Merritt Rd., Beamsville, ON   L0R 1B1   E-mail: grapevuw@npiec.on.ca

$70S $75D $15Child $20Add.person $105F $100Ste   🍽Meals   ► 9
From QEW take Exit 64 and Ontario St South into Beamsville. Turn left at King St. Proceed
3.6km, turn left at Merritt Rd.

🍳 Full, homebaked   ⌂ Rural, 2-storey, acreage, view from guest
rooms, porch, quiet   ■ 2D,1F,1Ste (upstairs)   ⊨1Q,2K,1P,cot
⟶1Sh.w.g, 1ensuite   ★ Air,F,TV in 1 guest room, jacuzzi in
suite, off-street parking   ✋ Designated smoking area, no pets
∾ Lithuanian
🕴 Bruce Trail hiking, caves, rock climbing, cycling, vineyards,
orchards, pottery shop, children's play area
🚐 Niagara Falls, Butterfly Conservatory, Marineland, Niagara-on-the-Lake (Shaw Festival)
🐾Charming country home with Victorian decor, surrounded by acres of vineyards in a peaceful
setting. Scrumptious country breakfast is served in the dining room overlooking the vineyards. Take
a stroll in the vinyards and sample fresh fruit in season. Hosts are happy to share interesting
stories about grape growing in Niagara. Visa ✓B&B www.tourismniagara.com/grapeview

Beamsville (cont'd)

Opperman, Norm & Jo Ann (The Vineyard B&B)   ☎ (905) 563-1052
4255 Mountainview Rd., Beamsville, ON L0R 1B2   E-mail: jopperma@becom.org

From QEW take Exit 64 (Ontario St/Beamsville) and proceed south to King St (Reg.Rd 81 - the
Wine Rte). Turn right (west) to Mountainview Rd, then left (south) for 1km .
$50S $60-75D $105F $15Add.person   ►8

🍴 Full, homebaked (self-serve before 7AM) 🏠 Rural, res.,
2-storey, older, acreage, view from guest rooms, pond at back,
porch, deck, quiet, secluded ■3(upstairs) ⊨2T,1D,1Q,1P,cot
⊐1Sh.w.g., 1sh.w.h. ★LF,TV in 2 guest rooms, off-street
parking ⌇ some French
🏃 Bruce Trail hiking, Mountainview Conservation Area, Niagara
Escarpment (World Biosphere Reserve), wineries, fruit & vegetable
stands, restaurants/bars

🚗 Historic towns & villages, antique shops, flea markets, Niagara Falls, N-O-T-L (Shaw Festival)
🚙 Large home nestled on the scenic Niagara Escarpment, on the Bruce Trail & adjacent winery
with magnificient views of Lake Ontario and southshore settlements. Hosts offer Eco-agri tourism
and golf excursions, as well as rides from bus/train stops or spots on the Bruce Trail. Campsites
available. Hostess can be contacted about the new Niagara Wine Country B&B Association. There is
a cat ✒BB www.bbcanada.com/1830.html

Belfountain   *(north-west of Brampton; see also Cheltenham, Erin)*

Raybould, Carrie & Terry (The Gingerbread Cottage)   ☎ (519) 927-3988
715 Bush St., Belfountain, ON L0N 1B0

From Hwy401 travel north on Mississauga Rd to Village of
Belfountain. Turn left on Bush St to house on left side.
$45S $60-70D 🍴Meals & packed lunches for hikers   ►4
🍴 Full 🏠 Village, 2-storey, hist., view from guest rooms, porch,
deck, quiet ■ 2D (upstairs) ⊨ 1D,1K(2T) ⊐ 1sh.w.g.
★Air,F,TV/VCR in guest rooms, off-street parking ⍟ No
smoking, no pets, children by special arrangement
🏃 Bruce Trail hiking, antique/gift shops, Gen.Store across road

🚗 X-c skiing at Terra Cotta, downhill skiing at Caledon, golfing, Orangeville, Guelph, Toronto
🚙 Charming pre-Confederation home with elegant decor and period antiques, situated near the
forks of the Credit River. Hosts are retired Teacher & Librarian and enjoy meeting people.
Breakfast may feature German Pancakes and is served on the deck overlooking the garden with its
trout pond and flowers (weather permitting). Take the resident golden retriever out for a stroll
around the little hamlet. There is also a cat in residence. www.bbcanada.com/1621.html

Blenheim   *(south-east of Chatham; see also Ridgetown)*

Huisman, Anneke & Rikus (Ridge Farm B&B)   ☎ (519)674-5934, Fax(519)674-3847
12061 Front Line, Blenheim, ON N0P 1A0   E-mail: rhuisman@MNSi.net

Located between Exits 101/109 on Hwy 401. Take Kent Rd15 to Lake Erie and proceed left in Troy.
$40S $50D $115Suite $5Child (plus tax)   ►6A

🍴 Cont/buffet 🏠 Farm, ranch-style, view from guest rooms,
deck, quiet, secluded ■2D,1Ste ⊨ 3Q ⊐ 1Sh.w.g.
★Air,KF,TV, private entrance, guest quarters are separate
⍟No smoking, no pets ⌇ Dutch, German
🏃 Golf Course
🚗 London, Windsor, Rondeau Park, Uncle Tom's Cabin,
Greenview Aviaries & Zoo, Lake Erie and beaches, Point Pelee
🚙 Warm welcome on cash crop farm in the rolling farmland
on the "ridge" near Ridgetown. Guests are welcome to stroll the garden, relax on the deck or enjoy
the gas barbecue. Breakfast is served in the guest breakfast room. ✒B&B

Belleville

(west of Kingston; see also Brighton, Consecon)

Porter, Katie & Ralph (Bell Creek Heritage House) ☎ (613) 968-4995, Fax (613) 968-6632
374 Airport Pkwy W., RR6, Belleville, ON   K8N 4Z6   E-mail: ralph.porter@sympatico.ca

Take Hwy 37 south at Belleville to College St.East. Turn right,
proceed 1km to Airport Pkwy W on right. Continue for 2.3km.
$45S $65D   ►6A
⬛Full   🏠 Rural, 5acres, 2-storey, older, swimming pool, patio,
porch, deck, quiet   ■3D(main/upper level)   ⊨2S,1D,1Q,R
⬗1Sh.w.h., 2ensuite   ★ Air,TV in 2 guest rooms, off-street
parking   ⊕ No smoking, no pets
🚗 Outlet Beach, Sandbanks Prov. Park, antique shops, Bayshore
Trail, Quinte Mall, Loyalist & Albert Colleges, Sports Centre, Shannonville Motorsport Park
🐾 Heritage house, originally a log structure, with deep window sills and stained wood trim,
located next to Bell Creek. Renovations have returned it to the charm of its period. Enjoy the
tranquil country setting. Host is a retired educator and hostess is active in the local school.
Breakfast is served in the cozy bright dining room. Visa   http://www.bbcanada.com/3097.html

---

Blind River

(east of Sault-Ste-Marie; see also Bruce Mines, St. Joseph Isle)

Bohren, Yvonne (A Taste of Home B&B) ☎ (705) 356-7165
29 Fullerton St., Blind River, ON   P0R 1B0

From east on Main St (Hwy17) in Blind River go north just after lights. From west look for house
before lights.
$40S $50D $5Child   ⌐8A,1Ch
⬛ Full   🏠 Downtown, 2-storey, older, porch   ■ 1S,3D,1Ste
(upst)   ⊨1S,4D,1R   ⬗2Sh.w.g.   ★Air,sitting room for guests,
separate entrance, off-street parking   ⊕ No smoking, no pets
🕴 Downtown, restaurants, shops, parks, marina
🚗 Blind River Museum (logging), scenic drives, golfing, Agawa
Tours (Sault-Ste-Marie)
🐾 Friendly welcome in comfortable ancestral home, situated in picturesque little town. House
has been in host's family since the early 1900. Good location for catching popular Agawa Canyon
Train leaving from Sault-Ste-Marie on day trips into the northern wilderness.Visa ⌐B&B

Horeck, Brian & Shirley (Head to Toe B&B & Esthetics) ☎ (705) 356-7892 or 0242
241 Woodward Ave., Blind River, ON   P0R 1B0   E-mail: headtotoe@on.aibn.com, 1-877-226-2852

From Hqy 17, turn at Royal Bank, then right onto Woodward Ave.
$50S $65D   (plus tax)   ►6A
⬛ Full   🏠 Res, 2-storey, view, river at back, deck, patio, quiet,
secluded   ■ 3D (ground level)   ⊨ 2D,1Q   ⬗ 1Private,
1sh.w.g.   ★ F,TV/air conditioners/ceiling fans in guest rooms, 2
hot-tubs, weight room, boat launch, gazebo, firepit on water's edge,
paddle boats, off-street parking   ⊕ Smoking outside, no pets
🕴 Quaint little town main street area, Blind River with boardwalk & water fountain, shopping, gift
stores, snowmobile trail
🐾 Warm welcome in soothing stress-free environment. Plan a package for a day or two of
personal services for adults. Relax in the out-door hot-tub overlooking scenic Blind River. There is a
cat in residence. Various packages available. Visa,Int.   http://www.bbcanada.com/2829.html

Bloomfield

(south of Belleville; see also Wellington, Consecon, Picton)

Evans, Frank and Bonnie (Cornelius White House) ☎ (613) 393-2282
8 Wellington St., Bloomfield, ON K0K 1G0

On Hwy 401 from Toronto, take Wooler Rd S to Hwy 33. Continue to Wellington, then Bloomfield.
From Kingston, take Hwy 401 west and Hwy 49 south to Picton, then Hwy 33 to Bloomfield.

$65S $80D $80F ►8A,2Ch
🍽 Full 🏠 Village, hist., acreage, patio, quiet ■4(upst)
⊨2T,2Q,1K 🛁4Private ★TV, parking
🧍 Restaurant, artisan studios, pottery/antiques and craft shops,
bicycling
🚗 Sandbanks Provincial Park, golf course, Lake Ontario
🐎 Early 1862-built house for a Dutch Quaker family is located in
quaint, quiet, but industrious farming community, close to clear
water & beautiful beaches. "Prince Edward County hospitality with European charm". Visa ✓B&B

Bognor

(south-east of Owen Sound; see also Clarksburg, Meaford)

Crawford-Weishar, Blue & David (Solstice b&b) ☎ (519) 371-1440
RR1, Bognor, ON N0H 1E0

Take Hwy 6 north towards Owen Sound. Turn east at Rockford, Grey Rd18. Proceed 12km to
Bognor/Walter's Falls turn-off. Turn south, following Grey Rd29 uphill, to B&B on left.

$65S $75D $10Add.person 🍽 Meals ►5-7
🍽 Full 🏠 Rural, hist., former church, acreage, view from guest
rooms, patio, deck, quiet ■ 2(main floor) ⊨2D, cot (incl.
antique sleigh bed) 🛁 1Sh.w.g. ★ TV,F(sunken),ceiling fans,
separate entrance, guest quarters are separate ♥ Ⓢmoking
outside, no pets, children welcome, peanut-free environment
⌇Some French, sign language
🧍 Bruce Trail hiking (Sydenham Tract: map29), bird watching,
on-site artisan studio & gallery, outside children's play area, Spring migration of spawning fish
🚗 Golfing, horseback riding, excellent downhill & x-c skiing, Duncan Caves, Inglis Falls, museum,
Symphony Series & Theatre, galleries, cycling trails, Georgian Bay/Lake Huron beaches, fishing
🐎 Renovated, spacious country church (ca 1868)perched atop a hill with a panoramic view of the
Niagara Escarpment & Queens Valley and surrounded by flora/fauna and forests with abundant
wildlife. Hostess is a stained-glass and mixed media artist. Breakfast is served in one of many dining
areas. Gourmet dinners (incl.Asian/curry cuisine) & packed lunches available. Pick-up & drop-off
service to points on Bruce Trail & Bus Terminal. There are 2 children in the host family and many
petting animals outside. Visa ✓CC http://www.bbcanada.com/3121.html

---

Bracebridge

(s/of Huntsville; see also Pt.Carling, Windermere)

Parsons, Donald and Jean (Parsons Bed & Breakfast) ☎ (705) 645-6009
RR1, Bracebridge, ON P1L 1W8

From Hwy11 exit at Bracebridge onto Muskoka Rd4. Turn left on Muskoka Rd15. Turn left at
Maplewood Rd. Turn left again at fork to 2nd house on the right. 911 is No1045

$40S $60D $10Child ►2A,4Ch
🍽 Full 🏠 Rural, bungalow, riverfront, patio ■2D,1S (main
& 2nd level) ⊨2D,2S(guest bunkie) 🛁 1Sh.w.g. ★TV,
parking
🧍 Santa's Village & Rudolph's Funland, x-c ski trails at back door
🚗 Downtown Bracebridge, sandy beaches, park, Muskoka Lakes,
artisans studios/shops, boating, canoeing, golfing, Segwun
steamship cruise
🐎 Spacious open-concept home is located on the scenic Muskoka River. Enjoy the outdoors,
including the private sandy beach and a cool dip in the river after a busy day of travelling. ✓ CC

Bracebridge (cont'd)

Bourdages, Marie & Gilles (Bourdages B&B-PTL Maple Syrup Farm) ☎ (705) 645-3711,
1123 Clear Lake Rd., RR3, Bracebridge, ON   P1L 1X1 ☎ (905) 728-4845

From Hwy 11, exit east on Hwy 118. Continue 25 km and turn left on Black River Rd for approx.
1km. Turn on Clear Lake Rd and follow signs to white bungalow.

$30S $45-50D   🍽 Meals ▶5
🛏 Choice, homebaked   🏠 Rural, bungalow, res., acreage, patio,
quiet   ■2 (ground level)   ⊨1S,1Q,1D   ⊒1sh.w.g.   ★TV/fridge
in guest living rooms, parking   👋No smoking, no pets
〰English (household language is French)
🏃 Public safe sandy beach, boat ramp, fishing/nature trails, x-c
ski/skidoo trail in front of house, visit sugar shack (when sap is
running), Happy Wanderer (Prov.snowmobile trail) at door
🚗 Bracebridge, Santa's Village, Lady Muskoka cruises, Algonquin Park, Fall colour cavalcade
🛋 Large, comfortable home situated on 28-acres of maple trees. Hosts produce maple syrup and
breakfast is always served with maple syrup. Relax, watch the birds and deer and enjoy the quiet,
invigorating country atmosphere "a home away from home". There is a cat in the house. Also 27ft
self-contained trailer available. Children welcome. ✓B&B

Streeter, Bob & Margaret (Streeters Landing B&B) ☎ 1-800-300-6252, (705) 385-2131
RR2, Utterson, ON   P0B 1M0 E-mail: streeter@vianet.on.ca

From Bracebridge go north on Hwy 11 for 19 km to left turn on Hwy 141. Proceed 7km to stop sign
and turn left on Hwy 35, then right to 1124 Windermere Rd and 1km to B&B on right.

$65-85DS/D ▶6A,3Ch
❋ Summer only   🛏 Full, homebaked   🏠 Rural, acres, view
from guest rooms, swimming pool, porch, deck, quiet, secluded
■ 3Ste (ground level)   ⊨ 2T,1Q,1K   ⊒3Ensuite   ★ TV,
private parking, host quarters are separate   👋No smoking,no pets
🏃 Nature trails, private ponds, birds sanctuary
🚗 Boat rentals, beaches, swimming, fishing, Algonquin Park
🛋 New, elegant country home with high vaulted ceilings
specifically built for B&B and situated on 5 acre parkland setting. Breakfast is served in separate
screened lani with a panoramic view of beautiful Muskoka pines, soft wood maples and mighty oaks.
Hosts are retired professionals and world travellers. Scottish heritage house specialty is "eggs of any
style" and other baked goodies. Visa ✓B&B   htpp://bbhosting.com/streeter

---

Yudin, Sandy and Norman Yan (Century House B&B) ☎ (705) 645-9903
155 Dill Street, Bracebridge, ON   P1L 1E5 E-mail: centurybb@muskoka.com

From Hwy 11, take Hwy 118 west towards Bracebridge. Go over the bridge at the first traffic light
to Dill (2nd St on right). Turn right to B&B.

$45S $70D $10-15Child $20Add.person ▶6
🛏 Full   🏠 Res., older, patio, quiet   ■ 3(upstairs)
⊨2Q,1S,1R   ⊒Sh.w.g.   ★ Air,TV in guest living room
👋No smoking, no pets
🏃 Waterfall, river beaches, picnic area, boat tour of Muskoka
Lakes, shopping, canoe rentals
🚗 Craft studios & galleries, Summer Theatre, Provincial Parks
🛋 Restored Century home in Ontario's premier recreational
lakes district. Hosts are lovers of nature, conversation and fine food. A friendly dog. Visa ✓B&B
www.bbmuskoka.com/centuryhouse

Bradford

(north of Toronto; see also Cookstown, Alliston)

Kay, Lorne & Carol (Blossom The Clown's B&B) ☎ (905) 775-0088, Fax 775-3883
Box 363, Bradford, ON   L3Z 2A9   E-mail: simonekay@interhop.net

Located at 33 Mulock Dr in Bond Head and off Hwy88, betw. Hwys27/400. From Hwy88 turn right
on Brown's Lane to Mulock Dr.

$40S $50D $10Child.Add.person $90F   🍽 Meals   ▶ 4A,2Ch

🍲 Full, homebaked   🏠 Rural, village, raised bungalow, acreage,
patio, porch, decks, pond   ■ 2D (main floor)   ⊨ 2T,1D
🛏1Sh.w.g.   ★ Air,KF,LF,F,TV, snooker table, hot-tub, sauna,
off-street parking   Ⓦ Designated smoking area, no pets
🕴 Quaint House Dining Room, antique stores, Aberle Potters,
restaurant, Sterling Salon, churches
🚗 Newmarket, Cookstown Antiques & Outlet Mall, Lake Simcoe,
Casino Rama, Holland Marsh, GO Train/Bus to Toronto

☛ Cheerful family home of a working Professional Clown, decorated with her collector clown
trivia, including books, videos, balloons and magical things in the decor. Situated in a quiet village
subdivision. Fitness equipment in ground level rec-room available for guests. Breakfast is served in
the quiet dining room or in the bright kitchen overlooking birds.✓B&B www/clownb-b.to

---

Braeside

(west of Ottawwa; see also Pakenham, Almote)

McGregor, Steve and Noreen (Glenroy Farm) ☎ (613) 432-6248
RR1, County Rd. 6, Braeside, ON   K0A 1G0

From Arnprior, take River Rdll km west. From Renfrew, take Cty
Rd6 off Hwy17 & signs "McGregors Produce" or "Glenroy Farm".
$40S $50D(and up)   🍽 Meals   ▶ 8A,3Ch
🍲Full, homebaked   🏠Farm ■5(main & upst.) ★TV ⊨T,D,
crib,cot 🛏2Sh.w.h.,1sh.w.g ⓌNo pets, no smoking, no alcohol
🚗 Renfrew, Storyland, Ottawa River Rafting, Ottawa, Lumber
Baron Festival, Bonnechere Caves, Arnprior, Cobden Logos Land
☛ Quiet setting in 100-year-old stone house on working farm.

Parents of Arnprior Hockey School Students welcome. Host family is very proud of their Scottish
roots. Families with children welcome.

Brighton

(east of Oshawa; see also Colborne)

Clark, Shona (Apple Manor B&B) ☎ (613) 475-0351
Box 11, 96 Main Street, Brighton, ON   K0K 1H0   E-mail: aplmanor@reach.net

From Hwy 401 take Hwy 30 south to traffic lights in town. Turn right on Main St (Hwy 2)
and continue 2 blocks.

$55S $70D $15Child   ▶ 8

🍲 Full, homebaked   🏠 Century 2-storey, veranda, pool, patio,
quiet   ■4D(upst)   ⊨2T,1D,2Q,1R   🛏 2Sh.w.g.
★Air,F,TV in guest rooms, electronic air cleaner, library,
parking   Ⓦ Smoking in designated area only, no pets
🕴 Great restaurants, antiques & craft shops, farmer's market,
Proctor House Museum, Applefest in September

🚗 X-c skiing, hiking/cycling trails, fishing, Presqu'ile Prov. Park (sandy beaches, swimming,
bird-watching), boat charters, Brighton Harbour, Gateway to Prince Edward County
☛ Located on the Apple Route, gracious and elegant Century Home (built in 1843) with warm
and relaxing ambiance and authentically decorated with period furniture and original artworks.
Delight in specialty breakfasts. Passes for Presqu'ile Prov. Park can be arranged. Host's bicycles
may be borrowed. Two Siamese cats "Keeta" & "Sasha" offer their own warm welcome. ✓B&B
www.bbcanada.com/1249.html

Bridgton (cont'd)

Friedrichkeit, Burke & Ken Bosher (Butler Creek B&B)   ☎ (613) 475-1248
RR7, Hwy 30-202, Brighton, ON   K0K 1H0   E-mail: obbrs@reach.net, Fax (613) 475-5267

Located 3 km south off Hwy 401 on Exit 509 to Brighton.
$55S $65D $85F   ► 8
🍴 Full   🏠 Village, 2-storey, hist., 9-acres, view from guest
rooms, porch   ■ 4D (upstairs)   ⊨ 2T,2D,1Q   ⌐ 1sh.w.g.,
1ensuite   ★ F,TV in guest lounge, off-street parking, ceiling fans
in each room, host quarters are separate   ⊛ No smoking, no
pets   ⌘German, French
🏃 Hiking, x-c skiing on property & adjoining Prov. Park
🚗 Beaches at Presqu'ile Park, Sandbanks at Prince Edward County, Lake Ontario, antiquing
📣 Long-time, experienced B&B hosts in new location (formerly Burken Guest House in
Toronto). White Victorian house with elegant furnishings, yet cozy atmosphere, perches over 9
acres of trees, meadows, gardens and bubbling brook (Butler Creek runs through property).
Breakfast is served in the formal dining room. Enjoy the congenial hospitality. There is a dog in
residence. MC/Visa ⌐B&B

Le Ber, Elizabeth & Charles (Sanford House B&B)   ☎ & Fax (613) 475-3930
Box 1825, 20 Platt St., Brighton, ON   K0K 1H0

From Hwy 401, take Exit 509 and Hwy 30 south for 5 km into town. At traffic light turn right onto
Main St. Go 3 blocks to Platt St, turn right to 2nd house on left.
$45S $55D   ► 6
🍴 Full, homebaked   🏠 Village, res., 2-storey, hist., view, porch,
quiet   ■3D(upstairs), separate guest quarters   ⊨2T,2Q
⌐Sh.w.g.   ★TV/VCR/games in guest lounge, air-conditioned
guest rooms, ceiling fans, electronic air cleaner, off-street
parking   ⊛No smoking, no pets
🏃 Restaurants, shops, farmers' market, antique auctions, Proctor
House Museum & Conservation Area, hiking/x-c ski trails
🚗 Presqu'ile Provincial Park (sandy beaches, swimming, birding, marsh board walk, cycling
📣 Warm welcome in stately red brick Victorian home (ca1895) featuring large, comfortable,
bright rooms with period furniture and sunny round turret room with view of town & Presqu'ile
area. Delectable homebaked breakfast is served in separate dining room. ⌐B&B

Payne, Linda & Jim (Harbour Haven B&B)   ☎ (613) 475-1006
44 Harbour St., RR3, Brighton, ON   K0K 1H0

From Hwy 401 take Exit 509 to Brighton via Hwy 30 south. Go
south through village down Prince Edward St to Harbour St.
$55S $65D   ► 5
🍴 Full, homebaked   🏠 Rural, res., swimming pool, patio, deck,
quiet   ■1S,2D(main floor)   ⊨1S,1D,1Q   ⌐1Sh.w.g.   ★F,TV,
ceiling fans, separate entrance, guest quarters are separate
⊛No smoking, no pets, children min. age 12
🏃 Marina, Lake Ontario boating & tours, fishing, restaurants
🚗 Presquile Park, museum, skiing, tennis, golfing, CFB Trenton, Prince Edward County, beaches
📣 Spacious contemporary home located by the Bay on the waterfront trail. Relax by the pool or
in the private sitting area or join the hosts in the cozy family room with fireplace. Breakfast is
served formally or by the pool. Hosts love to pamper their guests, particularly for celebrations and
special occasions. Visa,MC ⌐CC

Brighton (cont'd)

OBBRS (Ontario Bed & Breakfast Reservation Serive)   ☎(613)475-0266,Fax475-5267
RR7, Hwy 30-202, Brighton, ON   K0K 1H0   E-mail: obbrs@reach.net

(Burke Friedrichkeit, Owner/Operator)
Rates: $50-95S $55-165D $85-185Stes   (including full breakfast)   〜German,French
OBBRS provides one-stop reserving a Bed & Breakfast in Ontario without a service charge. With
one telephone call or fax or e-mail a room with any of the member homes will be reserved. Homes
are located throughout Ontario and represent a wide variety of styles and conveniences. All homes
comply with the Service's "Code of Ethics" and adhere to the "Standards & Procedures". To confirm
a reservation a credit card is required. Cancellation policy for urban centres is 48 hours and 7 days
for country properties. www.bbreservationsontario.com

Brinston   *(north-east of Brockville; see also Williamsburg, Iroquois)*

Westervelt, Gerry and Johanna (Westergreen Farm)   ☎ (613) 652-4241
RR2, 11245 Smail Rd., Brinston, ON   K0E 1C0

Take Exit 738 off Hwy 401 at Iroquois. Follow County Rd 1 north for 4 km to Irena Rd, turn right.
Continue 4 km to Brinston Rd (CRd 16), turn left. In Brinston turn right on Henderson Rd, right

on Bell Rd, left on Smail Rd to first farm (2nd house) on left.
$25S $35D $5Child (under age 12)   ►5
🍴 Choice, Farm, patio, quiet, a small orchard   ■1Ste,1F (main
floor) ⊨1S,2D ★TV, separate entrance ⬅1Private,
1sh.w.h. ✋No pets 〜Dutch
🚗 Upper Canada Village, Iroquois Seaway Locks, Fort
Wellington at Prescott, Thousand Islands vacation area, Ottawa
🐖 1825 grey stone house on a 60 milking cows dairy farm and located in the heart of Eastern
Ontario Vacation Wonderland. Hosts welcome young and old. ⌒CC

Brockville   *(see also Athens)*

Clarke, Keith & Sylvia (Underwood House B&B)   ☎ (613) 345-2797, Fax (613) 345-5810
402 King St. West, Brockville, ON   K6V 3S6

From Hwy 401, take Exit 696 and follow signs to Hwy 2 (King St.West). Turn right for 1km.
$45S $55-75D   15Add.person   ►6
🍴 Full, homebaked 🏠 Downtown, res., 3-storey, older, porch,
quiet ■ 3D(upstairs) ⊨ 1T,1D,1K,1R,1P ⬅ 1Sh.w.g.
★TV,off-street parking, guest quarters are separate   ✋ No pets,
designated smoking area, children minimum age 12
🏃 Theatre, museum, harbour & 1000 Islands boat tours, shops,
Fulford House (museum), St.Lawrence River
🚗 Gananoque, Fort Henry (Kingston), Upper Canada Village
(Morrisburg), murals (Athens), Hershy's (Smith Falls), US border
🐖 Victorian home (ca 1895) comfortably furnished with family heirlooms and collections, located
on old Hwy 2 (King St) with many older homes. Breakfast is served in the dining room or in the
glass-enclosed front veranda. Retired from the hospitality industry, hosts are interested and active
in the "World of Dollhouse Miniatures" and welcome other enthusiasts. Free pick-up/delivery for
bus, train or waterway travellers. Visa

Brockville (cont'd)

Logie, Dixie & John (The Calico Cat B&B)
193 Brockmere Cliff Dr., Brockville, ON   K6V 5T3
☎ (613) 342-0363
E-mail: dlogie@recorder.ca

From Hwy 401, take Hwy 2 Exit 687 (10km west of Brockville).
Look for B&B on Brockmere Cliff Rd (1km from exit).
$65S $80D   ►3
🍲 Full, homebaked(gourmet)   🏠 Riverfront, 2-storey, 1acre,
river view from guest rooms, patio, dock   ■ 2   ⊨ 1T,1Q
🛁1Sh.w.g.   ★ F,TV in guest room, private entrance, parking
♿ No smoking, children min. age 12
🏃 Bicycle path (50 km on 1000 Islands Parkway), bikes available
🚍 Town of Athens (11 murals), Gananoque & 1000 Islands Boat Tours, Professional live theatre
🚙 Home is situated among lovely gardens with 50 varieties of hostas, sculptures (by artist host)
and a waterfall, looking across to NY State. Located on the St. Lawrence River and surrounded by
the beautiful and popular 1000 Islands, a convenient stopover for travellers from Toronto to
Montreal. Breakfast is served on the stone patio or dockside (weather permitting). Enjoy a cup of
tea while watching the ships go by. Hosts are world travellers and recently retired. Bicycle & boat
tours can be arranged. There is a cat. www.bbcanada.com

Nash, David & Linda (Gosford Place B&B)
RR1, North Augusta, ON   K0G 1R0
☎ (613) 926-2164
E-mail: gosfordplace@recorder.ca

From Hwy401, take Exit698 and proceed north past the OPP. Turn left on North Augusta Rd (Cty
Rd6) at 4-way intersection and proceed 14.3km to Gosford Rd. Turn right to 2nd laneway on right.

$70S $75D   ►16
❄ Not at Christmas time   🍲 Full, homebaked   🏠 Rural,
heritage stone house, acreage, view patio, heated pool, quiet,
isolated   ■ 4D,2Ste (upstairs), includes log cabin guesthouse
⊨2T,1D,5Q,2P   🛁1Private, 2ensuite, 2sh.w.g.   ★Air,F,TV in
guest lounge, separate entrance   ♿No smoking, no pets, inquire
about children   ∾French
🏃 X-c skiing, jogging/walking/hiking on country roads, watch
maple syrup being made, church suppers, neigbouring Asparagus & Honey Farm
🚍1000 Island, Gananoque, Upper Canada Village, auctions, antiques, Bridge to USA, Ottawa
🚙 Rambling 155-year-old English country stone home with original red pine floors, tin ceiling,
Findlay Cook stove and antiques in quiet secluded country setting with English gardens. Relax by
the inground heated pool and go back in time and find some country serenity with todays comforts.
Ideal place for a romantic getaway or special occasion or a country retreat. ✒CC
http://wwwbbcanada.com/3182.html

Slack, Betty (Misty Pines B&B)
1389 Heritage Hwy 2, RR3, Brockville, ON   K6V 5T3
☎ (613) 342-4325
E-mail: bslack@recorder.com

In Brockville, take Hwy29 to King St. Turn right and continue for 3km on divided Hwy to B&B.

$60-85S/DD   🍽 Meals   ►9
🍲 Full   🏠 Rural, 2-storey, acreage, view, riverfront, patio,
quiet, secluded   ■ 4(upstairs)   ⊨ 2Q,1D,2T,1S,cot
🛁2Sh.w.g.   ★F,TV, ceiling fans, guest bikes available, off-street
parking   ♿No smoking, no pets, check re children
🏃 Walking path to St.Lawrence River, bike path at end of
driveway, museum, Fulford Mansion, golfing, boating, cruises,
swimming, River Festival (June/July), scuba diving, train tunnel
🚍 Thousand Island Parkway, theatre, Capital City Ottawa, Fort Wellington, Kingston
🚙 Warm welcome in modern executive French Provincial home. Enjoy the view of Molly's Gut (a
deep & narrow passage between island and mainland), situated on original homestead land owned
by hosts' ancestors. There is a resident cat calico "Patchie". ✒B&B www.bbcanada.com/1704html

Bruce Mines

(e/of Sault Ste Marie; see also St.Joseph I, Blind River)

Kersey, Christine and James (Beacon Inn B&B) ☎ (705) 785-9950
Box 250, 5 Mitchell St., Bruce Mines, ON P0R 1C0 E-mail: kerz@earthling.net

Located in Bruce Mines behind the museum, one block off Hwy 17 (75 km east of Sault Ste.Marie)

$80-125D ► 8
May-Nov (all rooms & cottage), Jan-Mar (cottage only)
Full Village, 2-storey, view, lakefront, large waterfront property, marina & private beach ■3D(upst) + cottage 4D 4Ensuite(3jacuzzi) ★Air,F,separate entrance, parking, canoe/rowboat for guests,spa on waterfront deck, large waterfront gazebo No smoking, no children, no pets
Extensive Museum/Archives next door, best snowmobile trails in ON outside front door, restaurants, Simpson Mine Shaft (1840's CopperMine),
Agawa Canyon Train from Sault Ste. Marie, Fort St. Joseph, Lock Tours
Bright and airy, beautiful new home overlooking the Bay; decorated with antiques and original art throughout and an atmosphere of comfort and elegance. Rooms & cottage are named after the 4 Canadian Great Lakes ("Superior, Huron, Ontario, Erie") with 6ft high windows looking onto the water. Breakfast is served by candlelight with lake views. Rumcake is served at 10pm. Ideal spot for honeymooners, special occasions & snowmobilers . Visa ✓CC

Burlington

(w of Toronto;see also Waterdown, Hamilton, Oakville, Campbellville, Milton)

Glatz, Arlene (Cedarcroft) ☎ (905) 637-2491, (905) 637-2079
3273 Myers Lane, Burlington, ON L7N 1K6

From QEW take Exit 105 (Walkers Line) south to New Street. Turn right to Pine Cove Rd. Turn left to Myers Lane on right.
$35S $55D $10Child ► 4
Choice Res., quiet, swimming pool ■ 2D (upstairs)
1Q,2T 1Sh.w.g. ★Air,F,TV in guest rooms,parking
No smoking Small plazas, Lake Ontario
Burlington Shopping Mall, downtown Lakeside Park and trendy shopping, Royal Botanical Gardens, Toronto, NOTL
Unique cottage-like home, beautifully decorated and situated on a quiet court. Relax in spacious cosy sunroom and enjoy the warm "Home-away-from-home" atmosphere. ✓B&B

Hoepp, Anneliese (Haus Anneliese B&B) ☎ (905) 634-8918
970 Birchwood Ave., Burlington, ON L7T 2H8

From QEW take Brant St(Exit101) south to Fairview St. Turn right and continue (west) on Plains Rd to Birchwood. Turn left.

$40S $50D Meals ► 2
Full Res., 2-storey, older, quiet, porch ■ 1Ste(upst)
1Q Private ★ Air,TV in guest sitting room, off-street parking, guest quarters are separate No pets, designated smoking area, not suitable for children German
Lake Ontario Waterfront Trail, lovely park & marina
Downtown, restaurants, Mapleview Shopping Mall, Botanical Gardens, Dundurn Castle, Go Train Commuter to Toronto, McMaster University, Niagara Falls
Warm and friendly welcome in older home with Canadian-German hospitality. Upper floor is exclusive for guests. Relax on the porch or in the large yard. Hostess is experienced in the catering industry and very active in the local ethnic community. ✓B&B

Burlington (cont'd)

Rennie, Jim & Kathy (Renn's Nest B&B)   ☎(905)319-0938,Fax(419)735-6970
5292 Walkers Line, RR2, Milton, ON   L9T 2X6   E-mail: jkren@bserv.com

From Hwy 401, take Guelph Line Exit south to Derry Rd and east to Walkers Line south. From QEW, take Exit105 and Walkers Line north. Located across from Indian Wells Golf Course.

$55S $80D $10Child(free under age5)   🍽Meals   ► 6
🍳Full, homebaked   🏠 Rural, 2-storey, 2acres, view from guest rooms, swimming pool, patio, quiet   ■3D(upstairs)   ⊨1D,1Q, 2T(K)(x-long)   🛁2Sh.w.g.   ★ Air,F,TV,off-street parking, LF by special arrangement   🖐 No smoking, no pets
🕴 Bruce Trail at back of property, Rattlesnake Point and Look-Outs, Indian Wells Golf Course across the road
🚗 Burlingon Air Park, Kelso Conservation Park, Milton, Burlington, Lake Ontario, Hamilton, Niagara Falls, Mennonite Country, downtown Toronto
📣 A hearty welcome in warm Christian home situated on 2.5acres of virgin woodland and gardens on the slope of Mt.Nemo with a commanding view of Indian Wells Golf Course (tee time booking can be arranged). Hosts are Medical Professionals who have extensive experience in medical missions in Africa. Relax in the heated pool or in the hot-tub. Special packages available to Clergy & Missionairies for refreshment and renewal. Breakfast is served on the patio by the pool or in the solarium. There is a dog in residence. ✓B&B   www.bbcanada.com/2831.html

---

Wilkie, Nancy & Peter (Wilkie House B&B)   ☎ (905) 637-5553, Fax (905) 637-7294
1211 Sable Dr., Burlington, ON   L7S 2J7   E-mail: nancy.wilkie@sympatico.ca

From QEW, take Brant St Exit and proceed south. Turn right at Fairview St., left at Maple Ave, left on Maple Crossing Blvd and left on Sable Dr.

$55S $65D $5child   ► 4A,2Ch
🍳 Full, homebaked   🏠 Downtown, res., 2-storey, swimming pool, deck   ■ 1D,1F(upstairs)   ⊨ 3D   🛁 1Private,1ensuite
★F,TV in guest room, ceiling fans, off-street parking   🖐No smoking, no pets
🕴 Lake Ontario & Spencer Smith Park, Joseph Brant Memorial Hospital, museum, Burl Arts Centre, Mapleview Mall, Burlington Transit Buses and connection to GO Commuter Train (to Toronto)
🚗 Oakville, Hamilton, Dundurn Castle, Royal Botanical Gardens, Rockton Lion Safari, N.Falls
📣 Large executive home located in the core of Burlington. Hosts have welcomed B&B guests for several years and provide a warm and friendly family atmosphere. Fax and computer access available. Ideal place for business travellers. Breakfast is served in special guest breakfast room. There are school children in the host family and 1 dog is in residence. Visa ✓B&B
http://www.bbcanada.com/834.html

Cambridge   *(east of Kitchener)*

Barrie, Debra and Sandy (Spruceview Century Farm)   ☎ (519) 621-2769
RR4, Cambridge, ON   N1R 5S5

From Hwy 401 take Exit 268 and go east on RegRd 97 (Cedar Creek Rd) for 5 km, pass Reg Rd 47 and look for 2nd farm on right.
$45S $60D $10Child   🍽 Meals   ► 6A,5Ch
🍳Full   🏠Farm, hist., patio, quiet   ■3(upst)   🖐No smoking, no pets   ★F,TV   ⊨1S,2D,1Q,1R, crib   🛁 1Private,1sh.w.g.
🕴 Farm grounds, hiking (Grand Valley Trail through property)
🚗 Farmers'markets, African Lion Safari, Mennonite Country
📣 5th Generation family field-stone house on 250-acre active working farm (beef, sheep, corn, grains & maple syrup). Enjoy the warm hospitality and quiet relaxing atmosphere. Visa ✓B&B

Cambridge (cont'd)

Moyer, Joan (The Calico Cat Bed & Breakfast)
42 Gilholm Ave., Cambridge, ON N1S 1T4

☎ & Fax (519) 623-8689
E-mail: jmoyer@sentex.net

Phone for directions.
$45S $55D   ▶ 4A
🛏Full 🏠Res., older, quiet ■2D(upstairs) ⊨2T,1D 🖐1Sh.w.g.
★ Air,TV in small guest sitting room, off-street parking 🖐 No
smoking, no pets, not suitable for children
🚶 Downtown Cambridge (Galt), outlet stores, restaurants, hiking,
canoeing on the Grand River
🚗 Kitchener/Waterloo farmers' markets, Stratford Festival, Royal
Botanical Gardens, hiking trails, Mennonite Country, Bell Homestead, Doon Pioneer Village
🐾 Warm and friendly welcome in quiet home in the old part of town. Relax on the old-fashioned
veranda overlooking the garden and have another cup of coffee. Hostess is involved with
Soroptimist International Service Club. There is a Calico cat in residence. ✓CC

Sauder, Erika (Morning Glory Guest House)
1035 Riverbank Dr., Cambridge, ON N3H 4R6

☎ (519) 650-1042, Fax (519) 650-9154
E-mail: mglory_bb@hotmail.com

Take Hwy 401 to Kitchener and exit onto Sportworld Dr. Turn right on Hwy8 (King) to Riverbank
(1.8km), then turn right again to Morning Glory (2km).

$80D $20Child or Add.person (in loft)   ▶ 2-4
🍽 Cont., homebaked 🏠 Rural, hist., private guesthouse,
acreage, view, quiet ■ 1D+loft ⊨ 2S,1Q 🚗1Private
★KF,F, ceiling fans, private entrance, off-street parking, guest
quarters are separate 🖐 No smoking, no pets, children min. age
8, suitable for one party only ↝German
🚶 Private walking path around spring-fed ponds and wooded areas
🚗 Kitchener, Mennonite Country, Stratford and Theatres
🐾 "Step back in time!" 175 year old Blacksmith Shop has been lovingly converted into a charming
A-frame guest house filled with antiques. Enjoy a spectacular view from the private deck
overlooking the spring-fed ponds and an abundance of different species of birds. Relax in the peace
and tranquility. There is a dog in residence. ✓B&B www.bbcanada.com/3343.html

---

Campbellville   *(east of Toronto; see also Milton, Burlington, Oakville, Waterdown)*

McPhee, Dave & Martha (Maranatha Log House B&B)
Box 340, 125 Main St S (Guelph Line), Campbellville, ON L0P 1B0

☎ (905) 854-0444, 854-0535
Fax (905) 854-3390

From Hwy 401, take Exit 312 and follow Guelph Line south through Campbellville. Look for house
after railway tracks on left hand side. From QEW take Guelph Line North Exit 102.

$65-85S/D   ▶ 5A
🍽 Full, homebaked 🏠 Hist., log house, view from guest rooms,
deck ■ 2D,1S(upstairs) ⊨ 2T,1D,1Q 🚗1Sh.w.g.with jacuzzi
★F,TV, off-street parking 🖐 No smoking, no pets, no children
🚶 Unique historic village with many artisans/antique shops and
tea rooms. several conservation areas (swimming, hiking, maple
syrup wagon rides, skiing etc), adjoining flower & gift shop
🚗 Burlington, Oakville, Guelph, Cambridge, Hamilton, Toronto
🐾 Historic log home with the charm of yesterday but with modern conveniences of today.
Originally built around 1850, it was moved to its present location and has been featured on TV &
magazines, photographed and painted by many artists over the years. Browse through the flower &
seasonal decorating shop (hostess has won many awards for her unusual and beautiful designs) and
enjoy the peaceful backyard from the deck. There are birds and a dog. MC,Visa ✓CC

Campbellville (cont'd)

Raithby, Nancy (Winklewood Lane)   ☎ (905) 854-0527, Fax (905) 854-3901
RR2, Campbellville, ON L0P 1B0

Phone for directions.
$65S $85D   (Reservation preferred)   ▶ 4A
🍳 Full 🏠 Rural, ranch-style cottage, acreage, deck, quiet
■2D ⊨4T 🛏 2Private ★F,TV/VCR, parking ✋No
smoking, no pets, no children
🧍 Kelso and Hilton Falls Conservation Parks for hiking & rock
climbing, birdwatching, Glen Eden ski hills, Bruce Trail hiking
🚗 Farm Museum (Milton), Aberfoyle Flea Market, U of Guelph

🔫 Enjoy a rural retreat with typical English cottage atmosphere among 8 acres of wooded bliss
on 16-Mile Creek and backing onto Kelso Conservation Park. Part of property is classified as
"natural". Relax on the gorgeous deck over the creek and partake in the rural tranquility.
Well-travelled host enjoys theatre, music and nature.✍B&B

Cargill   *(east of Kincardine; see also Paisley, Mildmay, Walkerton)*

Moffatt, Elaine and John (Cornerbrook Farm B&B)   ☎(519) 366-2629,Fax(519) 366-2275
RR2, Cargill, Ontario N0G 1J0

From Hwy 21, take Co Rd 15 at Tiverton and go east 14.5 km through Glammis to farm on right
side (well marked). Or travel 12 km north of Junction 4 and 9 on Bruce 20 to County Rd 15. Turn

left, to first farm on left.
$40S $50D $75F 🍽 Meals   (Children half-price)   ▶ 6
🍳 Full 🏠Farm ■3D(upstairs) ⊨2T,2D,1Q 🛏2Sh.w.g.
★TV, Air (on main floor) ✋ Smoking on patio, no pets
🧍 Hiking, skiing, woodland and maple bush
🚗 Saugeen River, canoeing, fishing, swimming, Lake Huron,
farmers' markets, museum, anitques
🔫 200-acre mixed farm with large modernized century-home
with open staircases, restored hardwood and a spattering of antiques add a flavour of the past.
Located in the heart of Bruce County in quiet, scenic surroundings with relaxed atmosphere. Enjoy
Lake Huron's magnificient sunsets. Senior citizens, cyclists and canoeists especially welcome.
Cycling packages available. Visa ✍B&B

Cheltenham   *(w/of Toronto; see also Brampton, Georgetown, Erin)*

Craig, Stephen & Shelley (The Top of the Hill B&B)   ☎ (905) 838-3790
14318 Creditview Rd., Cheltenham, ON L0P 1C0   Fax (905) 838-4685

From Hwy 401, take Mississauga Rd. north for 20km to King St. Proceed one road east to
Creditview Rd.and turn left.
$50S $60D $5Child $10Add.person   ▶ 4
🍳 Full, homebaked 🏠 Rural, village, 2-storey, hist., 2acres,
view from guest rooms, swimming pool, patio, deck, quiet
■2D(upstairs) ⊨ 2D 🛏 1Sh.w.g. ★ Air,F,TV,LF,
off-street parking ✋ No smoking, no pets
🧍 Hiking (Bruce Trail or Caledon Trailway), scenic rural village
(country store & dam), fishing & canoeing
🚗 Brampton Flying Club, skiing, golfing, cycling, Terra Cotta Inn & crafts, Belfountain
🔫 Original family homestead (1830-built heritage home) with rooms appointed in period decor,
lovingly renovated and modernized; located in lush park-like setting of the beautiful Niagara
Escarpment. Relax by the fireplace or on the patio by the pool and enjoy the unique pastoral
atmosphere. Hostess is very knowledgeable of the area and will pick-up from Brampton Flying
Club. Ideal place for cyclists and nature lovers. Ask about Get-away packages. There is a dog on
premises. Visa http://www.bbcanada.com/2135.html

Clarksburg

(east of Owen Sound; see also Thornbury, Meaford, Bognor)

Stewart, Karen & Norm (Hillside Bed & Breakfast)   ☎ (519) 599-5523
Box 72, Clarksburg, ON   N0H 1J0

From Hwy 26 in Thornbury, turn south at light and follow Bruce St to Clarksburg. Heading up hill, turn left on Brook St. Proceed to No110 at corner of Marsh St.
$50S $75D $20Add.person   ▶ 7
🍳 Full, homebaked   🏠 Village, 2-storey, hist., acreage, view from guest rooms, porches, quiet   ■ 3D(upstairs), host quarters are separate   🛏️2T,1D,1Q,cot   🛁 2Sh.w.g.   ★TV,F, separate entrance, off-street parking   ✋ No smoking, no pets, children minimum age 8
🚶 Walks on 3.5 acres of terraced lawns (natural streams, park benches, lookout over the pond), Village of Clarksburg (bridges over Beaver River & fish ladders)
🚗 Excellent downhill ski resorts, Bruce Trail hiking, fishing, boating, windsurfing at beaches of Georgian Bay, fine dining, antique shops, x/c skiing
👉 Warm and friendly atmosphere in stately Victorian home, overlooking the village, with spacious rooms, period furnishings, deep wood trim, chandeliers and fireplaces. ✔B&B

Clifford

(west of Orangeville, Mildmay, Gorrie, Walkerton)

Hutchison, Georgie & Bruce (Country Lane B&B)   ☎ & Fax (519) 327-8236
9792 Creek Rd., RR3, Clifford, ON   N0G 1M0   E-mail: hutch@wcl.on.ca

Follow Hwy 9 north to the south-end of Clifford. Turn right on Cty Rd 2, then left on Creek Rd to first house on left.
$30S $45D $5Child   🍽️ Meals   ▶ 8
🍳 Full, homebaked   🏠 Rural, bungalow, quiet, view from guest rooms, porch, secluded   ■2D,1F(main & lower level)   🛁1Sh.w.g. 1sh.w.h.   🛏️2T,1D,bunks   ★TV,LF,KF,house keys, ceiling fans   ✋Designated smoking area, no pets, children min. age 6
🚶 Country roads with little traffic, Wetlands
🚗 Mt.Forest, Hanover, Guelph, Owen Sound, Southampton, Lake Huron beaches
👉 Warm welcome in comfortable home with large windows, situated amidst quiet farms, winding streams and woodlands. Hosts are active in the community, local craft market, country jamborees, historic fairs & church events and are very flexible to suit guests' schedules. Refreshments are always available. Enjoy the congenial get-together in the kitchen or on the veranda and unhurried atmosphere. Seniors' discounts available on Monday to Thursday.

Cobourg

(east of Oshawa; see also Port Hope, Colborne, Brighton)

Duncan, Jayne and John (Victoria View)   ☎ (905) 372-3437
198 Church Street, Cobourg, Ontario   K9A 3V9

From Hwy 401, take Exit 474 and Hwy 45 south to Cobourg. At King St (Hwy 2) turn left to Church St and right to 4th house on left.
$55S $75D $10Child   🍽️ Meals   ▶ 4A
🍳 Full   🏠 Downtown, res, 2-storey, view, patio, quiet   ■2D(main & uper level))   🛏️1Q,2T(1K)   🛁1Sh.w.g.   ★Air,KFF,TV in guest rooms, ceiling fans, private entrance, off-street/street parking, guest quarters are separate   ✋Smoking outside, no pets
🚶 Victoria Park adjacent, beach/boardwalk, Waterfront Trail, downtown, restaurants, harbour, library, churches, Via Rail, Greyhound bus
🚗 Toronto, Rice Lake, Bay of Quinte
👉 Warm welcome in Tudor Style Home, furnished with a mixture of antiques & period pieces and located in the downtown Heritage discrict.

Cobourg (cont'd)

Thompson, Cathryn & Ian Woodburn (Mackechnie House B&B) ☎ (905) 372-6242
173 Tremaine St., Cobourg, ON   K9A 2Z2   E-mail: bandb@eagle.ca

From Hwy 401 at Cobourg, exit on the Burnham St cut-off and follow downtown signs to King St.
Turn right (west) and continue 2 blocks to Tremaine St. Turn left to 4th house on right.

$60S $100D   ◉Meals (plus tax)   ▶6
🍲 Homebaked   🏠 Downtown, hist., 2-storey, small acreage
■3 (down/upst), host quarters are sep. ⊨1D,3Q (two 4-poster)
🛁2Ensuite,1sh.w.g ★LF,parking ✋Smoking on porch
🚶 Sandy beach on Lake Ontario, multitude of south-eastern
Ontario historic buildings, Cobourg main street & Victoria Hall
🚗 Antique shops, Toronto, Trent River, Rice Lake, fishing
📢 Bright, spacious 1843 home, one of the most interesting
examples of domestic Greek Revival Architecture in Ontario, with most of the original features
intact and beautifully decorated, surrounded by lovely gardens, maple & chestnut trees. Hostess is a
prof. Caterer and serves interesting and above average meals. A friendly bagpipe playing "ghost" is
occasionally present. There is a young teenage boy in the host family and a friendly cat. Visa,Amex
✔B&B www.eagle.ca/market/mackechnie

Colborne   *(east of Oshawa; see also Brighton, Cobourg)*

Baird, Lori & Dorothy Fade (Treasure House B&B)   ☎ 905-355-1803, 1-888-655-5591
Box 707, Colborne, ON   K0K 1S0   E-mail: treashse@eagle.ca

Located at 4 North St in Colborne. From Hwy401 take Exit497 at Colborne (The Big Apple) and go
3km south to Hwy2 (Queens Hotel). Continue 1 block south on Division, turn left on North St.

$55S $65D   ▶6
🍲 Full, homebaked   🏠 Village, 2-storey, hist., porch, veranda
■3D (upstairs)   ⊨ 2T,1D,1Q   🛁 1Sh.w.g.,1sh.w.h.   ★F,TV,
off-street parking   ✋No smoking,no pets,not suit.for children
🚶 Walking tour of historic village (ca 1793), Art Gallery, antique
shops, farmers' market, stroll the wonderful .5 acre grounds
🚗 Presqu'ile Prov.Park (birdwatching/fishing/beaches), Cobourg
Rail Station (pick-up if needed), Brighton, Port Hope, Picton
📢 Retired sisters team in elegant Century home decorated with antiques and other treasures,
situated on spacious grounds on the "Apple Route". Relax in the reading room with books, music or
movies, or in the parlor with piano & fireplace, or sit on the spacious veranda. Delicious breakfast
is served in the gracious dining room. Visa ✔B&B

Consecon   *(south of Belleville; see also Wellington, Bloomfield)*

Banks, Rosemary (The Marsh House B&B)   ☎ (613) 394-5319
Box 143, 60 Mill St., Consecon, ON   K0K 1T0

$40S $55D $15Add.person ◉Meals (Deposit required) (Winter rates available)   ▶ 6A
From Hwy 401 take Exit 522 at Wooler Rd and continue on Hwy 33 to Rte 29. Look for house
opposite Post Office.

🍲 Full, homebaked   🏠 Rural, village, hist., older, acreage,patio,
quiet ■ 3D   ⊨ 3D,1T,1R 🛁1Sh.w.h.,1sh.w.g.   ★Air,TV,F,
fans ✋No pets, no smoking
🚶 Weller's Bay, Lake Ontario, Consecon village, United Church
(built in 1820)
🚗 North Beach Prov. Park and beautiful sandy beaches, fine
dining, Art studios, antique hunting, berry picking, museums, Bloomfield, Wellington, Brighton
📢 Friendly hospitaly in "Queen Anne"style home (ca 1876) furnished with some antiques, set in
a large attractive garden on the north end of the village next to the old stone church. Relax on the
outside patio or in the cozy guest lounge. Visa ✔CC

Coldwater *(north of Barrie; see also Waubaushene, Vict.Hbr, Moonstone, Midland)*

Wychers, Nancy & Hans (Heigh Head B&B)
RR4, Box D701, Coldwater, ON   L0K 1E0

☎ (705) 835-5386
E-mail: heighead@hotmail.com

Take Hwy400 north past Barrie to Exit 117 & Horshoe Valley Rd. Proceed 2km east past
Horseshoe Resort to 11 Trillum Trail in Oro Hills.

$55S $70D ►4A
🍳 Full, homebaked - 🏠 Rural, bungalow, hillside, acreage, view
from guest room, patio, porch, deck, quiet, secluded   ■2D(ground
level)   ⊨ 2T,1Q   🛏1Private, 1sh.w.g.   ★ Air,F,TV in guest
lounge, off-street parking, guest quarters are on separate level
Ⓦ Smoking outside, no pets, no children
🕴 Horseshoe Golf/Ski Resort,Mt.St.Louis skiing, Hardwood Hills
x-c skiing & mountain biking, local artisans, fine dining
🚗 Barrie, Orillia Midland, Georgian Bay
☛ Attractive open-concept Cape Cod-style home surrounded by 50acres of private parkland with
hiking, biking & ski trails. Relax in the private guest sitting room with fireplace, TV,VCR, guest
fridge and coffee bar. Host is a woodcarver. There is a dog and a cat in residence. Visa ⌐B&B

Cookstown *(south of Barrie; see also Alliston, Bradford)*

Baues, Gisele & Alfred (Victoria House B&B)
38 Victoria St.East, Cookstown, ON   L0L 1L0

☎ & Fax (705) 458-0040
E-mail: vichse@bconnex.net

Phone for directions.

$65D ►4A,2Ch
🍳 Full   🏠 Village, 2-storey, view from guest rooms, deck,
quiet   ■ 2D(main & upper level)   ⊨ 2Q,2R   🛏2Ensuite
★ Air,F,TV, off-street parking, private walkout deck, private
sitting area in one room, guest quarters are separate   Ⓦ Smoking
on decks, children min. age 8
🕴 Cookstown village with antique/craft/artisan shops, retaurants
🚗 Cookstown Outlet Mall, Lake Simcoe, Wasaga Beach, Orillia (Casino, Opera House), Toronto
☛ Bright Board & Batten home, of older origin (too large for Empty Nesters), nicely upgraded
and furnished with traditional to eclectic pieces and situated on large lot close to village centre.
Congenial hosts invite guests to relax on the private deck or in the guest living room with cathedral
ceiling. Breakfast is served in guest breakfast room. There are cats in residence. ⌐CC

Cornwall *(see also St.Andrews W.,Lancaster, Apple Hill, Williamstown)*

Johnson, Edward and Michelyne (Riverdale House B&B)
1002 Pescod Ave., Cornwall, ON   K6J 2J9

☎ (613) 933-0398

From Hwy 401 take Exit 789 (Brookdale) and drive to traffic circle. Take 7th St west and continue
onto Queen St. Turn right on Pescod Ave.

$40S $50D ►4
🍳 Full   🏠 Res., cedar deck, quiet   ■2D (upstairs)   ⊨T,Q
🛏2Sh.w.g.   ★Air,LF,TV in guest lounge   ⌁French
🕴 Pitt Street Mall shopping, St. Lawrence Seaway, Wood House
Museum, Inverarden Regency Cottage, Museum, bicycle path
🚗 Morrisburg (Upper Canada Village), beaches, Bird Sanctuary
☛ Comfortable contemporary home, beautifully decorated
including some antiques and conveniently located in quiet residential area of town. Well-travelled,
retired hosts with many interests enjoy visitors and showing them around Ontario's most easterly
City situated right on the St. Lawrence Seaway. More space available for special events.

Cornwall (cont'd)

Biggs, Carol & Peter (Blakely House B&B)   ☎& Fax (613) 933-6528
1712 Blakely Dr., Cornwall, ON   K6J 5L3   E-mail: blakelyhouse@sympatico.ca

From Hwy 401, take Exit 789 (Brookdale) to traffic circle. Take 7th St west straight onto Queen St, right on Riverdale, left on Grant then right on Blakeley Dr to 4th house on right.

$50-65S/D   ► 4A
🔲 Full, homebaked   🏠Res., 2-storey, deck, quiet, secluded
■1D,1Ste(upst)   ⊨4T   ⊒1Ensuite,1private   ★Air,LF,TV in upst.lounge, off-street parking   🖐No smoking, no pets, not suitable for children
🔥 Pitt Street shopping, Inverarden & Wood House Museum, scenic waterfront park with 35km recreational cycling path to Ingleside, public transportation to downtown
🚗 Morrisburg (upper Canada Village), Provincial parks and marinas, Montreal, Ottawa
🔫 Stylish home furnished with exceptional comforts, many collectibles and art. Located in a park-like setting near downtown. Well travelled hosts are former Toronto residents who enjoy meeting people from all over the world. There is a cat named "Smokey" in residence.

Lounsberry, Darlene and John (By the Sea B&B)   ☎ (613) 931-3041
19000, Hwy 2, RR1, Cornwall, ON   K6H 5R5   E-mail: berry@cnwl.igs.net

Located on Hwy 2, west of Summerstown and 8 km east of Cornwall. Exit 804 off Hwy 401. Phone or write for directions.
$50-60D $70Ste $10Add.person   🍽 Meals   ► 8
🔲Cont.   🏠Rural, 2-storey, hillside, view, patio, quiet, riverfront
■2(ground level)plus lower level suite   ⊨3D,1Q   ⊒2private, 1sh.w.h.   ⌇French   ★TV,F,KF,LF, private entrance, parking   🖐No smoking, no pets, children min age 10
🔥 Fishing/swimming/boating, St.Lawrence Seaway ships
🚗 Upper Canada Vill., Montreal, Coopers Marsh, Glengarry
🔫 Home is situated on the St. Lawrence Seaway. Watch International ships sail by and enjoy the park-like surroundings on the Seaway. Boat tours (fishing charters, sightseeing to the islands) & canoeing. Keno Japanese Massage and magnetic bed experience available upon request. MC ⌇CC

St.Germain, Marie Rose (Angel's Rest B&B)   ☎ (613) 938-0358
3370 Bruce St., Cornwall, ON   K6K 1M6

From Hwy 401 take Exit789 (Brookdale) north to Cornwall Center Rd. Turn right to 2nd street on left. From Hwy 138, turn right at stop light (Cornwall Center Rd), turn right at Bruce St.

$45S $55D $10Add.person   ► 5
🔲 Full   🏠 Res., courtyard, quiet   ■ 2D,1S   ⊨ 1S,1D,2T
⊒1Sh.w.g.   ★ TV,LF   🖐 Smoking outside, no pets, children min.age 10
🔥 Shopping Mall, restaurants, city bus stop, Studio/Gallery
🚗 USA & NY State, Casino, shopping, Upper Canada Village (historic 1800 Pioneer Village), golfing, Montreal
🔫 Comfortble artist's home with an eclectic collection of Canadian art and antiques intermixed with some 14th Century furniture and surrounded by grounds with sculptured park setting. There is a 15ft resurrection tree (perpetual in bloom) and Angels and creativity abound in this haven of tranquility and regeneration. Guests are invited to enjoy a soothing relaxation therapy by exploring their creativity with clay or paint. Relax by the campfire or read a book beside the waterfall. Breakfast is served elegantly in the Art Gallery/dining room, or under a canopy of maple leaves in the courtyard beside a trickling waterfall. Hostess delights in sharing her passions for her unique art. Holistic therapies are available upon request.

Creemore

(south of Collingwood; see also Maxville, Mansfield)

Cholvat, Carol & John (Mulmur House B&B)
Box 101, Honeywood, ON L0N 1H0

☎ (705) 466-3834
E-mail: mulmurhouse@georgian.net

From jct of Hwys 89/50, go west to Airport Rd (stop light). Turn north 15.5 km to Dufferin Cty Rd 21, then turn west 7.5 km to B&B on south side.

$50-65D $10Add.person   ▶ 6A,2Ch
🍽 Full, homebaked   🏠 Rural, older, acreage, view from guest rooms, patio, porch, deck, quiet   ◼ 3D (main & ground level)
⊨ 2T,1Q,1K   🛁 3Ensuite (1jacuzzi)   ★F, guest kitchen, private entrance, host quarters are separate, wheelchair access
✋ No smoking, no pets
🧍 Bruce Trail hiking & x/c skiing at back door
🚗 Collingwood, Wasaga Beach, excellent downhill skiing & groomed x-c ski trails, golfing
🚐 Newly retired teachers in 1905-built Ontario Gothic house nestled in the Mulmur Hills. The recent complimentary addition has received the Niagara Escarpment Environment Achievement Award. Enjoy the quiet retreat in any season - especially attractive in the fall with the blazing colours of nature. Breakfast is served at the pine harvest table in the large dining room. Leave the car at a Bruce Trail finishing point and get a ride to the starting point.

Smart, Jean & John (Blacksmith House B&B)
7 Caroline St.W., Box 130, Creemore, ON L0M 1G0

☎ (705) 466-3373, Fax (705) 466-2886
E-mail: jsmart@mail.transdata.ca

From Barrie, travel west on Hwy 90 and north on Simcoe Rd No10. At Simcoe Rd No9 turn left and proceed to Creemore. Turn left at Mill St and right at Caroline St.

$58S $68D   ▶ 5A
🍽 Full,homebaked   🏠 Village,2-storey,hist.,patio,porch,deck   ◼ 2D (upst)   ⊨ 2Q,1T   🛁 1Sh.w.g.,1sh.w.h.   ★Air,F,LF,TV,ceiling fans, off-street parking   ✋ No smoking,no pets,not suitable for children
🧍 Antique shops, artist studios, quaint village shops, North America's smallest Jail (1892), Creemore Springs Brewery (tours), unspoilt beauty of Purple hills (walking, bicycling), Bruce Trail hiking, local auctions
🚗 Downhill skiing at Devil's Glen & Blue Mtn ski areas, golfing, swimming & sailing on Georgian Bay, South Simcoe Railway steam train
🚐 Victorian home (ca 1895) located in a picturesque village nestled in the valley of the Mad & Noisy Rivers. Relax and enjoy afternoon tea in the cozy sunporch or on the back deck/patio overlooking the lovely private garden. Well informed hosts will provide information/maps/brochures of the area. Friendly Siberian Huskies "Keegan" & "Buddy" are outdoor pets. Visa ✔B&B

Dorion

(east of Thunder Bay)

Buckley, Kathy & Paul (Wolf Den Bed & Breakfast)
Box 21, Dorion, ON P0T 1K0

☎ (807) 857-2913
Fax (807) 857-1237

$40S $55D $10Add.person   (child free under age 6)   (groups rates available)   ▶ 6A,2Ch
Phone for directions.
🍽 Full, homebaked   🏠 Rural, 2-storey, acreage, deck, secluded, quiet   ◼ 1D,1S,1F(main & upper floor)   ⊨ 1Q,1D,1S+1Dfuton   🛁 1sh.w.g., 1sh.w.h.   ★ F,TV   ✋ Restr.smoking, no pets
🧍 Lake Superior and north shoreline, Wolf River, Coldwater Creek, Dorion Bible Camp, trails through property
🚗 Ouimet Canyon, Amethyst Mines, downhill skiing, walking trails in Nipigon Red Rock, golfing, Thunder Bay
🚐 Pleasant & comfortble open-concept home with screened summer sun room nestled in 109 acres of beautiful wooded area which borders the Wolf River. Hosts are outdoor enthusiasts. There are 3 small children in the host family & a Golden Retriever. Reservations appreciated. ✔B&B

Dundas
(west of Hamilton; see also Troy, Ancaster, Waterdown)

Pieper, Betty & J. (Walnut Grove Bed & Breakfast) ☎ (905) 627-0578
Box 83, 219 Hwy 8, West Flamborough, ON L0R 2K0

From QEW take Hwy 403 to Hwy 6 and follow to Hwy 5. Turn left, continue to Brock Rd, left again to Hwy 8 & right. House on left. $33S-40S $55-60D $10Child $20Add.person ☜Meals ▶ 7A,2Ch ☜ Full, hombaked ♠ Rural, village, 2-storey, older, .5acre, view from guest rooms ■ 2D,1F(upstairs) ⊨1S,2D,1Q,cot ⊲1Sh.w.g.,1sh.w.h. ★ LF,TV in guest living room, guest kitchen with extra provisions, private entrance, wheel-chair access to one room, host quarters are separate, window air-conditioners, off-street parking ♥ ⊛No smoking,no pets,children welcome
🏃 Webster's Falls & park, Borer's Falls, Christie Conservation Area (swimming, boating, picnics), charming rural walks & rugged hiking trails, interesting local village, Sulphur Springs Cons.Area
🚗 African Lion Safari, Flamborough Downs (harness racing), Dundurn Castle, hist. Whitehearn
🔫 Post & Beam (1848) house, built in New England Salt Box- style with comfortable decor and peaceful surroundings. Hosts are B&B world travellers and will act as a guide and/or driver to local points of interest. Pick-up can be arranged. Meals are served in elegant and leisure manner and special diets can be catered. There is a budgie in the house. Specialty: catering to wedding guests.

Dyers Bay
(south of Tobermory; see also Lion's Head, Hope Bay)

Girouard, Jean-Denis & Céline (Plumica B&B) ☎ & Fax (519)795-7499
1024 Dyer's Bay, Miller Lake, ON N0H 1Z0

Located in the Bruce Peninsula, south of Tobermory. $75-100S $85-110D $150F ☜ Meals ▶ 8 ☜ Choice ♠ Rural, 2-storey, view from guest rooms, lakeback, patio, porch, large deck, quiet, secluded ■2D,1F (upstairs) ⊨4Q ⊲ 3Private ★ TV in guest living room, small guest fridge, guest quarters are separate, private balconies, gazebo ⊛No smoking, children min. age 14 ⊶English (household language is French)
🏃 Bruce Trail hiking, Niag.Escarpment, Larkwhistle Gardens, Devils Monum./FlowerPot Rock
🚗 Tobermory, ferry to Manitoulin Island, Cabot Head Lighthouse
🔫 Newly-built French Country-style home furnished with antiques/contemporary and rattan pieces and nestled between 300ft of shore (crystal water) and the 90ft cliff of the Niagara Excarpement & Bruce Trail. Ideal place for hikers, nature lovers and small seminars or workshops. Hosts are a retired Journalist (also Big Band musician) & Watercolor Artist. After a day of hiking & exploring the Escarpment, relax with a book or magazine from the collection on Environment. There are a cat & a dog in residence (on the Welcome Committee). Longer stay discounts. ↙B&B

Steckley, Bill and Merrill (Merrill's Upper Deck) ☎ (519) 795-7714
Dyers Bay, RR1, Miller Lake, ON N0H 1Z0

Phone for directions. $50S $60D $75Ste ▶ 6A ☜ Full, homebaked ♠ Rural, 2-storey, view, lakefront, patio, quiet, decks ■ 1D (main floor), 1Ste (upstairs) ⊨ 2D,1P ⊲1Private, 1sh.w.h. ★F,TV in guest room ⊛ No smoking, no pets, adult accommodation
🏃 Bruce Trail, Lake, swimming, country walks
🚗 Tobermory, ferry to Manitoulin, Lark Whistle Gardens, Cabots Head Lighthouse
🔫 Enjoy waterfront hospitality and a true retreat in quiet country home, designed built by host family, elegantly furnished and tastefully decorated with beautiful quilts made by the hostess, overlooking clean Georgian Bay. There is a private upper deck ensuite. Enjoy the most beautiful view. A rock-lovers paradise. Specialty of the house is coffee cake, muffins and rice pancakes. ↙CC

Eganville

(south of Pembroke; see also Barry's Bay)

Verch, Miss Beatrice (Stonehedge Bed & Breakfast)   ☎ (613) 628-6901
RR2, Eganville, ON K0J 1T0

Located at 1271 Risto Rd. Take Rd512 off Hwy41 at Eganville to Nelson's Supermarket. Follow
Sand Rd for 5km to stop sign. Turn left at Silver Lake Rd for 0.2km Turn right at Risto Rd and
right at Red Plow on mailbox.

$20S $30D   ► 5
🛏 Full   🏠 Farm, quiet, older, view ■1S,2D(upst) ⊢◁2D,1S
◹2Sh.w.g.   ★TV,KF ✋no pets 〰 German (Flemish)
🚗 Bonnechere Caves, Golden Lake
📢 Gracious hostess invites guests to spend some time in rustic
country log house with quiet and relaxed atmosphere. Enjoy the
views of flower and vegetable gardens and awaken to the roosters'
crow. Long-time B&B hostess is involved with Red Cross Home Support Work. There is a dog in the
house. Most easily reached in early morning or evening. ✓B&B

Elmira

(n/of Kitchener; see also Elora, Fergus, St.Jacobs)

Milliken, Rodger and Doris (The Evergreens)   ☎ (519) 669-2471
RR1, Elmira, ON N3B 2Z1

In Elmira, take Arthur St. north towards Alma to Woolwich Rd 3, turn right to house on right.

$40S $50D $10Add.person/Child(age 5-16)   ► 4A,2Ch
🛏 Full, homebaked   🏠 Rural (fruit farm), backsplit, acreage,
view, patio, inground swimming pool, quiet, isolated   ■ 2D
⊢◁2D   ◹ 2Sh.w.g.   ★ F,TV,LF, parking   ✋No smoking
🏃 Wooded walks, 300 acre forest, x-c skiing
🚗 Elmira, shopping, Elora, St.Jacobs, Stratford Festival,
Kitchener (Octoberfest and famous farmer's market)
📢 Retired hosts in quiet location in the heart of Old Order Mennonite Country. House is set
among large evergreens. Relax on the pleasant large covered porch (upper level). A great place to
rest and enjoy the country atmosphere. There is a dog in residence. ✓B&B

Smith, Vivian and Gerrie (Teddy Bear B&B Inn)   ☎ (519) 669-2379, Fax (519) 669-5350
Wyndham Hall, RR1, Elmira, ON N3B 2Z1

From Elmira turn left at the 3rd set of lights (Church St also road 86). Go 1.5km to road 19. Turn
right and continue through Floradale to old schoolhouse on left at top of hill.

$65S-$80D   (Reservations please)   ► 6A
🛏Full 🏠Hist.1907 schoolhouse, acreage ■3D ⊢◁2D.2T(K)
◹2Ensuite,1private ★TV/VCR in rooms ✋No smoking,no pets
🏃 Antiques, Canadiana display, gift/collectables for sale, hiking
🚗 Elora Gorge, Fergus Highland Games, St.Jacobs
📢 Adults Magical Getaway. Beautifully remodelled 1907
choolhouse, retaining many of its original pine floors and pressed
tin ceilings. uniquely decorated with many antiques and
Teddy-Bear decor. Located in the heart of Mennonite countryside, B&B-Workshops/Consultations
available. Visa,MC ✓B&B

Elmira (cont'd)

Watson, Lindy & Clive (Bristows Inn)   ☎ (519) 669-1604, 1-877-669-1604
80 Arthur St S., Elmira, ON   N3B 2N4

Take Hwy 401 to Hwy 8 (Kitchener/Waterloo), then Hwy 86 north to Waterloo, leading into Elmira (becoming Arthur St).

$85S $95-110D $15Add.person   (plus tax)   ▶ 14A
🍴 Cont., homebaked   🏠 Village, 2-storey, hist., view from guest rooms, porch, quiet   ■ 7D (main & upper level)   ⊨ 1D,6Q (incl. 4-poster, brass & sleigh beds)   ⚫ 7ensuite   ★Air,TV & phone in guest rooms, private entrance, off-street parking, guest quarters are separate   Ⓦ Smoking outside, no pets, children min. age 14   ᴍ some French
🕴 Elmira Syrup Festival, Elmira Race Track

🚗 West Montrose (only covered bridge in ON), St.Jacobs, Mennonite Country, farmers markets
🚙 Designated historic and restored 1860 Gothic Revival-style home with modern comforts and amenities, period decor, nine foot Carpenter Gothic windows and ornate trim work in the Gables, providing a peaceful and soothing escape from the stresses of today. Located in the heart of Mennonite country. Breakfast, a delightful repast, is served in the guest breakfast room. There is a cat in residence. Well informed hosts will gladly point out the many things to see and do in the area. Afternoon tea or coffee is served. Visa,MC ⤿B&B www.bristowsinn.com

Elora   *(north of Kitchener; see also Fergus, Elmira)*

Bustard, Marilyn (The Sem Wissler House B&B)   ☎ (519) 846-2130, Fax 846-9332
17 George St., S1, Box 9, Elora, ON   N0B 1S0

From Guelph take Hwy6 to CtyRd7 and to 2nd set of lights in Elora. Turn right on Woolwich St and over the bridge, left on Washington and right on George St. Look for sign in front of house.
$55S $85D $145F $25Add/person   (reduced rates available)   ▶ 11A

🍴 Full   🏠 Village, 2-storey, hist., patio, deck, quiet   ■4D (upstairs) + 1Ste (main floor)   ⊨ 1S,1D,3Q, large futon
⚫4ensuite   ★ TV in guest sitting area and in suite, off-street parking   Ⓦ Smoking outside (in sunroom in winter), no pets
🕴 Elora Gorge, unique & interesting shops, artist studios, hiking trails along the river and gorge, fishing, Irvine River, music & theatre festivals
🚗 Guelph, Kitchener/Waterloo, farmers' markets, Stratford

🚙 150-year old stone house built by Sem Wissler (founder of Salem - a suburb of Elora) with a Bell Tower & it's operating bell. Situated in a small enclave of historic homes. The rambling house is flooded from its many windows & 3 sun porches and is presently being restored to it's old ambience. Breakfast is served either in the conservatory or in the dining room. There are 2 cats and a dog in residence. Visa ⤿ B&B

Hornsby, Lewis and Ethel (Ethel's Bed & Breakfast)   ☎ (519) 846-9763
231 Queen Street N., Box 33, Elora, ON   N0B 1S0

Travel north on Hwy 6 to Elora cut-off (County Rd 7). Continue across bridge in Elora. At flashing light turn right onto David Street, then continue to Queen Street. Turn right to 2nd house on left.
$40S $50D $5Child $10Add.person   ▶ 6A,3Ch
🍴Full   🏠 Village, res., bungalow, sunroom, deck, quiet   ■3D (main & upper level)   ⊨2T,2D,1P,cot
⚫1Private,1sh.w.g.,1sh.w.h.   ★Air,F,TV in 1 guest room, parking   ⓌNo smoking, no pets
🕴 Popular boutique and gift shops, Elora Gorge and park, Grand & Irvine Rivers, Elora Community Centre, cross-country ski trails
🚗 Elmira/Floradale, St-Jacobs, Mennonite country, craft shops

🚙 Well travelled hosts have stayed in many B&B's, are semi retired and have lots of time to spend with guests. Children welcome. ⤿B&B

Elora (cont'd)

Hendriks, Margaret & Harry (Trail's End B&B) ☎ (519) 846-5800
36 David St East, Elora, ON   N0B 1S0

Phone for directions.
$75-95D 🍽 Meals   ► 6A
🍳 Full   🏠 Village, 2-storey, hist., 0.5acres, quiet ■3D(upst)
■3Q   🛏 1Private, 2ensuite   ★Separate entrance, guest room
air conditioners, off-street & street parking, guest quarters are
separate   🚭No smoking, no pets, children by special
arrangement   ᔄ Dutch
🧍 Elora gorge, Irvine & Grand Rivers (fishing), Elora Cataract
Trailway, charming village shops, antique warehouse, Elora Festival, theatre, fine restaurants
🚗 Kitchener, Guelph, St.Jacobs Farmers Market, Elmira's Maple Sugar Festival, famous Kissing
Bridge, Stratford, Forks of the Credit, Hamilton, hiking trails
📣 Bright and cheery large Century Victorian home with warm simple elegance, some antiques
and a replica of an old cookstove in the kitchen. Breakfast (using herbs and garnishes from the
garden) is served in the bright sunroom or in the formal dining room. Ideal place from which to
explore the beautiful Mennonite countryside (watch out for horsedrawn buggies). There are two
Red Factor Canaries in the house, which like to entertain guests. Visa,Amex,Enroute ✓CC

Potter, Don & Jeanette (The Old Bissell House) ☎ (519) 846-6695
84 Mill St.East, Elora,ON   N0B 1S0   E-mail: potters@netcom.ca

From Hwy 401, take Exit295 (Hwy6) north to Fergus & Cty Rd18
west to Elora.
$75S $85D   (plus tax)   ► 10
🍳 Full   🏠 Village, hist., view, porch, quiet   ■5D (upstairs)
🛏2T(K),1D,3Q   🛁3Ensuite,1sh.w.g.   ★Air,F,priv.entrance,
off-street parking, guest quarters are separate, large guest living
room   🚭Smoking on back porch, no pets,children min.age 12
🚗 Kitchener, Mennonite Country/farmers' markets, St.Jacobs
🧍 Bissel Park across the street (hot air balloons in summer), shops & restaurants, downtown,
beautiful Elora Gorge, Elora Quarry & Conservation Park, Cataract Railway bike path, Theatre on
the Grand, fishing on the Grand River
📣 Historic 1856 stone house, beautifully restored, decorated with antiques, pine & oak
furnishings, overlooking Bissell Park and the Grand River. Breakfast is served by candlelight in the
dining room. Early retired hosts have been collecting antiques for many years and offer warm and
friendly hospitality. Visa,MC   www.bbcanada.com/2481/.html

Veveris, Ingeborg-Petra (Gingerbread House) ☎ (519) 846-0521
22 Metcalfe St.South, Elora, ON   N0B 1S0

From Hwy 401/403, take Hwy 6 north and then country Rd7 (Elora Rd) to Elora. At flashing light,
turn east (downtown) to B&B on left side.

$60S $70D $150-$200Ste $15Add.person   ► 20
🍳Full (Gourmet) 🏠Downtown, hist., 1 acre, quiet, 4 porches
■5D,2Ste (main & upper level)   🛏 S,D,Q,P,R   🛁 2Ensuite,
4sh.w.g.   ★ Air,F,separate entrance, guest dressing gowns &
slippers, common areas, jacuzzi, parking   🚭No smoking, no
pets   ᔄ German
🧍 Downtown Elora with many craft/pottery/souvenir shops,
restaurants, Elora Gorge nature walks
🚗 Mennonite country & markets, covered bridge, Kitchener/Waterloo, Maple Syrup Festival
📣 Gracious Century Manor, filled with antiques (historic reg'd building and 1st prize winner of
the Home-builders Assoc in 1991) situated in quaint & cheerful town full of interesting limestone
architecture. Breakfast is served on fine china and linen. ✓B&B
www.eic.elora.on.ca/b&b/gingerbread

Erin

(n/w of Toronto; see also Bellfountain, Cheltenham)

Edwards, Ginny (Cedarbrook Country Inn & B&B) ☎(519)833-1000,Fax(833-1004,
5483 Trafalgar Rd.(Wellington Cty Rd 24), Erin, ON   N0B 1T0   1-800-837-6599

From Hwy 401, take Trafalgar Rd north. Proceed 1km past Hwy 24 towards Hillsburg.

$75S $95D $25Add.person   🍽 Meals   (plus tax)   ► 22
💷 Full   🏠 Rural, hillside, 12acres, view from guest rooms,
patio, porch, deck, quiet, secluded   ■ 2D,6F (upstairs & ground
level)   ⊨ 4S,2T,2D,4Q,3R   ⊒ Private   ★ F(also in one guest
room),Air,LF,TV in guest lounge & in one guest room, sauna, large
& small meeting rooms, guest quarters are separate   ✋ Smoking
outside, no pets, children min. age 10   〰 French
🏃 Walking trails on property

🚗 Bruce Trail, Elora/Cataract Cycle Trail, theatres (Orangeville/Fergus), golfing
🔫 Warm, inviting, country mansion situated on wooded acreage overlooking the Caledon Hills &
Niagara Escarpment. Hostess is a Certified Reflexologist & Health Educator & artist, whose works
are displayed in-house. Treatments available, if booked in advance. Weekend workshops (wellness
education, quilting etc.) are available. Ideal place for a country wedding, conference, spa get-away or
a place to unwind. Breakfast is served in special guest breakfast room. Visa,MC ⌐B&B

Fenelon Falls

(north-west of Peterborough; see also Kleefiel)

Brown, Rondi & Rick (The Rhubarb Patch)   ☎ (705) 887-9586, 1-888-260-0927
30 Oak St., Box 474, Fenelon Falls, ON   K0M 1N0   E-mail: rhubarbpatch.bnb@sympatico.ca

From Lindsay (Hwy 7/35) proceed north on Hwy 35 to Hwy 121. Follow Hwy 121 to Fenelon Falls
Village. Cross bridge over Falls and turn left immediately on Water St, which becomes Oak St.

$85S/D   ► 8A
💷 Full, homebaked   🏠Village, 2-storey, hist., view from guest
rooms, patio, quiet, guest quarters are separate   ■4D(upstairs)
⊨2T,1D,1Q,1K   ⊒ 1Sh.w.g.   ★Air,F,TV,LF,KF, off-street
parking ✋No smoking, no pets,not suit.for young children
🏃 Boat cruise, hiking/cycling on the Victoria Rail Trail, Village
center, antique shops, boutiques, tea rooms, restaurants, Lock 34
Trent Severn Waterway, fishing, boating, beach, park

🚗 Kawartha Theatre, art galleries, Curve Lake Indian Reserve
🔫 Beautifully decorated and lovingly restored Victorian Century home with birdseye maple
wainscotting and pine/maple/cherry woodwork enhancing the many family treasures and antiques
displayed. Enjoy a view of the locks from 2nd floor veranda and breakfast (incl.rhubarb jams) on the
wrap-around porch. Have a pampered experience and relax in affordable elegance with a peaceful
country atmosphere. Specialty workshops available. Visa ⌐CC www.bbcanada.com/842.html

Lawrie, David, Helen & Patricia (The Victorian Well Country B&B)   ☎ (705) 887-9889
RR2, 1277 Cty Rd (Hwy121), Fenelon Falls, ON   K0M 1N0

Phone for directions.
$40-50S $50-60D $10Child/Add.person   ► 6A,4Ch
💷 Full   🏠 Rural, 2-storey, .85acres, view from guest rooms,
patio, porch, deck, quiet   ■1D,1F,1Ste (upst)   ⊨2T,1D,1Q,4R
(incl 4-poster)   ⊒1Sh.w.g., 1ensuite   ★Air,ceiling fans, sinks
in guest rooms, private entrance, guest sitting area & desk in suite,
off-street parking, guest quarters are separate   ✋ No smoking,
no pets, children min.age 12

🏃 Excellent trails for walking/cycling/skidooing/x-c skiing, bird-watching, boating, swimming,
fishing, golfing, Canal Locks, scenic rapids & drives
🚗 Lindsay, theatres, art galleries, antiques & crafts shops, Fenelon Falls, Bobcaygeon
🔫 19th Century Gothic-style home with quiet atmosphere & rural charm. Enjoy the view of
wooded areas and farm lands. Breakfast is served in special guest breakfast room.

Fenelon Falls (cont'd)

Schmidt, Kathy (Katie's Schoolhouse B&B)　　　　　　　☎ (705) 887-2525
RR2, Cameron, ON　K0M 1G0

Located at 350 Ranchers Rd, next to old white church. From Toronto travel east on Hwy 7 to
Lindsay, then north on Hwy 35 to Hwy 121 (turn-off at Fenelon Falls).

　　　　　　$40S　$55D　　　　　　　　　　　　　　　　　　　　　　▶5
　　　　　🍴 Full　🏠 Rural, hist., .5acres, view, patio, deck　■ 1S,2D
(upstairs)　🛏 1S,2D　🛁 1Sh.w.h.　★ TV,ceiling fans, front &
side sunrooms, off-street parking　🖐 No smoking, no pets, inquire
about children
🚗 Balsam Lake Prov.Park, boating, fishing, hiking, cycling,
horseback riding, cultural events & fairs, Trent Severn Waterway,
Kirkfield Liftlock

🔫 Former school teacher in charming, renovated brick schoolhouse (1878), featuring posts &
beams & guest rooms in the loft area. Located in popular Victoria Country in the Kawarthas.
Multiple skylights & large windows provide a bright, warm atmosphere. Guests are invited to
peruse Katie's collection of old schoolbooks. Hostess operated a B&B in North Vancouver for many
years.

Fenwick　　　　　　　　　　*(west of Welland; see also St.Anns, Niagara Falls)*

Schafer, Lore & Dieter (Schaferhof B&B)　　☎ (905) 562-4929, Fax (905) 562-3028
2746 Moyer St., RR3, Fenwick, ON　L0S 1C0　　　E-mail: schaferhof.niagara@sympatico.ca

Phone for directions.
$45-60S　$55-75D　$15Child　🍽 Meals　(plus tax)　▶6A
🍴 Full　🏠 Hobby farm, 15acres, raised bungalow, view from
guest rooms, patio, deck, quiet, secluded　■ 3D (main building)
plus 2D in sep building　🛏 2D,1Q　🛁 2Sh.w.g.　★ F,TV,
barbeque, guest quarters are separate　🖐 No smoking, no pets
〰German　　　　　　　　　　　　　　　　🕴 Bruce Trail, golfing
🚗 Ball's Falls, wineries, Lakes Ontario & Erie, Niagara Falls, Niagara-on-the-Lake, Hamilton
🔫 A hearty European welcome in farm home, surrounded by extensively landscaped grounds in
the fruit and wine growing region of the Niagara Peninsula. A wonderful place to relax and
rejuvenate. Enjoy the bonfire and weekend barbeque, watch fabulous sunsets and humming birds
from the large deck. Breakfast is served in special guest breakfast room. Guided bicycle wine-tours
and eco-tours can be arranged in advance. Vegetarian meals available. Airport pick-up can be
provided. Visa,MC ✓B&B http://www3.sympatico.ca/schaferhof.niagara

Fergus　　　　　　　　　　*(north of Kitchener/Waterloo; see also Elora, Elmira)*

Morrison, Douglas & Emily (Fergus Lee Bed & Breakfast)　　☎ (519) 843-5936
RR4, Fergus, ON　N1M 2W5

Located 3.3km east of Fergus. Phone for directions.
$50S　$75D　　　　　　　　　　　　　　　　　　▶6A
🍴 Full, homebaked　🏠 Rural, 2-storey, hist., patio, quiet　■3D
(upstairs)　🛏 2T,1D,1Q　🛁 Sh.w.g.　★ F, off-street parking　🖐 No
smoking, not suitable for children
🕴 Stroll through downtown Fergus along the Grand River, tour historic
Templin Gardens, Fergus Market, Theatre on the Grand, Fergus Highland
Games (world known), Cataract Trail, fly-fishing
🚗 Wellington County Museum & Archives, Elora (Elora Gorge & Mill),
hiking, whitewater rafting, unique shops, Mennonite Country, Stratford
🔫 Warm welcome in 1860's farmhouse with period flowered wallpapers, unusual antiques, wide
pine floors & cozy country look. Located on 100 acres 3km. east of Fergus. Enjoy tea on the veranda
or by the crackling fire and a memorable stay. ✓B&B

Fergus (cont'd)

Juergensen, Helen & Chris (Fly-in B&B)   ☎ & Fax (519) 843-1487
RR1, Beatty Line 6868, Fergus, ON   N1M 2W3

From Fergus take Hwy 6 north (towards Arthur). Turn left on roadsign "Nichol SideRd 5" to Beatty Line, then first left again and look for house on right.

$40S $60D $10Child(under age 12) $20Add.person   🍽 Meals   ► 6A,1-2Ch

Not March   Full, homebaked   Farm, rural, 2-storey Cape Cod, 100acres, view from guest rooms, indoor swimming pool, deck, quiet   3(upstairs)   2T,1Q,1P,cot   1Sh.w.g.   ★Air,TV in guest room, sep entrance, guest balcony, sep guest quarters   Designated smoking area, no pets   German
🏃 Walking, skidooing, x-c skiing, airplane tours
Large variety of restaurants, Elora Gorge (Musical Festival, antique stores), Fergus (week-end market, Highland Games)
Semi-retired farmers (cashcrop) in new farmhouse, an ideal place for relaxation. Enjoy the year-round warm indoor swimming pool and the wind protected sundeck or balcony. Hosts offer day tours in their private plane wherever guests desire to go (at hourly rate). Official registered runway is on property (Fergus airport). Country supper on request ✈B&B

Flesherton   *(south-west of Collingwood; see also Maxwell, Kimberley)*

Richter, Barbara & Hans (Bed & Brunch at Lake Eugenia)   ☎ (519) 924-9922
RR4, 150 Stanley Dr., Flesherton, ON   N0C 1E0   E-mail: bedbruncheugenia@hotmail.com

From Hwys 10 & 4 in Flesherton go east on No4 to Grey Rd13 and proceed through village of Eugenia to SRd31. Continue 2km east, turn right at Point Rd/Plantts Point signs and follow to Stanley Dr. Turn right.

$75S $85D $95F $10Child $20Add.person   🍽Meals   ► 16A,4Ch

Full(self-serve-buffet)   Rural, raised bungalow, 2acres, view from guest rooms, lakefront, deck, quiet   1S,1D,1F,2Stes (main & lower level), +cottage   2S,2T,2D,3Q,1K, cot, crib   2Private, 3sh.w.g., 1shw.h., 2ensuite   ★KF,LF,F,TV & ceiling fans in guest rooms, off-street parking, guest quarters are separate   Smoking outside   German
🏃 Private lake for swimming, boating & fishing, country roads for hiking or biking (boats & bicycles available n/c)
Beaver Valley/Collingwood/Talisman Ski Resorts, Georgian Bay/beaches, golfing, Bruce Trail
New house on the shore of beautiful Lake Eugenia. Relax on the private deck or private beach or by a campfire or fireplace, row or paddle a boat or canoe - (available for guests; n/c). Hosts may take guests for a boat-tour. There is a dog in residence. members.tripod.com/richters_eugenia

---

Gananoque   *(east of Kingston)*

Bounds, Jocelyn & George (Manse Lane Bed & Breakfast)   ☎ 1-888-565-6379
465 Stone St. South, Gananoque, ON   K7G 2A7

From Hwy 401, take Exit 645 and go south to traffic lights. Then straight ahead for 4.5 blocks.

$50S $55-130D $125F $10-30Add.person   ► 8A,1Ch

Full   Res., hist., Century home, pool, quiet   4(upst)
2T,3Q,cot   1Sh.w.g., 2ensuite   ★ F,TV, sinks in guest rooms, indoor bike storage, Air (window units), parking, swimming pool   No smoking, no pets, children min. age 6   some French
🏃 1000 Islands boat tour & playhouse, Gananoque Museum, St.Lawrence River, marina, excellent dining, shops
Old Fort Henry, bicycle paths, Fort Wellington, Kingston
Stately brick Victorian home with casual elegance and warm hospitality situated in popular vacation area. Hosts can provide theatre reservation/Boat Line tickets.CCards ✈B&B

Forest
(north-east of Sarnia; see also Parkhill, Grand Bend)

Selby, Diana (Hickory House on the Beach B&B) ☎ & Fax (519) 899-2227
RR5, Box5, 4766 Mack Ave., Forest, ON N0N 1J0   E-mail: hickoryhouse@xcelco.on.ca

From London & Toronto, take Hwys401/402 to Exit65 (Hwy81). Turn left on Millsboro Rd right on Scott and right on Mack Ave. Located 0.5km west of the town of Forest and 20km fron Sarnia.

$99S $178D $60Add.person 🍽Meals   ►10
🍴Full, homebaked, buffet 🏠Rural, 2-storey, older, acreage,view from guest rooms, lakefront, patio, porch, deck, quiet,secluded
■1Ste in Manor House plus 2 in Bank Cottages (all upstairs)
⊨2T,3D,1Q,1P ⚷1Sh.w.g., 1ensuite ★Air,KF,F,TV in guest rooms, ceiling fans, private balcony, hot-tub, private entrance, off-street parking, guest quarters are separate ♿Designated smoking area, no pets, children min. age 13

🏃 Private sandy beach, hiking, canoeing, x-c skiing, fishing
🚗 Five golf courses, Grand Bend (popular summer resort town), Bayfield, Huron Cty Playhouse
🚙 Luxurious retreat with finely chosen amenities, including everything required for the ultimate pampering experience, ideal for a romantic getaway, special occasions, garden parties & open-air concerts. Couples may choose dinner served by the house chef, followed by a hot-tub & massage - or just walk on the beach. Enjoy the spectacular sunsets (declared one of the best by Nat.Geographic). For fitness buffs, there is a fully equipped gym. Breakfast is served in special guest breakfast room. There is a dog and a cat in residence. Visa ✓B&B www.xcelco.on.ca/~hickory

---

Georgetown
(west of Toronto; see also Acton, Rockwood, Cheltenham)

Singleton, Ruth & Wayne (Victorian Rose Bed & Breakfast) ☎ (905) 702-0166
34 Cindebarke Terrace, Georgetown, ON L7G 4S5   E-mail: wayne@stn.com

From Hwy 401 take Trafalgar Rd north to Maple St in Georgetown. Turn right, then right on 8th Line, right again on Cindebarke Terrace.

$45S $55-60D $75F 🍽Meals   ►4A,2Ch
🍴 Full 🏠 Res., village, 2-storey, acreage, view, river at back, porch, deck, quiet ■2D(upstairs) ⊨1D,1Q ⚷1Sh.w.g.
★ Air,, off-street parking ♿No smoking, no pets
🏃 Golf Course, hiking trails, trout stream
🚗Scenic little hamlets, Int. Airport, Toronto, Lake Ontario
🚙 Comfortable home decorated with traditional & carefully blended Victorian-style accents. The house backs onto a meadow and bush area with a stream that brings with it a feeling of peace and quietness. Relax in the large spa under the stars. Congenial hosts enjoy helping guests with itineraries for theatre & events in southern Ontario. ✓B&B

Goderich
(on Lake Huron west of Toronto; see also Bayfield)

Beyerlein, Kathi (Kathi's Guest House) ☎ (519) 524-8587
RR4, Goderich, ON N7A 3Y1

From Hwy 8, take Hwy 1 to Benmiller & Huron Rd31 for 1.5km to B&B on left past Benmiller Inn.
$50S $60D $5Child(free under age 2) (Special longer stay rates)   ►4A,2Ch

🍴 Full 🏠Farm, separate guest house, patio, quiet
■2D(mainlevel) ⊨2Q,1R,crib ⚷2nsuite ★KF,separate entrance, small guest veranda ♿No pets 〰German
🏃 Village of Benmiller, Benmiller Inn & gift shop
🚗 Lake Huron & beaches, Goderich, Blyth Summer Theatre
🚙 Separate and self-contained cottage on working farm situated in beautiful rolling hill area. Suitable especially for families or a group of four. Enjoy breakfast in guest house. ✓B&B

Goderich (cont'd)

Davidson, Sandi (Copper Beach B&B)   ☎ (519) 524-8522, Fax (519) 524-8622
148 Victoria St.N., Goderich, ON   N7A 2S6

$45S $60D $15child/Add.person   ▣ (packed lunch)   ▶ 6A,1Ch

Phone for directions.
🕮 Full, homebaked   🏠 In center of town, 2-storey, hist.,porch
◼ 1S,3D(upstairs)   ⊨ 2T(K),1D,1Q,R   🛁 1sh.wg., 1ensuite
★ Air,LF,TV, off-street/street parking, bicycle & equipment
storage, guest quarters are separate   🖐No smoking, children
min age 5
🕯 Heritage Walking Tour, beach, downtown, hiking & cycling
trails, museum, Tourist Information Centre, fine dining
🚗 Point-Farms & Pinery Provincial Parks, Huron County Playhouse, Blyth Festival Theatre,
Stratford Theatres, London
☛ Warm welcome in comfortable home situated in beautiful Port Town. Relax in the pleasant
gardens behind the house. Breakfast is served in guest breakfast room. Lunches provided for small
groups of cyclists and hikers. CCards ✓B&B

Kraft, Hiltraud & Udo (Woodbine Farms & B&B)   ☎ & Fax (519) 529-3590
RR1, Dungannom, ON   N0M 1R0   E-mail: woodbinefarms@hotmail.com

Located 1 concession north of Dungannom (Cty Rd1). Turn left on the hill to 1st farm after bridge.

$30S $50D $5Child   (Reservations are preferred)   ▶4A,1Ch
🕮 Full   🏠 Farm, 2-storey, hist., porch, quiet
◼ 2D(upstairs)   ⊨ 1Q,1K   🛁 1Sh.w.g.   ★ F,TV,ceiling fans
in guest rooms   🖐 Designated smoking, no pets   ∾ German
🕯 Fishing, hiking, x-c skiing
☛ Warm welcome and friendly hospitality in old, beautiful stone
house located close to Lake Huron. Relax by the stone fireplace or
in the sitting room. ✓B&B

Strote, Argelyn (Twin Porches)   ☎ (519) 524-5505
55 Nelson St.E, Goderich, Ontario   N7A 1R7   E-mail: astrote@odyssey.on.ca

From the interesection of Hwys 8/21, go north 5 blocks to Nelson St (1st house west off Hwy 21).
$45S $55D   ▶ 6A
❄ May-Oct.   🕮 Choice, homebaked   🏠 Downtown, res., hist.,
patio, quiet   ◼ 3D (upstairs)   ⊨1D,2Q   🛁 1Sh.w.g.
★Air,F,TV, guest lounge and piano, host quarters are separate,
in-house collectibles (for sale)   🖐No smoking, no pets
🕯 Tourist Bureau across street, L.Huron beach/harbour, golfing,
tennis, lawn bowling, horse races, public swimming pool, fine
restaurants
🚗 Blyth Theatre, Huron Country Playhouse, Benmiller, Stratford Festival
☛ Congenial hosts in gracefully refurbished Victorian home with antique furnishings and
beautiful landscaped gardens located in the heart of Goderich. Relax on one of the small porches
after a busy day of travelling. ✓CC http://www.bbcanada.com/3694html

Goderich (cont'd)

Tanguay, Kathy & Al (Maison Tanguay)   ☎ (519) 524-1930,Fax (519) 524-8553
46 Nelson St.W, Goderich, ON   N7A 2M3   E-mail: tanguay@adyessy.con.ca

From Stratford, take Hwy 8 to end (Goderich). Turn right on Hwy 21 and drive 5 blocks north to
Nelson St. Turn left 2 blocks to house on right. Located 1.5block west of Hwy21 at Tourist Office.

$65(and up) 🍽 Meals   (Reservations recommended)   ▶ 6A
🍷 Full   🏠 Downtown, res.,quiet, large front veranda, deck (off
one guest room)   ■ 2D,1Ste (upstairs)   ⊨2T,1D,1Q
🛁3Private   ★Air.F,TV,LF,library of videos & games &
books,parking   🐾No pets, no smoking   〰French
🚶 Unique Town Square, downtown, shopping, fine restaurants,
Lake Huron beaches and harbour, golfing, tennis, museums, x-c
skiing/biking trails (complimentary bikes available)
🚗 Stratford Festival, Grand Bend, Huron Country Playhouse, Blyth Theatre, Bayfield
📣 Elegant, turn-of-the-Century Victorian home extensively renovated, tastefully decorated,
located on a quiet tree-lined street in the city's Heritage District just off town square. Relax on the
large front veranda and enjoy small-town living. Well travelled hosts delight in exchanging travel
experiences with guests. Business travellers welcome. Longer stay & off-season discounts. ✔ B&B
www.bbcanada.com/686.html

Gorrie   *(east of Goderich; see also Clifford, Mildmay, Blyth)*

Bott, Larry & Shirley (Walk-A-Bott Creek B&B)   ☎ (519) 335-3234, Fax (519) 335-3099
RR1, Gorrie, ON   N0G 1X0

Phone for directions.
$40S $50D $5Child $60F   🍽 Meals   ▶ 8
🍷 Full   🏠 Farm, 2-storey, view from guest rooms, riverfront,
porch, quiet   ■ 4D(upstairs)   ⊨ 4D   🛁 1Sh.w.h, plus
separate shower for guests)   ★F,TV, paddle boat & canoe for
guests   🐾No smoking
🚶 Playground, walks on riverbank, canoeing, paddleboating
🚗 Kitchener, Goderich & Lake Huron beaches, Blyth
📣 90-year old farm house situated on a hill overlooking the winding Maitland River. Relax under
the shade trees or in the gazebo and enjoy the tranquil scenery and wildlife. Savour meals in a
country-style atmosphere. There are also cozy gingerbread cabins. ✔B&B

Grand Bend   *(south of Goderich on Lake Huron)*

Hall-Grusska, Pamela & André (Lilacs & Lace Tower B&B)   ☎ (519) 236-7640
St.Joseph, RR2, Zurich, ON   N0M 2T0   E-mail: lilacbnb@hay.net

Located in St.Joseph at Hwy21/Rd10-11, between Grand Bend & Bayfield.
$75-150D   ▶ 8
🍷 Full, homebaked   🏠 Century home, 3-storey, hist.   ■ 2D,2Ste
(upstairs)   ⊨ 3Q,1K   🛁 2Private, 1sh.w.g.(2-person spa tub)   ★ F,TV,
ceiling fans, off-street parking   🐾 No smoking, no pets
🚶 Beach, ice-cream parlour, restaurant/lounge, St. Joseph Memorial Park
(walkway with historic signage)
🚗 Grand Bend Beach, Bayfield boutiques/antiques, Huron Country
Playhouse, Pinery Prov. Park, golfing, boating, x-c & jet skiing, drag racing
📣 Historic Victorian home with antiques, lace, original pine floors and
spacious, romantic guest rooms, located near beach. Enjoy the
relaxed atmosphere and the extensive perennial gardens with pond and waterfall. A former pipe
organ factory and ice house still stand on the spacious grounds. This home was visited by Brother
Andre, the founder of the famed Oratory of St. Joseph in Montreal. Outdoor Patio and Tea Room
open by reservation or chance. ✔CC www.bbcanada.com/2772.html

Grimsby

(south-east of Hamilton; see also Beamsville, Vineland, St.Anns)

Hunter, Patricia & John (Denwycke House At Grimsby)
203 Main St.E, Grimsby, ON   L3M 1P5

☎ (905) 945-2149,
Fax (905) 945-6272

From QEW, take Bartlett St Exit south to 1st stop sign (Main St East). Turn right, proceed 200ft to low stone wall and sign on right side.

$95S $125D $150F $15Add.person   ► 6

🍲 Full, homebaked   🏠 Village, hist., acreage, porch   ■ 2Stes (upstairs)   ⊨ 2K,2P   🛏 2ensuite   ★ Air,F,TV/phone in guest rooms, off-street parking, guest quarters are separate   🚭No smoking, no pets, children min. age 8   〰 French

🕴 Large garden featuring magnificient century old chestnut, black walnut and black locust trees

🚗Niagara Falls, NOTL, Bruce Trail, many wineries, superb dining, Lake Ontario, Hamilton

☛ Long-time and experienced B&B hosts (formerly in Ottawa) in new location. Luxurious suites in spacious heritage home, beautifully decorated, furnished with many antiques and located on the Niagara Wine Route. Well travelled hosts have collected many interesting momentos from their travells abroad. Relax under the trees in the garden or in the elegant living room. Breakfast is served in the formal dining room.   CCards ✍B&B-

---

Staz, Georgina & Barry (Maples of Grimsby)
3 Nelles Blvd., Grimsby, ON   L3M 3P9

☎ (905) 945-5719

From QEW take Exit74 south to Livingston Ave (flashing light), turn east 2km to Nelles Blvd on right.

$85S $95D $130(for 3)   🍽 Meals   ► 6A

🍲 Full, homebaked   🏠 Downtown, 2-storey, older, patio, porch, deck, quiet   ■ 3 (upstairs)(incl.1 bed-sitting room)   ⊨1S,2Q,1R,1P   🛏1ensuite, 1sh.w.g or private   ★Air,F,TV in guest room, ceiling fans, off-street parking   🚬Smoking on veranda, no pets, not suitable for children

🕴 Bruce Trail (UN Biosphere Reserve), museum, library, art galleries, wineries, local artists & potters, stained glass studio, Lake Ontario, Festival of Art, shops, restaurants

🚗 NOTL, Niagara Falls, Village of Jordon, R.Bot.Gardens, Pt Dalhousie/Henley Regatta, Toronto

☛ Warm welcome in charming home (1912), tastefully decorated, with award winning gardens and located on a quiet tree-lined boulevard in the heart of town. Breakfast is served in the formal dining room. Relax in the sunny rooms overlooking the pool area & garden or on one of the shaded little patios. One party only (3) in combined rooms (single & bed-sitting room). There is a canary in residence. ✍B&B www.bbcanada.com/2414.html

---

Guelph

(west of Toronto; see also Kitchener, Rockwood, Acton)

Gobbi, Ian & Teresa (Suffolk B&B)
115 Suffolk St.West, Guelph, ON   N1H 2J4

☎ (519) 823-1910, Fax (519) 823-8116
E-mail: ifarley@netcom.ca

From Hwy401, take Exit295 north to Paisley St. Turn east (right) to 4th traffic light (Yorkshire St). Turn left to first stop sign (Suffolk St). Turn right.

$65S $75D   ► 6

🍲 Cont. (self-serve on weekdays)   🏠 Downtown, res., 3-storey, hist., patio, porch, quiet   ■ 3D(upstairs)   ⊨ 2Q,2T,1P   🛏 1Sh.w.g. (whirlpool tub)   ★ KF,TV, off-street & street parking   🚬 Smoking outside, no pets, inquire about children

🕴 Downtown, boutiques, restaurants, pubs

🚗 University of Guelph, Fergus, Elora, Mennonite Country, farmers' market, St.Jacobs, Kitchener-Waterloo (Oktoberfest), Niagara F.

☛ Elegant, turn of the Century brick home with warm, relaxed atmosphere furnished with fine antiques and situated in historic and lively University town. Relax on the patio. Hosts enjoy helping guests with sightseeing tours of the City & surrounding area. There is a resident dog.   Visa www.bbcanada.com/suffolkbandb

Haliburton *(west of Bancroft; see also Minden, Wilberforce)*

Cleeland, Bonnie & Ken (Sunnyside Bed & Breakfast)   ☎ (705) 457-9173
Box 235, Sunnyside St., Haliburton, ON   K0M 1S0   1-888-345-5563

Take Hwy 35 or 11 north to Hwy 118 and east into Haliburton Village. Located on Sunnyside St & Maple Ave (Hwy 118), first house on left.
$50-65S/D ► 6
💲 Full, homebaked 🏠 Village, 2-storey, older, small acreage, view, quiet ■3D(upst) ⊨3D ⏁1Sh.w.g. ★F,TV, parking ⊛ No smoking, no pets
🏃 Haliburton Village, public park, beach & boardwalk on Head Lake, Haliburton School of Fine Arts, lake ice skating, Rails End Gallery, shops, great dining
🚗 Algonquin Prov.Park, biking & hiking trails, x-c & alpine skiing, golfing
📷 Comfortable home (ca 1905) located in popular Haliburton Highlands. Sit on the front porch and enjoy the quiet sounds of being away from the city. Take the opportunity and see Haliburton and its area from a more casual perspective. Perfect spot for people attending Sir Sandford Fleming College & School of Fine Arts. There is a small friendly resident dog.⌐B&B

Hamilton   *(s/w of Toronto; see also Burlington, Waterdown, Dundas, Ancaster, Grimsby)*

Hajas, Alex & Marvel (Westmount House B&B)   ☎ (905) 388-2250
18 Eldorado Ct., Hamilton, ON   L9C 2P9

From Hwy 403, take Mohawk Rd East Exit(Lincoln Alex.Pkway) and travel to Garth St. Turn left to Mohawk Rd, right on Millbank, left on Lynbrook, right on Montcalm, right on Eldorado.
$45S $55D   (Children welcome) ► 4
💲 Full, homebaked 🏠 Res., 4-level-split, view, patio, porch ■3D(upstairs) ⊨4T(2K),1D ⏁1Sh.w.g. ★Air,TV,LF,off-street parking ⊛No smoking,no pets 〰 Hungarian
🏃 Small Mall, churches, historic restored school museum, Westmount Recreation Centre across street (swimming)
🚗 Beautiful views from Hamilton Escarpment, downtown, McMaster U & Med Centre, hist Dundurn Castle, Rock Gardens
📷 Charming and friendly home, centrally located on beautiful Hamilton Mountain. Congenial hosts enjoy welcoming guests in their home and are happy to help with plans to see nearby attractions. Watch TV or relax in the lovely garden and patio after a day of travelling & sightseeing. Breakfast is served in the bright/relaxing dining room. ⌐B&B
www.bbcanada.com/650.westmounthouse

Lehnert, Sharon (Inchbury Street Bed & Breakfast)   ☎(905)522-3520,Fax(905)522-5216
87 Inchbury Street,Hamilton,ON L8R 3B7   E-mail: inchbury@lara.on.ca, 1-800-792-8765

From east on Hwy 403, exit at York Blvd, left at Rolph Gate (1st street past Dundurn traffic light), right on Kinnel, left on Inchbury. From west on Hwy 403 go east on Aberdeen, north on Locke, left on York and right on Inchbury.
$50S $65D $15Add.person ► 4A,2Ch
💲 Full, homebaked 🏠 Downtown, 2-storey, hist., quiet ■2D(upstairs) ⊨2D,1cot ⏁ 1Sh.w.g. ★ Air,LF,TV in guest lounge, street parking
⊛ Smoking outside 〰 German, French
🏃 Historic Dundurn Castle and waterfront park, Copps Coliseum, Hamilton Place, Convention Centre, downtown shopping, Art Gallery, restaurants
🚗 McMaster University, Royal Botanical Gardens, NOTL, Niagara Falls
📷 Late 19th Century home decorated with distinctive family art and English Garden, situated in a little enclave beside Dundurn Castle. Breakfast is served in the large dining room. Hostess is a runner, sailor & painter.
Visa,MC ⌐B&B www.bbcanada.com/inchbury

May, Gary & Anne (Galivants Rest B&B) ☎ (905) 575-5095
121 Dragoon Dr., Hamilton, ON   L9B 2C9

From Hwy 403 travel east on Lincoln Alexander Expressway to Upper James St. Proceed south to Stone Church Rd. Turn east to Upper Wellington, turn right and then left on Dragoon.

$50S $60D   ► 4A
⚏Full,homebaked   🏠Res.,2-storey,deck,quiet   ■2(upstairs)
⊨1D,1Q,1R   ⊨1Sh.w.g.   ★Air,TV,F,LF, off-street parking
✋No smoking, no pets, not suitable for children
☈ Shopping, restaurant, bus routes
🚗 Hospitals, lookouts with spect.views of the city, downtown
McMaster U, Copps Coliseum, Mount Hope Airport, Bruce Trail
📣 Large home located in the heart of Hamilton's mountain or
upper city. Hosts enjoy travel, birdwatching and theatre. MC ⤳B&B

Mordue, Bruce and Betty (East Mountain B&B) ☎ (905) 383-9517
61 East 43 St., Hamilton,ON   L8T 3B7

From Hwy 403 take Mohawk Road East Exit and stay to left for LINC (Lincoln Alexander Parkway). Take Upper Gage Exit, go left and 3 km to end. Turn right on Concession St and right on East 43rd St to house on left.

$50S $65D   🍽Meals   ► 4
✳ Not June/July/Aug.   ⚏ Full, homebaked   🏠 Res.,
bungalow, quiet   ■1S,1D (main level)   ⊨1Q,2T   ⊨1Sh.w.h.
★TV ✋No smoking, no pets
☈ Henderson General Hospital and Cancer Clinic, Mountain Brow,
Bruce Trail, city bus routes
🚗 Convention Center, Copps Coliseum, Hamilton General, St.Joseph's Hospital, Dundurn Castle
📣 Warm and friendly country-style atmosphere in cozy, quiet ranch-style home located one block
from Mountain Brow, which offers a panoramic view of the city and Niagara escarpment.⤳B&B

Roossien, Bert & Gale (Heritage House 1914) ☎ (905) 549-5247
202 St.Clair Blvd, Hamilton, ON   L8M 2P1   E-mail: beans@idirect.com

Take Hwy 403 to Main St East Exit and continue to St Clair Ave and then St Clair Blvd. Located 1 block east of Sherman.

$50S $60D   🍽Meals   ► 6A
⚏Full,homebaked   🏠Downtown, 3-storey, hist., view from
guest rooms, patio, porch,
quiet ■3D(upst) ⊨2D,1Q ⊨1Sh.w.g.   ★F,TV,fans, off-street
& street parking, host quarters are separate ✋Desig.smoking
area, not suit.for children
☈ Copps Coliseum, Hamilton Place, Gage Park, Football Hall of
Fame, downtown area, bus route at corner
🚗 Niagara Falls, Niagara-on-the-Lake, Lake Ontario, Kitchener, Lion Safari
📣 Designated Heritage Home (Edwardian Square home, built in 1914), furnished with antiques,
lots of character and warmth, situated on a beautiful quiet Blvd with gorgeous mature trees in a
very convenient location. Breakfast is served in special guest breakfast room. There is a dog in the
house. Visa ⤳B&B www.bbcanada.com/2943.html

Ross, Jim & Barb (Bay South B&B)   ☎ (905) 528-1959, Fax (905) 528-8894
279 Bay St.S, Hamilton, ON L8P 3J5

From Hwy 403 take Aberdeen Exit and proceed to Bay St. Turn left.
$55S $65D $15Child   ►5
🕮 Full   ♙ Downtown, hist., patio, porch, deck   ■ 2(upstairs)
⊨1S,2T,1Q   ⊲ 1Sh.w.g.   ★ F,KF,LF,TV in guest rooms,
air-conditioners, off-street parking   ⛛ No smoking
🕂 Hamilton Place, Copps Coliseum, Dundurn Castle, shopping
🚗 McMaster U, Lakes Ontario/Erie shorelines, Niagara Falls, Toronto
🚗 Large home situated in old neighborhood. Professional hosts have
excellent knowledge of local architecture and attractions. Breakfast is served
in special guest breakfast room. There is a dog and a cat. Visa ✒B&B

Hearst   *(northern Ontario - west of Timmins; see also Kapuskasing)*

Barrette, Rejeanne (Rejeanne's B&B)   ☎ (705) 362-4442
45A Houle St., Box 862, Hearst, ON P0L 1N0

Phone for directions.
$45S $55D $10Child (free under age 6)   ►6+
🕮 Full   ♙ Townhouse, tudor-style, duplex, patio, quiet   ■3(upstairs)
⊨3D,1R   ⊲1Sh.w.g.   ★TV,LF,separate entrance, parking   ⛛No
smoking, no pets   ⌇ English (household language is French)
🕂 Downtown Hearst, community and art centers, hospital, restaurants,
fitness trail along Mattawishkia River, Algoma Central Railway Station
🚗 Fairly new house with a French-Canadian atmosphere and situated in a
quiet hospital and residental zone. Free pick-up and delivery from Algoma
Central Station, airport and bus depot. Guided bus tour of the local sawmills
and surrounding area. Summer cottage available. ✒B&B

Levesque, Rita (Northwinds Bed & Breakfast)   ☎ (705) 362-4531
Box 2253, Lac Ste-Thérèse, Hearst, ON P0L 1N0

$60S $75D $10Child (free under age 12) $15Add.person   🍽 Meals   ► 8A,3Ch
From TCH11 in Hearst take Hwy 583N for 12 km to Lac St-Thérèse.

🕮 Full,homebaked   ♙ Rural, res., ranch-style, view, 7 acres,
patio, lakeside, quiet, isolated   ■ 1D,2F   ⊲ 1S,2Q,1K,2R,
crib   ⊲ 1Sh.w.g., 1ensuite   ★ F,TV, facilities for the disabled,
off-street parking   ⛛ No smoking   ⌇ French
🕂 Private dock for swimming, canoeing, pedal boating, fishing,
snowshoeing, snowmobiling
🚗 Golf course, X-c Ski Club, boat rentals, marina
🚗 Architecturally designed lakeside home with huge octagonal
living area with fireplace and view onto the lake and walkout to large patio. Enjoy the breathtaking
Northern sunsets. Access to main snowmobile trails on lake below. Dock is also suitable for
aircrafts. Canoe & pedal boat at guests' disposal. There is a cat in residence.

Hope Bay

(north of Wiarton; see also Pike Bay, Lion's Head)

Strang, Bill & Nancy (Cedarholme B&B) ☎ & Fax (519) 534-3705
108 Beech St., Hope Bay, RR6, Wiarton, ON   N0H 2T0

On Hwy 6 north of Wiarton, take County Rd 9 for 17 km. Turn right (east)
and proceed 1 km.
$45S $55-65D $10Add.person 🍽 Meals ▶6+
🍴 Full, homebaked 🏠 Rural, 3-storey, acreage, view from guest rooms,
patio, quiet ■1D,1F,1Ste(upstairs) ◀3T,2D,1Q,1P 🛏2Sh.w.g.,1ensuite
★F,TV, separate entrance, library, games, parking ✋ No
smoking 〜some French
🚗 Tobermory, ferry to Manitoulin I., scenic caves, Sauble Beach
🏃 Bruce Trail hiking, Hope Bay & sandy beach, volleyball/badminton court, Tea Room (May-Oct)
📣 Congenial hosts in spacious brick home on beautiful Hope Bay along the Niagara Escarpment.
Ideal place to stop over on the way to catch the Chi-Cheemaun Ferry from Tobermory or on a Bruce
Trail hike. There are also 4 winterized cottages available for families and pets. ✔B&B

Huntsville

(north of Orillia; see also Bracebridge)

Barter, Rod & Ginny (The Carriage House B&B) ☎ (705) 789-9434, Fax (705) 789-3222
22 Main St. West, Huntsville, ON P1H 2C3   E-mail: thecarriagehouse@hotmail.com

From Hwy 11 north exit at Muskoka Rd 3 and travel towards town center. (3km on left).
$50-65S- $65-75D $5Child(over age 10) $125F $10Add.person ▶ 6A,4Ch
🍴 Full, Homebaked 🏠 Downtown, 3-storey, older, view from

guest rooms, indoor swimming pool, patio ■3D(upstairs)
◀2T,1Q,2K,2cots 🛏1Sh.w.g.,1ensuite ★ F,separate
entrance, off-street parking, guest family room, guest quarters are
separate, sauna ✋No smoking, pets (by prior arrangement)
🏃 Shopping, fine dining, Muskoka Pioneer Village, Recreation
Centre, library, town waterfront, Mini Putt, boat tours
🚗 Golfing, tennis, downhill & x-c skiing, Algonquin &
Arrowhead parks, hiking, canoeing, mountain biking, boating
📣 Beautiful 1920's Georgian-style home with spacious accommodation, indoor swimming pool
and sauna near Huntsville's picturesque town centre. Enjoy a bayview breakfast before starting a
busy day of outdoor activities or sightseeing. There is a dog and a cat in residence. Visa ✔CC
www.bbcanada.com/3773.html

Cochran, Andy & Martha Mary (A Gingerbread B&B) ☎ (705) 789-4115
882 Riverlea Rd., Huntsville, ON P1H 1X5   Fax (705) 789-1272

$45S $60-80D $15Child/Add.person 🍽 Meals(lunch) ▶8
From Hwy 11 turn onto Muskoka Rd 3 into Hunstville. Proceed through town and turn south onto
Brunel Rd (Muskoka Rd2). Continue 2.7km to N.Mary Lake Rd. Turn right & follow pink reflective
B&B signs for 2.5km. Turn where the hand signals.
🍴 Full 🏠 Rural, waterfront, 2-storey, view, porch, deck, quiet,
secluded ■ 4(upstairs) ◀ 2T,3Q 🛏 1Ensuite, 2sh.w.g.
★TV, canoe for guests ✋ Smoking outside or in garage
🏃 Swimming/canoeing, driving range, trails (hiking, x-c skiing,
snowmobiling), boating, fishing, quiet road biking
🚗 Downtown, casual & fine dining on waterfront patios, shops,
Algonquin Nat.Park, Arrowhead Prov.Park, golfing, skiing
📣 Charming rural waterfront home with Gingerbread Trim on the porch, antiques inside and a
beautiful view in all seasons, situated on the sandy shore of the Muskoka River. Breakfast is served
in the sunny dining room or on the deck overlooking the water. Relax on the dock, swim or canoe,
and watch the loons, moose, mink & beavers as they drink on the far river shore. Enjoy dramatic
fall colours, pristene snow, spring flowers' fragrants and black & diamond-studded night skies.
There are 2 cats in residence. Visa ✔B&B www.bbcanada.com/2194

Huntsville (cont'd)

Rye, Robert & Dawn (Fairy Bay Guest House)   ☎ (705) 789-1492, Fax (705) 789-6922
228 Cookson Bay Cr., Huntsville, ON   P1H 1B2   E-mail: hosts@fairybay.ca, 1-888-813-1101

Located 7km east of jct of Hwys 11&60, off Deerhurst/Canal Rd.
$90-140S $105-180D $40Add.person (plus taxes)   ▶ 18A,6Ch
Full, homebaked   Rural, lakefront, 3-storey. acreage, view
from guest rooms, patio, porch deck, quiet, secluded   ■9
incl.1Ste(main/upper/lower levels) ⊨2T,6Q,1K,3P,foam-pads
1Sh.w.g., 8ensuite ★Air,KF,F, exercise room, tennis, sauna,
indiv.climate control, private entrance, guest quarters are
separate   Ⓦ Smoking outside, no pets

🕴 Beach, dock, boating, bicycling, fishing, hiking/nature trails, Hidden Valley Highlands ski area,
Grandview, Deerhurst Highland Golf course, trail & dog-sled riding, snowmobiling, fine dining, pub
🚗 Muskoka Pioneer Village, town of Huntsville, shopping, Algonquin Park, Santa's Village
🔪 Custom-designed country home, furnished and decorated as a B&B for the discriminating
traveller, and located on a quiet Bay with access to 40km of waterways in the heart of Muskokas
historic recreation region. Relax in the comfortable guest lounge or upstairs library, enjoy the view
of Fairy Lake through large windows, make use of the on-site equipment, or watch the Northern
Lights from the trellised deck. Breakfast is served in guest breakfast room. Visa,MC ✓CC
www.fairybay.ca

Von der Marwitz, Marina & Peter (Maplewood B&B)   ☎ & Fax (705) 635-1378
Hwy 60, Hillside, RR4, Huntsville, ON   P1H 2J6

$45S $60D $10Child $20Add.person $120F   ◖Lunch bag   ▶ 5A,2Ch

Located 11km east of Huntsville. Phone for directions.
� May-Oct   Full   Rural, 2-storey settler, hist., 4acres,
view, deck, gazebo   ■3 (upstairs)   ⊨ 1S,2T,1D,1P
1Sh.w.g., 1sh.w.h   ★TV, off-street parking   Ⓦ No smoking,
children min.age 10 or infants   ⌇ German

🕴 Golf Course, public beach, canoeing, kayaking, nature walks
🚗 Algonquin Park, 1000 Islands, Georgian Bay, x-c & downhill
skiing, European restaurants, Lehman's Animal Farm
🔪 Renovated former Post Office, historic settler's house with European hospitality. There is an
artist studio and unique outdoor gallery. Breakfast is served in formal setting. Relax in the library
and enjoy the walk pathways.

Iroquois   *(east of Brockville; see also Brinston, Morrisburg, Prescott)*

LeBlanc, Pierrette & Paul Taillefer (Blue Heron Bleu)   ☎ (613) 652-2601
11583 Lakeshore Dr., Iroquois, ON   K0E 1K0   Fax (613) 652-1112

From Hwy401,take Exit750 (Morrisburg),or Exit738 (Iroquois).Situated along the St.Lawrence R.

$50D   ▶ 5
Full, homebaked   Rural, ranch-style, view, lakefront, quiet,
private river terrace   ■3D(main & lower level)   ⊨2T,2D
2Sh.w.g.   ★ 2F,TVin guest rooms, parking, guest family room
with VCR/TV and library   Ⓦ No smoking, no pets, children min
age 12   ⌇ French
🕴 Apple orchards, berry picking, fishing in private Bay
🚗 Iroquois Seaway Locks, Carman House Museum, golf courses, Upper Canada Village, Ottawa
🔪 Relax in the sun-drenched breakfast room and enjoy ocean going ships and Lakers go by in the
St.Lawrence Seaway. Rest on the peaceful terrace at water's edge. There is a Silver Tabby cat in
residence. ✓CC   http://www.bbcanada.com/3175.html

Kapuskasing

(northwest of Timmins; see also Hearst)

Grzela, Marc & Miling (The Northern Oasis B&B & Specialty Suites)
62 Riverside Dr., Kapuskasing, ON   P5N 1A9   ☎ & Fax (705) 335-4818, 1-888-299-9494

From Hwy 11, turn on Riverside Dr. Or phone for directions.
$50-85SD   🍴 Meals   (plus tax)   ►6
🍷 Full   🏠 Downtown, res., 3-storey, porch
■3Ste(upstairs)   ⊨ 3Q,1R   🛏 3Private (with double
heartshaped red whirlpool tubs)   ★F, airconditioners,
TV/robes/hair dryers in guest rooms, off-street parking, guest
quarters are separate   ✋No smoking, no pets   ∾ French,
Fillipino, Spanish

🏃 Downtown, bus tours, Festival of Lights, Ron Morel Museum, Train Stn, Spruce Falls Paper
Mill, shopping, riverpark, leisure walks

🔫 Friendly Northern hospitality in historic house, (one of first houses built in town) recently
renovated, with river view and situated across from park. Semi-retired hosts have travelled
nationally & abroad and are happy to share experiences with guests and always give champagne
welcome. Breakfast is served in main dining room or in guest room, if requested. Honeymoon, Red
Carpet & Silver packages available. Free shuttle service from and to airport. Accommodation (up to
10) also available on the lake on private acreage. CCards

Kenilworth

(east of Orangeville; see also Clifford)

Pritty, Cyril & Margaret(Meg) (The Pritty Place B&B)   ☎ (519) 848-3598
RR4, Kenilworth, ON   N0G 2E0

Located at 8924 Wellington Rd 16 in Damascus. Travel 8km north of Hwy 109, 5km west of Arthur

(Hwy 6/109) and 15km west of Hwy 25 south.
$50S $55D $25Child $30Add.person   🍴 Meals   ►6
🍷 Full, homebaked   🏠 Village, log home, acreage, view from guest
rooms, quiet   ■ 1D,1F (upst)   ⊨ 2T,1D,1Q,crib   🛏2Sh.w.g.
★LF,F,TV, fans in guest rooms, piano, off-street parking, guest
quarters are separate   ✋ No smoking, no pets
🏃 Snowmobile Trail, Damascus Lake, Gen.Store(antiques/collectables)

🚗 Luther Marsh Conservation & Wildlife Area (hiking, canoeing, x-c skiing), Fergus, Elora
🔫 Very cozy and comfortable restored 1860 log home situated on landscaped 2acres with mature
trees and some bush adjacent to Damascus Lake. Enjoy warm and caring personal hospitality by
retired Professionals and "young in heart"

Kenora

(n/w of Thunder Bay near Manitoba border)

Sprague, Barbara & Curtis (The Kendall House B&B)   ☎ (807) 468-4645
127-5th Ave South, Kenora, ON   P9N 2A3

Phone for directions.
$60S $70D   ►6A
🍷 Full, homebaked   🏠 Downtown, hist., 3-storey, patio, porch,
quiet, gardens   ■ 3D(upstairs)   ⊨ 2T,2D   🛏 2sh.w.g.
★Off-street & street parking, guests occupy 2nd floor   ✋No
smoking, no pets, not suitable for children
🏃 Downtown, Lake of the Woods & Harbourfront, Shopping Mall,
museum, M.S.Kenora boat dock (cruising)

🚗 Kenora Airport, Bus station, Rushing River Prov.Park, hiking trails
🔫 Restored 1895 hist., award winning brick home decorated and furnished to the late 1800's on
extra large treed lot. Teacher & artist hosts are knowledgeable about the local history and are
interested in antiques, nature and photography. There is a resident cat.

Kenora (cont'd)

St.Hilaire, André & Eveline (Cozy Cove B&B)   ☎ (807) 468-6061, Fax 468-2301
415 Lakeview Dr., Kenora, ON   P9N 4H3

Located 200 m south of TCH at 2nd bridge west of downtown Kenora. Phone for directions.

$70S $75D   ► 4
Full, homebaked   In town, duplex, view from guest rooms,
lakefront, patio, deck, quiet, large gazebo, secluded   2D(ground
level)   2Q   2Ensuite   ★ LF,TV & pool table in lounge,
private entrance, guest quarters are separate   No smoking, no
pets, not suitable for children   French
Boat dock, walks along lakeshore to town
Norman Dam, boat rental, fishing, Paper Mill & tours, golfing
Retired teacher couple in comfortable home self-built by family members, with large deck and
beautiful landscaped grounds on Lake of the Woods. Entire floor exclusively for guests. B&B

Keswick   *(north of Toronto on Lake Simcoe)*

Eryavec, Amalia & Ivan (Bed & Breakfast By-The-Lake)   ☎ (905) 476-3624,
321 Lake Dr. North, RR1, Keswick, ON   L4P 3C8   Fax (905) 476-9692

$50-55S $60-70D   (Moderate weekly & midweek rates available)   ► 6A,2Ch
Hwy 404 ends at Davis Dr (Newmarket). Make a jog east to Woodbine,
proceed 20km north (Keswick business area). At the Esso Stn turn left
(west) onto Church St which runs into Lake Dr North. If lost, call collect.
Full, homebaked   Cottage country, 2-storey, acreage, view from
guest rooms, private lakefront, patio, deck, quiet   2D,1Ste(upstairs)
2Q,1K,1bunk,crib, playpen   1Sh.w.g., 1sh.w.h., 1ensuite, jacuzzi
★Air,F,LF,TV in guest rooms, fridge, host quarters are separate, guest
mountain bikes & canoes, off-street parking   No smoking, no pets, safe
place for children   Croatian,German,some Italian
Swimming, canoeing, golfing, tennis, restaurants, marinas, ice-fishing
Warm welcome in new spacious home by the water. "Toronto Riviera on the southern shores
of Lake Simcoe". From the west-view sundeck on the private lakefront, a boardwalk stretches out to
clear/sandy bottom water. Guest pick-up from Keswick GO Bus available. B&B

Kimberley   *(south-west of Collingwood; see also Maxwell, Flesherton)*

Stenhouse, Shareene & Brian (Stonehouse B&B)   ☎ (519) 599-6909, Fax 599-6910
RR1, Grey Rd. 7, Kimberley, ON   N0C 1G0   E-mail: stenhouse@bmts.com

From Toronto, take Hwy10 north - from Hamilton & Guelph take Hwy6 north - to Hwy4. Turn
east to Grey Rd13, then north to Grey Rd7(to Meaford). Proceed
3km and look for Firelane No 195688.
$75S/D   (plus tax)   ► 6
Full   Farm, hist. stone house, view from guest rooms,
100acres, swimming pool, porch, quiet, secluded   3(upstairs)
2D,1Q   1Sh.w.g. (or 1ensuite)   ★ TV/VCR in 2 guest
sitting rooms, fans in guest rooms, guest quarters are separate,
barbeque   No smoking, no pets
Hiking, skiing, golfing, cycling, canoeing, fishing, horsback riding, Bruce Trail crosses property,
Old Baldy, Beaver Valley & Beaver River, town of Kimberley
Collingwood, Owen Sound, Barrie, Beaver Valley Ski club, Talisman & Blue Mtn Resorts
Charming 1878 stone farm house, renovated to its original state, surrounded by The Valley's
natural beauty and peaceful environment, situated on property which is part of the Niagara
Escarpment (UNESCO Rerserve). Guests may relax and sip wine on the front porch, cool off in the
large pool or enjoy solitude by the creek's quiet spaces. Join the hosts around the fire pit on a starry
night. Hosts look forward to meeting people. Breakfast is served in guest breakfast room. There are
2 dogs and a cat (very friendly). Visa www.bbcanada.com/2852.html

Kincardine
(on Lake Huron north of Goderich)

Capeling, Pat & Ron (Wickens House B&B)
779 Princes St., Kincardine, ON   N2Z 1Z5

☎ (519) 396-3163
E-mail: wickenbb@primeline.net

Phone for directions.
$55S $65-75D   ► 6A
🍴 Full, homebaked   🏠 Downtown, res., 2-storey, hist., porch,
swimming pool, patio, deck, quiet   ■ 3D (upst)   ⊨3Q
🛏1Sh.w.g.,1sh.w.h   ★ F, ceiling fans, street parking, guest
quarters are separate   ✋ Smoking outside, no pets, not suitable
for children
🏃 Scottish Pipeband Parade (Saturday nights), Sunset Boardwalk,
Bluewater Summer Playhouse, Kincardine Summer Music Festival, Lake Huron and sandy beaches,
picturesque harbour, fishing derbies, water sports, golfing, x-c skiing, antiquing
🚐 Stratford, Owen Sound, Goderich, Port Elgin, numerous summer theatres
☛ Tudor style home (built in 1919) with front veranda, complete with pillars and wicker
furniture, located on a shaded street in historic section of town. Relax on the rear sundeck by the
swimming pool. Breakfast is served in guest breakfast room.

Wiebe, Art & Janice McKean (Glory Bed & Breakfast)
376 Nelson St., Kincardine, ON   N2Z 1X7

☎ (519) 396-7518

Phone for directions.
$40S/D   (monthly rates available)   ► 6
🍴 Full, homebaked   🏠 Res, 2-storey, hist., porch, acreage, quiet
■3D(upstairs)   ⊨2S,1D,1Q,2P   🛏1Sh.w.g.   ★TV,KF,LF,
sep.entrance, guest bicycles, off-street pkg   〰French, German
🚐 Blyth Summer Theatre
🏃 Lake Huron (sandy beaches, swimming, walking, fishing),
downtown, museum, lighthouse, golfing, trails for hiking/biking
on farm grounds, harbour (famous Sat/night March of Kincardine Scottish Pipe Band - July/Aug)
☛ Very quiet and peaceful 130-year old home surrounded by huge trees, flower gardens and
streams. Hosts have travelled world-wide and enjoy welcoming visitors from near and far. Breakfast
is served in guest breakfast room and includes produce from the veggie garden and farm. There is a
cat "Grey Bruce" who likes to curl up on visitors' laps. ✔CC

Kingston
(see also Amherst Isle, Gananoque)

Bruns, Ernie & Cynthia (Collins Lake Bed & Breakfast)
RR1, 3458 Buck Point Line, Inverary, ON   K0H 1X0

☎ (613) 353-1593
E-mail: clb-b@adan.kingston.net

From Hwy 401 take Kingston Exit 617 & Division St north 10.5km. Turn right at Buck's Corners
onto Holmes Rd then 2.2 km to Buck Point Rd & 1.5km to B&B.
$65S $75D $15Child/Add.person   ► 6A,2Ch
🍴 Cont., homebaked   🏠 Rural, log house, veranda, view,
lakefront, quiet   ■ 3F (upstairs)   ⊨2T,2S,2Q   🛏 2Sh.w.g.
★F,TV, launching facilities, canoe/rowboat for guest use   ✋No
smoking, no pets, children min. age 5   〰German
🏃 Fishing (Bass, Muskie) x-c skiing on lake, skating
🚐 Downtown Kingston, shops, restaurants, University, Ft Henry
☛ Log house with the ambience of a 19th Century country home with a beautiful view, situated
on grounds gently sloping to the lake surrounded by mature trees. Relax, enjoy the congenial
hospitality, watch the loons, herons and other lakeshore inhabitants. Hostess makes old-fashioned
jointed Teddy Bears. Canoe & rowboat available for guests' use.   www.bbcanada.com/827.html

Kingston (cont'd)

Campbell, Clare and Tom (Chart House) ☎ (613) 546-9026
90 Yonge St., Kingston, ON   K7M 1E6

Located across Olympic Harbour. Phone for directions.
$55-65S $65-75D (Reservations recommended) ▶ 8
🍴Full, homebaked 🏠Downtown, hist., view, patio, lakefront, very
quiet ■4D(upst) ⊨2D,2T,1Q,crib ⊯1Sh.w.g.,2ensuite, running
water in each room ★2F,TV in guest room, parking ⤳French
🏃 Kingston Portsmouth Olympic Harbour
🚗 Old Ft Henry, 1000 Islands, Prince Edward County
🐎 Warm welcome and friendly hospitality in completely
renovated historic 1848-built home, tastefully furnished with period pieces and a beautiful
English-style garden. Relax on the patio, where breakfast is served. Enjoy the beautiful view of the
harbour & watch the activities. ✏B&B

Franks, Carol A (Painted Lady Inn) ☎ (613) 545-0422
181 William St., Kingston, ON   K7L 2E1

From Hwy 401 take Division St Exit south into Kingston. Left on William St.
$98S $98-155D (plus tax) ▶ 14A
🍴 Full, homebaked 🏠 Downtown, res., 3-storey, hist., older, veranda,
balcony,, quiet ■ 7D(main & upper levels) ⊨ 2T,6Q
⊯7Private ★Air, private entrances, off-street parking, host quarters are
separate 🚭 No smoking, no pets, no children ⤳Spanish, Thai, German
🏃 Fort Henry, 1000 Islands boat cruises, restaurants, Bellevue House,
Queen's University, Royal Military College, museums
🚗 Gananoque, Smith Falls, US border
🐎 Stately brick home (built in 1872) as a church manse and tastefully
furnished with antiques. Breakfast is served in the formal dining room.
Relax on the Victorian veranda, on the balcony or in the parlor. Bridal suite & luxury rooms have
fireplaces & jacuzzis. Hostess is a former journalist, world traveller and trained chef. Gift
certificates available. CCards ✏CC www.paintedladyinn.on.ca

Grassby, Enid (Brakewater Reach B&B) ☎ (613) 634-2029
4244 Bath Rd., Kingston, ON   K7M 4Y7   E-mail: breakwater.reach@sympatico.ca

From Hwy 401, travel south on Rd 6 through Odessa and continue to Lake. Turn left and proceed

4.25 km to B&B.
$65S $75-85D $15Add.person 🍽 Meals ▶-
🍴 Full, homebaked 🏠 Res., hills-side (ravine), view from guest
rooms, lake at back, patio, porch, deck, quiet ■2D (ground &
lower level) ⊨ 1Q,1D, ⊯ 2Private ★F,off-street
parking 🚭 Designated smoking area, no pets
🏃 Lake Ontario, park, bus to downtown
🚗 Downtown Kingston, golfing
🐎 Charming home, decorated in a country Georgian style and nestled on the shore of Lake
Ontario just outside of the City. Relax on the private terrace or in guests sunroom and enjoy the
beautiful lake views. Breakfast is served on balcony or in the elegant dining room. There is a
resident dog. Visa ✏CC

Kingston (cont'd)

North, Mary Ellen (The North Nook)
83 Earl St., Kingston, ON K7L 2G8

☎ (613) 547-8061, Fax (613) 546-5857

From Hwy 401 take Exit 615 and Sir John A.MacDonald Blvd south to King St. Turn left, proceed
 to Earl St., turn left again.
$95S $115-135D (plus tax) ► 10A
■Full ■Downtown, 2-storey, hist., balcony, quiet ■4D,1F(upstairs)
╼D,Q ╼5Private ★ Air,TV/ceiling fans in rooms,street parking
◐No smoking, children min.age 12, small well-behaved dog welcome
⚘ Fort Henry, City Hall, Marine Museum, restaurants, 1000 Island Cruises,
Queens University Campus
🚗 Picton, Smith Falls, Brockville, Gananoque
📣 Historically designated (ca 1849) home with exposed limestone & brick walls, tin ceiling in
living room, filled with antiques passed down through generations. Located in the heart of
downtown. Knowledgeable hostess is in her second decade of welcoming B&B guests. Breakfast is
served in guest breakfast room. Long-term rates from Sept to May available. There are 2 small
resident dogs. CCards ╼B&B

O'Brien, Mary (The O'Brien House Bed & Breakfast)
39 Glenaire Mews, Kingston, ON K7M 7L3

☎ (613-542-8660
E-mail: mobrien@home.com

 From Hwy 401, take exit 615 (Sir John A.MacDonald) to Counter
St. Turn right, then left on Aberfoyle and right on Glenaire Mews.
Look for weathervane of horse.
$55S $55-95D ► 10
■Full ⚘Midtown, res., hillside ■3D,1Ste (upstairs & ground
level) ╼1K,3Q ╼2Ensuite, 1sh.w.g. ★TV in guest rooms,
parking ◐No smoking, no pets, children welcome
🚗 University, Military Academy, boat tours, shopping, dining
📣 Colonial-style brick home with Irish hospitality designed & decorated especially for B&B, in
nice residential area backing onto parkland. Enjoy the relaxed atmosphere. Visa,MC ╼B&B

Kirkfield

(west of Fenelon Falls)

Scott, Joan & Paul (Sir William Mackenzie Inn)
Box 255, Hwy 48, Kirkfield, ON K0M 2B0

☎ & Fax (705) 438-1278
1-800-266-6025

 Located in the village of Kirkfield on Hwy 48.
$65S $75D $20Add.person 🍽 Meals (plus taxes) ► 16
🍴 May1-Oct.20 ■ Full, homebaked ⚘Village,3-storey,hist.,
acreage, view from guest rooms, patio, porch, quiet ■7(upstairs)
╼3T,1D,3Q,2K,2P ╼ 7Ensuite ★ F,TV,LF, parking
◐Smoking area, no pets, children min. age 10 ⚘Sign language
⚘ Large beautiful grounds, conducted tour of 40 room Mansion
🚗 2nd largest liftlocks in the world, boat cruises, fishing, Casino,
swimming, Flea Market, bird-watching at Carden Plain
📣 Very large, historic (ca 1888) mansion on 13 acres featuring Sculpture Garden and nature
walk among spectacular 100-year old trees. Pick-up available for boating guests at Kirkfield Lift
Locks. Facilities for conferences & receptions. Golf package available (2 for 1). ╼B&B

Kitchener

eyebrow *(west of Toronto; see also Guelph, St.Jacobs, Guelph)*

Easton, Bill & Sheila (Dawn-Glo Inn & B&B)   ☎ (519) 653-9241, Fax (519) 653-4720
437 Pioneer Tower Rd., Kitchener, ON   N2G 3W6   E-mail: sheila@dawm-glo.on.ca

Located in Dawn-Glo Village. From Hwy 401 take Hwy 8 (Kitchener Exit). Proceed to Sportworld
Dr, turn right, through 2 lights, then immediately right on Pioneer Tower Rd.
$60S $75D   (Corporate & ext.stays discounts available)   ► 14

🍽 Full, homebaked   🏠 Village, 2-storey, acreage, hist., view
from guest rooms, riverfront, porch, quiet   ■ 5(main & upper
floor)   ⊨ 2T,4Q   ⌁ 3Sh.w.h.   ★ TV,KF   ⑭Designated
smoking area
🏃 Dawn-Glo village (horseback riding, hayrides, petting farm, bird
aviary, saddlery & craft store, walking/x-c skiing/snowmobiling
trails), hist. Pioneer Tower, Sports World Water Park, restaurants,
LuLu's Night Club

🚐 Kitchener/St.Jacobs farmers' market, Stratford Festival, covered bridge, Elora Gorge
🐎 Early 1800 farm house, restored to its original appearance, located in a park-like setting and
overlooking the Grand River & Valley known as "Little Paradise". Ideal place for weddings,
receptions, retreats or corporate meetings. Rest on the benches or walk on many trails or browse
through the craft shop filled with displays from local artists. CCards

---

Findlay, Jo-Anne (River Breeze Bed & Breakfast)   1-877-653-6756
248 Edgehill Dr., Kitchener, ON   N2P 2C9   ☎ (519) 653-6756 Fax (519) 653-6249

From Hwy 401 take Exit 278 and Hwy 8 west to Kitchener. Exit at Sportsworld Dr. Turn right and
through lights at King St. Proceed to 2nd driveway on right.
$40S $75D   🍽 Meals   ► 6A

🍽 Full, homebaked   🏠 Res, ranch-style, view, swimming pool,
patio, porch, quiet   ■3D(ground level)   ⊨2T(K),2Q
⌁1Ensiute, 1Sh.w.g.   ★Air,TV,F,LF, direct access to pool &
patio from each room, off-street parking   ⑭ Designated Smoking
area, no pets, not suitable for children
🏃 Sportsworld, horseback riding, new golf course across street
🚐 Farmer's markets, Oktoberfest, Mennonite Country, St. Jacobs, Elmira, Stratford Theatre
🐎 Unique U-shaped bungalow with extra-ordinary view of Grand River and Valley and large,
tempting inground pool in courtyard. Hosts, formerly active in the travel industry, are well
informed of the area. Enjoy homebaked goodies and preserves for a tantalizing breakfast served
indoors or out on the patio by the pool. ╱B&B

Holl, Frank and Maria (Austrian Home)   ☎ (519) 893-4056
90 Franklin St.N., Kitchener, ON   N2A 1X9

From Hwy 401 take Exit Kitchener Hwy 8 West to Exit
Fairway/Weber. Turn on Weber to 3rd light. Turn right.
$35S $50D $10Child   ► 4
🍽 Full   🏠 Res., patio   ■ 2D (upstairs)   ⊨2T,1D   ⌁Sh.w.h.
★ parking   ⑭ No smoking, no pets   〰German
🏃 Restaurants, bank, shopping centre
🚐 Downtown, Bingemann Park, Waterloo University, Stratford
🐎 Friendly Austrian-Canadian hosts welcome visitors to their
Austrian-style home with traditional handpainted decor, flower baskets, large backyard. Upper floor
is exclusive for guests. Enjoy the well-known October Fest activities in traditional style. ╱B&B

Kitchener (cont'd)

Krampitz, Alfred and Edith (Driftwood Home)
202 Driftwood Dr., Kitchener, ON   N2N 1X6

☎& Fax (519) 745-8010

Located in the west end of the City. Exit Fischer-Hallmann or Trussler Rd..

$40S $60-65D $10Child $15Add.person   ▶ 4A,2Ch
🍴 Full(German-style), homebaked 🏠 Res.,quiet ▦ 1F,1Ste(main floor) 🛏2T,1Q,R,cot ⬛1Ensuite, 1sh.w.h. ★TV,F,LF, parking ⊘No smoking, no pets 〰German, Polish
🏃 Sports Park, city of Kitchener, community trails, city bus stop
🚗 Waterloo University, Doon Pioneer Village, St. Jacobs/Elmira (Mennonite country), Niagara-on-the-Lake, Toronto, Stratford
🚩 Warm and friendly hospitality in raised bungalow Christian home with large treed lot and located on a quiet street. Enjoy the night city view, relax in the back yard or take a walk on the community trails. Toronto Airport pick-up available. ✍B&B

Loney, Endla (Rockway Drive B&B)
673 Rockway Dr., Kitchener, ON   N2G 3B5

☎ (519) 741-8718

Phone for directions. Located in the south end of town.
$45S $60D $15child   ▶ 4A,2Ch
🍴Full 🏠Res., 2-storey, older, quiet ▦2D (upstairs) 🛏1D,2T(large) ⬛1Sh.w.g. ★ Off-street parking, guest quarters are on upper floor ⊘ No smoking, no pets
🏃 Rockway Golf Club, Rockway Gardens, fine dining
🚗 St.Jacobs, Mennonite Country, Stratford (theatres), Chicopee skiing, Cambridge (factory outlet shopping), African Lions Safari, Waterloo Universiities
🚩 Comfortable home with cozy, warm atmosphere backing onto golf course & Rockway Gardens. Well travelled hostess is retired (former Interior Decorator and builder) and a hobby sculptor. Her works are displayed throughout the house. There are two small dogs "Tiny" & "Tha". ✍B&B

Mikolajewski, Gabi & Armin (Country House B&B)
35 Dodge Dr., RR2, Kitchener, ON   N2G 3W5

☎ & Fax (519) 748-6112

From Hwy 401 West take Homer Watson Blvd Exit and left on New Dundee Rd.
$40S $60D $100F $20Add.person 🍽 Meals   ▶ 4A,2Ch

🍴 Full 🏠 Sub., 2-storey, acreage, view from guest rooms, porch, deck, quiet ▦ 3(upstairs) 🛏 2Q,1K ⬛ 1Sh.w.g., 1ensuite ★F,Air,TV,LF,KF, off-street parking, quest quarters are separate ⊘ Smoking outside 〰 German
🏃 Pioneer Park Shopping Centre, Conestoga College Campus, walking trails through forest
🚗 Kitchener, St.Jacobs farmers' market, Stratford Festivals, African Lion Safari, Octoberfest, Niagara Falls, Toronto
🚩 Warm welcome in Christian based country house surrounded by mature nature setting with friendly German hospitality. Enjoy relaxation and comfort beside the fireplace or on the deck overlooking the garden.There are 2 friendly cats in residence. Hosts also offer Massage Therapy, Cranio Sacral Therapy through Reg. Massage Therapist (pre-booking recommended).
http://www.bbcanada.com/1481.html

Kitchener (cont'd)

Teal-Aram, Fay (Roots & Wings Bed & Breakfast) ☎ (519) 743-4557, Fax (519) 743-4166
11 Sunbridge Cr., Kitchener, ON N2K 1T4 E-mail: ia660@nonline.net, 1-877-743-4557

From Hwy 401, take Hwy 8 west & Hwy 86 north to University Ave E Exit. Turn right on Bridge
St, left on Bridle Trail, proceed to Sunbridge to first house on right.
$50S $75-100D $20Child(over age 10)   ► 8A,2Ch
🍴 Full   🏠 Sub., ranch-style, small acreage, view, swimming
pool, quiet   ■5D(main & lower floor)   ⊨2T,3Q,1K,1P,1R
🛁3Private,2shw.g.   ★F,LF,TV in lower level guest room, outside
jacuzzi sep.entr, wheel-chair access, parking 👋Desig smoking
🧍 Walking trails to Grand River, spring fed ponds behind house
(geese, heron & deer often seen)
🚗 Downtown Kitchener, popular farmer's market, shopping, restaurants, St. Jacobs, Elora
🐎 Retired School Principal in large comfortable home nestled in the heart of Central Ontario's
tourist region and Mennonite Country. Enjoy the easy-going country atmosphere. Hostess loves
motorcycling. There is a very gentle dog in residence. Children and pets welcome. CCards ⮑B&B
www.bbcanada.com/1039.html

Warren, Marg & Norm (Roses And Blessings) ☎(519)742-1280, Fax(519)742-8428
112 High Acres Cr., Kitchener, ON N2N 2Z9 E-mail: nmwarren@golden.net

From Hwy 401, take Hwy 8 to Hwy 7&8 West To Fischer Hallman,
left to Queen, left to Westheights, left to Blackwell to B&B.
$45S $50D $15child   ► 4A,1Ch
🍴 Full, homebaked   🏠 Res., back-split, patio, quiet   ■ 1D,1F
(upper and lower level)   ⊨ 1D,1Q,1R   🛁 2Private
★Air,LF,F,KF, TV & daily national newspapers in guest rooms,
hot-tub, guest quarters are sep., exercise equipment, off-street
parking   👋 No smoking, no pets   〰some French
🧍 Protected duck/wildlife pond, x-c ski trails, bus stop, plaza
🚗 Universities, farmers'market, Kitchener, St.Jacobs, Stratford, covered "Kissing Bridge"
🐎 Warm welcome in Christian home with cozy comfort and friendly hospitality. Sumptuous
breakfast is served in the candlelit dining room, featuring orchids & tropical plants. Relax by the
fireplace, in the hot tub or work out on the exercise equipment. Hosts love to pamper their guests
and are happy to assist with excursions and information about the Mennonite community. Guests
are provided with a special memento of their visit. Visa,MC ⮑B&B
www.bbcanada.com/rosesandblessings

Kleinburg *(north of Toronto)*

Clark, John and Rosalind (Humber House) ☎ (905) 893-9108
10555 Islington Ave., Kleinburg, ON L0J 1C0 E-mail: jwinderclarkk@home.com

From QEW, take Hwy 427 north to the village. (Islington Ave is the main street). Look for B&B on
right past main shopping area.
$40S $50D   ► 5
🍴 Full   🏠 Village, older, patio, quiet   ■ 3D (upstairs)
⊨1D,2T,1Q,P, crib   🛁1Ensuite, 1sh.w.g.   ★ TV   👋No
pets, non-smokers preferred
🧍 World renowned Art Gallery (McMichael Canadian Collection,
with guest exhibits, dining room and gift shop), fine dining at (The
Doctor's House) & other restaurants, gift shops, boutiques
🚗 Canada's Wonderland, Kortright center for Conservation, Toronto International Airport
🐎 Enjoy friendly hospitality in interesting 80-year-old home situated in charming village, very
close to Toronto Metropolis. Hosts have been welcoming B&B guests from all over the world for
many years. Enjoy the quaint village atmosphere. ⮑B&B

Lakefield

(north of Peterborough; see also Lindsay)

Crawford, Martha & Dan (Selwyn Shores Waterfront B&B)   ☎ (705) 652-0277, Fax 3389
2073 Selwyn Shores Dr.,RR3,Lakefield,ON K0L2H0   E-mail: selwyn@ptbo.igs.net,1-877-735-9967

From Buckhorn, travel south on Hwy 507/23 to Concession 20. Turn right, then right on 12th Line
to Selwyn Shores Dr. Look for 3rd house on right.

$65-85D $10Add.person   ► 10
Full, homebaked (buffet)   Rural, backsplit, view from some
guest rooms, lakefront, deck, quiet   4D,1F (main & ground
level walkout) 1T,2D,4Q,waterbed avail 2Sh.w.g.,2ensuite
F(3),LF,TV in guest room, piano, guest quarters are separate,
canoe/kayak/paddleboat for guests   No smoking, no pets
Dock/boat launch, fishing on Chemong Lake, x-c ski, skating,
snowmobiling, Art Gallery, Selwyn Conservation area
Peterborough Lift Locks, Canoe Museum, Zoo, Trent University, Petroglyphs (stone carvings)
Spacious home and a friendly atmosphere, with great sunsets over Chemong Lake situated on
the Trent Severn Waterway. Host is an expert professional bass fisherman who enjoys the
tournament trail all summer & hostess is an occasional professional Caterer. Both are involved in
many sports activities. Special diets accommodated with advance notice. Enjoy the huge collection
of cookbooks. Access to fax and Internet provided. Corporate long-stay guests welcome. MC
www.bbcanada.com/selwynshores

Lancaster

(east of Cornwall; see also Apple H., Williamstown, Alexandria)

MacRae, Guelda and Robert (MacPine Bed & Breakfast)   ☎ (613) 347-2003, Fax 347-2814
Box 51, Lancaster, ON K0C 1N0   E-mail: macpine@glen-net.ca

Travelling on Hwy 401, take Exit 814 at Lancaster. Go east on South Service Rd (1km from Esso
Gas Stn on the corner). Look for sign. Located 17 km from Cornwall.

$40S $45-50D $85Ste $15Child   ► 4A,2Ch
Full, homecooked   Farm,river-view, quiet   S,D(upst)
S,T,D,Q, cot, crib   Sh.w.g.   TV, sep.entrance, parking
Restricted smoking, no pets
Private cottage on St. Lawrence River (swimming, canoeing,
fishing for Lancaster perch), China Warehouse Outlet, antique and
craft and art stores, Cooper Marsh nature walks, birdwatching
Golfing, Upper Canada Village, Montreal, Cornwall, Ottawa
Modernized Century home tastfully decorated with hosts' own handwork (pieces of Folk Art
etc.) with a view of the St. Lawrence River and surrounded by large pine shade trees. Relax and
watch the ocean boats go by. Breakfast served in sunroom overlooking St.Lawrence River &
mountains in the distance. B&B   http://www.bbcanada.com/688.html

Leamington

(south of Windsor; see also Wheatley, Amherstburg)

Cowan, Margaret (Farm House B&B)   ☎ (519) 326-8384
319 Rd#14, RR5, Leamington, ON N8H 3V8

Located 10 km north of Leamington. By reservation only. Phone for directions.

$40S $45D   ► 6A,2Ch
Full,homebaked   Farm, view, patio, quiet   3D,1S(upstairs)
2D,2T,1S   1Sh.w.g.   Air,F,TV,parking   No pets
Point Pelee National Park, Jack Miner's Bird Sanctuary, Colasanti's
Tropical Gardens, Pelee Isle Ferry, Windsor
Several generation family, spacious red brick farm home and
old-fashioned parlour with woodwork from Oak trees cut down on the
farm. Relax by the fireplace or in the beautiful large back yard and
enjoy warm hospitality, clean air and quiet countryside. There is a cat in residence. B&B

Leamington (cont'd)

Collings, Berit & Tony (Do Drop In B&B)
202 Seacliff Dr.W, Leamington, ON   N8H 3Y6

☎ & Fax 519) 326-5558
E-mail: dodropin@mnsi.net

From Hwy 401 take Exit 48 and proceed south on Hwy 77 to Hwy 20 (Seacliff Dr. Turn right for 1.2km to Kenneth Dr. B&B located on corner. From Windsor take Hwy 3 to Leamington. At Ruthven, take Union Rd south to Hwy 18, turn left for 5km to B&B.

$40-45S $60D $10Add.person   ▶ 5-7
🍽 Full, homebaked   🏠 Res, split-level, patio, quiet   ■1S,2D
(upstairs   🛏 1S,2Q,1P,crib   🛁 2Sh.w.g.   ★ Air, off-street parking, guest quarters are separate   🚭 No smoking, no pets, children welcome   ∞ Swedish
🕴 Seacliff Park Beach (swimming, boating), marina, restaurants
🚐 Point Pelee National Park (biking, birdwatching, canoeing, hiking, swimming, sunbathing), Point Pelee-Sandusky (US) Ferry

🔫 Warm welcome in home with Swedish-English atmosphere, surrounded by trees, flower beds and many birds, located near popular tourist attractions and nature parks in Canada's most southerly point. Well travelled and informed hosts can provide help with itineraries.

Dick, Bob & Barb and Koop, Jay & Helen (Kingswood Inn)
101 Mill St.W, Kingsville, ON   N9Y 1W4

☎ (519)733-3248
E-mail: kingswd@mnsi.net, Fax(519)733-8734

From Detroit, take Hwy3 to Hwy29 and Mill St West. From Toronto, take Hwy401 to Hwy77. Take Rd20 and proceed to Division St South, then to Mill St West.

$95S $280D $40Add.person   (plus tax)   ▶ 10
❎ Not at X-mas & NewYears.   🍽 Full, homebaked, buffet
🏠Res., hist. view from guest rooms, acreage, swimming pool, patio, porch, quiet, secluded   ■ 5D(upstairs)   🛏 4Q,1D,cot
🛁4Ensuite, 1private   ★Air,F,TV, off-street parking, guest robes, whirlpool tub, guest quarters are separate   🚭No smoking, no pets, children min. age 12
🕴 Pelee Island Winery, Kingsville shops
🚐 Pt.Pelee N.Park, Colasantis Tropical Gardens, Jack Miner Bird Sanctuary, Windsor Casino
🔫 Gracious 1859 historic home, built in the octagonal style, with fine furnishings, antiques, art and personal treasures. Situated on 3acres of beautifully landscaped grounds surrounded by a stone wall. Relax in the spacious drawing room or watch a movie in the cozy library. Enjoy the oasis of tranquility and peacefulness. Perfect place for the ultimate romantic destination. Hosts love to pamper guests. Breakfast is served in the dining room or on the back porch (weather permitting). Gift Certificates available. Visa,MC ✍B&B www.lsol.com/kingswood

---

Dyck, Richard and Irene (Leamington Bed & Breakfast)
92 Oak St.East, Leamington, ON   N8H 2C9

☎ (519) 326-4378

Phone for directions.
$50S $60D   ▶ 4-5A
🍽 Choice, homebaked   🏠 Res., split-level,patio, quiet   ■2 (main & upper level)   🛏2D,1R   🛁2Private   ★Air,LF,TV in family room, parking   🚭 No smoking, no pets   ∞German
🕴 Beaches, stores, restaurants, marina, golfing, bus stop at door
🚐 Point Pelee National Park (swimming, canoeing, biking, hiking, birdwatching), Jack Miner's Bird Sanctuary, Colasanti's Tropical Gardens, Pelee Island Ferry, Amherstburg-Fort Malden, Windsor, Detroit
🔫 Bright & cheery split-level home with a lovely large patio located in an area with many beautiful atttractions. Enjoy a snack in the evening. ✍B&B

Leamington (cont'd)

Fegarty, Barry & Diane (Marlborough House B&B)   ☎ (519) 322-1395, Fax (519) 322-1444
49 Marlborough St.W., Leamington, ON   N8H 1V9

Located in central Leamington. Phone for directions.
$60S $75D   ▶ 6A
🍴 Full, homebaked   🏠 Res., 2-storey, hist., older, porch, quiet
■ 3D(upstairs)   ⊣ 2T,1Q,1K   ⊲ 2Sh.w.g., whirl-pool
★F,Air,TV in guest living room, ceiling fans, off-street & street
parking, guest quarters are separate   ✋ No smoking, no pets, no
children
🏃 Downtown area, shops, fine restaurants
🚗 Point Pelee Nat.Park (marsh boardwalk), Jack Miners Sanctuary, Tropical Gardens, wineries
📷 Enjoy comfort and hospitality in a recently renovated Victorian home on a quiet, centrally
located and tree-lined street. Hosts are retired Diplomats who have furnished the home with
Chinese & Russian antiques. A sumptuous breakfast served at guests convenience.MC,Visa ✓B&B

Gelinas, Linda & Tom (The Wedding House B&B)   ☎ (519) 733-3928, Fax (519) 733-9987
98 Main St.East, Kingsville, ON   N9Y 1A4   E-mail: wedding@mnsi.net

From Hwy 401 exit at Comber and take Hwy 77 south to Leamington. Turn right on Seacliff Dr and

proceed 14 km to Kingsville. (Seacliff Dr becomes Main St).
$65S $70-85D $5Child $10Add.person   ▶ 9
🍴 Full, homebaked   🏠 Downtown, 2-storey, hist., swimming
pool, porch, quiet   ■ 4D(upstairs)   ⊣ 4T(2K),1D,1Q,1R
⊲4Ensuite   ★Air,TV, off-street parking, guest quarters are
separate   ✋ No smoking, no pets
🏃 Ferry to Pelee Island, winery, shops, restaurants, churches
🚗 Point Pelee Nat.Park, Colasanti's Tropical Gardens, Heritage
Village, Jack Miner's Bird Sanct., John R.Park Homestead, Holiday Beach, Windsor, casinos
📷 Charming Victorian home, beautifully decorated and furnished with fine antiques and
collectibles, including old family pictures. Relax in the home theatre with complimentary movies.
Breakfast is served in guest breakfast room. There is a dog. Visa,MC ✓B&B
www.bbcanada.com/1953.html

Lindsay   *(west of Peterborough)*

Gilligan, Marje & Bert (Gilligan's Restful Haven)   ☎ (705) 324-9694
16 David Dr., Lindsay, ON   K9V 5G8   E-mail: m-b.gilligan@sympatico.ca

From Hwy401, take Exit Hwy35/115 and continue on Hwy35 to Hwy7. Turn left to 1st set of lights
(Angeline St). Turn right and proceed to David Dr. Turn left.
$45-50S $50-65D $10Child $20Add.person $80F   ▶ 10
🍴 Full   🏠 Res., back-split, acreage, gardenview from guest
rooms, swimming pool, patio, porch, quiet, deck   ■3D,1Ste
(upstairs & ground level)   ⊣ 2D,3Q   ⊲ 1Ensuite, 1shw.g.
★ Air,F,TV for guests, and in suite, ceiling fans, guest robes,
off-street parking   ✋ No smoking, no pets
🏃 Elgin Street Park, public transportation
🚗 Downtown, golf courses, tennis courts, Skylark VIII Boat
Tours, Academy Theatre (live entertainment), Drive-in Theatre,
museum, art galleries, Ken Reid Conservation Area, Trent Severn Locks
📷 Tastefully decorated home with beautiful gardens and large heated swimming pool, located in
a quiet neighbourhood. Wonderful breakfasts are served in guest breakfast room. Hosts like to treat
their guests like royalty. ✓CC

Lions Head

(south of Tobermory; see also Dyers Bay, Pike Bay, Hope Bay)

Bard, Ann & Don (Cape Chin North Connection) ☎ & Fax (519) 795-7525
RR4, Lions Head, ON   N0H 1W0

Phone for directions. Follow signs when in neighborhood.
$50S $60D $10Add.person   🍴 Meals ► 12
🍴 Full, homebaked 🏠 Farm, hist., acreage, view, patio, quiet,
isolated ■ 6 (loer level & upstairs) ⊨ 4Q,4T 🚿 3Sh.w.g.
★F,separate entrance, parking Ⓦ Restricted smoking, no pets
🏃 Bruce Trail & 18km ski trail on site, Devils Monument
🚗 Tobermory, Manitoulin I.Ferry, St.Margaret's hist.Chapel,
Cabot Head heritage lighthouse, Larkwhistle Gardens

🐾 Home was built in late 1800's, nestled in Maple Woods with rolling meadows and quiet peaceful countryside surroundings. Hosts have retired from operating a resort, have lots of time to enjoy their B&B guests and are members of "Home to Home cycling & hiking group" (includes all Bruce Peninsula). Ideal place for groups. Visa,MC ✔ Grey Bruce B&B, CC

Listowel

(north/west of Kitchener; see also Newton)

Bowman, Bartley & Audrey (Bartlane Farms B&B) ☎ (519) 291-1228
RR3, Listowel, ON   N4W 3G8 Fax (519) 291-2170

Located 5.6km east of Listowel on Line 86, Grid No 5224,
$35S $45D $60F ► 4-6
🍴 Full 🏠 Farm, 200-acres, 2-storey,
older ■1D,1F(upstairs) ⊨S,D 🚿1Sh.w.h.
★Air,TV,KF,LF, separate entrance, air-conditioners
Ⓦ Designated smoking area
🏃 Trails (for snowmobiling, x-c skiing, snowshoweing and bikes),
pond on farm grounds
🚗 Listowel (Paddyfest Irish Celebration), antique dealers &
auction places, fine restaurants, golfing, fishing, Festivals (Stratford,Blyth,Drayton)

🐾 Century red brick family farmhouse (ca 1863) with all of todays' comfort and yesterday's nostalgic atmosphere situated on large working cash-crop farm. Breakfast is served in the country kitchen or in antique furnished dining room. Tour around the pond, enjoy the herb & wild flower garden or relax under the shade tree. Guest are invited to trailer their snowmobiles, bring own skis or snowhoes or bikes and leave from the farm on groomed trail (guided tour available). There is a dog outside and cats in the barn.

London

(south-western Ontario)

Goodbrand, Stan & Verna (Goodbrand Retreat) ☎ (519) 453-2581
1172 Kaladar Dr., London, ON   N5V 2R5

Take Exit 100 from Hwy 401 W (Airport) and drive to Oxford St, turn west. Continue to Clark SRd and turn north. At 1st light, turn west on Cheapside St, right at Kaladar Dr.

$35S $50D ► 4
🍴 Full, homebaked 🏠 Res., split-level, swimming pool, patio,
quiet ■2D(upstairs) ⊨2D 🚿 Sh.w.g. ★Air,F,TV in one
guest room, ceiling fans, off-street parking Ⓦ Restricted
smoking, no pets ⌇ French
🏃 Fanshaw College, city bus
🚗 Airport, University Hospital, Pioneer Village and Fanshaw
Conservation area, golfing, shopping malls

🐾 Located in quiet northeast residential area of the city. Relax on the patio in park-like setting with coffee or tea in the evening. Hostess enjoys travelling, crafts and cooking for guests. ✔CC

London (cont'd)

Den Otter, Hanna & Peter (Sunny Weathers B&B)
15608 Ilderton Rd., RR3, Ilderton, ON N0M 2A0

☎ & Fax (519) 461-1457
E-mail: p.denotter@sympatico.ca

From Hwy 401 take Cty Rd23 (Highbury Ave) and proceed north of London to Ilderton Rd. Turn
right (east) to 2nd farm on left.

$48S $58D 🍽 Meals   ► 4
🍲 Full, homebaked   🏠 Farm, 200acres, 2-storey, older, view
from guest rooms, patio, porch, quiet   ■ 2D(upst)
🛏2T,1Q,1P 🛁1Sh.w.g.   ★ F,TV in guest sitting room, ceiling
fans in guest rooms, guest quarters are separate   ⓌDesignated
smoking area, no pets   ∾ Dutch
🕴 Winding walking trails through wooded area on farm property,
large fish pond (stocked with Bass), apple orchard

🚗 London, University of Western Ontario & Fanshawe College, golfing, dining, Stratford Festival
📢 Lovely renovated home on working cash crop farm located in one of the best farming areas in
Canada. Enjoy the relaxed atmosphere in a comfortable and peaceful retreat and ideal place for
nature lovers. A country breakfast is served in guest breakfast room. There are farm animals
outside. ✒B&B www.angelfire.com/country/sunnyweathers

Herbert, Theresa (Terry) and John (Cosy Corner B&B)
87 Askin St., London, ON N6C 1E5

☎ (519) 673-4598

Exit Wellington Rd off Hwy 401 (Exit 186). Turn left at Commissioners Rd,
right onto Wharncliffe and right onto Askin.

$35S $40D   ► 5A
🍲 Full   🏠 Downtown, hist.   ■ 1S,2D (upstairs)   🛏 1S,1D,1Q
🛁2Sh.w.g.(original tigerfoot tub), one on main floor)   ★LF,guest kitchen,
ceiling fans, electric blankets   ⓌNo pets   ∾French
🕴 Downtown shopping, restaurants, parks
🚗 Fanshawe/Springbank parks, Stratford Festival, Grand Bend, L.Huron
📢 Early retired couple in extensively restored 1871 spacious Victorian
home surrounded by many old churches & historic landmarks. Hosts are world travellers and enjoy
charing travel tales with guests. Breakfast is served in cozy family kitchen or dining room. ✒B&B

Humberstone, A. (Annigan's B&B)
194 Elmwood Ave. East, London, ON N6C 1K2

☎ (519) 439-9196

From Hwy 401 take Exit 186 (Wellington Rd) and go north to Grand Ave.
Turn left. Turn right at Ridout and immediate left onto Elmwood (one way).
Then look for 3rd house from corner on right side).

$45S $60D 🍽 Meals   ► 6
🍲Cont., homebaked   🏠 Downtown, res., hist., veranda ■3D(upstairs)
🛏2D,1Q (upstairs) 🛁1Sh.w.h., 1sh.w.g.   ★Air,F,TV, parking (off
street)   ⓌNo smoking, no pets
🕴 Downtown, Grand Theatre, Art Gallery, Thames Park, Galleria Mall
🚗 University of Western Ontario, Fanshawe College, hospitals, Stratford
Festival, Port Stanley

📢 Charming, Edwardian house with turret and interesting architecture owned by former
Interior Designer. "A taste of home with a touch of class". Long-term rates available.

London (cont'd)

Rose, Doug and Betty (Rose House)
526 Dufferin Ave., London, ON   N6B 2A2

☎ (519) 433-9978
E-mail: mperez@wwdc.com

Take Wellington Rd N Exit to Dufferin Ave. Turn right and 5 blocks past City Hall.

$40-65S/D   (Reservation recommended)   ►6
🛏Full   🏠 Downtown, 2-storey, quiet   ■3D   ⊨2D,1K
⊨1Ensuite, 1sh.w.h.   ★Air, off-street parking   ⊕No pets,
children min.age 12, no smoking
🧍 Downtown shopping, City Hall, dining, London Grand Theatre,
Richmond Row, parks, Art Gallery, excellent public transportation
🚗 University of Western Ontario, Fanshawe College, Stratford
🐾 Lovely, 130-year-old residence located in and area of historic
London homes. Active, retired hosts have been welcoming B&B guests from around the globe for
many years. Enjoy the congenial atmosphere and take a short stroll along tree-lined streets to the
downtown core. CCards

Van Boxmeer, Margaret (London's Little Inn B&B)
321 Dufferin Ave., London, ON   N6B 1Z3

☎ (519) 642-2323

From Hwy401, exit on Wellington Rd north & right at Dufferin
$56S $89D $8Child/Add.person   ►6
🛏 Full, buffet   🏠 Downtown, city centre, hist.   ■ 1D,2Ste
(main & upper level)   ⊨1D,2Q   🚗2Private, 1sh.w.g
★Air,KF,F,TV in guest rooms, ceiling fans, private entrance (1)
✋ Smoking outside
🧍 City Hall, Victoria Park, Grand Theatre, Centennial Hall,
Shopping Mall, Convention C, 5 major Cathedrals, Richmond Row
🐾 Charming Victorian Home with cozy front porch and enchanting garden oasis. Breakfast is
served in guest breakfast room. There is a dog and a cat in residence. Children welcome.   ↙ B&B

Lucknow
(north-east of Goderich; see also Gorrie)

Martin, Joan (Perennial Pleasures Guest Home)
Box 304, Lucknow, Ontario   N0G 2H0

☎ (519) 528-3601

Located at 558 Rose St & 3 village blocks north of Shell Garage
which is on Hwy 86 (Campbell St).
$35S $45D   ►9
🛏 Full   🏠 Village, modern bungalow, large deck, enclosed porch
at front   ■3 (main level)   ⊨3D,3R   🚗2Sh.w.g.   ★TV,LF,
electric heat & individual control, fans, handicapped
accessible   ♥   ✋Smoking outside, no pets
🧍 River, small park-walkway, pool, hockey, community complex, bowling green, good shops
🚗 Kincardine, Goderich, historic sites, Blyth Theatre, Bayfield, boutiques, fine fishing, beaches
🐾 Enjoy friendly hospitality in modern bungalow with comfortable and attractive rooms & large
deck and sheltered loggia. Visit the large garden of perennials (wide assortment for sale -
Grandma's favorites and new varieties).   ↙B&B

Manitoulin Island   *(north of Tobermory on Lake Huron/Georgian Bay)*

Arnelien, Barbara and Stan (Island Oaks)   ☎ & Fax(705) 368-2220 1-800-387-5723
Hwy 6, Sheguiandah, Manitoulin Isle., ON   P0P 1W0   E-mail: islandoaks@hotmail.com

Located 9km south of Little Current on Hwy 6 and 55km north of ferry dock in South Baymouth.

$50S $60D $80F $10Add.person   ► 8A,2Ch
🚗 Full, homebaked   🏠 Rural, ranch-style, 16 acres, quiet
■4(main & lower level) ⊨1K,2D,2T, 2cots 🛁Sh.w.g.(whirlpool),
(wheel-chair access)   ★ F,LF,KF,TV, wheel-chair ramp   ⓦNo
smoking, pets & children welcome   ⌇ Norwegian
🕴 Fishing, boat dock, historic village, swimming, hiking trail,
museum, antique store on property
🚗 Marina/beach,biking,horseback riding,museums,Pow-Wows

☛ Quiet guest home, decorated throughout in early Victorian splendor and surrounded by 16
picturesque acres in the hamlet of Sheguiandah. Truly a perfect retreat. Home is fully equipped for
the special needs of wheel-chair guests. Information on wheel-chair access places-to-go on hand.
Join the hosts at the round oak table and watch the natural beauty of small animals outside the
window while eating breakfast.

Daniels, Bob & Donna (Bay View B&B)   ☎ (705) 282-0741
Box 137, Kagawong, Manitoulin Island, ON   P0P 1J0

Take Hwy 540 to the village and look for B&B at 165 Main Street.
$40S $60D $20Roll-away   ► 7
📅May-Oct31(other by special arrangement) 🚗Full,homebaked
🏠Village, 2-storey, hist., view from guest rooms, lakefront, porch,
quiet, wrap-around deck   ■3D (upstairs) ⊨2T,2D,1R
🛁1Sh.w.g.   ★Air(upper level), TV in guest living room, ceiling
fans, separate entrance, off-street parking, his & her Mt. Bikes &
canoe for guests ⓦSmoking outside, no pets, children min. age 8
🕴 Lake across road with sandy beach, boat dock, swimming, fishing, marina, nature trails to Bridal
Veil Falls, tennis, library, restaurant next door
🚗 Manitoulin Island Day Excursions, historic point, museums, golfing
☛ Turn-of-the-Century Victorian home with widow's walk balcony and wrap-around porch (for
guests only) overlooking the beautiful Bay and North Channel of Lake Huron & beach. Retired
hosts are avid fishing persons and are involved in community activities and local Economic
Development Committee. Explore the wonderful Manitoulin Island from this central location.
Breakfast is served in private guest dining room. His-and-Hers mountain bikes and canoes for
guests available at nominal fee. There are 2 Min.Schnauzer (shedless) in residence.

Kay, Ron & Tammie (Happy Acres B&B)   ☎ & Fax (705) 859-3453
RR1, Tehkummah, Manitoulin Isle.,ON P0P 2C0   1-800-203-9028

Located 9km from South Baymouth ferry docks on Hwy 6, or 55 km from Little Current.

$40S $50D $60F $10Add.person   ► 9
🚗Homebaked 🏠Farm, older, quiet, 2-storey ■1D,2F(main &
upper level) ⊨1T,2D,2Q,1R ★TV,parking 🛁3Ensuite
ⓦNo smoking, no pets
🚗Museums, hiking trails, fishing, abundant wildlife, great native
crafts, annual pow-wow
☛ 3rd Generation family in completely renovated farmhouse
situated on popular vacation island. Children welcome.

ONTARIO   189

Manitoulin (cont'd)

MacDougall, Milton & Heather (MacDougall's B&B on Big Lake) ☎ (705) 377-4739
164 Coventry Rd, RR1, Bx16, S8, Mindemoya, Manitoulin, ON P0P 1S0

From South Bay turn left off Hwy 6 onto Hwy 542(Coventry Rd). Located 6km east of town.

$50-55S $60-70D $70-90Ste $10Add.person ▶ 8A
🌺 May1-Nov1 ⬛ Full 🏠 Rural, split-level, acreage,
lakefront, view from guest rooms, decks, quiet ■2D,1Ste (main
& ground level) ➤ 3Q,1R(D),1P ⬛1Sh.w.g., 1ensuite
★TV, ceiling fans in guest rooms, private entrance, off-street
parking, guest quarters are separate, guest sitting room in suite
🖐 Smoking outside, no pets, not suitable for children
🏃 Fishing off dock, birdwatching, walking or biking the Big Lake
Dam Rd, swimming, canoeing, worm catching (at night), loon watching & listening
🚗 All Island attractions and sights: golfing, hiking trails, churches, restaurants, Summer Theatre
🔫 Large country-style home with pine wood interior in charming park-like setting with
panoramic view of Big Lake and pastoral landscape. Hosts are a retired teacher and theatrical
"dahlink" and a retired Mining supervisor who enjoys telling mining & fishing tales and showing his
mining memorabilia. Scottish music and songs (Heather sings) upon request. Relax on one of the
two decks and savor the leisurely & carefree island pace and serene country setting. Enjoy a
country-style "can't-eat-lunch" breakfast, including prize-winning marmelade.✒CC

Martin, Marisa (Marisa's B&B) ☎ (705) 368-1260
45 Bay St, RR1, Little Current, Manitoulin Isle, ON P0P 1K0

From Little Current, take Hwy540 towards Gore Bay. Turn right on Honora Bay Rd to Bay St.

$40S $50D $10Child $25Add.person ▶ 6
⬛ Cont., homebaked 🏠 Rural, bungalow, view, patio, quiet,
lakefront ■1D,1F(main floor) ➤3T,1D,crib ⬛1Sh.w.g.
★F,TV,off-street parking 🖐 No smoking, no pets 〰Italian
🏃 Walking, swimming, Government dock, horseback riding,
indoor pool
🚗 Hiking/skiing trails, dining, shopping, marina, nature sights
and outlooks, Bridal Veil Falls,
🔫 Large, comfortable home on the water with a beautiful view of the Bay in quiet surroundings,
located at Honora Bay of picturesque Lake Huron. Enjoy the home-like and "environmentally
friendly" atmosphere.

Sheppard, Ron & Carol (Rockville Inn) ☎ (705) 377-4923, Fax (705) 377-5601
RR1, Mindemoya, Manitoulin Isle, ON P0P 1S0

From South Bay Mouth (ferry) on Hwy 6 turn left on Hwy 542, right onto Gibraltar Rd, right onto
Rockville Rd. Continue through onto Demmy Rd and right on Albert Rd. Look for signs.

$65-130S/D $15child (plus tax) ▶ 10A,2Ch
⬛ Full,homebaked 🏠 Rural, ranch-style, acreage, view from
guest rooms, lakefront, porch, quiet, secluded ■ 6D,1F (main &
upper level) ➤6Q ⬛ 6Private ★ F,KF/separate entrance
(in family accommodation) 🖐 Smoking outside, no pets
🏃 Hiking trail, boating, swimming, fishing, snowmobile trails
🚗 Restaurants, shops, golf course
🔫 Completely up-dated and remodelled ancestral farm home
(built by host's father in 1933) and situated on beautiful Lake Manitou with a spacious yard. Relax
in the common room by the fireplace and enjoy the peaceful country atmosphere. There is a large
country kitchen overlooking the lake. Rooms are decorated with nature themes i.e. "Morning Loon",
"Maple", "Birdsnest", etc. Snowmobilers can get a group rating. Weekly rates available. ✒CC
www.manitoulin-island/rockvilleinn

Manitoulin (cont'd)

Williamson, Harold and Sally (Mindemoya Lake View Farm)   ☎ (705) 377-5714
Mindemoya, Manitoulin Island, ON P0P 1S0

From Hwy 17, take Hwy 6 to Little Current. Then take Hwy 540 to West Bay and Hwy 551 to Mindemoya. Take Hwy 542 west to Lake Mindemoya, turn right onto lake shore road and look for 5th house on the right with lake on left. From South Baymouth ferry docks take Hwy 6 to Hwy 542.

$40S $45D   ► 6A,2Ch
🍴 Full   🏠 800-acre farm, lakefront, patio   ■ 3D   ⊨ 3D, cot, 2cribs   🍴 Sh.w.g.   ★TV,F   ✋ No pets, hunting guests welcome
🏃 Sandy beaches, fishing, swimming, beautiful sunrises & sunsets, Cup & Saucer hiking trail
🚗 Providence Bay, salmon fishing, Bridal Veil Falls, Ten-Mile Point scenic lookout

Located on the South-East shore of beautiful Lake Mindemoya (world's largest fresh-water island) and home of The Great Spirit Manitou. Excellent deer hunting packages (including permission to hunt) on property available. ⤙B&B

Manotick   *(south of Ottawa; see also North Gower)*

Chilvers, John & Heather (Chilvers B&B)   ☎ (613) 692-3731, Fax (613) 692-8221
5220 NcLean Cr., Manotick, ON K4M 1G2   E-mail: chilversbb@idirect.com

From Ottawa travel south on Hwy 16 to Rideau Valley Dr. Turn left and first left again on Barnsdale. Proceed over bridge to 4th house on right.
$40S $50D   ► 4A
🍴 Cont., homebaked   🏠 Village, 2-storey, view from guest rooms, riverback, patio, deck, quiet, private   ■ 2D(upstairs)   ⊨1D,2T   🍴 1Sh.w.g.   ★ F,TV,LF, ceiling fans, separate entrance, off-street parking   ✋ No smoking, no pets
🏃 Large park on Rideau River, boat access, restaurants, craft shops, art galleries, Canadian Guide Dogs for the Blind (tours)
🚗 Ottawa (direct route approximately 30km)
Comfortable home with view of extensive flower beds that sweep to the Rideau River. Enjoy abundant wildlife while eating a hearty breakfast. Relax in the guest sitting room or join the family. Hosts are active with Guide Dogs & involved in Community Groups/Service Clubs. There is a dog.

Mansfield   *(south of Collingwood; see also Shelburne, Alliston)*

Palmay, Sharon & Terry (The Palmay's B&B)   ☎ (705) 435-1556,
RR3, Mansfield, ON L0N 1M0   E-mail: palmays.bandb@sympatico.ca

From Toronto go north on Airport Rd (Dixon W). Cross Hwy 89 and proceed 2.5 km north. Take 1st left and continue .75 km . Turn right to 3rd house on left.

$55-75(S/D) $15Child   🍽 Meals   ► 12
🍴 Full, homebaked (special diets accommodated)   🏠 Rural, older, 2-storey, view, lakefront, patio, indoor swimming pool, spa, quiet   ■2Ste,4D(upstairs)   ⊨4T,3Q,1D   🍴2Ensuite,1Sh.w.h.
★TV,F,parking   ♥   ✋No smoking   💬French,Hungarian
🏃 Short walks around the pond or north to the Boyne River, hiking/skiing/fishing and snowmobiling at door step
🚗 Numerous golf courses, skiing, antiquing, Bruce Trail hiking, arts and craft studios, fishing
Lovingly restored Victorian home offering charm, warmth, elegance and distinction in the Hills of Mulmur. Enjoy a leisurely breakfast overlooking the pond, relax in the spa or do some lengths in the indoor pool. There are resident Chinese Shar-Pei show dogs and a Vietnamese potbellied pig. Kennel space may be available. Visa,MC ⤙B&B

Markdale

(south of Owen Sound; see also Kimberley, Flesherton)

Brown, Monica and Iain (Cozy Nook B&B)   ☎ (519) 924-2063
RR7, Markdale, Ontario   N0C 1H0

Located exactly halfway between Flesherton and Markdale on the east side of Hwy 10.

$39S $56D $20Child(under age 12) 📷Meals   ► 10
🍴 Choice, homebaked   🏠 Rural, village, hist., ranch-style, acreage, patio, quiet ■S,D,F ⊨S,T,D,Q,R,P, cot, crib 🛏1Private,1sh.w.g.,1sh.w.h. ★F,TV,KF, separate entrance, parking ✋Restricted smoking, no pets
🏃 Cross-country and downhill skiing, golfing, boating, tennis, Bruce Trail hiking, antique shops, boutiques
🔫 Warm hospitality in renovated and extended old schoolhouse (built in 1821) with beautiful gardens, patios, courtyard and greenhouse, situated in the very popular Beaver Valley area. Active hosts like golfing, tennis, cycling, swimming and skiing. ✓B&B

Charyk, Jean & Boris (Thornbrae B&B)   ☎ (519) 986-4502
486034 Grey Rd 30, RR4, Markdale, ON   N0C 1H0

Located 7km east of Hwy10 between Flesherton & Markdale.
$45S $55D $10Child   ► 8
🍴 Full   🏠 Rural, 2-storey chalet-type, 11.5acres, porch, deck, pond ■2D,1F (main & ground level) ⊨2T,2Q,1P 🛏1sh.w.g., 1private ★ F,TV, off-street parking, guest quarters are separate ✋ No smoking, no pets
🚗 The Beaver Valley (fishing, skiing, hiking),
🚗 Owen Sound, Collingwood, Orangeville, shopping, dining, entertainment areas
🔫 Warm and friendly welcome in chalet-type home filled with antiques and surrounded by pine & tamarack bush behind a natural pond. Breakfast is served in guest breakfast room.

Markham

(north-east of Toronto)

Cowan, Phyllis & John (Olde Towne B&B)   ☎ (905)294-7411, Fax 294-2983
63 Church St., Markham, ON   L3P 2M1   E-mail: cowanjs@sympatico.ca, 1-888-929-7411

From Toronto, take Hwy401 east to Markham Rd (Hwy48). Go north to Hwy7., turn right, proceed to Albert, turn left and continue to end. Turn right on Joseph, left on Maple, right on Church.

$75S $95D $150F 📷 Meals   ► 6
🍴 Full   🏠 Res., 2-storey, quiet ■ 2Ste,1F (upstairs) ⊨2T,1Q,1K 🛏 1Private, 2ensuite ★ Air,F,TV in private parlour, off-street parking, guest quarters are on separate level ✋ No smoking, no pets 〰 French, German
🏃 Markham Museum, Unionville Main Street (shops, restaurants) parks, swimming, skating, library, hospital, urban hiking, bike trails, public transportation to Toronto subway stops at door
🚗 Markham Theatre, downtown Toronto, Pearson Int.Airport, Seaton Hiking Trail, skiing
🔫 Freshly decorated large home in the heart of historic town. Hosts like to play bridge, tennis, travelling and are the publishers of the book called "Patron's Pick of Toronto's Favourite Restaurants". Also available accommodation in hosts' cottages in the Muskoka and Haliburton area - the Gateway to the North. Breakfast is served in guest breakfast room. There is a cat in residence. Visa ✓B&B www.bbcanada.com/oldetowne

Markham (cont'd)

Hall, Teil (Valley View House 109 B&B)　　　☎ (905) 472-3163, Fax (905) 471-0643
109 Robinson St., Markham, ON   L3P 1P2

From Hwy 401, take Hwy 404 north to Hwy 7, proceed east to Hwy 48, turn north to Robinson St.

Turn left to 5th house on left.
$60S $70D $15child　　　　　　　　　　　　　　　✔ 4-8
❿ Full　🏠 Sub., res., split-level, older, view from guest rooms,
patio, deck, quiet, secluded　■ 2Ste (lower level)　⊨2T,1Q,2P
⌒2Private,2sh.w.g.　★Air,F,TV,KF,sep.entrance,off-street
parking, hosts quarters are separate　🖐No smoking, no pets
🧍 Markham Village shops and restaurants, library, museum,
town parks, fitness clubs

🚗 Markville Mall, Markham Theatre, Unionville Main Street shops/dining, Toogood Pond

🐾 Suburban bungalow with lower area built into a hill on a large secluded, quiet & private treed lot in the centre of town. There is a small stream in shaded area with barbeque facilities. Breakfast is served in Canadiana furnished dining room or on the deck. Relax and enjoy the small town atmosphere in close proximity to the Metropolis. ✔B&B

Mattawa　　　　　　　　　　　　　　　　*(east of North Bay)*

Levitan, Mrs. Mary (Bear Creek Farm)　　　☎ (705) 744-2423, Fax (705) 744-5318
RR2, Mattawa, ON   P0H 1V0

From North Bay, take Rt 17 East to Valois Dr in Mattawa. Turn right at 1st road after railroad trestle (250 ft). Continue on Rue Belanger for 5km to single lane bridge and up hill to fork. Turn right to 2nd farm on left.
$55S $65D 🍽 Meals　　　　　　　　　　　　　　▶ 4A
❿ Full, homebaked　🏠 260-acre sheep farm, older, view, patio,
quiet　■2D,2S　⊨4T,futon　⌒1Ensuite,1sh.w.h.　★TV,F,KF
100 year old wood stove, spinning wheels, artesian well water
🖐prefer non-smokers
🧍 6km of hiking/walking trails on premises
🚗 Town of Mattawa/dining/shopping, beaches at Lake Papineau

🐾 Spendid solitude in rustic Century-old log home with lots of antiques & casual charm, situated on scenic hill with large herb and organic vegetable gardens near the pretty town on the river. Former art teacher spins, dyes, weaves wool from own sheep raised on hillside. There is a unique in-house folkart collection. Ideal place for summer/winter sports. ✔B&B

Maynooth

(north of Bancroft; see also Barry's Bay)

Exton, Bill (Ironwood Hill Inn B&B)   ☎ (613) 338-2032
General Delivery, Maynooth, ON K0L 2S0

Located 3.2km south of Maynooth on east side of Hwy 62.
$40S $50-60D $20Add.person   ▶9
🚘Full   🏠Rural, log cabin, 50-acres, views, quiet ■5(upst)
🛏1S,3D,1Q   ⊒3Sh.w.g.   ★LF, separate entrance, parking
🏃 Nature, hardwood bush & stream nice for walking, x-c skiing
🚗 Algonquin Park, Bancroft site of "Rockhound Gemboree
Mineral Show" (civic weekend)
📣 Large rustic log cabin located at the "hight of land" and providing an expansive view of rolling
forest hills, where shadow and light play, especially in the fall with a tapestry of colours, as far as
the eye can see (4 seasons of natural splendor). Active host enjoys camping, hiking, canoeing.

Meaford

(east of Owen Sound; see also Clarksburg, Thornbury, Bognor)

Avery, John & Bobbie (Irish Mountain Bed & Breakfast)   ☎ (519) 538-2803/538-2467
RR1, Meaford, ON N0H 1Y0   E-mail: hugo@log.on.ca

From Collingwood or Owen Sound, take Hwy 26 to 5 km west of Meaford. Then take Concession 9
north for 4km. Turn left at top of hill to house on left along the cliff.
$55-85S $69-99D $95-125F $20Add.person $10Dog   🍽 Meals   ▶8

🚘 Full (Gourmet),(also available in suite)   🏠 Rural, split-level,
acreage, fantastic view, swimming pool, patio, quiet ■1Ste,2D
(upst & ground level)plus cabin loft in the woods 🛏 2S,2Q,2K
⊒3Ensuite   ★Air,F,LF,VCR,TV in guest room, hot tub on
private deck, separate entrance, facilities for the disabled   ✋ No
smoking, pets outside (kennel & fenced run) ⬳some French
🏃 Great country restaurant, x-country ski & hiking trails, Irish
Mountain Look-out, M.T.S.C. Meaford
🚗 Georgian Bay (swimming, fishing, sailing), downhill ski resorts, antique & gift shops
📣 Spacious home (more California in style than rural Ontario) with soaring cathedral ceilings,
large picture windows and magnificient views. Hosts are hospitality professionals who formerly
operated one of the areas most popular restaurants, and well informed about hiking and eating
places. Host leads guided tours along the Bruce Trail. There is a cat in hosts' quarters. ✔B&B

Bourne, Ann & Bill (Ash-Berry Hill B&B)   ☎ (519) 538-2760
RR4, Meaford, (111 Penny Lane), ON N4L 1W7   Fax (519) 538-5303

Along South Georgian Bay, take Hwy 26 to Meaford and 2km S (at lights) on Grey CtyRd7. Turn
right (west) on John St (near top of hill) and right onto Penny Lane to end.
$65-80S/D $90-105F $10Dog   🍽 Meals   ▶8A,2Ch

🚘 Full, homebaked   🏠 Rural, res., hillside, 2-storey, 5acres,
view from some guest rooms, patio, deck, quiet   ■ 3D,1F(main &
lower level(walk-out) 🛏 3D,2Q   ⊒ 1Ensuite, 2sh.w.g.
★Air,KF,TV lounge with air-tight wood stove, guest quarters are
separate, wheel-chair ramp   ✋ No smoking, well-behaved pets
and children welcome when space allows
🏃 Bruce Trail & Georgian Trail, beaches, cycling, hiking, Meaford
Town Hall Opera and Play House (upstairs)
🚗Collingwood, Blue Mtn & Talisman Ski Hills, Bruce Trail, beaches, Scenic Caves, Harbour
📣 A home with a view! Spacious modern retreat with a panoramaic view of Georgian Bay and
countryside. Relax in the music/sitting room with grand piano or in the large TV-lounge with
kitchenette. Breakfast is served in the comfortable country kitchen or on the deck. Special diets can
be accommodated. People-orientated hosts will provide pick-up from the harbour, Georgian Trail or
provide luggage forwarding for hikers. There is a small dog in residence.✔B&B

Meaford (cont'd)

Young, Fred & Shirley (Glen Epping Country Home B&B) ☎ (519) 538-1968
RR4, Meaford, ON N4L 1W7   E-mail: glen.epping@bmts.com

Located 16 km south of Meaford and 1 km west of Grey County Rd 7, at Epping Side Rd 19.

$50S $65D $75F   ⬛$5Extra (cooked by hosts)   ► 5
⬛Full   🏠Rural, 2-storey, 100 acres, view, deck, patio, porch,
quiet, large pond   ⬛1Ste (first floor)   ⊨1D,1P,2S
⬛1Ensuite   ★Air,LF,F,KF, TV in suite, whirlpool avail,
sep.entrance, guest patio, parking   ⬤No smoking
🏃 Bruce Trail hiking, golfing, fishing, biking, canoeing
🚗 Excellent ski resorts (Blue Mtn, Talisman, Beaver Valley)
🐾 Century Home, completely remodelled and surrounded by
5 acres of landscaped gardens and ponds located in the Beaver Valley. Enjoy peaceful surroundings
close to major sports areas. Hosts are gardeners, hikers, bikers, skiers and birders. Ideal location for
Bruce Trail hikers. Guest quarters are in a separate wing of the house. Playground, bar-b-que &
firepit available. Children & pets welcome.

Midland   *(on Georgian Bay; see also Penetang, Waubaush, Victoria Hbr)*

Coulter, Marg & Mark (The Victorian Inn)   ☎ (705) 526-4441
670 Hugel Ave., Midland, ON L4R 1W9   E-mail: coulter@csolve.net, Fax (705) 526-4426

Follow Hwy 400 north to Hwy 93, turn right on Hugel Ave. (3rd
stoplight - Zellers) after Hwy 12.
$75-95S/D (Reservation, please)   ► 10
⬛ Cont.   🏠 Village, hist., 2-storey, veranda   ⬛ 5 (upstairs)
⊨ 2T,2Q,2K   ⬛3Ensuite,1sh.w.g.   ★ Air,TV/VCR, guest
sitting room, off-street parking   ⬤ Smoking outside
🏃 Downtown Midland, shops, restaurants, Midland Docks, 30000
Islands Boat Cruises, Little Lake Park with sandy beach, churches
🚗 Marty'rs Shrine, Ste-Marie-Among-the-Hurons, King's Wharf Theatre, Discovery Harbour
🐾 Victorian Century Home in prime downtown neighbourhood with large veranda for relaxation.
Enjoy the warm and friendly atmosphere. Hosts are well informed about area activities, eating
establishments and local entertainment. There is a small Cocker Spaniel (Frankie) who makes
everyone feel welcome. Pick-up from bus station available. Visa,MC www.victorianinn.on.ca

---

Hart, Jennifer & Milton Haynes (Little Lake Inn B&B)   ☎(705)526-2750, Fax526-9005
669 Yonge St., Midland, ON L4R 2E1   1-888-297-6130
                                           E-mail: info@littlelakeinn.com

From Hwy 400, take Hwy 93 north to Midland, turn right onto Yonge St.
$65-100S $75-110D $10Child $20Add.person   (plus tax)   ► 10A,3Ch

⬛ Cont,homebaked   🏠 Downtown, res, bungalow, hist., view
from 1 guest room, lake at back, porch, deck   ⬛ 2D,1F,1Ste
(main, ground & street level)   ⊨ 2T,3Q,2P,2cots   ⬛ 1Private,
3ensuite   ★ Air,F,TV/ceiling fans in guest rooms, private
entrance for suite, semi wheel-chair access, off-street parking,
guest quarters are separate   ⬤ Smoking outside, no pets
🏃 Downtown, shops, restaurants, Huronia Museum, Huronia
Indian Village, 30000 Island Boat Cruise, Little Lake Park, beach
🚗Martyr's Shrine,Sainte-Marie-Among-The- Hurons,Wye-Marsh Wildlife Ctr,Discovery Hbr
🐾 Deceivingly large Century home backing onto Little Lake Park, a unique parkside retreat,
situated in the heart of Midland. Experience the guest lounge with high, beamed ceiling, covered
veranda overlooking the water and the English Country Garden. Enjoy the casual, friendly
atmosphere. A healthy, hearty buffet breakfast is served by the fireplace in the parkside dining
room. Ideal place for business travellers (phone/desk/modem in suite). Pick-up from Bus Station
available. Gift Certificates available.Visa,MC ✓B&B hhttp://www.littlelakeinn.com

Midland (cont'd)

Hébert, Mrs. Ruth (G & R Hébert Bed & Breakfast) ☎ (705) 526-9474
Box 696, Midland, ON L4R 4P4

$40S $50D $5Child $10Add.person (Family rates available) 🍽 Meals ▶ 6A,5Ch

Phone for directions. Located 1km from Town Center.
🍲Homebaked 🏠 Rural, bungalow, quiet ■ 4 (main floor)
🛏 1Sh.w.h. ⊨2T,1D,1Q,2R,1P ★Air,TV,LF 🖐Designated
smoking area, no pets
🚗 Town Center, Georgian Bay (sailing, swimming, boating,
fishing), golfing, Saint Marie Among The Hurons, Martyr's Shrine,
Huronia Indian Village/Musum, 30000 Isls cruise, x-c skiing,
snowmobiling, ice fishing

🐾 Warm welcome in quiet comfortable home surrounded by 40 year-old pine trees. Relax & enjoy the homecooked meals. Hostess has a collection of interesting bells. Pick-up from bus/town. ⌐B&B

Lippert, Jane & Bob & Angela (A Wymbolwood Beach House B&B) ☎& Fax(705)361-3649
533 Tiny Beaches Rd South, RR1, Wyevale, ON L0L 2T0 E-mail: lippert@ngw.webgate.net

$60S $75-80D $15Add.person (special weekly rates available) ▶ 10
From Barrie, take Hwy 27 north to Elmvale and continue north on County Rd 6 to Wyevale. Turn

left at Con 5 to Tiny Beaches Rd. Turn right and look for sign.
🍲 Full, homebaked 🏠 Rural, split-level, hillside, view from
guest rooms, patio, decks, secluded, lake across street
■3D,1Ste,1F(main,upper and ground levels) ⊨ 2T,1D,2Q,2R
🛏1sh.w.g., 1ensuite ★ LF,F,TV in guest room, sauna, games
room, off-street parking & indoor parking for RVs, turn of the
Century piano in library-lounge, host quarters are separate
🖐Designated smoking area, no pets, inquire about children

🏃 Georgian Bay, sandy beaches, hiking trails, cycling, tennis, x-c skiing, snowmobiling
🚗 Midland, Penetanguishene, Wasaga Beach, Collingwood, historic sites, shopping, Casino-Rama
🐾 Escape to a secluded haven, nestled in the evergreens overlooking Georgian Bay - a
globetrotter's retreat or a couples' getaway paradise. Relax in the jacuzzi tub after a long day of
travelling or sight seeing and enjoy the charm and easy living. Phone and fax service available for
the corporate traveller. Inquire about the 2-bedroom suite. There is a resident Bichon Frisé. Visa
⌐B&B www.bbcanada.com/1743.html

Niblock, Gale & Hugh (B&B with the Artists at Galerie Gale) ☎ (705) 526-8102,
431 King St., Midland, ON L4R 3N3 E-mail: galeriegale@csolve.net, Fax (705)526-6229
From Toronto, take Hwy 400 to Hwy 93 to Hwy 12 to King St.

$60S $65D ▶ 6A
🍲 Buffet 🏠 Res., 3-storey, deck ■ 3D (2nd
floor) ⊨2T,2D 🛏1.5 Sh.w.g. ★ F/TV in guest lounge,
ceiling fans, off-street parking, guest quarters are separate 🖐No
smoking, no pets, not suitable for children
🏃 Little Lake Park (tennis courts, walking trails, jogging) YMCA,
museum, Indian Village, restaurants, downtown shopping, harbour
for Georgian Bay Boat Cruise
🚗 St.Marie Among the Hurons, Martyr's Shrine, Discovery Harbour, Wye Marsh Wild Life Ctr
🐾 Originally an art gallery, gracious large turn-of-the-Century home with modern and
traditional art displayed throughout. Enjoy warm hospitality in an artistic setting. Browse in the
small gift shop on premises. Host is a retired teacher and hostess is still active in her art & framing
business and both are active with golfing, tennis, canoeing and sailing. Breakfast is served in the
elegant dining area amid colourful original art by both hosts. Top floor contains the artists' studio
and their living quarters. CCards, ⌐B&B www.datatrav.com/galeriegale

Mildmay

(south-east of Kincardine; see also Clifford, Walkerton, Cargill)

Culbert, Shirley & George (Whispering Brook B&B)   ☎ (519) 367-2565,Fax (519) 367-5434
7 Jane St., Mildmay, ON   N0G 2J0   E-mail: culberts@bmts.com

Phone for directions.
$45S $50-60D $10Child/Add.person $10Cot   ► 6A,4Ch
🍴 Cont., homebaked   🏠 Res., village edge, split-level (3-storey),
2.5acres, patio, porch, deck, quiet, secluded   ■3(main & upper
level) ⇥2Q,1D, play pen with pad ⇥1Sh.w.g.,2sh.w.h. ★TV in
guest lounge, off-street parking 🚭Smoking outside, no pets
🏃 Stocked trout pond on property (watch 2 resident swans and
fish jump), feed deer in paddock on lawn, abandoned CNR rail-line
to explore,x-c skiing snowmobile trails, Village Christmas Lights Displays (well known)
🚗 Lake Huron beaches, ferry to Manitoulin Island, Blyth theatre town, Mennonite Country
👉 Warm welcome in comfortable, sunny cedar home in a park-like setting, situated in small and
friendly village ("where everyone knows everyone else") with interesting little shops and local crafts.
Relax in the park-like atmosphere & stroll among the flower beds. Sit on the lawn swing and watch
the deer. Breakfast is served in the country kitchen, on the large cedar deck, or in dining lounge.
Children welcome. ✔CC

Milton

(west of Toronto: see also Campbellville, Burlington, Oakville)

Sandlohken, Horst and Ille (Red Maple House)   ☎ (905) 878-5716
RR3, Milton, ON   L9T 2X7

From Hwy 401 take Exit 320 (Hwy 25) north and go 8 km to Reg Rd 15 (Service Station on corner).
Turn left and look for No 6190, 2km down road on left
$35S $60D   ► 2A
🍴 Choice   🏠 40-acre Maple Bush farm, ranch-style, tranquil,
isolated, swimming pool, very quiet   ■1D ⇥2T ⇥Ensuite
★Air,TV,F, separate entrance   🚭 no pets   〰 German
🏃 Maple bush, Bruce Trail for hiking and x-c skiing
🚗 Agricultural Museum, Glen Eden and Bronte Conservation
areas (summer and winter recreation), Crawford Lake (restored
Indian village), Milton, Rattlesnake Point (panoaramic views), Campbellville (quaint village
shopping), Lake Ontario, Burlington
👉 Warm welcome in contemporary, spacious country home with European atmosphere,
tastefully furnished and guest room located in separate wing. A wonderful place to wind down; relax
by the pool after a day of sightseeing and travelling. Situated on the Niagara Escarpment with own
maple bush at backdoor. Cash only, please. ✔CC

Minden

(south of Haliburton)

Howarth, Phyllis (The Stone House)   ☎ (705) 286-1250
RR3, Minden, ON   K0M 2K0

Located 3 km north of Minden on Hwy 35. Phone for directions.
$85S $95D $25Add.person   ► 12A
🗓 May15-Oct15   🍴 Full (hearty gourmet)   🏠 Rural, acreage,
view, quiet   ■2D,1Apt (main and upper floor)plus 2cottages in
the woods   ⇥T,D,K,Q ⇥ All private, plus outdoor shower
★F,LF, 2guest kitchens, parking   🚭No smoking
🏃 Swimming and boating on lake or river, golfing, trail hiking
👉 Secluded rustic hideaway with walking trails thru woods.
Relax in a "real piece of paradise and island of tranquility". ✔CC

Minden (cont'd)

Snyder, Nora (Minden House Bed & Breakfast)   ☎ (705) 286-4450
23 North Water St., Box 136, Minden, ON   K0M 2K0   1-888-745-8615

From Hwy 35 north, take first exit to Minden. Follow Main St over bridge, turn right immediately.
$60S $70D $10Add.person   ▶ 8A,2Ch
🍽 Full, homebaked   🏠 Village, hist., 1 acre, view from guest
rooms, quiet, riverfront, porch ■2(upstairs) ⊨ 2T(K),1Q
⛱Sh.w.g.   ★F,TV & coffee machine in guest lounge, off-street
parking   ⋓Pets welcome (in cottages only)
🏃 Downtown, shopping, churches, walking trails
🚗 Haliburton Highlands, Dorset, Algonquin Park, golfing, skiing
☛ Century home (circa 1850) with wrap-around porch situated
on the Gull River in small village. Enjoy the cozy and friendly atmosphere. Also available:
housekeeping cottages. There is a cat in residence.✔B&B

Mitchell   *(west of Stratford)*

Skinner, Doreen and Joe (Town & Country B&B)   ☎ (519) 348-8051
Box 211, 84 Frank St., Mitchell, ON   N0K 1N0

Take Hwy 23 south and continue to last street at south end of Mitchell. Turn right.
$30-40S $40-55D $15Child $15Add.person   ▶ 12A,4Ch
🍽 Full, homebaked   🏠 Acreage, view, quiet, split-level,balconies
■3D,2F (upstairs & lower level)   ⊨2D,4Q,1P, 2cots, crib
(playpen) -⛱3Ensuite, 1sh.w.g.   ★ Air,LF,TV in guest room,
parking ⋓No pets
🏃 Golf course, public swimming pool
🚗 Stratford Festival, Grand Bend Beach, Huron Country
Playhouse, Goderich Harbour and beach, Blyth Theatre
☛ Early retirement hosts are former dairy farmers. 1990-built
home designed with B&B in mind, situated on the outskirts of quiet town surrounded by peaceful
countryside & wide open fields. There is a small barn that houses the horses.

Moonstone   *(west of Orillia; see also Waubaushene, Vict. Harbour)*

Arbour, Ann & Paul (Arbourgate B&B)   ☎ & Fax (705) 835-5625
RR4, Coldwater, ON   L0K 1E0

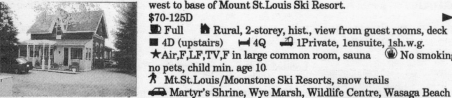

Located south Coldwater. On Hwy 400 north of Barrie, take Exit 131 & follow Mount St.Louis Rd
west to base of Mount St.Louis Ski Resort.
$70-125D   ▶ 8
🍽 Full   🏠 Rural, 2-storey, hist., view from guest rooms, deck
■ 4D (upstairs)   ⊨ 4Q   ⛱ 1Private, 1ensuite, 1sh.w.g.
★Air,F,LF,TV,F in large common room, sauna   ⋓ No smoking,
no pets, child min. age 10
🏃 Mt.St.Louis/Moonstone Ski Resorts, snow trails
🚗 Martyr's Shrine, Wye Marsh, Wildlife Centre, Wasaga Beach
☛ Warm welcome in B&B situated at base of ski hills. Relax in the common room by the
fireplace or on the 80 ft deck and watch skiing activities from the heated Florida Room. Visa

Mooretown

(south of Sarnia; see also Petrolia)

Blake, Robert(Bob) & Joanne (Moore Lodge)
1509 Moore Line, Mooretown, ON N0M 1M0

☎ (519) 864-1880
E-mail: wbobby@ebtech.net

From Hwy 402, take Modelane/Hwy 40 Exit and proceed to Plank Rd, turn left, then right on Kimball Rd, and left on Moore Line.

$50S $60D 🍽 Meals ►4A
❄ Summer only ☕ Full, homebaked 🏠 Farm, 2-storey, older, 100 acres, view from guest rooms, patio, quiet ■ 2D (upstairs) ⊨ 2D ⟶1Private, 1ensuite ★ Air,TV, ceiling fans 🚫 No smoking, no pets, not suitable for children
🏃 Grain fields, farming community, tennis courts
🚗 Lake Huron beaches, museums, several playhouses, golfing
🏴 Congenial & hospitable hosts in 5th Generatio, renovated

family farm home, tastefully decorated. Enjoy a relaxed country get-away and rest in the shade of maples & evergreens or stroll the grounds. Breakfast is served in guest breakfast room. Inquire about extended stays. www.bbcanada.com/2136.html

---

Morrisburg

(south-east of Ottawa on US border; see also Williamsburg, Brinston)

McCooeye, Gail & Peter (St.Lawrence B&B)
72 Lakeshore Dr., Box 547, Morrisburg, ON K0C 1X0

☎ (613) 543-3654
E-mail: mccooeye@mor-net.on.ca

Take Exit750 from Hwy31, and proceed south to Morrisburg.
$40S $50D ►6
☕ Full 🏠 Res, older, view from guest rooms, riverfront, patio, swimming pool, porch, quiet ■ 3D (upstairs) ⊨ 2S,2D
⟶1Sh.w.g. ★ Air, ceiling fans, off-street parking
🚬Designated smoking area
🏃 Upper Canada Playhouse, dock, beach, bike path, river access
🚗 Upper Canada Village, Iroquois Locks, Bird Sanctuary, Ottawa
🏴 Warm welcome by friendly and experienced hosts in large Edwardian house with view of St.Lawrence River. Relax by the pool or on the verandas and enjoy the garden. Breakfast is served in guest breakfast room. There is a dog in residence.

Newboro

(north-east of Kingston; see also Westport)

King, Charlene & Bob (Newboro House Bed & Breakfast))
31 Drummond St., Newboro, ON K0G 1P0

☎ (613) 272-3181
E-mail: bobking@rideau.net

From Hwy 401, take Exit 623 & Hwy 15 north. Turn left on Hwy 42 and go west 8 km to Newboro. From Hwy 7, turn south on Hwy 15 at Carleton Place and proceed to Hwy 42 and Newboro.

$70-75S/D (Picnic lunches) ►6
❄ Apr1-Oct31 ☕ Full 🏠 Rural, hist., acreage, quiet
■3D(main & upper level) ⊨ 2T,1D,1Q ⟶ 1Private, 1sh.w.g., 1ensuite ★ Separate entrance, parking, secure storage for bicycles 🚫 No smoking, no pets, not suitable for young children
〰 some French
🏃 Historic blockhouse at Newboro Locks, canoeing/boating on Rideau Waterway, popular cycling route, restaurants
🚗 Public golf courses, Foley Mt.Cons.Area (beach, self-guided walking tours, bird watching)
🏴 Second Empire Architecture home (1880) authentically renovated, with spacious rooms, tastefully decorated and surrounded by lawns & gardens for relaxing and sunbathing. Enjoy the warm and friendly atmosphere. Visa/MC ✓B&B

Newton

(north of Stratford; see also Listowel)

Streicher, Marlene and Ezra (Country Charm)   ☎ (519) 595-8789
RR1, Newton, ON   N0K 1R0

Located 0.75 km south of Newton. Phone for directions.
$30S $45D $5Child   🍽 Meals   ► 6A,2Ch
🍴 Full   🏠 Farm, quiet   ■ 3(upst)   ⊨T,D,Q   ⊒Sh.w.g.
★Separate entrance, parking, jacuzzi (in winter only) ⊛No
smoking,no pets   ᔕ Pennsyl.Dutch
🧍 Sawmill and buggy shop, store
🚗 Stratford, Millbank, bakery/cheese factory, Kitchener
🏹 Warm welcome by Amish Mennonite family in large country
home with new addition. Relax in the jacuzzi. ✔B&B

Niagara Falls

(see also NOTL,St.Cath.,Fenwick,Vineld,Grimsby,Beamsv,St.Anns)

Burke, Carolyn & Gary (Park Place Bed & Breakfast)   ☎ (905) 358-0279, Fax 358-0458
4851 River Rd., Niagara Falls, ON   L2E 3G4   E-mail: gbburke@vaxxine.com

$75-140S/D $90-100CarriageHouse $15Child $20Add.person (2nights rates avail.)   ► 8A,2Ch
Take QEW to Hwy 420 and continue to Clifton Hill, turn left and proceed to River Rd., left again 1.9

km to house on corner of Ellis St (entrance on Ellis St)
🍴 Full, homebaked   🏠 Res., 2-storey, hist., view, riverfront,
porch   ■2S,1Ste (upstairs)   ⊨ 1D,1Q,1K,2cots   ⊒ 2Private,
1sh.w.h.   ★ F,private entrance for guests, jacuzzi/sauna,private
balcony, host quarters are separate, off-street parking ⊛No
pets, smoking on porches only
🧍 The Falls, Skylon Tower, Imax Theatre, Victoria Pk, bicycling
🚗Butterfly Conservatory, Floral Clock, Botanical Gardens, wine
route, Marineland, Casino Niagara, boat/helicopter rides, Recreational Trail
🏹 Queen Ann-style Victorian home, designated historic and lovingly restored, with corner turret
and views of the Niagara River gorge, located on the Niagara River Parkway. Breakfast is served in
formal setting with silver, lace, linens and fine china and served to suite. Special diets will be
cheerfully accommodated. Pick-up from train or bus with prior arrangement. The carriage house
can accommodate a family and has cooking facilities. There is a large black Lab in residence. ✔B&B

Schafrick, Herbert and Martha   ☎ (905) 732-3170
27 Eastdale Cres, Welland, ON   L3B 1E6

From Toronto take QEW and Hwy 406. From Niagara Falls take Hwy 20, then turn left onto Hwy
406 south & follow to end. At stop light, turn right onto East Main
St and then left on Wellington St. Proceed to Eastdale Cr on right.
$40S $60D $10Child   ► 6
🍴 Full   🏠 Res., sub, patio, quiet   ■ 3D (main and upper floor)
⊨3S,1D,1Q,crib   ⊒1Private, 1sh.w.h.   ★ Air,LF, parking,
separate entrance ⊛No smoking, no pets   ᔕGerman
🧍 New Welland Canal, public swimming pool and playground
🚗 Niagara Falls, Niagara-on-the-Lake, wineries
🏹 Comfortable home situated in suburban Welland. Enjoy the relaxed, friendly atmosphere and a
selection of homemade jams from local fruits. ✔B&B www.bbcanada.com/obba.html

Niagara Falls (cont'd)

Siciliano, Luciana (Butterfly Manor Bed & Breakfast) ☎ (905) 358-8988
4917 River Rd., Niagara Falls, ON L2E 3G5   E-mail: b&bnotl@freenet.npiec.on.ca

From Toronto follow QEW to Hwy 420. Turn left on Stanley, right on Morrison, right again on
Zimmerman and 2 blocks to River Rd. From Buffalo cross Peace Bridge and follow Niagara River
Parkway to the Falls and to house 1.5 km north of Falls on the river.

$95-159S/D $10Child $15Add.person   ► 10+
🍴 Full, homebaked   🏠 Res., 2-storey, view from guest rooms,
riverfront,quiet ■5+(upstairs) ⊨Q3,4K(T) 🛏4Ensuite
★Air,F (in 2 guest rooms), separate entrance, off-street parking
👐No smoking, no pets   ∿Italian, German, French, Spanish
🏃 Mighty Falls, Niagara Falls/NY, downtown, restaurants, tourist
attractions, shopping, shuttle bus, train/bus stations
🚗 Niagara-on-the-Lake, Buffalo, NY

☛ Old Manor-type home with a delightful blend of old and new, overlooking the Niagara River,
situated in convenient location from the Falls and other points of interest on both sides of the
border. Breakfast is cooked and served in the very large open, modern kitchen with fireplace. This
B&B has been the receiver of the "Misty Award" several times. Special Rates for longer stays.
✍B&B http://vaxxine.com/bb

Niagara-on-the-Lake   *(north of Niagara Falls; see also St.Catharines, Vineland)*

Brown, Helen & Bill (Trillium House B&B)   ☎(905) 468-5649
6 Christopher St., Box 995, Niagara-on-the-Lake, ON L0S 1J0

From QEW take Exit38B onto Hwy 55 and continue 14km to Niagara-on-the-lake. Turn right on
John St, right on Charlotte St and left on Christopher St.

$95-120S/D   ► 6A
📅May-Nov 🍴Full 🏠Res., 2-storey, view from guest rooms,
0.5acre, swimming pool, patio,
quiet ■3D(upstairs) ⊨1T(K),2Q 🛏1ensuite,1sh.w.g. ★
Air,F, off-street parking   👐No smoking, no pets, not suitable for
children ∿French
🏃 Shaw Festival Theatre, Old Towne, shops, boutiques, galleries,
restaurants, Fort George, lakeside park and walkways, bicycle

and roller blade path linking up with Niagara Parkway to Niagara Falls, public transport
🚗 Golf courses, numerous wineries (wine tasting tours), Niagara River boat trips, Village of
Queenston, Weir Art Gallery, Butterfly Conservatory, Welland Canal (viewing platform/museum)
☛ Retired Professional couple in Williamsburg-style house with authentic decor and furnished
with antiques. Enjoy the peaceful setting and relax in the sunroom-lounge or quiet sitting room
overlooking the beautiful garden surrounding the swimming pool. Breakfast is served in the special
guest breakfast room. Rental bicycles available. ✍B&B

King, Helen and Mike (The King's Way)   ☎ (905) 468-5478
308 Nassau St, Box 684, Niagara-on-the-Lake, ON L0S 1J0

From QEW take the exit for N-O-T-L (Hwy 55) and follow through Virgil to Williams Street. Turn
left, go 2 blocks to Nassau Street, turn right on Nassau St.

$75-90D $10Child $15Add.person   ► 6A,2A
🍴Full 🏠Res, acreage, patio, quiet ■3D(upst) ⊨3Q,2cots
🛏1Private, 2shw.g. ★Air,F,parking, guest room balconies, guest
parlor 👐No smoking, no pets
🏃 Shaw Festival Theatres, golfing, shopping, restaurants
🚗 Art Park (Lewiston), US border, Fort Erie, hiking, N.Falls
☛ Enthusiastic host family in spacious modern home with
walk-out balconies, located on a quiet street within strolling distance of downtown, theatres and
shops. ✍B&B www.bbcanada.com/123.html

Niagara-on-the-Lake (cont'd)

Cummins, Bill & Lavender (Erinbeg Bed & Breakfast)   ☎ (905) 468-0040, Fax 0039
Box 1273, 156 Gate St. Niagara-on-the-Lake, ON L0S 1J0   E-mail: cummins@mergetel.com

Situated right in the old town at the corner of Gate & Prideaux Sts and 1 block north of Queen St.

$75S $85-105D $25Add.person   ► 7
Full, homebaked Downtown, res., 3-storey, hist., view, porch,
quiet 1Ste,2D (upst) 1R,2T,2Q 1Sh.w.g., 1ensuite ★ Air,
adjoining sitting room in suite, off-street pkg No smoking,no pets
Lake Ontario, 4 theatres, shopping, dining, golfing, Art Gallery
Niagara Falls, wineries (tours), St.Catharines, Marineland
Elegant, bright historic (1890) home situated among mature trees
& view of Lake Ontario reflects hosts' love of antiques and pewterware.
House specialty is Irish Soda Bread as well as hot Gooseberry Sauce &
Yogourt for potato pancakes. Visa ✓CC

Derry, Glenda & Bill (Cottonwood B&B Inn)   ☎ (905)-468-1236, Fax 468-8707
377 Johnson St., Box 1145, Niagara-on-the-Lake, ON L0S 1J0   188-663-3302
                                                          E-mail: cottonwood@sympatico.ca,
From Toronto or US border, take QEW to Hwy 55 and follow signs to Niagara-on-the-Lake (old
town). Proceed on Mississauga Rd to Johnson St, turn left.

$129-149S/D   (plus tax)   ► 6A
Full Downtown, res., 2-storey, quiet, secluded, porch
3D(upstairs) 2Q,1K 3Ensuite ★ Air,F, private
entrance, off-street parking, guest quarters are separate No
smoking, no pets, not suitable for childen
All Shaw Festival theatres, golf course (NA's oldest), historic
Fort Mississauga & Fort Niagara, historic Queen Street shopping,
fine dining, biking & hiking trails, picnic areas by the Lake
Estate wineries, Niagara Parkway scenic drive, Niagara Falls, Welland Canal, Casino Niagara
Retired Professional couple in spacious home, specifically designed for B&B and inspired by
the romantic architecture of the USA's Old South, with full width columned gallery, entry fanlight,
arched dormer windows and carved mantels. Relax in the gracious guest lounge or on the wide front
porch. Breakfast is served in special guest breakfast room. Visa,MC,Amex ✓B&B
www3.sympatico.ca/cottonwood

Hernder, Pat and Art (Hernder's Country Home)   ☎ & Fax (905) 468-3192
753, Line 3, RR2 Niagara-on-the-Lake, ON L0S 1J0   E-mail: hernder@idirect.com

From QEW take Exit Hwy 55 and proceed to Four Mile Creek Rd. At Virgil traffic light turn right,
continue to Line 3 and then left to 1st house on right.

$80-95S/D $20Add.person   ► 10
Full,homebaked Farm (vineyard), 2-level, view, quiet
4D,Ste(main & ground floor) 1K/2T,3Q 2Ensuite,
2private ★Air,F,large guest rec-room with
TV/fridge/microwave, large outside hot tub, screened gazebo
No pets,child. min. age 10, smoking outside only
Conservation area, tennis, wineries (tours and tasting), cycling
Downtown, theatres, restaurants, Niagara Falls, Casino
Spacious Colonial home viewing the Niagara Escarpment, situated on the wine route amidst
the cottage wineries, in the heart of Niagara's fruitland. Breakfasts always include fresh Niagara
fruits in season. Hosts'hobbies are handcrafted woodworks & Big-Band-Era memorabilia. ✓B&B
www.bbcanada.com/1166.html

Niagara-on-the-Lake (cont'd)

Ganim, Dr.Charles & Barbara(Post House B&B,ca1835)   1-877-349-POST,(905)468-9991
95 Johnson St., Niagaara-on-the-Lake, ON   L0S 1J0   E-mail: posthsebb@aol.com, Fax 468-9584

Take QEW & Hwy55 to end (Queen St), turn right, proceed to Victoria St and turn right. Park in
the double driveway at the trellis fence. Entrance to home is on Victoria St.

$160-340D $35Add.person(in suite only)   ►7
🍴 Full, homebaked (plus special health table)   🏠 Brick, hist. 2-storey,
pool   ■2D,1Ste (2nd floor)   ⊨2T,1Q,1K,1P   🛁 3Ensuite, jacuzzi
★ Air,F,LF,TV/Internet access/phone in guest lounge, hot-tub, off-street
parking available   Ⓢ Smoking by poolside, no pets, children min.age 12
🚶 Shaw Festival, theatre, shops, restaurants, Lake Ontario, Fort George
🚗 Niagara Falls, Casino, Brock University, St.Catharines, US border,
scenic drives, wine & fruit country, golfing
📣 Romantic, historic Georgian-style home, recently renovated to modern
amenities and decorated with George Bernard Shaw artifacts & antiques on
display, located in the Heritage District. Horse drawn carriages will
pick up guests for a ride to their favorite restaurant. Breakfast is served either poolside or in the
sun filled Conservatory overlooking the heated pool. Enjoy a special health table in addition to
hostess' "best muffins in North America". Special rates in off-season for business travellers.
Various special packages avail. CCards ✓B&B www.travelguides.cominnsfullon16.html

---

Landray,Elaine & Donna P. (Linden House B&B)   ☎(905)468-3923,Fax:(905)468-8946
389 Simcoe St., Box 1586, Niagara-on-the-Lake, ON   L0S 1J0   E-mail: linden@niagara.com

Take QEW and Hwy 55 into NOTL. Turn right on William St and proceed to house on corner of
Simcoe St. From Lewiston-Queenston Bridge, follow Niagara Pkwy into N-O-T-L. From Queen &
King crossroads, follow Queen St to Simcoe St, left to William St. Parking from William St.

$95-105D   ► 6A
🍴 Full   🏠 Res, 2-storey, deck, gazebo, quiet ■3D (upstairs
private guest wing)   ⊨ 2T(or 1K),2Q (incl. brass beds)
🛁3Ensuite   ★Air,TV/VCR/books in guest lounge, separate
entrance, off-street parking   Ⓦ No smoking, no pets
🗣Spanish, French
🚶 Shaw Festival (3 theatres), Fort George, museum, bicycle trail
(50 km from NOTL to Fort Erie), downtown Queen Street & shops
🚗 Ten wineries, Niagara Falls, Welland Canal Lock 3 (viewing & museum),
📣 Mother & daughter team in Cape Cod style home, built in 1990 especially for B&B and, as
such, affords privacy for guests and hosts, located in the old town. Retired professionals have
travelled extensively world-wide. Enjoy a sumptuous breakfast featuring Niagara fruits (no need for
lunch).✓B&B www.v-ip.com/linden

McMorrough, Yvonne (Avoca B&B)   ☎ (905) 468-5217, Fax (905) 468-1702
RR3, Niagara-on-the-Lake, ON   L0S 1J0   E-mail: avocanotl@aol.com

$130D $20Child $30Add.person   (Senior Discounts on certain days)   ► 6A,2Ch
Located at 3 Sentry Circle at Lakeshore and Garrison Dr.
🍴 Cont.,homebaked   🏠 Res., raised bungalow, 0.5acres groomed
gardens, lakeshore-view, patio, porch, deck, quiet ■3 (ground &
lower level)   ⊨ 6T(K)   🛁 3Private   ★ F,TV,LF, electr.
airfilter, 2 guest fridges, wheel-chair access in one guest room,
off-street parking   Ⓦ Smoking outside, no pets   🗣French,
Spanish, German
🚶 Golfing, tennis, Lake Ontario shoreline
🚗 Shaw Festival Theatre, Queen (Main Street shops, small theatres, restaurants), St.Catharines
📣 Elegant home with wheel-chair access (specially equipped and updated in 1995 by current
owner). Relax in the peaceful garden or settle down in the well-stocked library/lounge. Ideal place
for "literary addicts". Hostess has many years of exerience in hospitality & tourism (Ireland and
Canada). Visa,MC,JCB(Japanese) ✓CC members.aol.com/avocanotl

Niagara-on-the-Lake (cont'd)

Moyer, Marybeth & Jay (House on the River B&B)   ☎ & Fax (905) 262-4597
14773 Niagara River Parkway, Niagara-on-the-Lake, ON   L0S 1J0   E-mail: moyer@niagara.net

Phone for directions.
$110S/D $25Add.person   ► 8A
🍳 Full   🏠 Res., split-level, acreage, riverbank, deck, quiet   ■4
(ground level) ⊨4Q   🛏 4Ensuite   ★Air,F, private entrance
for 3 guest rooms,guest bicycles,parking 🚫No smoking,no pets
🏃 Niagara bike/walking path (56km from Fort Erie to the shores
of Lake Ontario), historic village of Queenston, The Weir Museum
& Gallery (Canadian Art)

🚐 Downtown shopping/dining, Shaw Festival Theatres, Niagara Falls, wineries (tours), golfing
🔫 Private and quiet home with a magnificient view overlooking the Niagara River to the village
of Lewiston NY and Art Park. Situated high on the Niagara River bank. Breakfast is served on the
river bank (weather permitting). ✏CC

Pellizzari, Imelda & Sergio (Comfort-on-the-Meadow B&B)   ☎ (905) 262-4112
976 Creek Rd, RR4, Niagara-on-the-Lake, ON   L0S 1J0   E-mail: comfort@mail.caninet.com

From QEW take Exit 38B (NOTL). Turn right at light to follow York Rd to St.Davids. Turn left at
4-way stop in St.Davids onto Four Mile Creek Rd. Look for 5th house on left past Line 6.

$65S $75-85D $20Child/Add.person   ► 6A,1Ch
🍳 Full   🏠 Rural, split-multi-level, acreage, view from guest
rooms, patio, porch, deck, quiet   ■ 3D(main & upper level)
⊨2T,2D   🛏1Sh.w.g.,1sh.w.h (ground level) ★Air,F,KF,LF,TV
in large guest lounge, ceiling fans, wood burning stove, separate
entrance, off-street parking 🚫Designated smoking area, no pets
indoor (kennel available) 💬 Italian, Spanish
🏃 Walks in gardens, orchards & vinyards

🚐 Old Town (Niagara-on-the-Lake), Shaw Festival Theatre, Niagara Falls
🔫 Bright and spacious home on 3acres of tranquil gardens & meadows and centrally located on
the Wine Route of the Niagara Peninsula. Enjoy a bountiful country breakfast (may include
homemade Italian sausage) before starting a day of sightseeing, theatre-going or travelling. ✏CC
http://www.bbcanada.com/1191.html

Runge, Katharina (Runge Residence B&B)   ☎ (905) 468-7515
844 East & West Line, RR3, Niagara-on-the-Lake, ON   L0S 1J0

Located between Virgil & NOTL, close to Hwy 55 across from Harvest Barn. Phone for directions.

$70-90S/D $20Add.person   ► 6
🌼 May-Nov   🍳 Full, homebaked   🏠 Rural, 2-storey, view
from guest rooms, porch, gazebo   ■ 3 (upstairs)
⊨2Q,2P,cot   🛏 3Private   ★ Air, private entrance, host
quarters are separate, off-street parking 🚫 Smoking oustide, no
pets, children min.age 5   💬 German
🏃 Harvest Barn across the street
🚐 NOTL, all theatres, Niagara Falls, US-border, wineries
🔫 Warm welcome in comfortable Cape Cod home with bright rooms & surrounded by orchards.

Niagara-on-the-Lake (cont'd)

Schankula, Mary (Amberlea)   ☎ (905) 468-3749
285 John St., Box 426, Niagara-on-the-Lake, ON   L0S 1J0

From QEW, take Hwy 55 to NOTL. Upon entering town, turn left at first cross street (John St) and look for 4th house on right.

$75-95S/D   ►6
🍳 Full 🏠Downtown, raised bungalow, patio, treed setting, quiet
■3D(lower level) ⊨1T,2K ⊶2Private, 1sh.w.h.   ★Air,F,TV in one guest room, parking 🚭No smoking
🏃 Unique shops, Shaw Festival and Courthouse Theatres, historic sites of Old Town, Lake Ontario picnic areas, walking, biking
🚐 Niagara Falls, Welland Canal, Ft Erie Race Track, Art Park (NY), Casino
☛ Located in a quiet, park-like area. Hostess is a history buff/art lover. Visa,MC ╰B&B

Smith, Kathy & Murray(Bruce Manor B&B)   ☎(905)468-4327, Fax468-2563(7:30-9:30AM)
602 Charlotte St.,Box 945,Niagara-on-the-Lake,ON L0S1J0   E-mail: brucemanor@networx.on.ca

From Toronto on QEW take Hwy 55 to NOTL. Turn right on John St and right on Charlotte. From US follow Hwy 190 across Queenston Lewiston Bridge. Exit immediate right on Niagara Parkway and continue to Niagara-on-the-Lake. Turn left on John St and left on Charlotte.

$80-90S - $90-100D $20-30Add.person   ►8A
🌼 April-Oct. 🍳 Gourmet, homebaked 🏠 Res., 2-storey, view from guest rooms, swimming pool, patio, decks, quiet, secluded
■2Ste,1D (upst) ⊨ 3Q,1R,1P ⊶ 1Private, 3ensuite
★Air,F,TV in guest room, 1 guest room air-conditioner, 2 ceiling fans, kitchenettes, bar-fridges & microwave in suites, private entrance, off-street parking, guest quarters are separate
🚭Designated smoking area, no pets, children min. age 10
🏃 Shaw Festival Theatres, downtown shops, Niagara River Steamboat, Fort George, N.River Pkwy
🚐 Niagara Falls, St.Catharines, wineries
☛ Large Georgian Style home located adjacent to the beautiful Bruce Trail. Retired teachers enjoy gardening, gourmet cooking, antique decorative interiors and entertaining. Relax in the extensive gardens surrounding the pool or on the patio against wooded backdrop of Bruce Trail. Breakfast is served poolside or in the dining room. (Fax operational only between 7:30 am and 9:30 am). Visa,MC ╰B&B www.bestnet.org/~brucemanor

---

Wiens, Egbert & Ingrid (Arbor Terrace)   ☎ (905) 262-5767
2014 York Rd., RR1, Niagara-on-the-Lake, ON   L0S 1J0

From QEW take Exit for Hwy 55 and proceed towards Niagara-on-the-Lake. At York Rd turn right.
$60-80S/D $10Child $110F $15Add.person 🍽 Meals   ►6A,2Ch
🍳 Full 🏠 Village, hillside, patio, deck, quiet, secluded
■1Ste(2D),1F (main & ground level) ⊨ 1K(2T),2Q,2S, cot, crib ⊶ 1Private, 1ensuite, whirlpool ★ Air,F,LF, private patio doors, wheel-chair access ⊶German, French, Russian, Dutch, some Italian
🏃 Queenston Heights Park, tennis courts, start of Bruce Trail (excellent hiking, mountain biking, cycling, rollerblading paths)
🚐 Shaw Festival Theatre (NOTL), Niagara Falls, Butterfly Conservatory, wineries, Lewiston US,
☛ Quiet and attractive guest home located in the historic village of Queenston. Host has been a teacher of modern languages for many years. Hostess is severely handicapped as a result of a stroke at age 33. Guests have been impressed by her charm and her graciousness which she is able to show despite her inability to speak. Breakfast is served on beautiful elevated terrace. Visa ╰CC
http://www.bbcanada.com/arborterrace

Niagara-on-the-Lake (cont'd)

Wisch, Uwe & Thea (Brockamour Manor)   ☎ (905) 468-5527, Fax (905) 468-5071
433 King St., Niagara-on-the-Lake, ON   L0S 1J0   E-mail: brockamo@vaxxine.com

Take QEW to Hwy 55 and follow signs to NOTL. Turn right at traffic light (Mary St) and continue
to last driveway at left before stop sign at King St. Look for large white house on corner.

$100-200S/D   ► 12
🍳 Full, homebaked   🏠 Res., hist., 1acre   ■6D(upstairs)
⊨2T,3Q,2K   🛁6Ensuite, jacuzzis   ★ Air,F in 2honeymoon
suites and one guest room, separate entrance, off-street parking
🌐No smoking, no pets   ∾German
🕺 Shaw Festival theatres, unique shops on Queen Street
🚗 Niagara Falls, Welland Canal, St. Catharines, US border,
bicycle trails, scenic drives, Fort George, wineries

🎏 Quiet, graceful elegance in lovely heritage Georgian home (circa 1812) with romantic, historic
past and a gracious present. Situated in beautiful park-like environment with huge old majestic
trees, waterfall and beautiful flowerbeds. Visa,MC ∠B&B   http://www.brockamour.com

---

North Bay   *(northern Ontario; see also Powassan, Mattawa)*

Persia, Marianne & Gary (Hummingbird Hill B&B)   ☎ (705) 752-4547, Fax 752-5150
RR1, 254 Edmond Rd., Astorville, ON   P0H 1B0   E-mail: mabb@vianet.on.ca, 1-800-661-4976

From Hwy17, take Hwy94 to Corbeil, follow signs to Astorville. From Hwy 11 (15km south of
North Bay) take Exit 654, turn left on Lake Nosbonsing Rd into village. turn right on Edmond Rd.

$60S $75D $15Child $20Add.person   🍴Meals   ► 6+
🍳 Full (choice:heart-smart/vegetarian)   🏠 Rural, 3-storey,
6acres, patio, porch, deck, quiet, secluded, screened gazebo
■3D(upstairs), plus loft   ⊨2T,2D,1Q   🛁2Ensuite, 1sh.w.h.
★ F,TV in guest rooms, private guest sitting area, sauna, hot tub,
solarium, off-street parking   🌐No smoking
🕺 Birdwatching, beaches, boating, artisan tours, hiking,
snowmobile trails, x-c skiing, ice fishing, deer feed in yard

🚗 Chief Commanda Boat cruise on Lake Nippising, Dionne Quints Museum, downhill skiing
🎏 Unique, geometric dome house with spiral staircases, cathedral ceilings, skylights, cedar
interior & exterior and beautifully decorated; surrounded by extensive perennial beds and water
garden. Enjoy the relaxing, charming and elegant atmosphere, relax in the hot tub on deck or in the
solarium filled with many tropical plants - a sunny & private place, with nature at it's best. In
summer breakfast can be served in cedar-screened gazebo. There is a dog and a cat in residence.
Ideal place for a spa weekend (spa & gourmet packages available). Visa ∠B&B
www.northbay-online.com/hummingbirdhill

North Gower   *(south of Ottawa,; see also Manotik)*

McDonald, Madeleine and Alfred   (Carsonby Manor)   ☎ (613) 489-3219
Box 6035 RR3, North Gower, ON   K0A 2T0

Phone for directions.
$45S $55-70D $8Child   ► 5
🍳 Choice (dietary needs can be pre-arranged)   🏠Rural, acreage,
quiet   ■1S,2D (upstairs)   ⊨1S,2D   🛁1Ensuite,2sh.w.g.
★Air,F,TV in guest room, in-ground swimming pool, separate
entrance, parking   🌐No smoking, no pets   ∾French
🕺 Manderley Golf Course, cross-country skiing

🚗 Village of Manotick, restaurants, Ottawa, Stittsville (Canada's largest flea market)
🎏 Large home in parkland setting with warm and friendly hospitality. Visa ∠B&B

Oakville

(west of Toronto; see also Burlington, Milton, Campbellville)

Kendall, Johanna & Wayne (Brass Lantern B&B)   ☎ (905) 337-0201
300 Lakeshore Rd West, Oakville, ON   L6K 1G1   E-mail: kendall@cgocable.net

Exit QEW at Dorval Dr (Exit 117)and proceed south to Lakeshore Rd. Turn right one block. Look
 for sign in front, on the south side.
$75S $85D   ►4
🍳 Full, homebaked 🏠 Downtown, res., ranch-style, view,
porch, deck ■ 2D (main level) ⊨ 2Q ⌁ 1Private,
1ensuite ★ Air,F,TV in guest rooms, off-street parking, guest
quarters are in separate wing ⬤ Smoking outside, no pets, not
suitable for children ∾ some Dutch & French
🧍 Downtown, shops, restaurants, theatre, library, Lake Ontario &
Oakville Harbour, Appleby Collage, Oakville Transit to "GO" Toronto Commuter Train at door
🚗 Toronto, Pearson Int.Airport, Niagara Falls area, antique shops in Campbelleville, Kitchener
🔫 Bright and spacious home with numerous large windows & skylights, vaulted ceilings and
lovely modern decor, located in desirable south-west area of town. Relax on the wrap-around deck
overlooking the wooded backyard with hugh oaks and maples or enjoy the birds, foxes, racoons from
the dining room window, while eating breakfast. Visa ✔ B&B www.bbcanada.com/1172.html

---

Webb, Philip & Janice (Valleybrook Bed & Breakfast) ☎ (905) 844-4138, Fax (905) 844-0617
1243 Valleybrook Dr., Oakville, ON   L6H 4Y1   E-mail: pwebb@cgocable.net

From QEW west of Toronto, take Ford Dr north & Upper Middle Rd west to Grand Blvd. Turn
 north, then west on Valleybrook Dr to 3rd house on right.
$50S $70D   ►4
🍳 Full, homebaked 🏠 Res., sub., 2-storey, swimming pool,
patio, deck ■ 2D(upstairs) ⊨ 1D,1Q ⌁ 1Sh.w.g.
★Air,LF,KF, TV/games in guest sitting room, off-street
parking ⬤ No smoking, no pets, children min. age 10
🚗 Downtown Oakville, shops, restaurants & fine dining,
Go-Communter Train, Toronto, Lake Ontario shores, Glen Abbey
🔫 Suburban executive home situated on the northside of East Oakville. Enjoy breakfast in
private formal dining room or poolside. Relax in the sitting room or take a dip in the pool. ✔B&B

Ohsweken

(south-east of Brantford)

Johnson, Lisa & Tim (The Bear's Inn B&B)   ☎ (519) 445-4133, Fax (519) 445-0439
Box 187, Ohsweken, ON   N0A 1M0   E-mail: bearsinn@wchat.on.ca

Located on 4th Line Rd in Ohsweken. From Hwy 401, take Hwy 403 west to Hamilton/Brantford,
exit Garden Ave., head sosuth, drive straight at first traffic light (Hwy 54/254) and proceed toward
Cayuga. Follow into the Six Nations Reserve. Turn right onto Chiefswood Rd, left onto 4th Line Rd
at traffic light, drive 0.8km and turn left at Inn.
 $49-69S/D   ► 18A,8Ch
🍳 Cont., homebaked 🏠 Village, 2 guest log homes, 3 acres,
quiet, isolated ■ 8Ste(main & upper floor), host quarters are in
two separate buildings ⊨D,Q,cots ⌁14Private ★Air,KF,TVin
guest room, sep.entrance, reading rooms, fax machine access,
exercise room, poole table, parking ★ No smoking, no pets
🧍 Ohsweken shopping district, restaurants, sports complex, Six
Nations Tourist Office, Pauline Johnson Home, golfing
🚗 Bell Homestead, Woodland Cultural Centre, Brantford, Hamilton, Niagara Falls
🔫 Experience Iroquois culture, art, history and hospitality in large white pine log homes located
on Six Nations Indian Reserve of the Grand River. Each house has a breakfast room. Each guest
room features a different theme dealing with Iroquois history & culture. Sightseeing tours to other
parts of the community available. Conference rooms. CCards ✔B&B

Orangeville

Proudfoot, Sandy & Jock (The Farmer's Walk B&B)   ☎ (519) 942-1775, Fax 942-0113
RR5,4th Line MonoTwp, Orangeville, ON   L9W 2Z2

Located between Hwy 10 & Airport Rd, north of Hwy 9 and south of Hockley Rd. On 4th Line of
Mono East, 5 country mail boxes north of the No5 Sideroad of Mono, on east side of the road.

$50S $65-70D   ▶ 5A
🍴 Full, homebaked   🏠 Rural, 2-storey, 10-acres, view from
guest rooms, swimming pool, patio, porch, deck, quiet, secluded
■2D,1S(upst) ⊨1S,1Q,2T ⊲1Ensuite, 1sh.w.g. ★F, hosts
quarters are sep.   ☝No smoking, no pets, no children
🏃 Bush walks, swimming, Bruce Trail, theatre, Hockley Valley
Resort (golfing, skiing), fine dining, antique shopping, x-c ski from
back porch, Mono Cliffs Park
🚗 Orangeville, Toronto International Airport, McMichael Gallery, Collingwood skiing
🚍 Warm welcome in quiet, secluded farmhouse-type family home, set well back from road and
overlooking the beautiful Hockley Valley. Hosts are a designer with in-house studio and retired Air
Canada pilot and Glider pilot. Hostess breeds some bantam Silkie chickens (enjoy fresh eggs for
breakfast). Equestrian facilities are available upon request. There is a dog and a cat in residence.
✔CC www.bbcanada.com

B&B Country Host, Reservation Service for Headwaters Country B&B Homes
RR5, Mono 5th LineEast, Orangeville, ON   L9W 2Z2   ☎ (519) 942-0686

Lesley Burns, President
Rates: $45S $65D (including full breakfast)   (Group discounts)
The Country Host B&B Reservation Service & Ski Host consists of a great variety of homes, such as
Victorian, heritage and restored Century homes, estates and horse farms. They are situated next to
Provincial parks or trailways including the Bruce and Caledon areas for hiking, biking, and near
antique shops, country markets, festival and live theatre. Some homes have swimming pools, spas,
home studios or workshops. Homes represented are located in Belfountain, Caledon, Cheltenham,
Collingwood, Hockley Valley, Tottenham, Meaford and Mono Mills. There is also a Villa and an
apartment available. For reservation call the above.✔CC www.countryhost.comm

---

Orillia

Bridgens,Betty & Tony(Betty & Tony's Waterfront B&B)   ☎1-800-308-2579,
677 Broadview Ave., Orillia, ON   L3V 6P1   Fax(705)326-2262
                                              E-mail: tony.bridgens@encode.com
From Hwy 12 in Orillia, take Couchiching Point Rd near Atherley bridge in the south-east end of
town and then turn right on Broadview Ave.

$75-89S $89-109D $10-15Add.person   🍽 Meals   ▶ 8A,3Ch
🍴 Full, homebaked   🏠 Res., modern 2-level custom built design,
view from guest rooms, 80ft Canal frontage, patio, deck, quiet
■3F(high lower level) ⊨2S,3D ⊲2Ensuite, 1private
★Air,LF,TV in guest lounge, library, guest coffee counter,
conference room (with copier, fax, computer), pedalboat & canoe at
dock, off-street parking ☝ No smoking, inquire about pets
⌇French, Norwegian, some German and Italian
🏃 Stephen Leacock Museum, Tudhope Park, restaurants, pike fishing in canal, biking
🚗 Kirkfield Lift Locks, Big Chute Marine Railroad, Casino Rama, Orillia Opera House, cruises
🚍 Modern home on Trent Severn Canal & Waterway in upper class parklike neighbourhood,
filled with family heirlooms. Relax in solitude in one of the sitting rooms, or socialize with congenial
hosts and other guests in another area. Use the lawnchair and enjoy the lakeview. Resident cat and
dog. Gift Certificates available. Visa,MC ✔B&B www.bbcanada.com/9.html

Orillia (cont'd)

Gregory, Judy & Freeman (Alexander House) ☎ & Fax(705) 326-1119, 1-888-873-0062
7 Alexander Dr., Orillia, ON   L3V 5L7

From Hwy 400 North take Hwy 11 to West St Exit. Proceed to
Fittons Rd, turn right to Alexander, right to 3rd house on left.
$60-65S $70-75D   ► 6A
✚ closed Dec24-26   ▣ Full, homebaked   🏠 Res., small town,
2-storey, older, patios   ■ 3D(upstairs   ⊨ 1D,2Q   ⊲1Ensuite,
1sh.w.g., (one jacuzzi)   ★ Air, TV in guest lounge,
air-conditioners, off-street parking, guest quarters are separate
ⓌNo smoking, no pets, no children

🕴 Shops, restaurants, churches, bus stop across the street, craft studio on premises
🚗 Rama Casino, Horseshoe Valley/Mt.St.Louis Ski Resorts, x-c ski trail, Orillia Opera House
📢 Unique Century Home (circa 1890) with many antiques, wicker, lace and collectibles. Enjoy
the elegance and charm of yesteryear with the convenience of modern day. Relax in the private
sitting room or on one of the outdoor patios overlooking lush gardens. Hosts are knowledgeable of
local attractions and happenings. Visa ⌐B&B

Guthrie, Pearl & Norm (The Verandahs Bed & Breakfast)   ☎ & Fax (705) 487-1910
RR2, Hawkestone, ON   L0L 1T0

Take Hwy 400 through Barrie, then Hwy 11 toward Orillia. Turn
east on Oro-Medonte Line 9, follow to end (3 km). House is on left.
$70S $80D   (Reservations recommended)   ► 6-7
✚May15Oct15/Dec27-Mar31 ▣Full, homebaked 🏠Rural, res,
3-storey, view from guest rooms, porch, quiet   ■3D(upstairs)
⊨3S,1Q,2K ⊲ 1ensuite,2private ★F/TV in guest lounge, guest
robes & slippers, guest bikes, off-street parking   ⓌNo smoking,
no pets

🕴 Park & safe sandy beach, boat launch, icefishing, snowmobiling from door
🚗 Ski resorts (downhill & x-c skiing), Barrie, Orillia, boat cruises, Mtn biking, golfing, Casino
📢 Lovely Victorian-style home with wide verandas. Bright welcoming ambiance, beautifully
decorated and situated 150 ft from Lake Simcoe. Relax on the verandas and enjoy the cool summer
lake breezes; in winter snuggle up under goose-down duvets. Well travelled hosts are retired and
enjoy welcoming guests in their spacious home. Deaf but friendly cat in residence. Visa,MC

Pidwerbecki, Mike (Siberi*inn Bed & Breakfast)   ☎ (705) 487-6456, Fax (705) 487-6459
RR2, Hawkestone, Oro, ON   L0L 1T0   E-mail: siberinn@barint.on.ca

Located 9km south-west of Orillia. Phone for directions.
$55-70S $65-80D $5Child(age 5-10) $10Add.person   ► 8
▣ Full, homebaked   🏠 Rural, 2-storey, acreage, view from guest
rooms, quiet, covered veranda   ■1D,1Ste   ⊨2T,2Q,1D
⊲1Private, 1ensuite   ★TV/2F/microwave in guest
lounge ⓌNo smoking, no pets, child min.age 5
🕴 Ganaraska Hiking Trail, snowshoe/snowmobile & x-c skiing (all
from doorstep)

🚗 Hardwood Hills/Horseshoe Valley/Moonstone/Mt.St.Louis & Snow Valley ski resorts,
equestrian farms, Casino Rama
📢 Comfortable custom-built home with covered veranda surrounding the house and situated in
the woods atop a hill. Relax in the peaceful setting of the panoramic hardwood forest. Take in the
fresh air and picturesque surroundings. Enjoy effection from the Siberian Huskies who run the
place. Unique decor includes Inuit souvenirs obtained by hosts on visit to Baffin Islands. Enjoy the
beautiful seasons including a great northern experience in the winter with plenty and the best snow
around!. Husky pets are not allowed in guest rooms. ⌐B&B www.barint.on.ca/~siberinn

Orillia (cont'd)

Taylor, Sioux (Panorama B&B)   ☎ & Fax (705) 326-1636
622 Moberley Ave., Orillia, ON L3V 6R6   E-mail: panorama.bandb@sympatico.ca

From Hwy 12 turn west onto Couchiching Point Rd. Look for 3rd street on right.
$70-80S $80-90D $20Add.person   🍽 Meals   ► 7
🍲 Full, homebaked   🏠 Res., split-level, view from guest rooms, lakefront, deck, quiet   ■3D
(ground & upper floor)   ⊨ 2Q,2T(K),1S   🛁 1sh.w.g., 1sh.w.h.   ★ F,KF,TV in guest room,
gas barbeque on deck, boat dock (to 25feet), firepit and lakeside seating, off-street parking, guest
quarters are separate   ✋ Smoking outside, no pets, children by special prior arrangement only
🏃 Clean/safe swimming, boating on Trent-Severn Waterway, Stephen Leacock Home/Museum,
fishing, Gordon Lightfoot hiking/biking Trail, Tudhope Park and restaurant
🚗 Casino Rama, Orillia Opera House (music/theatre), golfing, crafts/antiques, skiing
🐾 Modern, comfortable lakeside home situated in classic cottage setting. Hostess is well
informed about local happenings. Relax and enjoy the beautiful sunsets over Lake Couchiching from
the spacious deck and the restful atmosphere. Boats and canoe for guests. Free docking for boats &
seaplanes. "Naomi" a friendly Black Lab in residence. Weekly rates. MC,Amex ✓B&B

Templeton, Carol & Bob (Country Lane B&B)   ☎ (705) 487-5821, Fax 487-6097
1115 Old Barrie Ridge, RR2, Hawkestone, ON L0L 1T0   E-mail: clanebb@csolve.net

Take Hwy 400 through Hwy 11 North of Barrie, turn on Oro Line 9 right over highway, left on Line

9, and 6.6km to Old Barrie Rd. Turn right.
$70S $80D $10Child/Add.person   🍽 Meals   ► 6
🍲 Full   🏠 Farm, 2-storey, hist., view from guest rooms, porch,
deck, quiet, secluded   ■ 3D(upstairs)   ⊨2T,1D,1Q,cot
🛁2Sh.w.g.,1ensuite, jacuzzi   ★ Air,LF,F,TV in guest lounge,
ceiling fan in one room, off-street parking, guest quarters are
separate   ✋ Designated smoking area, children min.age 1
🏃 Ganaraska Trail, x-c skiing/bird watching/hiking on property
🚗 Casino Rama, Horseshoe Valley, Burls Creek Family Event Park, Orillia, Barrie, Mt.St.Louis
🐾 Charming Century farm house, fully modernized, ringed by 100 year old maple forests and
situated on 69 acres of farm land in the lovely hills of Oro-Medonte. Relax on one of 3 verandas or in
the gazebo nestled in a fruit orchard. Enjoy a hearty country breakfast with fresh farm produce and
eggs from the henhouse. There are dogs and cats. Visa,MC ✓B&B www.countrylanebb.com

---

Zardo, Jaqueline & Richard (Cavana House)   ☎ (705) 327-7759
241 Mississaga St. West, Orillia, ON L3V 3B7   E-mail: zardo@encode.com

Phone for directions.
$75-90S/D $25Add.person   ► 6
🍲 Full, homebaked   🏠 Downtown, 3-storey, hist., porches
■2D,1F(upstairs)   ⊨ 1D,1Q,1S   🛁 3Ensuite   ★Air,F,TV in
guest rooms, off-street parking, host quarters are separate   ✋No
smoking, children min. age 12
🏃 Downtown shopping, theatres, Opera House (heritage building -
live theatre/music all year), Casino, farmers markets, bus/train
🐾 Fully renovated & restored, traditional Victorian home decorated with anitques, old wicker,
paintings & traditional furnishings. Sumptious breakfasts served in gracious dining room. ✓B&B

Oshawa

(east of Toronto; see also Whitby)

Lutczyk, Robert & Michelle Whyte (Emerson Manor B&B)   ☎ (905) 579-3766
132 Stevenson Rd, Oshawa, ON L1J 5M5

From Hwy401 exit at Park Rd and proceed north to Gibb. Turn west to Stevenson Rd and north (2km) to B&B.
$65S $75D $100F $10Add.person   🍴Meals   ▶ 11A,2Ch
🍴 Full   🏠 Res, hist., view, patio   ■ 1D,3F (upstairs)
⊨3D,2Q,1P   ⊲ 4Private   ★ Air,F,TV, private entrance, off-street parking, extra large corner jacuzzi, piano, guest quarters are separate   👋 Designated smoking area   ᴡᴡ French, Polish
🏃 Major regional shopping mall, fine dining, city parks
🚗 Pearson International Airport, downtown Toronto, five Ski Resorts, several golf courses, Lake Ontario, Prince Edward County, Cullen Gardens, downtown Oshawa Murals, paved biking & roller blading trails, Oshawa Military & Canadian Automotive Museums
🏡 Elegant, restored Georgian Revival home, built in 1926, with unique features, period furnishings, many antiques and located in the heart of the city. Extensive renovations have been undertaken in the last year. Hosts are world travellers and enjoy meeting people. Gourmet breakfast is served in special guest breakfast room. Internet phone access in all rooms for business travellers. Visa www.bbcanada.com/3171.html

---

Ottawa

(see also Aylmer (Quebec), Manotik)

Ashworth, Dianna (Paterson House B&B)   ☎ (613) 565-8996, Fax (613) 565-6546
500 Wilbrod St., Ottawa, ON K1N 6N2   E-mail: paterson@cyberus.ca

From Hwy 417 (Queensway) exit at Nicholas St to Laurier, go east to Charlotte St and first right at Wilbrod.
$135S $195D   (plus taxes)   ▶ 8
🍴 Cont.   🏠 Downtown, res., hist., view from guest rooms, riverfront, porch, quiet   ■ 4Ste (upstairs)   ⊨ 1D,3Q
⊲4Ensuite   ★ Air,F,TV in guest rooms, private entrance, off-street parking & on site   👋 No smoking, no pets, children min. age 16   ᴡᴡFrench
🏃 Ottawa River, park with bicycle/pedestrian paths, Embassies, Diplom.residences/stately homes
🚗 Parliament Hill, Rideau Canal, Byward Market, museums, National Arts Centre, shopping
🏡 Magnificient historic Heritage mansion, beautifully restored to original elegance. Enjoy a tranquil and inspiring experience among traditional furnishings and Objects d'art. Deluxe Cont. breakfast is served in sunroom. There is a Health Centre for total mind/body rejuvination on the premises. CCards ⌐CC http://welcome.to/paterson_house

---

Bansfield, Anne-Marie and Irving (Le Gîte Park Ave. B&B)   ☎ (613) 230-9131
54 Park Ave., Ottawa, ON K2P 1B2

Take Metcalfe Exit off Hwy 417 (Queensway). Turn right (east) on Argyle and proceed 1 block to Elgin St(traffic lights). Turn left (north) and then right at Park Ave.
$55S $75D $10Child $20Add.person   ▶ 7
🍴 Full   🏠 Res., older, patio   ■ 2D,1F(upstairs)   ⊨ 3Q,1D,1S
⊲2Sh.w.g.,powder room in one guest room   ★Air,TV,F,LF, parking
👋No smoking   ᴡᴡ French
🏃 Rideau Canal (paths for jogging/cycling/ice skating, Winterlude Festivities, downtown, Parl.Buildings, Nat.Art Gallery, Elgin St & Byward Market, cafés, restaurants, boutiques, Museum of Civilization
🏡 Enjoy warm ambiance in 1904-built elegant home situated in charming residential area and very central location. House specialty is "delicious breads baked by Irving". Well-informed hosts will gladly help with itineraries and advise about local activities. Children welcome. Visa,MC

Ottawa (cont'd)

Coker, Midi (The Olde Bytowne B&B)   ☎ (613) 565-7939, Fax 565-7981
459 Laurier Ave East, Ottawa, ON   K1N 6R4   E-mail: midi@oldebytown.com

From Expressway (417) take Nicholas St Exit onto Laurier Ave. Turn right. From downtown, take
Laurier Ave, cross Canal to east. From Airport on Parkway/Bronson Ave to Laurier, turn right.
$65-69S $70-90D $10child   🍽 Meals   (plus taxes)   ► 14A,4Ch

🍳 Full, homebaked   🏠 Downtown, res., 3-storey, hist., small
acreage, view from guest rooms, riverfront, patio, porch, quiet
■2S,6D,2F (upstairs)   ⊨ 3S,6T,2D,5Q   🛏 3Ensuite, 1private,
2sh.w.g   ★ Air,F,TV,LF, piano, off-street parking   🚭 No
smoking, no pets   ⚓ French
⊼ Strathcona Park, Embassy Row, Rideau River, bus Rte #5,
Strathcona Fountain, Parliament Hill, National Arts Centre,
Ottawa University, walking path, downtown shops, restaurants
🚗 Gatineau Park, Upper Canada Village, Chateau Montebello
📷 Charming Victorian home with International ambiance & vintage decor, nestled among tall
trees along Embassy Row in the quiet downtown neighbourhood of Sandy Hill, facing fountain and
overlooking beautiful Strathcona Park and the idylic River. Enjoy the friendly hospitality,
cosmopolitan charm and afternoon teas. Ideal for honeymoon and special occasions. Hostess offers a
Hospitality Skills Training Programme on how to own and manage a Bed & Breakfast/Inn. Winner
of numerous tourism awards. ✒B&B www.midioldebytown.com

Faubert, Nicole (L'Auberge du Marché)   ☎ (613) 241-6610
87 Guigues Ave., Ottawa, ON   K1N 5H8

Phone for directions.
$60-90S $70-90D $25Add.person   ► 8A
🍳 Full, homebaked   🏠 Downtown, older, duplex, view
■3D,1Ste (main and upper floor)   ⊨1D,4Q   🛏 1Private,
1sh.w.g.   ★KF,sep.entrance 🚭No pets, no children ⚓French
⊼ Parliament Hill, National Gallery, Byward Market, Rideau
Canal and River, National Arts center, Canadian War Museum, ND
Basilica, Major's Hill Park, specialty shops, restaurants
🚗 Skiing, walking,hiking in Gatineau Hills
📷 Completely renovated turn-of-the-Century home beautifully decorated with truly Canadian
ambiance is located in the historic part of the city called "Byward Market", a 25-square-block area
containing all the interesting tourist attractions of Canada's Capital City. Hosts are in their 2nd
decade of welcoming B&B guests to their home. Guest quarters are in adjoining side of duplex.
Breakfast is served in host's quarters dining room. Visa ✒CC

Gervais, Richard (The King Edward Bed & Breakfast)   ☎ (613) 565-6700
525 King Edward Ave., Ottawa, ON   K1N 7N3

From Hwy 417, take the Nicholas Exit to Laurier Ave. Turn right, drive 3
blocks, then left on King Edward Ave. Located in the Sandy Hill District.
$65-80S $75-90D $10Add. person   ► 6
🍳Homebaked   🏠Downtown,hist.,deck,patio   ■2D,1Ste(upst) ⊨1D,2Q
🛏1Private,1sh.w.g.   ★Air,LF,TV in each room, 2 private balconies, second
floor is exclusive for guests, parking   🚭No pets, no smoking   ⚓French
⊼ Parliament Bldgs., Embassies, Byward Market, Sparks Street Mall, Nat.Art
Gallery, boat tours on Rideau Canal (also skating), UofOttawa, Museum of
Civilization, Nat. Arts Centre, Cdn Mint, bicycle paths, restaurants
🚗 Governor General & Prime Minister's residences, Museum of Science &
Technology, Gatineau Park & Meech Lake (hiking, skiing, beaches)
📷 Desig.heritage building, faithfully restored offering a uniqueness
of character & comfort found only in classic older homes, with spacious interior, high ceilings &
enormous bay windows in the tower. ✒B&B www.bbcanada.com/464.html

Khalsa,Harimandir & Siribandu(Natural Choice Vegetarian B&B)   1-888-3HO-YOGA
263 McLeod St., Ottawa, ON   K2P 1A1   E-mail: info@vegybnb.com, Fax 613-230-3043

Phone for directions.
$60S $70D $10Child/Add.person   ▶ 8A,2Ch
🍴 Full   🏠 Downtown, 2-storey   ■ 2D,2F (main & upper
floor)   ⊨6D, cots for children   ⊿2Sh.w.g   ★ Ceiling fans,
guest quarters are separate   🖐 No smoking
🍽 Canadian Museum of Nature, downtown attractions, shops,
restaurants
🔫 Majestic house, authentically designed rooms, decorated with
original artwork, a flourishing garden and relaxed atmosphere. Breakfast consists of organic
gourmet food incl.fresh baked organic whole-wheat breads and is served in guest breakfast room.
Special dietary needs are catered. Ideal place for weddings, honeymoon or special occcasions and
healty retreats. Massage Therapy available. There is a cat in residence. CCards   www.vegybnb.com

---

Mandoli, Ruth (Bye-the-Pond B&B)   ☎ (613) 236-5693, Fax 236-9302
18 Wilton Cr., Ottawa, ON   K1S 2T5   E-mail: survrent@compmore.net

Take Bank St. to Lansdowne Park Stadium and to Wilton Cr on north side of Bank St, crossing the
Rideau Canal.

$55S $75D $10Add.person   ▶ 5A
🍴 Cont.   🏠 Res., older, patio, quiet, view   ■1S,2D(upst)
⊨1S,2D,1R   ⊿ 1Sh.w.g.   ★ Air,F,TV & ceiling fans in guest
rooms, off-street parking   🖐 No smoking, no pets, children min.
age 12   ⤳French, German
🍽 Pathways alongside Rideau Canal, Lily Pond, unique shops &
restaurants, Civic Centre, bus stop (Nos 1/7)
🚗Parl.Hill, galleries, museums, Congress Centre, Universities, Casino de Hull, Gatineau Parc
🔫 Turn of the Century home with Victorian charm and European atmosphere, bordering on Lily
Pond & Rideau Canal and located in quiet residential Glebe District, a community known for its
unique shops and restaurants. Admire the tulip fields along the canal during Tuilp Festival (May)
or lace up the skates and join the skaters on the world's longest skating rink (Rideau Canal). An
imaginative & healthy breakfast is served in the sunroom or out on the patio overlooking the pond
& canal. There is a resident dog "Max".   www.bbcanada.com/3143.html

---

Przednowek, Krystyna & Rafal (By-the-Way Bed & Breakfast)   ☎ & Fax (613) 232-6840
310 First Ave., Ottawa, ON   K1S 2G8   E-mail: bytheway@magma.ca

From Hwy 417 (Queensway) take Bronson Exit south to Powell Ave. Turn left to Lyon St, right to
First Ave and right again to house on left.

$60-75S $70-85D $85-95Ste   ▶ 8
🍴Full, homebaked   🏠Downtown, res., 2-storey, quiet   ■3D,1Ste
(upper & lower level)   ⊨ 4T,2Q,1P   ⊿ 2Private,1sh.w.g.
★Air,TV in guest rooms, kitchen & separate entrance in suite,
central electronic filter, limited wheel-chair access, off-street
parking   🖐No smoking, no pets, children min. age 5   ⤳French
🍽 Civic Centre, Parliament, Lansdowne Park, Dows Lake/Park
(Tulip Festival), Rideau Canal (hiking, skating - winterlude), Bus Station, Carleton U.,museums
🚗 Gatineau Hills (hiking, skiing, cycling), Nat.Gallery of Canada & Arts Centre
🔫 Modern, smoke/pollen free, elegant house with warm and quiet ambiance located in the
central Glebe area, close to truly great amenities of downtown Ottawa - an ideal place for business
or pleasure travellers.Visa,MC ⤳B&B www.magma.ca/nbytheway

Rivoire, Robert & R.G Simmens (Haydon House)　　　☎ (613) 230-2697
18 The Driveway, Ottawa, Ontario　K2P 1C6　　　　　　　1-800-461-7889

Take Metcalfe Street Exit off Queensway to Somerset St. Turn right onto Somerset and to end.

House is at corner of Queen Elizabeth Driveway & Somerset St.W.
$60S　$80D　$90Ste　　　　　　　　　　　　　　　　▶6
⬛Full/Cont　🏠Downtown, res., hist., canal-view, porch ■3D
(upstairs) ⊨2T,2D　⬛1Private,2Sh.w.g. ★Air,F,parking,
sep.entrance, private outdoor portico sitting areas
🜨 Parliament Bldgs, Rideau Canal, Nat.Arts Centre, Nat.Gallery,
canal & river boat tours, Museum of Civilization, Ottawa U.
🚗 Embassies, Governor General/Prime Minister Residences
🜨 Victorian era mansion with traditional pine decor nestled in tranquil residential downtown district, beside the historic and picturesque Rideau Canal (put skates on inside and walk over to the longest skating rink in the world). Breakfast is served in dining room which has over 100-year-old church chairs from the province of Quebec. ✔B&B

Tsui, Helen (Helen House Bed & Breakfast)　　　　☎ (613) 789-8263
168 Stewart St., Ottawa, ON　K1N 6J9

Located west of Parliament Hill. From Hwy 417 exit at Nicholas, turn east
onto Laurier and north on Nelson to Stewart.
$55S　$68D　$90(for 3)　(Long stays available)　　　▶8
⬛ Full　🏠 Downtown, 3-storey, hist., quiet　■ 2D,1F (upstairs)
⊨2T,2D　⬛ Sh.w.g.　★ Air,F,KF,off-street/street parking　🖐 No
smoking, no pets　♥　〜 Chinese, some French
🜨 Parliament Hill, Rideau Centre, Byward Market, National Gallery,
University of Ottawa, restaurants, shops, various public transportation
🚗 Gatineau Park, Hull/PQ, Jacques Cartier Park, Laurentien resorts
🜨 Elegant Victorian home with warm ambience, located in the beautiful surroundings of Sandy Hill district. Breakfast is served in bright eating area.

Waters, Carol and Brian (Australis Guest House)　　☎ & Fax (613) 235-8461
35 Marlborough Ave., Ottawa, ON　K1N 8E6　　　　　E-mail: waters@intranet.ca

From Hwy 417, take Nicholas St Exit and turn right onto Laurier Ave East at first major
intersection with traffic lights. After 1 km turn right onto Marlborough. From Hwy 416 take Hwy

417East and follow as above.
$52-78S/D　$20Add.person　　　　　　　　　　　▶11
⬛ Full　🏠Downtown, older, view　■3 (upstairs)　⊨4D,3S
⬛1Private,2sh.w.g. ★TV 🖐No pets,no drinking,no smoking
🜨 Downtown, Parliament bldgs, Ottawa University, tourist sites
🚗 Gatineau Hills (skiing, water sports, beautiful foliage scenery)
🜨 75-year-old home with fireplaces and leaded windows situated
in beautiful older part of the City with many Embassies,
parkland and the Rideau River. Congenial hosts are winners of Fall Harvest Bake-Off Competition and hospitality Awards. Hostess has published a B&B Cookbook "Breakfast Companion & Whispered Recipes". ✔B&B www.bbcanada.com/1463.html

---

Ottawa Bed and Breakfast　　　　　　　　☎ (613) 563-0161, 1-800-461-7889
18 The Driveway, Ottawa, ON　K2P 1C6

(Mr. Robert Rivoire)
Rates: $49S　$59D　(including a full homecooked breakfast)
Ottawa B&B offers a professional reservation service and represents older homes situated right in the heart of the city, as well as suburban homes. The Agency represents 25 rooms in Ottawa and surrounding areas. For information contact the above.

Owen Sound   *(n/w of Toronto; see also Bognor, Meaford, Clarksburg, Thornbury)*

Breadner, Ron & Mickey (West Winds B&B)   ☎ (519) 376-9003
RR3, Owen Sound, ON   N4K 5N5   1-877-376-9003

Located south on 2nd Ave East & 3.4km from City Hall, just off Hwys 6/10/21.Phone for directions.
$65S/D $15Child/Add.person $75-100F   ⏺Meals   ► 8

🍴 Full, homebaked   🏠 Rural, bungalow, acreage, view from
guest rooms, swimming pool, patio, quiet, secluded   ■ 1D,1F
(main & lower level)   🛏 2D,2Q,1S,1cot   🛁 2Sh.w.g.,
1private   ★ Air,TV in guest room, ceiling fans, guest patio,
separate entrance, guest quarters are separate   Ⓦ Smoking
outside, no pets, call regarding children (age 10 & up)
🏃 Bruce Trail hiking, Inglis Falls, city bus, x-c skiing from door
🚗 Beaches, downhill skiing, snowmobile trails, golfing, ice &
salmon fishing,Maple Syrup/Pumpkin Festival,Celtic/Summer Folk F.,/ Northern Lights F,theatre
🐎 Warm and friendly welcome in spacious home adjacent to very popular Bruce Trail. Enjoy
breakfast overlooking the gardens and in front of a cozy fireplace. Caring hosts enjoy spoiling guests
and love flower gardening, woodworking & crafts. Consideration for vegetarians & food allergies.
Pick-up from buses and drop off/pick-up for hikers (extra charge). There is a very friendly
(non-shedding) Schnauzer ("Tiffany"). 🖊B&B

Burritt, Richard & Sylvia (Rolling Acres)   ☎ (519) 376-5440, (813) 938-4368(USA)
RR5, Owen Sound, ON   N4K 5N7

From Hwys 6 or 10 at Owen Sound take Hwy 21 (Blue Water scenic Rte from Sarnia) to Alvanley
Cross Roads and proceed to B&B next to Sutherlands Farm.
$35S $50D $75F   ► 4

❄ May 24-Nov30   🍴 Full, homebaked   🏠 Rural, ranch-style
bungalow, acreage, patio, deck, solarium, quiet ■2D (main level)
🛏2T,1Q   🛁 1Sh.w.g.   ★ F,LF,FV in guest room, separate
entrance   ⓌNo pets, designated smoking area if necessary,
children min. age 7
🚗 Bruce Trail and Niagara Escarpment, Southampton &
beautiful beaches, clean unpolluted lakes and rivers
🐎 Immaculate flower-filled home located in popular resort country. Enjoy the cosy and
comfortable atmosphere. Doll collectors welcome. Packed lunches for fishermen provided. Large
parking area for boats & trailers. Visa,MC 🖊B&B

Primmer, Philip & Wendy (The Highland Manor B&B)   ☎ (519)372-2699,Fax 372-1441
867-4thAveA W,Owen Sound,ON N4K 6L5   1-800-434-9372
                                E-mail: info@thehighlandmanor.com
Drive up the 9thSt West hill of Owen Sound. At the top, take the next 3 immediate lefts. 5th Ave

West, 8th StWest, then on to 4th Ave A West.
$69-79S $109-119D   ► 14
🍴 Full   🏠 Downtown, res., 3-storey, hist., view from guest
rooms, porch, quiet   ■ 3D,1F (upstairs)   🛏 5Q,1D
🛁4Ensuite   ★ TV/VCR,10F, guest suites are on separate 2nd
floor, elevator, private parking, bicycles free for guests, one-match
firelogs provided   Ⓦ No smoking, no pets
🏃 Bruce Trail hiking, skiing, cycling, live theatre, shops &
restaurants, farmers' market, Tom Thomson Art Gallery, Billy Bishop War Museum, harbour
🚗 Sauble Beach, antique markets, Bruce Peninsula, Inglis Falls, Harrison Park, skiing
🐎 4th Generation Owen Sounders in Canada's largest and oldest Victorian Mansion with 12-foot
high ornate plaster ceilings, stained glass windows, grand hallway, library and an elevator serving 3
stories. Nestled in mature maple trees atop the west hill of the city, with a spectacular view of
Georgian Bay & the historic harbour city below. Relax on the large wrap-around veranda. Breakfast
is served in 3-table estate dining room. There is a 1912 baby grand piano and organ in the music
room. Gift Certicates available. 🖊B&B www.thehighlandmanor.com

Paisley

(south-west of Owen Sound; see also Cargill)

Garton, John & Muriel (Gar-Ham Hall B&B)   ☎ (519) 353-7243
538 Queen St.N., Paisley, ON   N0G 2N0

Phone for directions.
$45-55S $55-65D $20Child   ▶ 10
🍴 Full, homebaked   🏠 Village, 3-storey, 2acres, patio, porch,
quiet   ■ 3D,1F (upstairs)   🛏 2T,1D,1Q,1K,1P   🛁 1Sh.w.g.,
2ensuite   ★4F(marble),TV in guest parlor, private entrance,
off-street parking   🖐 Designated smoking area, no pets
🕺 Heritage walk, canoeing (two rivers meet), museum, antique
shops, restaurants & tavern, specialty shops

🚐 Retired hosts in one of the village's prestigious Victorian homes elegantly decorated with
antiques & collectibles. Enjoy friendly hospitality, good conversation. ✍B&B

Pakenham

(west of Ottawa; see also Almonte, Braeside)

Gillan, Maureen and Art (Gillanderry Farms)   ☎(613)832-2317,832-2556,Fax832-2317
RR4, Pakenham, ON   K0A 2X0   E-mail: gillanfarm@sympatico.ca

Located 4 km north-east of Pakenham off Regional Rd 20 (joins Hwys 17/29). Look for Dominion

Springs Drive at the corner of Kinburn S.Rd (Reg.Road20).
$40S $50D   ▶ 4A,3Ch
🍴Full,homebaked   🏠500-acre farm, hist., view, quiet   ■3(upst)
🛏3Q,2R,1S   🛁1Sh.w.g.,1sh.w.h.   ★TV,F,LF   🖐No smoking
🕺 Dairy & crash crops, quiet country roads along Mississippi
River, spring-fed creek with mineral springs
🚐 Pakenham, 5-span stone bridge, craft shops, Mt. Pakenham
Ski Hill (downhill & x-c skiing), P.Highlands golfing, Ottawa

📣 7th consecutive generation family farm of Irish roots in 135-year-old, green-shuttered home of
limestone. Hosts' hobby is collecting and restoring antique farm tractors (farm museum). Hostess
is a "Decorative Painter". Enjoy generous farm breakfasts, a homey atmosphere and the beautiful
setting. Ideal location to use as a base to tour the Nation's Capital. There is a resident dog ("Bo").

Paris

(north of Brantford)

Courtemanche, Judy & Rick (The St.Andrew Cottage)   ☎ (519) 442-1652, 1-877-856-5558
23 St.Andrew St., Paris, ON   N3L 2W8   E-mail: jacri@golden.net

Take Hwy 403 to Hwy 2 to Paris, turn left at lights on Hwy 5. Follow Willow St to downtown
business section. Turn right on Grand River N to St. George St. Turn left and then left again on

Baird St and right to St. Andrew.
$35-45S $65-70D $10Add.person   🍽Meals   ▶ 6+
🍴 Full   🏠 Res., large exec home, hist., deck, quiet   ■5
🛏3S,2D,1Qcribs   🛁1Sh.w.g,3ensuite   ★LF,FK,F,TV/VCR in
some guest rooms, cozy guest living room, separate entrance,
private parking available, wheelchair friendly, tandom bike for
guests   🖐Smoking on deck, no pets
🕺 Mary Maxim's, "Grand Experiences" for canoeing on the Grand
River, boat rentals, Antique/Classic Car Assoc gathering, Christmas & crafts home tours
🚐 Adelaide Hunter Hoodless/Bell Homesteads, Sports Hall of Recogn., Wayne Gretzky Centre
📣 1880 circa, restored executive home located in heritage district. Spacious, separate guest
quarters have 10' ceilings and period furnishings. Hostess is Wedding Gown Designer and Interior
Decorator, specializing in period decor. Hosts are involved with antique & car restoration on the
premises. There is a resident cat named "Toi". Children's room available. ✍B&B

Parkhill

(north-west of London; see also Ailsa Craig, Forest, Grand Bend)

Rivard, Greg & Alene (Home Town Memories B&B)   ☎ (519) 294-1118
108 Main St., Box 842, Parkhill, ON N0M 2K0

From Hwy402 go north on Hwy81 to Parkhill. Located on Hwy81.
$75S $80D $8Child $10Add.person   ▶ 6A,1Ch
🍴 Cont. 🏠 Village, 2-storey, older, acreage, deck
■2D,1F(upstairs) ⊨3Q,P ⌐1Sh.w.g.,1ensuite ★Air,8F,TV,
ceiling fans in guest rooms, off-street parking ♨Designated
smoking area, no pets, children min. age12
🏃 Restaurants, Village stores, Sports Park, Community Centre
🚗 Golf courses, Summer Theatre, Grand Bend, Lake Huron & beaches, Sarnia, London, Stratford
🔫Fully restored, designated Heritage Home with 8 fireplaces, high ceilings and sweeping
staircase, surrounded by 1.4 acres and sculptured gardens. Hosts will be happy to explain the
heritage of their home. Relax under the majestic pines and feel the gentle breeze. Breakfast is
served in guest breakfast room. Visa ✔CC

Parry Sound

(west of Huntsville; see also Windermere, Port Carling)

Coomber, Sally & Rick (Pass The Thyme B&B)   ☎ 705) 746-8917
40 Cascade St., Parry Sound, ON P2A 1J9   E-mail: recoombe@hotmail.com

Travel north on Hwy 400 and Hwy 69 to Parry Sound. Turn left at McDonalds, continue to River St.
Turn right, cross William St, then River St becomes Cascade St. Proceed to top of hill to B&B.

$50S– $60D $10Add.person   ▶ 6
🍴 Full, homebaked 🏠 Res., hist., 3-storey, quiet ■ 3D,1Ste (2nd & 3rd
floors) ⊨ 2T,3D ⌐ Sh.w.h., 1private ★Air,TV, guest bicycles
available, private entrance/kitchenette in 3rd floor suite ♨ Smoking
outside, no pets
🏃 Town beach, Festival of Sound, 30000 Island cruises, museum
🚗 Provincial parks, hiking, x-c skiing, snowmobiling
🔫 Teacher host in designated heritage home filled with many
collectibles and located in a quiet, convenient area of town. Relax in the
lovely gardens beside the pond or on the porch. Pick-up from bus depot, train
station or town dock available.

Fischer, Heidi & Alex (Fischer's Lakeside Resort & B&B)   ☎& Fax (705) 342-7160
RR1, Shebeshekong Rd, Nobel, ON P0G 1G0   E-mail: fischers@vianet.on.ca

Travel north on Hwy69 past Parry Sound and Nobel. Continue for 12km. Take Woodsroad to the
end then turn right. Look for sign on right.
$50S $70D   ▶4A,2Ch
🍴 Full, homebaked 🏠 Rural, res., 80acres, view from guest
rooms, lakefront, balcony, quiet, secluded ■2D(upstairs) ⊨2Q
⌐1Sh.w.g. ★ TV, guest family room, off-street parking ♨No
smoking, no pets 〰 Swiss German
🏃 Private lake with sandy beach, fishing, boating, hiking, x-c
skiing (all on property), coffee shop/store
🚗 Prov. parks, Parry Sound, 30000 Island Boat Cruises, sightseeing by Air, Dinner Theatre
🔫 Country-style cedar home in family Resort surrounded by quiet nature. overlooking beautiful
Rainy Lake and located in the heart of the popular Parry Sound & Georgian Bay area. A nature
lover's paradise. Also 5 housekeeping cottages available and boat rentals. Winter weekend specials
available. There is a dog and a cat in residence.

Parry Sound (cont'd)

Wissel, Trudy (Blackwater Lake B&B)   ☎ (705) 389-3746, Fax (705) 389-3746
167 Blackwater Lake Rd., RR1, Parry Sound, ON   P2A 2W7   E-mail: trudy@zeuter.com

Take Hwy 69 to Hwy 518 and proceed east through Orrville to Blackwater Lake Rd.

$45-100F(for3) $20Add.person   🍽 Meals   ▶8
💷 Full   🏠 Rural, res., 7 acres, lake opposite, patio, quiet,
secluded   ■4(upstairs)   ⊨ 5S,1D   ⌐2Sh.w.h.,whirlpool
★TV,F,lakeview from 2 rooms,balcony   🖐No pets, not suitable
for small children ~German
🏃 Fishing, boating, swimming, canoeing
🚗 Hunting, hiking, Parry Sound (yearly Festival of the Sound)
🐎 Art/craft-oriented hostess in very homey and comfortable
house. Relax in the sunroom or deck and enjoy the beautiful view to three sides at the lake. Pick-up
at bus stop available. Fishing and paddleboat available at extra charge. Phone reservation
guaranteed until 5PM. ✓B&B   http://www.bbcanada.com

Pembroke   *(west of Ottawa; see also Eganville)*

Pilot, Bob & Lois (Pillars and Lace B&B)   ☎ (613) 732-7674
307 Maple Ave., Pembroke, ON   K8A 1L8   E-mail: boblo@webhart.net

From Hwys 17/41 exit on Paul Martin Dr (turns into River Rd). Cross over MacKay St and proceed

to Maple Ave. Turn left to 2nd house on right past Alfred St.
$55S $65D $10Cot   (Reservations requested)   ▶ 6A
💷 Full, homebaked   🏠 Downtown, 3-storey, hist., patio, quiet
■ 3D(upstairs)   ⊨ 3D   ⌐ 2Shw.g.   ★ LF,F,TV, off-street
parking, guest quarters are separate   🖐 No smoking, no pets,
not suitable for children
🏃 Historic Wall Murals, riverside walking & cycling trail, music in
the park, city buses, Champlain Trail Museum & Pioneer Village
🚗 Snowmobile & x-c ski trails, whitewater rafting & canoeing, entrance to Algonquin Park
🐎 Edwardian (ca 1904) brick home, winner of 1994 Architectural Heritage Award, with original
stained glass and woodwork and filled with antiques & art. Relax in the wicker furnished sunroom
or in the library by the fireplace and enjoy the lovely ambiance. ✓B&B   bbcanada.com/1245.html

---

Penetanguishene   *(on G.Bay west of Orillia; see also Midland,Waubaushene,Vict.Hbr)*

Maurice, Wendy (Chesham Grove Bed & Breakfast)   ☎ (705) 549-3740
72 Church St., Penetanguishene, ON   L9M 1B4   Fax (705) 549-5075

From Toronto take Hwy 400 north to Barrie & Hwy 93 to Penentanguishene. Turn right at 3rd
light (Robert St), then left on Fox St and right on Church St.

$40-50S $50-60D $10Child   ▶ 4A,1Ch
💷 Full, homebaked   🏠 Downtown, res, bungalow, view from
guest rooms, porch, deck   ■ 1D,1F (main floor) ⊨1Q,1D,cot
⌐1Sh.w.h. ★TV/VCR,wheelchair friendly,st/off-st.parking
🖐No pets, smoking in sheltered area outdoor ~some French
🏃 Downtown, shops, churches, restaurants, Penetanguishene
Bay, town dock, 30000 Island Cruise Boat (Georgian Queen),
Winterama (3rdwk/Feb), hiking/biking trails, Penetang Museum
🚗 Discovery Harbour (historic site & live theatre), Huronia Museum & Huron Indian Village
🐎 Quaint fieldstone bungalow with a pleasant & casual family atmosphere. Breakfast is served
in the breakfast nook overlooking McGuire Recreation Park & Penetanguishene Bay. Relax on the
veranda and enjoy the beautiful sunsets from the deck. Hostess is an avid gardener and cat lover
and would be pleased to assist with sightseeing plans. There are cats in residence. ✓CC

Penetanguishene (cont'd)

Robitaille, JP & Georgette (Chez Vous, Chez Nous Couette & Café & B&B)
160 Con16,RR3,Penetang(Lafontaine),ON L9M 1R3   ☎(705)533-2237,Fax (705) 533-1628

Located in Lafontaine. Phone for directions.
$50S $65D $10Child $15Add.person   🍴 Meals   ▶ 21
🍽 Full   🏠 Farm, village, 2-storey, older, view from guest rooms,
deck, quiet 🛏2D,5F(main & lower level) ⊨9S,5D,1Q,2cribs
🛁3Sh.w.g.   ★ TV, separate entrance   🖐 No smoking
〰English (household language is French
🏃 Farm grounds and farm animals, village craft shop
🚗 Beaches, historic sites, boat cruises, shopping malls, skiing
🐾 Spacious home with new extension for guest rooms (built by host), situated in a rare historic southern Ontario farmland environment and located in the heart of Huronia tourist country. After a busy day in the outdoors, relax and enjoy the friendly bilingual hospitality. 〰CC

Unsworth, Marion & Michael (Champlain Lodge)   ☎ (705) 549-3718
438 Champlain Rd., Penetanguishene, ON   L9M 1S5

Take Hwy400 north to Hwy93 and to Penetanguishene. Turn left at Robert and right at Champlain.

$50S $75-95D   ▶6A
🌐 May-Oct (other by special arrangement)   🍽 Cont., buffet
🏠 Rural, bungalow, hillside, view from guest rooms   🛏 3D
(main & lower level)   ⊨ 2T,2Q (incl.waterbed)   🛁 1Private,
1ensuite, 1sh.w.h.   ★Air,F,TV/VCR, private balcony in one
guest room, jacuzzi, off-street parking   🖐 Smoking outdoors, no
pets, not suitable for children 🚗 Discovery Harbour, Huronia
Museum, Huron Indian Village,
Wyemarsh Wildlife Ctre, St.Marie-among-the-Hurons, Martyr's Shrine, 30000 Islands boat cruises
🐾 Modern Log home overlooking Penetanguishene Bay and historic Discovery Harbour and
bordered on two sides by untouched woodland. Relax in the company of congenial hosts and their
pets, or enjoy the privacy in the guest room. Hosts are pleased to help plan sightseeing intineries.
There are 3 cats and a dog in residence. Visa,MC

Perkinsfield   *(north of Barrie; see also Midland, Penetang, Vict.Hbr, Phelpston)*

Houston-Ellery, Rosemary & Bill Ellery (Rosemary & Time B&B)   ☎ (705) 526-2793
5 Claudette Dr., Perkinsfield, ON   L0L 2J0   E-mail: roswil@esolve.net

From Toronto take Hwy 400 north to Barrie and Hwy 93 north to Midland. Proceed west 4km on
County Rd 25 (Balm Beach Rd) to St.Patricks Estates Subdivision in Perkinsfield. Turn left on

Claudette Dr. Look for sign on corner.
$65S $95D $10Child $15Add.person   ▶ 6A,3Ch
🍽 Full, homebaked   🏠 Village, res., raised bungalow, .5 acres,
porch deck, quiet   🛏3D,1F(main & lower level)   ⊨3Q,3cots
🛁3Ensuite ★ KF,LF,F,TV in guest rooms, ceiling fans, off-street
parking, whirlpool,guest sitting/dining area, microwave, fridge,
guest quarters are separate   🖐Desig.smoking area,no pets
🏃 Tennis court, beach
🚗 Historic Huronia, hiking (Trans Canada Trails), golfing, 30000 island boat cruises, skiing
🐾 Executive country home, tastefully decorated, situated in St.Patrick Estates in the hamlet of
Perkinsfield. Relax on the large deck and enjoy the simplicity of country life "Country
Hospitality....Time Well Spent". Breakfast is served in guest breakfast room. Ideal place for
extended stays. There is a mini Schnauzer (Rilly) in residence. Visa,MC 〰B&B
www.datatrav.com/rosemary&time

Perth

(south-west of Ottawa; see also Balderson)

Leach, Rick & Claire (Drummond House)   ☎ (613) 264-9175
30 Drummond St. East, Perth, ON   K7H 1E9

Phone for directions.
$60S $80D $15Add.person   ▶ 7A,2Ch
🍴 Full, homebaked   🏠 Downtown, 3-storey, hist., view from
guest rooms, riverfront, deck, gazebo ■3D(upstairs) ⟷3Ensuite
⊨2S,1D,1Q,1R   ★ Air,F,ceiling fans, TV in guest family room
🚭No smoking, no pets, children min. age 4   ⚑French
🕴 Restaurants, golf course, Tay River, downtown shopping, Great
Rideau Lakes Canal System, antiques
🚗 Ottawa, Westpoint Village, Lanark Mills outlets, Murphy Point & Silver Lake Prov. Parks
🐾 Spacious stone house (ca 1820), in the heart of beautiful historic town and featured in local
walking tour. Ideal place for boaters using the Rideau Lakes Canal System. There are cats.↗CC

McGuinness, Tom & Marty (Rivendell Bed & Breakfast)   ☎ (613) 264-2742, Fax 264-1568
RR4, (Hwy 7), Perth, ON   K7H 3C6   E-mail: plpinc@perth.igs.net

Located on Hwy 7,1.4 km southwest of Perth.ph for directions.

$45-70S $55-70D   🍽 Meals (Oct-Apr)   ▶ 5
🍴 Full, homebaked   🏠 Rural, log house, view, patio, porch,
quiet, acreage   ■ 2D,1S(upstairs), host quarters are separate
⊨1D,1Q,1S ⟷1Sh.w.g., 1ensuite ★LF,guest lounge with library
2nd floor reading area, separate entrance, guest fridge, parking
🚭No smoking, no pets, children by special arrangement ⚑French
🕴 Good restaurant, pond with aquatic wildlife on property, x/c
skiing, skating on pond
🚗 Lakes, parks, conservation areas, swimming, boating, hiking, fishing, downtown Heritage
Perth, factory outlets, antiques, museums, Lanark Rideau Cycle Trail (maps available)
🐾 Elegantly restored log house (ca 1830) with view of pond and creek, with antiques, numerous
wildlife prints, and large library. Breakfast is served in formal dining room. Enjoy the garden with
bugproof gazebo, aromatherapy herb garden, maze, walking paths, perennial garden and antique
shop. Safe bike storage. Pick-up at Rideau Trail/boats. There is a resident dog (not in B&B area).

Peterborough

(east of Toronto; see also Lakefield, Roseneath, Lindsay)

Bottcher, Paul & Karen (Armour Road Studio)   ☎ (705) 745-2071, Fax (705) 745-2943
1308 Armour Rd., RR9, Peterborough, ON   K9J 6Y1

From Hwy 7 By-pass exit at Ashburnham Rd. Turn left at stop sign and left again at next stop sign.
Proceed to Maria St., turn left and cross over bridge, then immediately right at Armour Rd.

$50-55S $60-90D $10Add.person   🍽 Meals   ▶ 11
❄ Apr-Nov 🍴 Full, homebaked   🏠 Sub. bungalow, view,2decks,
riverfront,sunporch ■5   ⊨1K,4Q   ⟷1Private/jacuzzi,
2sh.w.g.   ★Air,TV,F,KF,LF,parking 🚭No smoking ⚑French
🕴 Trent University, Riverview Park Zoo, river rowing, Sunday
afternoon concerts in the park, public route
🚗 Hydraulic Lift Locks, Buckhorn Art Festival, Petroglyphs
🐾Home is situated on the Otonabee River near Trent University
within city limits. Relax in the jacuzzi and enjoy the peace and tranquility of the countryside. House
specialty: "A touch of French cuisine". Free pick-up from Ptb.Airfield, Bus or Trent Severn Locks
may be available. Visa,MC ↗B&B

Peterborough (cont'd)

Bowers, Sam & Mary (DalaRose B&B) ☎ (705) 742-0877
203 Dahousie St., Peterborough, ON   K9J 2M1

Take George St North past Holiday Inn. Turn left on Dalhousie to B&B on left side.

$35S $50D $15Child   ►6
🍴 Full   🏠 Downtown, 2-storey, porch, deck, quiet   ■2F (upstairs)
🛏1S,2T,1Q,1R   🛁 1sh.w.g.   ★ TV in guest sitting room, KF in guest quarters, private entrance, off-street parking, host quarters are separate
✋Designated smoking area, no pets, children min age 10
🏃 Little Lake marina (waterfront Festival, lights showplace, concerts), downtown, antiques, shops, restaurants, Bus Terminal
🚗 Peterborough Lift Locks, Zoo, Trent U., golfing, Canoe Museum
📢 Comfortable home, situated in quiet part of downtown. . Hosts are knowledgeable about local tourism and willing to help with itineraries and attractions. Breakfast is served in the dining room and evening snack in the guest TV sitting room. "Elsie" the cat in residence. ⮑CC

Buchanan, Anna Jean (McLeod House) ☎ (705) 742-5330
486 Albertus Ave., Peterborough, ON   K9J 6A2

From Hwy 401 go north on Hwy 115 to Peterborough. Take Parkway exit and follow to end. Turn right onto Clonsilla which becomes Charlotte St and continue to Monoghan Rd. Turn left and proceed through 1st stoplight to Hopkins Ave. Turn left to Albertus and then right.
$40S $50D   (Discounts for longer stay available)   ►5

🍴 Full, homebaked   🏠 Res., older, multi-storey, garden deck, view, quiet   ■ 1S,2D(upstairs)   🛏1S,2T,1D   🛁 1Sh.w.g., 1sh.w.h.   ★ TV,F, parking   ✋ No pets
🏃 French cuisine restaurant, Trans Canada Trail (large park with hiking, cycling & ski trails), bus routes
🚗 Kawartha Lakes, Trent University, Hydraulic Liftlocks and boat cruises, Trent-Severn Waterway System, Summer Festival of Lights, Pioneer Village, Farmers' Market, Zoo & golf courses
📢 Friendly hospitality in gracious older family home, tastefully decorated and situated on a quiet street in the "Old West End" of the City. Transportation available to bus station & airport. ⮑CC

Hunter, Ruth & Terry (Hunter Farm B&B) ☎& Fax (705) 295-6253
RR9, Peterborough, ON   K9J 6Y1

Travel 7 km east of Peterborough on Hwy 7. Then proceed 3 km north on Hwy 134.
$40S $50D $15Child   🍽 Meals   ►5A,4Ch
🍴Full, homebaked   🏠Farm,2-storey, hist., acreage, view from guest rooms,porches,quiet,isolated   ■1S,2D(upst)   🛏1S,2D,1R,1P
🛁2Sh.w.h.   ★TV,parking   ✋No smoking, inquire about pets
🏃 Riding stable, bird watching, skiing, skating, sleigh riding, biking, boating & fishing in ponds (stocked with bass), sugar shack & walks in maple woods and Christmas trees, large barns, Apiary and wildlife Sanctuary, hill with viewpoint
🚗 Country Store, antique shops, flea markets, galleries, Petroglyphs (Indian Writings), Trent U.
📢 Congenial middle-aged hosts in spacious 1879 solid brick home, updated to include modern conveniences, while maintaining its original character and surrounded by 245 acre very private farm setting of ponds, fields, woods & wetlands in the popular Kawartha Lakes tourist region. Relax in the sunroom or on the large verandas and watch birds and wild animals in fields. Canada Geese & black swans are on the pond. There are a horse, a dog, cats, sheep, a miniature donkey, goats and pigs. A perfect child's get-away! ⮑B&B whokey.com/hunterfarm

Peterborough (cont'd)

Lindsay, Marlis (King Bethune Guest House)   ☎(705)743-4101,Fax(705)743-8446
270 King St.Peterborough,ON   K9J 2S2   E-mail: marlis@sympatico.ca, 1-800-574-3664

Located in downtown. From clock tower travel, south on George St, 1block, turn right on King St.

$74S $84-155D $20Add.person   (plus tax)   🍴 Meals   ▶ 10A,2Ch
🍲 Full(menu)   🏠 Downtown, 2-storey, hist., patios, porch, quiet
■ 2D,1Ste (upstairs and lower level)   ⊨ 1Q,2K,plus 1Q(futon)
🛁3Ensuite   ★ Hot-tub/F/TV/VCR/dataports/Casablanca ceiling
fans in guest rooms, room door locks, sauna, garden hot-tub, private
entrance for suite, garden fountain & fireplace, off-street parking
ⓌSmoking on porch
🕴 Library, P.O., restaurants, shopping, Little Lake (marina), art
galleries, bicycle/walking/nature trails, Trent Severn Waterway
🚗 Prov.Parks, Burleigh Falls & 4th-Line Theatre, lakes, hiking, skiing, Toronto
🐾 Spacious Victorian house situated in the heart of downtown with a beautiful walled English
garden (featured in 1994 Art Gallery Garden tour). Breakfast is served in the dining room, kitchen
or on the roofed garden patio at guests' schedule. Relax, read or socialize in the comfortable
surroundings. Office facilities & meeting space. Business travellers & Christmas holiday guests
especially welcome. Cycling route maps available. ✎CC   http://www3.sympatico.ca/marlis

---

Pollock, Elsie (By The River B&B)   ☎ (705) 742-7963
621 River Rd South, Peterborough, ON   K9J 1E6

From Hwy 7 take Lansdowne St West to River Rd South. From Hwy 115 proceed to Bensfort Rd.
Turn left to River Rd South and look for the sign of the rooster. Coming by boat, go south on East
Bank of Lock 19 on Trent Canal System and look for the sign of the ducks.

$40S $45-50D $5Child   ▶ 7
🍲 Full, homebaked   🏠 Res., split-level, riverfront   ■2D,1F
(upstairs)   ⊨ 2T,1D,1Q, cot   🛁1sh.w.g.   ★F,TV,off, street
parking, guest quarters are separate   ⓌNo smoking, no pets,
children min. age 2
🕴 Peterborough Lift Lock, restaurants, fishing, swimming,
boating, Festival of Lights, museums, x-c skiing, sporting events,
city bus route
🚗 Bethany Hills skiing, snowboarding, historic sites, art exhibits/gallery, churches
🐾 Spacious back-split suburban home situated on a large well-treet lot on the Trent Canal. Enjoy
the first cup of tea or coffee on the patio by the water's edge or wander through the gardens. In
winter warm up by the cozy fireplace.

Wilson, Sandie & Steve (Wisteria Bed & Breakfast)   ☎ (705) 749-5714
580 Gilmour St., Peterborough, ON   K9H 2K2   E-mail: swilson@lindsay.iqs.net

From downtown Peterborough, go north on Water, left on Charlotte, right on Monaghan and right
on Gilmour to house on left side.

$75-85S $85-95D $10Add.person   ▶ 4A
🍲 Full, homebaked   🏠 Downtown, 3-storey, older, verandas,
patio, swimming pool, balconies   ■ 2D   ⊨ 1Q,1K
🛁1Private, 1ensuite   ★ 3F, library, jacuzzi   Ⓦ No smoking,
no pets, no children
🕴 Restaurants, entertainment, shops, boat tours, Little Lake, Lift
Locks, Festival of Lights, Canoe Museum, Trent University, Sir
Sandford Fleming College, Art Gallery, hospital, historic walks
🚗 Curve Lake Indian Crafts, Buckhorn Wildlife & Art Festival, Lang Century Village, Caves
🐾 Warm welcome and friendly hospitality in luxurious Victorian home. Breakfast is served at
poolside or balcony or in the formal dining room with fireplace. After a busy day of travelling or
sightseeing, relax in the library or by the pool and enjoy the gardens. There is a 17 year old cat in
residence. ✎B&B   www.bbcanada.com/3840

Petrolia

(south-east of Sarnia; see also Mooretown)

Currah, Edgar & Carol (Wander Inn B&B)   ☎ (519) 882-1849, 1-888-892-6337
4107 Catherine St., Petrolia, ON   N0N 1R0

Take Hwy 402 to Hwy 21 cut-off and continue 13km to Petrolia Line. Turn left and proceed through Petrolia. Turn right on Eureka St and left on Catherine St.
$40S $50D $10Child/Add.person $65F   ► 6
🍴Full,homebaked 🏠Res.,hist.,2-storey,patio,quiet ■3D(upstairs)
╞═2T,3D 🛁 1Sh.w.g.(whirlpool) ★Air,TV,LF ceiling fans,
off-street parking ✋ No smoking, no pets
🚶 Shopping, antique shops, Victorian architecture, live theatre
🚗 Oil Museum of Canada, working oil fields (Petrolia Discovery),
Chemical Valley, St.Clair River Parkway, golfing, bridge to US
🔫 Warm welcome in comfortable home filled with antiques and crafts and located on a tree-lined street. Watch TV in the family room or relax on the veranda with a cup of coffee or seasonal beverage. Browse through the rustic craft corner (new little store at the back of the house). Breakfast is served in the dining room. There is a small dog in residence. ✍CC

Phelpston

(north of Barrie)

Van Casteren, Lynda & Nicholas (Nicholyn Farms B&B)   ☎ 1-888-203-8313
RR2, Phelpston, ON   L0L 2K0   Fax (705) 737-2972

Located 10km north of Barrie at 3088 Horseshoe Valley Rd West. Travel north on Hwy 400 to Horseshoe Valley Rd (Exit 117), proceed west 3km to top of hill. Or take Hwy 27 north to Horseshoe Valley Rd, proceed east 2km.
$50S $60D $10Child   🍽 Meals   ► 10
🍴 Full, homebaked 🏠 Rural, 130acres, 2-storey, hist., view
from guest rooms, porch, deck, quiet ■ 2D,1F(upper & lower
level) ╞═1S,3Q,4cots,crib 🛁 1Private, 2ensuite ★Air,F,TV
in guest rooms, off-street parking ✋ No smoking, no pets,
children welcome 〰 basic Dutch & French
🚶 Hiking (Ganaraska Trail), cycling, snowmobiling, x-c skiing,
birdwatching, walking on country roads, horseback riding, shops
🚗 Golfing, skiing, theatre, quaint shops, galleries, museums, dining, cruises, Wasaga Beach
🔫 Charming, completely renovated, spacious farmhouse surrounded by lawns, gardens and trees in a parklike setting and situated on a working hog farm. Breakfast is served in special guest breakfast rooms. Relax by the wood burning fireplace in the guest lounge or in the TV room and enjoy Ontario's popular resort area. Visa,MC ✍B&B www.nicholyn.com

---

Picton

(south of Bellev.; see also Bloomf, Wellington)

Allcorn, Donna & Sid (The Doll House B&B)   ☎ & Fax (613) 393-1744
RR1, Picton, ON   K0K 2T0   E-mail: ophasid@kos.net

From Hwy 401 take Hwys 33/62/49 south to Bloomfield. Continue south on Hwy 12 (West Lake Rd). Turn right at Isaiah Tubbs Resort. Proceed .8km to B&B. Look for sign.
$55S $60D $15Child $80-90F $15Add.person   🍽 Meals   ► 2A,2Ch
🍴 Full 🏠 Rural, bungalow, view from guest rooms, lakefront,
deck ■ 1(main floor) ╞═1D,1P,1R 🛁1Sh.w.h. ★Fan,
separate entrance ✋No smoking, no pets ❤
🚶 Private sandy beach, swimming, fishing, walking, gift shop on
premises (dolls & crafts), boat & sail rentals
🚗 Sandbanks Prov.Park, golfing (Picton), antiques, craft shops
🔫 Warm welcome in bright and spacious home with resort-like
surroundings, yet tranquil country life atmosphere. Breakfast is
served with a view of the Sand Dunes. There are 2 dogs and a rabbit in residence. ✍ CC

Picton (cont'd)

Carroll, Bob and Mary Lou (Carroll's Waterfront Bed & Breakfast)   ☎ (613) 373-2166
10922, Adolphustown, Hwy 33, Loyalist Pkwy, RR1, Bath, ON   K0H 1G0

Located 1.6km east of Glenora Ferry and 12km east of Picton.
$40S $60D   ► 8
🍽 Full, homebaked   🏠 Rural, bungalow, acreage, view, patio,
waterfront, quiet   ■3(main & lower level)   ⊨2T,2P(D,Q)
🛁1Private, 1sh.w.h.   ★TV,F,LF,KF, use of canoe, parking
👋Smoking on deck only, no pets
🏃 Swimming, canoeing, dock, fishing, Loyalist Cultural Centre,
Adolphustown Prov. Park, restaurants
🚗 Sandbanks Prov.Park, marina, Napanee, Picton, Kingston, Cheese factory, arts & antiques
🚗 Very bright and modern waterfront home situated on Adolphus Reach. Hosts have taken
bicycle trips in England/France and visited many delightful B&B places. Relax in the hammock in
the small orchard or on the deck and enjoy the view and friendly cottage-like atmosphere. ✔ B&B

Dobinson, Irene & Bill (Duck and Loon B&B)   ☎ (613-476-8167
630 Hwy 49, RR2, Picton, ON   K0K 2T0   E-mail: dobinson.res@sympatico.ca

From Hwy401, take Exit566 and Hwy49 south for 26km. From the west (Toronto) on Hwy401
travel to Belleville (Exit543) and Hwy62 south. Continue on Hwy33 east to stop sign in Picton.

Turn left on Hwy49 to B&B on right (2km)
$65-80S/D   ► 6A
✚May1-Oct15–   🍽 Full, homebaked   🏠 Rural, ranch-style,
1.5acres, view from one guest room, lakefront, deck, quiet,
secluded   ■3D(main floor)   ⊨2T,1D,1Q   🛁1Ensuite,1sh.w.g.
★Air,TV in one guest room & in guest family room, off-street
parking, guest quarters are separate   👋 No smoking, no pets,
not suitable for children
🏃 Golf Course, private acreage overlooking Picton Bay, watch sailboats and lake yachts pass by
🚗 Sandbanks, Lake on the Mountain, shopping, fine dining, antique shops, art studios, theatre,
museums, Yacht Club, scenic drives along Hwy33 to Glenora Ferry or along the water to Kingston
🚗Tastefully decorated ranch-style home overlooking beautiful Picton Bay. Breakfast is served in
the formal dining room with a breathtaking view. Relax and enjoy the beauty of the sun setting on
the Bay, as ducks splash in the water and the loons call out. Host is an antique car enthusiast and
hostess enjoys refinishing upholstery. There are 2 cats in residence. Visa

---

Dubyk, Pat & Ron (Ginkgo Tree Place)   ☎ (613) 476-1792,Fax (613) 416-4699
352 Main St. E, Box 4219, Picton, ON   K0K 2T0   E-mail: ginkgo@kos.net

For scenic road from Kingston, take Hwy 33 to Glenora Ferry.

$65-80S/D   ► 8
🍽Full   🏠Res., older, patio   ■4D(upst)   ⊨2T,1Q,2D   🛁2Sh.w.g.
★Ceiling fans, off-street parking, TV in guest sitt.room, 2 guest
verandas   👋No smoking, no pets, children min. age 10
🏃 Historic museums, shopping, yacht club, tennis, antique shops
🚗 Sandbanks beaches, excellent bicycling, ice fishing, skating
🚗 Classic, large Victorian home, beautifully decorated, in very
convenient location with large landscaped grounds and gardens
including a large "Ginkgo" tree. ✔ CC www.bbcanada.com/2429.html

Picton (cont'd)

Grondin, Carolyn (Tall Pines B&B) ☎ (613) 476-7424
41 Ferguson St., Box 995, Picton, ON K0K 2T0 E-mail: cgrondin@kos.net

From West, take Exit 522 (Wooler Rd S) to Hwy 33 (Loyalist Pkwy). Turn left to Picton and right
on Ferguson St. From East, take Exit 566 and proceed south on Hwy 49 to Picton. Turn left on
 Ferguson St.
$50S $60D $15Add.person ▶6
⏹Full 🏠Res, 2-storey, porch, quiet ■2D(upstairs) ⊨1S,2D
🛏1Sh.w.h. ★Air,TV, window fans, off-street parking ✋No
pets, designated smoking area
🏃 Downtown area, restaurants, unique shops
🚙 Sandbanks Prov.Park, Lake Ontario beaches, tour route for
bicycling/boutiques/antique shops, Lake on the Mountain
🔫 Warm welcome in quiet, central home, built ca 1880, located in historic town of Ontario's only
Island County which is surrounded by much history, winding roads & beautiful beaches. Delicious
breakfast is served in the dining room. A perfect place for a great holiday. ✍CC
www.bbcanada.com/1321.html, www.pec.on.ca

Malachowski, Marianne P. (Marianne's Bed & Breakfast) ☎ (613) 476-3992
127 Main St., Picton, ON K0K 2T0

From West (Toronto) on 401, take Exit 522 (Wooler Rd) and continue on Hwy 33 (Loyalist
Parkway) to Picton. From East on Hwy 401, take Exit 566 and proceed south on Hwy 49. Turn
right on Main St in Picton.
$45-50S $60-70D $10Child $15Add.person 🍽Meals ▶8
🔋 Full, homebaked (served buffet) 🏠 Downtown, 2-storey, hist., porch,
quiet, deck, pond ■2D,1F(upstairs) ⊨2S,2D,1Q,R 🛏 1Sh.w.g.,
2sh.w.h. ★ F,TV in guest family room, air-conditioners, ceiling fans,
off-street/street parking ✋Smoking outside
🏃 Regent Theatre (live Summer Festival), antique & craft shops, museums,
historic houses, restaurants, exceptional sailing, golfing, Picton Harbour
🚙 Sandbanks Provincial Park (miles of beach), guided walks along dune
trails, sport fishing, scenic drives in Quinte region
🔫 Spacious and charmingly decorated (ca1840) Quaker-style stucco & brick house with a blend of
unpretentious and sophisticated old-fashioned elegance, located on the main street in town. A
memorable Gourmet breakfast is served in the formal dining room or on the deck overlooking the
beautiful gardens with pond. Hostess is a retired Nurse and loves gardening and history. Relax by
the fireplace and enjoy country hospitality at its best. There is a dog in residence. Visa, ✍B&B

Williams, Bob and Helen (Wilhome Farmhouse B&B) ☎ (613) 393-5630
RR1, Picton, ON K0K 2T0 Fax: (613) 393-5108

Take Hwy 33 (Loyalist Parkway). Between Bloomfield & Picton, turn south on Cty Rd 32 for 1km,
watch for checkerboard road sign in yard.
 $45S $55-60D $10Child $20Add.person ▶6A,3Ch
❄May-Oct.(other by reservation) 🔋 Full,homebaked
🏠300-acre farm, hist., deck ■2D,1F(upstairs) ⊨2S,2D,1Q,1R,
playpen for child's bed 🛏 1Sh.w.g.,1sh.w.h. ★ TV,F, separate
entrance, parking ✋ No smoking
🏃 Walk on country roads, cycling, birdwatching, Bloomfield
🚙 Picton, antique/craft shops, museums, Sandbanks Prov Park,
beaches, fishing, fine dining, Belleville, Kingston
🔫 Circa 1850 Loyalist home (with original pine floors and woodwork throughout and antiques
abound, including the original bake oven/fireplace in the kitchen). Situated on rolling farmland,
now part of a working farm settled by the host's family in 1814. Relax on the deck overlooking the
countryside and be amazed by the star-filled skies. There are two cats in residence.

Picton (cont'd)

York, Marg (Log House B&B)   ☎ (613) 476-5978
Box 413, 2 Henry St., Picton, ON   K0K 2T0

Take Exit 522 from Hwy 401 (Wooler Rd South) and travel south on Hwy 33 to Picton. Upon entering town limits, turn left on first street to house on right.
$45S $75D $10Child   ▶ 4A,1Ch
🍴 Full, homebaked   🏠 Res., 2-storey, log home, .5 acres, view from guest rooms, porch, deck, quiet   ■ 2D (main & upper floor)   ⊨2T,1Q ⊲2Ensuite, whirlpool bath   ★Air,F,TV in 2 guest rooms,off-street park.,sunroom ⊛Smoking outside,no pets
⚑ Downtown Picton, harbour, antique & craft shops
🚐 Sandbanks Provincial Park, extensive Lake Ontario shoreline

🦯 New modern log home, built by hosts, with cathedral ceilings, open plan, lounge area with fireplace and landscaped flower gardens. Retired couple are natives of the area. Breakfast special is buttermilk pancakes served with fruit sauces, maple syrup; fresh preserves & sweet salsa. ✔B&B
http://www.bbcanada.com/1187.html

Pike Bay

Winters, Elinor & Bob (Winter's Wharf Bed & Breakfast)   ☎ & Fax (519) 793-3875
25 Purgatory Rd., RR1, Mar, ON   N0H 1X0   E-mail: bwinters@bmts.com

From Wiarton, take Hwy 6 north to Pike Bay Rd. Turn west to Whiskey Harbour Rd and north to Purgatory Point. Located near Pike Bay on the shores of Lake Huron (west side of the Peninsula).
$55S $65D $15Roll-away $10Add.person   🍽 Meals   ▶ 9
🍴 Full, homebaked   🏠 Rural, 2-storey, view from guest rooms, lakefront, private deck, quiet, isolated   ■ 3D,1F (upstairs)   ⊨1D,2Q,1R   ⊲1Sh.w.g., 1sh.w.h.   ★ F,LF,TV in common room, 6ft whirlpool tub   ✋ No smoking, no pets, no children
⚑ Lake Huron, nature walks, fishing, birdwatching, boating
🚐 Bruce Trail hiking, x-c ski/snowmobile trails, Lion's Head, harbours, shopping, Georgian Bay beaches, Bruce Peninsula National Park, Tobermory Ferry to Manitoulin Islands

🦯 Comfortable home with 2 large decks with panoramic view of Whiskey Harbour & Lake Huron and the tree-covered shore of the Bruce Peninsula. Relax on the 3nd-storey private deck. Enjoy the tranquil atmosphere and sleep to the restful sound of waves on the rocky shore. Breakfast is served on the wharf-like deck. There are 2 Golden Retrievers. Visa ✔B&B   www.bbcanada.com/465.html

Port Carling   *(west of Bracebridge; see also Windermere)*

Nicholson, Terry & George (Nicholson's Bed & Breakfast)   ☎ (705) 764-1095
RR1, Port Carling, ON   P0B 1J0

Located on Hwy 118 and 18 km west of Bracebridge (8 km from Port Carling). Look for sign opposite the Thom Wroe Rd.
$50S $60-70D   ▶ 6A
✖ not X-mas & New Years   🍴 Full   🏠 Rural, 2-storey, quiet, chalet-style,acreage, patio   ■2D,1Ste(upstairs)   ⊨2T,1Q,1D   ⊲1Ensuite, 1sh.w.g.   ★ F,TV,parking   ⊛ No children, no pets, restricted smoking, no food or beverages in guest rooms
⚑ Picnic area & beach on Lake Muskoka, boat launching ramp
🚐 Excellent restaurants, golf courses, steamship cruises

🦯 Spacious home surrounded by many trees, virgin bush and unusual rock formations and situated near a section of Lake Muskoka. Long time B&B hosts are originally from England and have travelled the B&B route in many different countries. ✔B&B

Port Carling (cont'd)

Mann, Wilsie & Bob (DunRovin B&B) ☎ (705) 765-7317
Box 304, Port Carling, ON P0B 1J0 E-mail: dunrovin@muskoka.com

Take Hwy 169 north to Mortimer's Point Rd (Muskoka Rd 26). Turn right and proceed 2 km to B&B on left. Look for sign and No 1197.

$110S/D ► 4A
Full, homebaked Rural, hillside, acreage, view from guest rooms, lakefront, sundeck on boathouse, quiet 2D(ground level) 2T,1Q (incl.romantic canopy) 2Ensuite
★Ceiling fans, separate entrance, off-street parking, guest quarters are separate No smoking, no pets, no children
Swimming, canoeing, paddle boating, x-c skiing
Artisans shops, boat cruises, boutiques, scenic drives, theatres, museums, Segwun boat tours
Picturesque home surrounded by a spacious deck overlooking the north bay of Lake Muskoka. Guests who come by plane, boat or car are welcome to enjoy the warmth and charm of a cottage with all the comforts of home. Relax in the hammock and watch the herons go by or in the hot tub in the winter after a day on the ski trails. Breakfast is served upstairs in great room or on deck overlooking the lake. Hosts are pilots and both know the local area well. ✓B&B
www.bbmuskoka.com/dunrovin

Port Dover

(on Lake Erie, s/of Simcoe; see also Waterford)

Koch, Lena & Fred (Dover Lodge) (519) 583-0729, Fax (519) 583-0302
224 St.George St. Box 269, Port Dover, ON N0A 1N0 E-mail: lenakoch@sympatico.ca

From Hwy403 travel to Simcoe and take Hwy24 south to Hwy6 to Port Dover. Located 1 road west of Main St.
$55-85S/D $20Add.person (longer stay discounts) ► 16+
Full, buffet-style (European) Village, 2-storey, hist.
3D,3F plus apt. 5D,2S,2Q 3Sh.w.g. ★TV/fans in guest rooms, quest quarters are separate Smoking outside, no pets, children min. age 10 German
Beach, Ligthhouse Festival Theatre, shops, restaurants
Brantford, Simcoe, Lake Ontario, Hamilton, Kitchener, London, Stratford, Toronto
Large, stately, Century home (ca 1858) with special character, furnished with old and timeless furniture and enhanced with charming German hospitality. Situated in attractive fishing town on the beautiful North shore of Lake Erie. Breakfast is served on the porch and is enjoyable in the morning air. Perfect place for a holiday or just a night or two. There is a cat in the house, but kept away from guests. http://www3.sympatico.ca/lenakoch

---

Port Hope

(east of Oshawa; see also Cobourg, Colborne)

McCormick, Diane and David Priest (Uppertowne Inn) ☎ (905)) 885-5694
187 Walton Street, Port Hope, ON L1A 1N7

From Hwy 401 exit at Hwy 2 or Hwy 28 for downtown Port Hope. Look for house near top of the Walton Street (Hwy 2) hill.

$45-55S $60-70D $10Child/Add.person ► 9
Full Downtown, hist., res., 3-storey, patio, quiet, large ravine lot 4D,1S(upst) S,T,Q,R 2Sh.w.g. ★Air,F,TV in guest room, parking No smoking
Antique shops, fishing
Beaches in Prince Edward County, Ganaraska Forest, good dining spots, civilized watering hole, excellent river/stream fishing
Gracious Georgian-style home dating back to 1857, (at the time serving as a hotel to horse and carriage travellers), is situated in attractive town which is largely 19-Century without being in any way artificial. Bicycle tours organized. There are 2 cats and a dog in the house. ✓CC

Powassan
(south of North Bay; see also Sundridge, Mattawa)

Hynd, Jo-Anne Elaine (Satis House Bed & Breakfast)
RR2, 258 English Line, Powassan, ON   P0H 1Z0

☎ (705) 724-2187
E-mail: satisbed@vianet.on.ca

From Powassan travel south on Hwy 11 and turn west (right) onto English Line for 1.5km. Located 10km north of Trout Creek.
$50-75S/D $25Add.person   🍽 Meals   ► 11
💧 Full, homebaked   🏠Rural, 100 acres, view, quiet ■4(upstairs)
⊨5T,2D,1Q   🛁 1Sh.w.g., 1ensuite   ★ TV,VCR   🚬Smoking outside only, children min. age 10   ↝ French
🏃 Hiking, snowmobiling, swimming
🚗 Nipissing/Trout/Nosbonsing Lakes, beaches, museums, antinque & craft shops, Almaguin Highlands, Algonquin Pk, North Bay waterfront attractions
🐎 Unique, new Georgian-style home with high ceilings and gorgeous view of open land, gardens and pine forest growing on site. Enjoy "the best butter tarts in the North". There is a cat in residence. Visa ↝B&B www.satishouse.com

---

Prescott
(south of Ottawa on US border; see also Brockville)

Cudlipp, Vivienne & Graham (Blue Heron Inn B&B)
RR1, Box Cr2, 1648 Cty Rd 2, Prescott, ON   K0E 1T0

☎(613)925-0562, Fax(613)925 0737
E-mail: cudlipp@cybertap.com

From Hwy 401 take Exit 716 south on Edward St into Prescott. Turn right on King St (Hwy 2) and proceed 1.9km out of Prescott to Inn on right side.
$65-100S/D $10Add.person   🍽 Meals   ►10-12
💧 Full, homebaked, buffet   🏠 Rural, 2-storey, hist., acreage, view from guest rooms, riverfront, swimming pool, patio, quiet
■ 5D (main & upper level)   ⊨ 2D,3Q,2R   🛁 5Private   ★Air (ground floor), 2F,TV in one guest room, ceiling fans, 2guest sitting rooms, off-street parking, guest quarters are separate 🚬No smoking, no pets,children min age 12
🏃 Prescott, Fort Wellington, Forwarder's Museum, scuba diving shop, wreck of "Rothesay" across street (lessons & boat dives), snowmobiling, x-c skiing, Prescott Marina (Sunday summer concerts)
🚗 Brockville, 1000 Islands, Upper Canada Village, Bridge to USA, summer theatres
🐎 1857 Quarried Stone House with 2 acres situated on edge of the St.Lawrence River. Enjoy the quiet sophistication and peaceful atmosphere and relax on the bench by the river to watch beautiful sunrises and sunsets, or take a dip in the heated inground pool. There is a dog in residence. Parking for boats & snowmobiles. Weekly rates available. Visa,MC   www.blueheroninn.on.ca

---

Ridgetown
(east of Chatham; see also Blenheim)

Ure, Margaret & Glen (Ridgeland Bed & Breakfast)
RR2, Ridgetown, ON   N0P 2C0

1-800-737-1897
☎ (519) 674-2461

From Hwy 401, take Exit 101, proceed south on Kent Rd 15 for.4km & look for 3rd house on right
$60S $85D   (Reservations please)   ► 4
💧 Full, homebaked   🏠 Farm, 2-storey, hist., acreage, swimming pool, patio, porch, deck, quiet   ■ 2D (main & upper level)
⊨2Q   🛁 2Ensuite, jacuzzi   ★ Air,F,TV in guest room, separate entrance, large common room with player piano   🚬 No smoking, no pets
🏃 Surrounding cash crop farm grounds
🚗 Country auctions, Uncle Tom's Cabin, golfing, Rondeau Park
🐎 Century home (built in 1873) purchased by the host family and moved to their farm grounds, completely renovated blending 1800's charm with today's amenities and tastefully furnished with authentic antiques. Congenial hosts love to tell the storey and historic facts of the home. Guest rooms are separate from host quarters. ↝CC

Rockwood
(west of Toronto; see also Acton, Guelph)

Isbrucker, Jane (Country Spirit)   ☎& Fax (519) 856-9879
RR5, Rockwood, ON   N0B 2K0   E-mail: cspirit@sympatico.ca

From Hwy 401, take Exit 312 north (Guelph Line) and continue for 16 km to Indian Trail (0.5 km past stop sign). Turn left and left again on Ash St to 2nd property on right side.

$50-$80S/D $25Add.person   ⦿Meals   (weekly rates avail)   ► 6

Full, homebaked   Rural, cedar home, country view from guest rooms, 5 acres, decks, quiet, pond, wooded area, secluded ▪ 2 (main and upper floor)   ⊨ 2Q,1D   1Ensuite, 1private ★ Air,TV, F, parking ⦿No smoking, no pets, not suitable for children ⤳French, Dutch, some German
🏃 Hiking, biking, x-c skiing, walks on country lanes & wooded acreage from back door
🚗 Exclusive boutique shopping, exc.dining, antiques, airport
📷 Spacious, elegant and comfortable country home surrounded by virgin woods and pleasant gardens and pond. Situated at the edge of the village of Eden Mills in the beautiful Eramosa River Valley. A "hidden jewel" and ideal spot for a relaxed mini-vacation. Active hostess is well informed and involved in local activities and happenings. Ideal place for cyclers. ✔B&B
www.bbcanada.com/1177.html

Roseneath
(south-east of Peterborough)

DeLaFigueroa, Sylvia   ☎ (905) 352-3552
RR4, Roseneath, ON   K0K 2X0

From Hwy401 take Hwy45 north and proceed 23km to Gulf Gas Station. Please phone from here for pick-up.
$80S/D $35Add.person   ► 2A,2Ch
❄Summer only   Full, homebaked   Rural,, hist.,acreage, loghouse, view from guest rooms, patio, screened sunporch, deck, quiet, secluded ▪ 1D,1S (upstairs) ⊨1Q,1S   1Ensuite, 1sh.w.g ★ TV, ceiling fans ⦿Designated smoking area, no pets, children min.age 10 ⤳ Spanish
🚗 Excellent fishing (Walley, Perch, Bass, Trout), boat rental, popular Alpine Resort, Cobourg
📷 Long-time hostess (formerly in Montreal) in new location. Large, new rustic/elegant loghome with beautiful staircase and furnished with antiques. Situated on Rice Lake, surrounded by 5acres of trees and lovely scenery. Feel the cool breeze from the lake. Hostess is an Abstract Artist and many of her works are displayed throughout the house. Ideal place for birding. Families with children may pitch tents. There is a dog and a cat in residence.

Sarnia
(on Lake Huron, west of London; see also Forest, Mooretown, Petrolia)

Robertson, Ellen & John (Bluewater Bed & Breakfast)   ☎ (519) 336-7457
21 Bradley Place, Sarnia, ON   N7V 4H6

From Hwy 402, take Christina St Exit and proceed north to Cathcart Blvd. Turn right to O'Dell, then left on Bradley Place.
$45S $55D   ► 6A
Cont, homebaked   Res., multi-storey, patio, quiet ▪ 3D (upstairs) ⊨2T,1D,1Q   1Shw.h., 1ensuite, 1private ★Air,F,TV/VCR in guest sitting room, parking ⦿ No smoking, no pets, children min. age 15
🏃 Sandy beach, Post Office, Mini Mall, Video Rental, park with hiking paths & picnic tables, boat launch & marina
🚗 Restaurants, hist.buildings, Petrolia Discovery, museums, Wetlands & bird watching, golfing
📷 Quiet, modern, owner-designed home filled with curios from around the world & a mixture of modern & 19th Century furnishings. Savour breakfast served on the garden patio. ✔CC

Sarnia (cont'd)

Ellis, Connie (Catalpa Tree B&B)   ☎ (519) 542-5008, 1-800-276-5135
2217 London Rd, Sarnia, ON N7T 7H2   E-mail: catalpa@ebteck.net, Fax (519) 541-0297

From Hwy 401, take 402 westbound and Mandaumin Rd Exit. Proceed to County Rd 22 (old Hwy 7 London Line). Turn right and then 5km to B&B on left. From Hwy 402 eastbound exit at Airport

Rd to County Rd 22 (Hwy 7) and turn left 2km to B&B on right.
$40S $51D $10Child 🍽 Meals   ▶6
🍹 Full(gourmet)   🏠 Farm, Century home, 2-storey, porch, quiet ■3D(upstairs) ⊨2T(K),1Q,1D ⊲🔲1Sh.w.g.
★Air,F,TV,LF, sep.entrance, guest quarters are separate, gas fireplaces in some guest rooms 🖑 Designated smoking area
〜some French
🏃 Golf Course across the road at end of lane

🚗 St.Clair River Parkway, Sarnia Bay, Lake Huron beaches, US border, Victoria Playhouse
👉 Victorian (ca 1894) home with a warm mix of contemporary and period pieces. Relax on the veranda, or play a game of croquet. Golf & gourmet weekends & interesting day tours can be arranged. Breakfast is served in special guest breakfast room or on the veranda. Pick-up at airport/bus/marina can be arranged. There is a resident Mini Schnauzer "Penny" and cat "Skipper".Visa www.bbcanada.com/3012.html

---

Sault-Ste-Marie   *(see also St.Joseph I., Bruce Mines, Blind Riiver)*

Brauer, Margaret & Bernt (Top o'the Hill B&B)   ☎(705)253-9041,1-800-847-1681,
40 Broos Rd, Sault-Ste-Marie, ON P6C 5S4   E-mail: brauerb@sympatico.ca, Fax946-5571,

From North on Hwy 17, turn right on Hwy 550(Second Line W). and proceed 7.4km to Broos Rd. turn right. From East take the Hwy 17 Bypass to Hwy 550 (Second Line and jct with Hwy 17 north (water tower). Follow Hwy 550 for 7.4km west to Broos Rd and turn right. House is up hill.

$45S $65-95D $15Child(under 16,free under 5)   ▶6
🏵 May-Oct 🍹Full, homebaked 🏠Sub., gardens, view from guest rooms, patio, quiet ■3D (upper level) ⊨ 2T,1K,1Q
⊲🔲1Sh.w.g.,1ensuite ★Air,F,TV, piano, parking, solarium with indoor fish pond 🖑No smoking 〜 German
🏃 Hiking and walking along creek and bush, Lily pond with fish
🚗 ACR Agawa Canyon Train, swimming, fishing, boating, hiking, Sault Locks

👉 Unique, large hill-top house with tranquil European ambiance and unhurried atmosphere is surrounded by picturesque gardens, which won the City Beautification Award in 1999 and located in District 9, Algoma. Enjoy the spectacular autumn colours and afterwards relax in comfortable home which was selected for 1990 Art Gallery of Algoma House Tour. Breakfast is served in the center dining room. There is a Golden Retriever "Meggie" in residence. Reservations requested. Visa〜B&B http://www3.sympatico.ca//brauerb

Sault-Ste-Marie (cont'd)

Duncan, Jim & Joyce (Knight Home B&B)   ☎(705) 949-3241, 1-877-949-4874
61 Lansdowne Ave., Sault-Ste-Marie, ON P6B 1K5   E-mail: knight@soonet.ca

From Sudbury on Hwy 17E continue into city (becomes Wellington St). At Bruce St, turn right to top of hill and right again onto Lansdowne. From Hwy 17N proceed into city (becomes Great Northern Rd), Turn right on Bruce and at top of hill turn left onto Lansdowne.
$40S $50-60D $5child $80F $10Add.person   ▶6
🍴 Full, homebaked   🏠 Res, 3-storey, older, porch, deck, quiet ■2(upst)
🛏 2T,1D,1K   🛁 1Sh.w.g.   ★ TV in guest room, ceiling fans, off-street parking, small guest sitting room   🚭 No smoking
🧍 Restaurants, shopping malls, Casino, Boardwalk, Agawa Tour Train, Sault Locks (tours), bus route
🚗 Int.Bridge, Airport, beaches, hiking trails, fishing, skiing, Kewadin Casino
🐾 Warm welcome in cozy modernized turn-of-the-Century built ancestral home, centrally located in a quiet area on the hill, overlooking the city's steel mill and International Bridge. Relax on the cozy front porch and reflect on the day's journey or anticipate the coming events. House specialty is a variety of French Toast dishes. Dog in residence. ✓B&B www.staycanada.com/Knight-Home/

Patriquin, Barb & Mike (Hiawatha House B&B)   ☎ (705) 759-0188, 1-888-848-9889
972-5th Line East, Sault-Ste-Marie, ON P6A 5K7   E-mail: info@hiawathahouse.com

From City Centre, follow Hwy17 north to 5th Line. Turn right (east) and proceed 1.6km to B&B.
$40-55S $50-65D $10Child   ▶7
🍴 Full(on weekends), Cont.(during week) 🏠Rural(within city limits),2-storey,acreage,view from guest rooms,patio,deck,quiet
■2D,1Ste(main & upper level) 🛏 1S,3Q 🛁1Ensuite, 1sh.w.g. ★LF,F,TV, off-street parking 🚬Smoking on Patio 〰French
🧍 Adjacent to Hiawatha Highlands Conservation Area (waterfall, small lake, x-c skiing/biking/walking trails), golfing, snowmobiling
🚗 City Centre, Agawa Canyon Tour Train, Int.Bridge to USA, northshore of Lake Superior
🐾 Spacious home with cathedral ceilings, and large sunken living room located in a beautiful conservation area with all the park-like amenities at the door. Enjoy the breathtaking autum colours and easy access to Hwy17 North (Trans Canada Highway). Breakfast is served in special guest breakfast room. Every effort is made to provide for special requests. CCards ✓B&B
www.hiawathahouse.com

Sutton, Maria (Brockwell Chambers)   ☎ & Fax (705) 949-1076
183 Brock St., Sault-Ste-Marie, ON P6A 3B8   E-mail: bed@ssm.ca

From North or East follow "Bridge to US" signs. Located 1block after road becomes one-way. From USA, follow "to Hwy 17" signs and turn left on Brock St (Tim Horton on corner).

$65-85S $75-95D (plus tax)   ▶8A
🍴 Full 🏠 Downtown, hist., porch ■ 4D (upstairs)
🛏2S(1K),3K 🛁 4Private ★ F,TV in guest rooms, ceiling fans, jacuzzi, phone with intercom in each room, off-street parking, guest quarters are separate 🚭 No smoking, no pets, not suitable for children 〰 Dutch, German
🧍 Downtown, Agawa Canyon Tour Train, Bush-plane Heritage Centre, waterfront boardwalk, Court House, Civic Centre, hospitals, Museum & Arts Council, Sault Locks & cruises, Roberta Bondar Park
🚗 Algoma Fall Festival, Sault & Kewadin Casinos, x-c & downhill skiing, golfing, boating
🐾 Pleasant, elegantly modernized 1905-built home with confortable furnishings, large sitting room and gas fireplace in central location. Hostess has an exceptional flair for making guests feel comfortable. Breakfast is served in large dining room especially furnished for guests. ✓B&B

Sault-Ste-Marie (cont'd)

Smith, Linda & Richard (Eastbourne Manor B&B)   ☎ (705) 942-3648
1048 Queen St., Sault-Ste-Marie, ON   P6A 2C7   E-mail: eastbournemanor@yahoo.com

$50-65S $65-85D $15Child $30Add.person   🍽 Meals   ▶ 6A

Approaching Sault-Ste-Marie follow signs to hospitals.
🍴 Full, homebaked   🏠 Downtown, res., 2-storey, hist., view, patio, porch, deck   ■3D (upstairs)   ⊨2T(K),1D,1Q, cot   ⊒1Sh.w.g., 1ensuite   ★ LF,F,TV,air conditioner & ceiling fans in guest rooms, off-street/street parking   ⊛ Smoking outside, no pets, children min age 10
🥾 Hospitals, shopping, fine dining, Court House/Civic Center, waterfront boardwalk, Sault Locks (tours), Agawa Canyon Train
🚐 Downhill/x-c skiing, golfing, boating, Kewadin Casino
🔫 Warm welcome in designated heritage house (ca1903), fully restored in its Victorian era and centrally located. Enjoy the comfortable and friendly hospitality and reside in a little piece of Ontario history. Breakfast is served in the formal Victorian dining room. Relax with coffee to the back garden terrace or the front veranda, with panaorama of the St.Mary's River through a hedge trimmed walkway. The rear garden fountain and waterfall are both lit for evening enjoyment. There are cats in residence. ✒B&B www.bbcanada.com

---

Tholberg, Lilja (Grand Oaks B&B)   ☎ (705) 254-3797 1-888-625-6686
9 Grandriver Cr., Sault-Ste-Marie, ON   P6B 3R9

From Hwy 17E to Bypass Hwy 550 proceed on Black Rd. Turn left onto McNabb and then onto St.Georges. Turn right at Grand Blvd, left on Grandriver Cresc.
$45S $65D   ▶ 5
🍴 Full, homebaked   🏠 Res., patio, quiet   ■ 1S,2D (main floor)   ⊨ 1S,2D   ⊒ 1Sh.w.g., 1sh.w.h., access to sauna
★Air,2F,TV in one guest room, separate entrance, off-street parking, guest quarters are separate   ⊛ No smoking, no pets, children min. age 10   ∾ Finnish
🥾 Agawa Canyon Train Tour, St. Mary's River boardwalk, Roberta Bondar Pavilion, fishing (Cohoe & King salmon), Bon Soo Winter Carnival
🚐 Public swimming (Pointe des Chenes), Hiawatha ski trails, Lake Superior scuba diving, Locks
🔫 Warm welcome in cozy home with cathedral ceiling, quiet comfort, and centrally located. Breakfast special is Finnish pancakes (crepes with fruit in season), including "Pulla" (Finnish coffeebread) served in guest breakfast room. Relax and rejuvenate after a steamy sauna. There is "Dick" the cat in residence. ✒B&B

Selkirk   *(on Lake Erie s/o Hamilton; see also Port Dover)*

Maguire, Darrell & Laura (The Broomtree Guest House B&B)   ☎& Fax (905) 776-1846
205 E Lakeshore Rd., RR1, Selkirk, ON   N0A 1P0   E-mail: dljrmaguire@kwic.com

$40-50S $50-60D $5Child $10Add.person   🍽Meals (plus tax)   ▶ 9
From Simcoe, take Hwy 3 to Reg Rd 53 into Selkirk. Turn right at East Lakeshore Rd and proceed 3 km. Situated on road leading to Selkirk Provincial Park.
🍴 Full, homebaked   🏠 Farm, village, 107 acres, view from guest rooms, deck, lakefront, quiet   ■1D,1Ste (upstairs in main house), 1D(in bungalow across lane)   ⊨2T,2Q,1P,cot,crib   ⊒1Private, 2sh.w.g.   ★ TV,LF, parking   ⊛ No smoking, no pets
🥾 Walks on country roads with view of lake, sandy beach across with shallow swimming area, tree farm/sugar bush trails
🚐 Museums, golfing/fishing, Pt Dover, Hamilton, Welland Canal
🔫 Tree farm with spacious old farmhouse with beautiful view of Lake Erie. Explore the farm or relax in the sunroom or under the awning on the deck and watch the waves. Excellent holiday location for windsurfers, bird watchers and families.Visa ✒ B&B

Sharbot Lake

(north of Kingston; see also Westport, Newboro)

Dinelle, Lettie & Denis (Rockhill B&B)
Box 99, Sharbot Lake, ON   K0H 2P0

☎ (613) 279-3006
E-mail: lettie-d@hotmail.com

From Hwy401, take Exit611 and proceed north for 65km on Hwy 38 to B&B on left. From Hwy7, take Hwy38 and proceed 3km to house on right.

$40-60S $60-90D $20Child/Add.person   ▶ 3
✚ Summer only (other by special arrangement)   ◐ Full
🏠Res., 2-storey, lakeview from guest rooms, lakefront, patio
■3D (upstairs)   ⊨ 2S,2T,1K,cot   ⛟ 3Private   ★Air,F,TV, private entrance, off-street parking, guest quarters are separate
Ⓦ No smoking, children min. age 5   ∾ Dutch, German, French
🕺 Restaurants, public beach, stores, swimming, canoeing
🚌 Bus stop (hosts will pick-up), historic Kingston, Lake Ontario,
Newly retired couple (from hotel industry) in new home with Dutch influence situated in a little village, where fishing is the main tourist attraction. Hosts love quilting, golfing, tennis and canoeing. Breakfast is served in special guest breakfast room. There is bike storage and boat docking for guests. Visa

---

Shelburne

(north of Orangeville; see also Mansfield)

Anderson, Robert & Eleanor (Anderson's Hilltop B&B)
RR1, Blind Line #595438, Shelburne, ON   L0N 1S5

☎ (519) 925-5129

Take Hwy 10 north from Orangeville to Primrose. Proceed west on Hwy 89 to Line 2 WHS (2km.), & south 2.8 km to No 595438.

$45S $50-55D   🍽 Meals   ▶ 10
◐ Full   🏠 Farm, 2-storey, acreage, view, patio, porch, quiet
■5D(ground & upper level)   ⊨ 2T,2D,2Q   ⛟ Sh.w.g. & private   ★F,TV,LF,KF,wheelchair accessible, parking   Ⓦ No smoking, no pets   ∾ French
🕺 Wooded area hiking/wildlife viewing, small stream, x-c skiing
🚌 Shelburne (Old Time Fiddlers Contest), Orangeville, Medieval Festival, Fall Fair and art tours & Summer Theatre
Large modern, red brick home on 100-acre beef farm with a scenic country view, situated on a quiet gravel road. Relax and enjoy the rural atmosphere. Special arrangements can be made for transportation and vehicle placement for Bruce Trail hiking. ✓B&B

St-Andrews West

(north of Cornwall; see also Williamstown, Lancaster, Apple Hill)

Peachey, Norma & Jan (Winook Farm B&B)
RR1, Rd6, 16997, St. Andrews West, ON   K0C 2A0

☎ (613)932-1161,Fax(613)932-7801
E-mail: aw575@glen-net.ca

From Hwy 401 take Brookdale Exit, turn right (north) to Hwy 138. Follow to St.Andrews West. OR From Hwy 417 take Cornwall Exit (south) on Hwy 138 to St.Andrews West. Turn west on Road 6 & proceed 2km to stone farmhouse on north side. Look for sign on approaches to St.Andrews W.

$40S $60D $15Child/Add.person   🍽 Meals   ▶ 6A,2Ch

◐ Full   🏠 Farm, 2-storey, hist., 150 acres, view from guest rooms, swimming pool, quiet   ■ 3(upstairs)   ⊨2S,2D,1R
⛟1Sh.w.g.   ★ TV,F, ceiling fans, separate entrance   ⓌNo smoking, no pets
🕺 Farm grounds suitable for walks, snowshoeing, x-c skiing, historic St.Andrews village with church/pub/restaurant
🚌 Upper Canada Village, Cornwall, Int. Bridge to USA, Maxville Highland Games (Aug), Ottawa, St.Lawrence Park (nature trails)
Historic stone farm house (ca 1823), tastefully restored, containing several wood stoves for extra comfort. Originally from Britain, hosts are widely travelled and interested in history and weaving. They maintain a flock of sheep and are fulltime honey producers. There are friendly Labrador Retrievers in their own area. ✓B&B www.bbcanada.com/2475html

St.Ann's
(south-west of St.Catharines; see also Beamsville, Grimsby, Fenwick)

Hatorp, Agnete & Poul (Hatorp Vacation B&B)   ☎ (905) 562-4016/688-0421
4171 Reg.Rd 69, St.Ann's, ON   L0R 1Y0   Fax (905) 688-1577

$45S $60D $10Child $15Add.person   🍽Meals   ▶ 7A,3Ch
From QEW take Victoria Ave (Exit57) and 24 to Vineland. Continue south to Reg.Rd69. Turn right and proceed 3km to B&B.

🍲 Full, homebaked   🏠 Farm, 44 acres, bungalow, hillside, view from guest rooms, riverfront, patio, porch, quiet, secluded   ■3F (main & ground level)   ⊨ 1S,1D,2K,1cots,crib   🛁 1Sh.w.g., 1sh.w.h.   ★ KF,F,TV in guest rooms, private entrance, off-street parking, wheel-chair access   ♨Designated smoking area, no pets   ∽ German, Danish
🕴 River (canoeing), pond, woods and trails, farm animals
🚗 St.Catharines, Niagara Falls, NOTL, Welland Canal, Butterfly Conservatory, 40 wineries
🐎 Warm welcome in large farm home situated in very convenient location. Hostess is interested in holistic medicine and organic gardening. Relax by the pond, enjoy the peaceful atmosphere and watch the ducks and geese. Breakfast is served in separate guest breakfast room. ∽B&B

St.Catharines
(see also NOTL, Niagara Falls, Vineland, Beamsville, Grimsby)

Gale, Ross & Carol (Inn on the Henley B&B)   ☎ (905) 934-5146 Fax (905)646-3937
360 Martindale Rd., St. Catharines, ON   L2R 6P9   E-mail: b&b@innonthehenley.com

On QEW at St.Catharines take 7th St Exit. At stop sign turn right, then left and follow service road to Martindale Rd. Turn left to house on right.
$85-150S/D   ▶ 8A
🍲 Homebaked   🏠 Res., hist., 3 acres, view from guest rooms, riverfont, swimming pool, patio, porch, deck, quiet   ■4D(street level & upstairs)   ⊨ 1D,2Q,1K   🛁 4Ensuite   ★F,TV, private entr, airconditioners, off-street parking   ♨Designated smoking area, no pets, not suitable for children
🕴 Starting line of Henley Regatta, boating, fishing, canoeing, swimming, Old Port Dalhousie, Martindale Pond with Canada Geese, bus stop at front door
🚗 Downtown, Brock University, N.Falls, US Border, x-c ski/bike trails, octagonal lighthouse
🐎 1840-built home, historically known as "Stokesdale", full of Canadiana antiques, overlooking the Regatta Starting Line on a quaint harbour which cherishes and preserves its early association with the Welland Canal. Well travelled hosts enjoy gardening/wood carving. Guests are invited to create Twig furniture. "Leave the stress behind and take a walk with nature". Rates may increase during the 1999 World Rowing Championship. ∽B&B

Versluis, Fran & Leo (Old Port B&B)   ☎ (905) 934-5761
73 Main St., St.Catharines, ON   L2N 4V1

$80-125S/D $10Child $15Add.person   (Discounts available for 3 nights plus)   ▶ 10
Located in Port Dalhousie. From QEW exit at Ontario St and go north to Lakeport Rd. Turn left and follow into Port Dalhousie. Turn left on Main St.

🍲 Full, homebaked   🏠 Res., 2-storey, older, patio, porch, deck, quiet   ■ 2D,1F(upstairs)   ⊨ 1S,1D,2Q,futon   🛁 1sh.w.g., 1ensuite   ★Air,TV,F, separate entrance, off-street parking
♨No smoking, no pets   ∽ Dutch
🕴 Lakefront park (with beach, pier, restaurants, shops, antique carousel ride), Rowing Henley course
🚗 Niagara Falls, ferry to Toronto (summer), NOTL, US Border
🐎 Comfortable home situated in the heritage part of town, just steps from the grandstand at the finish line of the Henley Rowing course. Breakfast is served in dining room. Relax on the front or side porch or on the backyard deck. There is a young school-age boy in the host family.

St.Catharines (cont'd)

Nunn, Ron & Barbara (Hayocks on the Lake B&B)   ☎ & Fax (905) 934-7106
43 Ann St., St.Catharines, ON L2N 5E9   E-mail: hayocks@sympatico.ca

From QEW at St.Catharines exit on 7th St North. Turn right on Lakeshore Rd and proceed

4km to Ann St. Turn left.
$90-150D $20Add.person   ►7
🍳 Full 🏠 Res., 2-storey, view from guest rooms, lakefront,
solarium ■ 3(upstairs) ⊨ 2T,1Q,1K,1P 🛏 3ensuite
★F, air-conditioners, guest quarters are in separate wing
Ⓦ Smoking outside, no pets, children min age 12
🏃 Old Port Dalhousie with lakeside park and sandy beach, craft
shops, restaurants, Henry Island, bus to downtown
🚗 Downtown, Niagara-on-the-Lake, Niagara Falls, Niagara Wine Rte, Welland Canal, Hamilton
🐾 Historic lakefront home (ca 1860) restored by present hosts, with period antique lighting
fixtures throughout the house, furnished with many antiques and located in the heart of Niagara
Wine Country. Relax in the solarium and enjoy the spectacular lake view. Well travelled hosts (he a
retired airline captain) enjoy meeting people. ✍B&B http://www.bbcanada.com/hayocks

---

Sax, Paul & Shirley (Henleyview B&B)   ☎ (905) 937-7525, Fax 937-8228
54 Canal St., St.Catharines, ON L2N 4S9   E-mail: pws1935@aol.com

Located in Old Port Dalhousie. From Toronto on QEW exit at 7th St. Go north to end, turn right
on Lakeshore (becomes Main), proceed to Brock St & right on Canal. (House on corner). From
Niagara Falls on QEW take Ontario St and go north to Lakeport. turn left & left on Brock.

$70-80S/D   ► 4A
✚ Summer only 🍳 Full, homebaked 🏠 Res, 2-storey, older,
view from guest rooms, lakefront, porch, deck, quiet ■ 2D
(upstairs) ⊨ 1D,1Q 🛏 1Sh.w.g. ★ Air, TV/VCR in extra
sitting room, ceiling fans, off-street parking Ⓦ Designated
smoking area, no pets
🏃 Lake Ontario, beach, eating & drinking establishments, Dinner
Theatre, Antique Carousel, marina, fishing
🚗 St. Catharines, Niagara on the Lake, Niagara Falls, Casino Niagara, wineries, Toronto, Buffalo
🐾 Retired hosts in friendly and comfortable home, decorated in the style of early 1900,
overlooking the Henley Rowing Course and located in quaint lakeside town. The Finish Line of the
Henley is seen from one guest room. Relax in the screened-in porch or in the patio garden area.
Hostess has done Chinese Painting for many years.

Woodward, Barbara & Wm. (Woodward House B&B)   ☎ (905) 646-3795
31 Centennial Dr., St.Catharines, ON L2N 6A5   E-mail: bknightw@becon.org

Take QEW to Ontario St (St.Catharines) and proceed north (towards Lake). Turn right at Linwell

Rd to 2nd St on right.
$55-65S $70-90D $140F   ► 6
🍳 Full, homebaked 🏠 Res., raised bungalow, view from guest
rooms, patio, quiet ■ 3D(upstairs, street & lower levels)
⊨2T,2Q 🛏 1Private, 2sh.w.h. ★ Air,F,TV, private entrance,
off-street/street parking Ⓦ Smoking outside, no pets, children
min. age 12
🏃 Port Dalhousie and beach, Antique Carousel, Henly Regatta
🚗 NOTL & Shaw Festival Theatres, Welland Canal, Wine Route, Brock University, Niagara Falls
🐾 Large, contemporary, raised bungalow, situated in the heart of Niagara in a very quiet
residential area. Full gourmet breakast is served in the dining room, using linens, china and crystal.
Hosts enjoy assisting guests with local itineraries. Visa ✍B&B

St.Jacobs

(north of Kitchener; see also Elmira)

Catton, Jeri-Lynn & Kevin (The Log House B&B)
RR1, Breslau, ON N0B 1M0

☎ & Fax (519) 648-9474
E-mail: info@theloghouse.on.ca

From Guelph, travel west on Hwy 7 and north on Rd86 to Rd51 at Ariss. turn west and proceed 5.2km to house on south side.
$125D ▶6
💭 Full 🏠Rural, log house, 50 acres, porch, deck, 2ponds ■3D (upst) ⊨3Q ⊇1Private, 1sh.w.g. ★LF,F,TV, off-street parking 🚭No smoking,no pets, not suitable for children 🏃 Walking/ski trails on forested acreage, Mennonite farms, ponds, horseback riding, wildlife

🚗 St. Jacobs, Cambridge, Kitchener/Waterloo, Stratford Theatres, Toronto Airport, African Lion Safari, Universities of Waterloo, Guelph & Sir Wilfred Laurier, golfing, Streamliner Railway
☛ Spacious hand-crafted, full scribe round log-style home with unique and interesting decor and cathedral ceilings and floor to ceiling wood burning stone fireplace. There are antiques and Giftware for sale. Relax by the ponds and watch the depth for bass, sunfish or turtles and waterfowl, walk or ski the quiet trails on site. Hosts are retired Police Officer turned teacher & financial adviser and are very knowledgeable about the area and attractions. Visa/MC www.theloghouse.on.ca

---

Feick, Lynne and Earl (Countryside Manor B&B)
Box 500, 39 Henry St., St. Jacobs, ON N0B 2N0

☎ (519) 664-2622, 1-800-476-8942

From Hwy 401, exit on Hwy 8 and go north to Hwy 86 North. Exit on King St north and proceed to St. Jacobs. Turn left at 1st street in town and continue over railway tracks to 1st house on left.

$60S $65D $15Child ▶4
💭Full 🏠Farm, older, patio, quiet,panoramic view ■2D(upst) in separate guest quarters ⊨2S,1D ⊇1Sh.w.g. ★Guest sitting room, private balcony 🚭no pets ∽German 🏃 St.Jacobs, farmers' market, lovely shops, walks along Mill Race 🚗 Kitchener/Waterloo, hiking, covered bridge ☛ 1917-built, renovated and tastefully decorated Victorian home with manicured gardens in park setting, situated in the
heart of Mennonite country. Enjoy breakfast on the patio to the sound of the fountain. Ideal place for Garden weddings. Visa ✓B&B www.bbcanada.com/349.html

---

Hill, Joyce & Neil (Village Bed & Breakfast)
61 Queen Street, St.Jacobs, ON N0B 2N0

☎ (519) 664-2890

From Hwy 401 exit on Hwy 8 toward Kitchener/Waterloo. Take Hwy 86 to Waterloo & proceed to 1st exit to St.Jacobs, turn left into town. Queen St is 1blk west of main street.

$65S/D $175Ste(2nights) ▶8
💭 Full 🏠 Village, res., older, 2-storey, quiet ■3D,1Ste (main & upper level) ⊨2S,4D ⊇1Sh.w.g.,1ensuite ★Air, parking 🚭No smoking 🏃 Village of St. Jacobs, shops, Mennonite Interpr.Center, excellent German/Mennonite eating places, walking trail, cycling, golfing 🚗 Mennonite farming area, only covered bridge in Ontario ☛ Retired professional couple invites guests to step into yesteryear
as the horse and buggies pass the window, while one block away the village bustles with visitors. Enj;oy homemade breads and jams. Minimum of 2 nights in suite. ✓B&B

St.Jacobs (cont'd)

Noice, Anne & Barry (The Old Flax Mill B&B)
50 Glasgow St.N., Conestogo, ON   N0B 1N0

☎ (519) 664-3600
E-mail: benoice@aol.com

From Hwy 401, take Hwy 8 north and continue on Hwy 86 north to Waterloo. Stay on Hwy to lights at Reg RD 17. Turn right to Conestogo (3 km). Turn left on Glasgow St, proceed to bottom of hill.

$70S $80D   ► 5
🍴 Full, homebaked   🏠 Village, 2-storey, 2-acres, view, quiet
■2D (upst)   ⊨ 2Q   🛏1Sh.w.g.   ★Air, woodstove, parking
✋No smoking,no children, no pets   ✎French,German
🏃 Quiet sitting area by stream, old livery stables on property, quiet walks in the village of Conestogo
🚗 Kitchener, Waterloo, St. Jacobs, farmers' market
🐽 Congenial hosts (retired teachers) in spacious Colonial-design home with elegant decor, surrounded by tall trees and large property in a tranquil, park-like setting. There is a Labrador in residence.✒B&B

St.Joseph Island   (s/of Sault Ste Marie; see also Bruce Mines, Manitoulin Isle)

Higgins, Paul & Rilla (Sunset Bay B&B & Studios)   ☎ (705) 246-2177, Fax (705) 246-0481
RR1, Richards Landing, St.Joseph Island, ON   P0R 1J0   E-mail: sunsetbay.bb@sympatico.ca

Phone for directions.
$40S $60D   ► 6A,2Ch
🍴 Full, homebaked   🏠 Rural, 2-storey, view from guest rooms, lakefront, quiet, deck, secluded   ■ 3D(upstairs)   ⊨ 2T,2Q
🛏 3Ensuite,2sh.w.g,1sh.w.h.   ✋ F,TV,guest balcony, photography studio   ✋ No smoking
🏃 Swimming, fishing, boating, cycling, hiking, views of shipping (westbound lane)
🚗 Sault-Ste-Marie, airport, Soo Locks (tours), Agawa Canyon Rail Tours, historic Fort St. Joseph, museums, shops, galleries, marinas, winter sports
🐽 Newly-built (1996) cedar home situated on 80acres. Relax in the scenic and serene atmosphere with abundant birds and wildlife. Former Travel Agent hosts from Alberta enjoy meeting people, love photography and are sports-minded. Relax in the sitting room/library or the indoor hot tub. Indoor studio- or outdoor-portraits can be arranged as a special momento of the B&B stay. Airport transfer service available for additional charge. There is a cat in residence. Visa,MC ✒B&B
www.bbcanada.com/1207.html

Smith, Phyllis (The Anchorage)   ☎ (705) 246-2221
RR1, Richards Landing, St.Joseph Isle, ON   P0R 1J0

Phone for directions.
$25S $45D $12Add.person   ► 10
✚ Summer   🍴 Choice   🏠Rural, acreage, view, seaway-front,quiet
■1S,1D,1Ste(upstairs)   ⊨2T,2D,1Q,R,P,crib   🛏1Sh.w.g.   ★TV in guest rooms, private guest driveway   ✋Restricted smoking
🏃 Walking trails (wildlife), miniature golf, sandy beach (private)
🚗 Fort St. Joseph National Historic Park, Island Museum, "Soo Locks", famous Agawa Canyon Train trips
🐽 Quiet, friendly B&B home is on the Seaway where ships from all over the world pass right in front. From the porch watch the water activities. Enjoy breakfast a stone's throw away from the Captain's wheel. ✒B&B

St.Marys
(south-west of Stratford)

Burgin, Aileen & Harold (Green Arbour B&B)   ☎ (519) 229-6671, Fax (519) 229-8572
5894 Perth Line 8, RR1, St. Marys, ON   N4X 1C4   E-mail: aburgin@quadro.net

From Kirkton on Hwy 23 (north-west of St Marys), turn east on Perth Line 8 and look for 1st

farmhouse on north side (Fire No 5894)
$55D   ►4-6
✳ Summer (other times by reservation)   🍴 Full, homebaked
🏠 100-acres farm, veranda, quiet ■2D(upstairs) ⊨1Q,2T(1K),
cot ⊒1Sh.w.g. ★ Air,TV 🚫 No smoking, no pets
🧍 Sugar bush, village of Kirkton, llama hikes, x-c skiing
🚗St.Marys & Quarry, Stratford Festival, London, Blyth,
L.Huron, River Valley Golf & Country Club with llama caddies

🔫 Quiet, homey Century farmhouse with veranda, renovated and lovingly maintained, set well
back from paved road on 3 acres of carefully tended lawns, and surrounded by hundreds of trees
planted on property by the family. Sour dough waffles with own maple syrup is a house specialty.
Hosts raise & train Llamas for caddying and hiking. There is a resident cat and a dog. Guests are
invited to bring suitable footwear to explore the 100 acre farm. Visa ↙CC
www.greenarbourbnb.on.ca

St.Thomas
(south of London)

Held, Nadine & Don (Victorian Rose B&B)   ☎ (519) 633-3274, 1-877-VICROSE
44251 Talbot Lines, RR3, St.Thomas, ON   N5P 3S7   E-mail: vicrose@execulink.com

From Hwy 401 at London, take Exit 189 (Highbury Ave) south to Hwy 3. Look for B&B beside

Family Flowers Garden Centre east of St.Thomas.
$55-60S $70-85D $15Child $90-100F   ►6A,3Ch
🍴 Full, homebaked   🏠 Hobby farm, 3-storey, hist.,porch
■1D,2F(2nd floor)   ⊨ 1S,2D,2Q,cradle (incl antique beds)
⊒1Sh.w.g.,1ensuite ★ Air,TV, ceiling fans, guest quarters are
separate 🚫 No smoking, no pets (can be boarded nearby)
🧍 Large Garden Center (next door), farm land with fruit trees
🚗 London, Grand Bend, Port Stanley & Port Burwell beaches,
local wineries, craft & antique shops, auctions, Hawkcliff (bird migration), Sparta
🔫 Victorian country home (1892) filled with ornate antique beds in guest rooms and many
antiques throughout. Relax on the spacious enclosed veranda, sit out in the large, sunny &
tree-shaded backyard, or stroll around the gardens with roses and plants from British Columbia,
Germany & Japan. Hosts create spectacular breakfasts for guests (choose from menu), served in
guest breakfast room. There are pets in residence (not in guest area).Visa,Amex ↙B&B
http://www.bbcanada.com/victorianrose

St.Thomas (cont'd)

Moczulski, Joseph & Lorraine (Rosebery Place B&B) ☎ (519) 631-1525, 1-800-878-6916
57 Walnut St., St.Thomas, ON   N5R 2Y7   E-mail: rosebery@execulink.com

From Hwy 401 exit at Hwy 4 and procesd south into St.Thomas. Turn right on Stanley St at top of
hill and continue to Walnut St. Turn right to house on left.

$55S $65-75D $10Add.person 🍽 Meals ► 16
💧 Full 🏠 Res., 3-storey, hist., acreage, porch, deck, quiet
■2S,5D,2F (upstairs) ⊨2S,6T,1D,2Q,1K ⊐2Sh.w.g. ★TV,
off-street parking, wheel-chair access with lift & ramp, guest
quaarters are separate 🖐 No smoking, no pets
🕴 Main downtown area, Jumbo Elephant Statue, Pioneer &
Military Museums, old English hist. church, Art Gallery, Princess
Theatre, historic walking tour

🚗 Port Stanley (fishing port, antiques, boutiques, theatre), Hawk Cliff (bird migration), Sparta
🐴 Gracious Century home (late 1800's) located on "the Hill" in historic area of town surrounded
by historic attractions. Relax in the cozy living room or the bright airy sunroom. Browse in the gift
shop, or make an appointment for the Tea Room. Ideal place for small weddings, family occasions,
workshops/seminars/meetings. Breakfast is served in the formal dining room or cheerful breakfast
room.Weekly & monthly rates available.Visa ⁓CC bbcanada.com/rosebery

---

Stratford   *(west of Kitchener; see also Baden, Mitchell, Wellesley)*

Cook, Roger & Elaine (Double CC Farm & B&B)   ☎ (519) 271-1978
4335, Rd 110, RR1, Stratford, ON   N5A 6S2

Take Hwys 7&8 between Stratford & Shakespeare. Turn north on Rd 110 and proceed 3.3km from
corner. Look for house No. 4335.

$80Ste $15Child 🍽 Meals ► 2
💧 Full 🏠 Farm, hist., view from guest rooms, riverfront,
porch, deck, quiet, secluded ■ 1Ste (main floor) ⊨ 1Q
⊐1ensuite ★ LF,F,TV, woodstove, ceiling fan, private
entrance, guest quarters are separate 🖐 No smoking, no pets
🕴 Hiking & x-c ski trails, skating on pond, Heritage Works
woodshop, miniature donkeys, farm animals

🚗 Stratford Festival Theatre, Shakespeare village, Mennonite Country
🐴 Heritage home (ca 1867) located on 200 acres farm. Award-winning hosts are very interested
in nature and conservation and have planted close to 10000 trees over the last decades. Watch them
work in the on-site workshop. Relax in the large screened-in porch or sit by the pond and take in
the tranquil country atmosphere and solitude. There is a fully operational circular Amulree
Sawmill (approx. 100 years old) on the property. ⁓B&B

Hrysko, Dianna & Mary Allen (Deacon House B&B)   ☎ (519) 273-2052, Fax (519) 273-3784
101 Brunswick St., Stratford, ON   N5A 3L9   1-877-825-6374

Take Hwy 7 to Stratford (from London or Kitchener). Turn south on Nile St (at east end of town)
and proceed 2 blocks to Brunswick St. Turn right.

$100-115S $115-125D $30Add.person (plus tax) ► 14
💧Full,homebaked 🏠Downtown,res.,hist.,large front porch
■6D(upst,incl 1Ste) ⊨2T,2D,3Q ⊐1private, 5ensuite
★Air (in guest rooms),F,KF,TV in guest reading room, large guest
kitchen, private balcony in one guest room, ample parking on
site 🖐No smoking, no pets, children min. age 9
🕴 Three Theatres (Avon/Festival/Tom Patterson), downtown
🐴 Well traveled hosts (Nurses) in large Queen Anne-style Heritage home with antiques &
Canadiana country whimsical details throughout. Escape packages available. There are cats in
residence. Visa,MC ⁓B&B www.bbcanada.com/1152.html

Stratford (cont'd)

Hopkins, Ray & Leonora (Avon & John B&B)
72 Avon St., Stratford, ON N5A 5N4

☎ (519) 275-2954, Fax 275-2956
E-mail: avonjohn@strat.net, 1-877-275-2954

In Stratford, take Huron St west to John St. Turn left, go 3 blocks to B&B on corner of Avon St.

$85-90S $90-95D   (plus tax)   ►6
🍲 Full, homebaked (special diets with ample notice) 🏠 Res., 3-storey, porch, quiet ■3D(upstairs) ⊨2T,2Q ⇋2Private, 1ensuite ★Air,F,TV, barfridge & coffeemaker in guest rooms, terry robes, off-street parking �🖐Smoking in outdoor lanai, no pets, children min.age 12 ⌇French, Dutch, German
🏃 Three theatres (Stratford Festival), downtown, shops, restaurants, River Avon with parks & gardens
🚗St.Jacobs (Mennonite Country), St.Marys (Stone Town), Shakespeare (antique lovers hamlet)
🚢 Beautiful Edwardian home, restored to its original elegance, with large manicured garden and located in a quiet park-like setting. Traditional English breakfast is served with full choice of hot dishes. Relax in the salon with a unique Wurlitzer Baby Grand Piano. Hosts have retired from the hospitality industry and provide all the amenities, with the warmth and hospitality of an earlier era, for today's discerning traveller.Visa,MC⌇B&B www.bbcanada.com/avonjohn

Sudbury

(northern Ontario)

Empie, Russel & Family (Lady Ashley Waterfront B&B)
919 Sunnyside Rd., Sudbury, ON P3G 1J3

☎ (705) 522-9800,
1-888-263 3389, Cell (705) 699-7832

Coming from Sault-Ste-Marie, take Hwy17-Bypass, turn right on Long Lake Rd. Proceed 1.8km, turn right on Sunnyside Rd and continue 1.4km to B&B

$50-125S/D $10Child   (Gift Certificates avail.)   ►6
🍲 Full, homebaked, self-serve 🏠 Res., ranch-style, lakefront, patio, deck, quiet ■3D (main floor) ⊨1D,2Q,cot
⇋2ensuite, 1private ★ Air,F,private entrance, microwave & bar-fridge avail., paddle boat, canoe & boat, off-street parking
�🖐Smoking outside, no pets, children min. age 10
🏃 Restaurants, IMAX Theatre, Science North, hospitals, Cancer Centre, South Ridge Mall, Sudbury Boat & Canoe Club, picnic area & B-B-Q, good fishing
🚗 Downtown, Airport, Bus & Train Station
🚢 Retired couple in all brick home situated on 17Mile Long Lake in a quiet prestigious area of the city. The beautiful romantic Bridal Suite overlooks the lake. Ideal place for Honeymoon and special occasion. Professional Bridal Consultant on premises. Limo service available. Breakfast is served in dining room or on patio overlooking the lake. Snowmobilers welcome. Free phone calls to anywhere in Canada. Shuttle service to & from airport, train or bus (May-Oct). ⌇B&B

Girouard, Carmel & Tom (Auberge-sur-lac B&B)
1672 South Lane Rd., Subury, ON P3G 1N8

☎ & Fax (705) 522-5010
1-888-353-6727

$60S $75D $5child $15Add.person $90F   🍽 Meals   ► 7A,2Ch

Located off Hwy69 south and 1.3km north of Welcome Centre.
🍲 Full, homebaked, self-serve, buffet 🏠 Rural, lakefront, acreage, view from guest rooms, executive-style bungalow, quiet, decks, secluded ■ 1D,1Ste,1F (main floor) ⊨1D,2Q,cot,crib
⇋1Ensuite, 1sh.w.g. ★ KF,LF,F,TV, double jacuzzi with view of sunset on the lake, paddle-boat for guests' use, off-street parking �🖐 Smoking outside ⌇ French, some Spanish
🏃 Bountiful blueberries free for the picking, dock with lounge chairs, swimming, fishing, birdwatching, listening to loon calls, public transit to City
🚗 Sudbury, Killarney Prov. Park, historic site (Voyageur Route on French River), Onaping Falls
🚢 Warm welcome in lakefront estate home with relaxing and tranquil environment and local and international art displayed throughout. For corporate travellers, there is a fully equipped office available. Relax on the large deck or dock. Hosts also have rustic cottages on Killarney Prov. Park. Bridal/Romance/Adventure Packages available. Visa,MC ⌇B&B www.cyberbeach.net/asl

Sundridge
(south of North Bay; see also Powassan, Huntsville)

Belrose, Barbara (Belrose B&B)   ☎ (705) 384-7504, Fax 384-9935
13 Lansdowne St., Sundridge, ON P0A 1Z0

In Sundridge, turn at Paget St (going into the subdivision). Follow 3 blocks to Lansdowne.

$50S $60D $15Child   ▶ 6A,2Ch
🍴 Full, homebaked   🏠 Village, bungalow, view from guest
rooms, patio, deck, quiet, secluded   ▦ 3 (main & lower level)
🛏 3Q,2P   🚿 2Sh.w.g., 1ensuite   ★ Air,LF,F,TV,ceiling fans
in guest rooms, off-street & street parking
🏃 Sandrose Decorative Art Studio (inhouse), Lake Bernard, riding
stables, snowmobile & hiking trails, golfing
🚗 Lake Bernard Girls Camp, Hockey Opportunity Camp, G.Bay
🗨 Warm welcome in country home filled with antiques and collectibles, "where cares drop away
at the door". Stroll in the extensive perennial gardens or through the adjacent tree-filled fields.
Relax in comfortable surroundings after day-tripping excursions, which are mapped out in the area
directing visitors to local craft/art and antique shops. This home enjoys the laughter of children.
There is a Cocker Spaniel in residence who loves kids. Visa ✔B&B

Thornbury
(east of Owen Sound; see also Clarksburg, Meaford)

Naish, Glenn & Karen (Glennkaren B&B by the Bay)   ☎ (519) 599-2186,Fax 599-3065
285 Sunset Blvd, Thornbury, ON N0H 2P0

From Thornbury, on Hwy 26, go west 5 km to Christie Beach Rd. Turn right to 39th Sideroad, turn
right down hill to Sunset Blvd, right again past Prime Shores Resort. Look for blue & white house
on Bay side.

$45S $75D $5-15Child   ▶ 7,1baby
🍴 Full, homebaked   🏠Rural, side-split, view, Bay-front, patio,
quiet   ▦ 2 (upstairs & ground level)   🛏 1D,1Q,1P,1S
(trundle)   🚿1Private, 1ensuite   ★ TV, bicycles & skis
available, separate entrance, parking   🚭No smoking, no pets
🏃 Georgian Bay & private beach, swimming, boating, surfing,
Georgian Trail & Bruce Trail hiking, bicycling, x-c skiing
🚗 Thornbury, good restaurants, Meaford, Collingwood, several ski resort, golf courses, fishing
🗨 Unique home, with stained glass windows, , carved furniture, modern conveniences, country
accents and homey ambiance. Situated on beautiful Georgian Bay. Relax on the private beach, or
view gorgeous sunsets from the 2nd storey deck. In summer breakfast is served on the deck
overlooking the Bay. 2nd night rates available.

Thunder Bay
(northern Ontario; see also Dorion, Atikoken)

Aylward, Linda & Arnie (Captain's Quarters B&B)   ☎ (807) 475-5630
RR1, South Gillies, ON P0T 2V0   E-mail: aylward@air.on.ca

From Thunder Bay Airport, travel 20km south on Hwy 61. Turn right onto Hwy 608 for 8.3km

to East Oliver Lake Rd., turn right, then left at first driveway.
$60-75D $15Add.person   ▶ 4A,2Ch
🍴 Full, homebaked   🏠 Rural, 2-storey, log house, acreage, deck
& veranda, quiet   ▦ 2D (main & upper level))   🛏 2Q,2T
🚿2Ensuite   ★ Air,TV,i ndoor storage for motorcycles.   🚭No
smoking, no pets, inquire about children under age 12
🏃 Birdwatching, golf practice range
🚗 US border (Grand Portage Casino), Kakabeka Falls, Old Fort
William, Candy, Loch Lomond & Big Thunder Ski Resorts, Kamview x-c ski area
🗨 Cordial hosts in quiet & charming log home that assures rest and relaxation in the natural
beauty of wood highlighted by 20 foot cathedral ceilings. Enjoy the flowers and well-kept grounds
from the veranda or deck. Breakfast is served with a gourmet flare. ✔B&B

Thunder Bay (cont'd)

Ellchook, Sandy & Betty (Sunrise Farms B&B)   ☎ & Fax (807) 935-2824
4123 Oliver Rd., RR1, Murillo, ON   P0T 2G0

Located between Murillo and Kakabeka Falls on the Oliver Rd. Phone for detailed direction.
$45S $55-65D $10Child (free under age 5) 🍴 Meals   ▶ 4A,2Ch

🍽 Full, homebaked 🏠 Beef/cattle farm, ranch-style, quiet, view from guest rooms, isolated ■2(ground level) 🛏1D,1Q,R,crib 🛁1Sh.w.h.,1private ★TV,LF, ample parking, wheel-chair access 〰some Ukranian
🏃 Ponds, snowmobile trails, walking/hiking on farmland pastures, "This Old Barn" (Tea Room & craft shops)
🚗 Kakabeka Falls, restaurants, swimming, hiking & x/c-skiing
📣 Comfortable open-concept hill-top home with a beautiful panoramic view of Thunder Bay region. Enjoy a delicious country-style breakfast and relax in tranquil surroundings. Hosts raise cattle. Bed & Bale for guest horses. ✓B&B

Hall, Nancy (Archibald Arbor B&B)   ☎ (807) 622-3386, Fax (807) 622-1540
222 South Archibald St., Thunder Bay, ON P7E 1G3   E-mail: nthall@norlink.net

Take Arthur St. Exit off Hwy 11/17 to downtown. Turn left on Archibald St to house on right.
$40S $55D $5Child $15Add.person   ▶ 6A,2Ch

🍽 Cont. 🏠 Downtown, older side by side duplex, quiet ■3D (upstairs) 🛏 2D,1Q,1P,2cots,crib 🛁 1Sh.w.g.(incl deep-footed tub)
★ Air,TV,private entrance, street parking, guest quarters are separate
🚭No smoking, no pets
🏃 Thunder Bay Museum, restaurants, art galleries,International Friendship Gardens, bicycle rentals, farmers' market, unique downtown stores, McKellar Hospital, main Bus Terminal
🚗 Sleeping Giant Prov.Park, Old Fort William Historic Fort, Kakabekka Falls, Ouimet Canyon, Amethyst Mines
📣 Comfortable character brick duplex with relaxing decor situated in convenient downtown location. Reflexology/Therapeutic Touch is offered as additional service in a treatment room. Breakfast is served in the bright and spacious guest living/dining room. There is a Siamese cat (not in guest area). CCards✓B&B

Isaksen-Sitch, Sonja (Sleeping Giant B&B)   ☎ (807) 475-3105
532 Cambrian Cr., Thunder Bay, ON P7C 5B9

$50S $60D $85F 🍴 Meals (special weekly rates available)   ▶ 4+
From Hwys 11/17 turn onto Harbour Expressway. Turn right on Golf Links Rd, right on James St, right on Redwood Ave and right on Cambrian Cr.

🍽 Full 🏠 Res., bungalow, view from guest rooms, patio, deck, quiet ■ 2 (main floor) 🛏 1T,1D,1Q,1P 🛁 1Sh.w.g., 1sh.w.h. ★ F,TV,LF, off-street parking 🚬 Smoking on deck, no pets, inquire about children 〰 Danish
🏃 Extensive walk/bike trail begins at Conf.College, city bus
🚗 Golfing, x-c & downhill skiing, airport, restaurants, fine dining
📣 Newly decorated, elegant & spacious home with French doors leading to double-tierd deck, surrounded by award winning gardens, and situated on a quiet tree-lined street. House specialty is Danish "abelskivers". World travelled hostess has a diploma in travel & tourism administration, and takes pleasure in welcoming guests. Breakfast is served in formal dining room. There is a Border Canary "Casey" in residence. Business travellers welcome. Quiet work area available. Visa ✓F0BBA

Walker, Karen & Robert (McVicar Manor B&B)   ☎ (807) 344-9300
146 N.Court St., Thunder Bay, ON   P7A 4V2   E-mail: rtwalker@tbaytel.net

Follow Hwy17 to Hwy102, turn south onto Red River Rd (Hwy102) and proceed 3km to Algoma St. Turn left, follow 0.6km, turn right onto Harrington Ave. Turn right onto Emmerson Ave, and to Ray Ct. Look for sign on coach house.

$55-110S $85-110D $15Add.person   (plus tax)   ▶9
🏠 Full, homebaked 🏠 Downtown, 3-storey, hist., view from guest rooms, riverfront, porch, secluded ■ 3F (upstairs)
▬3Q   ▬1Private, 2ensuite (1whirlpool) ★ LF,F,off-street parking, TV/VCR on request, guest quarters are separate
Ⓦ Smoking outside, no pets, inquire about children
🧍 Harbour Front Park, Casino, Magnus Theatre (NWO's only Prof.Theatre), fine dining, fishing charters, Canada Games Complex (NA largest indoor pool), auditorium, shops, Cinema Complex, hospitals, Cancer Clinic, Court House
🚗Old Fort William,Sleeping Giant,Agate Mine,5 Amethyst Mines,Ouimet Canyon,Lakehead U.
🎞 Stately and quiet (1906-built) red stone mansion with large parlor, and sweeping oak staircase leading from the foyer & dining room and view of Lake Superior.. Situated on an acre of parkland at creek side in secluded park setting. Relax in the solarium. Breakfast is served in guest breakfast room. There are 2 cats in residence. Visa,MC ✔ B&B www.bbcanada.com/

Weber, Armin & Sara Jeffrey (Pinebrook Bed & Breakfast)   ☎(807)683-6114,Fax8641
RR16, Mitchell Rd., Thunder Bay, ON   P7B 6B3   E-mail: pinebrok@baynet.net

On Hwy 17 and 4km east of Thunder Bay, turn north on Hwy 527 to Mitchell Rd (4km). Turn west 1 km, then south onto Pine Dr following B&B signs.

$45S $50D $15Add.person   (plus tax)   ▶ 10A,4Ch
🏠 Full 🏠 Rural, 2-storey chalet-style, view from guest rooms, acreage, riverfront and back, deck, quiet ■ 4D,1F (ground and main floor) ▬2S,3D,2Q ▬3Sh.w.g.,1ensuite,jacuzzi whirlpool ★F,TV,LF,woodfired Finnish Sauna by river,excellent reading & video library, x-c skiis/canoe/mountain bikes Ⓦ Designated smoking area, children & pets welcome 〰German
🧍 Walking/mountain bike & ski trails, riverside
🚗 Old Fort William, Mt.McKay, Kakabeka Falls, Sleeping Giant Prov. Park, Ouimet Canyon
🎞 B&B Chalet & property with a unique, friendly and tranquil environment, yet very close to the city. Enjoy the quiet nights and truly relaxing retreat atmosphere. Retired teacher hosts have been active in tourism and enjoy helping guests with itineraries. There is a dog and a cat in residence (all very friendly). CCards ✔B&B

Tillsonburg   *(south-east of London; see also St.Thomas)*

Coy, John & Bev (The Open Door B&B)   ☎ (519) 842-9184
109 Queen St., Tillsonburg, ON   N4G 3H4   E-mail: mcoy@oxford.net

From Hwy401 take Hwy19 south at Ingersoll-Exit to Tillsonburg.
$50S $60D $5Child   ▶5
🏠 Full, homebaked 🏠 Split-level, patio, swimming pool, quiet
■ 1S,2D (upstairs) ▬ 1S,1D,1Q ▬1Ensuite, 1sh.w.g
★F,TV,fans in guest rooms, off-street parking Ⓦ No smoking, no pets, inquire about children
🧍 Restaurants, shops, Sports Complex, lovely Lake Lisgar, historic Annandale House & Museum
🚗 Golfing, hiking trails, antique shops, theatre, hist.driving tours & rich agricultural heritage
🎞 Comfortable, quiet get-away in centrally located family home, attractively decorated and situated in park-like setting. Relax by the pool and in the picturesque gardens. Hosts have a good knowledge of Tillsonburg and the surrounding area. Breakfast is served in guest breakfast room. There is a cat "Perkins" in residence. www.bbcanada.com/3352.html

Tobermory
(north of Owen Sound; see also Dyer's Bay, Lion's Head)

Buchanan, Libby & Allen Potvin (Dogwood Point B&B) ☎ & Fax (519) 596-2671
97 Eagle Rd, RR1, Tobermory, ON N0H 2R0

From Hwy 6 (south of Tobermory), turn west on Warner Bay Rd. Proceed 7km to "T" intersection, turn left 3km to B&B.
$60S $70-80D $30Add.person ► 9
⬛Full 🏠Rural, 2-storey, view, lakefront, porches, decks, quiet, secluded ■3D,1F(main & upper floor) ⨝3S,1D,2Q ⌒2Sh.w.g.
★TV in guest common room, wheel-chair access, purified drinking water ⬤No smoking, no pets, not suitable for children
🚗 Bruce Trail, Tobermory (15km), Ferry Term., boat tours
🧍 Swimming & snorkeling from lakeside deck in Lake Huron (on property), view bird/wildflowers
🏡 Modern waterfront home with quiet atmosphere, nestled in wonderful trees and gardens. The Bruce Peninsula is a unique "back-to-nature" experience. Relax on one of two level porches overlooking the lake, enjoy the sound of the waves, the smell of the balsam/cedar trees and the sparkle of the sun off the water. Guests are advised to bring old shoes for swimming (rocky shore) and hiking boots for exploring the Bruce. "And don't forget the camera!". There are 2 cats in residence. ✒B&B www.dogwoodpoint.on.ca

---

Smith, Bob & Linda (Vista Hermosa B&B) ☎ (519) 596-8065
119 Eagle Rd.E, RR1, Tobermory, ON N0H 2R0   E-mail: vistatob@kanservu.ca

Take Hwy 6 north to Warner Bay Rd. Turn left and proceed past airstrip. Follow paved road to stop sign, then turn left to B&B.

$55S $70D 🍽 Meals ► 4A
✴ Not winter ◗ full, homebaked 🏠 Rural, raised bungalow, 1acre, view, lakefront, deck, quiet, secluded ■2D(main & ground level) ⨝ 2D ⌒ 1Sh.w.g., 1Ensuite(2pce) ★ F,TV,ceiling fans, private entrance, off-street parking ⬤ No smoking, no pets, no children
🧍 Hiking & strolling along shoreline or on trails, swimming, birdwatching, local arts & craft shops
🚗 Chi-Cheemaun Ferry Dock, Bruce Peninsula National Park, Bruce Trail, Fathom Five National Marine Park, glass bottom boat tours, Flowerpot Island
🏡 Retired couple in Cedar home (inside & out), tastefully decorated and large wrap-around deck overlooking Lake Huron. Relax in the common room for a game of cards, watch TV/movies or enjoy outdoor activities. Hosts have welcomed many International students over the years and are active with stained glass work and oil painting. "Vista Hermosa" means "Beautiful View" in Spanish. There is a cat in residence.

Toronto
(see also Kleinburg, Oakville, Markham, Whitby)

Bird, Ed & Louise (Cavendish House B&B) ☎ (416) 921-3644
5 Linden St., Toronto, ON M4Y 1V5   E-mail: cavendish@sprint.ca

Take Hwy 401 to Don Vallery Pkwy. Go south and take Bloor St Exit west to Sherbourne. OR QEW to Jarvis St, north to Bloor St and east to Sherbourne.
$75S $95D ► 6A
⬛Full 🏠Downtown, 3-storey, hist.,quiet ■3D(upst) ⨝3D ⌒2Sh.w.g.
★ F,TV & air conditioners in guest rooms, street parking, guest quarters are separate ⬤No smoking, no pets, not suitable for children
🧍 Major shopping, theatres, restaurants, Gallery district, trendy urban area, subway system
🚗 CNTower, Casa Loma, Domes Stadium, Toronto Zoo
🏡 1890-built home has retained its Victorian charm, furnished with many antiques and paintings (all for sale) and located near Yonge/Bloor in the heart of the city. Hosts are originally from Ireland. Breakfast is served in special guest breakfast room. There is a gentle dog ("Betty") in residence. CCards ✒B&B
http://www.lizworks.com/cavhouse.html

Toronto (cont'd)

Boake, Audrie (King-Rie)   ☎ (416)226-3283/484-0107   Fax (416)484-1510
163 Franklin Ave., Willowdale (Toronto),ON   M2N 1C6   E-mail: kbab@sympatico.ca

Located in the Yonge and Sheppard area, north of Hwy 401.
$60S $70D $10Add.person   ▶ 4
🍳 Full(provided - make yourself)   🏠 Res., bungalow, quiet
■ 1Ste(lower level)   ⊨ 2T,1P   ⤴ Ensuite   ★ TV in guest
lounge, KF, separate entrance   ⊛ No smoking, no pets
🏃 Yonge Street subway, shopping center, laundromat,
restaurants, North York City Center
🚗 Golf Club, Science Center, Toronto Zoo, downtown, Airport
🐾 Cozy bungalow close to ravine with lots of flowers in the garden and an English-type front
yard. Accommodation is self-contained. There are 2 cats ("Tiger" & "Miss Maple") in the house.

Buer, Carol & Paul (The Mulberry Tree B&B)   ☎ (416) 960-5249, Fax (416) 960-3853
122 Isabella St., Toronto, ON   M4Y 1P1   E-mail: mulberry@istar.ca

From Hwy 401 take Don Valley Pkwy south to Bloor Exit. Proceed to Sherbourne,turn left, then
right on Isabella. From QEW take Jarvis St Exit north to Isabella & right.

$70-85S $85-110D $25Add.person   🍽 Meals   ▶ 8
🍳 Full, homebaked   🏠 Downtown, 3-storey, hist.   ■ 3D,1F(upstairs)
⊨ 1S,2T,3Q,2cot   ⤴ 1Ensuite, 1private, 1sh.w.g.   ★ Air conditioners &
ceiling fans in guest rooms, TV and small balcony in guest lounge, off-street
parking, guest quarters are separate, in-room data ports/phone/desks.
⊛ No pets, no smoking, not suitable for children   ↬ French, German
🏃 Royal Ontario Museum, Yorkville, Cabbagetown, Eatons Centre,
Reference Library UofT., restaurants, TTC
🚗 CN Tower, Harbourfront, Art Gallery, Toronto Isles, Chinatown
🐾 Spacious heritage home, tastefully renovated and filled with original art
located in tree-lined neighbourhood downtown. Enjoy the friendly, homey atmosphere and relax in
the courtyard. There is a photography gallery onsite. Breakfast is served in the gallery cafe. Well
travelled hosts provide lively breakfast conversation. Ideal place for business travellers with access
to fax/laser printer/business services. There is a cat. Visa,MC ↩B&B

Buer, Michelle & Paul-Antoine (Les Amis B&B)   ☎ (416) 591-0635
31 Granby St., Toronto, ON   M5B 1H8   E-mail: les-amis@istar.ca, Fax (416)591-8546

Located 1 block south of College subway at Yonge St.
$65-85 $75-95 $15Child $20Add.person   ▶ 7
🍳 Full   🏠 Downtown, res., townhouse, patio   ■ 1S,2D(upstairs)
⊨ 1S,1D,1Q   ⤴ 2Sh.w.g.   ★ Air,TV in guest rooms, guest quarters are
separate, street parking, indoor parking available   ⊛ No smoking
↬ French, some Spanish
🏃 College Park, Maple Leaf Gardens, Eaton Centre, shops, restaurants,
theatres, College Subway Station
🐾 Young Parisian couple in green B&B located in quiet downtown
neigbourhood, will help guests discover the sites/sounds & taste of the City.
Gourmet Vegetarian breakfast and certified organic foods are a house
specialty and served on the roof deck, weather permitting. Visa ↩B&B

Toronto (cont'd)

Charbonneau, Suzanne (Terrace House Bed & Breakfast) ☎ (416) 535-1493, Fax 9616
52 Austin Terrace, Toronto, ON   M5R 1Y6   E-mail: terracehousebandb@sympatico.ca

From East on Hwy 401 exit at Bathurst, turn right on Wilson and right again on Bathurst. From West on Hwy 401 exit at Allen Rd S and go east on Eglinton, then south on Bathurst. From QEW exit at Spadina Ave, go north to Davenport Rd, turn west and then north on Bathurst.

$65-89S $80-107D $20Add.person   ► 6
🍽 Full (Gourmet)   🏠 Res., 3-storey, hist., deck, quiet   ■3D(upstairs)
⊨2T(1K),2Q,1P   🛁 1sh.w.g., 1ensuite   ★ F,TV, airconditioner in rooms, street & off-street parking, host quarters are on top floor 🚭No pets, no smoking, inquire about children ⚐French
🕴 Casa Loma, Spadina Historic House, Bloor Street cafes, Terragon Theatre, St.Clair West Subway Stn, U of T, ROM/AGO, Yorkville, ROM
🚗 Metro Zoo, Ontario Place, CNE, McMichael Museum
🐾 1913-built home, richly furnished with antiques, stained/leaded glass windows and scrolled living room ceiling, situated in Forest Hill, a quiet residendial neighborhood in the Casa Loma area. Well travelled hostess has lived in Europe, US and Africa, and enjoys exchanging travel experiences and memories. There are 2 cats in residence. Visa,MC ✓B&B   http://www3.sympatico.ca/terracehousebandb

---

Coxe, Jennie (Alcina's Bed & Breakfast)   ☎ (416) 656-6400
16 Alcina Ave., Toronto, ON   M6G 2E8   E-mail: alcinas@idirect.com

Located south of St.Clair and west of Bathurst.Phone for directions.
$75S $80-85D $10Child $20Add.person   ► 6A,2Ch
🍽 Cont.   🏠 Downtown, res. 3-storey, older   ■ 2D,1Ste (upstairs)
⊨2T,2Q   🛁3Ensuite   ★ Sit-in garden, guest coffee-nook, off-street parking 🚭 No smoking
🕴 Historic Casa Loma and Flower Gardens of restored Spadina House (tours), exclusive Wychwood Park neighbourhood, St.Clair West Subway Stn, Bathurst, bus, shopping
🚗 Downtown, University, Harbourfront, Science Centre, Yorkville, Theatre district, Lake Ontario
🐾 Gracious old Victorian house with "good bones", tastefully renovated and centrally located. Enjoy the casual elegance of warm wood, stained glass, soft period furnishings in a bright and airy setting with a quiet, private English flower garden. The loft suite is a delightful retreat. There is "Cina" the resident cat.✓B&B www.bbcanada.com/alcinas

---

Dallimore, Rob (Dallimore Residence)   ☎ (905) 822-3540, Fax (905) 823-5212
2110 Varency Drive,Mississauga, ON L5K1C3

Phone for directions. Located in west of Toronto, close to Junction of QEW & Erin Mills Pkwy.

$40S $60D   (Minimum stay 2 nights)   ► 6
🍽 Full   🏠 Res., sub., acreage, patio, quiet   ■ 3D (upstairs)
⊨2T,1D,1Q   🛁Sh.w.g.   ★Air,parking 🚭Restr smoking
🕴 Large shopping Centre, good restaurants, excellent local bus service to City Centre
🚗 Lake Ontario shoreline & parks, downtown Toronto, "GO" Commuter Train to TO (free parking at station), Niagara Falls
🐾 English-style hospitality in large modern home located on large treed property. Well travelled hosts enjoy discussing mutual adventures from all over the world. Special rates for 7days or more. Airport pick-up with minimum 3days stay. ✓B&B

Toronto (cont'd)

Eby, Daniel (Daniel's Musical Hideaway B&B)
118 Isabella St., Toronto, ON   M4Y 1P1

☎ (416) 929-2715, Fax 929-5632
E-mail: dmhbb@home.com

Located east of Jarvis St. and south of Bloor St.
$75S $85D $15Child/Add.person $100F   ▣ Meals   ► 15
🍴 Full   🏠 Downtown, townhouse, view from guests room, patio, porch   ■ 2S,2D,2Ste,2F (upper,ground & lower levels) plus 2cottages   ⊨ 4T,1D,6Q,1K,5P   🚽4Private, 2ensuite, 2sh.w.g.
★Air,KF,LF,F,TV in guest rooms, ceiling fans, private entrance, off-street parking, guest quarters are separate   ✋Designated smoking area, no pets   ～Italian, German, Russian
🕴 Skydome, Eaton Center, Casa Loma, Royal Ontario Museum, AGO, Chinatown, Bata Shoe Museum, 3 subway stops   🚗Kleinburg, Acton, Port Perry, Lake Simcoe
🚙 Warm welcome in spacious modern townhouse with elegant decor and artistic atmosphere, located in the hub of the city. Host is an Operatic Baritone, who teaches singers. Breakfast is served in special guest breakfast room. Special rates & extended stay discounts available during off season (Nov-May). There is a cat in residence. MC ↙B&B www.datatrav.com/daniels

---

Getgood, David & Marcie (Amblecote B&B)
109 Walmer Rd., Toronto, ON   M5R 2X8

☎ (416) 927-1713,Fax 927-0838
E-mail: info@amblecote.com

Locaed 3 blocks north of Bloor St, just west of Spadina Rd.
$65-105S/D   ► 8
🍴 Cont. (Full/gourmet on weekends)   🏠 Downtown, res.,hist.   ■ 5   ⊨ 2Q,3D   🚽 2Ensuite, 2sh.w.g.   ★TVs,Fs, parking, guest fridge, bath robes, hair dryers, air conditioning in guest rooms   ✋ No smoking, no pets, children minimum age 14, minimum stay 2 nights
🕴 Museums, University of Toronto, Casa Loma, Spadina House,
Kensington Market, Chinatown, restaurants, shopping, Yorkville, Spadina subway station
🚗 CN Tower, Eatons Centre, SkyDome, Lake Ontrio waterfront and beaches, theatres, Zoo
🚙 Rambling, historic Edwardian home in the English cottage style with elegance and charm furnished with antiques and Persian rugs. Located in superb and wonderful, eclectic Annex neighbourhood. Distinctive breakfast is served in the formal dining room, by candlelight or in front of a cheery fire. Guests are invited to enjoy the pleasures of an earlier time in tranquil setting. Hoagy Carmichael, the dog, in residence. www.amblecote.com

---

Jarvie, May (Feathers' B&B)
132 Wells Street, Toronto, ON   M5R 1P4

☎ (416) 534-1923

Located 2 blocks north of Bloor Street and 1/2 block east of Bathurst.
$55-75S $75-85D $15Add.person $5(extra for 1 night booking)   ► 4A,2Ch
🍴 Cont.(lavish)   🏠 Downtown, older   ■ 1D(upstairs), 1Studio apt(downstairs for honeymooners or families)   ⊨ 2T(1K),1D,1T
🚽1Private, 1sh.w.h.,1private   ★ Air,LF,TV in guest room, parking
✋No pets,no smoking   ～Dutch,French, some German
🕴 Bathurst Subway and streetcar, Bloor Street dining and entertainment area, Royal Ontario Museum, Casa Loma, Mirvish Village, antiques and bookstores, bus stop on corner
🚗 Eaton's Center, Yorkville, Toronto Harbourfront, Science center
🚙 Charming Victorian family home situated in a super downtown location called "Annex". Antique furniture, oriental tapestries and original artwork
lend a unique atmosphere to interesting and beautifully renovated house. Steps away from a delightful area of affordably priced cosmopolitan restaurants and outdoor cafés. Studio apartment is great for honeymooners or families. ↙B&B

Toronto (cont'd)

Kavanagh, Pat & John (Kavanagh B&B)   ☎ (905) 277-2696
1208 Greening Ave., Mississauga, ON   L4Y 1H5

From QEW take Cawthra Rd north (Exit 134), then right on North Service Rd. to Stanfield Rd (first light). Turn left and proceed 2 blocks to Greening, turn right.

$45S $60D $15Add.person   ► 4A
🍴 Full   🏠 Res.,1.5-storey, patio, quiet   ■2D(main & upper level)   ⊨2T,1Q   🛁1Sh.w.g.   ★ TV,private entrance, fans in guest rooms, off-street parking, guest quarters are separate
✋No smoking, no pets, no children
🚙 Shopping Centers, downtown Toronto, Ontario Place, Toronto Airport, Royal Botanical Gardens, Lake Ontario and lakefront trails, good restaurants, theatres

🐎 Warm welcome in lovely suburban home. Knowledgeable, long-time hosts will be happy to help with itineraries. A small craft shop is located in the guest family room. On pleasant mornings enjoy a full Canadian breakfast on the patio or in separate guest breakfast room. There are 2 outdoor cats. ✔B&B

Ketchen, Donna and Ken (Orchard View)   ☎ (416) 488-6826
92 Orchard View Blvd., Toronto, ON   M4R 1C2   E-mail: ketchen@istar.ca

Centrally located, 1block north of Eglinton Ave & 1block west of Yonge St.
$60S $70-75D   ► 4A
🍴Full   🏠Uptown, res., 3-storey, patio, quiet   ■2D(upstairs)   ⊨2T,1Q   🛁1Ensuite, 1sh.w.h.   ★Air,parking   ✋No smoking, no children
🚶 Subway Stn (Eglinton/Yonge 2blks) to City center & all major city attractions, good shopping, excellent restaurants, library, North Toronto Mem.Centre

🐎 Renovated, spacious 1911-built home is uniquely decorated for the 1990's and centrally situated . "Park the car and discover Toronto"! Friendly, helpful hosts have been welcoming B&B guests for many years. There is a resident cat called "Schubert". ✔ Travelinx   www.bbcanada.com/925.html

---

Maguire, Dorothy (Craig House)   ☎ (416) 698-3916, Fax (416) 698-8506
78 Spruce Hill Rd., Toronto, ON   M4E 3G3

From Hwy 401, take Victoria Park Exit and go south to Queen St. Turn right and at 1st stop light turn right again on Beech. Proceed to Sycamore (first left) to Spruce Hill Rd. From Gardiner Expressway, exit at Lakeshore Rd and travel to Woodbine St. Proceed to Queen St, turn right,

continue to 3rd stop light, turn left at Beech, then as above.
$55S $70D $95Apt $15Add.person   ► 6A
🍴 Full   🏠Beaches Res., 3-storey, guest sundeck   ■3D (1st/2nd level),1Ste(upst with lounge)   ⊨2D,1R,2Q   🛁1Sh.w.g.,1private
★Air,F,sep.entrance,guest kitchen,parking   ✋No smoking,no pets
🚶 Board-walk-by-the-lake, parks, pubs, boutiques, sidewalk cafés, 24hr public transportation on corner
🚙 Eaton Centre, C.N.Tower, Harbour-front, Sky Dome,
🐎 Traditional Beaches home featuring stained glass and leaded bay windows, surrounded by flowers and a forest of stately oaks and located in a neighbourhood with the air of a small resort town by the lake. Breakfast is served in the dining room looking on to the garden.

Toronto (cont'd)

McGregor, Gail (Marlborough Place Bed & Breakfast)　　　☎ (416) 922-2159
93 Marlborough Ave., Toronto, ON　M5R 1X5

Located north of Bloor/Yonge Sts. Phone for directions.
$65S　$115D　　　　　　　　　　　　　　　　　　　　　　▶4
🍲 Cont.(lavish)　🏠 Hist., townhouse, 3-storey, decks on each level　■ 1S,1F (upstairs)
🛏1S,2T　🛁1Ensuite, 1sh.w.h. (jacuzzi)　★ Air,LF,TV, guest sitting & reading areas, private
deck, parking　🖐 Restricted smoking, no pets
🏃 Bloor Street, Yorkville, Royal Ontario Museum, Parliament Bldgs, Rosedale or Summerhill
Subway Stations, excellent shops & restaurants, Toronto Lawn Tennis Club
🔪 Comfortble, newly renovated 1900 Victorian townhouse with open staircase on third floor loft.
Enjoy the view of the garden from the private deck. Long term rates available in winter. ✔B&B

McLoughlin, Katya and Bernie (Beaconsfield B&B)　　　☎ & Fax (416) 535-3338
38 Beaconsfield Ave., Toronto, Ontario　M6J 3H9　　　　E-mail: beacon@idirect.com

Located near Queen St West & Dovercourt St. From Gardiner Expressway, take Jamesen Exit &
go north to Queen. Turn right, past Dufferin to Beaconsfield Ave and left.
$79S/D　$119Ste　$20Add.person　　　▶6-8A
🍲 Choice, homebaked　🏠 Downtown, res., hist., decks, front veranda
■2D,1Ste (upstairs)　🛏1S,2T(1K),2Q, 2cots　🛁1Private,1sh.w.g.
★Air,KF,LF,TV in guest room, Mexican honeymoon suite with tree-top
terrace, parking　🗣Spanish, Slavic languages, some French
🏃 City transit streetcar (24-hour service), Queen Street West (trendy shops,
ethnic restaurants), Canadian National Exhibition, Ontario Place
🚗 Eaton's Centre (10 min.trolley ride), Sky Dome, CN Tower, theatres
🔪 Artist hosts (painting and film acting) in large 1882 Heritage home
with imaginatively decorated rooms full of colour, art, books, antiques and
plants ("eclectic, un-conventional and fun"). Well travelled and informed
hosts will help with itineraries for sightseeing, entertainment and dining. A generous breakfast is
designed around guests' food preferences. There is a resident cat in host quarters. ✔B&B
http://www.bbcanada.com/beaconsfield

Pedersen, Jean & Paul (The Red Door B&B)　　　☎ (416) 604-0544
301 Indian Rd., Toronto, ON　M6R 2X7　　　　E-mail: reddoor@idirect.com

From Hwy 401, take Hwy 427 south, then take the Gardiner Expressway east. Exit at Lakeshore
Blvd and proceed to Parkside Dr and to Bloor St. Go east 2 blocks and south 2 blocks to B&B.
$60-90S　$90-110D　$20Child/Add.person　$150F　　　▶7A,3Ch
🍲 Full　🏠 Res., 3-storey, hist., quiet　■ 1S,2D,1Ste
(upstairs)　🛏 1S,3Q,cot　🛁 1Shw.g., 2ensuite
★F,TV/air-conditioners in guest rooms, off-street parking
🖐No smoking, no pets, children min. age 10　🗣 French
🏃 High Park, Lakeshore Park, restaurants, shops, Bloor West
Village, Roncesvalles Village, Keele Subway Station
🚗 Train/Bus station, Royal Ontario Museum, Toronto Zoo,
Science Center, Lake Ontario, CN Tower, International Airport
🔪 Elegant 1912 home on a quiet, tree-lined residential street, ideally located with quick access to
downtown. Gourmet homecooked breakfast is served in the dining room where guests from
virtually any part of the world meet. Hostess is an artist whose passion for painting and interior
design gives the home its unique & gracious ambiance. Host is a musician, who composes music
and teaches at UofT. They hope that guests find "the decor inviting, the beds comfortable, the
breakfast appetizing and the atmosphere warm and friendly". Visa ✔ B&B
http://webhome.idirect.com/~reddoor/

Toronto (cont'd)

Perks, Dave & A.Tanner-Hill (The House on McGill)   ☎ & Fax (416)351-1503
110 McGill St., Toronto,ON   M5B 1H6   E-mail: mcgillbb@interlog.com, 1-877-580-5015

Located near intersection of Church & Carleton Street.
$50-70S $65-85D $15Add.person (discounts for long-term stay)   ▶ 9A
🌙 Cont+, self-serve   🏠 Downtown, 3-storey, townhouse, view from guest
rooms, porch, quiet   ■ 6D(upstairs)   ⊨1D,4Q,1K(2T) ⌂2Sh.w.g.
★Air,F,LF, street parking, microwave/fridge/coffeemaker for guests,
bicycles on loan, internet access, guest garden/deck, guest quarters are
separate   ⓌNo smoking, no pets, no children   ∽ French, Australian
🕏 Eaton Center, University of Toronto, Maple Leaf Gardens, Yonge Street,
theatre district, Allen Gardens, St.Lawrence Market, Yorkville, Church
St.Village, Carleton Cineplex, Ryerson U., Cabbagetown, streetcar/subway
🚗 Ontario Place, ROM, AGO, Science Centre, Toronto Isls, Harbourfront
📸 Elegantly restored 1894 Victorian Townhouse with stained glass windows and modern
conveniences, located in quiet shady enclave in the heart of the bustle of the City. Host will be
happy to guide guests in their own car on a tour of the city. Breakfast is served in special guest
breakfast room. Ideal place for business travellers. Visa,MC   www.interlog.com/~mcgillbb/

Snelson, Karen & Ken(Mayfair B&B)   ☎ (416) 769-1558, Fax (416) 769-9655
78 Indian Grove, Toronto, ON   M6R 2Y4   E-mail: ksnelson@compuserve.com

Located half a block south of Bloor Street and one block east of Parkside/Keele St.

$70S $80-90D $15Add.person   ▶ 8A,3Ch
🌙 Full, homebaked   🏠 Res., older, quiet   ■ 3Stes (upstairs) plus effic.
suite   ⊨2T,2Q,1cot   ⌂ 4Ensuite   ★Air,TV in guest room, parking
Ⓦno pets, no smoking
🕏 High Park, shopping and restaurants, subway stop
🚗 Downtown Toronto, Canadian National Exhibition, Ontario Place
📸 Elegant, 1911 Edwardian home furnished with antiques and persian
carpets with many leaded and stained glass windows and beautiful oak
panelling. Located in a quiet residential area close to downtown. Congenial,
well travelled hosts enjoy helping guests with plans.Visa ∽B&B

Vallance, Philomena & Dave (Philomena & Dave B&B)   ☎(416)962-2786,Fax964-8837
31 Dalton Rd., Toronto, ON   M5R 2Y8   E-mail: valladp@echo-on.net, 1-888-272-2718

Located near Bloor St & Spadina Ave. By prior reservation only.
$50S $70D   (Discounts for long stay & off-season)   ▶ 4A
🌙 Full   🏠 Downtown, res., 3-storey, quiet, deck   ■ 2D(upstaires)
⊨2T,1Q   ⌂1Sh.w.g.   ★ TV in guest rooms, guest kitchen for light
snacks with morning sun-deck, off-street parking   ★ Designated smoking
area, not suitable for children   ∽ German, Italian
🕏 Royal Ontario Museum, Chinatown, subway & streetcar, various
restaurants, University of Toronto
📸 Friendly hospitality in comfortable home with stained glass, leaded
windows and original oak, located in the pleasant downtown community
called the "Annex". Enjoy the very quiet atmosphere, yet close proximity to
Bloor Street with large selection of stores and restaurants
operated by many nationalities. Breakfast is served in enclosed cozy sun room. There is a
cat.∽B&B   http://www.bbcanada.com/2072.html

Toronto (cont'd)

Vanderkooy, Joan (Vanderkooy Bed & Breakfast)   ☎ (416) 925-8765
53 Walker Ave., Toronto, ON   M4V 1G3

Phone for directions. Located in the Yong/St.Clair area.
$50-65S $70-80D   ►6
🍽 Full   🏠 Downtown, res., 2.5-storey, patio, deck   ■ 3D (upstairs)
🛏 4T(1K),1D   🛏 1sh.w.g., 1Ensuite   🚗 Air,F,TV,off-street parking,
beautiful waterfall and pond in garden   🖐 Smoking outside
🏃 Popular restaurants and shops on St Clair Ave, Yorkville Ave & Bloor St.,
Summerhill Subway Station to downtown attractions
🚗 Ontario Place & Lake Ontario Harbourfront, Eaton Centre, CN Tower
🐾 Bright and cheerful home with a friendly, casual atmosphere and filled
with fine touches, including stained glass and original art. Breakfast is served
in open dining room overlooking the garden. Relax on the flower filled deck in
warmer weather. There is a resident cat. ✍B&B

Wong, Anita & Jonathan (An 1871 Historic House B&B)   ☎ (416) 923-6950, Fax 1065
65 Huntley St., Toronto, ON   M4Y 2L2   E-mail: an1871hist@interlog.com

Phone for directions.
$65-135S/D $20Child/Add.person   🍴Meals   ►14
🍽 Full, homebaked   ■ Downtown, hist., city view from guest rooms
■3D (upstairs), plus coach house   🛏 4T,2Q,1K,2R,2P   🚗 1Sh.w.g., 2
Ensuite   ★ Air,F,TV in guest rooms, ceiling fans, private entrance,
off-street parking, guest quarters are separate   🖐 No smoking, no pets
〰Manadrin
🏃 Bloor St & Yorkville Ave with trendy shops, Bata Shoe Museum, Royal
Ontario Museum, Greek Town Village, Gardiner Ceramic Museum, Ontario
Art Gallery, Eaton Center, Chinatown, subway stations on Bloor St.
🚗 MacMichael Art Gallery, Canada's Wonderland, Metropolitan Zoo
🐾 New owners in well established downtown B&B. Unique character home built in 1871 with
lovely finials, original moldings & millwork, 11ft high ceilings. Breakfast is served in the formal
dining room. The coach house is at the back of the property. ✍B&B   www.bbcanada.com/3021

Bed & Breakfast Homes of Toronto   ☎ (416) 363-6362
46093, College Park PO, Toronto, Ont. M5B 2L8

Rates: from $45S   from $60D   (including breakfast and parking)
Bed & Breakfast Homes of Toronto is an established B&B association with a difference: a
cooperative of 10 friendly, independent homes allows travellers to speak directly with the host
before booking. Standards are high, yet room rates are low. Call or write for free brochure
describing homes throughout the city. ✍B&B

Toronto Bed & Breakfast Inc.   ☎(416)588-8800/927-0354,Fax(416)927-0838
Box 269, 253 College St., Toronto, ON   M5T 1R5   E-mail: beds@torontobandb.com

(Marcia Getgood, President)
Rates: $60-105S $70-120D   (including breakfast)
A professional reservation service of quality inspected Bed & Breakfast accommodation, providing
high level of safety, comfort, cleanliness & hospitality. Toronto's longest running urban B&B
Service. Advance reservation recommended. Free brochure on request. CCards.

Toronto (cont'd)

Downtown Toronto Association of B&B Guest Homes   ☎ (416) 368-1420/Fax 368-1653
Box 190, Stn. B, Toronto, ON   M5T 2W1

(Mrs. Linda Lippa, Co-ordinator)
Rates $45-65S $55-75D $80-120Stes   (Full/gourmet breakfast)
The Downtown Toronto Association & B&B Guest Homes is a professionsl reservation service, representing Toronto's largest selection of fully inspected and privately owned Victorian homes in downtown Toronto, all within 10 minutes of major tourist attractions. All hosts are active in the arts or hospitality industries and proudly feature distinctive homes in downtown locations, with access to 24 hour transit. Some homes offer fireplaces and jaccuzzis. Free brochure with map of the city and home descriptions available. ✏B&B

Troy   *(west of Hamilton; see also Dundas, Ancaster, Waterdown)*

Cornell, Lillian & Carl (A Slice of Home B&B)   ☎ (519) 647-2082
1927 Hwy 5West, Troy, ON   L0R 2B0

Located 6.6km west of Peter's Corners and 16km west of Clappison's Cut.
$35S $45-55D   🍽 Meals   ▶ 5A,2Ch
◨Full 🏠Rural, ranch-style, view from guest rooms,quiet ■3(main level) ⊨1D,1K,1P,1S, 3cribs,1cot ⏁1Sh.w.h. ★KF,LF,F,TV, off-street parking ⚲No smoking, no pets
🐾 Warm welcome and friendly hospitality in quiet country home comfortably decorated. Enjoy the water gardens from the solarium and relaxing country atmosphere. There are 2 resident cats.

Victoria Harbour   *(north of Barrie; see also Midland, Penetang., Waubaushene)*

Barron, Frank & Joyce (Daisy's Place)   ☎ (705) 534-4601
7 Bayside Ave, RR1, Box 189, Victoria Harbour, ON   L0K 2A0   E-mail: barronjoyce@hotmail.com

Take Hwy 400 north to Hwy 12 West and to Victoria Harbour, Park St. Proceed to Davis Dr (2nd on right) and then to Bayside Ave. Turn right.
$50S $60D $30Add.person   ▶ 6
◨ Full 🏠 Rural, bungalow, lakefront, patio, deck, quiet ■3D (main & ground level) ⊨2S,2D ⏁2Sh.w.g.,1ensuite ★F,TV, separate entrance, wheelchair friendly ⚲No smoking, no pets
🏃 Georgian Bay, country walks, x-country skiing, ice fishing
🚌 Moonstone & Mt.St.Louis Ski Resorts, Huronia Museum & Indian Village, Martyr's Shrine, Wyemarsh Wildlife Centre
🐾 Friendly hospitality in modern home on the water. Relax in the recreation room with pool table, TV, piano, games Enjoy breakfast in the dining room overlooking beautiful Georgian Bay.CC

Vineland   *(west of St.Catharines; see also Beamsville, Grimsby, St.Anns, N.Falls, NOTL)*

Dunnink, Janet and Bert (Travellers Home)   ☎& Fax (905) 562-5656
RR1, Jordan, ON L0R 1S0

Location: 2666-8th Ave, Vineland. From QEW Exit57, turn off on Victoria Ave towards Vineland.
Go through stoplights. After 4km turn left on 8th Ave and continue to No2666.

$45S $70D $10Child/Add.person (weekly rates)   ▶ 6A,2Ch
🍽 Full   🏠 Rural, res., 1.5-storey, wooded lot, patio, quiet
■1S,2D(upper
level) ⊨2S,1D,1Q,1R ⬛3Ensuite ★Air,F,KF,TV in guest room,
separate entrance, parking, private guest sitting room ✋No
smoking, no pets ∽Dutch
🏃 Balls Falls historic park, Bruce trail hiking, Prudhommes
Landing (Wet & Wilds), golfing, several wineries (tours & tasting)
🚗 Niagara Falls, Marineland, quaint town NOTL, Welland Canal, Lake Ontario
🐾 Spacious home with Dutch hospitality on quiet property located in Ontario's "Fruit Belt" with
plenty of fruits in season. Entire upper level is for guests. Located 20km from Niagara Falls.

Tieman, Jane & André (Tintern Vacations B&B)   ☎ 1-888-298-7291, Fax (905) 563-3446
2869 Tintern Rd, RR1, Vineland, ON L0R 2C0   E-mail: tintern.vacations@on.aibn.com

From QEW take Exit 57 (Victoria Ave/RR24) and proceed south to Spring Creek Rd. Turn right to
Tintern Rd and then left.

$60-90D $10Child $15Add.person 🍽 Meals   ▶ 18
🍽Full, homebaked   🏠Rural, village, bungalow, hillside,5-acres,
view from guest rooms, swimming pool, river at back, quiet, deck
■4D(main & ground level) ⊨4D,1K,2Q,2T,2cots,crib
⬛3Ensuite, 1sh.w.g. ★Air ✋Desig smoking area ∽some
Dutch & French
🏃 Canoeing, cycling, golfing, country walks, churches
🚗 35 wineries, Niagara Falls, Casino, Niagara-on-the-Lake, Bruce Trail hiking, Butterfly Cons.
🐾 Fruit hobby farm with beautifully decorated large family home, situated on lush acreage in the
heart of Niagara's wine region. Ideal place for outdoor enthusiasts. Explore the area by canoe,
paddle boat or tandem bike. There are teenagers in the host family. Large play area and volley ball
court and pool. Hosts are founders of Wine Country B&B Assoc. There is a talking parrot in
residence and llamas, calves and chickens on the grounds. ✔B&B www.bbcanada.com/1778.html

---

Walkerton   *(east of Kincardine; see also Cargill, Paisley, Mildmay,)*

Huygen, Ruby (Silver Creek Bed & Breakfast)   ☎ (519) 881-0252
17 Yonge St S, Walkerton, ON N0G 2V0

In Walkerton, at junction of Hwys 4/9 proceed 1 block south of Main Street. Watch for signs.

$35S $45D   🍽 Meals   (Family rates available)   ▶ 6
🍽 Full, homebaked   🏠 Downtown,res.,older,.75acreage,quiet
■3D(upst) ⊨3D ⬛1Shw.g.,1shw.h. ★TV,F,parking
✋Smoking outside
🏃 Downtown shopping, parks, Saugeen River (canoeing, fishing),
Walkerton Ski Hills, cross country and snowmobile trails
🚗 Lake Huron and beaches, Kincardine, Blyth Theatre
🐾 Comfortable country-style home near downtown surrounded
by spacious lawns and flower gardens with the Silver Creek running through property. Enjoy a
hearty breakfast with homemade jams and tea biscuits. There is a cat outside. ✔B&B

Waterdown

(west of Toronto; see also Burlington, Hamilton, Dundas)

Sherwood, Anne & Eric (Sherwood Rockhaven B&B)
6 Faircrest Dr., Waterdown, ON   L0R 2H1

☎ (905) 689-8814, Fax 689-1625
E-mail: a.sherwood@sympatico.ca

Phone for directions.
$50S $60D $10Child/Add.person   ► 4A,2Ch
🍲 Full   🏠 Village bungalow, porch, deck, quiet   ■2D (lower level)   ⊨ 2D,1Q   ⊒1Sh.w.g.,plus powder room   ★ Air,TV in guest rooms, off-street parking, excercise room, guests quarters are separate   🖐 No smoking no pets
🧍 Downtown, antique & charming village shops, good restaurants & pubs, seasonal Village Players, Antique Car Shows, Bruce Trail
🚗 Burlington, Lake Ontario, major shopping malls, Flamboro Downs Race Track, Hamilton, McMaster University, Royal Botanical Gardens, scenic country drives, Mennonite Country
☛ Warm welcome in new home with bright ambiance, located in quiet neighborhood of charming village, with easy access from major routes. Retired hosts are well travelled and enjoy meeting people from all parts of the world. Relax on the wrap around deck & veranda or in the cozy backyard surrounded by many beautiful plants and flowers. Vegetarian diet catered. Gourmet breakfast is served from menu indoors or outdoors on the patio. Fax/Internet facilities for corporate guests available. There are 2 friendly cats "Burt & Ernie" in residence. Visa ✓B&B
http://www.bbcanada.com/2415.html

Waubaushene

(on Georgian Bay, north of Barrie; see also Penetang.,Vict.Hbr.,Midland)

Boyd, Jan & Bev (Lamplight B&B)
1163 Gratrix Rd, RR1, Waubaushene, ON   L0K 2C0

☎ (705) 835-5622

From south take Hwy 400 north past Barrie to Exit 141 at Coldwater. Turn left onto Vasey Rd and continue to Gratrix Rd (app.2.5km) Turn right and look for 3rd house on right.

$40S $50D $10Child $100F   🍽 Meals   ► 5
🍲 Full, homebaked   🏠 Farm, hist., 2-storey, view from guest rooms, quiet   ■ 1S,2D(upstairs)   ⊨ 1S,2D   ⊒ 1Sh.w.g.
★KF,LF,TV, ceiling fans, off-street parking   🖐No smoking, no pets, not suitable for children
🧍 Walking, biking, x-c skiing, horseback riding, boat rentals
🚗 Huronia Museum & Huron-Quendat Village, Discovery Hbr, Casino Rama, St.Leacock Museum, Big Chute Marine Railway
☛ 4th Generation family in Century farm home, recently redecorated, filled with antiques, surrounded by 50acres of farmland & large flower/vegetable/herb gardens, and located in the midst of popular vacation destination. Hosts enjoy "talking gardening...", are knowledgeable about the local area and have done extensive boating locally and sailing in the Bahamas. Breakfast is served in the country kitchen. Special diets available with advance notice. ✓B&B

Carpenter, Mary & John (Waubaushene Heritage House B&B)
Box 429, 337 Pine St., Waubaushene, ON   L0K 2C0

☎ (705) 538-1857

Take Hwy 400 and Hwy 69 crossing Hwy 12 into Waubaushene.Travel 1 block on Pine St to top of hill and to B&B beside Waubaushene Heritage store.
$40S $50D   ► 6A,2Ch
🍲 Full, homebaked   🏠 Village, 2-storey, hist., lakeview, porch   ■ 3D (upstairs)   ⊨ 2T,1D,1Q   ⊒ 1Private, 1sh.w.g.   ★Air, separate entrance, off-street parking   🖐 Smoking on front porch
🧍 Beach, boat rental, marina, churches
🚗 Discovery Bay (Penetanguishene), Big Chute (railway boat crossing) on Severn Waterway, Wye Marsh, St.Marie Among the H.
☛ Newly renovated 1881 house with a view of the lake in popular resort district. Hosts are well informed about this historic area and enjoy helping guests with plans. Enjoy fishing or lunch on the porch or a day at the beach.Visa,MC ✓CC

Jones, David & Kay (Wawa Lakeshore Bed & Breakfast) ☎(705)856-1709,Fax1785
1 Gold St., Wawa, ON P0S 1K0   E-mail: dhjones@onlink.net

Located 225km north-west of Sault-Ste-Marie on Hwy 17 north.
$55D   ▶6
🍽Cont/deluxe 🏠Downtown, res., 3-storey, lakefront, view from
guest rooms, patio, deck, quiet ■1Ste(upstairs) ⊨2D,1Q
🛏1Sh.w.g.   ★ F,KF,TV/VCR/phone in guest sitting room,
separate entrance, off-street parking, balconies, guest quarters are
separate ⚇No smoking, one party only ⚭Finnish

🏃 Lakeshore walkway displaying historic plaques, shallow sandy beach, snowmachine trails
🚐 Scenic High Falls, Agawa Pictographs, Magpie Valley Badlands, old mine sites
🐾 Warm & friendly hospitality in lovely open-concept home located on the beach overlooking
scenic Wawa Lake. Guest quarters are in two upper floors with loft on third floor. Ideal place for a
family or up to 3 couples travelling together. Reduced rates for extended stays.

Burford, Ed & Dr.Norma Sanders (Goose Down Inn)   ☎ (705) 856-7003
37 Klondike St., Wawa, ON P0S 1K0   E-mail: nsanders@onlink.com

Turn off Hwy 17 and follow Hwy 101 into Wawa. Proceed past Wally's Restaurant & turn right onto
1st street (Klondike St). Look for white house with blue shutters & geese on the front deck.

$40S $50D $60F   ▶ 4A,2Ch
❄May15-Oct15 🍽Full,homebaked 🏠 Res., ranch-style,
quiet ■3D (main level) ⊨1K,2T,2R 🛏Sh.w.g. ★LF, guest
dining/sitting room, parking ⚇No smoking, no pets

🏃 Wawa Lake (spring fed), swimming, Wawa Goose Monument
🚐 Magpie High Falls, hiking trails, Lake Superior, miles of sandy
beaches Old Woman Bay
🐾 Retired professional hosts in comfortable home decorated
with family antiques and art. House specialty is Ed's homemade pork sausages and wild blueberry
jam. Host is very knowledgeable of the area and its resources. There is a Hungarian Puli dog named
"Panya" in residence. ⌐B&B www.bbcanada.com/goosedownbb

Paulencu, Cathie & Joe Lynett (Superior Avenue B&B)   ☎ (705) 856-7479
120 Superior Ave., Wawa, ON P0S 1K0

From Hwy 17 turn into Hwy 101 & follow into Wawa. Proceed past Wawa Motor Hotel, turn left on

Nipigon St (1 block to Superior Ave), follow curved street for 1km.
$50-55S $55-65D   ▶4
❄ May-Sept (other by reservation) 🍽 Full 🏠 Res.,
bungalow, hillside, view from guest rooms, patio, quiet ■2D
(main floor) ⊨ 1D,1Q 🛏1Private, 1ensuite ★ F,TV in
guest living room, off-street parking ⚇ Smoking outside, no
pets, not suitable for children
🏃 Public beaches, local parks, downtown, shopping

🚐 Golf Course, Lake Superior, scenic High Falls, old mine sites, hiking trails
🐾 Brick bungalow, tastefully decorated overlooking public golf course. Hosts are knowledgeable
about the area and enjoy golfing, gardening, roller blading and good conversation. Breakfast is
served in the comfortable dining room. ⌐B&B www.bbcanada.com/2731.html

Wellesley

(north of Stratford; see also Baden)

Hafemann, Adolph and Emily (Firella Creek Farm B&B) ☎ (519) 656-2974
1666 Hutchison Rd., RR2, Wellesley, ON   N0B 2T0

Take Hwy 401 to Kitchener and then Hwy 7/8 West. Turn right onto Rd 5 (just past Baden) and continue to Wellesley. Turn left onto Queen St W. At the end turn right and proceed 1 km to farm.

$40S $55-65D $10Child   🍽 Meals   ► 6A,2Ch and baby
🔲Full   🏠98-acre farm,2-storey,view,patio,quiet   ■3(upper & main floor)   〰German   🛏2T,1D,1Q,1P,crib   🛁1Sh.w.g.,1ensuite, 1private   ★Air,TV,F, parking   ✋No smoking, no pets
🏃 Trout pond, nature trails, wooded areas, stream, meadows and wildlife, cross-country skiing and hiking on farm grounds
🚗 Local Cider Mill, Wellesley Apple Butter & Cheese Festival Stratford theatres, St.Jacobs farmers' market

📣 New comfortable house is equipped with climate control and located in the heart of Mennonite farming country. Relax by the cheery fire with a hot apple cider. Hosts cater to special dietary needs. Children welcome.✓B&B

Wellington

(south of Trenton; see also Consecon, Bloomfield, Picton)

Haeberlin, Elaine & Richard (Tara Hall Bed & Breakfast) ☎ (613)399-2801, Fax 399-1104
Box 623, 146 Main Street, Wellington, ON   K0K 3L0   E-mail: tarahall@intranet.ca

From Hwy 401, take Wooler Rd (Exit 522) & Hwy 33 (Loyalist Pkwy) south to Wellington.
$50-60S $62-85D   ► 7A,3C
🔲 Choice   🏠 Village, hist., view, lakefront, patio, deck, quiet, parking   ■1S,2D,1F(upst)   🛏2T,1K,2Q,1R   🛁3Sh.w.g.
★Air,7F,LF,KF, TV in common & most guest room, jacuzzi
✋No smoking indoors
🚗 Sandbanks Provincial Park, Lake on the Mountain, Picton
🏃 Lake Ontario sandy beach, fishing, boat launch, golfing, antiques/crafts, hist.sites, restaurants
📣 Spacious, c1839 historically designated, majestic home. Rooms have luxury decor & fireplaces & overlook Lake Ontario and West Lake. Hot breakfast served in formal dining room.Visa ✓B&B
www.intranet.ca/~tarahall

Waterfall, Jean & Jim (Bridies Bed & Breakfast) ☎ (613) 399-2376
307 Main St., Wellington, ON   K0K 3L0   E-mail: bridiebb@reach.net

From Hwy 401E take Exit 522 (Wooler Rd) and proceed south on Hwy 33 into the village.

$50S $60D $15Add.person   ► 8A,4Ch
🔲 Full   🏠 Village, res., 2-storey, hist., view from guest rooms, lake at back   ■2D,1F(upstairs)   🛏3D,2R,1P,crib   🛁1Sh.w.g., 1sh.w.h.   ★ TV, street parking   ✋ No smoking, no pets
🏃 Tea Room, numerous antique and craft shops, artisans and historic museum, beach on Lake Ontario
🚗 Provincial Parks, Sandbanks, North Beach, pottery studios
📣 Beautiful 1860-built house, once the village Doctors home, situated in picturesque Lake Ontario village. Stroll down to the waterfront, sit on a bench or rock and enjoy the breathtaking scenery. Hosts display precious Royalty plates and other collactables and visitors may enjoy the model trains. Visa ✓B&B

Wellington (cont'd)

Whittaker, Pat & Roger (Rose & Thistle Bed & Breakfast)   ☎ (613) 399-1413
Box 615, 306 Noxon Ave, Wellington, ON   K0K 3L0

From Hwy 401, take Exit 522 (Wooler Rd) and follow Hwy 33 to Wellington. Turn north off Main St. at West St and proceed 1 block.
$45S $55-75D $15Add.person   (Family rate available)   ▶ 6
🍲 Full, homebaked   🏠 Village, older, 3-storey, quiet, veranda
■3D(upst) ⊨2T,1D,1Q,1R ⊐1Sh.w.g.,1ensuite ★Air,TV, upstairs library/den for guests, compl.bicycles & locked storage
🚭No smoking
🏃 Lake Ontario, beach and lakefront parks, craft & gift shops, fishing, boating, cycling, antiques, museum, x/c skiing, hiking
🚗 Sandbanks & North Beach Provincial Parks, Bloomfield, Picton, cheese factory
📣 Renovated and restored Queen Anne-style home with spacious guest rooms complete with mini-libraries. Situated in the heart of the village two blocks from Lake Ontario, which offers an everchanging scenery. Enjoy the breeze from the lake on the wrap-around veranda. Cycling tours can be arranged. Two cats are unobtrusive co-hosts. Visa

Westport   *(north of Gananoque; see also Newboro)*

Bradley, Anne & Robert (A Bit of Gingerbread B&B)   ☎ (613) 273-7848
27 Bedford St., Box 183, Westport, ON   K0G 1X0

From Hwy 401 at Kingston, take Exit 617 and then Rte 10 north. Located in the village.
$35S $45-75D $15Add.person   ▶ 6A,1Ch
🍲Full 🏠Village,hist.,2-storey,quiet ■3D(upst) ⊨4T,1Q,1R
⊐1Sh.w.g.,1ensuite ★TV,library, separate guests quarters & entrance, off-street parking 🚭No smoking, no pets
🏃 Rideau District Museum, historic village walking tour, harbour & island picnic site on Rideau Waterway with marina, Rideau Trail, Foley Mt. Conservation Area, Spy Rock Lookout, beach at Sand Lake, boutiques, antique shops, restaurants, boat trips
🚗 Five Locks on Rideau Canal & historic Jones Falls Dam, hiking, cycling, canoeing
📣 Century home in picturesque village. Ideal place for exploring the Rideau Lakes area. Transportation to trails and excursions to places of interest or dining can be provided. Receiver of accredited ON Superstar 1999 Tourism Award. Visa,MC ⌐B&B

Cowan, Terry and Mary (The Cove Country Inn)   ☎ (613) 273-3636
General Delivery, Westport, ON   K0G 1X0

From Hwy 401, take Exit 617 (Hwy 10) north to Westport. Look for Inn on the corner of Main and Bedford St on the water.
$50-120D(Summer) $40-95(Winter) 🍽 Meals   ▶ 12
🍲 Full 🏠 Village, hist., view, lakefront, patio, quiet ■ 6D (incl 4jacussi suites) ⊨6T,3D,R ⊐ 4Ensuite, private
★Air,F,LF,2F, ceiling fans in guest rooms, piano lounge, hot tub & sauna, parking separate entrance ♥ 🚭Restricted smoking
🏃 Boating, swimming, fishing, dining, entertainment, windsurfing,fish sanctuary, skating, sleigh rides, x-country skiing
🚗 Rideau Lake Locks, Old Fort Henry, historic Perth, Kingston
📣 Antique and historic setting in popular vacation village. Cross-country ski packages, boat cruises and bicycle tours can be arranged. Visa,MC, ⌐B&B

Westport (cont'd)

Rothwell, Kathy & Margot (The Rothwells' Stone Cottage B&B)   ☎ (613) 273-3081
Box 368, Westport, ON K0G 1X0

From Hwy 401 take Westport Exit & proceed on Hwy 10 to village
$70-90D $105F   ◧Meals   ► 8A,2Ch
▣ Full   ♠ Village, hist.,acreage, 2-storey, view, lakefront, oval
in-ground pool, patio, porch, quiet ■4(main & upper floor)
⊨4T,2D,2cots ⊒2Sh.w.g.,1ensuite ★Air,2F,LF,KF,TV in one
guest room, separate entrance ⓌDesignated smoking area
🏃 Hiking & x-c ski trails on lake & Foley Mountain, lake skating
🚗 Perth, Smith Falls, Kingston, Merrickville

🐎 Historic home, decorated in an elegant style that befits its heritage and furnished with family
heirlooms. Guests are welcome to sit on the screened veranda or on the tree-shaded patio
overlooking the Upper Rideau Lake. Canoe available for lake exploration. Breakfast is served on the
veranda in the summer. All inclusive weekends can be arranged for small groups. MC ⌐CC

Wheatley   *(south-east of Windsor; see also Leamington, Amherstburg)*

Dent, David & Elizabeth (By the Bay B&B)   ☎ (519) 825-7729
RR1, Box1, S7,Wheatley, ON N0P 2P0

From Hwy 401 take Exits 56 or 63 and proceed south on Rd1 from Tilbury to Wheatley.

$55S $85D $10Child $15Add.person   ► 4
▣ Full, homebaked   ♠ 2-storey, view, patio, porch, quiet
■2D(upstairs)   ⊨ 2T(K), 1D   ⊒2sh.w.g.   ★ Air,F, ceiling
fans, off-street parking, canoe and bikes for guests   Ⓦ Smoking
outside, inquire about children   ⌁ Dutch
🏃 Lake Erie and sandy beach, Wheatley Prov.Park (walking,
canoeing, cycling)
🚗 Point Pelee Nat. Park, Leamington, Hillman Marsh, Windsor

🐎 Warm welcome in unique open-concept, architect designed house with lovely garden and small
Carolinian forest behind, nestled near the waters of Wheatley Prov.Park. Hosts are retired
educators who love to travel, read and enjoy theatre, gardening and backyard birding. Enjoy
sumptuous breakfasts. Visa ⌐B&B www.wincom.net/~ddent

Patterson, Bea & Bruce (B&B's Bed & Breakfast)   ☎ (519)825-8008,Fax 825-7737
216 Erie St.S., Wheatley, ON N0P 2P0   E-mail: brucep@mnsi.net, 1-800-851-3406,

From Hwy401 take Hwy2 Exit into Tillbury and turn south on Erie St. Continue 22km south.
$85S/D $10Child/Add.person   (plus tax)   ► 8A,4Ch
▣ Full, homebaked   ♠ Village, hist., 3-storey, swimming pool,
patio, porch, deck, quiet   ■ 3D,1F (main & lower level)
⊨2T,1D,2Q, cot   ⊒ 1Private, 3ensuite   ★Air,satTV in sitting
area, private entrance, off-street parking, pool table, guest quarters
are separate   Ⓦ Designated smoking area, no pets, arrival after
3pm and departure before 11am
🏃 Talbot Trail, shops, beaches, churches, restaurants
🚗 Hillman Marsh, Point Pelee National Park, Windsor Casino, Chatham, Leamington, birding,
golfing, sport fishing, scuba diving, antique hunting and auctions
🐎 Warm welcome and friendly hospitality in comfortable home with antique furnishings, located
in pleasant village. Hosts are avid birders. Guided tours are available at extra cost. A country
breakfast is served in the guest breakfast room. Box lunches can be provided on request. There is a
dog and a cat in residence. Visa,MC ⌐B&B www.mnsi.net/~brucep

Whitby

(east of Toronto; see also Oshawa)

Stapleford, Ann (St.John's Inn B&B) ☎ (905) 666-4514
508 John St.W., Whitby, ON   L1N 2V6

Exit Hwy 401 at Hwy 12 (Brock St) and proceed to John St. Turn left and continue to Palace St.

Look for house on corner with 8ft hedge & entrance on Palace St.
$65-85S/D $85Suite   ► 5-7
❋ Spring-Fall   Full, homebaked   Downtown, res., hist.,
converted church, decks, quiet, isolated   1S,2D (main & upper
level)   2S,1D,1Q,1R   1Sh.w.h., 1ensuite   ★F,TV in one
guest room & in large upper level rec room, parking   No pets
Lake Ontario, Whitby Hbr, downtown, restaurants, Pearson
Lanes shopping, Pickering Flea Market (Sundays), golfing
Cullen Gardens & Miniature Village, Yacht Club, Toronto Commuter Train, two ski areas
Unique home (ca 1902), with 32 ft ceilings, stained glass windows and furnished with many
antiques, served as the Catholic Church until 1959. Enjoy the friendly casual atmosphere and relax
among extensive grounds. Hosts are well travelled and knowledgeable of Whitby's historic past.
There are two well-trained resident dogs who love children. Visa

---

Wood, Mary & Ted (Ezra Annes House 1836)   ☎ (905) 430-1653,1-800-213-1257
239 Wellington St., Whitby, ON   L1N 5L7   E-mail: mwood@durham.net, Fax (905) 430-3341

From Hwy 401 exit at Brock St/Hwy 12 and go north to Burns. Turn left to Annes St. Turn right
and continue north over Dundas/Hwy2 to Gifford. Turn left to Wellington and then right.

$60S $95D   ► 4
Full, homebaked   Downtown, res., 2-storey, hist., view from
guest rooms, stone terraces, quiet   2D(upstairs)   1D,1Q
2Ensuite   ★ Air,TV,F,LF, sauna room, off-street
parking   No smoking, not suitable for children   some French
Lake Ontario shores, ravine and park
Cullen Gardens, Go-Train/bus to Toronto, Bird sanctuaries
1836-built home is filled with antiques, books and the grace
of a bygone era. The English perennial garden has stone terraces, a water garden and rose arbour.
Host is a Mystery Writer. Enjoy the elegant hideaway with gourmet breakfasts, afternoon tea on
the terrace, good conversation, and gracious, friendly atmosphere. Visa ✔B&B ezraannes.com

---

Wiarton

(north of Owen Sound; see also Pike Bay, Hope Bay, Lion's Head)

Christensen, Jorn and Elsie (Bruce Gables)   Fax (519) 534-0779
410 Berford St., Box 448, Wiarton, ON   N0H 2T0   ☎ (519) 534-0429/winter 0933

Hwy 6 passes through Wiarton and is known as Berford Street. Located at the northwest corner of
Berford and Mary Streets. Parking off Mary Street.

$45S $55D $5Child $10Add.person   ► 9
❋ May-Oct   Full   Village, view   3(upstairs)
1D,2Q, cot   1Sh.w.h.,1sh.w.g.   ★F,TV,parking (off Mary
St)   No smoking   French, German, Spanish, Danish
Bruce Trail, swimming in Colpoy's Bay, sailing, fishing, golfing,
restaurants, village centre
Bruce Peninsula National Park, Tobermory Island Ferry
Spacious, turn-of-the-Century Victorian home restored to its Victorian splendour with bay
windows overlooking Wiarton and the clear blue waters of Colpoy's Bay, decorated with momentos
of hosts' stay in Switzerland and world travels. Enjoy the European atmosphere. ✔B&B
www.bbcanada.com/948.html

Wiarton (cont'd)

Cox, Gord & Ellie (Down A Country Lane B&B)
RR3, Wiarton, ON N0H 2T0

☎ (519) 534-3170
E-mail: gefcox@bms.com

Located in Oliphant. From Owen Sound, take Hwy6 north to Hepworth and continue west to Sauble B. Proceed on Bruce County Rd13 north to stop sign. Turn right, proceed to 5th house on right.
$45-55S $50-60D $10Child $10Add.person 🍽 Meals (weekly rates avail) ▶ 4A,3Ch
🍴 Full, homebaked 🏠 Rural, split-level, acreage, lakeview, porch, quiet ■3D(upper level) ⊷ 3Q,3R ⌁ 1Ensuite, 2sh.w.h. ★ TV & ceiling fan in guest lounge, sep.entrance, campfire area & barbeque Ⓦ No smoking, no pets
🚶 Walk through lawns with rose beds
🚗 Lake Huron shoreline, Sauble Beach, Wiarton, Bruce Peninsula highlights. x-c skiing, hiking, birding, Bruce Trail
Warm welcome in picturesque country home situated in very quiet, peaceful surroundings. Relax on the covered wrap-around porch and enjoy the lovely view of Spry Lake and the beautiful sunsets. Weekends only Sept-June. ⌐CC www.bbcanada.com/1055.html

---

Cumming, Mary (Shoreline B&B)
RR1, Eastnor Twsp, Pike Bay, Mar, ON N0H 1X0

☎ (519) 793-4197

From Wiarton take Hwy 6 north to Pike Bay Rd. Turn left 6.6km to corner store. Turn left, then right at 1st road to 2nd house on left.

$45S $50D $5Child $60F $15Add.person ▶ 8A,2Ch
🗓July-Aug(other weekends only) 🍴Full, homebaked 🏠Rural, 2-storey, acreage, lakefront, patio, porch,deck, quiet ■3D,1F,1Ste (upstairs) ⊷1S,1D,3Q,1P,2cots ⌁1Private,1sh.w.g.,1sh.w.h.
★Air,F,TV,KF, canoe & bicycles for guests ⓌDesignated smoking area, children min. age 5, small outside dog pen available
🚶 Lake Huron, canoeing, fishing, biking, nature walks, x-c skiing, birdwatching, snowmobile trails
🚗 Sauble Beach, Bruce Peninsula Nat.Park, Tobermory (ferry to Manitoulin Isle), Bruce Trail
Spacious, comfortable home with large veranda and deck, located on 2.5 acres waterfront on quiet cove off Pike Bay, overlooking Lake Huron. Ideal place for nature lovers to enjoy the rustic beauty of the Bruce Peninsula. Breakfast is served in special guest breakfast room. Hostess loves gardening and "lazy dog Jessica loves watching". ⌐B&B http://www.bbcanada.com/2183.html

---

Last, Victor (Hillcrest B&B)
394 Gould St., Wiarton, ON N0H 2T0

☎ & Fax (519) 534-2262

Enter Wiarton from south and descend the hill. Turn left at Mary St. Located at 1st intersection with Gould St (south-west corner)
$45S $55D (Children's rates available) ▶ 4
🍴Full 🏠Rural, village, hist. ■2D,F(upst) ⊷T,D ⌁1Sh.w.g. ★F, wrap-around veranda ⓌNo pets, no smoking 〰French, some German
🚶 Bruce Trail, Niagara Escarpment, Colpoy's Bay, Bluewater Park, Wiarton village center, restaurants, Bruce's Cave, Oxenden
🚗 Oliphant (sandy beach), warm shallow water
Spacious and comfortable, former (1880's) timber baron's house - a good base for interested naturalists and travellers who would like to explore the many attractions in this part of the Peninsula. Host is well informed about the area's history, geography and is active with nature photography and field naturalist groups. Guided Eco-Tours available. ⌐B&B

Wiarton (cont'd)

Paquin, Doloris (The Green Door Bed & Breakfast)　　　☎ (519) 534-4710
Box 335, 376 Berford, Hwy 6, Wiarton, ON　N0H 2T0

Travel on Hwy 6 through Wiarton (Berford St). Located 1/2 block north of Elm St on west side.

$50S　$75D　　　　　　　　　　　　　　　　　　　　　　► 8
🍳 Full, homebaked　🏠 Downtown, village, historic, 3-storey,
view, patio　■ 4D (upstairs)　↦ 2D,1Q,2T　🚗 1Ensuite,
1sh.w.g.　★Separate entrance, parking　✋ No smoking
🚶 Antique shops, restaurants, park at Colpoy Bay (swimming,
walks), Bruce Trail hiking, hospital
🚙 Lark Whistle, the Caves, The Herb House, pottery shops
🐚 Red brick turn-of-the-Century home, restored to its original
Victorian splendor and tastefully decorated with antiques. Lounge in the spacious living room or sit
outside and enjoy the maple shaded deck and barbeque facilities. There is a resident dog.

Peer, Rosemary & Evelyn (Rosecliffe B&B)　　☎ (519) 534-2776, Fax (519) 534-1160 *77*
502435 Island View Dr., RR2, Wiarton, ON　N0H 2T0　　　　E-mail: roserep@bmts.com

Located 10km east of Wiarton on Frank St (Island View Dr.) across from Wiarton Golf Course.

$35p.person　　　　　　　　　　　　　　　　　　　　　　　► 8
🍳 Full　🏠 Rural, ranch-style, view from guest rooms, acreage,
lakefront, patio, veranda, quiet　■ 1S,1D,1F (ground
level) ↦2S,2D,2Q　🚗 1sh.w.g., 1sh.w.h.　★ TV,F in Asiatic
Room　✋ Smoking on patio, no pets, no children
🚶 Hike the Bruce Trail, explore caves (Unesco World Biosphere
Niagara Escarpment), cycle & stroll on scenic roads, swim &
sunbathe on shore, visit potteries, antiques & artisan studio
& shops, Wiarton Blue Water Park & marina, scenic lookouts at Skinners Bluff & Graham's Hill,
seasonal stream/waterfall on property
🚙 Fathom-5 Underwater Nat Park, Tobermory/Chi-Cheemaun ferry to Manitoulin, Sauble B.
🐚 Spacious waterfront home nestled in a quiet woodland escarpment setting with a spectacular
view over Colpoy's Bay to THE Island. Hearty country fare served outdoors on the ledge-rock stone
patio (weather permitting). Packed lunches available upon prior request. Mother & daughter host
team enjoy meeting international guests and folks with rural roots. A Haven for hikers, cyclists and
naturalists and a serene retreat; "Be spoiled naturally". Gift Certificates available. ✔B&B
http://www.bbcanada.com/1199.html

Veerman, Joanne & Michael Pearson (Long Lane B&B)　　☎ & Fax (519) 534-3901
RR2, Wiarton, ON　N0H 2T0　　　　　　　　　　　　E-mail: longlane@bmts.com

From Hwy 6 in Wiarton, turn east onto Frank St for 4.5 km. Turn right at Oxenden and proceed 7

km to "T". Turn left for 2 km and right to 2nd farm.
$40-45S　$55-60D　🍽 Meals & packed lunches　　　　► 8
🍳Full,homebaked　🏠Farm,older,deck,porch,quiet　■1S,2D,1F
(upstairs)　↦2T,1D,2Q　🚗 1Sh.w.g., 1sh.w.h.　〰Dutch
★TV,Elmira wood stove　✋Smoking outside only
🚶 Bruce Trail hiking (Skinner's Bluff), bird watching, star gazing,
x/c-skiing, walking/cycling on country roads, Bruce Caves
🚙 Bruce Peninsula, Tobermory, Keppel Croft & Gardens
🐚 Lovely Century home, featured in the 1997 Wiarton Area House Tour, surrounded by 104
beautiful acres, far from any traffic or noise and easy to find. Enjoy the warm hospitality in the
large farm kitchen, relax on the porch with complimentary tea & coffee. Gift Certificates available.
Vegetarian option available. ✔B&B　www.bbcanada.com/1524.html

Wiarton (cont'd)

Vickers, Sally & Leighton
Box 298, Wiarton, ON N0H 2T0

☎ (519) 534-3504, Fax 534-4036
E-mail: sally-leight@log.on.ca

Located 7km north of Wiarton on Hwy 6 (on right side).
$40S $60D $10-15Child   🍴 Meals   ▶ 8A,2Ch
🍶 Full   🏠 Rural, acreage, patio, quiet   ■ 2D,1F (upstairs &
ground level)   ⊨3D,1K,2cots   ⊶2Ensuite,1private   ★ TV,F,LF,
KF,guest lounge, parking   ✋ No smoking
🚶 Walking & x-c ski trails on 50 acres of cedar bush at door
🚗 Tobermory ferry dock, swimming, boating, fishing, Bruce Trail

🐾 Large country home.Enjoy a visit or relax in upstairs sitting area. There is a friendly dog
oustide. Visa ✓B&B

Wilberforce

(west of Bancroft; see also Haliburton, Minden)

Clark, Hilda (The House in the Village)
Box 63, Wilberforce, ON K0L 3C0

☎ (705) 448-3161/448-2018

From Peterborough take Hwy 28 north. Turn left on Dyno Rd (North of Apsley) and left on Hwy
121. Turn right on Hwy 648. Located in the village across from Agnew's General Store.

$35S $45-50D $10Add.person   ▶ 9
🍶Homebaked   🏠Village, older, acreage, patio, quiet   ■5(main
and upper level)   ⊨2T,1S,1Q,1D   ⊶1Sh.w.h.,2sh.w.g.   ★TV,
parking, wheelchair access in one room   ✋No pets, no smoking
🚶 General store, mineral shop, crafts, museum, lake, Gov't dock,
park, tennis & basketball courts, snowmobile trails, restaurant,
church, library, canoeing, boating, fishing
🚗 Public beach, museum & art galleries (Haliburton, Bancroft),

School of Fine Arts, Sir Sams ski area, x-c ski trails
🐾 Retired teacher in comfortable & homey place, nestled in a quiet village of the south-eastern
Haliburton Highlands. Relax, enjoy doing nothing by the beautiful hills, forests & lakes. Ideal spot
for small groups & for overflow from cottages or visiting friends.✓B&B

Williamsburg

(west of Cornwall; see also Brinston, Morrisburg)

Allard, Marcel & Victor Dupuis (The Village Antiques/Tea-Room & B&B)
4326 Hwy 31, Williamsburg, ON K0C 2H0

☎ (613) 535-2463, 1-877-264-3281

From Hwy 401 take Exit 750 & proceed north on Hwy 31 for 10km.
$50S $55D $12Add.person   (plus tax)   🍴Meals   ▶ 8A
🍶 Full, homebaked   🏠 Village, 2-storey, older, patio, quiet
■2D,1F(main & upper level)   ⊨ 2T,3D   ⊶ 2Sh.w.g.
★Air,TV & air-conditioner in guest rooms, ceiling fans, guest
lounge, off-street parking, guest quarters are separate
✋Designated smoking area, no pets, no children   ⤳ French
🚶 Historic site, churches, shopping, golfing, library, res.park

🚗 Upper Canada Village, theatre, St.Lawrence River, Botanical Gardens, Iroquois Locks, Ottawa
🐾 Comfortble home, originally a harnesmaker shop, built around 1860, has retained the charm
of yesteryear, yet offers all modern convenience. Peruse the antique shop, enjoy an oasis of charm &
hospitality in the heart of Eastern Ontario. Dinner-Theatre B&B Packages available. Breakfast is
served in special guest breakfast room, and Dinner is available from the Tea Room menu.. There is
a cat. CCards ✓B&B http://www.bbcanada.com/1181.html

Williamstown *(n/e of Cornwall; see also Lancaster, Apple H, Alexandria, St.Andrews W.)*

Caron, Mary & Michael (Caron House 1837)   ☎ (613) 347-7338
Box 143, Williamstown, ON   K0C 2J0

From Hwy 401, take Exit 814 north to Lancaster Village and west on Pine St. Go 7 km (and 2 centuries) through Williamstown to four corners, turn left and continue over bridge, then left again

to 3rd house across from St. Mary's Church. Look for sign
$45S $55D   (Reservations recommended)   ▶ 4A
🍴 Full (Gourmet)   🏠 Village, hist., acreage, veranda, patio, gazebo, Victorian & herbal gardens,quiet   ■2D(upstairs)   ⊨2D   ⊐1Sh.w.g.   ★ 3F,TV, separate entrance, entire upper floor for guests only, parking 🚭No smoking, no pets   ⚮French
🏃 Tennis court, village with historic sites, ideal for cycling
🚗 St.Raphael's Ruins (1821), Coopers Marsh, Upper Canada Village, Montreal, Ottawa
🏹 Historic brick home with charming blend of the unpretentious and the sophisticated, offering old-fashioned elegance, antiques, bright chintzes, candlelight gourmet breakfasts and turn-of-the-Century hospitality in the finest tradition of a small elegant country inn. Weather permitting, guests may dine alfresco in the gazebo or on the brick patio. Entire upper floor can be booked for one party only. ✔B&B

Wert, Wendy & Les (Capricorn Capers B&B)   ☎ (613)347-3098, Fax (613)347-1112
5480 County Rd 19, RR2, Williamstown, ON   K0C 2J0   E-mail: capricorn@cnwl.igs.net

From Hwy 401, take Exit 814, turn left on Hwy 34 to Pine St (3rd after rail tracks). Turn left on Pine (County Rd 17) for 7 km to village of Williamstown. Turn right on County Rd 19 (towards St. Raphael), to 2nd house on left after leaving village.

$35S $60-70D   ▶ 6
📅May-Oct 🍴Full, homebaked 🏠Rural, res. ■2D(upstairs), 1Ste (main level)   ⊨2T,1K,1Q, crib   ⊐ 3ensuite   ★F,TV in study, separate entrance, parking, wheel-chair access   🚭No pets, no smoking
🏃 Historic village of Williamstown, nature trails in sugar bush & meadowlands, hiking, x-c skiing, cycling
🚗 Upper Canada Village, golfing, Cooper Marsh Visitor Centre, fishing in St.Lawrence River, Cornwall, Ottawa, Montreal
🏹 A Glengarry welcome in comfortable stone-brick home with beautiful gardens and nestled in the hardwoods of Eastern Ontario. A delightful spot for nature lovers & bird watchers. Families, seniors, honeymooners welcome. There is a dog in residence.✔B&B   www.countryhosts.on.ca

---

Windermere   *(s/w of Huntsville; see also Pt Carling)*

Webb, Marlene & Bill (Twisted Acres B&B)   ☎ (705) 769-3003, Fax (705) 769-3664
Box 116, Windermere, ON   P0B 1P0   E-mail: tabandb@vianet.on.ca

From Bracebridge, take Muskoka Rd 4 to Windermere. In the village, look for No 2411 on left side.
$55S $70-85D   (inquire about children rates)   🍽 Meals   ▶ 8A,4Ch

🍴 Full, homebaked   🏠 Village, 2-storey, 55acres, view from guest rooms, porch, quiet, secluded   ■ 3D,1Ste (main & upper level)   ⊨ 1D,3Q,2R,1P   ⊐ 2Sh.w.g., 1ensuite
★Air,KF,F,TV in guest rooms, private entrance, wheel-chair access, off-street parking, guest quarters are separate
🚭Designated smoking area, inquire about pets, children welcome
🏃 Beach, swimming, golfing, tennis, boating, x-c skiing, trails
🚗 Algonquin Park, Pioneer & Santa's Villages, down-hill skiing
🏹 Warm welcome in new, spacious home with large veranda and country atmosphere, surrounded by peaceful scenery. Hosts are family oriented, community minded (Lions & W.I) and enjoy welcoming guests in their home. Relax in a quiet haven minutes away from attractions & action. Breakfast is served in guest breakfast room. Visa www.angelfire.com/on/twistedacres

Windermere (cont'd)

Dutton, Barbara & John (Top House Retreat B&B)
Box 134, Windermere, ON P0B 1P0

☎ (705) 769-3338
E-mail: tophouse@muskoka.com

From Bracebridge, take Muskoka Rd 4 to Windermere. Turn left at Longhurst Rd to 1st on left.
$60S $65-70D $10Child/$10Add.person   (over age 5)   🍽 Meals   ▶ 7A,1Ch

🍲 Full, homebaked   🏠 Rural, village, 2-storey, older, 31 acres, view from guest rooms, porch, quiet   ■ 3D,1F (upstairs)   ⇥3Q,1P,crib   🛁 2Sh.w.g.   ★ F,TV,LF, off-street parking   ⓦDesignated smoking area, no pets
🔥 Groomed walking trail on property (a Muskoka Heritage Stewardship wood lot), tennis, golfing, public beach with rental facilities, x-c skiing from door, snowmobile trails
🚗 Scenic roads, villages, beaches of Muskoka Resort region,
📷 3rd Generation Muskoka family home in park-like setting overlooking Lake Rosseau. "A house that likes guests". Relax in the tranquil atmosphere and enjoy the great lookout view from the covered porch. Hosts are world travellers and well informed about the local history & attractions and will give guided tours & nature walks through the property. A naturalist's paradise. There is a cat and a hedgehog. Visa ✓B&B

Rowntree, Ruth & Gid (Rowntree Cottage)
RR2, Utterson, ON P0B 1M0

☎ (705) 769-3640/off season:(416) 231-6631
E-mail: rowntree@muskoka.com, rowntree.home@sympatico.ca

Location: 1182 Dawson Rd. in Windermere, Muskoka. From Hwy 118 West, take Muskoka Rd 25 for 8.5 km to Dawson Rd. Or from Muskoka Rd 4 west, take Rd 25 for 1.2 km to Dawson Rd, 1km to

B&B. Seasonal address: 11 Herne Hill, Etobicoke, On M9A 2W9
$40S $75D $30Add.person   ▶ 9
📅Late Spring-Thanksgiving   🍲 Full   🏠 Rural, village, hist., acreage, view, lakefront, boat dock, quiet, screened/glass porch   ■1D,2F(upstairs)   ⇥ 3D,3S   🛁 Sh.w.g., wash vanities in all rooms   ★Air(in guest rooms), F,TV,video, free paddle boat/canoe & horse-shoe pitch   ⓦNo pets,restr.smoking,child min.age 8
🔥 Lake Rosseau sandy beach swimming (1000 ft wooded
shoreline), free docking for boat (no jets),(bring windsurfer/bicycle), scenic nature walks
🚗 Resort area, golfing, tennis, gift shops, restaurants, Summer Theatre, boat/craft tours
📷 Charming, restored Century Victorian home, antique filled, Muskoka Cottage with stone fireplace; situated on sparkling Lake Rosseau, has been in host's family for over 70 years, (the original ice house, chicken house and stone root house are still on the property), and surrounded by beautiful scenery and quiet elegance. Relax on the screened (glassed-in) porch overlooking the lake. Hosts have completed their first decade of B&B hosting. A "Destination B&B"! Visa ✓B&B

Woodstock

(east of London)

Littlejohns, Ina & Harry (Heritage Guest House B&B)
594766 Hwy 59 South, RR4, Woodstock, ON N4S 7V8

☎ (519) 456-8721

From Hwy 401, take Exit 232 and Hwy 59 south for 0.5km. Look for sign and house on left.
$55S $65D   🍽 Meals   ▶ 4

🍲 Full, homebaked   🏠 Rural, res., bungalow, 0.3acres, quiet, secluded   ■ 2D (main floor)   ⇥2Q   🛁 1Ensuite, 1private   ★ Air,F,TV, separate entrance, off-street parking   ⓦNo smoking, no pets, children min. age 10
🔥 Public golf course, restaurants, specialty shops, artist's studio, candy making operation
🚗 Downtown Woodstock, Pittock Conservation Area, London
📷 Warm welcome in"1953 Cottage that has grown into an extended rural bungalow". Retired hosts in mediterranean-style home with comfortable antique country furnishings, enjoy welcoming B&B guests from worldwide. Relax in front of the fireplace in the large lounge/craft shop and breakfast area, which served until recently as a popular Tea Room. Watch the variety of birds in the secluded backyard from the bay-window area. Visa, ✓B&B

Quebec

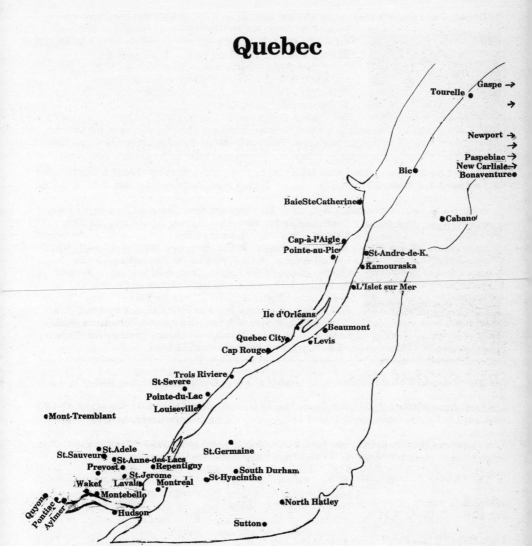

Gaspe →
Tourelle →
→

Newport →
→
Paspebiac →
New Carlisle →
Bonaventure →

Bic

Cabano

BaieSteCatherine

Cap-à-l'Aigle
Pointe-au-Pic

St-Andre-de-K.
Kamouraska

L'Islet sur Mer

Ile d'Orléans
Beaumont
Quebec City
Levis
Cap Rouge

Trois Riviere
St-Severe
Pointe-du-Lac
Louiseville

Mont-Tremblant

St.Adele
St.Sauveur
St-Anne-des-Lacs
St.Germaine
Prevost
Repentigny
St.Jerome
South Durham
Wakef
Laval
Montreal
St-Hyacinthe
Montebello
Quyon
Pontiac
North Hatley
Aylmer
Hudson
Sutton

Tourisme Québec
CP 20000, Québec, QC G1K 7X2

toll-free 1-800-363-7777

Aylmer

(near Ottawa ON; see also Pontiac, Wakefield, Quyon)

Bergeron, Guy & Denyse (Maison Bon Repos)   ☎ (819) 682-1498
37 Cedarvale, Aylmer, QC   J0X 2G0

In Ottawa cross any bridge north to Quebec and turn left on Hwy 148 west into downtown Aylmer.

Proceed 5km, turn left on Rue Terry Fox and right on Cedarvale.
$40-45S $50-55D $10Child   ▶ 6A,1Ch
🍴 Full   🏠 Sub., riverfront, quiet   ■ 3D(main & upper floor)   ⊨2Q,1D   ⊒2Private, 1sh.w.h.   ★ LF,TV in guest room, ceiling fans, storage for guests' sports equipment
♨Designated smoking area, no pets, children min. age 7
🏃 Restaurant, Ottawa River
🚗 Ottawa, Parliament Hill, cycling path, ski hills

📢 Warm welcome in comfortable mezzanine home. Enjoy the magnificient view of the Ottawa River and the tranquil natural surroundings. Delicious breakfast served in the dining room.✔B&B

Charron, Lise & Rhéal (L'Escapade B&B)   ☎ (819) 772-2388, Fax 772-4354
912 Aylmer Rd., Aylmer, QC   J9H 5T8   E-mail: escapade@mondenet.com, 1-877-882-7755

Located app.15 min. from Ottawa/ON. On Hwy 417 West take Exit 123 (Island Park Dr.). Crossing

Champlain Bridge, turn left on Aylmer Rd. and continue 2km.
$50-60S $60-70D $10Add.person   ▶ 4A,1Ch
🍴 Full, homebaked   🏠 Res., sub., view   ■3D(upst) ⊨1D,1Q,1T cot ⊒1Sh.w.g.   ★Air,F, parking   ♨ No smoking, no pets, children min.age 6   ﹌ English (Household language is French)
🏃 Golfing, biking and x-c ski trails, skating on Canal
🚗 Ottawa (Capital City), Hull, Gatineau Park

📢 Elegant traditional home well situated on large treed lot, a short scenic drive away from Parliament Hill. Winner of Agricotours Award of Excellence (96/97). Hostess serves full breakfast in dining room or on the terrace overlooking a lovely garden. Enjoy an all-season peaceful hideaway. ✔B&B   http://www.bbcanada.com/279.html

Baie-Ste-Catherine

(north side of St.Laurence, across from Riviere du Loup)

Savard, Anne-Marie & Real (Gîte Entre Mer et Monts) ☎ (418) 237-4391, Fax (418) 237-4252
476 Rte 138, Baie-St-Catherine, QC   G0T 1A0   E-mail: entremeretmonts@fjard-best.com

From Quebec City, take Rte 138 east toward LaMalbaie & bridge to Tadoussac. Then proceed 2.8km

to No 476. From Tadoussac, drive 4km from ferry.
$40S $50D $15Child $20Add.person   🍽 Meals   ▶ 10
🍴 Full, homebaked   🏠 Village, bungalow, view from guest rooms, river at front, patio, quiet   ■2D,3F(upper and lower level)   ⊨3S,5D   ⊒1Sh.w.g., 1sh.w.h.   ★ F,2V,2private entrances, off-street parking   ♨ No smoking, no pets   ﹌ English (household language is French
🏃 Walks along St.Laurence riverbanks and woods and forests, picnic areas, horse-back riding, snowmobiling, x-c skiing

🚗 La Malbaie, Baie-St-Catherine, beach, Sagawney Fjord, parks, biking trails, Pointe Nova Beluga whale observation and Interpretation Centre, Tadoussac

📢 Hostess is the proud owner of the regional Agricotour du Quebec Hospitality Award Winner and offers Quebecois Cuisines (table d'hote d'Anne Marie). There is a dog, Visa,MC ✔B&B
fjard-best.com/entremeretmonts

Beaumont

(east of Quebec City; see also Lewis)

Fournier, Michèle & Jean L'Heureux (Au Gré du Vent) ☎(418)838-9020,Fax(418)838-9074
220 Chm. St-Roch, Beaumont, QC G0R 1C0   E-mail: augreduvent@msn.com

Phone for directions.
$50-60S $55-65D $15Child/Add.person   ► 6A,2Ch
⚕ closed Oct and April   ⚙ Homebaked   ⌂ Rural, 2-storey,
hist., patio, quiet, secluded   ■ 2D,1F(upstairs)   ⊨3D,1R,crib
🛁1sh.w.g., sinks in 2 rooms   ★ F,TV in guest living room, wood
burning stove, guest quarters are separate, off-street parking
🚭No smoking,no pets   ⤳English(household language is French)

🚐 Ferry, Old Quebec, Gross Ile (Irish Mem Nat Historic Site)

🚙 Warm and friendly hospitality in bicentenary traditional Quebec-style home with country
decor and period furnishing. FAQ Excellence prize winner 1998. Breakfast is served in the dining
room. There is a dog and a cat in residence. Ideal stop betw. Ontario & Maritimes. Visa ╱B&B

Bic

(north-east of Riviere du Loup)

Parceaud, Judy (Aux Cormorans Bed & Breakfast)   ☎ (418) 736-8113, Fax (418) 736-4216
213 chemin du Golf, Bic, QC G0L 1B0   E-mail: cormoran@globetrotter.qc.ca

From Quebec City take Hwy 20 past Riviere du Loup, then Rte 132 past Bic to "Aux Cormorans"
Exit (right turn). At the theatre turn left and follow B&B signs to the point. Look for last house on
left at seashore.

$40-55S $55-75D $10Child/$10Add.person   ► 12
⚙ Full, homebaked   ⌂ Rural, 2-storey, hist., view from guest
rooms, oceanfront, porch, quiet   ■4D,1F(upstairs)   ⊨2T,5D,2R
🛁2Sh.w.g.,1ensuite   ★ F, guest quarters are separate, off-street
parking   ⚙ Smoking on porch, no pets   ⤳French
🏃 Walks along the beach from the calm of the Bay to the wild &
natural coastline of the St.Lawrence Estuary

🚐 Bic Golf Club, Bic Provincial Park, Metis Gardens, Bic Theatre

🚙 Sea-side home (ca 1896) with cottagy decor, overlooking Massacre Island and snuggling close
to the south shore of the St.Lawrence River in Bic Bay. Relax on the encircling verandas and
observe a continuous spectacle of sea birds following the eternal ebb and flow of tides. Hostess is a
native of Windsor, England and has spent many years in Northern Quebec. Visa,MC╱B&B
www/bbcanada.com/2982.html

Bonaventure

(south-shore Gaspé; see also New Carlisle, Paspebiac, Newport)

Hall, Helen (Bay View Manor/Manoir Bay View)   ☎ (418) 752-2725, (418) 752-6718
395 Rte132 Bona.E., Box 21, New Carlisle, QC G0C 1Z0

From Quebec City follow Rte 20 and Rte 132 south to Matapédia and then east to Gaspé Peninsula.
Located beside Fauvel Golf Course in Bonaventure East.
$25S $35D $5Child (under age 12) $10Add.person   ► 15A,5Ch
⚕ April1-Nov30   ⚙ Full, homebaked   ⌂ Rural, 2-storey,
hist., view from guest rooms, oceanfront, deck, quiet   ■ 1D,5F
(main & upper level)   ⊨ 5T,5D,1R, crib   🛁1Private,2sh.w.g.
★ TV, picnic tables, camping on grounds   ⚙Smoking outside,
no pets, ideal place for children of all ages   ⤳ French
🏃 Fauvel Golf Course, picnic grounds, quiet private beach, corner
store, crafts, birdwatching, Bonaventure East lighthouse
🚐Acadian & United Empire Loyalist Museums, Perce Rock

🚙 Comfortable home, once served as a country store and rural post office. Listen to the sound of
the waves washing up on the shore, view the spectacular sunrises, watchful lighthouse beacon and
breathtaking sunsets over the water. Hostess is a retired teacher. ╱B&B
http://www.bbcanada.com/1012.html

Cabano
(east of Rivière-du-Loup)

Emond, Roger (Au Ranch du Soleil Levant)　　　　☎ (418) 854-2983
69 Rte 232 Est, Cabano, PQ　G0L 1E0

Phone for directions. Located 1.6km from Trans Canada Hwy.
$40S　$50D　$5Child　$10Add.person　　　　► 10
⬭ Homebaked　🏠 Rural, ranch-style, lakefront, patio, porch,
quiet, secluded　■ 5D (ground level)　⊨2T,4D　🛏 2Sh.w.g.
★ TV,LF, private entrance, guest quarters are separate, off-street
parking　ⓦDesignated smoking area　⌇ English, Spanish
(household language is French)
🚗 Golfing, fishing, hunting, restaurants
🏃 Hist.Fort Ingall, fishing, beach, bicycle path "Petit Temis" (130km along Lake Temiscquata)
🐾 Congenial hosts in recently built ranch-home with country-style decor, surrounded by woods
and trees and facing gorgious Temiscouata Lake. Relax and enjoy the tranquil atmosphere. Ideal
place for a short visit or a vacation. Located halfway between Ontario & PEI.

Cap-à-l'Aigle
(north side of St.L.River east of Québec City; see also Point au Pic)

Villeneuve, Claire　　　　☎ (418) 665-2288
215 Rue St-Raphael, Cap-à-l'Aigle, QC　G0T 1B0

Located on north side of St. Lawrence River. On road 138 at La Malbaie cross the bridge, turn right
and continue to village and to St.Raphael St on right side.
$30S　$50D　$15Child (over age 5)　　　　► 11
⬭ Full, homebaked　🏠 Village, hist., view, riverfront, quiet
■4D,1F(upstairs)　⊨2T,4D,1S　🛏 2Sh.w.g.,1shower only
★TV,KF, separate entrance, parking　♥　⌇ English
(household language is French)
🏃 St. Lawrence River, beach, wharf and marina
🚗 La Malbaie/Manoir Richelieu/Baie Ste Catherine, Casino
🐾 Warm welcome in comfortable home with quiet and relaxing surroundings including the oldest
thatched barn in Quebec (over 150 years). Hostess enjoys welcoming guests from worldwide. ↝B&B

Cap Rouge
(south of Quebec City)

Denis, Yvan (L'Hydrangée Bleue)　　　☎ (418) 657-5609, Fax (418) 657-7918
1451 Rue du Golf, Cap Rouge, QC　G1Y 2T6

From Hwy 20 at Quebec, cross Pierre Laporte Bridge and exit chm St.Louis West. Turn right on
chm Louis Francoeur and turn left on chm St.Foy to the river. Turn right on Rue St.Felix and

continue to rue du Golf.
$45S　$50-60D　$10Child　$15Add.person　　　► 4
⬭ Full　🏠 Res., 3-storey, patio, quiet　■2D(upstairs)
⊨2D　🛏1Private, 1ensuite　★ TV,LF, ceiling fans, off-street
& street parking　ⓦ No smoking, no pets　⌇English
(household language is French)
🏃 Golf course, marina, x-c ski trail, St.Lawrence River banks
🚗 Shopping Centre, Old Quebec, historic Montmorency Falls
🐾 Teacher hosts in large modern home situated on a quiet street. Enjoy the warm and friendly
atmosphere. ↝B&B

Gaspé

(Gaspé region; see also Newport, Paspébiac, New Carlisle, Bonaventure)

Beriault, Helen & Denis (Gîte La Canadienne)   ☎ & Fax (418) 368-3806
201 MGR Leblanc St, Gaspé, QC   G4X 1S3

From Hwys 132/198 take Prov.Rd 60 to Gaspe donwtown. Continue on Jacques Cartier or Rue de la Reine to rue de la Cathedrale. At the Bells Tower (church) proceed on MGR Le Blanc St to B&B

$45S $55D $10Child   ▶ 12
✲ June-Aug.   ⌻ Full   🏠 Downtown, res., bungalow, patio, quiet   ■5(ground level)   ⊨5D,2R   ⏚5Private   ★ KF,LF, private entrance, off-street and street parking, guest quarters are separate   ⛚ No smoking, no pets   ∾ French
🏃 Restaurants, Shopping Center, Baie of Gaspé, Jacques Cartier Cross, museum, marina, walking trails, bus stop
🚗 Forillon Nat.Park, Percé Village (Copper Mine)

☛ Warm welcome in comfortable home with Canadian atmosphere and situated in a quiet neighbourhood in the beautiful Gaspé area with many activities and interesting sights. Hosts are a teacher and hospital worker and like to meet people from all corners of the world. There is a small dog in residence. Visa ✔BB

Fortin, Blanche & Roland (Gîte Baie Jolie)   ☎ (418) 368-2149
270 Montée Wakeham, Rte 198West, Gaspé, PQ   G4X 1V5

Take Rt 132 East all the way to Gaspé. At the Gaspé Bridge keep going straight for 1.5 km along the Bay (198 Rd W), to house on right side or phone for directions.

$45S $45-55D $10Child/Add.person   ▶ 9
✲ May to Nov15   ⌻ Homebaked   🏠 Res., view, bungalow, patio, quiet   ■ 4D(main and lower level)   ⊨3D,1Q,1R,1P   ⏚2Sh.w.g.   ★KF,TV in 2 guest rooms, parking   ⛚ No pets, rest.smoking   ∾ some English (household language is French)
🏃 Cathedral Christ the King, Jacques Cartier Cross, Soldiers' Memorial Monument, museum, golfing, salmon fishing
🚗 Parc Forillon, Percé Rock

☛ Warm and friendly Québec Hospitalité in comfortable home situated on the Bay of Gaspe(aigue09r). Relax and enjoy a lovely view of water and mountains. Hosts have many years experience in the tourist trade.Visa ✔B&B

Hudson/Heights   *(west of Montréal)*

Henshaw, Naomi and Fred (Riversmead)   ☎ (450) 458-5053
245 Main Rd, Hudson, QC   J0P 1H0

Take Hwy 40 west from Montreal towards Ottawa and any Hudson Exit to Main Rd.

$60-100S/D   ▶ 6A
⌻ Full (English)   🏠 Village, acreage, hist., view, lakefront, patio, swimming pool, quiet   ■ 3D   ⊨2T,2D   ⏚ 2Sh.w.g.
★ 2F   ⛚No smoking   ∾ French
🏃 Fine restaurants, swimming, golfing, tennis, bicycling, riding, x-c skiing, shops, riding, sailing, maple syruping
🚗 Historic Georgian brick home filled with family antiques and situated on large grounds with access to Lake of Two Mountains.
Delicious breakfast is served either on screened porch or in the Victorian dining room.

Bouffard, Mariette & Jean-Marc (Aux Capucines B&B)   ☎ (418) 829-3017
625 Ch Royal, St-Laurent, Ile d'Orléans, QC G0A 3Z0

From Quebec City, take Hwy 40 east to Ile d'Orléans Exit. Proceed
over bridge and continue 12km to house on riverside.
$50S $60-65D $25Add.person   ► 6A,1Ch
🍽 Full 🏠 Rural, acreage, river-view from guest rooms, patio,
riverfront, quiet, secluded ■ 1S,2D,1F(upstairs)
⊨1T,1D,1Q 🛁1Sh.w.g. ★ F, entire 2nd floor for guests
🚭 No smoking, no pets, not suitable for children ∾ English
(household language is French)
🏃 Fine dining in historic building, golfing with beautiful scenery of St-Laurence River, shore
walking trails, tennis, kayaking,artisans/crafts   🚗 Quebec City
🐾 Retired couple in very large, beautiful Colonial home, by the shores of the St.Laurence River
and set back from the road among mature maple trees and Nasturtium (capucines) beds. Hosts are
well travelled & enjoy exchanging stories with guests. Experience beautiful Ile d'Orléans.∕B&B

Dumesnil, Yolande & Claude (Le Mas de l'Isle Bed & Breakfast)   ☎ & Fax (418) 829-1213
1155 Chemin Royal, St.Jean, Ile d'Orléans, QC G0A 3W0   E-mail: sorciere@total.net

From Quebec City, take Rte 138 east toward St-Anne-de-Beaupre and Ile d'Orléans Exit. Travel
over bridge, at traffic light continue for 17.5 km and turn left at B&B sign. Look for house on right.

$55S $60D $20Child(under age12) $30Add.person   ► 9
🍽 Full 🏠 Rural, view from guest rooms, quiet, deck ■2D,1F
(upstairs) ⊨ 1S,3D,2R 🛁 1Sh.w.g., 1sh.w.h. ★F,TV,
books & games 🚭 No smoking, no pets ∾ English (household
language is French)
🏃 Village of St. Jean (founded in 1679) with well established
historic homes, boutiques, restaurants, 1732-built church and
cemetery, 1858-built quay, beach, swimming pool
🚗 Historic villages on the island, Montmorency Falls, Cap Tourmente Nat Wildlife area
🐾 18th Century replica farmhouse situated on a cliff overlooking the St.Laurent River. Relax
and enjoy the peaceful surroundings. Winter rates available.There is a resident cat. Visa ∕B&B

Lambert, Gérard & Lucie (Le Giron de l'Isle)   ☎ (418) 829-0985, Fax (418) 829-1059
120 Chm des Lièges, St-Jean, Ile d'Orleans, QC G0A 3W0   1-888-280-6636
                               E-mail: giron@iname.com
From Quebec City take Hwys40 or 440 east to Ile d'Orleans. Cross bridge and proceed through
traffic lights towards St.Laurent & St.Jean villages. Continue 2.4km past St.Jean's church,
turn right on Chm des Lieges.

$59-85S $69-95D $30Add.person   ► 10A
🍽 Full, homebaked 🏠 Rural, 2-storey, view from guest rooms,
riverfront, patio, quiet, secluded ■ 4(upper & main floor)
⊨2T,3Q 🛁 4Private ★TV,F,LF, ceiling fans, jacuzzi in suite,
off-street parking 🚭 No smoking, no pets ∾ English
(household language is French)
🏃 Shore walks, art galleries, shops, pond fishing, bird watching
🚗 Quebec City, Mont St-Anne, Montmorency Falls, St-Anne de Beaupré Shrine, golfing, skiing
🐾 Newly built island home with modern comfort located by the majestic St.Lawrence River with
its impressive boats and breathtaking sunrise and moonlight. Relax on the veranda, patio or private
balcony. Retired hosts are knowledgeable about the region. A private tour of the beautiful gardens
can be arranged. Visa,MC ∕B&B

Ile d'Orléans (cont'd)

Lapointe, Louise & Hughes L'Heureux (Le Vieux Presbytère) ☎(418)828-9723
1247 MgrD'Esgly,Saint-Pièrre,Ile d'Orléans,QC G0A 4E0   Fax(418)828-2189

$50S $60-100D $15Child/Add.person 🍽 Meals   ► 12
Take Rte 440 from Quebec City to Ile d'Orléans. After crossing bridge, turn left at traffic light. Go
2 km, turn left between two churches in the centre of village.
🛏Full 🏠Village, farm, hist., view, quiet ■5D(upst & ground
level)+2 cottages ➤2T,4D,1P,2R ➤2Sh.w.g.,1private ★TV,
parking ⚬English (household language is French)
🧍 Hist. church, craft shop, bicycle rentals, public pool
🚗 Quebec City, golfing, museum, skiing, Montmorency Falls
🔫 Large and beautiful ancestral residence (200-year old stone
house) with warm and cozy atmosphere near the oldest church in
Québec, located on large property with buffalo, wappitis, goats etc. Visa,MC www.presbytere.com

---

Lettre, Francoise (Jardin d'Antan)   ☎ (418) 829-3834
556 Chm Royal, St-Laurent, Ile d'Orléans, QC G0A 3Z0

From Quebec City take Hwy 40 or 440 to Ile d'Orléans, cross bridge and proceed 12km.
$55S $68D $15Child(under age 12) $125F $20Add.person   ► 6A
🛏 Full, homebaked 🏠 Village, hist., acreage, view from guest
rooms, swimming pool, patio, quiet, secluded ■ 3D(main &
upper floor) ➤ 3D ➤1Private, 1sh.w.g. ★ TV in guest
living room, sep.entrance, off-street parking Ⓝ No smoking,no
pets ⚬English(household language is French)
🧍 Golfing, walking trails, handicraft & art boutiques, fine cuisine
in old Water Mill
🚗 Old Quebec, Montmorency Falls, Mount Ste-Anne ski area
🔫 Charming 17th Century stone house furnished with antiques and with a 4-sided roof that
bears witness to the earliest French settlement. Enjoy the large old-style country garden and
intimate atmosphere of yesteryear. www.gites-classifies.qc.ca/jarant.htm

---

Kamouraska   *(s-w of Rivière-du-Loup; see also L'Islet sur Mer, SteAndre)*

Bossé, Nicole & Jean (Chez Nicole & Jean)   ☎ (418) 492-2921
81 Ave Morel, Rte 132, Kamouraska, QC G0L 1M0

From Hwy 20, take Exit 465 to Kamouraska. In the village, turn left on Morel Ave (132 Rd) to 2nd
house on left past church.
$45S $55-65D $10Child $20Add.person   ► 7A,1Ch
🛏 Full, homebaked (Gourmet) 🏠 Village, res., 2-storey, hist.,
view from guest room, riverfront, patio, wrap-around
balcony,quiet ■4D(upstairs) ➤3D,3T ➤1Private,
1sh.w.g.,1sh.w.h. ★TV, parking, solarium Ⓝ No smoking, no
pets,children min.age 5 ⚬some English (household lang French)
🚗 Rivière-du-Loup, La Pocatière, Saint Pascal
🧍 Restaurant, museum, dock fishing, bicycle/walking on panoramic path along the shore, golfing,
summer theatre, horseback riding, birdwatching, sea kayaking, hiking, rock climbing
🔫 Early retired couple in 19th Century home on south shore of the St. Lawrence River in
320-year old historic village with typical architecture. In K"amour"aska, nature lovers will be
impressed by the sunsets over the water and the view of the surrounding fields and woods. Visa
↙B&B www.total.net/~stefnat/gite.html

Laval
(north of Montreal)

Trudeau, Louise (Gîte du Bord de l'Eau)
495 des Patriotes, Laval, QC H7L 2L9

☎ (450) 625-3785, Fax (450) 625-8235
E-mail: gita_d_eau@hotmail.com

Located 8.5km east of Hwy13/Exit17, 3.5km east of Hwy15/Exit16.
$47S $62D $5-15Child $20Add.person (plus tax) ► 4
❑Full 🏠Res., riverfront, 2-storey, swimming pool,deck,quiet
■1F(street level) ◄ 2D plus foam mattress ⏁1Private
★F,TV in guest room, off-street parking ✋No smoking, no
pets ⌣English, Spanish (household language is French)
🏃 Canoeing/bicycling/fishing/skating/x-c skiing from property,
restaurants in the old village of Ste Rose, bus from Montreal
🚗 Laval, shopping centers, golf courses, Space Science Center, Mille-Isle River Park, Montreal
📣 Long time hosts have welcomed guests from many different countries over the years.
Delicious breakfast is served with a wonderful view of the Mille-Iles River. Admire the truly
spectacular sunsets. Visit a truly French Canadian family and enjoy friendly atmosphere and good
conversation.- http://www.info-internet.net./~trudeau

Lévis
(across the river from Quebec City; see also Beaumont)

Pelletier, Véronique & Emile (Gîte Des Bosquets B&B)
162 Rue des Bosquets, Lévis, QC G6V 6V7

☎(418)835-3494,Fax 835-0563
1-888-335-3959

$35-40S $50-60D $15Add.person $80F 🍽 Meals ► 8A,4Ch
From Quebec City or Riv-du-Loup take Exit 327 from Hwy 20 and turn right on Mgr Bourget. Go
1km and turn left on Champagnat. At 2nd stop turn right on Des Bosquets. From Ferry in Levis,
turn right on Côte du Passage, after 1st light turn left on Champagnat. Pass 6 stops and turn left
on Des Bosquet.
❑ Full, homebaked 🏠 Downtown, res., townhouse, view from
guest rooms, riverfront, patio, quiet ■1S,2D,2F(upstairs &
lower level) ◄1S,2T,5D ⏁2Private, 1Sh.w.g. ★Air,TV,
private parking, bicycle storage ✋Desig. smoking area, no pets,
child min.age 10 ⌣English (French is household language)
🏃 Famous restaurants, public swimming pool, golfing, KL
Theatre, Fort de la Martinière and Fort No1 (Nat.hist.site - with
mysterious tunnels, amazing blockhouses & caponiers), ferry boat, Rue St.Laurent/riverfront
📣 Comfortable home facing Old Quebec with a nice view of St.Lawrence River and situated in a
quiet area of historic town. Relax on the terrace & admire dancing lights at night.Visa,MC ⌐B&B

L'Islet-Sur-Mer
(s/side of St.Lawrence east of Quebec;see also Kamouraska)

Caron, Marguerite and Denis (Auberge La Marguerite)
88 Des Pionniers Est, CP 101, L'Islet-Sur-Mer, QC G0R 2B0

☎ (418) 247-5454
1-877-788-5454

On Hwy 20 East (from Montreal), travel past Quebec City and Montmagny and exit at Hwy 285
North (Exit 400). Travel 4 km through L'Islet village to intersection of Rt 132 (in village of
L'Islet-Sur-Mer), turn right and continue for 1 km to house on right side. Look for sign.

$69-134S $84-148D (Children's rates avail.)🍽Meals ►12A,2Ch
❑ Full 🏠Village, historic, acreage, view, patio, quiet ■6
(upstairs,including family suite) plus 2 downstairs ◄2T,2D,5Q
⏁8Private ★Air,F, comfortable guest sitting room, separate
entrance, parking ⌣English (household language is
French) ✋No smoking, no pets
🏃 Scenic St.Lawrence River, historic church
🚗 Quebec City, artisan villages along the St. Lawrence
📣 Very spacious 180-year-old home, well-kept and pretty with large garden to walk, read, relax,
and located in the heart of a 300-year-old historic village on the St.Lawrence River. Rooms are
named after schooners built in the area. Meals are served in the bright large dining room.

Louiseville
(west of Trois Rivières; see also Pointe-du-Lac, St.Sévère)

Gilbert, Michel (Gîte de La Seigneurie B&B)   ☎ & Fax (819) 228-8224
480 Chemin du Golf, Louiseville, QC   J5V 2L4

From Quebec City take Hwy 40 east and Exit 166. Take Rte 138 east to Rte 348 west. Turn left and

drive 1.5 km to 7th road on right.
$45S $60D $15Add.person 🍽 Meals (plus tax)   ▶ 12A,4Ch
🍞 Homebaked 🏠 Farm, hist., quiet, isolated 🚿2Sh.w.g.
■1S,2D,1Ste,1F(upstairs) ⊨ 2S,5D,4R 🚿 2Sh.w.g., 1Private
in suite   ★F, private balcony in suite 🚭 No smoking, no pets,
children min. age 12 〰English (household language is French)
🕺 Golf courses, cycling paths, farm activities, c-x skiing
🚗 Zoo, museums, Ste.Ursule Water Falls, St.Lawrence cruise
📣 Comfortable Victorian home (built in 1880) with Victorian Garden on 14 acres. Relax on the
veranda & enjoy country life with a calm/cozy atmosphere. House specialty: "forfaits" (inquire
please). Hosts are music & flower lovers. Artist Lithograph atelier on site. Also available
full-equipped separate house on property for longer stays. ✔B&B

Mont-Tremblant
(north of Montreal)

Lachance, Pierre & Sylvie Senécal (Auberge Le Lupin B&B)   ☎(819)425-5474,Fax6079
127 Pinoteau, Mont-Tremblant, QC   J0T 1Z0   E-mail: lelupin@lelupin.com

From Montreal, take Hwys 15/117 north past St-Jovite. Turn right on Montée Ryan and continue
to end. Turn left along lake to 2nd street on left. Look for B&B sign.

$59-85S $79-109D $15Child $25Add.person (plus tax) ▶ 18
✴ not Xmas holiday period 🍺 Full, homebaked 🏠 Resort
town, 2-storey, log house, patio, quiet ■ 4F,5D (main, upper &
lower levels) ⊨ 4S,9Q,cot 🚿 9ensuite ★F,TV in 7 guest
rooms, wheel-chair access, off-street parking 🚭Designated
smoking area, no pets 〰 French
🕺 Lake (with limited beach access), boat cruises, golfing, tennis,
Tremblant ski lift, hike/ski/bike path at door, dog-sledding
🚗 Mont Tremblant Park (canoeing, hiking, horseback riding), hydroplane tours, Fish Hatchery
📣 Splendid log home (built in 1945) with spacious rooms and cozy atmosphere, nestled in the
center of Mont Tremblant recreational playgrounds. Relax by the massive stone fireplace and enjoy
a natural setting outside the window. There is a dog and a cat. Reservations recommended, inquire
about winter rates. CC's ✔B&B www.lelupin.com

Montebello
(east of Ottawa ON)

Lacasse, Suzanne (À l'Orée du Moulin Bed & Breakfast)   ☎ & Fax (819) 427-8534
170 Joseph Lucien Malo, Papineauville, QC   J0V 1R0

Phone for directions.
$45S $60D $20Child $30Add.person 🍽 Meals ▶ 6A,2Ch
🍺 Full, homebaked 🏠 Village, 2-storey, hist., swimming pool,
patio, porch, deck, quiet ■4D(upstairs) ⊨1Q,2T,2D,2cots,1P
🚿2Sh.w.g. ★ Separate entrance, off-street parking 🚭Not
suitable for children, designated smoking area 〰English
(French is household language)
🕺 Ice-fishing on the Outaouais River
🚗 Chateau Montebello (largest log structure in the world), fine dining in village, Domaine Omega
📣 Historic home built around 1850 beautifully restored with wrap-around porch and situated on
the northshore of the Outaouais River. Golf packages available.Visa
www.destinationquebec.com/ftpdocf/oree/oreea.htm

Montréal

(see also Hudson, Laval, Hudson)

Alacoque, Christian (Alacoque Bed & Breakfast) ☎(514)842-0938,Fax 842-7585
2091 St.Urbain, Montréal, QC H2X 2N1   E-mail: christian.alacoque@sympatico.ca

Located west of St.Laurent & south of Sherbrooke Sts. Phone for directions.
$40S $60D $10Child $20Add.person (plus tax)   ▶ 9
🍲 Full 🏠 Downtown, 3-storey, view, quiet ■ 1D,1Ste,1F (ground
level) ◄ 4D,1Q,1R ⊡ 1Sh.w.g., 1private ★ Air,LF,KF,TV in guest
room, private entrance, off-street & street parking, (garage available), host
quarters are separate ⤳ English (household language is French)
🕇 Place des Arts, Chinese Quarter, Conference Centre, McGill U., Old
Montreal, Latin Quarter, subway station (St.Laurent/Place des Arts)
🚗 Botanical Garden, Biodome, Olympic Stadium
☛ 1830-built home with original wood finishes & elegant furniture.
Gourmet breakfast is served in the guest breakfast room. Visa,MC ↙B&B
www3.sympatico.ca/christian.alacoque

Bilodeau, Pierre & Dominique Bousquet (Pierre & Dominique)   ☎ (514) 286-0307
271 Square St-Louis, Montreal, QC H2X 1A3   E-mail: info@pierdom.qc.ca

Phone for directions.
$45-50S $70-80D $15Child   ▶ 7+
🍲 Full, homebaked 🏠 Downtown, townhouse, hist., view from
guest rooms, quiet ■ 1S,1D,1F(ground level) ◄ 1S,2D,1Q
⊡ Sh.w.g. ★ TV, fans, private entrance, street parking(free),
guest quarters are separate 🚳No smoking,no pets ⤳French
🕇 McGill University complex, UQAM, boutiques, restaurants,
theatres, museums, Palais of Congrès, Old Montreal, Sherbrooke Metro Stn, Voyageur Bus Term.
🚗 Montreal Dorval Airport, Laurentian Mountains
☛ Warm welcome in the heart of the Latin Quarter in a charming Victorian house on the
Saint-Louis Square which has captivated several generations of poets and artists. Enjoy the
tranquility of the country in downtown and relax in the park to the sound of birds. Hosts are very
knowledgeable of the City & provide "off-the-beaten-track" itinerary. ↙B&B www.pierdom.qc.ca

---

Blondel, Lena (Montreal Oasis B&B)   ☎ (514) 935 2312, Fax (514) 935-3154
3000 Breslay Rd., Montréal, QC H3Y 2G7

Follow directions to downtown/center-ville Montréal, do not take the Bonaventure Express Rd, but
exit at Atwater and continue to Breslay Rd/Chemin de Breslay, turn left to
1st house with turquoise door.
$60-75S $70-90D $10Child $25Add.person   ▶ 8+
🍲 Choice, homebaked (Gourmet) 🏠Downtown, res.,large garden
■3D(upst) ⊡2Sh.w.g. ★TV 🚳No pets ⤳Swedish, French, some
Spanish, German
🕇 Various restaurants/fine dining (Crescent, St.Cahterine & Sherbrooke
Sts), Museum of Fine Arts, Cdn. Center for Architecture, Mt Royal Park (a
short hike up hill), Montreal Forum, Alexis Nihon Plaza (part of
underground City), Old Montreal, The Latin Quarter, subway stop
☛ Spacious home, decorated with Swedish & Quebec furniture, located in
downtown's beautiful "Priest Farm district" (once a holiday resort for priests). There are original
lead windows and slanted ceilings. Swedish hostess is world travelled and loves all kinds of music
and African Art. There is a beautiful blue-cream Siamese cat & a collection of Bergman movies &
videos. Hostess also operates "A Montreal Oasis B&BA" a small quality B&B Network.

Durand, Lise & Jean Pierre (Gîte "Le 6400" B&B)   ☎ (514) 259-6400, Fax (514) 255-4692
6400 Rue Lemay, Montreal, QC H1T 2L5

From Mirabel Airport take Hwy 15 south to Hwy 40 East. Exit at Lacordaire Blvd and proceed
south to Rosemont Blvd. Turn right to Lemay. From Dorval Airport take Hwy 520 east to Hwy 40

East and continue as above.
$35-45S $55-65D   (plus tax)   ► 4
🕮 Full   🏠 Res., 2-storey, patio, swimming pool, quiet   ■2
(main floor)   ⊨ 2S,1D   🛏 1Sh.w.g.   ★ Air,LF,TV,street
parking   🖐 No smoking, no pets, not suitable for children
〰English (household language is French)
🚶 Biodome, Botanical Gardens, Olympic Stadium & Tower,
mueum, golfing, cycle path, bus No131, Metro L'Assomption

🚗 Old Port (cruising jet-boating), Old Montreal, Cathedral, St.Josph Oratory
🐾 Warm welcome in comfortable home. Bicycles for guests available. Breakfast is served in the
salle à manger. Relax in the reading/ TV room or on the patios by the pool. ✔B&B

Fischer, Alexander (Chez Alexandre Le Bienheureux B&B)   ☎(514)282-3340,Fax 3973
3432 Hutchison, Montreal, QC H2X 2G4

Phone for directions.
$60-85S $75-95D $15Child/Add.person (plus tax)   ► 8
🕮 Full   🏠 Downtown, 3-storey, hist., quiet   ■ 2D,1Ste(upstairs)
⊨2S,2Q,1P   🛏 1Sh.w.g., 1sh.w.h.   ★Air,KF,LF,2F,TV,fans in guest
rooms, private entrance, off-street and street parking, guest quarters are
separate   🖐Desig.smoking area, no pets, children min.age4
〰French,German
🚶 Downtown area and Underground City, Central Station, Bus Terminal,
museums, Place des Arts, McGill University, Chinatown, shops, restaurants,
Jazz Festival, trepidating nightlife, buses No24/80, Metro Stations
🚗 Laurentian Mountains, Eastern Townships
🐾 Quiet Victorian House with high ceilings and large luxurious interior, situated in the middle
of Cosmopolitan Montreal. Retired University Professor, assisted by his dynamic team of young
Montrealers, will make certain that guests enjoy and experience the well-being and happiness of
their stay. Breakfast is served in the elegant dining room. Relax in the quiet atmosphere by the
fireplace or in the little garden. Hosts live in lower level. Visa,MC

Hornby, Linda Michelle (Angelica Blue B&B)   ☎ (514) 844-5048, Fax 448-2114
1213 Ste.Elisabeth St.,Montreal,QC H2X 3C3   E-mail: info@angelicablue.com, 1-800-878-5048

Phone for directions.
$55S $65D $80F $10Add.person   ►15
🕮 Full, homebaked (self-serve)   🏠 Downtown, 3-storey, Victorian
Row-house, patio, quiet   ■4D,2Ste(upstairs)   ⊨ 2T,3D,5Q,3K,3P
🛏1Private, 2ensuite, 2sh.w.g.,1sh.w.h.(incl 2antique claw tubs)   ★KF&
microwave,LF,TV, ceiling fans, bicycles, off-street & street parking
🖐Designated smoking area   〰French
🚶 Chinatown, Old Montreal (port), downtown shopping, Convention Centre,
wonderful restaurants, underground shops, American Consulate, subway
🚗 Skiing, snowmobiling, Casino, Mt.Royal Olympic Station, Biodome
🐾 Historic home (ca 1890) with spacious sunny rooms, recently decorated
in different themes, original wood floors and brick walls exposed. Located in the heart of downtown
Montreal. Relax in the comfortable TV & sitting room. A scrumptious breakfast is served in cosy
bistro. Children welcome. CCards www.angelicablue.com

Montreal (cont'd)

Jacques, Micheline & Fernand (Gîte Maison Jacques) ☎(514)696-2450, Fax 2564
4444 Paiement St., Pierrefonds, QC   H9H 2S7   E-mail: gite.maison.jacques@sympatico.ca

From Hwys 20/40 exit at Blvd Saint-Jean (Exit 50N) and continue north to Blvd Pierrefonds. Turn
 left to Paiement St and left again.
$43-46S $59-63D $6-12Child   ▶ 7A,1Ch
✚ closed Dec & Jan   ◑ Full, homebaked   🏠 Res., sub.,
bungalow, patio, porch, quiet   ■3 (main and lower level)
⊷S,T,D,Q,R,cot   ⊷3Private   ★ Air,TV,F, off-street
parking   ⓌNo smoking, no pets   ⋙ French
⚲ Village center, restaurants, services, churches, shopping
centers, recreational parks, skating rink, bus routes #68 & #215
🚗 Downtown Montreal, Mirabel/Dorval Airports, skidoo trails, Laurentians, St. Laurence Seaway
📢 Retired teachers in comfortble home located in a peaceful suburb in the "West Island" and in
excellent proximity to the city and skiing/cycling/swimming/golfing areas. Enjoy the quiet
seclusion and relax in the backyard, the lawn swing or the screened veranda after a day of
sightseeing or travelling. Breakfast is served on patio weather permitting.C.Cards ⌐B&B
www.maisonjacques.qc.ca

Logan, Andrée (Marmelade B&B)   ☎ (514) 876-3960, Fax (514) 876-3926
1074 Rue St-Dominique, Montreal, QC   H2X 2W2   E-mail: marmelad@total.net

 Phone for directions.
$65S $75-110D $10Child $14Add.person   (plus tax)   ▶ 16
✚ closed Jan   ◑ Full, homebaked   🏠 Downtown, hist., 3-storey, older,
patio   ■5D,3F(upper & ground level)   ⊷2T,4Q,1K,2R,1P   ⊷1Sh.w.g.,
1sh.w.h.   ★ LF,2TV guest lounges, ceiling fans, separate entrance,
off-street & street parking   ⓌDesignated smoking area, not suitable for
children   ⋙ English (household language is French)
⚲ Montreal & Old Port, Convention Center, Place des Arts, Chinatown,
sites of Jazz & Film Festivals, Latin Quarter, underground shopping,
riverfront bicycle paths, Metro Stations (subway), major bus routes
🚗 Botanical Gardens, Olympic Site, Casino, US Border, Laurentian
Mountains and resorts (skiing)
📢 Charming older (1870) home, recently renovated in contemporary style and tastefully
decorated, situated in the heart of downtown. Works of local artists are on display throughout the
house. Hostess is former Hospitality & Tourism Exec. and willing to help guests with itineraries.
Enjoy a hearty gourmet breakfast."Farley" the friendly resident Bearded Collie is eager to welcome
guests. Also apartment available for longer stay.Visa ⌐CC www.total.net/marmelad

---

Messier, Nicolas (Au Gît'Ann B&B)   ☎ (514) 525-3938, Fax (514) 879-3236
1806 St-Christophe, Montreal, QC   H2L 3W8   E-mail: augite@cam.org

From the Voyageur Bus Terminal exit on Berri St North, turn right on Ontario St, right again on
St-Christophe.
$50-60S $65-75D $15Child $20Add.person   (plus tax)   ▶ 5A,4Ch
◑Cont.   🏠Downtown, townhouse, quiet   ■4(upstairs)   ⊷2S,2D,1K   ⊷1Sh.w.g.   ★KF,TV,
ceiling fans, street parking   ♥   ⓌDesign.smoking area   ⋙ French,Spanish
⚲ Downtown core area with shops, boutiques, restaurants, entertainment, Universities, Congress
Center, Old Port of Montreal, subway station, bus connection to airport
📢 Active and knowledgeable young host in comfortable home located on a calm street in the
heart of the village. Enjoy the peaceful ambience. Children welcome.

Montreal (cont'd)

Ritchot, Gilles (B&B Turquoise)
1576 Alexandre de Sève, Montreal, QC H2L 2V7

☎ & Fax (514) 523-9943

Located 1 block north of Ste Catherine St E and 2 blocks west of Papineau St.
$60S $70D $15Add.person   ► 10
🍽 Buffet 🏠Downtown, 2-storey, older, patio, deck, quiet ■5D(main &
upper floor) 🚪5Q 🛁2Sh.w.g.   ★ Private entrance, street parking,
guest quarters are separate 🖐Designated smoking area, not suitable for
children 〰 French
🕴 Montreal's Gay Village (bars & restaurants), Old Montreal, Latin
Quarter, downtown business district, museum, subway/bus stations
🚗 Olympic Park/Botanical Gardens, Casino, Mount Royal Observatory
📷 Colourful home with a quiet, warm and friendly atmosphere, Victorian
interior situated in the heart of the Gay Village. The exterior balconies lead
to a sunny flower garden and goldfish pond. Knowledgeable host will provide necessary information
on cultural activities and sightseeing. Breakfast is served in guest breakfast room. 〰CC

Schilling, Rosemarie (The Gable B&B)
56 Gables Court, Beaconsfield, QC H9W 5H3

☎ (514) 697-3609
E-mail: rosemarieschilling@hotmail.com

From autoroutes 20 or 40, exit at Saint Charles and go south to Beaconsfield Blvd. Turn right to
4th street then left to B&B.

$55S $75-85D $40Add.person   ► 4A,1Ch
🍽 Full, homebaked   🏠 Res., hist., riverview from guest rooms,
private lakefront, swimming pool, tennis court, patio, quiet
■2(upstairs) 🚪2T,1Q 🛁1Private, 1sh.w.h.   ★ F,TV in guest
room, parking 🖐No smoking, no pets 〰French, German
🚗 Downtown Montréal, Laurentiens, Ottawa, Quebec, Vermont
🕴 Quaint village, boutiques, on bus route (No200/211) from
City, McGill & McDonald colleges, Fairview Center shopping, riverfront restaurants.
📷 Home is situated in a private Country Club & decorated Laura Ashley-style with antiques &
paintings. Located on the St Lawrence River with its own swimming pool, tennis court and boating
facilities. World travelled hostess (a former Stewardess) is now an Art & Antique Collector.
Breakfast is served in the formal dining room. Min.2-nights stay. "Herzlich Willkommen!"

Touchburn, Gisela (St-Annes Bed & Breakfast)
27A Perrault Ave,Ste-Anne-de-Bellevue,Montréal,QC H9X 2E1

☎ (514) 457-9504, Fax 457-8881
E-mail: touchburn@sympatico.ca

From Montréal, take Hwy 40 and Exit 41. From Hwy 20 take Exit St-Anne de Bellevue, follow Rue
St.Pierre south to Rue Ste-Anne. Turn left and proceed to Ave Perrault.

$40-60S $50-70D $15Add.person   ► 6
🍽Full, homebaked   🏠Res., village, 2-storey, swimming pool,
patio, quiet ■2(upstairs) 🚪1S,2T,2Q 🛁1Private,
1Sh.w.g. ★TV,F,parking 🖐No smoking 〰French, German
🕴 Boardwalk & bicycle path along lakeshore (& x-c skiing), fine
restaurants, swimming, sailing, tennis, shops, train & bus stops
🚗 Downtown Montreal, Dorval Int Airport, Laurentiens resorts
📷 Enjoy high quality, inexpensive accommodation in a pleasant
neighbourhood near the Macdonald Campus of McGill University and John Abbott College. 〰B&B
http://bbcanada.com/376.html

A Bed & Breakfast Downtown Network
3458 Laval Ave., Montreal, QC H2X 3C8

☎ (514)289-9749,Fax(514)287-7386,1-800-267-5180
E-mail: bbdtown@cam.org

(Bob Finkelstein, Co-Ordinator)
Rates $35-55S $45-65D $10Child $110F $20Add.person   (including full breakfast)
A Bed & Breakfast Downtown Network is in its 15th year of operation and represents 80 homes
(specializing in the center-city, Latin Quarter and Old Montreal. For reservation call the above.
www.bbmontreal.qc.ca

Montreal (cont'd)

A Montreal Oasis Bed & Breakfast Network   ☎(514) 935-2312, Fax (514) 935-3154
3000 Breslay Rd., Montreal, QC H3Y 2G7

(Lena Blondel)
$40-80S $55-90D   (including breakfast - some gourmet)
A Montreal Oasis Bed & Breakfast Newtork is a small network of quality homes, situated in the
heart of the city, the "Latin Quarter", in the "Old City" or near the Universities. Hosts are artists,
composers, performers & professionals with many and varied interests and abilities. Some are
native to the city, others have come from different parts of the world. Each has been carefully
chosen. Most travelled worldwide & have a wealth of experience to tell. The Network will remain
small in order to maintain the quality service it is known for. Call for information/reservation.

New Carlisle   *(on Gaspé south-shore; see also Paspebiac, Newport, Bonaventure)*

Sawyer, Aaron (Bay View Farmhouse B&B)   ☎ (418) 752-6718/752-2725
337 Rte 132, Main Highway, Box 21, New Carlisle, QC G0C 1Z0

From Quebec City follow Rte 20 east and then Rte 132 to Gaspé Peninsula. Located on Rte 132.
$25S $35D $5Child $10Add.person   ► 10A,5Ch
❄ May-Oct.   ⚙ Full, homebaked   🏠 Farm, 2-storey, hist., acreage,
view from guest rooms, porch, deck, quiet   ■ 2D,3F (upstairs)
⊨4S,5D   ⊒1Sh.w.g., 1sh.w.h.   ★ TV, parking   ⚓Smoking outside,
no pets   ⤳French
🏃 Beach, walking, birdwatching, bus route
🚗 Tennis, boat cruises, Fauvel Golf Course, Acadian & United Empire
Loyalist museums, British Heritage Centre, St. Elzéar Archaeological Caves, Maguasha Fossil Site,
Percé Rock, Bonaventure Island Bird Sanctuary
🏹 Warm welcome and quiet Gaspésian country hospitality in comfortable farmstead with
un-ending and breathtaking mountain-sea vistas. Memorable copious farm breakfasts served.

Newport   *(south shore of Gaspé; see also Paspebiac, New Carlisle, Bonaventure)*

Lambert, André & Guylaine Michel (Auberge les Deux Îlots)   ☎ (418) 777-2801
207 Rte 132, CP 223, Newport, QC G0C 2A0   1-888-404-2801, Fax (418) 777-4719

$40-55S $50-65D $5-10Child $15Add.person   (plus taxes)   ► 12A,4Ch
From Quebec City take Hwy 20 east and Rte 132 to Newport. Look for B&B located 1.5km west of
church on seaside facing the rest area looking over two islets.
⚙ Full, homebaked   🏠 Village, 3-storey, older, 34 acres, view
from upstairs guest rooms, oceanfront, quiet   ■3D,2F(upper
level)   ⊨5D,1Q,2R,crib   ⊒ 2Private, 2sh.w.g.   ★F,KF,TV in
guest sitting room, private entrance, guest quarters are separate,
off-street parking   ⚓ No smoking, no pets   ⤳English
(household language is French)
🏃 1km beach on property, Bolduc Museum, fishing harbour
🚗 Centre d'interpretation du Bourg de Pabos, Percé Rock, Musée Acadien de Bonaventure,
historic site du Banc de Paspébiac.
🏹 Spacious house, once the estate of a wealthy merchant, with old-fashioned charm, enchanting
decor and cozy comfort, situated on property including the most beautiful beach in the township.
Tucked between Percé and Bonaventure, an ideal place for a longer stay, quiet nights and days filled
with discovery. Breakfast ("a pleasure for the palate") is served in guest breakfast room. Special
packages, including dinner are available in the family restaurant. Visa ✔ B&B
http://www.bbcanada.com/lesdeuxilots

North Hatley *(south of Sherbrooke)*

Fleischer, Ann and Don (Cedar Gables) ☎ (819) 842-4120
Box 355, 4080 Magog Rd., Rt 108, North Hatley, QC J0B 2C0

From Sherbrooke, Montreal points west and north, take Autoroute 55 South and exit Rt 108 East
to house before center of village. From Eastern USA, take I 91 North to Quebec Autoroute 55 N

$64-104S $73-104D (off-season discounts) ▶ 10-12
🍴 Gourmet(famous) 🏠 Res., village, older, view, lakefront,
patio, dock, lakeside deck, sunporch ■ 4D,1Ste (ground & upper
floor) 🛏 4K,1D,P, futon 🚿 5Ensuite ★ 3F,VCR, tape
deck, piano, 2canoes, rowboat, parking ⋙ some French
🚗 Piggery Theatre, 7 alpine ski areas, riding stables, Orford
Festival, 2 Universities
🏃 English-style pub, village center, summer concerts,
watersports, swimming, cycling, fishing, gourmet/casual dining
🔫 Large, tastefully appointed turn-of-the-Century home on Lake Massawippi in the beautiful
Eastern Townships. Hostess is an expert spinner and weaver and has a few surprises, host is a
brewer & winemaker. Visa,MC,Amex ✔B&B

Paspébiac *(south-shore Gaspé; see also New Carlisle, Bonaventure, Newport)*

MacWhirter, Anne and Gordon (Macdale B&B) ☎ (418) 752-5270
365 Rte 132, Hope Paspébiac, QC G0C 2K0 E-mail: agmacwhirter@hotmail.com

Phone for directions. Weekly rates available.
$45S $50-60D $10Child(under age 12) 🍽 MealE-mail: ✔ 10
🍴 Full, homebaked 🏠 Farm, older, view, multi-storey, quiet,
oceanfront ■3F (upstairs) 🚿1Private(in loft), 3sh.w.h.
🛏2S,3D,1P,cot ★TV in guest room, parking 🚭No smoking,
pets outdoors only ⋙French
🏃 River, beach, playground/park with mini golf, tennis courts,
canteen, fishing, churches, walking trail, ski-dooers welcome.
🚗 Historic site (Paspébiac), Acadian museum, Loyalist Village, golfing, Thallasotherapy
🔫 5th Generation farm with cow/calf operation along with chickens (which supply brown eggs).
Host is a retired High School Teacher, while hostess continue to teach Grade One. ✔B&B
www.bbcanada.com/399.html

Pointe-au-Pic *(on north side of St.Lawrence east of Québec City; see also Cap-à-l'Aigle)*

Vermette, Raymonde & Adolf Frizzi (La Maison Frizzi B&B) ☎(418)665-4668
8 Côteau-sur-mer, CP 526, Pointe-au-Pic,, QC G0T 1M0 Fax (418) 665-1143

Phone for directions.
$65-75D $15Child $25Add.person ▶ 11
🍴 Full, homebaked 🏠 Village, res., Austrian-style, view, patio,
oceanfront, quiet ■2D,2F(upstairs) 🛏S,Q,cots
🚿2Sh.w.g. ★F,TV,LF, separate entrance, parking
⋙English, German, Italian (household language is French)
🏃 Manoir Richelieu Hotel, restaurants, St-Laurent River, golfing,
museum & art gallery, swimming, sailing, fishing, riding
🚗 Whale watching tours, Hôtel Tadousac, Cap Eternité, Mont Grands Fonds (skiing, skating)
🔫 Typical Tyrolian-style house with very charming & friendly hospitality "à la Québecoise" and
a beautiful view of the St-Laurent River. Relax on the outside terrace where breakfast is served
weather permitting. Hosts' daughter helps with B&B chores. There is a Golden Retriever called
"Max" in residence.Visa,MC ✔B&B

Pointe-du-Lac

(west of Trois-Rivières; see also Louiseville, Saint Sevère)

Piccinelli, Barbara and Jacques (Gîte Baie-Jolie)   ☎ & Fax (819) 377-3056
711 Notre Dame, Rte 138, Pointe-du-Lac, Trois-Rivières, QC   G0X 1Z0   Fax (819) 377-3056
E-mail: jacques.piccinelli@baie-jolie.com

From Montréal, take Hwy 40 East and Exit 187. Continue on Rte 138 east for 7 km. Look for B&B sign. - From Quebec City, take Hwy 40 West. Exit to Hwy 55 and then take Notre Dame Exit and continue on Rte 138 west for 5 km.

$35S $55-60D $10-15Child   ► 6A,4Ch
🍳 Full, homebaked   🏠 Village, res., ranch-style, swimming pool, view, riverfront, quiet   ■1D,2F (main & upper level)
🛏4D,1S   🛁 3Private   ★ F,LF,TV in 2 guest rooms, separate entrance, parking facilities for the disabled, bicycles available
✏French, German, Italian
🕴 St.Lawrence River, Lake St. Pièrre

🚐 Old Center of Trois-Rivières, cruises to Montréal and Québec, National Park of the Mauricie
🐾 Comfortable home with warm hospitality is situated on a magnificient site on the banks of the St. Lawrence River and Lake St. Pierre, 10km away from the "old Center" of Trois Rivière. Relax in the garden with picnic table & barbeque. Enjoy a copious breakfast with delicious French pancakes, maple syrup & homemade breads. There is a resident dog. Children welcome. Visa ✓B&B

Pontiac

(west of Ottawa; see also Quyon, Wakefield)

Fisher, Ken (Wanaki-on-the-Ottawa B&B)   ☎ (819) 455-9295, Fax (819) 455-9213
133 Ave des Plages, Pontiac (Luskville), QC   J0X 2G0   E-mail: kfisher@magi.com

$45S $55D $5Child (under age 13) $70F $15Add.person   🍽 Meals   ► 10A,4Ch
Phone for directions.

🍳 Full (gourmet)   🏠 Rural, 2-storey, view from guest rooms, riverfront, 3acres, deck, quiet, secluded   ■2D,1F (ground level)
🛏6S,2T,1D   🛁 2Sh.w.g.   ★ Air,F,TV, LF,KF, indoor swim spa & exercise room, separate entrance, guest quarters are separate   🚭No smoking   ✏ French
🕴 Extensive, private and secluded beach with view of open water, canoeing or x-c skiing on the river

🚐 Ottawa, Hull, Casino, Luskville Falls, Gatineau Park, Prov. snowmobile trail
🐾 Large, new house surrounded by woods overlooking private beach and the Ottawa River. Sumptuous meals range from traditional to vegetarian. Relax in the swim spa or by the campfire. Breakfast is served in special guest breakfast room. Meeting room for 20 available. There are very friendly dogs in residence.   www.bbcanada.com/612.html

---

Prévost

(north of Montreal; see also Ste Anne des Lacs, St.Adele, St.Sauveur)

Laroche, Francois (Aux Berges Fleuries)   ☎ (450) 224-7631, Fax (450) 436-5997
1028 Principale, Prévost, QC   J0R 1T0

From Montréal take Hwy 15 north and Exit 55. Cross bridge and turn right on Rue Principale. Look for B&B on left side.

$45S $65D $20Add.person   ►9
🍳 Full, homebaked   🏠 Village, hist., patio   ■ 5 (main floor)
🛏3S,2D,1Q   🛁 3Private, 1Sh.w.g.   ★LF,TV in guest lounge, parking   ✏English(household language is French)
🕴 Restaurants, flea market, art gallery, park (river & woods), hiking, canoeing, golfing at back door, cycling, fishing, x/c skiing
🚐 St-Sauveur (shopping, theatres) excellent downhill skiing
🐾 100-year old red brick country house located in quiet village at the beginning of the Laurentian Mountains. Rooms are named after important painters (Monet, Van Gogh, Renoir, Picasso, Cezanane). Experience the very special house breakfast, enjoy an ideal get-away from the hectic life in the city around the outside fireplace. Visa,MC ✓CC

Quebec City
(see also Ile d'Orléans; see also Cap Rouge, Beauport, Levis)

Blouin, Gilberte "Mimi" (Bienvenue Chez Mimi) ☎ (418) 524-9161, Fax (819) 843-7627
70, rue Fraser, Québec City, PQ G1R 2B6

Entering City on Hwy 20, cross bridge & take Blvd Laurier (becomes La Grande Allée). Turn left on
Cartier and right on Fraser.
$50-55S $65-70D $15Add.person   ▣ Meals   ► 6+
🖢 Full, homebaked   🏠 Res., 3-storey, hist., deck, quiet
■1S,2D(upstairs)   ⊨ 1S,2T,1Q,2R   ⌁ 1sh.w.g., 1sh.w.h.   ★Individual
air-conditioners, TV in guest rooms, piano, parking   🚭Restricted smoking
🚶 Center of Old Québec City, lively district of rue Cartier, hist. Plains of
Abraham, easy access to buses #11 & #801
🚗 Chutes Montmorency, Ste-Anne-de-Beaupré, Ile d'Orléans, Mont
St-Anne skiing, Charlevoix
🐎 Cozy, comfortable home with a wonderful balcony shaded by a stately maple tree, situated in
central location. Breakfast is served in the dining room. Enjoy the friendly atmosphere.
http://ww.bbcanada.com/577.html

Bourgault, Ginette (Bourgault Centre Ville)   ☎ (418) 525-7832
650 Dela Reine, Quebec City, QC G1K 2S1

Phone for directions.
$55S $65D   ► 10A,2Ch
🖢 Full, homebaked   🏠 Res., townhouse, 3-storey, patio, quiet
■5D,1Ste(upstairs)   ⊨ 2T,1D,3K,cots   ⌁ 2private, 3sh.w.g.   ★LF,KF
with microwave,TV in guest room, bike rack, garage for motorcycles/canoes,
barbeque, picnic table, parking   ∾ English (French is household language)
🚶 Old walled city of Québec, Museum of Civilization, Art Gallery,
restaurants and shops, train & bus station
🐎 Spacious renovated Century home with bright, large courtyard and
flower garden in back. Also apt-studio available.

Lafleur, Gilles (La Maison Lafleur B&B)   ☎ (418) 692-0685, Fax (418) 694-0551
2 Rue de Laval, Quebec City, QC G1R 3T9

From Hwys 20/40, follow signs to Old Quebec. Located inside Walls.
$65S $85D $120F $15Add.person   ► 8
🖢 Full   🏠 Downtown, 2-storey, view from guest rooms, quiet   ■2D,1F
(upstairs)   ⊨ 2D,1Q,1R,1P   ⌁ 1sh.w.g., 1sh.w.h   ★ TV,off-street
parking   🚭No smoking, no pets   ∾ French
🚶 Downtown area with tourist attractions, restaurants, services, bus/train
🚗 Ski resorts, Cote-de-Beaupre, Ile d'Orléans, maple sugar cabins
🐎 Comfortable home with stone walls and interior decoration of style and
harmony situated in peaceful location in the heart of the old Latin Quarter,
surrounded by exceptional views of 17th and 18th Century architecture.
Host is a longtime resident of Old Quebec and will gladly suggest many unforgettable places to visit
(all within walking distance). Visa

Saint-Aubin, Monique and André　　　　　☎ (418) 658-0685, Fax (418) 658-8466
3045 rue de la Seine, Ste-Foy, QC　G1W 1H8　　　　　E-mail: staubin@qbc.clic.net

From Montreal, take Hwy 20 east to Quebec City and Pierre Laporte Bridge. Exit on Laurier Blvd.
At 1st traffic light turn right to rue Lavigerie, and right on rue de la Seine (3rd street).

$45S　$60D　$10Child(under age 12)　　　　　▶9
🍽 Full　🏠 Res., multi-storey　■2D,1F(upstairs & main
level)　⊨ 2T,2D,1Q　🛁3Sh.w.h.　★ Air,TV,F,parking
🚭No pets　〰English (household language is French)
🚶 Shopping Center, bus and railway station, Laval University
🚗 Old Quebec City, museum, Art Gallery, Summer Festival,
golfing, Zoo, downhill skiing, Ile d'Orléans
　　　🔫 Comfortable Canadian-style home located in quiet residential
neighbourhood. Sightseeing tours and excursions can be arranged with pick-up at the
house.✒B&B　http://www.bbcanada.com/2696.html, htt;://www.qbc.clic.net/~staubin

---

Saint Gelais, Marie Denise (A L'Etoile de Rosie"　　☎ (418) 648-1044, Fax 648-0184
66 Rue Lockwell, Quebec City, QC　G1R 1V7　　　　E-mail: etoilerosie@sympatico.ca

From Pierre Laporte Bridge on Hwy20, take Exit134 East via Quebec and
proceed on Blvd Laurier which becomes Grand Allee. Continue to Cartier St,
turn left to Ste-Foye, right to Turnbull, right to Lockwell and right again.
$70S　$85D　$15Add.person　　　　　▶8
🍽 Homebaked　🏠 Upper town, 2-storey, view from guest rooms
■2D,1F(upstairs)　⊨ 2T,2Q,1R　🛁 1Sh.w.g., 1sh.w.h.　★ Street
parking (4pm to 10am)　🚭 No smoking, no pets, children min. age 6
〰English (household language is French)
🚶 Rue Cartier & Saint Jean Street shopping, Congress Centre, Musee du
Quebec, Old City, bus route
🚗 Chateau Frontenac, Citadelle de Quebec, Plaines d'Abraham, Parliament
🔫 Comfortable Centennial townhouse (ca 1920) exuding great energy and situated on a quiet
tree-lined street near the artists quarters of Saint Jean Baptiste and Montcalm in an area with
European atmosphere. Enjoy the superb view of the Laurentians from the solarium. Breakfast is
served in special guest breakfast room. Hostess is knowledgeable about the sites and happenings in
the City and will gladly help with plans.　www.bbcanada.com/2165.html

---

Tessier, Gaétan & Sylvie (B&B Bedondaine - Couette et Café)　　☎ (418) 681-0783
912 Ave Madeleine de Verchères, Quebec City, QC　G1S 4K7

Coming from Hwy 20 over Pierre Laporte Bridge procced on Blvd Laurier toward Quebec City.
Continue past Laval University, turn left on Blvd René Lévesque, then left on Ave Madeleine de V.
$40S　$60D　$10Child　$15Add.person　(special rate for longer stays)　　▶4A,2Ch

🍽 Full,homebaked (selfserve)　🏠 Res., raised bungalow　■2D
(lower level)　⊨ 1D,crib　🛁 1Sh.w.h.　★ F,LF, storage space
for guest bicycles and skis　🚭 No smoking, no pets　〰English
(household language is French)
🚶 Jardin Coulange, Domaine Cataraque, Rue Maguire (Sillery),
restaurants, shops, Laval University, x-c skiing, tennis, bus route
🚗 Old City of Quebec, Ils d'Orléans, Chute Mont Morency, Mont
St.Anne downhill skiing, Museum de la Civilization
🔫 Comfortable family home situated on a calm street. Enjoy warm and friendly Quebec
hospitality. Host is an English Teacher & hostess is a Librarian. Healthy breakfast is served in the
dining room with beautiful music. There is a cat in residence. Ask about pick-up in summer.

Quebec City (cont'd)

Tim, Guitta & Greg (Maison Historique James Thompson)　　　☎ (418) 694-9042
47 Rue Sainte-Ursule, Old Quebec City, QC　G1R 4E4

Entering the City via 175 north, tun left on 2nd street inside Saint-Louis Gate.
$65D　$10Add.person　(plus tax)　🍽 Meals　　　　　　　　　▶ 10

🍳 Full, homebaked　🏠 Downtown, 3-storey, hist., quiet
■1S,1D,2F(upstairs)　🛏 5D,1futon　🛁 1Sh.w.g., 1sh.w.h -
★TV in guest lounge, ceiling fans, off-street & street parking,
guest quarters are separate　✋ No pets　〰 French
🕴 Chateau Frontenac, Citadal, fortified Old Towne, bus & train
station, harbour, horse buggyrides
🐎 Historic home (ca 1793) in the heart of Old Quebec. Breakfast
is served in the dining room at guest's choice of time.✍CC

Quyon　　　　　　　　　*(west of Ottawa,ON; see also Paspebiac, Aylmer, Wakefield)*

Marcotte, Gilles & Christine (Hillside B&B - Lit et Gîte de la Colline)　☎(819)458-2324
315 Clarendon St., RR4, Quyon, QC　J0X 2V0

$35S　$50D　$15Add.person (child under age 5 free)　🍽 Meals　(plus tax)　▶ 8

Follow Hwy 148 west and 3.3km west of Quyon.
🍳 Full, homebaked　🏠 Farm, 2-storey, view from one guest
room, patio, quiet　■ 2F(main level)　🛏 2D,2P,cot
🛁1Sh.w.g., 1ensuite　★ F,TV,private entrance, wheel-chair
access, guest quarters are separate　✋ No smoking　〰 French
🕴 X-c skiing, snowshoeing, tobogganing, skidoeing trails (Reg &
Trans Quebec No13), hiking
🚗 Golfing, skiing, Luskville Caves, Gatineau Park, boating
🐎 Large, newly renovated home with country decor and beautiful view of the Gatineau Hills.
Relax by the warm fire in the evening either outside or in. Enjoy the quiet and relaxing atmosphere
after a day of travelling or sightseeing or hiking in the bush. Fresh pizza available from onsite
pizzaria. Breakfast is served in large central eating area. There is a resident dog (not in B&B area).

Repentigny　　　　　　　　　　　　　　　*(north-east of Montreal)*

Cloutier, Denise & Claude Neveu (La Villa des Fleurs)　　☎ (450) 654-9209
45 rue Gaudreault, Repentigny, QC　J6A 1M3　　E-mail: lavilladesfleurs@sympatico.ca

From Montreal or Quebec City on Hwy 40, take exit 96E and 640 east. Turn left on l'Assomption
Blvd, right at Perreault St and left on Gaudreault. From Rte 138 in Repentigny, turn on Claude
David St and right at L'Assomption Blvd, then as above.
$40S　$50D　$10Add.person　　　　　　　　　　　　　▶ 12
🍳 Full, homebaked　🏠 Res., sub., split-level, swimming pool,
patio, deck　■ 3D,1F (main, ground & upper level)
🛏2S,3D,1Q　🛁 2Sh.w.g.　★ F,TV,KF,LF, off-street parking
✋Designated smoking area　〰 French
🕴 Shopping, cinema, church, bicycle way, restaurants
🚗 Olympic Stadium, Botanic Garden Biodome, St. Helene Island
🐎 Warm and friendly welcome in large modern home. Enjoy the congenial hospitality. ✍B&B

Sainte-Adèle   *(n of Montreal; see also Ste Anne des Lacs, Prevost, St.Sauveur, St.Jerome)*

Belanger, Helga & Jaques (Auberge La Girouette des B&B)   ☎ & Fax (450) 229-6433
941 rue Ouimet, Ste-Adèle, QC   J8B 2R3   E-mail: la.girouette@securenet.net

$50-70S $65-100D $140F $20Add.person   (plus tax)   ► 14

From Montreal, take Hwy15 north and Exit67 (Ste-Adele Blvd). At
4th traffic light, turn left on rue Morin to 4ht street left.
🍲 Homebaked   🏠 Village, hillside, 3-storey, .5acres, view, patio,
deck   ◼ 3D,1Ste(upst & ground level)   ⊨ 10S(3K),2D,(extra
long),cot   🛁5Ensuite   ★ Air,LF,F,TV/VCR in guest living
room, indoor spa, off-street parking   👋 No smoking, no pets, not
suitable for children   ⌇ French, German
🚗 Downtown Montreal, Mont Tremblant Resort

🏃 Lake, beach, skiing golfing, bicycling, jogging, x-c skiing, restaurants & fine dining, cinemas, art
galleries, antique shops, concerts, festivals, public transportation to downtown Montreal
📢 Warm welcome in small European-type Inn perched on the mountainside and high above the
valley with splendid views of mountains all around. Ideal place for a well deserved TLC rest, for
celebrations & anniversaries or for small business meetings (seminars, working groups). Breakfast
is served in special guest breakfast room. CCards, ⌐B&B www.bbcanada.com/2491.html

---

Boorne-Durivage, Louise & Robert Parizeau (A L'Oreé du Bois B&B)   ☎ (450) 229-5455
4400 Rue des Engoulevents, Sainte Adèle, QC   J8B 3J8   E-mail: aloreedubois@sympatico.ca

From Montreal take Autoroute 15 north and Exit 67. Proceed 7km on Hwy 17N. Turn left on
Chemin du Moulin at Lac Millette and continue 2km to Rue des Engoulevents. Turn right up hill to
private road and stay left.
$60-100S $80-125D $20Child/Add.person   (plus tax)   ► 13A

🍲 Full, homebaked   🏠 Rural, waterfront, hillside, 2-storey,
acreage, view from guest rooms, natural swimming pool, patio,
deck, quiet, secluded   ◼ 3D,1F(upst),1Ste(main level) (weekly)
⊨ 1S,1D,4Q,3cots, hideaway   🛁 2Sh.w.g., sinks in rooms,
1private   ★ F,TV, private entrance, off-street parking, guest
quartes are separate, KF/LF/TV in suite   👋Designated smoking
area, no pets, children min. age 12   ⌇English, (household
language is French)
🚗 Airports (Dorval & Mirabel)

📢 Well travelled hosts in distinctive Canadian home with rustic ambiance, professional decor and
surrounded by 7acres of landscaped domain with flowing river and magnificient panoramic vista.
Ideal place to relax and take part in outdoor activities winter or summer and in daily "Happy Hour".
Enjoy a delicious breakfast of smoked salmon, paté Mediteranean served in guest breakfast room
(not included in suite). There are 2 dogs (not in B&B area).MC ⌐B&B pages.infinit.net/jpmenard/

St-André-de-Kamouraska   *(west of Rivière-du-Loup; see also Kamouraska)*

Robert, Yvon & Isabelle Poyau (Auberge La Solaillerie)   ☎ (418) 493-2914
112 Rue Principale, St-André-de-Kamouraska, QC   G0L 2H0   Fax (418) 493-2243

$45-85S $55-90D $20Child $25Add.person 🍴Meals (plus tax) (Off-season discounts)   ► 24

From Hwy 20, take Exit 480 toward St-André. In the village, turn
right on Ave Principale. Look for house next to Post Office.
✚ Summer only   🍲 Full   🏠 Village, hist. 3-storey, acreage,
view from guest rooms, riverfront, patio   ◼ 11 (main & upper
level   ⊨5D,6Q   🛁 6Private, 2sh.w.g., footbath and sink in
three guest rooms   ★ Separate entrance, guest quarters are
separate   👋Designated smoking area, no pets   ⌇ some
English (household language is French)

🏃 Hiking, golfing, summer theatre, boat cruise, horsback riding, bird watching
📢 Spacious historic home built in 1853 with authentic period decor and view of the St.Lawrence
River. Breakfast is served in the onsite period restaurant. CCards ⌐B&B

Saint-Hyacinthe *(east of Montreal, see also St German de Grant, South Durham)*

Avard, Bernard & Carmen (Le Jardin Caché B&B) ☎ (450) 773-2231, Fax (450) 773-9099
2465 Ave Raymond, Saint-Hyacinthe, QC J2S 5W4   E-mail: jardencache@sympatico.ca

From Montreal or Quebec City take Hwy 20 and Exit 130 Blvd Laframboise to the Arch. Turn
right on Bourdages, right on Bourassa, left on Raymond.
$40-50S $55-65D $15Child $80F (plus taxes) ▶ 6A,1Ch
🍴 Full, homebaked 🏠 Res., 2-storey, patio, porches, quiet
■3D(upstairs) ⊨2T,1D,1Q,1R 🛏 2Sh.w.g. ★F,TV,ceiling
fans, separate entrance, off-street & street parking, spa, guest
quarters are separate ✋ Designated smoking area, no pets,
English (household language is French)
🧍 Retro Rock/Roll Music Festival (Aug), Agricultural Fair, golf
courses, walking/cycling paths, x/c skiing, bus & train, Medieval Food Fair (Labour Day wkd)
🚗 Montreal, Dorval Airport, Drummondville Folklore Festival
🚩 "Young" Bell Canada pensioners and well travelled hosts in family ancestral home filled with
antiques and paintings, located in the heart of the city. Winners of the Montérégie Hospitality
Excellence Prize (96/97). Relax in the outside spa situated in the English garden with fish pond.
"Scrumptious breakfasts are worth the detour"! Visa,MC ✔B&B bbcanada.com/lejardincache

---

St-Germain-de-Grantham *(south of Drummondville, see also South Durham)*

Levasseur, Juliette (Le Madawaska B&B) ☎ (819) 395-4318
644 Rte 239, St-Germain-de-Grantham, QC J0C 1K0

From Montreal on Hwy 20, take Exit 166. turn right onto Hwy 239 North. From Quebec City take
Exit 166 and turn left onto Hwy 239. Proceed 3km.
$40S $55D $10Child ▶ 6
🍴 Homebaked 🏠 Rural, older, multi-storey, large flowered
grounds, wrap-around veranda ■3D(upper/lower level) ⊨2T,1D
🛏Sh.w.g. ★Parking ✋ No smoking, no pets ∿ English
🚗 Drummondville (historic village), Folklore Festival (July)
🚩 Large warm country home ca1916, with simple comforts/sunny
atmosphere. Enjoy true warm Acadian-Québec hospitality. ✔B&B

St-Jérôme *(n of Montréal; see also Prévost, Ste Anne des Lacs, Ste Adele, Se.Sauveur)*

Lemay, Marie-Thérèse et Gérard (L'Etape) ☎ (450) 438-1043
430 Melançon, St-Jérôme, QC J7Z 4K4

From Montréal or Mirabel Airport, take rte 15 north & Exit 43 east for St-Jérôme. Proceed along
DeMartigny St to City center. Turn right on Blvd Labelle & just before the park in front of the
Cathedral turn left on DuPalais. Proceed to Melançon on left

$40S $55D $12Child $20Add.person ▶ 6A,1Child
🍴 Full, homebaked 🏠 Res., older, large acreage, quiet
■3D(main & upper level) ⊨1S,4T,1K 🛏 3Sh.w.h.
★TV,F,LF,KF ✋ Restricted smoking ∿English (French is
household language)
🧍 City center, Cultural Center, art galleries, popular concerts in
the park, shops and restaurants, church, baseball/football field,
Petit train du Nord, cycling trail
🚩 Stone-brick house is a cottage in the New-England style with 2 columns framing the front
door, built by a renowned architect and situated adjacent to a municipal park. Hosts are
professional retirees and active in local cultural and sociological groups. ✔B&B

St.Sauveur

(north of Montreal; see also St-Anne-des-Lacs, Prevost, Ste-Adele)

Desruisseaux, Noelle & Jon Threlkeld (Le Petit Clocher)   ☎ (450) 227-7576
216 De L'eglise, St.Sauveur, QC   J0R 1R7   Fax (450) 227-6662

E-mail: lepetit.clocher@sympatico.ca

From Montreal, take Rte15 north and Exit 60 to center of town. Located 1km from church.

$125S $150-195D   (plus tax)   ► 8A
🍴 Full   🏠 Village, hillside, 2-storey, hist., acreage, view from
guest rooms   ■ 4D (main & upper level)   ⊨ 4Q
🛁 4Ensuite   ★ F,TV in guest rooms, private entrance, off-street
parking, guest quarters are separate   ♨ Designated smoking
area, no pets, not suitable for children   ⌇ French
🎿 Skiing (day & night), hiking, bicycle paths, theatre, Art
Festivals, boutiques, restaurants
🚗 Montreal, Mt. Tremblant, scenic drives

🦅 Spacious home with warm elegant decor, nestled on 4 acres with panoramic view of ski slopes
and the village of St.Sauveur des Monts in the popular resort area of the Laurentians. CCards
📖B&B   www.bbcanada.com/lepetitclocher

Turgeon, Mirelle(Mimi) & Benny(Aux Petits Oiseaux B&B)   ☎(450)227-6116,Fax 6171
342 rue Principale,St.Sauveur,QC   J0R 1R0   1-877-227-6116

E-mail: auxpetitsoiseaux@sympatico.ca,

From Montreal take Hwy15 north. Turn left at Exit60 (Rte364North). Turn right, 2nd set of lights,

turn right again on rue de la Gare, then left on rue Principale.
$60-90S $65-115D $10-25child $150-165F   (plus tax)   ► 12A
🍴 Full, homebaked   🏠 Village/Resort, 2-storey, hist., view from guest
rooms, swimming pool, patio, deck quiet   ■ 4 (upper & lower level)
⊨1T,3D,1Q,R,cot   🛁 4Private   ★ Air,F,TV in guest rooms, ceiling fans,
off-street/street parking, guest quarters are separate   ♨No smoking, no
pets   ⌇English, Spanish, Danish, German (household language is French)
🎿 Restaurants, boutiques/shops, alpine/x-c skiing, bike/walking trails,
Summer theatre, well-known Mt.St.Sauveur Ski Resort & Aquatic park, bus
🚗 Downtown Montreal, Mt Tremblant Ski/Golf Resort, Ste-Agathe
🦅 Charming & traditional Quebec home with original wood panelling and
large natural stone fireplace, richly furnished with antiques and filled with round-the-world
souvenirs and artifacts, offering a restful and cozy atmosphere. Located in the center of a very
picturesque Laurentian village. Candlelight breakfast is served with a splendid view of the ski hills
of Mt St.Sauveur and the lovely landscaped garden and pool. CCards 📖B&B www.bbcanada.com

---

St-Sévère

(west of Trois-Rivières; see also Louiseville, Pointe du Lac)

Héroux, Lise (Au Bourgainvillier)   ☎ & Fax (819) 264-5653
83 Rue Principale, St-Sévère, QC   G0X 3B0

Located halfway between Montréal and Québec City. From Hwy 40 take Exit 180. In Yamachiche at
flashing light, proceed towards Shawinigan and continue on Rt 153
for 3 km. Then follow signs to St-Sévère for 5 km.
$35S $50D $10Child $15Add.person   ► 8A,3Ch
🍴 Full   🏠 Village, older, quiet   ■ 4 (upstairs)   ⊨4D
🛁2Sh.w.g.   ★ TV,LF, parking   ♨ No pets   ⌇ English
(household language is French)
🎿 Watch farming activities, walking in village "promenade"
🚗 Art Gallery, museum, summer theatre, boat cruise, skiing
🦅 Sixth-Generation family (Héroux and Bourgainville) in rustic, spacious, 170-year-old home
with antique furnishings situated in an agricultural village projecting a taste of yesterday. Relax on
the wrap-around porch and enjoy the peaceful, quiet country atmosphere. 📖B&B

Ste-Anne-des-Lacs *(n/w of Montreal; see also Prevost, St Jerome, Ste Adele, St.Sauveur)*

Swerdlow, Anne   ☎ (450) 224-5401
39 Chemin des Lilas, Sainte Anne Des Lacs QC J0R 1B0

From Montréal, take Hwy 15 north and Exit 57 at Ste-Anne-des-Lacs. Turn left and proceed 5 km

to Chemin des Lilas (opposite gas station). Turn left.
$30S $35D $6Add.person ◙ Meals   ▶ 4
◫ Full, homebaked 🏠 Village, view, patio, lakefront, quiet
■2D(upstairs) ⊨ 1S,2T,1D ⊒ Sh.w.g. ★ TV,F,KF,
parking, space for ski equipment 🚭No smoking
🏃 Lake directly in front of house, swimming, canoeing, woodland
strolls, x-c skiing
🚗 Several major resorts for winter sports, esp.downhill skiing
🖝 Well travelled hostess in very spacious comfortable family home overlooking the lake and
situated in beautiful wooded area surrounded by the Laurentien Mountains. Enjoy the close
proximity (7km) to popular St.Sauveur Ski Resort, jewel of the Laurentien ski area.

South Durham   *(south-east of Drummondville, see also St.Germain)*

Carson, Norman & Heather Lunan (La Sixième Génération B&B)   ☎ (819) 858-2539
415 Ch.Mooney, Durham-Sud, QC J0H 2C0   E-mail: 6genb+b@dr.cgocable.ca, Fax(819)858-2001

From Montreal, travel east on Hwy 20 to Exit 147. Follow Hwy 116 east to Durham-Sud. Proceed
2.5km past village on Mooney Rd. From Hwy 10, take Exit 88 and follow Hwy116 to Mooney Rd.
$40-45S $55-60D $10Child $15Add.person (plus taxes)   ▶ 6A,2-3Ch

◫ Full, homebaked 🏠 Farm, 2-storey, hist., view from guest
rooms, swimming pool, patio, porch, deck, quiet ■2D,1F(main &
upper level) ⊨ 2T,1D,1Q,1P ⊒ 1Sh.w.g. ★ F,TV, guest
quarters are separate 🖐 Designated smoking area 〰 French
🏃 Children's play area, river/fields/woods, skidoo trails, x-c skiing
🚗 Historic Woolen Mill, museums, x-c ski club, concert halls,
golfing, antiquing, cycling
🖝 Warm welcome in enlarged & extended 1865-built home on
Sixth Generation farm, surrounded by peace & beauty. Ideal place from which to view exquisite fall
foliage. Join the host family in the original beam accented living room for social time. There is a cat
and a dog. ✔B&B www.slxiemegeneration.qc.ca

Sutton   *(south of Granby near US border)*

LeBaron-Watson, Pat & Allan Watson (Willow House)   ☎ (450) 538-0035
30 Western Ave., Box 906, Sutton, QC J0E 2K0

From Montreal, take Eastern Township Auto Rt 10 and Exit 60 onto Hwy 139 to Sutton. Turn

right off Principale at Foyer Sutton to Western Ave.
$30S $50D $20Child $20Add.person ◙ Meals   ▶ 8
◫ Choice 🏠 Village, hist., view, patio, quiet ■4D(upstairs)
⊨4T,1D,1K ⊒Sh.w.g. ★TV,LF, guest den 🖐 Designated
smoking area 〰French
🏃 Boutiques, Art Sutton, library, antiques, fine restaurants,
gorgeous fall colours, public transportation to downtown Montreal
🚗 Mount Sutton ski hill, x-c skiing, Vermont Border, golfing
🖝 Lovely Old Loyalist home with a view of running brook and pond. Situated in the hub of
artisans environment with many arts/craft shops nearby. Enjoy homebaking for breakfast and
afternoon tea. Pets welcome. ✔CC

Tourelle

(on northshore of Gaspé area, east of Matane)

Miville, Bibiane & Rino Cloutier (Au Courant de la Mer)   ☎ & Fax (418) 763-5440
3 Rue Belvedere, Box 191, Tourelle, QC   G0E 2J0   1-800-230-6709

$35-50S $50-60D $7-12Child $12Add.person $12Priv.Bath   ▶ 12A,3Ch

From Quebec City take Hwy 20 and Hwy 132 east to Tourelle. From the Rest Area drive 0.2km and turn left at white house.
❖Mar-Nov ◐ Full 🏠3-storey, patio, oceanfront ■2D,2F(upst) ⊨1Q,2D,4T plus hide-away ⊿ 2Sh.w.g.+watercloset&sink ★ TV in guest room, off-street parking ✋Smoking in Den, no pets
~English (household language is French)
🚶 Stroll by the sea, stores, restaurant, Sea Food Canteen
🚐 Parc de la Gaspèsie (Mont Jaques Cartier), Explorama, Mont Albert
🐾 Retired teacher/med.service hosts in large home by the sea with warm & friendly atmosphere & a superb view of the St.Laurence River. Relax by the rythm of the waves breaking on the beach & enjoy the peaceful environment.Longer stay rates available. Visa ✒B&B

Trois Rivière

(east of Montreal; see also Point du Lac, Louisville, Saint Severe)

Loiselle, Michele (Le Gîte Loiselle B&B)   ☎ & Fax (819) 375-2121
836 des Ursulines, Trois-Rivières, QC   G9A 5B9   1-888-552-2121

Phone for directions.
$50-60S $60-70D   ▶ 11
◐ Homebaked 🏠 Downtown, 3-storey, hist., patio, quiet ■4D,1F (upstairs & lower level ⊨ 3S,4Q ⊿ 5Private
★Air,TV, private entrance, off-street parking, guest quarters are separate ✋ No smoking, no pets ~ English (household language is French)
🚶 Cruises on St.Maurice & St.Laurence Rivers, golfing, beaches, marinas, bicycle roads, antique dealers, shops, restaurants
🚐 National Park La Mauricie & historic site, Pulp & Paper Industry Exhibition Centre
🐾 Large home built in 1899, restored over the years and located in the historic city area. Hosts are proud receivers of the City's Heritage Restoration Award. Visa,MC ✒CC

Wakefield

(north of Ottawa,ONT; see also Pontiac, Quyon)

Mercier, Madeleine and Jacques (Les Trois Erables)   ☎ (819) 459-1118, 1-877-3ERABLE
801 Riverside Rd., Box 852, RR2, Wakefield, QC   J0X 3G0   E-mail: troiserables@cyberus.ca

From Ottawa, take MacDonald-Cartier Bridge across Ottawa River and Hwy 5 north to temporary end. Proceed on Hwy 105 to Wakefield (follow Maniwaki signs).
$55S $65D $80Ste   ▶ 8-10
❖ Closed Nov.and April ◐Full 🏠Village, hist., 3-storey, acreage, view, river, patio ■3D(upstairs),2Ste ⊨2T,4Q,1D ⊿4Ensuite ★ Air,F,TV in guest room, sep.entrance, parking
✋Rest. smoking ~English (household language French)
🚶 Gatineau River, Gatineau Park, restaurants, shops, x-country & alpine skiing, lake swimming, windsurfing, canoeing, hiking, mountain biking, nature trails, rhapsody of legendary fall colours
🐾 National Capital Region Heritage home, built around the turn of the Century, tastefully restored and renovated to enhance the craftsmanship of years gone by and provides guests with superior sleeping and relaxing facilities. Enjoy a hearty breakfast with the sun filtering through the stained glass windows or on cold mornings feel the warmth from the unique fireplace.Visa,MC ✒CC http://www.bbcanada.com/1346html

New Brunswick

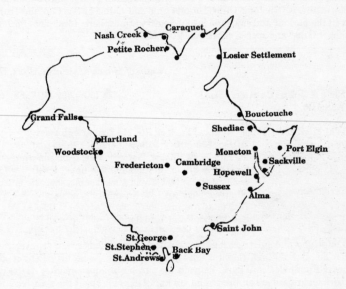

Tourism New Brunswick
Box 12345, Fredericton, NB   E3B 5C3

toll-free 1-800-561-0123

Albert

(south of Moncton; see also Alma, Hopewell Cape)

Tingley, Cyril and Mary (Florentine Manor) ☎(506)882-2271,Fax882-2936,1-800-665-2271
RR2, 356 Hwy 915, Albert (Harvey), Albert Co., NB E0A 1A0   E-mail: florainn@nbnet.nb.ca

$60S $79-99D $12Child $129(Ste) 🍽 Meals   (plus tax)   ▶ 16A,4Ch
Located at 356, Hwy 915. Take Rt114 at Moncton towards Fundy Nat.Park. At Riverside-Albert
take Rt915 past old Bank of NB for 3.5km to Harvey Corner on Fundy Coastal Drive.

🏠Full,homebaked 🏠Rural, acreage, hist. pastoral views from
guest rooms, quiet ■6D,1F,1Ste (main & upper floor) 🚪Private
(2 with whirlpool tub) ⊨6T,5D,2Q,2K,2R ✋No pets, no
smoking ★F,TV,LF,KF, private entrance in suite, guest robes,
🏃 Country lanes for leisure walks, prime birdwatching location
🚗 Shepody Bay Hemispheric Shore Bird Reserve at Mary's Point,
Fundy Nat.Pk, Hopewell, Cape Rocks world's largest flower pots
📣 Spacious (1860) house with extreme high ceilings (11ft),
full of antiques, speaks of the grandeur of a past era when sailing ships were built and launched in
the shipyards nearby. A "Customs Office" at one time and visited by Sea Captains from all over the
world. Relax in the parlour and enjoy the lovely country atmosphere. Ideal place for large groups
(biking, birding, hiking) and special occasions. Visa, MC ✓B&B

Alma

(south of Moncton; see also Albert, Hopewell Cape)

O'Regan, Elsie & John (Captain's Inn)   ☎ (506) 887-2017, Fax (506) 887-2074
Alma, NB E0A 1B0

Take Rte 114 at Moncton to Fundy National Park or Rte 114 Exit after Sussex.

$61S $75-80D $10Add.person   (plus tax)   ▶ 21
🏠 Full   🏠 Village, 2-storey, view from some guest rooms,
quiet ■ 8D,1F (ground, main & upper level) ⊨ 9Q,1D,1S
🚪9Private ★ F,TV in guest rooms, separate entrance,
off-street parking ✋No smoking, no pets
🏃 Fundy National Park, world's highest tides at Bay of Fundy
🚗 Mary's Point Bird Sanctuary, Hopewell Rocks, Cape Enrage,
Moncton, golfing, fishing, well groomed x-c ski trails
📣 Very comfortable and quiet spacious house with a homey country atmosphere, overlooking the
mighty tides of the Bay of Fundy (highest tides in the world), in quaint little fishing port near East
Gate entrance of Fundy National Park. Relax in the parlour or sunroom after a busy day outdoors.
Hosts were born and raised in the village and are knowledgeable about the area. Visa,MC ✓B&B

Back Bay

(south of St.George)

Matheson, Peggy & Murvin (The Beach House B&B)   ☎ (506) 755-2675, 754-5662
34 Madison Rd., Back Bay, NB E5C 2Y9   E-mail: peggym.@nb.sympatico.ca, Fax (506) 755-6688

From Hwy 1 (Exit 43), follow Rte 172 & Deer Island Ferry signs for 14km to B&B. Look for signs.
$40S $65D $15Add.person   ▶ 7

🏠Full,homebaked 🏠Village,raised bungalow, hillside,oceanfront,
acreage,view from guest rooms,patio,deck,quiet ■2D,1Ste (main
& ground level) ⊨1D,2Q,cot 🚪1Shw.g.,1sh.w.h. ★TV,private
guest deck,off-street parking ✋Smoking outside
🏃 Ocean beach, stroll along water's edge collecting sea shells &
driftwood, lobster pound, Sardine Canning Plant, fishing wharf
🚗 St.Andrews-by-the-Sea, Saint John, lighthouses, three islands
ferries, Aquaculture sites, bicycling the "Quoddy Loop", US border
📣 Large ocean home with waterfront deck. Watch the tides rise & fall in an everchanging
panorama of beauty. Hosts know the area well, have been involved with the local fishing industry
for 30 years and can tell many "sea lures and tales". A hearty Maritime breakfast is served on the
deck or in the dining room while watching loons, cranes, eagles & ducks. Visa,MC ✓B&B

Bouctouche

(north of Moncton; see also Shediac)

Haché, Eveline (Domaine-sur-Mer)
Box1, S13, RR3, Bouctouche, NB E0A 1G0

☎ (506) 743-6582
E-mail: domaine@auracom.com

Located in Saint-Thomas on Rte 535 on the shore road and 10km south of Bouctouche.

$65-100S/D   (plus tax) ▶4
🍴 Full 🏠 2-storey, oceanfront, 2acres, view ■2(upstairs)
🛏2D ⬛2Private ★ F,TV,off-street parking 🖐No pets, no
smoking 〰English (French is household language)
🏃 Quiet beach, wooded trails, clam digging, 2wharfs
🚗 Bouctouche (with 13km of sandy dunes), Kouchibouguac,
Shediac, Moncton, Confederation Bridge to PEI
🐾 Warm welcome and friendly hospitality in Acadian home
surrounded by gardens and ocean across the road. Enjoy the uplifting frontal view of the sea and the
tranquil environment. Hostess is knowledgeable about Acadian culture and history. Take in a day at
"The Pays de la Saguine" & "The Acadian Culture". ✎B&B

Cambridge Narrows

(west of Moncton; see also Sussex)

Steeves, Susan & Greg (Cambridge-Narrows B&B)
RR1, Cody's, NB E0E 1E0

☎ (506) 488-2000

From TCH 2 at Jemseg, take Rte 695 to Cambridge Narrows. Turn right before bridge (Rte 715).
From east, take Rts 710/715 at Coles Isle, continue to Cambridge N. & then 1km on Rte 715.

$29S $49-54D $59Ste $5Add.person ▶ 6A,2Ch
🍴 Homebaked 🏠 Farm, acreage, 2-storey, view, lake across
road ■ 2D,1Ste(upstairs) suite has loft 🛏1D,1Q,1K,R,P,crib
⬛ Sh.w.g., 1ensuite ★F,LF,KF,TV, separate entrance 🖐No
smoking, no pets, families welcome
🏃 Restaurant, store, campground (beach, pool, dock, Rec Hall)
🐾 Renovated older home, situated on a little hill overlooking
Washadehoak Lake, surrounded by pastures & forests. Relax on
the wrap-around veranda and enjoy the peaceful country atmosphere. Two-seater bike for rent.
Breakfast in suite available at extra charge. Hosts operate the large campground and services on
the property by the lake. ✎B&B http://www.bbcanada.com/2276.html

Caraquet

(east of Bathurst; see also Losier Settlement, Petit Roger)

Dugas-Landry, Martina E (La Maison Touristique Dugas)
683 Boul.St Pierre Ouest, Caraquet, NB E1W 1A1

☎ (506) 727-3195,
Fax (506) 727-3193

Located on Rt 11 and 6.5 km west of downtown Caraquet.
$29.95S $38D $9.95Add.person   (plus tax)
🍴 Choice 🏠 Res., village ■ 8S,3D,2Ste(upstairs), including sep.
house, plus cabins 🛏2T,15D,2cots ⬛3Sh.w.g.,1sh.w.h.
★TV,KF, parking 🖐Restricted smoking 〰English
(household language is French)
🏃 Wooded road leading to beach, excellent swimming
🚗 Village Historique Acadien, Aquarium, Pope Museum
🐾 Comfortable, 1926-built, spacious family home still has the orginal woodwork and is furnished
with antiques. Relax on the old-fashioned front veranda. ✎CC

NEW BRUNSWICK   291

Fredericton

Fowler, Betty & Doug (Fowlers Bluff B&B)   ☎ (506) 450-6173
48 Crestline Dr., McLeod Hill, NB   E3A 6B1

Travel off Rte 105 from Fredericton or on Hwy 2 at MacTaquac to Royal Rd/Stanley and exit to
McLeod Hill on right. Proceed 4km to Hillview Dr. Turn right on Sunset and right on Crestline. Or
call for directions from Royal Rd/Stanley.

$50S $60D   ► 4A
❖ Summer only   ◖ Full   ♠ Rural, 2-storey, view from guest
rooms, 2.5acres, deck, quiet, secluded   ■2D(upst)   ◄2D
◢1Sh.w.g.   ★ KF,F,TV,ceiling fans, off-street parking
Ⓦ Smoking outside, pets outside, not suitable for children
♀ Walking path through woods, viewpoint on ancient Volcanic
Cliff, wood turning demonstrations (display & sale of items)
🚗 Historic Fredericton Centre, beaches, shopping, diving, Kings
Landing, Govt.House, hunting, fishing, canoeing, cruises, golfing, tennis
📣 Relaxing Cape Cod home nestled on treed acreage overlookng the Nashwaksis Valley, that
boasts the most spectacular sunsets north of Florida. Hosts enjoy various hobbies, including wood
turning, gardening, motorcycling, canoeing and historic military re-enactment. Breakfast is served
in separate guest breakfast room.

Gorham, Frank and Joan (Carriage House Inn B&B)   ☎ (506) 452-9924
230 University Ave., Fredericton, NB   E3B 4H7   E-mail: chinn@nbnet.nb.ca, Fax 458-0799

Located off Hwy 2 and 102. Take Exit 295. Phone for directions.

$65-70S $75-85D $15Add.person (plus tax)   ► 20
◖ Full, homebaked   ♠ Downtown, res., hist., quiet, open and
screened verandas, adjacent river   ■D,S(main & upper levels)
◄2T,7D,6Q,3cots   ◢11Private   ★Air exchanger,
TV,F,KF,LF,parking, solarium, fax/computer, phones in rooms,
♀ Saint John riverfront biking & walking path, farmer's market,
Art Gallery, Prov. Legislature, Playhouse Trans Canada Trail
🚗 King's Landing (1780-1830 re-created village)
📣 3-storey Victorian mansion, built in 1875, surrounded by huge Elm trees. Spacious rooms are
furnished with antiques. Gracious mahogany staircase winds to 3rd floor and new sky-lit library.
Breakfast is served in solarium. Children welcome. CCards ✔B&B

Hawkins, Kathleen and Lorne (The Hawks Nest B&B)   ☎ (506) 363-3645
150 Rocky Rd., Keswick Ridge, NB   E6L 1V2

From Trans Canada Hwy 2, take Exit 274 and cross the Mactaquac Dam. Turn into 2nd road on

right. Proceed up the hill to house on left (1km).
$45S $60D   ► 6
◖ Full, homebaked   ♠ Rural, acreage, patio, quiet   ■3D(main
& upper level)   ◄2D,1Q   ◢1Sh.w.g.+1/2sh.w.g   ★F,TV,LF,
parking   Ⓦ No smoking, no children
♀ Mactaquac Provincial Park (boating, beaches, golfing, marina,
fine dining, c/c skiing, skating, sleigh rides), salmon/bass fishing
🚗 Kings Landing, Woolastook Park, Fredericton, Crabbe Mtn
📣 Colonial country home situated near the beautiful St. John River in the most breathtaking
scenic area of NB. Enjoy a full country breakfast with all the homemade fixings. Host is active with
the large family building business, hostess is an experienced toll/art painter, and both are
knowledgeable about the area. Enjoy the lovely decor and the congenial and relaxed atmosphere.
House motto: "Come as a stranger, leave as a friend". There is a large friendly dog called "UBU".

Fredericton (cont'd)

Myshrall, Elsie (Appelot B&B)   ☎ (506) 444-8083
1272, Rte 105 Hwy, Douglas, NB E3A 7K2   E-mail: appelot@nbnet.nb.ca

From Hwy2, take Exit for Mactaquac Park and first right onto Hwy105 South to house on left (9km). From Fredericton, take Westmorland Bridge 105 North and continue approximately 14km

to house on right. Look for signs.
$50-55S $65-70D   ▶ 6
🍴Full, homebaked 🏠Rural, older, riverfront, view,sunporch
■3(upstairs) ⊨2Q,2T(extra length) ⊷1Sh.w.g.,1sh.w.h.,
1private ★TV,VCR, fans, picnic table, gas BBQ, parking
🚳No smoking, no pets
🧍 Orchards & woodlands, St. John River, Trans Canada Trail
🚗 Kings Ldg, Mactaquac Prov. Park, Beaverbrook Gallery

🐾 Completely renovated 1905-built attractive farmhouse situated on hillside with sweeping view of river and surrounding countryside. Full scrumptious breakfast served in spacious enclosed sunporch with view of the beautiful valley. ✒B&B http://bbcanada.com/187.html

---

Grand Falls   *(south of Edmundston at US border)*

Coté, Noel and Norma (Cote's B&B)   Fax (506) 473-1952
575 Broadway Blvd West, Grand Falls, NB E3Z 2L2   ☎ (506) 473-1415, 1-877-444-2683

From Hwy 2, take Exits 75/76 or 81 to Broadway St.
$40S $65D $15Add.person   ▶ 13
🍴 Full, homebaked 🏠 Downtown, res., older, 2-storey, patio,
quiet ■5(4upstairs) ⊨5Q,1K ⊷5Ensuite ★TV,KF,LF,
ceiling fans & air-conditioners, sep entrance, 2private balconies,
parking 🚳No smoking ∿French
🧍 Falls & Gorge, Wells In Rocks, museum, swimming, tennis, ball
field, gift shops, restuarants, downtown
🚗 USA border, Danish Community (largest in Canada), golf course

🐾 Home is situated in the quiet part of downtown. Enjoy a complete breakfast in the dining room, evening snack on the patio. Hosts have a collection of "Precious Moments", Decoupage artwork and needlepoint in the house. Enjoy homemade jam and NB maple syrup. Visa,MC ✒B&B

Crawford, Rachel (Maple Bed & Breakfast)   ☎ (506) 473-1763
142 Main St., Grand Falls, NB E3Z 2V9

From Hwy 2, take Exits 76 or 81 into Grand Falls.
$75-90S/D $15Child   ▶ 8
🍴Full, homebaked 🏠Downtown, res., older, patio, quiet ⊨T,D,R
■3(upstairs) ⊷3Private ★ F,TV and sink in each guest room,
guest housecoats, ceiling fans, 1 private balcony 🚳 No smoking,
children min age 6
🧍 Restaurants, stores, gift shops, scenic Grand Falls and beautiful
Gorge with walking trails, swimming pool
🚗 Golf Clubs, tennis courts, Danish settlement, Madawaska Weavers, swimming pool

🐾 Congenial hosts in 1934-built home, with lots of charm and personality, uniquely decorated and elegantly furnished - "a comfortable home away from home". Hostess likes candles and there are many of them in the house. Visa✒ B&B

Hartland

(north-west of Fredericton; see also Woodstock)

Campbell, Rosemary (Campbell's B&B) ☎ (506) 375-4775
7175,Rte 105, Upper Brighton (Hartland), NB E7P 2P7

From Rt 2 (Trans Canada) take Exit 170 to Rt 105 north for 2km.
$40S $50D $5Child $10Add.person ► 8A,4Ch
🍴 Cont, homebaked (help yourself) 🏠Farm, large wrap-around
veranda, riverview, quiet ■3D,1F (main and upper level)
🛏3S,4D,2R,crib 🛁1Private,1sh.w.g ★Air,KF,LF,TVin guest
living room, separate entrance ⊛No pets, rest.smoking, large
quilt display ⋙some French
🕴 Saint John River, canoeing, fishing, hunting, snowmobiling
🚐World's longest covered bridge, golfing, Fredericton, US Border (Maine), tennis, swimming
🐗 500-acres family farming operation on original farmstead, situated along the Saint John River
Valley in New Brunswick's "Potato Belt". Large rooms are decorated with family antiques. The
entire house is available for guests. Host lives in smaller building on the property. ✒ NB B&BA

Hopewell Cape/Hill

(south of Moncton; see also Albert, Alma)

Holmstrom, Stephen & Elaine (Peck Colonial House B&B & Tea Room) ☎(506)882-2114
Hopewell Hill, Albert Co., NB E0A 1Z0

Located on Rte 114, east of Riverside Albert. Phone for directions.
$40S $50-55D $10Add.person 🍽 Meals ► 6
🍴Full, homebaked 🏠Farm, 3-storey, hist.,view from guest
rooms,quiet,isolated ■2D,1F(upstairs) 🛏2T,1S,2D,crib
🛁2Sh.w.g. ★ TV, parking ⊛ No smoking, no pets
🕴 Walk in 340 acres of field and forest with small creek
🚐 The Rocks, Fundy Nat.Park, Mary Pt. Bird Sanctuary, Cape
Enrage lighthouse, Albert County Museum, covered bridges
🐗 Comfortable, 9th Generation 200-year old ancestral Colonial home (on original land grant),
filled with handwoven rugs (by hosts) and surrounded by gardens. There is constant restoration in
progress. Hosts are very knowledgeable about local history and events. Enjoy breakfast or a light
evening snack in the unique 19th Century cozy in-house Tea room, also featuring chowders. ✒B&B

Losier Settlement

(east of Bathurst; see also Caraquet)

Losier, Jocelyne (Chez Prime) ☎ (506) 395-6884
8796 Losier Settlement, Rte 11, NB E1X 3C1

Located on Rt 11 in the Acadian Peninsula and 5 km north of town Tracadie-Sheila.
$30S $45-50D 🍽 Meals(Acadian Foods) ► 6A
🕱 July/Aug 🍴Full 🏠Rural, acreage ■3D(upstairs)
🛏2T,2D 🛁2Sh.w.h. ⊛No pets, no smoking ⋙English
(Household language is French)
🕴 Peaceful blueberry farm surroundings, country walks, country
store, Christmas tree plantation
🚐 Acadian village at Caraquet, Marine Center at Shippagan, Bird
Sanctuary at Miscou, public beaches, fishing, airport, train station
🐗 4th Generation Losiers (family has been on property since 1854), is taking great pride in
preserving their heritage and keeping the original decor in the house. There is a very old Thomas
Organ and a huge hat collection. Discover Acadian history and traditions firsthand. Hosts will
celebrate their 15th Anniversary of welcoming guests to their B&B. www.gov.nb.ca/tourism

Moncton

Langille, Gladys and Carson (Park View B&B)
254 Cameron St., Moncton, NB   E1C 5Z3   ☎ (506) 382-4504

Going East on Trans-Canada Hwy 1, take Exit 488 and continue on Mountain Rd turning right at Cameron St(8km). Going West, take Exit 511A and continue on Rte 132 onto Main St

(15 km). Turn right on Cameron St.
$45S $55D $8Child $10Add.person   ► 6A,2Ch
🅓 Choice, homebaked 🏠 Downtown, older, view, quiet
■3(upstairs) ⊨ 2S,2D,1Q   ⌐ 1Sh.w.g. ★Air,F,TV,LF,
parking ⍟No pets, no smoking
🔨 Victoria Park, Moncton Museum, Thomas Williams House,
Tidal Bore, Acadian Museum, Art Gallery, Highfield Square
🚗 Magnetic Hill & Game Farm, Rocks Provincial Park, beaches
🐾 Spacious, Art Deco home located in the center of the City and across from beautiful Victoria Park. Retired host is active in the local Duplicate Bridge Club and a painter, whose pictures and that of other local artists are displayed throughout the house. Hostess is a teacher. Enjoy the congenial atmosphere and a delicious breakfast served in elegant dining room. ⌐B&B

Martin, Jeremy (Bonaccord House)
250 Bonaccord St., Moncton, NB   E1C 5M6   ☎ (506) 388-1535 Fax (506) 853-7191

$40-45S $50-58D   from$55Ste(for 2) $10Add.person   ► 16-18
Located in downtown at the corner of John St. From Main St turn north on Bonaccord St or from

Mountain Rd turn south on Bonaccord St.
🅓 Full, homecooked 🏠 Downtown, res., older, patio, upper and lower verandas ■5(main & upper levels) ⊨6S,1D,4Q,1R
⌐2Sh.w.g.,3Private ★F,guest slippers,parking ⍟No pets, no smoking ⌁French,some Spanish
🔨 Downtown, restaurants, theatre, Moncton Museum/Art Gallery, shopping, University of Moncton, Victoria Park & Tidal Bore viewing, hist.Thomas Willams House, farmer's market
🚗 Magnetic Hill, Hopewell Rocks, Shediac beaches with warmest water north of Carolinas
🐾 Large yellow, 3-storey, turn-of-the-Century residence with a double living room, complete with fireplace and bay window, offering a convivial atmosphere in which to meet fellow travellers or just sit quietly and read. Centrally located and an ideal place from which to explore downtown Moncton and southeast New Brunswick. Visa ⌐B&B

Nash Creek   *(west of Bathurst; see also Petit Roger)*

Hayes, Kathleen & Allan (Haye's House B&B)
22 Hayes Rd., Nash Creek, NB   E8G 1A8   ☎ (506) 237-5228/237-2252
E-mail: hayesbb@nbnet.nb.ca

From north on Hwy11 take Campbellton Exit357. From south on Hwys11 or 134 take Bathurst Exit357.
$57S $67D   ► 6A
❄ April-Nov. 🅓Full, homebaked 🏠 Rural, village, 3-storey, hist., view from guest rooms, oceanfront ■ 3(upstairs)
⊨T,D,Q   ⌐ 2Sh.w.g. ★ F,TV in guest living room, portable fans in rooms, private entrance, off-street parking ⍟ No smoking, no pets, inquire about children ⌁French
🔨 Bay of Chaleur, beach, scenic view points of Gaspe, Mont St.Joseph, Heron Island Park
🚗 Acadian Trail (scenic route), golfing, watersports, fishing, museums, Festivals, parks
🐾 Warm welcome in elegant ancestral home (1910) with spacious grounds and veranda, offering full view of Bay Chaleur and mountains of Gaspe and continuing to serve the family traditions. Breakfast is served in guest breakfast room. Visa,MC ⌐B&B

Petit-Rocher

(north of Bathurst, see also Nash Creek)

Landry, Laurina & Lionel (Auberge D'Anjou)
587 Rue Principale, Petit-Rocher, NB E8J 1H6

☎ (506) 783-0587, Fax (506) 783-5587
E-mail: auberge.anjou@nb.aibn.com

From Hwy 11, take Exit 326 to Petit Rocher. Located on Rte 134.
$60S $65D $5Add.person   (plus tax)   ◙ Meals   ► 18
🍴 Full   🏠 Village, 2-storey, hist., deck   ■14D,1Ste, (main &
upper level)   ⊨4T,14D,1Q,2P, cot   ⊷12private, 6sh.w.g
★Air,KF,LF,TV in guest room, ceiling fans, kitchenettes in 3
buildings, off-street parking, host quarters are separate
ⓦDesignated smoking area, no pets   ⌇ English (household
language is French)

🏃 Bay of Chaleur, mining museum, art gallery, beautiful church, fisherman wharf, tennis
🚗 Parc Atlas (trout fishing, scuba diving, cycle trail), Pabineau & Tatagouche Falls, Daley Point
(nature trails), canoe excursions, golfing, public beaches, Acadian historic village
📷 Large hist.family resort buildings (large main building, & old convent) completely renovated
and located in picturesque village on the Acadian Coastal Drive. Hosts have an apartment in the
former Convent. CCards   www.sn2000.nb.ca/comp/auberge-d'anjou

---

Port Elgin

(east of Moncton)

Flad, Anne (Indian Point B&B)
323 Fort Rd., Port Elgin, NB E0A 2K0

☎ & Fax (506) 538-7586
E-mail: flad@nbnet.nb.ca

$50S $60D $6Add.person

(Child under age 10 free)   (plus tax)   ◙ meals   ► 18A,6Ch
Situated 1.5 km from Hwy into Port Elgin.ph for directions.
🍴 Full, homebaked   🏠 Farm, bungalow addition to farm house,
view, oceanfront, quiet   ■ 2D,3F,2stes, host quarters are in main
building   ⊨12D,2P,cot   ⊷5Private,2ensuite   ★TV,KF,LF,phone
in guest room, separate entrance, picnic tables, parking, barbeque
ⓦDesignated smoking area, no pets   ⌇German
🏃 Shallow beach on property, village shopping, restaurants,
walking trails connected to the property
🚗 New Confederation Bridge to PEI, scenic coastline of Northumberland Strait,
📷 Enjoy German hospitality in the Maritimes. Accommodation is in large extension to the main
farm house, with a beautiful view across to Nova Scotia and located at the Green Bay ("the warmest
Bay north of Florida"). The atmosphere is one of peace and serenity. Breakfast is served in separate
guest breakfast room in the main house. There is a resident dog. ✏B&B www.indian-point.nb.ca

---

Sackville

(south-east of Moncton)

Young, Bill & Jean (The Savoy Arms B&B)
47 Bridge St., Sackville, NB E4L 3N8

☎ & Fax (506) 536-0790, 1-800-583-5133

From TCH 2 take Exit 541 & Hwy 106 (Bridge St) to B&B on right.
$58S $70D   ► 8
🍴 Full, homebaked(buffet-style)   🏠 Village, 2-storey, hist., porch,
deck, quiet   ■4D(upstairs)   ⊨2T,2D,1Q   ⊷4Private
★F,LF,TV/VCR in three guest sitting rooms, private entrance,
piano/games in library/den   ⓦ No smoking, no pets,
🏃 Sackville Waterfowl Park, Mount Allison University
🚗 The Rocks at Hopewell C., Parlee Beach, Shediac, PEI Bridge
📷 Retired Prof. couple in beautifully decorated 19th Century home with elegant decor and with
theme relating to Gilbert & Sullivan operettas. Relax on the spacious deck, in the cozy upstairs
sitting alcove or in the the common rooms. Breakfast is served in guest breakfast room/lounge.
There is a cat in residence. ✏B&B

Saint John

Holyoke, Ralph & Karen (Homeport Historic B&B)   ☎ (506) 672-7255, Fax (506) 672-7250
80 Douglas Ave., Saint John, NB   E2K 1E4   E-mail: stay@homeport.nb.ca, 1-888-678-7678

From City Centre & Harbour Station follow signs to Reversing Falls onto Main St. Proceed through
3rd set of light (past McDonalds) and take quick left onto Douglas Ave.
$70-120S $80-125D $15Child/Add.person   (plus tax)   ► 8A,2ch

🍴 Full, homebaked (gourmet)   🏠 Res., 3-storey, hist., acreage,
view from guest rooms, river/ocean at back, patio
■5(upstairs)   ⊨5Q,cot, crib   🚿 Private, ensuite   ★LF,TV,
air-conditioners, fans, guest robes, fainting couch in one guest
room, host quarters are separate, off-street parking   ⍟ No
smoking   ⌇French, German
🚶 City Centre, shopping, restaurants, Reversing Falls (world
famous) Tourist Centre, historic up-town walking tours, bus stop
🚗 Fundy coastal villages, swimming, adventure tourism, quiet country picnics, whale watching
🚩 Restored, spacious ship-builders mansion (ca 1858) richly furnished with quality antiques &
local art, located high on a hill with breathtaking views of city, harbour, tidal flats & Bay of Fundy.
Relax in the opulence of a by-gone era. "Rise & Dine" gourmet breakfast is served in formal dining
room with very formal table setting. There is a resident dog. CCards ✓B&B   www.homeport.nb.ca

---

Marks, Diane (Garden House B&B)   ☎ (506) 646-9093, Fax (506) 652-8425
28 Garden St., Saint John, NB   E2L 3K3

$50-60S $65-85D   7-10child/Add.person   🍽 Meals   (plus tax)   ► 10
Phone for directions.

🍴 Full, homebaked   🏠 Downtown, hist.   ■ 1S,2D,1Ste (main
& upper level)   ⊨ 2S,3D,1Q,2cots   🚿4Ensuite   ★ LF,F,TV in
guest rooms, ceiling fans   ♥
🚶 Uptown area, City Market, walking tours, museum, Harbour
Station arena, Imperial Theatre, good restaurants
🚗 St.Martins, St.Andrews, Fundy Nat.Park, Irving Nature Park
🚩 Friendly "downeast" hospitality in wonderfully appointed
1900's Victorian home, elegantly furnished with antiques and with high ceilings. Relax by the
fireplace or in the library. Breakfast is served in elegant surroundings and helps start a day the
right way. There is a cat in residence. Visa,MC ✓B&B

Molloy, Linda & Gregg (Linden Manor B&B)   ☎ (506) 674-2754, 1-877-674-2754
267 Charlotte St. West, Saint John, NB   E2M 1Y2   E-mail: linden@fundy.net

From Hwy 1, take exit 109 for 6 blocks to Charlotte St West. Turn right and proceed 2 block to
corner of Charlotte and Lancaster Sts. From Digby Ferry go 4 blks on Lancaster St.

$65-70S $70-75D $15Add.person   ► 6A
🍴 Full, homebaked   🏠 Res., hist., quiet   ■1D,1F (main &
upper level)   ⊨ 1K,2Q(incl. poster beds)   🚿3Ensuite   ★LF,TV in
common area, parking   ⍟No smoking, no pets
🚶 Nova Scotia Ferry Terminal, Carleton Martello Tower,
world-famous Reversing Falls & Rapids
🚗 Farmer's market, art galleries, museums, Loyalist House,
Cherry Brook Zoo, Rockwood Park, nature park, theatre
🚩 Large Colonial home, built in the early 1800's. Stroll through the house and view original
paintings and prints by the host-artist. Enjoy good company in the large family kitchen, which has a
huge cozy fireplace. Breakfast is served in the formal dining room. Visa,MC ✓B&B
http://user.fundy.net/linden

Shediac
(east of Moncton)

Pyke, Pauline & Christopher (Auberge Belcourt Inn) ☎ (506) 532-6098
310 Main St., Box 631, Shediac, NB   E0A 3G0   E-mail: belcourt@nbnet.nb.ca, Fax (506) 533-9398

Phone for directions.
$79-115S/D   (plus tax)   ► 14
🍴 Full   🏠 Downtown, hist., porch   ■ 7D(main & upper
level)   ⊨ 2S,4D,1Q   ⚓ 1Private, 2sh.w.g., 4ensuite
★Air,off-street & street parking   ⊛ Designated smoking area,
no pets, children min. age 7   ⋙ French, Cantonese
🕺 Downtown area shopping, restaurants, canoeing, beaches,
marina, fish market, ocean cruises
🚗 Parlee Beach Prov.Park, Confederation Bridge to PEI, Hopewell Rocks, Bouctouche (board
walk) Fundy & Kouchibouguac Nat.Parks, Moncton (Tidal Bore/Magnetic Hill)
🚚 Elegant, spacious & meticulously restored Victorian home with stained-glass windows,
furnished throughout with period antiques and located in beautiful coastal town. Breakfast is
served on fine china in the oval dining room. House specialty is authentic home-cooked Chinese
meals. Enjoy the cozy, warm atmosphere provided by two large fireplaces and relax in one of several
elegant drawing rooms or on the veranda. Ideal place for corporate meetings and the perfect setting
for intimate and elegant weddings. CCards ⌙ B&B

St. Andrews
(west of SaintJohn;see also St.George,St.Stephen,Back Bay,St.George)

Barton, Carole & Walter (The Mulberry B&B) ☎ & Fax (506) 529-4948
96 Water St., Box 332, St. Andrews, NB   E5B 1A5

Phone for directions.
$70S $80D   (off season rates available)   ► 5
🍴Full   🏠2-storey, hist.,waterview from guest rooms,veranda
■3D(upstairs), guest quarters are separate   ⊨2Q,1T
⚓2Private   ★TV in guest rooms, parking   ★No smoking,
pets by prior arrangement
🕺 Shops, restaurants, wharf, market quare, museums, golfing
🚗 Scenic drive to Saint John, whale watching, sea kayaking, Deer Isle, Grandmanan, Campobello
🚚 Charming Georgian home (ca 1800), well decorated interior, some antiques, situated in
picturesque resort town, designated as a national historic district (first Seaside Resort). Relax on
the large veranda and enjoy the waterview and the friendly hospitality of well travelled hosts.

Everett, Jura & Robert Estes (Harris Hatch Inn B&B) ☎ (506) 529-4713
142 Queen St., St.Andrews, NB   E5B 1E2

Phone for directions.
$95S/D   🍽 Meals   ► 4
❎ Summer only (other on special request)   🍴 Full   🏠 Res.,
hist., 3-storey, patio, quiet ■2Stes(upst) ⊨2Q ⚓2Ensuite
★Air,LF,F/TV/coffee maker in each guest room, off-street &
street parking   ⊛No smoking, no pets, not suitable for children
🕺 Downtown shops and galleries, museums, historic homes,
beautiful churches, waterfront, Kingsbrae Gardens
🚗 Ministers Island, Campobello Island, Passamaquoddy Bay Loop
🚚 Beautiful, stately brick home built in 1840 with high ceilings and recently completely restored,
blending modern conveniences with historic design. Breakfast is served in special guest breakfast
room. Relax in the living room or enjoy a stroll about town. Hosts also operate the St.Andrews
Lighthouse Restaurant and extend discounts for guests. Special arrangements for late arrivals.
There is a dog in residence. Visa,MC ⌙B&B

St.Andrews (cont'd)

Remer,Jay & Greg Cohane(The Windsor House of St.Andrews) ☎(506)529-3330,
132 Water St., St.Andrews,NB E5B 1A8   Fax (506)529-4063,1-888-890-9463
                                                  E-mail: gregjay@nbnet.nb.ca,

Take Rt1 to Rt127 into St.Andrews and proceed to Water St.
$225S/D   (plus tax)   🍴 Meals   ▶ 12A
🍲 Full   🏠 Downtown, hist., view from guest rooms, patio,
porch, deck, quiet   ■6D (upstairs)
⊨2T,1D,4Q   ⇨6Private   ★F,TV in guest rooms, off-street &
street parking, guest quarters are separate   Ⓦ Designated
smoking area, no pets, children min.age 16

🕴 Algonquin Golf Course, Kingsbrae Horticultural Gardens, superb whale watching, kayaking
🚗 Kings Landing Historic Settlement, Atlantic Salmon Federation, St.Andrews Biological Station
🐾 Elegant historic Inn, fully restored former loyalist home, furnished throughout with museum
quality antiques and works of art. Ideal place for a romantic get-away, small weddings, business
meetings and relaxation. Enjoy the view from the outer veranda of the St.Andrews Harbour and
watch the 28tft tides of the Bay of Fundy. Hosts specialize in spoiling their guests. There is a
"therapy" dog in residence. Breakfast and dinners served in the formal dining room. CCards
www.townsearch.com/windsorhouse

St.George   *(west of Saint John; see also Back Bay, St.Andrews)*

Dougherty, Eleanor and Harvey (Bonny River House B&B)   ☎ (506) 755-2248
960 Rte 770, Bonny River, NB E5C 1C8   E-mail: bonnyriverbb@hotmail.com

Coming from East or West on Hwy1 bypass St.George Exit and take Manor Rd. OR take St.George
Exits off Hwy1. Continue on Main St and look for Rte770 opposite large white church. Proceed

north approx 9km. Located in Bonny River.
$55-65S $65-75D   ▶ 6
🍲 Full, homebaked   🏠 Rural, acreage, view, riverfront, patio,
quiet, isolated   ■3 (upst)   ⊨ 2T,1D,1Q   ⇨ 3Private
★TV, parking   Ⓦ No smoking   ∿French
🕴 Canoeing and boating, fishing, birdwatching, beautiful fall color
spectrum, x-country skiing,skating, excellent hunting, cycling
🚗 Saint John, Fundy Isles, Calais (US)

🐾 Renovated Century farm house on large acreage overlooking the Magaquadavic River and
grounds reaching down to the riverbank on three sides. Relax in peaceful and tranquil surroundings
on the water's edge or on the sunny patio. Ideal place for honeymooners "or get-away from it all".
Bring a bicycle (do the loop across a covered bridge & natural canal).Visa ✓B&B
http://www.bbcanada.com/92.html

Sussex   *(west of Moncton; see also Cambridge N.)*

London, Bertha & Lloyd (Jonah B&B Place)   ☎ (506) 433-6978
977 Main St., Sussex, NB E0E 1P0

Phone for directions.
$55S $65-85D   🍴 Meals   ▶ 6
🍲Full   🏠Downtown, hist.,acreage, patio, deck, quiet,
secluded   ■3D(upstairs)   ⊨ 3D   ⇨Sh.w.g   ★F,TV,
off-street parking   Ⓦ Smoking outside
🕴 Downtown Sussex, shops, retaurants
🚗 Fundy Nat.Park, Hopewell Cape Rocks, Saint John, Moncton
🐾 Charming home built in 1884 with original 12ft ceilings,
moulding and fireplaces, having maintained much of its original character. Enjoy a quiet evening on
the veranda surrounded by mature trees and garden. Breakfast is served in guest breakfast room.
There is a resident cat.

St. Stephen
(west of Saint John, St. Andrews, St. Georges, Back Bay)

Whittingham, David & Judy (Blair House Heritage Breakfast Inn)   ☎ (506) 466-2233,
38 Prince William St., St. Stephen, NB   E3L 1S3   1-888-972-5247, Fax (506) 466-1699
                                                                         E-mail: blairhse@nbnet.nb.ca
Located near Visitor Information Center and 3rd house east of Christ Church, 0.4km off Rte 1.
$55-85S $60-95D $10-15Add.person   ▶ 10A,2Ch

🍴 Full, English   🏠 Res., acreage, hist., quiet, 3-storey,
riverview ■5D(main & 2nd floor) ⊨2T,1D,3Q,2R
�washroom 5Ensuite ★F,TV, off-street parking, ceiling fans, some
air-conditioners 🚭 No smoking inside, pets outside only
🚶 Prov.Visitor Information Centre, Chocolate Museum, 25+ft
tidal St.Croix River, waterfront retaurants & pub, craft & souvenir
shops, rail-to-trail pathway, churches, Canadian-US border
crossing (Calais/ME), duty-free store
🚗 Fundy Tides (25+ft), whale-watching beaches, Deer & Campbello Islands (Roosevelt's cottage),
ferry to Grand Manan, Moosehorn Nature Wildlife Refuge, Charlotte County museum, St.Andrews
☛ Spacious, elegant mansion standing back on treed grounds was built in 1850's and overlooks
the historic St.Croix River, located in quiet town setting. A relaxing stop-over along the Bay of
Fundy Coastal Scenic Drive. Ideal base for exploring Passamaquoddy Bay (on wheels or water).
Fundy Isles on both sides of the Int.border. Tea & cookies served in guest living room at 9pm.
Annual Chocolate Fest & Int. Festival with Calais, ME (1st week in Aug). There is a dog in host
quarters. CCards ✔B&B www.blairhouseinn.nb.ca

Woodstock
(north-west of Fredericton; see also Hartland)

Froehlich, Elfriede and Edgar (Chalet Swiss B&B)   ☎ (506) 328-6751
4064 Rte 105, Box 4205, Woodstock, NB   E7M 6B6

Take Trans Canada Hwy 2 and exit at Woodstock or Upper Woodstock. Cross the Saint John River
on Grafton Bridge, turn right (south) onto Hwy 105 and drive 9 km along river to Chalet. Look for
sign at access to drive up hill.

$49S $54D $15Child/Add.person   ▶ 7
📅 May-Oct 🍴 Homebaked 🏠 Rural, hillside, view, acreage,
quiet, secluded ■ 2F (ground level) ⊨2S,4T(K),2D
🚿2Private ★TV,LF, separate entrance, hosts quarters are
separate, parking 🚬 Designted smoking area ⋯ German
🚗 World's longest covered bridge (Hartland), Kings Landing
Historical Settlement, Fredericton, Woolastook Wildlife Park
☛ Enjoy a quiet and relaxing atmosphere in Swiss-style Chalet with typical European decor and a
"Kachelofen" in the comfortable living room. Situated high on the hill guests can enjoy the
commanding and breathtaking views over the Saint John River Valley from the windows or while
eating breakfast on the large sunny deck. There is a very friendly and entertaining Miniature
Schnauzer in the house. German hosts enjoy "serving special people in a special way". ✔B&B

Prince Edward Island

P.E.I. Visitor Services Division
"Dial-the-Island" and Marine Atlantic Ferry schedule
Box 940, Charlottetown, PEI C1A 7M5
Northumberland Ferry schedule (Pictou/NS to Wood Islands/PEI)

toll-free 1-800-565-0267
toll-free 1-800-463-4734

toll-free 1-800-565-0261

Albany

Rogers, Jim & Sue (The Captain's Lodge)
Seven Mile Bay, RR2, Albany, PEI C0B 1A0

☎ (902) 855-3106, 1-800-261-3518
E-mail: captains.lodge@pei.sympatico.ca

From Confederation Bridge, turn left on Rte 10 (Blue Heron Drive) and proceed 7 km to St. Peters
Church. Turn left at 4th house past church, go on gravel road 1km towards water, turn right to

green house.
$85D (plus tax) (Sen.discounts & off-season rates)   ▶ 6A
▓ May-Oct (other by special arrangement)   ⬚ Full   ⌂ Rural,
2-storey, hist., view from guest rooms, porch, quiet, veranda near
warm beach ■3D(ground & upper level) ⊨2T,2Q ⊒1Private,
2ensuite ★F,TV room, guest robes/slippers, parking   ⊛No
pets, no smoking, not suitable for children ⌇French
⚲ Walks to lovely red sandy beach, beachcombing, Seven Mile Bay

🚗 New Confederation Bridge, Hist.Charlottetown, live theatre
🛥 Large home built by a sea captain, furnished with antiques, and beautiful rustic-elegant decor,
surrounded by potato, grain & clover fields and many flowers (spectacular Lupins in June/July), on
the quiet serene side of PEI, where the sea is warm and inviting. Relax on the cozy sunporch and
veranda or curl up by the wood stove and enjoy evening deserts and good conversation. There are
resident pets (Lab "Snoop", cat "Ziggy", bunny "Precious". Visa,MC ⌐B&B
www3.pei.sympatico.ca/captains.lodge

Albion Cross

Foster, Fred (Needles and Haystacks B&B)
RR2, St-Peter's Bay, Albion Cross, PEI C0A 2A0

☎(902)583-2928,Fax(902)583-3160,
E-mail: ffoster@auracom.com, 1-800-563-2928

Located 500m off Rt 4 on Rt 327 in Albion Cross. Look for signs.
$65-110D ▣ Meals (plus tax) (Reservation preferred) (weekly rate available)   ▶ 8

▓May1-Oct31 ⬚Full,homebaked ⌂Rural, 2-storey, hist., view,
mansard roof, 5 acres, quiet ■4(upstairs) ⊨2T,3D ⊒2Ensuite,
1sh.w.g.,1sh.w.h. on main floor ★TV,KF,LF, two woodstoves,
bicycles for guests, enclosed sundeck with hot tub, parking   ⊛No
smoking ⌇French
⚲ Apple orchard, bicycling, excellent for long walks
🚗 Lobster fishing ports, white sandy beaches ("singing sands"),
Magdalen Islands Ferry, golf courses
🛥 Large 1880's home furnished with antiques provides romantic setting in Dundas farm
country. Enjoy a cool drink in the orchard or on the swing with a book and relax on the sun deck
with spa. House specialty: blueberry pancakes. Host is world-traveller and skier and has produced
the "Bays & Dunes Drive" travelling cassete for visitors of East PEI. CCards ⌐B&B

Bideford

Trowsdale, Janice & Wayne (Hilltop Acres Bed & Breakfast)   ☎ & Fax (902) 831-2817
Bideford, Box 3011, Ellerslie, PEI C0B 1J0   E-mail: wjt_hilltop@pei.sympatico.ca,1-877-305-2817
www3.pei.sy;mpatico.ca/wjt_hilltop
From Summerside, follow Hwy 2 to Miscouche. Take Rt 12 (Lady Slipper Dr) to Tyne Valley and Rt

166 through Bideford. Look for house on right.
$40-45S $50-60D $15Add.person (Longer stay rates)   ▶ 7
▓ June1-Sept30 (off-season by reservation)   ⬚ Full   ⌂ Rural,
2-storey, acreage, panoramic view,quiet, riverfront ■4D(upst)
⊨2D,1Q,1R ⊒1Private,1Sh.w.g. ★TV in guest L-room,
parking ⊛No smoking
⚲ Fisheries Research Stn & Shellfish Museum, picnic site & a
Lucy Maud Montgomery's house, biking & walks down to river
🚗 North Cape Wind Test Site, Lennox Island Indian Reserve & Craft shop, Elephant Rock
🛥 Beautifully renovated 1930's home situated on 50 acre farm in historic community,
convenient to any point on the island. Enjoy an excellent view of Goodwood River & Malpeque Bay
from second storey balcony. Host has LM Montgomery family ties (documented).

Brackley Beach

(north of Charlottetown; see also South Rustico)

Zember, Em & David (Red Island B&B)
RR9, Winsloe, Brackley Beach, PEI C1E 1Z3

☎ (902) 672-2242, 1-800-698-5530
E-mail: zember@isn.net

$50-90S $55-95D $65-105F 5Child(free under age 5) $10Add.person (plus Taxes) ▶ 20

Located on Rte 6 between Rtes 15 and 7.

🍵 Cont.+ (self-serve) 🏠 Farm, 2-storey, quiet ■2D,4F(upst & outside main house) ⊨8D,2Q ⬛2Private,4ensuite,whirlpool ★AirLF,TV/VCR/ceiling fans in guest rooms, private entrance in suites, guest quarters are separate ⊕No smoking 🚶 Walking trails on property & in wooded area, private "natural" beach on Rustico Bay, bird watching, Country General Store

🚗 Brackley Beach, Charlottetown with shops, restaurants & theatres, National Park, Cavendish & Anne of Green Gables, Lobster Suppers, golf courses, airport, Confederation Bridge
🔫 Large, remodelled 19th Century farm home with spacious, shaded grounds and guest convenience kitchen, centrally located. Hosts are a young family and professional dog trainers (dogs have separate living quarters/entrance). Breakfast is served in special guest breakfast area. There are 4 dogs and a cat (not in guest common or private areas). Off-season rates before June18 & after Aug16. Visa,MC ⌐B&B www.redisland.com/bbguide

---

Cavendish

(north-east of Kensington; see also Stanley Br., Park Corner, Stanley Bridge)

Dorgan, Gloria & Patrick (Wild Rose Country Home B&B)
Cavendish Rd., RR2, Hunter River, PEI C0A 1N0

☎ (902)-963-3324
1-800-794-3324

Located on the Cavendish Rd., Rte 6 and 3km east of Cavendish intersection.
$95-110S/D $8Add.person (Off-season rates Sept21-June21) ▶ 18

🍵 Cont. 🏠 Rural, new, veranda, quiet ■ 6(upstairs) ⊨6D,2Q,2T ⬛ 6Private ★Air,LF,TV in guest rooms, barbeque, separate entrance, parking ⊕ No pets, no smoking 🚗 National Park (great walking and cycling trails), Anne of Green Gables House, Golf course, Cavendish Beach, Lobster Suppers, restaurants, deep-sea fishing, Charlottetown
🔫 Modern, newly renovated home, a quiet country retreat located in rural Cavendish. Enjoy the fantastic sunset view from the veranda and friendly island hospitality. Visa,MC ⌐B&B

Brewer, Ruth & Dede Brewer-Wilson (The Country House Inn)
Gulf Shore Rd., RR2, Hunter River, PEI C0A 1N0

☎ & Fax (902) 963-2055
1-800-363-2055

Centrally located in Cavendish Nat.Park on the North Shore Gulf Shore Rd. Phone for direction.
$50-87S/D $12Add.person 🍽 Meals (plus Tax) (3-nights minimum) ▶ 21

🏖May-Oct. 🍴Full(buffet) 🏠 Rural, hist., acreage,oceanfront, sea-view from guest rooms ■5,+2 apts, 2nd/3rd level) ⊨2S,2T,5D,2P,cots (including canopy bed in studio) ⬛2Sh.w.g., 1ensuite, 2private, 2shw.h. ★KF, TV in guest room, jacuzzi available, separate entrance for ground floor studio (wheel-chair friendly), small fridge in rooms, some facilities for the disabled, barbeques, bicycle rental, free entrance to Park for house guests ⊕No smoking

🚶 Cavendish National Park, beaches, hiking, jogging, cycling, birdwatching, walks along the cliff
🚗 Cavendish, golfing, theatre, Island sites, day trips in any direction of the island, biking
🔫 Mothere & daughter team in charming spacious old Island home, tastefully decorated with antiques and heritage furniture and panoramic view overlooking the Gulf of St. Lawrence. Situated high on a hill on spacious grounds in the National Park. Breakfast is served in sunporch facing the Gulf. Relax in the music room or enjoy the large LM Montgomery library. Guests are exempt from Park entry fees. Weekly rates available. ⌐CC http://www.town.cavendish.pe.ca/countryhouseinn

Cavendish (cont'd)

MacLure, Naomi (MacLure Bed & Breakfast)   ☎ (902) 963-2239
Cavendish Rd., RR2, Hunter River PO, Cavendish, PEI   C0A 1N0

Located on Rt 6 and 3 km east of Cavendish intersection and 15km from Hunter River.

$45-55 per room $5Add.person   🍽 Meals   ▶ 9
🍳Cont,homebaked   🏠Rural, older, patio, quiet   ■3(upstairs)
⊨1S,4D,cot   ⌘1Sh.w.g.,1sh.w.h.(on main floor)   ★LF,TV in guest room, sep.entrance, parking   ⊕ No pets, no smoking in bedrooms
🚶 Country roads for walking, National Park, great cycling area
🚗 Anne of Green Gables House, golf course, Cavendish Beach, deep-sea fishing, restaurants, Lobster suppers, Charlottetown
🐚 Remodelled Century farm house, featuring a large sun deck, perfect for lounging, situated in a tranquil farming community in fairly central location.

Morris, Edward & Ann (Willow Cottage Inn)   ☎ (902) 963-3385
Hunter River, RR1, Cavendish, PEI   C0A 1N0   E-mail: willow.inn@pei.sympatico.ca

From Charlottetown go west on Rte 2 to Rte 13, north to Rte 6 and west to Memory Lane on left.
$60-100S $68-105D $10Add.person   (plus taxes) (off-season rates available)   ▶ 18

📅 May15-Oct15   🍳 Full, homebaked   🏠 Rural, 2-storey, quiet, older, acreage porch   ■ 7F,plus family suite(main & upper level)   ⊨T,D,Q   ⌘1Private, 6ensuite ★Air, F/TV/VCR in guest sitting room, refreshment counter in guest rooms, veranda & TV in two guest rooms and suite, LF/service, separate entrance for suites ⊕No smoking
🚶 Anne of Green Gables house (next door), tennis courts, golfing, beach & dunes, hiking & bicycling (rental nearby)
🚗 Charlottetown, Confederation Bridge, north/southshore beaches, good restaurants, fishing
🚗 Cozy family-owned Inn decorated in homey old-fashioned Victorian manner. After a day of sun /sand/exploring this enchanting Island, spend some lazy time in the charming guest sitting room or on the shady veranda. Hosts are very proud of their Island and love to share this enthusiasm. Breakfast is served in guest dining room. There is a dog & a cat in hosts' private area.Visa,MC
www.peionline.com/al/willow

Charlottetown   *(see also Cornwall, Marshfield, Rice Point)*

Barnes, Lee, Peggy & Elaine (Taste of Home B&B)   ☎ (902) 566-9186
Box 6674, 33 Marianne Dr., York Point, PEI   C0A 1H0   E-mail: barnes@isn.net, 1-877-201-7003

Located 1km off TCH. Turn towards York Point on Hwy 248 at the North River traffic lights.
$50-55S $55-60D $6Child(free under age 5) $10Add.person   ▶ 12

📅 May1-Nov30   🍳 Full, homebaked   🏠 Rural, split-level, patio, quiet, secluded   ■2D,2F(main & lower level) ⊨2S,3D,1Q, cot,crib ⌘3Private   ★KF,LF,F,TV in guest rooms, hot tub, ceiling fans ⊕Restricted smoking area, no pets
🚶 Nice quiet area for walking
🚗 Downtown Charlottetown, beaches, golfing, Cavendish and northern beaches, Summerside, Confederation Bridge from NB, Wood Island ferries to NS
🐚 Warm welcome in modern comfortable home. Relax in the large (for 6) hot tub on the patio and enjoy the large private backyard. Families welcome. Courtesy pick-up at airport and bus station. There is a Highland White Terrier, but not permitted in guest quarters. ✓B&B
http://www.isn.net/~barnes/

Campbell, Maida (Campbell's Maple Bed & Breakfast) ☎ (902) 894-4488
28 Maple Avenue, Charlottetown, PEI C1A 6E3

From Borden on Hwy 1, turn left on Belvedere Ave through one
traffic light. Maple Ave is the next street on the left.
$55-65D $7.50Child $15Add.person (plus Tax) ► 8
✚ May24-Oct31 ⬛ Full, homebaked ⬛Res.,sub.,acreage,patio,
quiet ■4(upper & lower level) ⊨S,D,cot ⊒2Private, 1sh.w.g.
(lower level) ★TV,F,parking
⚹ Shopping centres, restaurants, park
⬟ Charlottetown downtown, beaches & most Island attractions
⬛ Situated in residential area, this suburban home has a large
backyard and deck for relaxation. Enjoy a comfortable home atmosphere and the company of
knowledgeable retired professional hosts. Courtesy pick-up at airport & downtown. Convenient
location upon entering the City. ⤙B&B

Lefebvre, Margaret & Jim (Charlotte's Rose Inn) ☎(902)892-3699, 1-888-237-3699
11 Grafton St,Charlottetown,PEI C1A1K3 E-mail: charlottes.inn@pei.sympatico.ca, Fax894-3699

Phone for directions.
$115-145S/D (plus tax) ► 8A
⬛ Full ⬛ Res., 3-storey, patio, porch, deck, quiet ■ 4D(upstairs)
⊨2T(K),3Q ⊒ 4Private ★ KF,LF,TV & ceiling fans in guest rooms,
off-street/street parking, phone/fax available, guest quarters are on 2nd
floor ⬤ No smoking, no pets, children min age 8 ⤳ French
⚹ Historic downtown (2blocks), shopping, theatres, movies, excellent
restaurants, art galleries, ocean & boardwalks (1block), Confederation
Centre of the Arts, Harbour, SMT line
⬟ Cavendish, Souris, Summerside, Argyle shore, Anne's House and
L.M.Montgomery's house
⬛ Warm welcome in heritage Victorian home built in 1884 and located in the center of town
with elegant decor and comfortable parlour. Hosts aim to exceed their guests' expectation.CCards
⤙B&B www.peisland.com/charlottesinn

Newcombe, Paul & Joyce (Reddin House Bed & Breakfast) ☎ & Fax(9-5): (902) 892-7269
90 Brighton Rd., Charlottetown, PEI C1A 1V1   E-mail: pnewcomm@auracom.com

From Bridge, take Rt1 (TCH) to Charlottetown & North River Rd. Turn right on Brighton.
$65-70S/D ◨ Meals (plus tax) ► 4
⬛ Full, homebaked ⬛ Res., hist., view, quiet ■2D(upstairs)
⊨2Q ⊒ 1Private, 1ensuite ★ F,TV, fans, bicycles & tennis
racquets avail,parking ⬤No pets,restr.moking ⤳some French
⚹ Walking trails, tennis courts, swimming pool, downtown area
⬛ Historic home built in 1915, near the harbour and nestled in
beautiful surroundings of Victoria Park. There is a Newfoundland
dog in residence. ⤙CC www.peiland.com/reddin

Charlottetown (cont'd)

Roper, Ken & Marilyn (Hillside House B&B) ☎ 1-888-892-3640
25 Hillside Dr., Charlottetown, PEI C1A 6H9   E-mail: hillsidehouse_roper@pei.sympatico.ca

Take Rte 1 to Belvedere Ave. Turn left to Mt Edward Rd, left again to Hillside, turn right.

$110S/D (plus tax)   ► 2A
🍴 Cont., homebaked   🏠 Res., 3-storey, hist., 2acres, deck, quiet,
wrap-around veranda   ■ 1Ste (3rd floor) ⊨1D
⊒1Ensuite   ★LF,TV in guest room, ceiling fans,
air-conditioner, off-street parking, mountain bikes for guests,
guest quarters are separate   ⚘ No smoking, no pets
🏃 Bicycle/walking trails, City Centre, shopping, theatre,
museum, craft stores, parks, marina, dining
🚗 Golfing, Lobster Suppers, Green Gables house, beaches, trails and boardwalks, harbour tours
🚐 Large comfortable home with Gingerbread trim, furnished with many antiques and beautiful
wrap-around veranda situated on large grounds. Hosts like to spoil their guests and offer after
theatre trays and lots of home-made snacks. ✔ B&B

Cornwall
(south Charlottetown; see also Rice Point)

Gilbert, Barbra & Michael (Safe Haven Guest House)   ☎ (902) 675-2623, Fax 675-4259
16358 Trans Canada Hwy, New Haven, PEI C0A 1H0   E-mail: barbra.gilbert@pei.symatic.ca

$59S $69D $10Child/Add.person (plus tax)   🍽 Meals   ► 12
Located just west of Charlottetown on Hwy 1.
🍴 Full   🏠 Village, 2-storey, hist., patio, porch   ■ 4D(main &
upper floor) ⊨2D,2Q,2R ⊒2Sh.w.g.   ★Air,LF,TV,private
entrance, off-street parking, guest quarters are separate with
guest living & dining room ⚘Smoking outside, children min. age
7
🏃 Walk in beautiful gardens, horseshoe pits, badminton,
Encounter Creek Water Park
🚗 Charlottetown, Victoria By the Sea, Cavendish Resort,
Summerside, north/south & east beaches, Wood Isle Ferry, Confederation Bridge
🚐 Warm welcome in comfortable home with convenient access to all major Island attractions.
Hosts are very eager to please their guests and enjoy pampering them. Breakfast is served in guest
dining room. There is a dog and a cat in residence. Visa,MC ✔B&B
www3.pei.sympatico.ca/barbra.gilbert

Crapaud
(south-west of Charlottetown; see also Victoria, Alberny)

Wells, Dennis & Kathleen (Simple Comforts B&B)   ☎ (902) 658-2951
Box 122, Crapaud, PEI C0A 1J0

$24.95S $40D $10Child(over age 6)/Add.person (plus tax) 🍽Meals   ► 12
Take Trans Canada Highway east of the Confederation Bridge
towards Charlottetown. Located just outside of Victoria by the Sea.
✖ Off season by reservation   🍴 Full   🏠 Rural, 2-storey, hist,
acreage, view from guest rooms, deck, quiet, secluded ■3F plus
4 hostel rooms(upstairs) ⊨3D,2T ⊒ 2Sh.w.g. ★ off-street
parking, TV, ceiling fans ⚘ No smoking ∿ little French
🏃 Villages of Crapaud and Victoria-by-the-Sea, outstanding
Playhouse theatre
🚗 Summerside, Anne of GreenGables, Cavendish, Charlottetown
🚐 1853 Church Manse and renovated Horse Barn Hostel. A delicious breakfast is served in
eclectic camp style dining hall. Comfortable bicycles available for rent. Families with young children
welcome. There are 3 dogs and 3 cats, ✔B&B

Elmira

Rose, Elora & Robert (Lakeville B&B & Cottage)   ☎ & Fax (902) 357-2206
RR1, Elmira, PEI   C0A 1K0   1-877-385-2206

Travel east on Rte 2 to Souris, then Rte 16, left on Rte 16A to North Lake Hbr, 3rd house on right
$45-60S/D $70-80Ste $10Add.person 🍴Meals (plus tax)   ▶ 8A,2-4Ch

Summer only(off-season by special arrangement) 🔲Full,
homebaked 🏠 Farm, 2-storey, older, view, lakefront, oceanback,
patio, quiet ■3D,1Ste(main & upper level) ⊨2Q,2D
⊒2Sh.w.g,1sh.w.h., 1private ★TV,KF,sep.entrance,
wheel-chair access for cottage 🖐Designated smoking area
🧍 White sandy beach on property, fishing village, deep-sea (tuna)
fishing charters, Confederation Trail hiking and biking
🚐 Souris, Magdalin Island Ferry, Provincial park restaurants
📣 Spacious home on potato & grain farm surrounded by lake and ocean with a wonderful view.
Hosts are happy to show guests around the 250 acre farm. There is a resident dog"Lindy".Visa
www.peisland.com/lakeville/cottage.htm

Georgetown

Taylor, Joan & Ken (The Georgetown Inn)   ☎(902)652-2511, Fax(902)652-2544
19 Kent St., Box 192, Georgetown, PEI   C0A 1L0   E-mail: unicorn@pei.sympatico.ca

From Charlottetown travel east to Hwy 3 to Georgetown. Located on the main street and one block
up from the harbour. From Wood Island Ferry take Rte 315 to Montague, follow Hwy 4 to Pooles
Corner and turn right. Or take the scenic Hills & Harbours Drive.
$85-120D $15Child/Add.person   (plus tax)   Off-season discounts 🍴Meals   ▶ 14A,2Ch

🔲 Full, homebaked 🏠 Res., village, 3-storey, hist., harbour
view from guest rooms, ocean at back, deck ■ 7(upst) ⊨7Q
⊒7Ensuite ★ LF,TV in some guest rooms, ceiling fans, private
deck overlooking the harbour, off-street parking 🖐Designated
smoking area, no pets, children min age 6
🧍 Kings Playhouse, beach, cycling trail, boat launch, trout &
lobster fishing, small shipyard (guiding ocean going tugs)
🚐 Charlottetown, Wood Island Ferry, Montague, Singing Sands
📣 150 year old spacious home, has served as a post office, bank, lodge and a tea room over the
years, is fully remodelled and located one block from the finest sheltered harbours on the East
Coast (Lobster Harbour). Very hospitable hosts (one-time entertainers) offer "theme nights" on
request. Relax in the Victorian Garden. Breakfast is served in guest breakfast room. Weekly rates
and off season rates available from Oct1-June 14th.
CCards http://www3.pei.sympatico.ca/unicorn

Hunter River

MacInnis, Kathy (Hunterlea Hill B&B)   ☎ (902) 964-3088
RR2, Hunter River, PEI   C0A 1N0

Located on Rte13 in Hunter River, 1km south of Hwy Rte2 and 15km from Cavendish.
$50S $80D $10Child/Add.person $90F   (plus tax)   ▶ 6

🔲 Full 🏠 Farm, hist., view from guest rooms, porch, quiet
■2D,1F(upstairs) ⊨ 1D,2Q,R ⊒ 1Private, 1ensuite,
whirlpool-tub ★ LF,TV in guest rooms, ceiling fans, private
entrance, off-street parking 🖐 No smoking
🧍 Farm grounds with farm animals, Confederation Trail borders
on farm property
🚐 All Island attractions, Cavendish, Summerside, Charlottetown

📣 Enjoy PEI's rural beauty and tranquility in character farm
house with barns (over 100 years old), overlooking picturesque country village. Hosts raise horses
and chickens and enjoy welcoming families with children. Breakfast is served in guest breakfast
room. There is a dog. ✔ B&B

Kensington

(north of Summerside; see also Park Corner, Stanley Bridge)

Thompson, Valerie and Don (Thompson Tourist Home) ☎ (902)836-4160,1-800-567-7907
Kensington, RR6, Margate, PEI C0B 1M0   E-mail: thomtour@atcon.com

From Rte 6 turn left on Thompson Point Rd and proceed 1.4 km. Located 5 km north-east of

Kensington in Margate.
$35S $40D $70Ste $5Child $70F (3nights/wkly rates) ▶ 10
✚ Summer only ◐ Cont. ♞ Farm, older, quiet, riverfront,
multi-storey, view ■3D,1Ste(upstairs) ⊨3T,2D,1Q
⌁1Private, 1sh.w.g., 1sh.w.h. ★TV ⍟Pets on leash
♝ Small boat launch, beach, swimming, clam digging
🚙 Woodleigh Replicas, Lucy Montgomery Museum, deep-sea
fishing, Cavendish National Park, Anne of Green Gables
☛ Restored farm home in picturesque setting. Relax on the balcony and enjoy the scenic
waterview. There are 3 cats in the house.Visa http://mypage.direct.ca/d/dgthomps/

Marshfield

(north of Charlottetown)

Wood, Wallace and Doris (Woodmere)   ☎ & Fax (902) 628-1783, 1-800-747-1783
Marshfield, RR3, Charlottetown, PEI C1A 7J7

Located 6 km from Charlottetown on Rt 2 East. Look for signs.

$75D $15Child/Add.person (plus tax)   ▶ 12A,4Ch
◐Full, homebaked ♞Horse farm, 2-storey, rose garden
■2D,2F (upstairs) ⊨ 4T,2Q ⌁ 4Ensuite ★ TV in guest
rooms, separate entrance ⍟ No pets
♝ Mares and foals graze in pasture close to house, Hillsborough
River, rose garden
🚙 Golfing, harness racing, Charlottetown, fine dining, airport
☛ Spacious, new Colonial home was built especially for B&B,
furnished with custom-made pine furniture from the Maritimes and situated on large grounds in
convenient location. Long time B&B hosts raise standard bred horses. Horses love guests'
attention. Enjoy the extensive rose gardens. Off season rates Sept15-June15. Visa,MC ⌐B&B
http://www.bbcanada.com/725.html

Murray River

(south-east of Montague)

MacSwain, Joan (Coastal Homestead B&B)   ☎ 1-800-817-5294
High Bank, RR4, Murray River, PEI C0A 1W0

Located 14km east of Wood Island Ferry on Hwy 18 and 5km from Murray River.
$36-45S $50D $10Child $12Add.person   (plus tax)   ▶ 6A,4Ch

✚ May-Oct30 ◐ Full, homebaked ♞ Rural, 2-storey, hist.,
2acres, oceanfront, quiet ■1S,2D,1F(upper & ground level)
⊨ 1S,2T,2D,2cots ⌁ 1Sh.w.g., 1sh.w.h. ★ TV,private
entrance, off-street parking, fans ⍟ No smoking, no pets, no
alcohol ⌇ French   ♝ Cliffs
🚙 Light Houses, craft/antique stores, Ceilidhs, beaches,
churches, seal & birdwatching boat tours
☛ Cozy and quaint 4th Generation 1880-built family home,
decorated with antiques and African Art and beautiful view of Pictou Island and Nova Scotia.
Hostess is a native Islander who has returned from living abroad. Relax in the reading nook and TV
room with videos. Enjoy the quiet and tranquil atmosphere. Breakfast is served in separate guest
breakfast room. Off-season rates available. There is a dog and a cat in residence (not allowed in
guest area). Visa ⌐B&B

New Glasgow
(north-west of Charlottetown, see also South Rustico, Hunter River)

MacLean, Garth & Ann (Lowlands Inn)　　　☎ & Fax (902) 964-2490
New Glasgow, RR2, Hunter River, PEI　C0A 1N0　　　E-mail: lowlandsinn@pei.sympatico.ca

From Confederation Bridge, turn right off Hwy 1 onto Rte13 and continue to New Glasgow.

$95S/D　$120-140Ste　$15Child/Add.person　　(plus tax)
⬛ Full, homebaked　🏠 Rural, hillside, 2-storey, view from guest rooms, acreage, riverfront, patio, porch, deck, quiet, secluded　■8(ground level)　⊨ 6Q,2K,2R,8P,crib　⚏ 8Private
★Air,KF,TV,ceiling fans, private entrance, wheel-chair access, off-street parking, guest quarters are separate　♥　🖑No smoking, no pets
🏃 Lobster Suppers, fine dining
🚗Cavendish Beach, Anne of GreenGables, golfing, Charlottetown

☛ Newly constructed, spacious home with beautiful waterviews of the River Clyde and large cozy sitting room off the lobby. Breakfast is served in the brightly lit dining room with scottish decor. Enjoy "A wee bit of Scotland on Bonnie Prince Edward Isle". There is a dog in residence. Visa,MC www.peionline.com/al/lowlands

New Perth
(north of Montague)

Van Dyke, John & Lorraine (Van Dyke's Lakeside B&B)　　☎ (902) 838-4408
New Perth, RR3, Montague, PEI　C0A 1R0

Located on Hwy 3 and 12km from Montague. Look for round house on right just before the water.

$75-90S/D　$10Child　(plus tax)　⬛3.50Each (Full)　　　　► 12A,2Ch
🌺 Summer only　⬛ Cont., homebaked　🏠 Farm, 2-storey, lakeview from guest rooms, 102 acres, lakefront, deck, quiet ■4 (upstairs & main level) plus new addition　⊨2D,4Q　⚏1Sh.w.g., 1ensuite with jacuzzi, 1sh.w.h., 1private　★TV,KF,LF, separate entrance, large parking area, barbeque, wheel-chair access, host quarters are separate 🖑No pets
🏃 Wooded path along lake, trout fishing
🚗 Salt water beaches, historic Ch'town, Wood Island ferry

☛ Newly renovated, enlarged 1885 house beside a quiet lake, with unique dining/living room (the actual old house) and bright and cheerful modern guest quarters. New gazebo equipped to do outdoor cooking. Relax on the large patio and enjoy breakfast in the beautiful surroundings. There are family pets outside. Visa ✓B&B

Orwell Cove
(east of Charlottetown)

Currie, Audrey (Ar Dachaidh By The Sea B&B)　　☎ (902) 659-2028, 1-888-235-4570
Orwell Cove, RR2, Vernon Bridge, PEI　C0R 2E0　　　E-mail: acurrie@pei.sympatico.ca

Located off Hwy 1, between Charlottetown & Wood Island Ferry.
$75-110D　$10Add.person　(plus tax)　　　► 6A,5Ch
⬛ Full, homebaked　🏠 Rural, ranch-style, 1.5-storey, acreage, view, oceanfront, quiet, secluded　■ 2Ste,+studio apt (main & upper level)　⊨ 1D,2Q,R,2P　⚏3Ensuite, jacuzzi ★KF,LF,TV in guest rooms, ceiling fans, guest quarters are separate
🖑Smoking on outside decks　〰 French
🏃 Wooded trails & beach, riding lessons on site

🚗 Beaches, golfing, theatres, seal cruises, deep sea fishing, shops and fine dining, Charlottetown
☛ Executive waterfront, glass and beam cedar home with spacious stylish comfort, situated on a hill overlooking open water. Relax on one of the 2decks and enjoy the inspirational view. Golf and honeymoon packages available. There are 2 saddle horses, a dog and a cat. CCards ✓B&B
www.peisland.com/orwell

Park Corner

(north of Kensington; see also Stanley Bridge)

Williams, Hank & Clara (Beds of Lavender Bed & Breakfast)   ☎ (902) 886-3114
Park Corner, Rte 20, RR2, Kensington, PEI   C0B 1M0

Located in Park Corner. From Confederation Bridge proceed to Summerside and Kensington. After traffic light, turn left on Rte 101 and continue to Park Corner at end of road. Turn right on Rte 20, cross over Lake of Shining Waters to first house on right. Look for illuminated sign next to road.

$25S $40-50D $10Child   (plus tax)   ▶ 6
🔲 Summer only   🔲 Cont. plus   🏠 Rural, acreage, view from guest rooms, lakefront, deck, quiet   ■ 1S,2D (upstairs)
🛁1Sh.w.g.   ★ TV   🚫 No smoking, no pets
🧍 Sandy beaches, quiet walks along country roads or through Lavender Gardens on property, historic homes, fishing
🚐 Ch'town, Summerside, Cavendish Resort, Confederation B.
🐾 Friendly and informal new (1993-built) home with balcony off one guest room, furnished with Shaker-style furniture, overlooking Lake of Shining Waters in a quiet rural setting and in the heart of Lucy Montgomery historic country. Guest quarters are on 2nd floor. Experience the still evening from the deck and enjoy the beautiful smell of lavender in and around the house. Hosts are happy to share their knowledge of the island.

Rice Point

(south of Charlottetown; see also Cornwall)

Burdett, Louis & Marina (Straitview Farm B&B)   ☎ (902) 675-2071
Rice Point, RR2, Cornwall, PEI   C0A 1H0

Take Rte19 off Trans Canada Hwy to DeSable. From Wood Island Ferry take Rte1 to Cornwall and then Rte19 for 10km.
$40S/D $2.50🔲Each $5Add.person   ▶5
🔲 May1-Nov30   🔲 Full   🏠 40-acre farm, raised bungalow, view from guest rooms, patio, quiet   ■ 1Ste (above ground level)   ⇥ 2D,1S   🛁 1Private   ★ Private entrance   ♥
🧍 Farm grounds and farm animals, ideal area for cycling
🚐 Beaches, golf courses, Charlottetown, Rocky Point
🐾 Warm and friendly welcome in home with large front and back yards and a wonderful view of Northumberland Strait. Join congenial hosts in the living room for coffee/tea/conversation.🛏B&B

Richmond

(west of Summerside; see also Bideford)

Gaudet-MacArthur, Mrs. Erma (Mom's Bed & Breakfast)   ☎ (902) 854-2419
Richmond, PEI   C0B 1Y0   1-888-666-7999

Located in at intersection of Rte 2 & Hwy 127, and 3 km off Lady Slipper Drive.

$45-80S/D $10Add.person   🍽 Meals (plus tax)   ▶ 10
🔲 May15-Oct15   🔲 Full, homebaked   🏠 Village, rural, acreage, quiet, 2verandas   ■3D,1F(upst)   ⇥5D   🛁2Sh.w.g.
1Private   ★TV in guest room, secure bicycle storage, parking
🚫 Smoking on veranda only, no pets
🧍 Village, craft stores, churches, Confederation Trail
🚐 Sandy beaches, Le Village Pionnier Acadien, museums, beaches, Mill River Resort, golfing
🐾 Century home with antique furniture & unique heirlooms and an atmosphere of modern comfort and the cherished past. Guests are welcome to enjoy the parlour with piano and relax on the veranda. Weekly rates on request. Reservations recommended. Off-season rates available. CCards 🛏B&B

South Rustico

(north-west of Charlottetown; see also Brackley B., New Glasgow)

MacDonald, Judy and Gary (Barachois Inn)
mailing: Box 1022, Charlottetown, PEI   C1A 7M4

☎ (902) 963-2194
E-mail: barachoisinn@pei.sympatico.ca

Located in South Rustico on Church Rd (Rt 243).
$135-185D $35Add.person   (Deposit required)   ▶ 13
❊❊ May 1-Oct.31   ⬢ Full   🏠 Village, historic, acreage, view,
quiet ■2D,2Ste(upst) ⊨2Q,2D,2S,1P(Q),cot ⬛Private ⓌNo
smoking,no pets ★Sitting rooms in suites,parking ⤳French
🚶 Seashore, clam-digging, golfing, horseback riding, Farmers'
Bank of Rustico (1869) and St. Augustine's Church (1838)
🚗 Charlottetown City center, theatres, Province House

☛ Spacious Victorian house, located in a beautiful historic community, has lovely vistas
including a view of Rustico Bay, Winter River and surrounding countryside. Built in 1870, and
restored to its former graciousness without sacrificing modern comforts. Visa,MC ⤳B&B
http://www.metamedia.pe.ca/barachois/

St. Peters Bay

(north-east coast; see also Albion Cross)

Ross, Alan & Cori (Hearts Ease Dining & B&B)
Box 17, St. Peter's Bay, PEI   C0A 2A0

☎ (902) 961-3387
E-mail: hearts@isn.net

$75D $15Child/Add.person

(plus taxes)   🍽 Meals   ▶ 6A,3Ch
Phone for directions.
⬢ Full   🏠 Village, 2-storey, hist, acreage, view from guest
rooms, lakefront, porch, deck, quiet ■3D(upstairs)
⊨3Q,3cots ⬛ 3Private   ★ TV,ceiling fans, off-street
parking, guest quarters are separate ⓌNo smoking, no pets
⤳French
🚶 Churches, restaurants, convenience store, post office,
Confederation Trail, golfing, beaches
🚗 Souris, Charlottetown, Montague

☛ Award winning Heritage Home built in 1860 has been completey restored to it's original
beauty and located on beautiful south shore of the Island. Gourmet breakfast and fine dining (by
reservation) is featured. There are a dog and a cat in residence. CCards www.isn.net/heartsease

Stanley Bridge

(north-east of Kensington; see also Cavendish, Park Corner)

MacEwen, A.S.(Buddy) & Helen (Linden Cove Farms)
Stanley Bridge, Box 737, Kensington, PEI   C0B 1M0

☎ (902)836-3222, Fax(902)836-3700
E-mail: linden.cove@pei.sympatico.ca

Located at 222 Campbelllton Rd on Rte 238, off Hwy 6. Phone for
directions.
$60-75S/D $8Add.person   (plus tax)   ▶ 12+
❊❊ Summer only   ⬢ Cont, homebaked   🏠 Farm, 2-storey,
view, riverfront ■4D,1F(ground and upper floor)
⊨2T,5D,R,crib ⬛Private   ★TV in guest rooms, parking
ⓌDesignated smoking area, no pets
🚶 Stores, Marine Aquarium, deep sea fishing boats, artist's
paradise surroundings, browse through the antique store on site
🚗 Restaurants, pub, craft shops, pottery studios, Summerside, Charlottetown, lobster suppers
☛ 70-year old ancestral home, well maintained and surrounded by huge Linden trees (same age
as the house) on 100 acre grain & potato farm. Relax on the shaded lawns and enjoy the superb
view of New London Bay and sanddunes. Housekeeping apartments & cottage on property also
availaible. ⤳B&B www.bbcanada.com/644.html

Stanley Bridge (cont'd)

Weeks, Adelaide (Blue Heron Tourist Home)   ☎ (902) 886-2319
RR6, Stanley Bridge, Kensington, PEI   C0B 1M0

Take Rt 238 off Hwy 6 in Stanley Bridge. Turn by the Aquarium and follow signs and private road
all the way to house in the trees and by the water.
$25-30D   🍽 $2Each   ▶ 6A
🔲 Reservation required after Sept.   🍽 Choice   🏠 Res., acreage, riverfront, view, patio
■3D (main and upper level)   ⊨ 3D   ⊒ 1Private, 1sh.w.g.   ★ F,TV in one guest room,
separate entrance, parking, pool table
🏃 Stanley River beach, Marineland Aquarium, licenced dining room
🚗 Cavendish, Lobster suppers (June-Oct), deep-sea fishing
📣 Long time hosts make visitors feel right at home in comfortable house by the river. Relax on
the large deck and enjoy the beautiful view overlooking the Stanley River and shallow beach. ✍B&B

Herbert, Penny & Rod (Silver Fox B&B Inn)   ☎ (902) 436-1664
61 Granville St., Summerside, PEI   C1N 2Z3   E-mail: herberts@pei.sympatico.ca,1-800-565-4033

From Confederation Bridge take Hwy1A, then Hwy11 to Summerside. Turn north on Granville St.

$75-125S/D $10Add.person   (plus taxes)   ▶ 12
🍽 Cont.,homebaked   🏠 Res., hist., porch, deck, quiet   ■ 4D,2F (2nd &
3rd floor)   ⊨ 2T,3D,2Q,2S   ⊒ 6Private   ★ TV in guest sitting room,
off-street parking   ⍟ Smoking outside, no pets, children min. age 10
🏃 Live Theatre, Exhibition Centre, shopping, walking tour, antique & craft
shops, entertainment on Harbourfront, Museum
🚗 Golfing, north & southshore beaches, Confederation Bridge to NB, deep
sea fishing, seal watching
📣 Warm welcome in historically & architecturally significant Victorian
home, carefully updated to preserve the character while adding modern
facilities. Situated central 2rto the business and shopping district. Associated with blue Barn
Antiques, the home features much period furniture and many collectible items, most of which may
be purchased. www.silverfoxinn.net

Tignish   *(north-west part of the Island)*

Arsenault, Jackie & Elmer (Maple St. Inn Bed & Breakfast)   ☎ (902) 882-3428
214 Maple St., Tignish, PEI   C0B 2B0

Turn left off Hwy 2 (runs into Phillip St.) onto Church St and proceed to Maple St. Go past

church and look for house immediately after Recreation Center.
$35S $45D $10Child/Add.person   (plus tax)   ▶ 8
🔲June1-Sep.30   🍽Full, homebaked   🏠Village,2-storey,3acres
■3D (upstairs)   ⊨ 2T,1D,1Q,2cots   ⊒ 1Sh.w.g.   ★TV,LF,
pool table in guest sitting room, off-street parking   ⍟ No
smoking, no pets
🏃 Museum across street, Roman Catholic Church, downtown
🚗 Fishing port, sandy beaches, tip of Province with longest
natural reef in Eastern Canada, wind test site
📣 School Teacher hosts in cozy & comfortable new modern family home, well decorated. Enjoy
the spacious guest quarters, friendly hospitality and congenial ambience. Relax in the cozy little
guest sitting room in the upper hallway. There are school children and a cat in the house. ✍B&B

Victoria

(east of Borden; see also Crapaud, Albany)

Wood, Kay (Dunrovin Lodge - Cottages & Farm)   ☎ (902) 658-2375
Box 40, Victoria, PEI   C0A 2G0

$40S $50D $6Child $60F $25Add.person   (plus tax)   🍽 Meals   ► 10
Phone for directions.

🌞Summer to Sept30   ⬤Full, homebaked   🏠Farm,2-storey, hist., 100acres, view from guest rooms, patio, quiet   ▦ 4 (upper & ground level), incl. tower room   ⊨ 2S,4T,2D   ⬤1Private, 1sh.w.g.   ★ F,separate entrance, guest quarters are separate   🖐Designated smoking area, no pets in lodge, families welcome   🜊 Churches, playhouse & museum, Chocolate Factory, wharf development, craft and art shops, lobster dinners, beaches, golfing   🚗Charlottetown, Summerside, "Anne Country", Cavendish beaches, Int.Doll House, Car Museum   📷 Warm and friendly Island hospitality in historic (ca 1802) Heritage home and only farm to contain a village (Victoria). Hostess has welcomed many renowned guests over the years and is well informed about local history. She is involved with various organizations and has received many honours. Enjoy the many recreational facilities on the grounds, the warmer southshore waters and take in the picture of rural life and its delights. There are 2 cats and a much loved Sally dog outside.

West Point

(on south-west coast, south of O'Leary)

MacDonald, Audrey & Lynwood (Stewart Memorial House B&B)
RR2, O'Leary, West Point, PEI   C0B 1V0   ☎ (902) 859-1939, (902) 859-2970

From Confederation Bridge bear left on main Hwy to Coleman Corner or O'Leary Corner and follow signs to West Point.
$60-75S/D   ► 7A,2Ch
⬤ Full   🏠 Rural, 2-storey, hist., view from guest rooms, patio, quiet   ▦ 4(upstairs)   ⊨4D,2cots   ⬤ 3Sh.w.g., 1ensuite   ★ TV,LF,KF,separate entrance, wheel-chair access   🖐Designated smoking area   🜊 West Point fishing harbour & wharf, trail to Light House restaurant & gift shop, beautiful Northumberland Strait beach area, newly erected World War II Memorial   🚗 Summerside, Mill River Golf Course & Resort, Alberton, O'Leary, Tignish   📷 Large new modern house full of historic artifacts of West Point area. First Generation Settlers, hosts (Mother & daughter team) and family live across the street and are very knowledgeable of the area's geneology. A Dictionnaire généalogique des familles acadiennes is available for research. Host is a fisherman and docks his boat at the wharf a few steps from the house. Visa,MC 🛏B&B

Nova Scotia

(including Cape Breton Island)

Tourism Nova Scotia and Check Inns Reservation Services
Box 130, Halifax, NS   B3J 2M7   toll-free 1-800-565-0000

Annapolis Royal

(on west coast; see also Paradise, Barton)

Lahey, Dorothy & Dick (The Turret B&B) ☎ (902) 532-2770
372 St.George St., Box 497, Annapolis Royal, NS   B0S 1A0

Take Hwy 101 and Exit 22 North. Follow St.George St to traffic light. Look for house with B&B sign on right.

$55-65S $65-75D   ▶ 6A
🍳 May-Oct (other by special arrangement)   🍽 Full, homebaked
🏠Downtown, village, hist., view, verranda   ■4D(main & upper level) ⊨2T,2Q,1K (incl.four-poster)   🛁 1Private, 1sh.,w.g., 1ensuite
★ TV,F, guest sitting alcove, off-street & street parking, host quarters are separate   🚭No smoking, no pets, not suitable for children
🚶 Annapolis Tidal Power Plant, Historic Gardens, Fort Anne, historic grave site with candlelight tours, restaurants, shops, bus route to Halifax
🚗 Port Royal Historic Site, Upper Clements Park, whale watching (Brier Island) Digby and ferry to NB
🐾 Retired couple in registered Historic home decorated and furnished

to the Victorian era. Well travelled hosts were born in NS and are very knowledgeable of the local and Atlantic regions. Relax by the window in the little turret guest sitting room. 🛏 B&B

McGinis, Jim & Jean (The Carriage House B&B)   E-mail:mcginis@ns.sympatico.ca
643 Upper St.George St., Box 164, Annapolis Royal, NS   B0S 1A0   ☎ (902) 532-5156

From Hwy 101 take Annapolis Royal Exit and follow St.George St into town.

$65S $75D $10Add.person   ▶ 5
🍳May1-Oct31(other by special arrangement) 🍽Full,homebaked
🏠Res, hist. porch   ■ 2(upstairs ⊨ 2Q,1R 🛁2Ensuite
★TV,F, off-street parking   🚭 No smoking, no pets
🚶 Annapolis Royal Historic Gardens, Fort Anne Nat.Park, Candlelight Graveyard Tour farmer's market, King's Theatre, Tidal Power Station., downtown (exquisite shops, fine dining, museums, waterfront boardwalk)
🚗 Kejimkujik Nat.Park, Upper Clements Wildlife Park, excellent bass fishing, wilderness hiking trails, whale watching, golfing, Lester B.Pearson Int.Peacekeeping Centre, Digby & ferry to NB
🐾 Retired R.C.M.P. Officer family in 1890's heritage home situated in small historic town at the mouth of the Annapolis River. Enjoy casual elegance & warm hospitality. Breakfast is served in the formal dining room. Relax in the screened sunporch or by the fireplace on a cool evening. Indoor storage available for bikes and motocycles. There is a resident cat (not in guest area). Visa 🛏CC
www3.ns.sympatico.ca/mcginis

Susnick, Donna and Michael & Faye McStravick (The King George Inn) ☎(902)532-5286
548 Upper St. George Street, Annapolis Royal, NS   B0S 1A0   1-888-799-KING

Turn off Hwy 101 at Annapolis Royal Exit22 or: off Hwy 1, 1 km from light.
$59-159S/D $108-168Ste $10Add.person   ▶ 10
🍳 May15-Oct15   🍽Full(country-style) 🏠Res.,hist.,acreage,view, decks, picnic area ■8 (upper & lower level) ⊨S,D,T,Q,crib 🛁8Private, jacuzzies ★F,TV in guest rooms, phone in parlour, classic movies, lawn games, bicycles 🚭 No smoking 〰 French
🚶 World's highest tides, wharf and waterfront walkway, restaurants, antique and craft shops, Fort Anne, Historic Gardens, Tidal Power Project, gift shop on premises
🐾 1868 restored grand Victorian sea captain's mansion (designated a "Registered Heritage Property"), comfortably furnished with antiques,

ornate fireplaces & leaded glass windows. suites are suitable for honeymoon and families. Vacation packages. Whale watching & golfing can be arranged. Bus & bicycle groups welcome. Visa, MC 🛏B&B http://www3.ns.sympatico.ca/dms/king.htm

Antigonish

(east of New Glasgow)

Bekkers, Sisca & John (Bekkers Bed & Breakfast) ☎ (902) 863-3194
Clydesdale Rd., RR2, Antigonish, NS B2G 2K9

Take Exit 32N to Main St., left at Hawthorne (Rte 245). Proceed
3km, turn left on Clydesdale Rd to B&B on left with sign.
$35S $50-60D $5Child ► 7
✹ June1-Oct31 ⬤ Full 🏠 Rural, ranch-style, acreage, view
from guest rooms, riverfront, deck, quiet ■ 3 (main & ground
level) ⊨ 2T,2Q,1P,crib ⬱ 1Private, 1sh.w.g. ★ TV
🚭No smoking, no pets ⤳ Dutch
🚗 Canso Causeway to Cape Breton Island, Sherbrooke Village
🐾 Former Dairy Farmer hosts offer warm welcome in quiet country setting with scenic view of
valley and rolling hills. There is a dog. ↳B&B

Baddeck

(on Cape Breton Island - central)

Stephen, Murdena & Bob (The Stephen's B&B) ☎ & Fax (902) 929-2860
RR4, Baddeck, NS B0E 1B0 E-mail: stephensbandb@ns.sympatico.ca

Located in North River Bridge. From TCH 105, take Exit 11 and proceed 19.2km north on The
Cabot Trail to North River Bridge. Turn right onto Murray Rd and continue 2km.

$50S $60D ► 6A
✹ May-Oct31 (off-season by special arrangement) ⬤ Full,
homebaked 🏠 Rural, 2-storey, view from guest rooms,
riverfront, porch with veranda, quiet ■ 3(upstairs)
⊨2T,1D,1K(2T) ⬱ 1Sh.w.g., 1sh.w.h. ★ F,sat/TV,VCR and
movies,ceiling fans 🚭Smoking on veranda, no pets, no children
🕴 Walks along the water (3km long), trout & salmon fishing,
hiking, kayaking, sailing
🚗 Gaelic College, Baddeck, Alexander Graham Bell Museum
🐾 Retired, professional couple in beautifully restored country home situated high on the bank of
the Murray River with magnificient view. Located near famous Cabot Trail (a spectacular drive
around the northern part of Cape Breton Island). Host is a retired member of the Royal Canadian
Mounted Police. The beautful setting and house was featured by a BBC Television (Scotland) crew
when shooting a Gaelic speaking programme (1993). Visa,MC ↳B&B www.bbcanada.com/1847

Barton

(south of Digby)

Dechênes, Laurette (The Barton House) ☎ (902) 245-6695
Box 33, Barton, Digby County, NS B0W 1H0

Located on Hwy 101 in Barton directly across the street from the Barton Post Office.

$45S $50D $90Ste $10Child/Add.person ► 12
⬤ Full 🏠 Rural, hist., older, view from guest rooms, patio,
quiet, oceanfront ■3D(main & upper floor) ⊨4T,3D
⬱1Ensuite, 2private ★ TV in guest rooms, LF,KF, deck with
whirlpool, parking in yard ⤳French
🕴 Beach and Provincial Park
🚗 Ferry to New Brunswick, Upper Clements Theme Park, Digby
museum, Digby Fleet shopping
🐾 Beautifully remodelled 200-year old home with friendly atmosphere, situated in a convenient
location overlooking the ocean and beautiful St. Mary's Bay. ↳B&B

Cape North

(on northern tip of Cape Breton Isle)

McEvoy, Hansel and Sharon (Oakwood Manor)
North Side Rd., Cape North NS B0C 1G0

☎ & Fax (902) 383-2317
E-mail: oakwood.manor@ns.sympatico.ca

At Cape North, take road to Bay St.Lawrence for 1.6km & Northside Rd (0.4km).

$60-65S $70-90D $15Add.person   ► 14

🏵 May1-Oct31   ◑ Full, homebaked   🏠 150-acres farm,
3-storey, view, quiet, isolated ■4D,2F(on 2nd & 3rd floor)
⊨2Q,5D,2T(K),P ⊞Ensuite with jacuzzi ★Air,F,TV/movies in
guest lounge, B-B-Q, host quarters are separate, private
entrance ♿ No smoking, no pets
🚶 Enjoy the vast surrounding farmland and tranquil countryside,
take a leasure stroll in apple orchard or the private path to the
base of the mountains

🚗 Hiking trails, beaches, museums, whalewatching, bicycle rentals, restaurants, gift shops
🚤 150 acre farm nestled beneath the shadow ot the North Mountain in beautiful Sunrise Valley.
The home was built in 1930 by the owners father from local wood cut and milled on wooded area of
the farm. in a pretty valley. Longtime B&B hosts are of Irish descent. Enjoy a stay "in the woods".
Breakfast is served on the 9ft table in the kitchen. Videos of local scenes and some wildlifethe
frequent that farm at different seasons. Visa ⌐B&B

Chester

(west of Halifax; see also Mahone Bay)

Fraser, Suzan (Mecklenburgh Inn)
78 Queen St., Box 350, Chester, NS B0J 1J0

☎ (902) 275-4638
E-mail: frnthrbr@atcon.com

Located next to the Post Office. Phone for directions.
$55S $65-75D $115Ste $20Add.person   ► 10
🏵 May24-Oct31   ◑ Full, homebaked   🏠 Village center, hist.,
water view, covered balcony ■ 3D(upstairs)plus suite on main
level ⊨2T,2D,2Q,4P ⊞3Sh.w.g.,1private ★ 2F,TV,VCR,
private entrance for suite ♿Smoking on balcony, no pets,
children min age 10 ⁓French
🚶 2blocks from ocean, tennis courts, golf club by the ocean, yacht
clubs, summer theatre, public wharves, ferry to Tancook Island
🚗 Airport, Mahone Bay, City of Halifax, Bluenose II, Peggy's Cove, Lunenburg Fisheries Museum
🚤 Large home (c.1890) in the heart of seaside village with cozy/informal atmosphere, painted
period furniture and paintings by local artists. Young hostess has spent many years travelling
around the world and is a Cordon Bleu trained chef and an experienced sailor. Visa,Amex ⌐B&B

Zinck, Maureen (Blandford Inn B&B)
Lighthouse Rte No 329, Blandford, NS B0J 1T0

☎ & Fax (902) 228-2016

From Halifax follow Hwy 103 to Exit 6, turn left toward Hubbards, then along ocean side to B&B.

$60S $72D $20Child 🍽Meals   ► 16
🏵 May-Oct   ◑ Buffet   🏠 Rural, village, hist., view from guest
rooms, deck, quiet, secluded ■ 4F(upper & ground
level) ⊨8D ⊞4Private ★ TV,F,LF, wheel-chair access in
ground floor guest room, bicycles and fishing rods for guests,
off-street and street parking ♿No smoking, inquire about pets
🚶 Beautiful Bayswater Beach, oceanside meanders, horseback
riding, nature trails, hiking paths, fishing from the wharfs
🚗 Historic seaports of Chester, Mahone Bay, Lunenburg, dining, shopping
🚤 Charming Cent ıry house with a new addition located by the ocean providing a good place to
relax, unwind, relieve stress and restore the mind and body. Enjoy the tranquil and peaceful
atmosphere. Hostess was born and raised in the area and is knowledgeable of sites and events.
Breakfast is served in the sunroom overlooking the harbour. Small groups for weddings or special
occasions can be accommodated. Visa,MC ⌐CC www3.ns.sympatico.ca/blandford.inn

Folly Lake
(north-west of Truro; see also Masstown, Tatamagouche)

Younger, Angela (The Winnett House at Folly Lake) ☎ (902) 662-4197
Folly Lake, RR1, Londonderry, NS B0M 1M0

Phone for directons.
$35S $40-45D 🍽 Meals   (plus tax) ▶ 6
🍴 Full, homebaked 🏠 Rural, lakefront, 2-storey, older, acreage,
view from guest rooms, patio, porch, deck ■ 3D (upstairs)
⊨2T,1D,1Q 🛁 1Sh.w.g. ★ F,LF,TV/VCR, piano in guest
living/library room, indivi.thermostats 🚫No smoking, no pets
🚶 Folly Lake, hiking trails, loon nestings, Snowmobile Club
(Fundy) and trails, blueberry fields, maple sugar camp
🚗 Bay of Fundy (highest tides and Tidal Bore), beaches (clam-digging, rock-hounding, fossil cliffs
📮 Older-style home furnished with antiques and country-style decor, overlooking Lake and Folly
Mountain. Hostess is originally from New Zealand and travelled many years before settling down in
this beautiful area. Relax on the deck or sunroom overlooking the lake and enjoy the spectacular fall
colours in season. Special diets considered with notice. Winter packages and rates for skiers and
snowmobilers are very popular. ✓B&B

Grand Pré
(east of Wolfville; see also Windsor, Kentville)

Halbrook, John & Cally Jordan (Inn the Vineyard) ☎ (902) 542-9554,1-800-565-0000
Box 106, Grand Pré, NS B0P 1M0 E-mail: jhalbrook@bigfoot.com, Fax(902)542-1248

Located at 264 Old Post Rd in Grand Pré. From Hwy 101 follow
Exit 10 and signs.
$69S $77-95D $20Add.person ▶ 7
✤ Summer only 🍴 Full 🏠 Village, hist., acreage, quiet ■3
(upper & lower level) ⊨1S,2D 🛁3Ensuite ★F,TV,parking
🚫No smoking ∿French
🚶 Grand Pré Nat.Hist.Park, Covenaters Church, orchards
🚗 Wolfville, Acadia University, fine restaurants, elegant shops, Evangeline Beach, Cape Split
📮 Registered Heritage house, locally known as the "Stewart House", has been in host family for
200 years, with classic Colonial-style that retains its original layout, character and charm. Enjoy
the relaxing atmosphere. Writer-host is well informed about the Annapolis Valley region. ✓B&B

Halifax
(see also Prospect, Peggy's Cove))

Ellis, Bruce & Anna (Caribou Lodge B&B) ☎ (902) 445-5013, 1-877-445-5013
6 Armada Dr., Halifax, NS B3M 1R7

Phone for directions.
$85-100S/D $15Add.person ▶ 8
🍴 Cont., homebaked, buffet 🏠 Sub., 2-storey, hist., view from
guest rooms, patio, porch, quiet, secluded ■ 3 plus 1Ste(main &
upper level) ⊨ 2D,1Q,1R 🛁 1Private,2ensuite, whirlpool in
suite ★ LF,TV in each guest room, wheel-chair access, separate
entrance & porch in ground level suite, off-street parking, guest
quarters are separate 🚬 Designated smoking area
🚶 Hemlock Ravine Park, "Titanic" Cemetary, numerous restaurants, Art Gallery, Duke of Kent
Music Room (Nat.Hist.Site), bus routes Nos12/80/14
🚗 Downtown Halifax, Int.Airport, Acadian Museum, Peggy's Cove, Shubenacadie Wildlife Park
📮 Spacious Century home with warm period furnishings and art gallery/gift shop. Watch
hostess "A.J.Scanlan" work at her easel in the gallery and gift shop. Host offers professional
expertise in both the region's civilian and military heritage. Breakfast is served in special guest
breakfast room. Group & extended stay terms available. Perfect place for honeymoon and special
occasions. There are 2 dogs in residence. Visa,Amex http://www.achilles.net/~bb/572.html

Halifax (cont'd)

MacDonald, Innis and Sheila (Fresh Start B&B) ☎ 902) 453-6616, Fax (902) 453-6617
2720 Gottingen St., Halifax, NS   B3K 3C7   1-888-453-6616

Located 1 block north of MacDonald Bridge, across from Maritime Command Museum.

$60-65S $65-70D $85Ste (Off-season Rates available) ► 22
⚫Full, homebaked 🏠Downtown, 3-storey, hist. ■7D,1Ste
(upstairs) ⊨4T,2Q,6D,2cots
⨼2Private,3sh.w.g. ★TV,F,KF, parking, meeting
facilities ⚫No smoking ⌇some German
🕴 Maritime Command Museum, Citadel Hill, historic Halifax
waterfront, shopping, fine restaurants, site of Halifax Explosion,
public swimming pool, Maritime Museum of the Atlantic
🚐 Picnic area, fresh/saltwater beaches, windsurfing, Peggy's Cove, Fundy Tidal Bore
🐾 Modest Victorian Mansion which has retained much original woodwork and glass. Experienced
sister-team hosts have been receiving guest for many years. Though close to downtown, the location
is very quiet. Business travellers welcome. There is a cat on premises. CCards ⌐B&B

Kentville   *(see also Wolfville, Pt.Williams, Grand Pre)*

Snow, Richard & Sandra (The Grand Street Inn B&B)   ☎(902)679-1991,1-877-245-4744
160 Main St., Kentville, NS   B4N 1J8   E-mail: grandstreetinn@ns.sympatico.ca

Phone for directions.
$65S $75D $10Child/Add.person   ► 10
⚫ Full 🏠 Res., 3-storey, acreage, swimming pool, view, patio,
porch, deck ■2D,1F(upstairs) ⊨ 2T,3D,1P,crib ⨼2Private,
1ensuite ★F,TV, ceiling fans, separate entrance, off-street
parking ⚫ Smoking ouside, no pets ⌇ French
🕴 Agricultural Centre, museum & nature trail, downtown,
shopping, dining, entertainment, Courthouse Museum
🚐 Hall's Harbour, Lobster Pond, Acadian University (Wolfville), Atlantic Theatre Festival, Bay of
Fundy (highest tides in the world), scenic drives, Halifax and Int.Airport
🐾 Completely renovated spacious Queen Anne Revival Century home, tastefully decorated and
situated in the heart of the Annapolis Valley. Rooms are on 2nd & 3rd floor. Early retired Air Force
hosts were born in Newfoundland & Northern Ontario. Relax in the large common rooms or
outside by the pool. Breakfast is served in formal dining room. There is a young school boy in
residence. Children welcome. Visa,MC ⌐B&B

Louisbourg

(on Cape Breton Island south of Sydney)

Doyle, Judy & John (The Manse)   ☎ (902) 733-3155 or 733-3694
10 Strathcona St., Louisbourg, NS B0A 1M0

Follow Hwy 22 straight into town of Louisbourg & continue down
Main Street. Turn left at Mariner Hardware to 1st house on right.
$45-55S/D $15Add.person   (plus tax)   ► 6A
🍴 Full   🏠 Downtown, res., hist., view from 2 guest rooms,
oceanside   ■ 3D (upstairs)   ⊨ 3D,3R   ⊒ 1Sh.w.g.,1sh.w.h.
(on main floor)   ★ Parking   ⍟ Not suitable for children
🏃 Downtown, restaurants, shops
🚗 Fortress, city of Sydney, scenic lighthouse, historic beach

🐾 Spacious, turn-of-the-Century home with large rooms, many antiques, collectables and a
panoramic view of harbour and ocean. Host is a retired Army Officer. Both hosts have travelled
extensively in N.America/Europe/Middle East & enjoy sharing their home with guests. ✎B&B

Ferguson, Hazel (Sunlit Valley B&B)   ☎(902)562-7663,Fax 562-2222,1-877-808-8883
821 Brickyard Rd, Albert Bridge, NS B0A 1P0   E-mail: hazelferguson@ns.sympatico.ca

From Port Hawkesbury, take either Rt 4 or Rt 105 to Sydney area. From Sydney take Hwy 22 tow.

Louisbourg, crossing the Mira River, take 1st left, then 3 km.
$40S $50-60D $16Add.person   ► 7
🌼May 1-Oct.30   🍴Full   🏠Farm, view, riverfront, quiet, deck
■4(main & lower level)   ⊨4D,1S   ⊒2Sh.w.g.   ★F,TV room
🚗 Fortress of Louisburg, Provincial Park, swimming beaches,
camping & picnicking, NFLD ferry, Glace Bay Miners Museum,
Marconi Museum, "Rita MacNeil Tea Room", Sydney,
🐾 Very social and congenial atmosphere in comfortable Cape

Breton home overlooking the Mira River. Well-informed hostess will help with travel plans.
✎B&B   http://sunlit.hypermart.net/sunlit/

MacLeod, Harvey and Mona (MacLeod's B&B)   ☎ & Fax (902) 733-2456, 1-888-989-0880
5247 Hwy. 22 Louisbourg, NS B0A 1M0

Located 10 km before Louisbourg on Rt 22 and 23 km from Sydney.

$30-40S $45-55D   ► 6
✚ May1-Sept30   🍴 Full   🏠 Rural, acreage, patio, quiet
■3D(upstairs)   ⊨3D (upstairs)   ⊒1sh.w.g., 1ensuite
★TV,F, parking   ⍟Restricted smoking, no pets
🚗 Fortress of Louisbourg, Miners Museum, Newfoundland
Ferry, Sydney Airport
🐾 Cape-Cod home in a very quiet country area. Enjoy the
interesting birds on the property. Very convenient location. Visa
✎B&B

Lunenburg

(west of Halifax; see also Mahone Bay, Riverport)

Albo, Rafel & Peter Fleischmann (Hillcreoft Café & Guest House)
Box 1665, 53 Mountague St., Lunenburg, NS B0J 2C0 ☎ & Fax(902)634-8031

From Halifax take Hwqy 103 west and Exit 10 (Mahone Bay). From Yarmouth take Hwy 103 east and Exit 11 via Blockhouse. Located 1 block from Lunenburg Harbour.
$50S $65D (plus tax) ► 6
April-Dec Cont, homebaked 2-storey, hist. 3D(upst)
2T,2Q 2Sh.w.g. (incl.one ground level) ★Air, fans in guest rooms, private parlour with library and piano, street parking, guest quarters are separate Smoking outside, no pets some Italian, Spanish, French
Atlantic Fisheries Museum, Art Gallery, Harbour cruises, restaurants, horse & carriage ride, guided town walking trail
Beaches, Hiking, The Ovens National Park
Restored 1850's home with international decor throughout of the owners unique collection of folk art with an international twist. Enjoy the international cuisine of creative meals from fresh local ingredients, served in two small intimate dining rooms. Visa,MC

Heubach, Merrill and Al (Blue Rocks Road B&B) ☎ & Fax (902) 634-8033
RR1, #579 Blue Rocks Rd., Lunenburg, NS B0J 2C0 E-mail: nika@tallships.ca, 1-800-818-3426

From Hwy 103, take Exit 11 towards Lunenburg and travel on Rt 324S for approx. 10 km. At stop sign, turn left towards Blue Rocks. Turn left again at next stop sign, proceed to 4th house on left.

$50-70S $60-80D $20Add.person ► 6
closed Nov-March Full, homebaked Rural, res., hist., acreage, oceanview, quiet 3(upstairs) 2T,2D
1Private,1sh.w.g. No smoking,no pets German, French
Bicycle shop on premises, Lunenburg Centre, fine restaurants, galleries, shops, scenic surrounding countryside, beautiful uncrowded beaches, fishing, whale-watching, sea-kayaking.
Mahone Bay, Halifax, Kejimkujik Nat.Park, Peggy's Cove
Artfully restored, comfortable 19th Century home with veranda overlooking Lunenburg Bay and gardens. and surrounded by a cyclist's paradise. Enjoy awesome breakfasts and the friendly relaxed atmosphere. Hosts operate the Lunenburg Bicycle Barn (day-trip plans, maps, bicycle rental, accessories, full service available). There is a very friendly dog in residence. Visa ✓B&B

Jennings, Tom & Judy (Commander's Bed & Breakfast) ☎ & Fax (902) 634-3151
56 Victoria Rd., Box 864, Lunenburg, NS B0J 2C0 1-800-550-4824 (Reserv.only)

From Halifax, take Hwy 103 south-west toward Yarmouth and Exit 11. Continue on Hwy 324 to Lunenburg and proceed to house on left prior to harbour.

$60-90S/D $15Add.person ► 10
Full Village, hist., 3-storey, view, oceanfront, patio, porch, deck, quiet 4F(upstairs) 3Q,2T,4P 4Private ★F,3TV,LF 2lounges,Fax/photocopier/word processor, sitting areas in all rooms, library, iron/blower avail., parking Designated smoking area, young adults 12 & over welcome
Sports Park, Exhibition grounds, tennis, swimming pool, picnic area downtown & historic district, restaurants, local craft shops Fisheries Museum, fishing.
Halifax, Mahone Bay, Peggy's Cove, scenic south-shore drives & coastal villages
Elegant turn-of-the-Century home, retaining all of its original character. Interesting naval memorabilia collected by host during navy career, as well as an extensive library, ship/airplane models, working model railway & a unique "pig" collection. CCards ✓CC
www.destination-ns.com/lighthouse/commande.ns

Mahone Bay

(west of Halifax; see also Lunenburg, Chester)

McHugh, Patricia & John (Mahone Bay B&B)
558 Main St., Mahone Bay, NS B0J 2E0

☎ (902) 624-6388, Fax 624-0526
E-mail: mahonebaybbns@istar.ca

Located in the centre of town on the Lighthouse Route.
$60-80S $75-95D $160-170F   🍽 Meals   ▶ 8
🍴 Full, homebaked   🏠 Village, 2-storey, hist., view from guest
rooms, oceanfront, porch, balcony ■4D(upstairs) ⊨2T,1D,2Q
🛏2Private, 1sh.w.g.   ★Air,KF,LF,4F,TV/VCR in guest rooms,
ceiling fans, private entrance, off-street parking, guest quarters are
separate   Ⓦ No smoking, no pets   ⤳Basic French & German
🚗 Lunenburg (UNESCO Heritage Site), Chester Bay, Halifax

🕴 "The Three Churches" (most famous photographed scenery in all of Nova Scotia), Art Galleries,
Main Street, shops, restaurants, Mimi's Restaurant
📢 130-year old Cape Cod home furnished with French & English antiques, chinz fabrics and an
antique china collection (English Blue Willow). New location for experienced hosts (formerly in
Toronto, where they have welcomed many travel writers and business travellers over the years).
Relax on the comfortable wicker-filled wrap-around balcony and enjoy the beautiful oceanview
across the street. Hosts is a well-known retired Toronto businessman (coffee houses) and hostess
has her own Interor Design Co. Breakfast is served in the formal dining room. There is a cozy
proper English Tea Room, where Afternoon Tea is served daily. ✐B&B
www.bbcanada.com/mahonebaybb.ns

O'Brien, Rose & Allan (The Manse at Mahone Bay Country Inn)
88 Orchard St., Box 475, Mahone Bay, NS B0J 2E0

☎ (902) 624-1121
Fax (902) 624-1182

Approaching from the east look for house next to first of 3 famous churches. Look for yellow house
with white trim.
$85S $105D $15Add.person   🍽 Meals   (plus tax)   ▶ 10
🍴 Full, homebaked   🏠 Village, hist., view from guest rooms,
oceanfront, deck, quiet   ■ 4D(ground & upper level)incl.carriage
house   ⊨ 2T,3Q   🛏 4Private   ★ F,TV in guest rooms,
ceiling fans, off-street parking   ⤳ French
🕴 Shops, galleries, restaurants, fishing, sailing
🚗 Halifax, Peggy's Cove, Chester, Lunenburg, Wolfville

📢 Elegant, restored 1860's manse (former parson's house) with all modern amenities, great art,
books, eclectic music and a wonderful view of the Bay, situated on a tree-lined street. Relax on the
deck or by the fireplace. Ideally suited for weddings and special occasions. Visa,MC ✐CC

Piccolo, John & Faith (Amber Rose Inn)
319 West Main St., Box 397, Mahone Bay, NS B0J 2E0

☎ & Fax (902) 624-1060
E-mail: amber@amberroseinn.com

From Hwy 103 take Exit 11, turn right at Blockhouse (4-way stop) and proceed 2km. From Hwy 3,
turn up, away from the water at intersection with monument, proceed 1km.
$95-115S/D $15Child/Add.person   (plus taxes)   ▶ 8A
✠ May-Oct   🍴 Cooked   🏠 Village, 2-storey, hist., patio,
porch, deck   ■ 3Ste (upstairs)   ⊨ 2D,2Q   🛏 3Private,
whirlpool tub   ★TV/fridge/coffee machine/guest robes in suites,
airconditioner, guest quarters are separate, private entrance
Ⓦ No smoking, no pets, not suitable for children   ⤳ Italian
🕴 Waterfront & harbour, shopping, park, wooded area with trails,
restaurants, churches

📢 Originally a General store, one of Mahone Bay's best preserved architecture of Heritage
buildings, has been renovated and expanded to modernize facilities, while maintaining the look and
feel of the original house. Experienced hosts operated a B&B in Lunenburg for many years. Enjoy
luxury decor, spacious lawn & gardens. Breakfast is served in the guest dining room. CCards
www.amberroseinn.com

Margaree Forks
on west coast of Cape Breton; see also Mar.Harbour)

Harrison, Robin & Marilyn (Harrison Hill B&B)   ☎ & Fax (902) 248-2226
Box 561, Margaree Forks, NS   B0E 2A0   E-mail: harrisonhill@capebretonet.com

From Rte 19, turn right at T junction toward Baddeck. Continue past Co-op/Fire Hall & Dept of
Fisheries to B&B sign. From Baddeck, follow Cabot Trail from Red Barn past Doyle's Rd.
$60D $10Child/Add.person   (plus taxes)   ▶6

🍳 Full   🏠 Rural, village, 3-storey, older, acreage, view from
guest rooms, patio, porch, deck, secluded   ■ 3D(upstairs)
🛏2T,2D,1Q,P,R   🛁 2Sh.w.h.   ★ LF,TV,off-street parking
🚭No smoking, no pets
🏃 Salmon fishing (Margaree River), beaches, on-site gift corner
🚗 Cheticamp (Acadian Village), Baddeck (Alexander Bell
Museum), Centre Bras d'Or Festival, Fortress of Louisbourg, Cape
Breton National Park

👉 Elegant, romantic and old world charm in restored large older home with spacious grounds set
in tranquil surroundings of beautiful scenery. Relax on the wrap-around veranda. Host is a Concert
Pianist. Special interest is music, drama and travel. Enjoy the entertainment in the music room,
soirees or outdoor theatre in the back garden (Sat & Thurs evenings July15-Aug15). Visa,MC

Margaree Harbour
(on west coast of Cape Breton; see also Margaree F.)

Taylor, Francis and Mary (Taylor's Bed & Breakfast)   ☎ (902) 235-2652
Margaree Harbour, Civic No10038, Inverness County, NS   B0E 2B0

Located 1.5 km south of Margaree Harbour bridge on Cabot Trail.
$40S $50D $5Child $10Add.person   ▶ 6A,2Ch
❇ June-Dec.   🍳 Full, homebaked   🏠 Farm, hist., view, quiet,
oceanfront, veranda   ■ 3D(upstairs)   🛏3D,2cots   🛁Sh.w.h
★TV, parking
🏃 Beaches, restaurants, gift shops, laundromat, hiking trail
🚗 Deep-Sea Fishing
👉 Comfortable Century farm house overlooking St. Lawrence
Gulf/Margaree River. Native hosts are well informed, & happy to help with travel plans. ✔B&B

Wheeler, Jan & Bob (Chimney Corner B&B & cottages)   ☎ & Fax (902) 235-2104
2581 Shore Rd,Margaree Harbour, NS   B0E 2B0   1-888-211-9061
E-mail: 2352104.trans@tourism.ca

From Canso Causeway take Ceilidh Trail (Rte 19) and proceed beyond Inverness. Turn left at Shore
Rd (Rte 219). Travel north for 13km and turn left into long driveway at B&B sign.

$65-85S/D   (Reservations preferred)   ▶ 4A
❇ May15-Oct15 (other by arrangement)   🍳 Gourmet,(may
cater to dietary requirements)   🏠 Rural, split-level 3storey,
25acres, view, oceanfront, deck, quiet, secluded   ■ 2D (ground &
upper level)   🛏 2D   🛁 2Private   ★ F,TV,LF, beach towels
for guests, barbeque   🚭 No smoking, no pets
🚗 Cabot Trail, AGB Museum (Baddeck), CB Highlands Nat.Park,
whale watching, salmon fishing, canoeing, boat tours

🏃 Wooded trails, private beach on grounds, Chimney Corner Beach (famous "singing sands")
👉 Unique A-frame house built and decorated by hosts situated on the ocean. Each guest room is
on a separate level, adding to a feeling of privacy. Hosts are retired educators with many and varied
educator interests and abilities. Ideal place for honeymoons, special occasions, anniversaries. Also
on property 2 deluxe housekeeping cottages. CCards ✔B&B   www.bbcanada.com/2264.html

Masstown

(west of Truro, see also Folly Lake)

Eisses, James & Ellen (Shady Maple Bed'N Breakfast) ☎ & Fax(902) 662-3565,
RR1, Debert, Masstown, NS B0M 1G0 E-mail: emeisses@ns.sympatico.ca, 1-800-493-5844

From Truro on Hwy 104 take Exit 12 to Masstown, turn on Hwy 2 and travel 5 km. Or from Hwy
102 take Exit 14A, turn left to Masstown and go 11.8 km to white farmhouse with 2 silos by barn.
$50S $60-90D $5Child(free under age 3) $10Add.person ►8A,4Ch
▧Full ﬔFarm,patio,quiet,inground pool & spa ■3(upst) ⊨3Q,cots,crib
🛁1Ensuite, 1sh.w.g., whirlpool bath ★TV,F,LF,Tidal Bore Video ⊛No
smoking ⌁Dutch
ℵ Woodland walking trails, extensive farm grounds, view of Bay of Fundy
🚗 World famous Tidal Bore viewing site, Halifax Airport, Parrsboro, Truro
🐾 Working farm with large recently renovated and restored Century farm
house, but still maintaining "that down home" feeling. Guests are
welcome to view and visit farm activities. House specialty is candlelit breakfast.

Middleton

(west of Kentville; see also Paradise, Annapolis R.)

Griffith, Richard & Shae (Fairfield Farm Inn) ☎ & Fax (902) 825-6989
10 Main St., Box 1287Middleton, NS B0S 1P0 E-mail: griffith@glinx.com, 1-800-237-9896

Located in Middleton at west end of Main Street on Hwy 1.
$55-70S $60-75D 🍽 Meals (plus tax) ►10
▧ Choice ﬔ Hist.,110acres, 2-storey, mountain view, patio ■5D
(main & upper level) ⊨1D,3Q,1K 🛁5Ensuite ★Air-conditioners
& ceiling fans, LF,TV/radio & hairdryers in guest rooms, separate
entrance, large guest kitchen, parking ⊛ No smoking, no pets
ℵ Annapolis River with trail for walking (on property), pitch & putt golf
& practice putting green on property, historic 1790 Loyalist church across
the street, MacDonald Museum, boutiques, restaurants, Tourist Bureau
🚗Bay of Fundy shore, hist.Annapolis Royal, Nat.Parks, whale watching
🐾 Historic hospitality in elegant 1886 Victorian Country Inn with period antiques and modern
amenities. Situated on 110 acres in the "heart of the Annapolis Valley". Ideal base from which to
explore the historic and scenic valley and South Shore of the province. Very suitable for groups,
retreats and special occiasions. Hosts live in separate building on the property. CCards ✓B&B
www.valleyweb.com/fairfieldfarminn/

Musquodoboit Harbour

(east of Halifax)

Skaling, Randy & Judy (Wayward Goose Inn - B&B) ☎ & Fax (902) 889-3654
343 West Petpeswick Rd, Musquodoboit Harbour, NS B0J 2L0 1-888-790-1777

From Dartmouth, take Hwy 107 to Rte 7 at Musquodoboit Harbour. Turn right for 1.7 km to West
Petpeswick Rd and right again 1.7km to Inn.
$52-73S $58-83D $5Child $15Add.person ►6A,4Ch
📅May24-Sept30 ▧Full,homebaked ﬔRural,2-storey,acreage,
waterview,patio,quiet,private ■3D(upst)incl.honeymoon suite &
whirlpool bath, guest quarters are seprate ⊨2T,2Q, foams and
sleeping bags for children 🛁2Ensuite,1private ★F,TV/VCR &
stereo, canoe/rowboat/daysailer,separate entrance ⊛No pets, no
smoking, 2-night minimum by reservation
ℵ Walking/cycling trails, water activities, birding
🚗 Sandy beach, craftshops/antiques, restaurants, golfing, scenic drives along the coast, Halifax
🐾 Spacious, quiet Inn overlooking the magical Petpeswick (saltwater) Inlet. Enjoy traditional
Maritime Hospitality on Nova Scotia's undiscovered Maritime Folklore. Eastern shore. Hostess is a
water colour artist. Browse in "Judy's Art Works Studio" in the barn. Lessons available. Hosts are
very knowledgeable about local sights and events. Ideal place for honeymoon and special occasion.
Visa,MC ✓B&B

North Brookfield *(west of Bridgewater)*

Harlow, Les & Emma (The Big Oak Tree B&B)
mailing: RR1, South Brookfield, Queen's Co., NS B0T 1X0

☎ (902) 682-2783
Fax (902) 682-3399

From Halifax on Rte 103, take Exit 13, turn right on Hwy 325, left on Rte 208 to North Brookfield.
Continue on Rosette Rd to Harlow Rd and follow signs.

$35S $45D $10Add.person (over age 12)   ► 6A,2ch
🍳 Full, homebaked   🐄 Farm, hist., view from guest rooms,
lakefront, deck, quiet, secluded   ■ 2D,1F (upstairs)
⊨3D,1Q   ⊒1Sh.w.g.   ★ TV in guest sitting room, ceiling
fans, private entrance   ⓦ Designated smoking area, no pets
🏃 Lake swimming with beach, canoeing, fishing, nature trails,
biking, Wilderness camping (island), golf course
🚗 Kejimkujik National Park, Bridgewater, Digby, Peggy's Cove

📣 5th Generation ancetral farmhome (built in 1827 and completely renovated), located on a
Peninsula between Little and Big Tupper Lakes. Breakfast is served in special breakfast room.
Hosts are proud owners of an award given in 1992 for the largest hardwood tree in the province. (A
giant red oak located 75 ft behind the house). Visa ✓ B&B

Paradise *(west of Kentville; see also Middleton, Annapolis Royal)*

Grimard, Kim & Claude (The Paradise Inn, B&B)
116 Paradise Lane, Box 24, Paradise, NS B0S 1R0

☎ 902) 584-3934, 1-877-584-3934
E-mail: grimard.kc@ns.sympatico.ca

From Hwy 101 take Exit 19, then west on Rte 1 to Paradise Lane.
$65S $70D $15Add.person   (plus tax)   ► 7
🔆 May15-Aug30 (other by special arrangement)   🍳 Full,
homebaked   🐄 Rural, village, 2-storey, hist., view from guest
rooms, deck, quiet   ■ 3D(upstairs)   ⊨ 2T,2Q,cot   ⊒1Private,
1sh.w.g.   ★ Terry bathrobes, fans, clock radios, private guest
parlour, secure bicycle & canoe storage, off-street parking   ⓦNo
smoking, no pets   〰 French
🏃 Eden Golf & Country Club, Annapolis Valley Exhibition (early Aug), Annapolis River canoeing
🚗 Annapolis Royal, Fort Anne, King's Theatre, World famous Bay of Fundy, Oaklawn Farm Zoo
📣 Unique home (ca 1876) situated next to the Annapolis River with a brook running through
property. Formerly called the Paradise Hotel and used as an Inn for many years, now converted into
a comfortable, luxurious B&B. Located on the scenic Evangeline Trail in the heart of NS farmland.
Breakfast is served in the cozy dining room and evening refreshments are served in parlour. Browse
through the craft cupboard of tiny stitchery and crafts. CCards ✓CC www.paradiseinn.ns.ca

---

Port Mouton *(on south coast near Liverpool)*

Adams, Judy and John ("Apple Pie" B&B)
Box 32, Central Port Mouton, Queens Co., NS B0T 1T0

☎ (902)683-2217,Fax683-2180
1-888-72-APPLE (722-7753)
E-mail: applepie@aurocom.com

Located 1.5 km off Exit 21 from Hwy 103. Look for sign.
$75S/D $20Add.person   🍽 Meals   ► 2+
🍳Full 🏠Village, hist., 3-storey, oceanfront,quiet ■1D(upstairs)
⊨2T(or1Q) ⊒1Private ★F,TV,LF, library, music room
ⓦNo smoking, no pets, unsuitable for small children
🏃 Beautiful white sandy Carter's Beach, birdwatching, hiking and
biking trails, family restaurant
🚗 Liverpool town, Kejimkujik Park, Halifax, Yarmouth

📣 Warm welcome in turn-of-the-Century home with a cozy pellet stove in the living room,
overlooking Mouton Harbour and the Atlantic Ocean. Enjoy the pleasant atmosphere of a Victorian
Country Tea Room in the bright and spacious sunporch (June-Sept) or browse in the little gift
shop. Host is a cabinet maker & musician & sign carver. The workshop is always open to visitors.
House specialty: delicious lobster chowder & steamed mussels (on request). Visa,MC

Peggy's Cove

(west of Halifax; see also Prospect)

Webb, Karl & Shelley (Havenside B&B)   ☎ & Fax (902) 823-9322, 1-800-641-8272
225 Boutilier's Cove Rd., Hackett's Cove, NS   BOJ 3J0   E-mail: kwebb@ns.sympatico.ca

$75-175S $85-195D   ► 6-7A,2Ch
From TCH103 take Exit 5, follow signs to Rte 333 & Hackett's
Cove. Located 10km from Peggy's Cove.
✚ May1-Oct31 (off season by special arrangement)   🍽 Full,
homebaked   🏠 Rural, village, 1.5 storey, acreage, view, 3decks,
oceanback, quiet ⬛3(main floor)+1Ste(2nd floor) ⊨4Q
⬛3Ensuite (1whirlpool) ★F,LF,TV, gathering room, games room
with pool table, square grand piano & organ, ample parking
ⓌNo smoking, no pets, 2nights minimum in suite
🏃 Walks in scenic area, sailing charters, whale & bird-watching, canoeing, swimming, deep-sea
fishing, restaurants, churches, barbeques, picnics
🚗 Peggy's Cove, Halifax, South Shore of Nova Scotia, Mahone Bay, Chester, beautiful beaches
🐾 Spacious new home, tastefully decorated, overlooking picturesque cove. Knowledgeable and
gracious hosts are retired educators and delight in welcoming appreciative guests from all parts of
the globe. Ideal base from which to explore the historic and scenic area, and a wonderful retreat for
those with relaxation in mind. Relax in the gathering room on the ground level or on the waterfront
decks. Enjoy NS writings and art works (some for sale). Breakfast (which makes lunch redundant)
is served in the guest breakfast room. Visa,MC ✓B&B http://www3.ns.sympatico.ca/kwebb

---

Prospect

(west of Halifax; see also Peggy's Cove)

Prsala, Helena & Stephen O'Leary (Prospect B&B)   ☎& Fax (902) 852-4493, 1800-7258-732
1758 Prospect Bay Rd., Prospect, NS   B3T 2B3   E-mail: dynamic.realty@ns.sympatico.ca

From Hwy 103 take Hwy 3 and then Hwy 333 following signs for Peggy's Cove and Prospect.
Proceed to Prospect Village and continue all the way to end of road at the water. Look for B&B sign.

$75-125D $10Add.person 🍽 Meals (plus tax)   ► 12
🍽 Full, homebaked   🏠 Village, hist., 2-storey, view from guest
rooms, oceanfront, deck, quiet ⬛ 3D,2F(main & upper floor)
⊨ 1D,4Q,2S ⬛5Ensuite ★ TV, canoe & kayaks for
guests ⓌNo smoking, no pets ᚛Czech, some German,French
🏃 Magnificient walking trails along coastline, small sandy private
beach behind house
🚗 Peggy's Cove, City of Halifax, deep-sea fishing, boat tours
🐾 Professional couple in unique, restored Century-old former Convent overlooking scenic
Prospect Bay and situated at water's edge in very quiet location. (featured in Nat.Geographic in
1975). Relax by the water or in the large sitting room and enjoy the pleasant informal atmosphere.
There is a school-age boy in the host family. Perfect place for honeymoon and special occasions.
Private Island picnics and Eco Adventure Tour packages can be arranged. Visa,MC ✓B&B
http://www.destination-ns.com/lighthouse/prospectbnb/

Port Williams

(west of Wolfville; see also Kentville, Grand Pre)

Buckley, Ron & Carol (The Old Rectory Bed & Breakfast)   ☎ (902) 542-1815, Fax 2346
1519 Hwy 358, RR1, Port Williams, NS   B0P 1T0   E-mail: orectory@fox.nstn.ca

From Hwy 101 take Exit 11 to Rte 1 and then to Hwy 358. Located 3 km beyond Port Williams.

\$50S   \$60-75D   \$15Add.person   ► 8
May1-Oct31(other by arrangement)   Full,homebaked
Farm, 2-storey, hist., orchards, porch   3D (upstairs)
2T,1D,1Q,2R   2Private,1ensuite   ★F,TV,LF, guest
sunroom   No smoking, no pets
Stroll or sit in the surrounding apple orchard
Look-Off, fishing village with "Lobster on the Rocks", hiking
trails, rockhounding, historic Prescott House, Grand Pré Park

Retired professional couple in spacious, fully restored Victorian Century home nestled in tall
trees with 3 acres of orchard and garden with over 40 varieties of roses - located in the heart of
apple growing and market gardening area. Well informed hosts like to share their knowledge of the
local area. Retired Geologist host will take guests on geological tours in the area (at small fee).
Restored 1925 Model T on display. Home has been featured in various magazine. Visa ✔B&B

McMahon, Mary (Carwarden B&B)   ☎(902)678-7827,Fax0029,1-888-763-3320
640 Church St., RR1, Port Williams, NS   B0P 1T0   E-mail: carwarden@ns.sympatico.ca,

From Hwy 101 take Exit 11 to Rte 1 & right to Hwy 358. Proceed
4.4km to Church St, turn left and 2.2km to B&B.
\$50-55S   \$60-65D   \$15Add.person   ► 9A
May1-Oct31   Full, homebaked   Rural, 2-storey, hist.
view from guest rooms, 3 acres, veranda, quiet   3D,1F
(upstairs)   2D,1Q,3T   1Sh.w.g,2ensuite   ★LF,F,
separate entrance, large rooms, fans, off-street parking   No
smoking, no pets, not suitable for children

Bay of Fundy shores (tides, agate, driftwood, lobsters), Cape Split hiking trail, museums,
galleries, Acadia University, Theatre Festival, golfing, antiquing, fine dining

Restored 1910 Heritage home with great character. antique furnishings and beautiful view
across sweeping Canard Dykelands. Relax on the wide veranda, shaded by magnificient elms, a cool
& pleasant retreat for conversation, reading or idling. Savour a decadent breakfast in formal guest
dining room with fireplace, beamed ceiling - tea & crumbs in evening. Hostess is a former teacher,
30-year resident and thoroughly familiar with the area. There are dogs & cats. Visa,MC ✔B&B
http://www.bbcanada.com/1427.html

River Bourgeois

(on Cape Breton Isle east of Canso)

Chilvers, Glyn & Sharon (Grandma's House B&B)   ☎ (902) 535-2512, Fax 535-3713
RR1, River Bourgeois, Richmond County, NS   B0E 2X0   E-mail: sharon.chilvers@ns.sympatico.ca

From scenic Hwy 104 take Exit 47 to route 4. Located 6.6 km west of the town of St. Peters.
\$55S   \$65D   (off season rates available)   ► 6

Full, homebaked   Rural, 2-storey, 50acres, view from guest
rooms, riverfront, patio, quiet   3D (upstairs)   3D
1Sh.w.g.   ★Private entrance, hosts quarters are separate,
off-street parking   No smoking, no pets   English
(household language is French)
Nature path on property, Antique & Gift shop on premises
St. Peters, Port Hawkesbury, Rita MacNeils Tea Room, route
to Cabot Trail and Louisbourg

Retired couple in beautiful large 1912-built Victorian home decorated with antiques. Hostess
was born here and returned to operate a B&B. Breakfast is served in the elegant dining room
overlooking the river. Guests receive a discount on any purchase in the gift shop. Visa,MC ✔B&B
http://www3.ns.sympatico.ca/sharon.chilvers/grandmashbb.htm

Riverport
(west of Halifax; see also Lunenburg, Mahone Bay)

Driver, Margo & Derek (Heronwell B&B) ☎ (902) 766-1220
Box 17, 167 Lower LeHave Rd, Riverport, NS B0J 2W0   E-mail: heronwell@tallships.ca

From Bridgewater or Lunenburg, follow scenic Lighthouse Rte332
to Riverport. Look for sign at "T"jct by bridge.
$50-55S $55-60D (plus tax) ►6
🍽 Full, homebaked 🏠 Rural, village,,2-storey, older, view from
guest rooms, riverfront, patio, quiet, deck ■ 3D(upstairs)
🛏2T,2D(extra long) ➡ 1Sh.w.g., 1ensuite ★ F,TV, off-street
parking 🖐 Designated smoking area, no pets, not suitable for
children ⌇ some German & French
🏃 Fishing charters, Lahave Island & Marine Life Cruise, bird watching (Salt Marsh or River)
🚗 Lunenburg, Fishery Museum, Mahone Bay, Bridgewater, Chester, Peggys' Cove, many sandy
beaches, Ovens Natural Park
🚆Tastefully decorated Victorian home (ca1869) with the charm & character of the 19th Century
retained throughout, located on the water in historic village. Unwind and enjoy the glorious sunsets
& scenic view of the LaHave River. Well travelled young hosts enjoy sharing their home and
providing a friendly haven for the weary traveller. There is "Sophie" the Airedale dog in residence.
Visa ✓B&B www.bbcanada.com/1852.html

Sydney
(on Cape Breton Island's east coast; see also Sydney Mines)

McEwen, Evanel & Lloyd (Park Place B&B) ☎ (902) 562-3518, Fax (902) 567-6618
169 Park St., Sydney, NS B1P 4W7   E-mail: lemcewen@highlander.cbnet.ns.ca

From Hwy 125 take Exit 8 and turn right at 2nd set of lights. Turn
left again at Park St and proceed up 3 blocks.
$45S $50-60D $5Child $10Add.person ►6
🍽 Full, homebaked 🏠 Downtown, res., 3-storey, hist.,patio
■3D(upstairs) 🛏2T,2D ➡Sh.w.g. ★TV ♥ 🖐No pets
🏃 Bus Station, park, town/shopping center, hospital, Steel Mills
🚗 Louisbourg, Glace Bay, Miners Museum, historic North End
🚆 Interesting 1905-built home with curved walls in front hall
and living room. Congenial hosts have travelled and lived in many countries and display souvenir
artifact in the home. Enjoy the warm, genuine hospitality. VIP Service. Visa,MC,JVC

Sydney Mines
(on Cape Breton Isle east coast north of Sydney; see also Sydney)

Matthews, Clifford J. (Gowrie House Country Inn) ☎ (902)544-1050
139 Shore Rd,Sydney Mines,NS B1V 1A6   Fax(902)736-0077,1-800-372-1115

From Rt 105 (Trans Canada Hwy) take Exit 21 and follow Rt 305 north for 3 km.
$109-155S $119-155D $145-195Ste $239-295Cottage 🍴Meals ►15+

📅 May-Oct. 🍽 Full 🏠 Hist., acreage, quiet ■5D(upst),
plus deluxe caretaker's cottage 🛏2T,3Q,1K 🚗4private
★Air,Parking 🖐 Small pets only
🚗 Nfld Ferry, Louisbourg Fortress, Glace Bay Miners Museum,
Nfld Ferry Terminal, Cabot Trail
🚆 1825-built home enhances the feeling of comfortable elegance.
Reserve dinner for 4-course repast which may include delicacies
from waters, fields & gardens of NS. Visa,MC,Amex ✓B&B

Tatamagouche

(north of Truro; see also Wallace)

LeFresne, Shelley & James (Train Station Inn) ☎(902)657-3222,Fax(902)657-9091
21 Station Rd., Tatamagouche, NS B0K 1V0   E-mail: train.station@ns.sympatico.ca

$68.75(Station) $98-149(Caboose) $5Child   🍴(Full extra)   (plus tax)

From Amherst, take Hwy 6 (Sunrise Trail) east.
🍴 Cont., homebaked   🏠 Village, 2-storey & railway cars, view
from guest rooms, 2nd storey deck, , acreage, riverfront, patio,
porch, deck, quiet   ■ 4F(upstairs), plus suites in 7 caboose
╟5S,5D,7Q,3R(incl berths under the cupola)   🛁 10Private
★Air,TV,LF,KF, ceiling fans, separate entrance, air-conditioners,
off-street parking   ⊛ Smoking outside
🏃 Wander or cycle along abundant rail-trail beside the river, Train
Museum, Fraser Culture Centre, Tatamagouche Creamery-Coffee House & Market, camp fires
🚙 Village of Tatamagouche, Pictou, Truro, vineyards, Northumberland beaches, golfing, skiing
🚗 Historic Train Station & railway cars, tastefully restored, furnished with beautiful antiques
which capture the historical aura overlooking the green hills and the Waugh River on NS's Scottish
Sunshine Coast. Guest rooms are in the former station & railway cars and the former waiting
rooms are converted into a railway museum/cafe, where breakfast is served, while the station clock
tick-tocks away. Breakfast may be delivered to the caboose. Caboose mini suites area ideal for a
romantic get-away and family vacations. CCards ✒B&B www.trainstation.ns.ca

Wallace

(east of Amherst on northern shore; see also Tatamagouche)

Dominy, Daphne & Leslie (Jubilee Cottage Country Inn) ☎(902)257-2432,Fax 257-2510
Box 269 Hwy 6, Wallace NS B0K 1Y0   E-mail: jcottage@auracom.com, 1-800-481-9915
                                                        www.bbcanada.com/jubileecottage

Located on Rte 6 in the village of Wallace. Look for Civic No 13769.
from $60-95D $15Add.person   🍽 Meals   ► 7
❋ May-Oct   🍴 Full   🏠 Village, 3-storey, hist., acreage, view
from guest rooms, ocean at back, quiet   ■ 3D(upstairs)
╟1D,2Q,cot   🛁 3Ensuite (incl.2whirlpool)   ★ TV,F & ceiling
fans in guest rooms, private entrance, off-street parking, guest
quarters are separate   ⊛ No smoking, children min. age 10
🏃 Wallace Bay, watch Blue Herons and Canada Geese
🚙 Natural wildlife area(hiking trail), golfing Jost Vineyard Farm with winery store
🚗 Tastefully decorated home (ca 1912) located in historic village on the Sunrise Trail near the
warmest salt water beaches north of the Carolinas. Relax in the screen house. Ask about romance
and golf packages. Hosts were nominated for 1997 Accommodation Award of Excellence for NS.
Five-course candlelight dinners a house speciality; recommended by "where to eat in Canada".
Breakfast is served in guest breakfast room. There is a cat in residence. Visa, MC ✒B&B

Windsor

(north-west of Halifax; see also Wolfville, Grand Pre)

Boegel, Sharon & Terry (Boegel's Bed & Breakfast) ☎ (902) 798-4183, Fax (902) 798-1063
145 Dill Rd., RR1, Windsor, NS B0N 2T0   E-mail: boegelbb@glinx.com

Take Hwy 1 to Exit 5 & Hwy 14 west to Chester Rd, left on Dill Rd.
$40S $50-60D $10Add.person (plus tax)   ► 4+
🍴 Full, homebaked   🏠 Rural, split-level, acreage, view, patio,
deck   ■2D(upstairs)   ╟4T,2cots   🛁1Sh.w.g.   ★F,TV/VCR,
barbeque, ceiling fans in guest rooms, ramp to front door, host
quarters are separate   ⊛ No smoking, no pets
🏃 Walks by nearby pond with ducks, turtles & spring peepers,
Birthplace of Hockey
🚙 Annapolis V., Halifax, southshore beaches, highest tides
🚗 Comfortable hillside home with a nice view of the valley, situated just outside the City on 1.75
acres and in a very quiet area. Relax and feel just like at home. Hostess is a hobby quilter. Fax
service available (fee charged outgoing). There is a cat in residence. Visa,MC ✒B&B

Wolfville

(north-west of Halifax; see also Pt.Williams, Kentville, Grand Pre)

McKenzie, Brian & Lisa (Garden House B&B)   ☎ (902) 542-1703
150 Main St., Box 412, Wolfville, NS B0P 1X0

From Annapolis Royal/Digby follow signs to Annapolis Valley on Hwy101 nd take Exit 11 into
Wolfville. Drive through town and look for B&B located 2 blocks from Tourist Information Centre.

$50-65S $60-80D $15Add.person   ► 6A,2Ch
Apr1-Dec15 (other by special arrangement)   Full   Downtown,
res, 2-storey, hist., view, 1 acre, quiet   3(upstairs)   2D,1Q,1P
1Private,1sh.w.g. ★TV in guest parlour, sep.entr., on-site parking No
smoking indoors, no pets, certaian dates 2nights minimum   French,
German, Dutch
Downtown area, Acadia University, Atlantic Theatre Festival, shops,
restaurants, antiques, historic properties, strolling on dykes & bird watching,
cycling, Acadia Bus Line and city bus
Various swimming "holes", beaches, hiking, historic Center Grand Pré,
40ft tides (world's highest), Cape Split Lookoff, Blomidon Prov.Park
Professional hosts in comfortable heritage home (ca 1830) (former Minister's house), nestled
amids stately elms and a sunny cottage garden with a sweeping view over fields of hay, Minas Basin
and Cape Blomidon, and located close to center of town. Host also teaches B&B courses in nearby
college and hostess is an airline stewardess. There are school-age boys (17&13) in the family, plus a
golden retriever dog. Breakfast is served in quaint guest breakfast room. Visa,MC ✓B&B

Yarmouth

(on south-west coast of NS)

Semple, George & Joan (Murray Manor)   ☎ & Fax (902) 742-9625
225 Main St., Yarmouth, NS B5A 1C6   E-mail: mmanor@auracom.com

Located across from Ferry Terminal and Tourist Bureau on the
main street in town.
$55S $75D   ► 6A
Full, homebaked   Downtown, 2-storey, hist.,
acreage,historic, quiet   3D(upstairs)   2T,1D,1Q,1R (incl.
4-poster)   2Sh.w.g.(incl.1on main level) ★ Separate
entrance, extensive library, harbour view from 2 guest room prayer
windows (Gothic), robes & towel/showermat caddy for each room,
off-street parking, secure garage for motorcycles and bicycles   French (Acadian)
Ferry to Bar Hbr. & Portland, bus/airport terminals, shops, restaurants, on hist.walking tour
Lighthouse, Look-out/old Finnish cemetery, golfing, large shopping area, scenic coastal drives
Retired military family & Yarmouth natives in beautifully maintained Gothic Regency
Heritage house (ca 1825), surrounded by lovely grounds with Rhododendrons (over 100 years) &
green house tucked in behind flowering shrubs & stone wall. Complimentary pre-dinner wine prior
to 6pm. A wonderful place for honeymoon and special occasions. Pick-up and delivery to airport,
bus & Halifax Shuttle. One room environmentally friendly. Visa ✓B&B
www.auracom.com/cts/mmanor

Newfoundland & Labrador

Cape Onion

Engle

Rocky Harbour
Woody Point

Change Isle
Hillgrade
Fogo
Roberts Arm

Lewisporte

Corner Brook
Stephenville

Glovertown
Eastport
Port Blandford
Trinity

Port-aux-Basques

English Hbr.West

Heart's Delight
St.John's

Mount Carmel

Government of Newfoundland/Labrador
Dep't of Development (Tourism Branch)   toll-free 1-800 563-6353
Box 8730 St. John's, NF   A1B   4K2

For CN Marine Ferry schedules and rates contact:
Reservation Bureau, Maritime Atlantic   toll-free 1-800 341-7981 USonly

Box 250, North Sydney, NS B2A 3M3   (902) 794-5700

Cape Onion

(northern tip of Nfld)

Adams, David and Barbara (Tickle Inn at Cape Onion) ☎ (709) 452-4321 (709) 739-5503
RR1, Box 62, Cape Onion, NF A0K 4J0

Take Rte430 (Viking Trail) all the way north to Rte436 (in direction of L'Anse aux Meadows) and
continue past Pistolet Bay. After a short distance, turn left onto Rte437, and then left to Raleigh
and Ship Cove, Cape Onion. At Raleigh turn right and proceed 10km to B&B.
$50-55S $55-65D $10Add.person 🍽 Meals (plus tax) ►8

🌺 June-Sept. 🍵 Cont., homebaked 🏠 Rural, hist., 3-storey,
9-acre, view, oceanfront, quiet ■3D,1F 🛏2T,3D,2cots
🛁2Sh.w.g.,1sh.w.h. ★F,KF,LF,TV in parlour with antique organ,
separate entrance, parking 🚭Smoking outside, pets (may be
considered with special arrangement)
🚶 Beachcombe, watch whale/iceberg, nature walk/hike trails,
🚗 L'Anse aux Meadows (World Heritage Site), St.Anthony (Grenfell
Museum, fishplant, outport communities
📣 Fourth generation family in historic home, attractively restored, traditionally decorated and
located in beautiful pastoral setting on beachfront property. Enjoy the warm Newfoundland
hospitality. Relax in the parlour around the Franklin stove and listen to the legends and music
traditional to the area and Province. Fall asleep to the sounds of seabreezes and waves lapping the
shore. House specialty: Local seafood dishes. Reduced rates for 2 or more nights stay. 🖊B&B

Change Islands

(on north coast north of Gander; see also Fogo, Hillgrade)

Oake, Beulah & Eddie (Seven Oakes Island Inn & Cottages) ☎ (709) 621-3256
Box 57, Change Islands, NF A0G 3R0 off season (709) 635-2247

From TCH East of Gander, take Rte 330, turn left onto Rte 331 then right onto Rte 335 to
Farewell. Or: from TCH West, take Rte 340 to Lewisporte, turn right onto Rte 331, then left onto
Rte 335 to Farewell. Relax on the 20 min scenic boat ride to Change Islands.
$49-69S/D $85D(Cottage) $10Add. person 🍽 Meals 🍷 Extra ►16+

🌺 May-Oct(extended upon request) 🏠 Village, res, 3-storey, hist.,
6-acres, view from guest rooms, ocean-front, patio, deck, quiet
■8(upper & lower level) + cottages, guest quarters are separate
🛏T,D,Q 🛁 Private ★ F,LF,TV room & Nfld books & crafts,
phone/fax service, row-boats & bicycles rentals,boat charters to Fogo,
parking 🚭No smoking, no pets
🚶 Playground/picnic area, hiking/walking trails, explore miles of
shoreline, cod-jigging, whale-watching, iceberg-viewing
📣 Warm and friendly welcome in spacious, restored historic 110-year old former merchant's
home, a chosen location by artists & honeymooners, situated on the original site of the "Squid
Jiggin Ground". Relax on the large wrap-around deck with a breathtaking panoramic ocean view or
in the parlor by the open fireplace. Enjoy traditional Newfoundland meals in the spacious dining
room. Small tours & dinner meetings can be accommodated. Also available housekeeping cottages
by the ocean. 🖊 CC

Corner Brook
(on west coast of Province;see also Woody Point, Rocky Hbr)

Swyer, Edna and Eldon (Humber Gallery Hospitality Home)   ☎ & Fax (709) 634-2660
Box 15, Corner Brook, NF   A2H 6C3   E-mail: eldonswyer@thezone.net

Located 15 km east of downtown on the TCH (Exit 10) in Little Rapids at 26 Roberts Drive.
$50S $55D $10Add.person (child free under age 5) 🍽 Meals (Senior Discounts) ►6
⚜ June-Sept.(Feb/March for skiing) 🍷 Cont. 🏠 Rural, quiet,
acreagae, deck ■ 3D (main and upper floor) ⊨1T,2D,1R
🛁Sh.w.g. ★F,KF,TV, barbecue 🖐No pets 〰some French
🕴 Humber River, nature & x/c ski trails, fall colour spectacles,
U-pick strawberry farms
🚙 Corner Brook, Marble Mountain Ski Resort,beaches on Deer
Lake, Gros Morne National Park, Bay Island sites
🐾 Very impressive home with Cathedral ceilings and finished in cedar, pine, BC Fir in the heart
of the Scenic Humber Valley Reserve. Excellent place for an overnight stop when going or coming
from Gros Morne Nat Park. Relax on the sundeck, enjoy the spectacular view. Guide for salmon or
trout fishing available. The Brit.Royal family has visited this area many times.Visa ✔B&B
http://www.bbcanada.com/3304.html

Wilton, Claude & Ulah (Wilton's Bed & Breakfast)   ☎ & Fax (709) 634-5796
Marble Drive, Steady Brook, NF   A2H 2N2

Phone for directions.
$35S $45-50D $10Child   ►6
🍷 Homebaked 🏠 Village, 2-storey, 3 acres, view from guest
rooms, patio, deck, quiet ■ 2D,1Ste(main & upper floor)
⊨2S,1D,1K 🛁 1Ensuite, 1sh.w.h. ★ Guest TV room, private
entrance, host quarters are separate, off-street parking 🖐 No
smoking, no pets
🕴 Great Atlantic Salmon Humber River, Marble Mountain skiing
🚙 Gros Morne National Park, explore the Bay of Islands, Blow-me-Down Mountain, C.Brook
🐾 Warm & friendly hospitalty in spacious modern home with deck & garden. Enjoy the close
proximity to Water Falls and Ski Mountain. Licensed fishing guide available. ✔B&B

Eastport
(south-east of Gander; see also Glovertown)

Pinsent, Lillian & Walter (Pinsent's B&B & Art Studio)   ☎ (709) 677-3021
Box 85, 17 Church St., Eastport, NF   A0G 1Z0

From TCH, take Rte 310 Exit to Eastport at west entrance to Terra Nova Nat. Park. Drive through
park and through Sandringham. Turn left at T-Intersection in Eastport enroute to Salvage and to
3rd house on right. Situated near Credit Union.
$40S $50D $10Add.person   🍽 Meals(Oct-Apr)   ►4
🍷 Full, homebaked 🏠 Rural, village, older, 2-storey, salt-box
design home, view, patio, quiet ■ 2D(upstairs) ⊨2D,1R
🛁1Sh.w.g. ★TV,LF, parking 🖐Smoking area provided
🕴 Stroll on banks to 2 beautiful beaches, art-studio/frame shop,
Family Funland with Fairground tours & pond, over 100-year old
Anglican Church, x/c skiing from doorstep, camping
🚙 Gander Airport, Terra Nova Park, hiking, beautiful fjords, boat tours, whale watching, ferry
🐾 Delightful, quaint saltbox house (ca 1905) is surrounded by whispering aspens and gardens
located where the mountains meet the sea. Enjoy the salt sea breeze rising from Salvage Bay. Enjoy
happy memories and a restful night. Hostess from Saskatchewan and host, an ex-mountie turned
artist, delight in "talking up Newfoundland". Guests are invited to view the studio exhibits in a
separate building on the premises. There is a resident cat. ✔B&B

Stephan, Lynn & Larry (Laurel Cottage B&B)   ☎ (709) 677-3138, Fax (709) 677-2979
41 Bank Rd., Eastport, NF   A0G 1Z0   E-mail: laurel@nf.sympatico.ca, 1-888-677-3138

From Trans Canada Hwy exit onto Rte 310 to Easport (road to the beaches). Turn left at stop sign
and proceed to ocean. Turn left on Bank Rd and watch for sign.
$52-65S $55-65D   🍽 Meals   ► 6

🍴 Full   🏠 Rural, village, 2-storey, older, view from guest rooms,
oceanfront, wrap-around veranda, porch, quiet ■ 3D(upstairs)
⊨2T,1D,1Q ⟶1Private,1sh.w.g. ★F,TV,LF ⓦDesignated
smoking area,not suitable for children
🧍 Sandy beaches with lagoon (Eastport & Sandy Cove),
beachcombing, surfing, canoeing, Summer Beach Festival, local
arts & crafts, Art Gallery with artist in residence, birdwatching,
hiking/snowmobiling/x-c skiing from doorstep, sea kayaking
🚗 Gander Airport, Terra Nova Nat. Park, Twin Rivers Golf Club, White Hills Ski Resort,
whale/dolphin watching tours, spectacular sea coast scenic drives, ferry to St.Brendan'Island
🔫 Lovingly restored English-style Cottage (ca 1920) with antiques and eclectic furnishings. An
abundance of natural light that spills into the rooms combined with fine china & art work &
fireplace create a memorable ambiance. Enjoy the spectacular view of the intrinsic beauty of the
coastline. Breakfast is served in the guest breakfast room overlooking the ever-changing sea. Visa
✒B&B www3.nf.sympatico.ca/laurel

Englee   *(on north-east coast south of St.Anthony)*

Reeves, Holly & John (Reeve's Ocean View B&B)   ☎ (709) 866-2531
Box 217, 69 Church Rd., Englee, NF   A0K 2J0

From TCH take Rte 430 north to Plum Point and then travel east on Rte 432 and 433 to Englee.
$45S $50D $5Add.person   🍽 Meals   ► 6

🍴Full 🏠Res, multi-storey, view from guest rooms, patio, quiet,
oceanfront ■3D(upstairs) ⊨3D,1cot ⟶2Ensuite, 1sh.w.h.
★KF,LF,TV in guest room, parking ⓦNo pets
🧍 Whale watching and iceberg viewing from front patio
🔫 Newfoundland hospitality in quiet and private surroundings.
Relax and enjoy beautiful views. Hosts will take guests on a boat
tour to photograph icebergs and whales. Visa ✒B&B

English Harbour West   *(on southshore (Fortune Bay))*

Petite, Debbie (Olde Oven Inn)   ☎ (709) 888-3461, (709) 888-4402
Gen.Del.,English Harbour West, Fortune Bay, Nfld   A0H 1M0   Fax (709) 888-3441

From Trans Canada Hwy (Rte 1), take Rte 360 at the Bishop's Falls junction and travel all the way
to Dept. of Hwys. Depot. Turn left onto Rte 362 and keep following the signs to Inn.
$40S $50D   (plus Tax)   🍽 Meals   (Rates for longer stays/off season)   ► 8A

🍴 Cont. 🏠 Rural, older, view, patio, quiet, oceanfront ■4D
(upstairs) ⊨ 4D,1R,1P ⟶2Sh.w.g. ★ LF,KF,TV in guest
room, parking ⓦ No smoking
🧍 Hiking, rowing, berry picking, outdoor lobster boil-up avail.
🚗 Yarn Point Craft shop, trout & salmon fishing, lighthouses
(St.Jacques, Sagona Isle.)
🔫 Built in 1920, charming home retains many of its original
features with a super view of the harbour and located in a small
pretty fishing community. Arrangements can be made to take guests out fishing for cod, lobster,
salmon etc. Guests can also go on the private longliner to visit remote communities where the
people were re-located. Pick-up to/from Gander airport available. CCards ✒B&BA

Fogo
(on Fogo Island - north-east coast; see also Change Isle)

Payne, Mrs. John (Payne's Hospitality Home)   ☎ (709) 266-2359
Box 201, Fogo, NF   A0G 2B0

Take Fogo Ferry (5 return trips daily in summer) to Fogo Island from Farewell (near Stoneville).

$28-32S $56D   ▶7
🍵 Cont.   🏠 Townhouse, quiet, view   ■3(upstairs) ⊨3S,2D
cot, crib   ⌁1.5Sh.w.g.   ★TV   🐾No pets.
🎣 Store, church, watch fishing boats and icebergs (in season) from
nearby hills, whale watching,
🚗 Ferry dock, sandy beaches, crab factory tours
🗝 Enjoy the Atlantic Ocean view and lovely breezes from the
hill tops in comfortable island home located in historic settlement on rugged, scenic Island. Guests
can participate in the local Folk Festival (August).

Glovertown
(east of Gander; see also Eastport, Port Blandford)

Churchill, Doug & Linda (The Lilac Inn B&B)   ☎ & Fax (709) 533-6038
Pinetree Rd., Rte 310, Box 221, Glovertown, NF   A0G 2L0   E-mail: lilacs@thezone.net

$50-55S $60-65D $65F $10Add.person   ▶9

From Hwy1 take Exit 25. Drive through town, keep right for 3km.
Turn left on Pinetree Rd.
🍵 Full, homebaked   🏠 Res., village, hist., 3-storey, view from
guest rooms, veranda, quiet   ■2D,1F(upstairs)   ⊨1S,1D,2Q,1R
⌁2Private, 1ensuite   ★ F,LF,TV avail.in guest rooms, off-street
parking   🐾No pets, no smoking
🎣 Bird watching, "Whimsicals" store/café, Tickleview Restaurant
🚗 Terra Nova Nat.Park, scenic drive around Eastport Peninsula,
Splash'n Putt Amusement Park, Twillingate, quaint fishing village of Salvage
🗝 Warm welcome and friendly Newfoundland hospitality in restored Victorian home, nestled in a
lovely garden with lilac trees and old-fashioned rose bushes; situated on a quiet street in the centre
of town. Relax on the beautiful veranda. There is a cat in residence. Visa ✓B&B

Heart's Delight
(west of St.John's)

Colbourne, Eric (The Beacon B&B)   ☎ 1-877-388-2850
Box 283, Heart's Delight, NF   A0B 2A0

$55-65S/D $5Child $10Add.person $75F   🍽 Meals   ▶8
Phone for directions.
🍵 Full   🏠 Village, raised bungalow, view, oceanfront,
deck,quiet, secluded   ■3D,1Ste (main & ground level)
⊨2S,2T,2Q,cot   ⌁4Private   ★LF,TV in guest room, ceiling
fans, off-street parking   🐾No smoking
🎣 Whale watching, hiking trails
🗝 Warm welcome in comfortable home overlooking the town of
Heart's Delight and Trinity Bay within a beautifully landscaped
setting. The home contains a collection of Aboriginal and Newfoundland art, as well as a small
library. Enjoy fine Newfoundland cuisine and true Newfoundland hospitality. Breakfast is served in
guest breakfast room. There is a dog in residence. Visa,MC

Hillgrade

(north of Lewisporte; see also Fogo; Change Isle)

Gidge, Dora & Alvin (Sunset Bed & Breakfast) ☎ & Fax (709) 628-5209
General Delivery, Hillgrade, NF A0G 2S0

Located on the road to the Isles New World Island, 10km from Twillingate.

$40S $45D $10Child/Add.person Meals ► 6A,2Ch
Summer only Full, homebaked Rural, split-level, view from guest rooms, patio, porch, quiet, oceanfront 2D,1F (main & upper level) 3D,1T,cot 3Private ★ LF,TV in sunroom, ceiling fans, off-street parking No smoking
Beach and Pier, new hiking trail overlooking Friday's Bay, occasional whale watching and iceberg viewing, berry picking
Twillingate
Warm welcome and friendly Newfoundland hospitality in quiet peaceful area with large garden for adults and children. There is a telescope for star-gazers. Enjoy the beautiful sunset from the patio or sunroom. Breakfast is served in the sunroom overlooking Friday's Bay. Visa ✓B&B

Lewisporte

(west of Gander; see also Roberts Arm)

Leschied, Carl and June (Northgate B&B) ☎ (709) 535-2258, Fax (709) 535-2239
106 Main St., Lewisporte, NF A0G 3A0

Travelling on TCH from Grand Falls proceed to Notre Dame junction. Proceed 10km on Hwy 340 to Lewisporte.
$40S $55D $10Add.person Meals ► 8
Homebaked(wholesome) Res.,view,older,1.5-storey, oceanfront 4D(upst) 2T,3D 3Private ★F,large veranda, parking No smoking German
Labrador Ferry Terminal, museum and craft shop, restaurants, whale watching and fishing tours
Two major salmon rivers, strawberries "u-pick" in July and August, Provincial parks, historic Twillingate (view icebergs in May and June)
Large home decorated in country style, overlooking Lewisporte Harbour. Relax on the veranda and enjoy the harbour activities or warm up by the cozy fire on cool evenings. Hosts operate a 27 ft tour boat, featuring trips with lunch beside icebergs (in season), to Beothuk Indian Island haunts, cod jigging & island cookouts (overnight at remote island cabin).Visa ✓B&B
http://www.bbcanada.com/3130.html

Mount Carmel

(south-west of St.John's)

Jardine, Rosalind (Salmonier Country Manor - The Convent Inn) ☎ & Fax (709) 521-2778
Main Road, Mount Carmel, St.Mary's Bay, NF A0B 2M0 Fax (709) 521-2788

From St.John's on Rte 1 (TCH), take Salmonier Line (Rte 90) onto Rte 93 to Mount Carmel.
$69S $79-99D $10Child/Add.person Meals (plus tax) ► 18+
May-Nov Full, homebaked Rural, hillside, 2-storey, hist., view from guest rooms, riverfront, deck, quiet 8(upstairs) 2T,1D,5Q,4R Private ★ LF,F,TV in guest rooms, jacuzzi, fans, off-street parking, guest quarters are separate No smoking, no pets
Nature hiking trails and walkways, riverbank leading to ocean
St.Mary's Bay Ecological Center, Cataract Falls, Salmonier Nature Park, golf course, caribou gazing, Avalon Wilderness Reserve, Argentia (ferry to Nova Scotia), 7 scheduled Salmon Rivers
Former Convent owned by Presentation Sisters who taught school in the community, located 1 hour scenic drive from St.John's. Country breakfast and traditional NF foods served in the dining room. House feature: "Christmas and the Mummers" (July & Aug) a NF traditional skit with NF Christmas dinner (reservations required). Browse in the gift shop featuring Newfoundland artisans. Catering to specialty affairs. Gift Certificates.Visa,MC ✓ B&B

Port-aux-Basques

(south of Corner Brook)

Gibbons, Elizabeth and Henry (Caribou Bed & Breakfast)   ☎ (709) 695-3408
Box 53, 30 Grand Bay Rd., Port-aux-Basques, NF A0N 1K0   E-mail: douglasg@thezone.net

Located 5 min drive from the Gulf Ferry linking Newfoundland to the Mainland.
$43-48S $49-54D $6-10Child $10Add.person (Cots extra)   ► 10A,4Ch
⬛ Summer only ⬤ Cont.(extensive) 🏠 Res., ranch-style,
quiet ■ 4(main level) ⊨ 2S,4D,4R ⬜ 2Private,
1sh.w.g. ★ TV,F, parking ⬤ No smoking
🕴 Shopping center, churches, seafood restaurants, Provincial
Interpretation center, sea, beaches
🚗 Ferry to Nova Scotia, Regional Museum, ancient Rose Blanche
Lighthouse, Dorset Eskimo Site, long stretches of Cape Ray
beaches and large sand dunes, scenic Codroy Valley
🐾 Convenient location at the Gateway to Newfoundland. Informative adult-occupied home is a
great starting point for a trip to the rest of Newfoundland and Labrador. Breakfast is served in time
to catch the ferry boat. Free brochure on request. Visa,MC ✓B&B home.thezone.net/~gibbons

Port Blandford

(south of Glovertown; see also Trinity)

Parsons, Rhoda & Vernon (Terra Nova Hospitality Home)   ☎ (709) 543-2260
Gen.Del,Port Blandford,NF A0C 2G0   E-mail: terranova@nf.sympatico.ca, Fax(709)543-2241
Located 2km east of Terra Nova National Park.
$45S $55D $65F $8Add.person 🍴 Meals   ► 14
⬤ Full 🏠 Rural, 3-storey, view from guest rooms, oceanfront,
patio, deck, quiet ■ 1S,5D,1Ste(ground, main & upper level)
⊨2T,5D,2Q,2R,cot, crib ⬜ 5Private, 1sh.w.g., 1shw.h.
★Air,F,TV,LF,KF, exercise room, sauna/hot tub, wheel-chair
access ⬤ Designated smoking area, no pets
🚗 Terra Nova National Park with many walking trails
🐾 Friendly hosts in spacious new home built especially for B&B and cozy hospitality. Relax in
the Great Room by the fireplace or in the sauna. Also self-cont. cabins (incl. honeymoon &
anniversary cottage) on site. Guiding service for snowmobiling, ice fishing, hiking etc. available.
Ideal place for larger groups, business meetings etc. ✓CC www.terranova.nfld.net

Roberts Arm

(north of Grand Falls; see also Lewisporte)

Warr, Evelyn and Bruce (Lake Crescent Inn)   ☎(709) 652-3067/3568, Fax (709) 652-3327
Box 69, Roberts Arm, NF A0J 1R0

Located 26 km off Hwy 1 on Rte 380 and approx. halfway between Port aux Basque and St. John's.
Drive along the beautiful Beothuk Trail to Roberts Arm. (1st residence when entering town)
$32S $37-45D $10Add.person 🍴 Meals   ► 12A,2Ch
⬤ Cont.(healthfood conscious) 🏠 Rural, res., multi-storey, view, lakefront, patio, quiet
■3D,1F(main and upper level) ⊨ 2T,4D,1S,1P ⬜ 2Private, 2Sh.w.g.,1shower ★ TV
parking, wheel-chair access, whirlpool ⬤ No pets
🕴 Crescent Lake Beach (see "Cressie, the Lake Monster"), Medical Clinic, stores, library, quiet
beaches for strolling, Hazelnut Adventure & Hiking Trail, Boardwalk (great for birdwatching)
🚗 Iceberg viewing & whale-watching (in season), fine dining, scenic Tommy's Arm River
(Atlantic Salmon fishing), quaint & interesting fishing villages, Long Island (5min ferry ride), old
mining town of Pilley's Island & Heritage Centre
🐾 Enjoy sights of icebergs and the "Upside Down Tree" on your drive to the B&B. Modern home
overlooks Crescent Lake (guests are invited to bring the camera, in case the "Lakemonster"
appears). Relax in the whirlpool and enjoy a quiet talk or visit the antique room. A great place to
use as a base from which to explore the beautiful area and vast, rugged scenery. Boating trips can
be arranged. CCards ✓B&B

Rocky Harbour

(north of Corner Brook; see also Woody Point)

Wentzell, Sarah (Evergreen B&B)   (709) 458-2692, 1-800-905-3494
General Delivery Rocky Harbour, NF A0A 4N0

Follow Rte430 (Viking Trail) north from Deer Lake for 70km. At first intersection to Rocky Harbour, turn left and proceed 1km to B&B.
$35S $40D $5Child $10Cot   🍴 Meals   ►8
🍲 Full, homebaked   🏠 Res, bungalow, patio, quiet, secluded   ■4(main & ground level)
🛏2T,3D   🛁2Sh.w.g., 1sh.w.h.   ★ KF,LF,TV,off-street parking, guest quarters are separate
🚭No smoking, no pet
🕴 Recreation Complex, numerous trails for young & old, bus from Corner Brook and airport
🚐 Deer Lake Airport, Corner Brook, Gros Morne National Park & World Heritage Site, indoor swimming pool with hot-tub,
☛ Spacious home surrounded by beautiful scenery and centrally located. The perfect place to visit Gros Morne National Park or to take a trip up Western Brook Fjord and Bonny Bay (by boat). Relax on the large patio or in the backyard and enjoy great Newfoundland hospitality from the heart. Breakfast (including a variety of NF jams) is served from menu in bright and sunny breakfast area. Visa,MC ✔ B&B

St. John's

(on east coast)

Badrudin, Trish (Waterford Manor)   ☎ (709) 754-4139, Fax (709) 754-4155
185 Waterford Bridge Rd., St.John's, NF A1E 1C7   E-mail: info@waterfordmanor.nf.ca

Phone for directions.
$80-165D   (plus tax)   ► 14
🍲 Full   🏠 Res., sub., hist., river at back, quiet   ■ 3D, 3Ste
(upstairs)   🛏 4D,2Q,1K   🛁 3Private, 3ensuite(jaccuzi)   ★F
(in suites), TV in guest rooms, table fans, off-street parking, guest
quarters are separate   🚬 Designated smoking area, no pets, not
suitable for children
🚐 Downtown, shopping mall
🕴 Park-like setting with gazebo and river on property, bus route, Bowering Park
☛ Victorian-style B&B in authentic Heritage house built in 1870 with period furnishings and conducive elegant atmosphere. Ideal place for special occasions and meetings. Breakfast is served in special guest breakfast room. CCards ✔B&B www.waterfordmanor.nf.ca

---

Holden, Bob and Cindy (Compton House)   ☎ (709) 739-5789, Fax (709) 738-1770
26 Waterford Bridge Rd., St. John's, NF A1E 1C6   E-mail: comptonhouse@nf.sympatico.ca

Located downtown and west of water street. Phone for directions.
$59-189S $69-199D $15Add.person   ► 16A
🍲 Full, homebaked   🏠 Downtown, res., hist., patio, acreage,
quiet   ■ 5D,3Ste (main and upper floor)   🛏4D,5Q,2P,2R
🛁1Private, 5ensuite   ★9F,Air,KF,3whirlpools, separate entrance,
TV and phones in guest rooms, parking, sunroom   🚭No pets, no
smoking, no children
🕴 Downtown St. John's, shopping, business section, restaurants
and night life on George St., Harbour Charters and boat tours,
Bowring and Victoria Parks, on main bus route
🚐 Cape Spear and Signal Hill National Historic Pks, Bird Island and Cape St. Mary's Bird Sanct.
☛ Designated a Heritage home, elegant Victorian Mansion is set in a large garden and has been beautifully restored and furnished with antiques. Full English-style fireside breakfasts are elegantly served in the formal dining room. Hosts are very knowledgeable about local history and their home town and welcome any inquiries. CCards ✔B&B

St. John's (cont'd)

Keating, Patrick (The Roses B&B)   ☎ (709) 726-3336, 1-877-767-3722 (ROSES BB)
9 Military Rd., St. John's NF   A1C 2C3

From Hwy 1 take downtown Exit; from airport go to Nfld Hotel & look for B&B 2 blocks west.

$60S $75-85D $10Add.person   (plus tax)   ► 16
🍴 Full (self-serve weekends)   🏠 Downtown, hist., view from guest rooms,
patio, porch, quiet   ■ 2D,3F (main, upper & lower levels)   ⊨ 8D
2Private,2ensuite,1sh.w.g.   ★ F,TV in guest rooms, separate entrance,
off-street parking   No smoking, no pets
🧍 Downtown, churches, museum, waterfront, Colonial Bldg. restaurants,
walking trails, Quidi Vidi Lake, Commissary House, bus stop
🚗 Signal Hill, Cape Spear, Quidi Vidi Village, harbour & waterfront
Classic turn-off-the-Century home fully restored maintaining its
originality & furnished with many antiques, situated in central location.
Enjoy the beautiful view of the St.John's Harbour from the top floor. Breakfast is served in guest
breakfast room. CCards ✔B&B

Knoechel, Jill & Roy (McCoubrey Manor)   ☎ (709) 722-7577, Fax 579-7577
6-8 Ordnance St., St.John's, NF   A1C 3K7   E-mail: mccmanor@nfld.com, 1-888-753-7577

Located directly across from Hotel Newfoundland.
$69-139S/D $10Add.person   (plus tax)   ► 14+
🍴 Homebaked, buffet   🏠 Downtown, res., hist., 3-storey,
harbour view from guest rooms, porch, deck   ■ 7 (plus one apt)
(main, upstairs & ground levels)   ⊨D,Q   Ensuite
★KF,LF,F,TV/VCR/phone & ceiling fans in guest rooms, double
jacuzzi, indiv.thermostats, private entrance, off-street parking,
guest quarters are separate   Smoking on veranda, no pets, children min.age 8
🧍 Downtown shops, restaurants, Government House, Provincial Archives, NFld Museum, art
galleries, Memorial University   🚗 Signal Hill, City Hall, the Harbour, nightlife of George Street
Queen Ann-style heritage home with spacious rooms, graced with antiques, wide wood trim,
high ceilings and bay windows. Enjoy the relaxing breakfast atmosphere and wine & cheese in the
evening. Rest on the front veranda with its unique garden setting right in the heart of downtown.
Deluxe suite is perfect for honeymoon or special occasions. Also available: housekeeping apts for
longer stays or for families. CCards, ✔B&B   www.mccoubrey.com

Morrison, Maxine (Pleasant Mem'ries)   ☎ (709) 753-2378, Fax (709) 781-0065
110 Pleasant St., St. John's, NF   A1E 1L4   1-877-853-2377

Located in downtown, near waterfront & near Delta Hotel.
$39S $57D $10Child   off-season rates (Sept-May) available.   ► 6
🍴 Full, homebaked   🏠 Downtown, hist., 3-storey, view, patio, quiet   ■ 3 (upstairs)
⊨2T,2D,P   1Sh.w.g.   ★ TV in 3rd-floor common area with view, street parking
Smoking on patio, no pets
🧍 Waterfront & Harbour, Signal Hill, Water St & Duckworth St, Quidi Vidi Village, Apothecary
Hall, churches, museum, Murray Premises
Warm and friendly welcome in quiet and cozy home, built in the late 1800 and elegantly
furnished, hovering a few minutes stroll from the excitement and adventure of downtown. Enjoy
the splendid full view of the historical waterfront with the harbour and Signal Hill. "This B&B
experience promises to be a melange of legendary hospitality that lulls the mind and calms the
spirit as the guests spend time in the capital city during vacation or on business".Visa ✔ B&B

St. John's (cont'd)

Peters, Janet & Arie Vander-Reyden (Prescott Inn B&B)   ☎ (709) 753-7733,
Box 204, 19 Military Rd., St. John's, Nfld A1C 2C3   E-mail: jpeters@nfld.com, Fax (709) 753-6036

Phone for directions.
$50-105S/D $90-120Ste(with kitchen)   ▶ 14A,3-4Ch
🍳 Full   🏠 Downtown, res., hist., view, patio, quiet ■ 6D,3Ste
(main/upper floor) ⊨2S,2T,5D,1P ⊐3Sh.w.g.,1ensuite,
whirlpool ★KF,F & TV in guest room, sep.entrance, parking
🚭Restricted smoking ⌇German, Dutch, some French
🧍 Downtown St. John's, historic St. Thomas' Church, Hotel Nfld,
Commissariat House, Lieut Gov's Residence, Prov Archives
🚗 Scenic Marine Drive, Marine Biology Laboratory, Quidi Vidi Village, Puffin Bird Sanctuary
🐾 Tastefully decorated home is centrally located and contains a small collection of
Newfoundland/Labrador novels and literature as well as an extensive Art Collection (for viewing
and purchase). Hosts "keep on top" of all local entertainment and are very knowledgeable about
Provincial and local happenings and can assist with plans. Hosts also operate "On your own
Itinerary Tours" Also avail. cottage (2suites) with a "million $ view" of St.John's Harbour. ✐B&B
www.prescottinn.nf.ca

Trinity
(north-east of Clarenville)

Gow, Tineke (Campbell House Bed & Breakfast)   ☎ (709) 464-3377, 1-877-464-7700
High Street, Trinity, Trinity Bay, NF A0C 2S0   E-mail: tgow@campbellhouse.nf.ca

From TCH in Clarenville, turn onto Rte 230 (Discovery Trail) and proceed 70 km. Take Rte 239 to
Trinity Bay, turn left and follow road to village.
$75S $89-95D $150-190Ste $10Add.person (plus tax)   ▶ 10

📅 May-Oct 🍳 Full, homebaked 🏠 Village, 2-storey, hist.,
older, acreage, view from guest rooms, oceanfront, patio, deck,
quiet ■ 3D(upstairs)plus 2 guest houses (2bedroom suites)
⊨2T,2S,3D,3Q ⊐ Private or ensuite ★F,KF,TV,separate
entrance, sinks in some guest rooms, off-street parking 🚭No
smoking, no pets, children min. age 7 ⌇Dutch
🧍 Walking trails with breathtaking views of land and seascape,
restaurants, craft shops, museums, Interpretation Centre, wharf
🚗 Abandoned fishing villages, local boat tours to view Nfld marine wildlife.
🐾 Three Heritage homes, built in 1840, completely restored, furnished with period pieces and
magnificient views of the ocean, located in the centre of the village (the "jewel" of the island). Hosts
are ardent gardeners & musicians and have often shown guests a real Nfld "Time" with a healthy
repertoire of traditional fiddle music. Icebergs may be seen from the guest room windows. Ideal
base location from which to explore the Bonavista Peninsula. CCards
http://www.campbellhouse.nf.ca

Woody Point
(north of Corner Brook; see also Rocky Harbour)

Parsons, Jenny & Stan (Victorian Manor Hospitality Home)   ☎ (709) 453-2485
GrosMorneNat.Park,Box165,Woody Point,NF A0K1P0E-mail: vmanor.grosmorne@nf.sympatico.ca
$50-125S/D $7Add.person 🍳$4.75Each 🍽Meals (winter)   ▶ 8

At Deer Lake on TCH1, take Rt430 to Wiltondale then Rt431.
Located in Gros Morne Nat.Park, a World Heritage Site.
🍳Choice,homebaked 🏠Village,hist.,acreage,view,oceanfront,
sunporch ■7 ⊨6D,1Q ⊐4Private,2sh.w.g.,1jacuzzi ★F,TV in
guest room, sep.entrance, parking 🚭No pets, no smoking
🧍 Seashore, whale watching tour boat
🚗 Lookout Hills Trail, Gros Morne Mountain & trails (Green
Garden's Trail with Sea Caves/Tablelands trail & rare plants)
🐾 4th Generation owners in unique Victorian Home still contains many artifacts and is rich in
history and Newfoundland culture with scenic panorama of Gros Morne and Bonne Bay. Fishing
and boat excursions can be arranged. ✐B&B www.grosmorne.com/victorianmanor